Politics and Power in the Multinational Corporation

The current financial and economic crisis has negatively underlined the vital role of multinational companies (MNCs) in our daily lives. The breakdown and crisis of flagship MNCs, such as Enron, WorldCom, Lehman Brothers, Toyota and General Motors, does not merely reveal the problems of corporate malfeasance and market dysfunction. It also raises important questions, both for the public and the academic community, about the use and misuse of power by MNCs in the wider society, as well as the exercise of power by key actors within internationally operating firms. This book examines how issues of power and politics affect MNCs at three different levels: the macro-level, the meso-level and the micro-level. This wide-ranging analysis shows not only that power matters but also *how* and *why* it matters, pointing to the political interactions of key power holders and actors within the MNC, both managers and employees.

Christoph Dörrenbächer is Professor of Organizational Design and Behavior in International Business at the Berlin School of Economics and Law, Berlin.

Mike Geppert is Professor of Comparative International Management and Organization Studies and Director of the Research Centre for Comparative Studies on Organizational Learning in International Settings (COLIS) at the University of Surrey, Guildford.

Politics and Power in the Multinational Corporation

The Role of Institutions, Interests and Identities

Edited by

Christoph Dörrenbächer

and

Mike Geppert

CAMBRIDGE
UNIVERSITY PRESS

CAMBRIDGE UNIVERSITY PRESS
Cambridge, New York, Melbourne, Madrid, Cape Town,
Singapore, São Paulo, Delhi, Mexico City

Cambridge University Press
The Edinburgh Building, Cambridge CB2 8RU, UK

Published in the United States of America by Cambridge University Press, New York

www.cambridge.org
Information on this title: www.cambridge.org/9781107406650

First published 2011
First paperback edition 2012

A catalogue record for this publication is available from the British Library

Library of Congress Cataloguing in Publication Data
    Politics and power in the multinational corporation : the role of institutions, interests and
    identities / [edited by] Christoph Dörrenbächer, Mike Geppert.
        p.   cm.
    ISBN 978-0-521-19717-5 (hardback)
        1. International business enterprises–Political aspects.   2. Corporate power.
    I. Dörrenbächer, Christoph, 1961–   II.   Geppert, Mike.   III.   Title.
    HD2755.5.P637 2011
    338.88–dc22
    2010051116

ISBN 978-0-521-19717-5 Hardback
ISBN 978-1-107-40665-0 Paperback

Contents

Part I Introduction

Part II Politics and power in MNCs: institutions, social embeddedness and knowledge

Part V   Conclusions

Figures

Tables

Contributors

Paul W. Beamish is Canada Research Chair in International Business at the Richard Ivey School of Business, University of Western Ontario, Canada. He has authored or co-authored 49 books, and more than 100 articles or contributed chapters. He has received best research awards from the Academy of Management, the Academy of International Business (AIB) and the Administrative Sciences Association of Canada (ASAC). In 1997 and again in 2003 he was recognized in the Journal of International Management as one of the top three contributors worldwide to the international strategic management literature in the previous decade. He served as Editor-in-Chief of *Journal of International Business Studies* from 1993–97 and is on numerous editorial boards. He is a fellow of the Royal Society of Canada, Academy of International Business and the Asia Pacific Foundation of Canada.

Florian August Arthur Becker-Ritterspach is Assistant Professor of International Business and Management at the University of Groningen, the Netherlands and is co-organizer of the special interest group International Management at the European Academy of Management (EURAM). Next to knowledge transfer and learning, his research has focused on issues of power, politics, conflict and intra-firm competition in multinationals. He has published his work in the *Journal of International Management*, *Management International Review*, and *Critical Perspectives on International Business* among others, and has recently published a book on transfer and hybridization in multinationals.

Susanne Blazejewski is Professor of Management and Organization at the Alanus University of Arts and Social Sciences, Alfter/Bom, Germany. Her current research interests focus on conflict and micro-politics in multinational corporations, organizational cultures and practices transfer in international contexts. Her work on conflictual processes and politics in MNCs has been published in the *Journal of World Business*, *Competition & Change* among others and she has written several books and book chapters.

Hyunghae Byun is a PhD Student in the Department of Culture, Organization and Management of VU University Amsterdam, the Netherlands, supported by the NWO Mosaic Grant program. She was born and raised in South Korea but has been living in the

Netherlands since 1987. This personal background has triggered her interest in intercultural interactions among different national/cultural groups. Since obtaining her master's degree in 2001, she has worked on the research project "Japanese–Dutch Encounters in an Organizational Context," which was supported by the Netherlands Institute for War Documentation and VU University Amsterdam. Her PhD research focuses on processes of identity formation in cross-boundary situations within multinational companies. The comparative study of intercultural interactions between Japanese and Dutch nationals in different organizational contexts is the central theme in her research.

Jean-Luc Cerdin is Professor in the Management Department at ESSEC Business School Paris–Singapore. He has served as a visiting professor at Rutgers University and University of Missouri St-Louis, and is a visiting scholar at Wharton. He researches, publishes and consults in three primary areas: human resource management in multinational organizations, international assignee management and career management.

Andrea Daniel studied psychology at the University of Regensburg, Germany before she joined ESCP Europe, Berlin, Germany. There, she worked as a research assistant at the Department of International Management and Strategic Management with Stefan Schmid. Together with Stefan Schmid, she was involved in a research project on internationalization of top management which was financed by the Bertelsmann Foundation. Andrea Daniel completed her PhD on perception gaps between headquarters and subsidiary managers in 2009. Since January 2009, she has been working as a consultant at Bain & Company in Amsterdam and Munich.

Christoph Dörrenbächer is Professor of Organizational Design and Behavior in International Business at the Berlin School of Economics and Law (Faculty of Business and Economics), Berlin, Germany. Previously he worked as a consultant and research fellow at various organizations in Germany and abroad, including the Social Science Research Center, Berlin and the University of Groningen, the Netherlands. Visiting appointments were with the United Nations Centre on Transnational Corporations (New York), the Central European University (Budapest) and the Manchester Metropolitan University. He holds a PhD from the Faculty of Social Sciences of the Free University, Berlin. His current research focus is on knowledge transfer, subsidiary role development, headquarters–subsidiary relationships and careers in multinational corporations. He has published widely in renowned international academic journals including the *Journal of World Business*, *Management International Review*, *Journal of International Management*, *Competition & Change* and *Personnel Review*. He is associate editor of *Critical Perspectives on International Business*.

Mark Fenton-O'Creevy is Professor of Organizational Behavior at the Open University Business School, UK. He has a long-standing research interest in the cross-national translation of management practices. He is Co-director of the Centre for International Management Practice, Education and Learning, and Director of the Centre for Practice-Based Professional Learning at the Open University. He received a National Teaching Fellowship from the UK Higher Education Academy in 2007, and was made Senior Fellow of the Higher Education Academy in 2010 in recognition of his work on practice-based learning. Other research is focused on the work, decision-making and behavior of traders in investment banks. Publications related to the topics of the book and book chapter have been published in *Journal of International Business Studies, European Journal of International Management, European Journal of Industrial Relations, International Review of Management Studies* and *Beta: Tidsskrift for bedriftsokonomi* [Scandinavian Journal of Business Research].

Jens Gammelgaard is Associate Professor at the Department of International Economics and Management at Copenhagen Business School, Denmark. He researches the strategic development of foreign subsidiaries. Furthermore, he has published within areas such as M&A and knowledge management. He has recent publications in *Journal of World Business, Management International Review, Journal of International Management, International Journal of Knowledge Management*, and *Behavioral and Information Technology*. He is a national representative and board member in the European International Business Academy and is Program Director for the Bachelor of International Business program at the Copenhagen Business School.

Mike Geppert is Professor of Comparative International Management and Organization Studies, and Director of the Research Centre for Comparative Studies on Organizational Learning in International Settings (COLIS) at the University of Surrey, Guildford, UK. Since 2010, he has been an elected Board member of the European Group for Organization Studies (EGOS). His most recent research is on cross-national comparisons of management and organization, socio-political issues in multinational companies and transnational institution building. His work has been published in books, book chapters and academic journals, such as *Human Relations, Industrial Relations Journal, Journal of International Management, Journal of Management Inquiry, Journal of Management Studies* and *Organization Studies*, reflecting his multidisciplinary research interests and commitment to interdisciplinary work. He is currently the leader of an international comparative research project on "Work and employment relations of European multinational grocery retailers – discounters and hypermarkets."

Paul N. Gooderham is Professor of International Management at NHH, the Norwegian School of Economics and Business Administration. He is Director of the GOLD project which focuses on the role of social capital in enhancing knowledge transfer within multinational enterprises. He is also Research Director at SNF – the Research Foundation at NHH – and a visiting professor at Nottingham Business School.

Publications related to the topics of the book and book chapter have been published in *Journal of International Business Studies, Knowledge Management Research & Practice* and *International Review of Management Studies.*

Graham Hollinshead is Reader in International Human Resource Management at the University of Hertfordshire, UK. He has published widely in the field of international business and human resource management, including articles in *Human Resource Development International, Human Relations, Journal of World Business, Management Learning* and *European Journal of Education.* He is also author of a number of successful textbooks, the most recent being *Human Resource Management: an International and Comparative Perspective.* He teaches "Managing and Working Across Cultures" on the MBA program at the University of Hertfordshire Business School and has acted as a consultant for the German GTZ in upgrading management capacities in Serbia. He is a fellow of the Chartered Institute of Personnel and Development (CIPD). His current areas of research interest relate to critical management and employment issues in the off-shoring of financial services and software development.

Alexei Koveshnikov is a doctoral candidate at Hanken School of Economics in Helsinki, Finland. He is writing his dissertation on issues of politicking, power struggles, trust and legitimacy in multinational companies. His other interests include research on multinational companies from emerging markets, nationalism and cultural stereotyping in organizations, and critical perspectives on globalization.

Mairi Maclean is Professor of International Management and Organization Studies at Exeter University Business School, UK. She was previously Professor of International Business at Bristol Business School, UWE, and before that Reader in International Business in the School of Management, Royal Holloway, University of London. She holds an MA and a PhD from the University of St Andrews and an MBA from the University of Bath. Her interests include business elites, corporate governance, business history and comparative organization studies. Her books include *Business Elites and Corporate Governance in France and the UK* written with Charles Harvey and Jon Press, and funded by the Leverhulme Trust and Reed Charity; and *Economic Management and French Business from de Gaulle to Chirac.* She is the author of four books, and editor of a further four. Recent publications include contributions to *Organization Studies, Human Relations, Business History, Business History Review* and the *Sociological Review.*

Glenn Morgan is Professor in the Human Resource section at Cardiff Business School, UK. Prior to this he was based at Warwick Business School. He is one of the editors of the journal *Organization* and a Visiting Professor at the International Centre for Business and Politics, Copenhagen Business School. He is a member of the Executive Committee of the Society for the Advancement of Socio-Economics (SASE) and has been one of the convenors of the EGOS Standing Working Group on Comparative Economic Organization. Recent edited books include *The Oxford Handbook of Comparative Institutional Analysis* (with Campbell, Crouch, Pedersen and Whitley) and *Images of the Multinational Firm* (with Collinson). He has published in a range of journals on multinationals, globalization, institutional change and more recently on the regulation and governance of international financial markets.

Rune Rønning is Chief Researcher at AFF (Administrative Research Institute) at the Norwegian School of Economics and Business Administration. He also has worked as an organizational consultant for the same organization since 1991. He holds a doctorate (DMan) in complexity and organizational change from the University of Hertfordshire in the UK. He has a long-standing relationship with the Tavistock Institute of Human Relations and is a member of A Working Alliance, a UK network of organizational consultants and researchers. His current interests include international leadership, social capital and here-and-now consultancy work with organizations.

Katja Rothe is an organizational sociologist (MA). She was previously a research fellow at the Social Science Research Center Berlin, Germany in the Internationalization and Organization unit, conducting research on knowledge sharing in organizations, working conditions, and internationalization and L&D. She has also worked as a self-employed trainer in social skills and organizational development for companies in the field of further qualification for adults. At the moment she works as a training manager at the employee academy of a hospital cooperative in Berlin.

Stefan Schmid is Professor of International Management and Strategic Management at ESCP Europe, Berlin, Germany, where he is also head of the department. He studied business administration in Augsburg, Paris, Oxford and Berlin. Prior to joining ESCP Europe, he was affiliated with the Catholic University of Eichstätt-Ingolstadt, Germany. His research focuses on strategies of internationalization, headquarters–subsidiary relationships and international corporate governance. His work has been published in journals such as *International Business Review, Management International Review, Thunderbird International Business Review, International Journal of Management Reviews* and *Marketing Theory.* He is also author of several books and numerous case studies. The textbook *Internationales Management* (co-authored with Michael Kutschker) is the best-selling textbook in the German-speaking countries and reached seven editions within nine years. Stefan Schmid served as Vice President of the International Management Division of the German Academic Association for Business Research from 2006 to 2008, and was President from 2008 to 2010. Stefan Schmid teaches in MSc, MBA, PhD and executive education programs and is Academic Dean of the Master in European Business (MEB) program at ESCP Europe.

Andreas Schotter is Assistant Professor of Strategy at the Thunderbird School of Global Management, Glendale, Arizona USA. His primary research interests are the management of the MNC headquarters–subsidiary interface, emerging markets, corporate strategic change, global innovation and technology management, the management of environmental sustainability across borders, and poverty alleviation in lesser-developed countries through micro-enterprise evolution. His research and cases have been published in leading academic and practitioner journals. He has received scholarly and conference awards in recognition of his work. Before embarking on an academic career, he was a senior executive with several multinational corporations in the automotive, industrial equipment and consumer goods industries. He has lived and worked in Europe, Asia, Australia and North America. As an entrepreneur, he jointly owned and operated a manufacturing business in Australia together with a Chinese partner. He has consulted with numerous corporations in the manufacturing, retail and service industries.

Arndt Sorge is the acting Director of the Internationalization and Organization unit of WZB (Wissenschaftszentrum Berlin für Sozialforschung, Germany), and François Sellier Professor of International Business and Management at the University of Groningen, the Netherlands (until the end of 2010). He continues as an honorary professor at the Faculty of Economics and Social Science, University of Potsdam, Germany. He has mainly worked in international comparisons of management, organization, human resources, industrial relations and technical change, in universities or research institutes in the Netherlands, Germany, Britain and France. He edited the organization section of the *International Encyclopedia of Business and Management* and was Editor-in-Chief of *Organization Studies*. His last individual book was *The Global and the Local*. He was made an honorary member of EGOS (European Group of Organization Studies) in 2010. From an earlier life as a glider pilot in his youth, and from making maps from aerial photography in the German Federal Army, he has retained a lifelong interest in aviation and aeronautical engineering, to which he only now came back to with the present paper and others. With colleagues in several countries, he started ICAROS (International Consortium for Airline Research and Organizational Studies).

Christopher Williams is Assistant Professor of International Business at the Richard Ivey School of Business, University of Western Ontario, Canada. His research interests include entrepreneurship in international firms, knowledge creation and transfer in international firms, and offshore outsourcing of knowledge-intensive work. His work is published in academic journals such as *Research Policy, Information Systems Journal, Journal of World Business, International Business Review, R&D Management, Journal of International Management* and *Journal of Interdisciplinary Economics*. Christopher has over two decades of industry experience in international companies including GEC Research, Midland Bank, Informix Software and IMS Health.

His work in industry was mainly in international innovation projects, information systems and product development.

Karen Williams is Senior Lecturer in Comparative Employment Relations in the School of Business and Economics, Swansea University, Wales. Her background is in linguistics (German and French) and international relations. She completed her PhD on conflict resolution in the German and British manufacturing industry at the University of Surrey. Research interests include the transfer of employment relations strategies and practices in multinational companies, and the influence of different societal and organizationally based systems of employment relations on the world of work. She has worked with Mike Geppert and Dirk Matten on an Anglo-German study of change management in the engineering industry, which has led to publications in the *Journal of Management Studies, Human Relations* and a co-edited book. She is currently part of an international team researching into the internationalization strategies of food retail multinational companies in Europe and the effect on working conditions and employment relations, funded by the Hans Böckler Foundation.

Sierk Ybema is Associate Professor in the Department of Culture, Organization and Management, VU University Amsterdam, the Netherlands. His research centers on processes of politics, identity and sensemaking, with empirical settings ranging from amusement parks to newspaper offices and multinational corporations. He has published widely on culture and conflict, relational and temporal identity talk, managerial discourse and "postalgia", intercultural communications, inter-organizational relationships, and organizational change and crisis. This work has been published in such journals as *Human Relations, International Journal of Cross-Cultural Management, Organization Studies* and *Journal of Managerial Psychology*. He is co-editor of *Organizational Ethnography: Studying the complexities of everyday life* (with Dvora Yanow, Harry Wels and Frans Kamsteeg) and *Organizational Culture* (with Dvora Yanow and Ida Sabelis). He also co-edited a number of Special Issues, one of which was on *Constructing identity in organizations* in a 2009 issue in *Human Relations*. He has co-organized a number of conferences and sub-themes, including EGOS *Upsetting Organizations* conference in Amsterdam 2008, and the bi-annual conference on *Organizational Discourse*.

Foreword

The MNC as a political organization

Ram Mudambi, Temple University

I will argue that the business firm is properly viewed as a political system and that viewing the firm as such a system both clarifies conventional economic theories of the firm and ... suggests some ways of dealing with classical problems in the theory of political systems generally. (March 1962: 663)

Organizations, particularly large ones, are like governments in that they are fundamentally political entities. To understand them, one needs to understand organizational politics ... (Pfeffer 1992: 29)

The above quotes exemplify the reality of the functioning of all large and complex organizations. Large business firms in general and multinational corporations or companies (MNCs) in particular form a large and important set within this group. Yet most theories aimed at explaining the functioning of business firms, both in strategic management and economics either ignore the political dimension of the organization, or treat it as an aberration. In the mainstream literature, the strategy of business firms has traditionally been accepted to be the creation and maintenance of competitive advantage.

As noted by Mintzberg (1979), the operation of a business firm gives rise to both cooperation and conflict. Conflicts can arise between owners and managers in the division of the value created by the firm as well as amongst managers in the struggle for power and control rights within the firm. It is this latter set of conflicts that is the subject of this very topical volume. These conflicts have been analyzed within two quite disparate perspectives, namely agency theory and resource dependency theory. Both of these perspectives have been extensively developed in independent literatures. However, while these literatures have much to offer each other, these links have hitherto been underdeveloped.

Within the agency perspective, conflict amongst managers has been framed as one where managers at headquarters are the principals and managers in operating divisions are their agents. It is recognized that MNC subsidiaries pursue their own interests and are not a mechanical instrument of headquarters' will. More importantly, "the local interests of the subsidiaries may not always be aligned with those of the headquarters or the MNC as a whole" (Nohria and Ghoshal 1994: 492). However, while the agency perspective incorporates autonomous decision-making by subsidiary managers, their decision-making autonomy may be categorized as discretion in the sense of Williamson (1996). Headquarters delegates or "loans" decision rights to subsidiary managers, but retains the power of veto, i.e. the ability to overrule any subsidiary decision.

In contrast, the analysis of power in the management literature has been based on the basic notion that "power is the ability to get others to do something that they would not otherwise do" (Dahl 1957) and that the successful exercise of power requires that it be based on a set of "legitimating principles" that are specific to the organization (Weber 1968). This is the basis of resource dependency theory, which posits that power is (a) based on the control of resources that are considered strategic within the organization (Pfeffer and Salancik 1978); and (b) is often expressed in terms of budgetary and resource allocations (Mudambi and Navarra 2004). Resource dependency theory is externally focused in the sense that "power is held by divisions that are the most important for coping with and solving the critical problems of the organization that arise from its environment" (Pfeffer and Salancik 1978). Organizational survival in a competitive environment provides a logical basis for this position, since organizations that fail to address their critical problems will disappear.

On the basis of the foregoing discussion, it is clear that agency theory and resource dependency theory are two pillars upon which to understand decision-making by managers in MNCs. Both these theories find voice in the constituent chapters of this volume. But the editors of the volume go further, by recognizing that applying these theories to the MNC requires acknowledging its unique contextual subtleties. These arise from the fact that the MNC is embedded in multiple local contexts, giving rise both to opportunities and challenges (Meyer et al. 2011). These local contexts can generate firm-specific advantages ranging from R&D and marketing-based knowledge (Mudambi 2008) to efficient employee relations (Tüselmann et al. 2006; Williams and Geppert, this volume).

The multiple embeddedness perspective (Meyer *et al.* 2011) provides a cohesive framework to view the three constituent parts of this volume. First, the strategies and functioning of German MNCs cannot be understood without recognizing their social embeddedness. Second, ignoring contextual issues, headquarters–subsidiary relations reduce to a simple conflict between global (headquarters) versus local (subsidiary) optima. Recognizing the importance of local contexts emphasizes the role of rationalization (Dörrenbächer and Gammelgaard, this volume) and hence the importance of boundary spanners (Mudambi and Swift 2009, Schotter and Beamish, this volume). Third, national identities and home and host country culture are critical issues underlying MNC political processes and decision-making.

All three sections of this collection provide us with novel approaches to understanding decision-making within MNCs. Hence they give us new insights into the functioning of the world's largest business enterprises.

Philadelphia, Pennsylvania, 2010

REFERENCES

Dahl, R.A. 1957. "The concept of power," *Behavioral Science*, 2: 201–18

March, J.G. 1962. "The business firm as a political coalition," *Journal of Politics*, 24(4): 662–678

Meyer, K., Mudambi, R. and Narula, R. 2011. "Multinational enterprises and local contexts: the opportunities and challenges of multiple embeddedness," *Journal of Management Studies* (in print)

Mintzberg, H. 1979. *The Structuring of Organizations*. Englewood Cliffs, NJ: Prentice-Hall

Mudambi, R. 2008. "Location, control and innovation in knowledge intensive industries," *Journal of Economic Geography*, 8(5): 699–725

Mudambi, R. and Navarra, P. 2004. "Is knowledge power? Knowledge flows, subsidiary power and rent-seeking within MNEs," *Journal of International Business Studies*, 35(5): 385–406

Mudambi, R. and Swift, T. 2009. "Professional guilds, tension and knowledge management," *Research Policy*, 38(5): 736–745

Nohria, N. and Ghoshal, S. 1994. "Differentiated fit and shared values: alternatives for managing headquarters–subsidiary relations." *Strategic Management Journal*, 15(6): 491–502

Pfeffer, J. 1992. "Understanding power in organizations," *California Management Review*, 34(2): 29–50

Pfeffer, J. and Salancik, G.R. 1978. The External Control of Organizations: A Resource Dependency Perspective. New York: Harper & Row

Tüselmann, H., McDonald F. and Thorpe, R. 2006. "The emerging approach to employee relations in German overseas affiliates: a role model for international operation?" *Journal of World Business*, 41(1): 66–80

Weber, M. 1968 trans. *Economy and Society: An Outline of Interpretive Sociology.* Edited by G. Roth and C. Claus Wittich. New York: Bedminster Press

Williamson, O. 1996. *The Mechanisms of Governance.* Oxford University Press.

Part I

Introduction

1 Politics and power in the multinational corporation: an introduction

Mike Geppert and Christoph Dörrenbächer

The current financial and economic crisis has negatively underlined the vital role of multinational corporations (MNCs) in our daily lives. The breakdown and crisis of flagship MNCs, such as Enron, WorldCom, Lehman Brothers, Toyota and General Motors, does not merely reveal the problems of corporate malfeasance and market dysfunction but also raises important questions, both for the public and the academic community, about the use and misuse of power by MNCs in the wider society, as well as the exercise of power by key actors within internationally operating firms. Given these and previous similar developments, it is surprising that questions about organizational power and politics have not had a more central role in the study of the MNC.

Historically, research on the MNC was focused on studying the influence and changing role of headquarters (HQ) management (e.g. Stopford and Wells 1972; Vernon 1966), with, for example, Hymer (1970) actually predicting that more geographical dispersion of MNCs would lead to greater concentration of decision-making power at the center. As long as HQ management was seen in the driving seat, the role of lower level managers, e.g. in local subsidiaries, and of other employees was mainly reduced to adaptation either to centrally set strategies or to external environmental pressures. Later, studies on the "evolution" of the MNC stressed that MNCs can hardly be managed top-down, especially if "diversification" and internationalization are increasing, but they did not "dare" shed more light on power relations and organizational politics. Instead, they preferred to apply an apolitical language, referring to "barriers" to evolutionary changes (Bartlett and Ghoshal 1989). Nohria and Ghoshal (1997) went even further and saw no need to make any references to organizational politics, asserting that the adoption of differentiated network structures in the transnational corporation might even have pacifying effects. Indeed, most IB (International Business) studies are focused on helping MNC management to overcome strategic and structural misfits in responding to environmental pressures. From this perspective, political behavior and resistance by certain actors and groups of actors are seen as dysfunctional, and the task of "good" management is to overcome these organizational "barriers."

Despite this broader trend, a few scholars have actually predicted that the increased diversification of strategies and structures of MNCs observed by evolutionary scholars might have some organizational political consequences, and that "influence and power of how the trade-offs between multiple stakeholders and multiple perspectives are made" (Doz and Prahalad 1991: 46) needs to be considered in future research. This call was taken up slowly and only by a certain stream of research, e.g. by Birkinshaw and his colleagues studying subsidiary entrepreneurship (2000) and mandate changes (1996). These studies show that subsidiaries develop their own strategies in order to influence decisions about resource allocation and compare strategic approaches which lead either to the gain or loss of subsidiary mandates. In short, managerial strategies are in the center of this research and political interests are mainly interpreted as (bounded) rational, concentrated on improving the power position for themselves and the subsidiary in the MNC when fighting for, for example, enhancements of their mandates. In line with early micro-political approaches it is assumed that subsidiary management is "self-interested" and follows (bounded) rational strategies when playing "games" to gain mandates and thus power (see e.g. Crozier 1964; Doz and Prahalad 1991). Power is understood as being directly related to the control of "uncertainty zones," which affect the performance of other members of the MNC, and to "critical resources" on which other actors are dependent (Crozier and Friedberg 1980; Pfeffer and Salancik 1978). To sum up, resource dependency, and to a smaller extent micro-political approaches, have been the core theoretical building blocks for a rather small number of IB studies focusing on power and politics within the MNC. But to date, the role of power is conceptualized in a rather simplistic way: (a) individual and collective actors possess power because they control critical (scarce) resources and (b) actors who can gain and control more critical resources have more power (see also Clegg *et al.* 2006).

What is missing in the IB debate, however, is a more nuanced sociological understanding of power and politics in which questions are asked about: *what* forms or constitutes "self-interests" in MNCs, *for whom* are certain managerial strategies effective or efficient (Hinings and Greenwood 2002), and *who* is actually benefiting from the implementation of more standardized transnational structures, benchmarking systems or best practices, which are crucial issues in MNCs nowadays. The fact that actors have different interests regarding the implementation of such measures, and that they might resist the implementation of certain measures or try to renegotiate proposed measures, is hardly considered in mainstream debates on power in MNCs. The conceptualization of agency is reduced to the questions of who has what power and who has power over whom (Clegg *et al.* 2006: 127). The role of institutions, interests and identities of actors who engage in political games in and around MNCs is neglected. We propose that power is not a property of certain powerful actors but should be understood as a "relational effect" (Clegg *et al.* 2006: 222), which means that power has to be studied in reference to the social context in which political strategies are embedded. Institutionalist scholars have addressed the problem of embedding agency and knowledge within different social and societal settings of MNCs (Redding 2005) and stress that the institutional duality between HQ and subsidiaries (e.g. Vora *et al.* 2007) might trigger political struggles and conflicts. Moreover, the role of political interests and social identities has also been stressed by Morgan (2001), who suggests that MNCs should be studied as "transnational social spaces" and by Bélanger and Edwards (2006), who are skeptical about attempts to conceptualize the MNC as "placeless" transnational corporations, suggesting instead the study of the MNC as a "contested terrain" (Edwards and Bélanger 2009).

The chapters in our book build on these recent conceptual developments while bringing together two typically separated theoretical debates: first, about the institutional and cultural embeddedness of social relationships in the MNC, and second, about the role of agency and diverse interests and identities of key actors, which constitute the MNC as a "political system" (Bélanger and Edwards 2006; see also Morgan and Whitley 2003). In short, the contributions of our book fit well under the rubric "emergent critical perspectives" within a framework recently provided by Barner-Rasmussen *et al.* (2010), which compares key IB perspectives on "contemporary multinationals" (see also Andersson and Holm 2010). The authors distinguish between mainstream "design," "network," "institutional" (which we call institutionalist in this chapter) and critical perspectives. The chapters of our book study politics and power in the MNC at three levels (see also Bélanger and Edwards 2006). First, they look at politics and power in the MNC at the *macro-level* of (national and international) society, where the role of societal institutions and the cultural and political influences of stakeholders such as shareholders, governmental agencies, non-governmental pressure groups and civic movements are studied. Second, they examine power and politics at the *meso-level*, where the MNC itself, as a more or less politicized organization, is the focus of analysis, along with its key players in managerial positions (both within the HQ and the subsidiaries) and its employment relations. Third, the chapters in this volume examine power and politics at the *micro-level*, i.e. among individual actors, especially at the subsidiary level, which are studied as political systems where strategic decisions of MNCs have to be legitimized (Kostova and Zaheer 1999), leading to political game-playing, resistance and negotiations between managerial groups and between managers and employees.

Our introductory chapter unfolds as follows. First, we review in detail how power and politics have been discussed in the mainstream IB as well as in institutionalist literature. Second, we introduce alternative approaches to how power and politics has been defined and analyzed, referring to emerging debates about the MNC as a "transnational social space" (Morgan 2001a), "contested terrain" (Edwards and Bélanger 2009) and spaces for certain "types of micro-politics" (Morgan and Kristensen 2006). While especially referring to the role of institutions, which are not just structural and cultural constraints to agency, but also trigger or enable certain political strategies, we will in particular shed some light on the diverse and sometimes contradictory socio-political interests and identities of actors and groups of actors constituting transnational social spaces (Becker-Ritterspach 2006; Becker-Ritterspach and Dörrenbächer 2011; Clark and Geppert 2006; Dörrenbächer 2007; Dörrenbächer and Becker-Ritterspach 2009; Dörrenbächer and Geppert 2006, 2007, 2009a, 2009b, 2010; Geppert and Williams 2006). Finally, we will introduce the contributions of our book, which cover different levels of analysis and relate to the role of institutions, interests and identities in the exercise of power and politics in MNCs.

Power and politics in the MNC: mainstream rationalistic IB and sociological institutionalist approaches

MNCs have become essential parts of our daily lives. As customers, employees, shareholders and interested and/or critical citizens we are dealing with them either as a stakeholder or as multiple stakeholders. We typically see multinationals as monolithic organizations. But, like any institution in society, they are not. They are geographically, socially, culturally and institutionally diverse organizations, which raises issues of politics and power. This volume deals with this complexity, focusing in particular on issues of politics and power, an underdeveloped area of study in mainstream analyses of multinational corporations.

An increased specialization of social sciences, especially from the 1950s onwards, led to the establishment of IB as academic discipline and the dominance of economic and rationalistic[1] perspectives in the study of the MNC, intellectually driven mainly by political economists and economists. Sociological studies focused historically not so much on the MNC itself as unit of analysis, but rather on the spread and crisis of production models, such as Fordism and post-Fordism, throughout capitalist societies (see e.g. Lash and Urry 1987). Only recently have MNCs as unique organizations received the attention of some, mainly organization sociologists interested in the role of institutional influences on MNC structures and capabilities. However, as we will see, both camps – economic and rationalistic mainstream IB approaches as well as institutionalist sociological studies of the MNC – either neglect the role of politics and power in the MNC or address it only in a limited way. Next, we will discuss how the first, IB camp, treats politics and power in MNCs. We focus on two leading approaches, the so-called eclectic and evolutionary paradigms. Then we move on to the second, institutionalist camp, and distinguish between North American neo-institutionalist and European comparative institutionalist approaches.

The eclectic paradigm: apolitical economic view with unexamined political implications

Mainstream economic research focuses on the efficiency of managerial control when studying foreign direct investment (FDI) and how MNCs internationalize. Drawing on ideas of transaction cost economics, it is asserted that either market-oriented or hierarchical forms of control (or some combination of them) are applied to control international ventures. One highly influential approach in this academic camp is Dunning's eclectic OLI theory, which explains FDI and the existence of the MNC by arguing that international operating firms are mainly interested in maintaining and gaining "ownership," "locational" and "internalization" advantages (e.g. Dunning 2000; Dunning and Rugman 1985). According to this scheme, *ownership* advantages refer to a company's specialized home country capabilities, such as human capital, patents, technologies, intellectual property rights, brands and reputation. It is assumed that these assets must be hierarchically

---

[1] Rationalistic theorists, either implicitly or explicitly, believe that managerial decision-makers are able to replace 'irrationality' with technical or economic rational decisions. Such a perspective assumes that better managers and organizational designs will help to avoid irrational decisions (see e.g. Fischer 2005).

controlled when replicated by MNCs in new international market environments, with a key question being how to transfer knowledge and management practices efficiently. *Locational* advantages are mainly seen as cost-saving activities such as labor costs and transport costs, as well as being close to customers and efficiently tackling trade barriers (tariffs and quotas). Finally, *internalization advantages* are seen as the ability of a firm to organize its international business activities in a more transaction cost-efficient way than its local competitors.

The OLI theory has been developed further, mainly with reference to the so-called "knowledge economy." For example, Dunning and Lundan (2009) argue that resource-seeking and market-seeking activities are not sufficient and that strategic assets are more knowledge intensive than originally assumed in IB studies of the MNC. They suggest that instead of transferring just "hard technologies," the transfer of "soft technology" such as organization structures and work practices becomes increasingly important and requires rethinking of traditional approaches to studying MNCs. However, this approach does not go as far as considering issues of political processes and power in the creation of knowledge assets in the MNC. This is because the eclectic paradigm is an *apolitical* tool, both for researchers and managers, designed to inform internationalization decisions, and shares the basic assumptions of transaction cost theorists such as Williamson (1985). As a result, some highly significant implications about power relations in MNCs are ignored, or minimized as simply a factor of principal–agent relationships (see e.g. Perrow 1986 for critique). Economic rational actors are typically seen as the drivers of internationalization, and managers (agents) need to be controlled by owners (principals) because of the potential risk of opportunistic behavior and the threat of selfish, profit and career-enhancing behavior, especially if "assets" are highly specific and "uncertainty" is high. A key problem with such basic assumptions about human nature and agency is that economic rationality of agents is understood as being universal, neglecting the social context, the social embeddedness of economic actions (Granovetter 1985) and the influence of diverse contextual rationalities (Morgan 2001a). Moreover, the conceptualization of MNCs as predominantly economic decision-making systems is misleading. Rationality is not only "sub-optimal" because of incomplete contracts and opportunistic manager behavior, but also because of the political nature of decision-making processes. Decision-making in the MNC, as in any other organization, is based on political coalition building and therefore often "bounded," as stressed by organizational theory pioneers Cyert and March (1992: 226–30).

In summary, we believe that economic studies neglect politics and power in the MNC, despite the fact that they implicitly assume that selfish and cheating actors need to be controlled either by effective contractual or hierarchical arrangements in order to efficiently control the management of international ventures, including MNCs. While these studies refuse to acknowledge that politics and power are a natural aspect of MNC decision-making, they indirectly bring power and politics into the picture, in a very limited but sound way.

The evolutionary model of the MNC: rationalistic and normative view on power and politics in the MNC

While the economic approaches described above developed a rather simplistic understanding of the management of MNCs, the so-called *evolutionary* theory of the MNC paints a more sophisticated picture by examining how internal organizational design and management structures are linked to internationalization in MNCs. Whereas the former approach conceptualizes the organization of the MNC simply according to different degrees of hierarchical or market coordination, the latter concentrates on the management of MNCs, which is still seen as bounded (rational), with the HQ in the driving seat. Grounded in a mixture of both evolutionary and contingency theory based ideas, this approach asserts that the task of management is to "select" the best organizational forms and internationalization strategies to "fit" specific external environmental requirements (see e.g. Westney 2009 for an overview). A key argument is that the management of MNCs faces a "dilemma" as they increasingly internationalize their business activities. This dilemma emerges because MNC management needs to balance the demands of being *globally efficient* – an argument which largely follows the assumption of economic theories – and the *demands of the local host environments* the subsidiaries operate in, especially when autonomy and thus power resources of host country managers are not in line with the external environment. In the highly influential work of Bartlett and Ghoshal on the evolutionary model of the MNC, the role of power relations is hardly explicitly mentioned but implicitly understood as being instrumental for the management of the MNC. The key question is *how much power needs to be centralized at the HQ level* and how much power needs to be shared with subsidiaries in order to be able to effectively manage the international operations. This question becomes even more prominent in the authors' discussion about the final so-called transnational stage of "evolution," when balancing global efficiency and local adaptation is seen not just as a task of structural change but also as a task of managing culture and building "global mindsets" to enhance coordination and control (Bartlett and Ghoshal 1989). The bias towards top-down power structures and the neglect of political processes in mainstream evolutionary studies becomes apparent when considering the case of ABB, which was seen as the closest ideal-typical model of the transnational firm (Bartlett and Ghoshal 1989). But the company then ceased to experiment with transnational matrix structures. Ironically, as Westney stresses, the "influence of host country management 'waned' from the mid-1990s on, and the much-vaunted balance of business, geography and function eroded" (2009: 129). In short, balancing global and local demands within the MNC is a dynamic political process which is capable of both reinforcing and undermining established power structures, issues which have been widely ignored by mainstream evolutionary scholars.[2] Additionally, Bélanger et al. (2003) stress, also in reference to Bartlett and Ghoshal's study, that the research methods of their study are not suitable for critically reflecting on power relations and politics within MNCs, criticizing that the applied "methodology appears to be dependent on the intentions and formal discourse of the main corporate leaders" (Bélanger et al. (2003: 473). Unfortunately, further developments of the evolutionary framework, e.g. by Nohria and Ghoshal (1997), who suggest studying MNCs as "differentiated networks," seem to even further neglect the role of power and politics in the MNC. Based on the normative mantra it is assumed that managers can learn to effectively create and manage transnational cultures, and that as a consequence of improved "effectiveness" of management "inter-functional and cross-divisional conflicts, the dysfunctional effects and illegitimate aspects of politics and power will hardly ever appear – they may even disappear" (Dörrenbächer and Geppert 2006: 253).

To summarize, mainstream evolutionary approaches to the study of the MNC opened up the black box of hierarchical structures within the MNC by focusing on how internationally operating firms can be better managed and organized. However, because of a bias towards efficiency and the normative, rather simplistic belief that political "dysfunctions" can be eliminated through more effective management, this approach overlooks the dynamics of political processes and the role of social agency.

---

[2] There are of course exceptions, as we will discuss later. Here we refer in particular to the seminal paper of Doz and Prahalad (1991) and the work of Birkinshaw and colleagues on subsidiary mandate change. Most of the work of the latter scholars, however, remains closely linked to the evolutionary model of the MNC, and theory building on politics and power in the MNC has been limited.

Research on subsidiary entrepreneurship: explicit focus on power and politics in the MNC but still largely drawing rationalistic views

The work of Hedlund (1986) was pioneering as well as inspiring for IB schol-ars, including Bartlett and Ghoshal, when developing their ideas about the evolution of MNC strategies and structures. In comparison to mainstream IB research, Hedlund made us aware that the strategic approaches of MNCs are more dynamic and might switch back and forth between more or less hierarchical control and coordination mechanisms, which he called "heter-archy" (see also discussion in Collinson and Morgan 2009). It is important to note that *heterarchy* is not the same as what economic studies discuss under the label of market coordination, but instead points to the strategic choices and roles of subsidiaries, which cannot be fully controlled by the HQ. This observation is picked up and developed further by IB scholars, including Birkinshaw (1996, 2000). Accordingly, Andersson *et al.* (2007: 802) suggest conceptualizing MNCs not as a hierarchies, but as "federations," where both HQ and subsidiaries "are involved in a perpetual bargaining process."

A key contribution of these IB studies in terms of politics and power within the MNC is their emphasis on the fact that subsidiary managers actively influence relations with HQ when negotiating charter changes, rather than just passively responding to HQ demands. It is also stressed that subsidiaries have and develop different roles, which provide them with *critical resources* for increasing their mandates when bargaining with the HQ (e.g. Birkinshaw 1996). An illustrative example of how MNC power relations and the political strategies of subsidiaries to gain influence at the HQ level is conceptualized and analyzed in this research stream is provided in the study of Birkinshaw and Ridderstråle (1999). Conceptually, the authors draw on ideas of organ-izational power found in contingency and resource dependency theories. They introduce the metaphor of the "corporate immune system" within the MNC to demonstrate how established power relations influence entrepre-neurial initiatives by subsidiaries and why some initiatives are accepted and others are rejected by the HQ. The functioning of the corporate immune sys-tem is explained at three levels: (1) the power of the HQ, (2) the power pos-ition of the subsidiary with the MNC in comparison to fellow subsidiaries and (3) internal and external market success of initiatives. Even when sub-sidiary power is seen as crucial for entrepreneurship within the MNC, the HQ is understood – in reference of Weber's (1947) classical definition of bureaucratic power (Birkinshaw and Ridderstråle 1999 – as the holder of central *authority-based power*, having an ultimately "legally granted authority

… in that the legal charter of an organization allows shareholders to grant a CEO and the CEO may push this authority further down the organization" (Birkinshaw and Ridderstråle 1999: 152).[3] The relative *power position* of the subsidiaries in relation to the HQ is explained in reference to resource dependencies; subsidiaries, it is assumed, will gain and/or lose power in their attempts to bargain charter developments (e.g. Birkinshaw 1996). The success of these initiatives and of the negotiations with the HQ is seen as closely linked to the question of whether they are able to control scarce resources on which other subunits of the MNC (including the HQ) are dependent. It is assumed that all subunits of the MNC are in competition for resources, which can be both internally and externally based, but that external *market support* is crucial to explain the success of initiatives. Comparing the success and failures of subsidiary management initiative-taking showed that the corporate immune system appears to be highly conservative. In the study of Birkinshaw and Ridderstråle (1999), HQ managers remained quite powerful in blocking internal initiatives, and the HQ and other subunits "within the system prefer to work within existing routines, throw their support behind low-risk projects, and resist ideas that challenge their own power base" (Birkinshaw 1996: 154). On the other hand, subsidiaries that could gain more external support and economic success for their initiatives were more powerful and better equipped to bargain with the HQ, because of "avoidance of all parts of the corporate immune system" (Birkinshaw 1996: 175).

In summary, these studies on subsidiary initiative-taking and entrepreneurship are quite important for understanding the role of power and politics within the MNC, issues which have either been neglected or only indirectly approached in mainstream IB research as discussed above (see also Dörrenbächer and Geppert 2006). Especially the most recent work of Bouquet and Birkinshaw (2008) goes far beyond the mainly rationalistic arguments of previous studies, providing a more eclectic and broader view on the dynamics of power and politics within the MNC. Combining economic and sociological ideas this paper studies why and how subsidiaries and actors in lower power positions are able to gain influence on HQ decision-making. Moreover, their findings about the role of external resource-building activities can be linked to comparative institutionalist studies, which show how local actors' (both managers and employees) political approaches are interlinked with

---

[3] This quote also shows that ownership control is conceptualized in a rather specific way. However, not all MNCs are listed on the stock market, which might have different effects on HQ authority and power relations, as stressed by comparative institutionalist studies. This is an issue we shall come back to in our next section.

power resources provided by local institutions (see e.g. chapters of Sorge and Williams and Geppert in this volume). However, most of the work on subsidiary initiatives and entrepreneurship maintains a rationalistic view and avoids "stepping too far beyond the boundaries of the firm" (Collinson and Morgan 2009: 12). This prevents deeper insights into the social and institutional constitution of the MNC and the interplay of institutions, interests and identities that constitute power relations and political interactions within the MNC, issues that will be discussed next.

Institutionalist studies of the MNC

Institutionalism stresses the role of social institutions and different institutional environments for the social constitution of the MNC. There are two main streams of institutionalist approaches to studying the MNC. Both stress that organizations need to adapt and respond to their institutional environments, but they come to very different conclusions about how organizational forms and management practices are transferred across societal borders and about the degree and impact of pressures for global standardization of managerial and organizational practices in MNCs (see e.g. Geppert *et al.* 2006; Tempel and Walgenbach 2007). The first stream has been brought forward, e.g. by Westney (1993) and by Kostova and colleagues (e.g. Kostova 1999; Kostova and Roth 2002; Kostova and Zaheer 1999), and draws heavily on neo-institutionalist organization theories developed in North America. The second stream draws on a mixture of ideas brought forward by European comparative institutionalists such as the political science related "varieties of capitalism" approach and sociological perspectives on "divergent capitalisms." Compared to the three mainstream IB approaches, which apply rationalistic ideas of how MNCs operate and function, institutionalist research argues that no organization can be understood without understanding its social embeddedness in the wider society. Thus rationality is understood as being socially constructed, and scholars need to take into consideration the role of social institutions when analyzing the behavior of MNCs.

North American neo-institutionalism: contextualized but tortuous views of power and politics in the MNC

North American neo-institutionalists are largely interested in the diffusion, adoption and institutionalization of organizational practices and structures across national borders. It is assumed that universal ideologies and management ideas diffuse across the globe as "best practices" and will be adopted by organizations, including MNCs, because their adoption ensures the survival of the organization. The adoption processes leads to isomorphism of organizations populating the same organizational field (e.g. Meyer 1994). Neo-institutionalists believe that organizations adopt certain managerial ideas and organizational practices not so much because they are seen as efficient, which is linked to economic success in rationalistic approaches, but because adoption is seen as crucial in order to enhance an organization's legitimacy and thus its survival within its institutional environments (DiMaggio and Powell 1991; Scott 2001).

It is further emphasized that similar organizational ideas and practices are not just spread across certain societies or industrial sectors, but become increasingly globally standardized (e.g. Meyer 2000; Tempel and Walgenbach 2007). Regulative, normative and cognitive-cultural institutional pressures are seen as the three key mechanisms for the transfer of organizational practices across the globe (Kostova 1999; Scott 2001). The *regulative* mechanism refers to the influence of transnational regulatory bodies and organizations such as the World Trade Organization (WTO); the *normative* mechanism refers to the increased professionalization of management and organizations based on certificates such as MBAs; and the *cognitive-cultural* mechanism refers to the increasing impact of globally shared ideas and ideologies, such as liberalization of markets, which are understood as leading to an increased diffusion of global best practices which are both adopted and spread by MNCs. At the same time, it is argued that MNCs must comply with the different institutionalized expectations of the various institutional environments in which they operate when adopting and implementing certain management ideas and practices across national borders (Kostova 1999). Similarly to evolutionary studies, which point to the need of MNC management to balance the demands of both global and local market environments, institutionalists believe that managers face two *conflicting isomorphic pulls*: (1) the international pull of the overall strategies and structures of the MNC which need "approval" of stakeholders across the world, and (2) the national pull of expectations within the host countries where the MNC operates (Westney 1993). The neo-institutionalist idea of isomorphism is applied to the MNC as follows: MNCs always require legitimacy, hence they must seek the acceptance and approval of constituents at various levels and in various institutional environments. That means external institutional pulls from home and host countries lead to tensions based on diverse institutional pressures, and internal isomorphic pulls lead to convergence, meaning the adoption of similar organizational strategies and structures across the MNC (Westney 1993; see also Kostova and Zaheer 1999). However, the political consequences of these conflicting isomorphic pulls for the MNC have not been considered systematically by neo-institutionalists because of their over-socialized conception of actors. Thus they have been criticized for ignoring the socio-political dimension of local adoption of managerial practices, i.e. all the questions of who pulls, why and how (see e.g. Geppert and Williams 2006: 52–4).

A key argument brought forward in neo-institutionalist studies of the MNC is that conflicting isomorphic pulls are especially a problem when *institutional distance* between the home country of an MNC (where organizational practices originate) and the host country (where organizational practices are transferred) of one of its subsidiaries is high, resulting in a situation where regulatory, normative and cognitive-cultural pressures are very different for the HQ than they are for the subsidiary (Kostova and Roth 2002; Xu and Shenkar 2002). This problem is discussed as *institutional duality* between home and host country contexts and leads to problems in transferring knowledge across the MNC and for subsidiaries to adopt best practices locally. The role of power relations in these processes is at least mentioned, but only in a very limited way. It is argued that the "dependency" of a subsidiary on its HQ will influence the degree to which the subsidiary "adopts," "implements" and "internalizes" practices and ideas transferred by the HQ. Four patterns of adoption by subsidiaries are distinguished: "active," "minimal," "assent" and "ceremonial." In this framework, power and politics are conceptualized as a side issue, coming into play mainly when subsidiaries "feel high dependence" on the HQ (Kostova and Roth 2002: 230).

In summary, politics and power relations in the MNC has only randomly been addressed by neo-institutionalist scholars. Their focus on institutional isomorphism and an over-socialized view of actors has hindered the development of a detailed understanding of the political dynamics triggered by conflicting isomorphic pulls and institutional duality. The different interests and identities of actors involved in legitimizing and/or de-legitimizing certain organizational practices, and the political implications of these processes, are hardly acknowledged. Neo-institutionalist studies of the MNC neglect to relate their key constructs, such as institutional distance and duality, to societal differences in power distribution between various stakeholders, which have an important impact on power relations within the MNC. Addressing this issue is a central contribution of comparative institutionalist studies, as we examine in the next section.

European comparative institutionalist studies: explicit but static view of power and politics in the MNC

European comparative institutionalist studies assume that the degree of social and societal embeddedness differs significantly between capitalist societies, so that "best practices" developed in the home country are shaped by that country's institutions and must be adapted locally when transferred to other countries. Leading comparative institutionalists question evolutionary scholars' belief that transnational models of the MNC based on the emergence of global structures and "mindsets" will encourage learning across borders, stressing that this "is only likely to happen under particular, rather limited, conditions" (Whitley 1999: 146). Alternatively, Whitley proposes that the MNC is "a distinct organizational form," emphasizing that influences of distinct national "institutional factors mean that most MNCs do not share significant amounts of decision-making across national borders nor do they develop global careers that could facilitate extensive and long-term collaborative learning across countries" (Whitley 1999: 162).

In comparison to North American neo-institutionalists, research by these scholars is not so much focused on isomorphic institutional pressures leading to various degrees of adoption of organizational practices, but rather on how home and host country institutional features, such as the financial, corporate governance, industrial relations, training and skill development and innovation systems, are interrelated with work and employment systems within the MNC (see e.g. Geppert at al. 2003; Whitley 2001). Moreover, environmental institutional influences are not so much discussed in terms of institutional distance, e.g. between home country of the MNC and host country of subsidiaries, but in terms of societal distinctiveness of national institutional regimes, which Whitley calls national business systems. A key question is how societally distinct combinations of market and non-market related forms of coordination (e.g. forms of ownership control, skill development and involvement of lower-level managers and employees in decision-making) influence capability building and authority sharing within firms, including the MNC (Whitley 1999). Jackson and Deeg (2008) argue that European institutionalists have "developed a theory of comparative institutional advantage in which different institutional arrangements have distinct strengths and weaknesses for different kinds of economic activity" (Jackson and Deeg 2008: 541). They suggest that societal institutions create distinct and coherent types of capitalism. The most popular typology (actually a dichotomy) demonstrating institutional diversity of capitalist economies is based on the seminal work of political-economists Hall and Soskice (2001), which distinguishes between liberal and coordinated market economies. Another, more sophisticated and sociologically based typology which deals directly with MNCs has been developed by Whitley. He also makes the distinction between various degrees of coordination in capitalist economies, and classifies six types of capitalism: two more liberal types with low impact on non-market coordination mechanisms (called fragmented and compartmentalized), and four more coordinated types of national business systems (called industrial districts, state organized, collaborative and highly coordinated) (Whitley 1999). He suggests that coordinated market economies have a comparative advantage in manufacturing, because their distinct societal institutions support the specialization of firms in diversified quality production (e.g. Sorge and Streeck 1988), which requires long-term corporate finance, incremental innovations, high skills, more collaborative modes of organizing the supply chain, interdependent arrangements between managers and employees and employee involvement (Hall and Soskice 2001; Whitley 1999). In contrast, it has been shown that the particular institutional features of liberal market economies such as the USA have supported more radical innovations and the specialization of firms in other industries, e.g. the software and entertainment sector (Hollingsworth 1997).

Differences in national institutional regimes are seen as the basis of historically distinct patterns of industrialization, leading to different forms of industrial sector specialization and development of firm-specific capabilities. It is assumed that these developments explain not only differences in the internationalization strategies of MNCs (Whitley 2001), but also how authority is shared within the MNC (Whitley 1999) and how the HQ controls its subsidiaries (Harzing and Sorge 2003). Accordingly, for European institutionalists, power relations in MNCs are largely shaped by distinct home country institutional features. Whitley (1999) conceptualizes power in terms of Weber's ideas on legitimate authority, reflected especially in how authority is shared: (a) between owners and top managers both in the HQ and at the subsidiary level, (b) between HQ and subsidiaries, and c) between top management and lower level employees and groups of employees at the work systems level (Whitley 1999, 2001). Liberal market economies, it is assumed, are characterized by the direct control of owners (e.g. reflected in strong shareholder value orientation) and the weak influence of other external stakeholders (such as employer and employee associations), combined with strong authority of top management and weak influence of lower level management and employees (Hall and Soskice 2001). Accordingly, this research has shown that MNCs from liberal market economies (such as the USA), because of lower degrees of social commitment to power sharing with various internal and external stakeholders and pressure from stock owners to meet short-term financial goals, have developed more standardized organizational practices and transfer them internationally as "best practices" (Almond and Ferner 2006; Geppert *et al.* 2003). In comparison, MNCs originating from coordinated market economies are understood to have more difficulties in standardizing and transferring their home-country-developed idiosyncratic organizational practices, due to greater social commitments with stakeholders and because host countries often do not "offer" the same high level of institutional support as the home country in terms of skills development for lower level managers and employees (Whitley 1999). Moreover, it is suggested that the lack of "complementarities" between home and host country institutions has led to "avoidance strategies," i.e. MNCs from liberal markets avoid investing in coordinated markets such as Germany because of "constraining" host country institutions (see e.g. Tempel 2002). Research also found evidence that German MNCs only selectively transfer home-country work and organizational practices to subsidiaries in less coordinated emerging market economies, avoiding institutional "constraints" of the home country (Bluhm 2001; Dörrenbächer 2004).

In summary, European comparative institutionalists assert that the distribution of authority and power within MNCs cannot be understood without reflecting their societal institutional features and foundations, which differ significantly across countries. This is an important message that is hardly addressed in mainstream IB literature, including in neo-institutionalist studies of the MNC. They argue that the rationalistic assumptions in eclectic IB research about the need of owners to control managerial opportunism and its political implications for conceptualizing power in MNCs must be treated with caution, because the specific societal context of such models is ignored.[4] The same is true for the work of scholars studying subsidiary initiatives and entrepreneurship, which assumes that internal and external markets are sufficient to understand the success or failure of mandate development and whether subsidiaries gain or lose power when negotiating with the HQ. Both power resources and criteria for success cannot be fully

---

[4] It has been stressed that key assumptions of transaction cost economics as well as principal–agency theory are biased because they reflect ideal-typical features of a liberal market economy. Non-market coordination is only considered in terms of suboptimal outcomes by rationalistic scholars.

understood without considering their interrelationship with home and host country specific institutions.

Like the other approaches discussed above, comparative institutionalism neglects to bring power relations in HQ and subsidiaries to life and shed more light on the "contests" and dynamic political processes that both sustain and undermine authority of powerful managers and other stakeholders. Power and politics are conceptualized in a rather static and over-socialized way, i.e. interests and identities are understood as being ingrained in the key features of the national business systems which have developed in a path-dependent way. Both North American neo-institutionalist and European comparative institutionalist scholars have only recently begun to understand power and politics within the MNC in a less deterministic and rigid manner, a trend that we will come back to in our next section.

Studying power and politics in the MNC: the role of institutions, interests and identities

Power and politics in MNCs: towards a more bottom-up and more actor-centered perspective

In the former sections we have argued that leading concepts either have little to say about power in MNCs or conceptualize it in a very specific managerialist and/or functionalist manner. In our view, this is related to the fact that the role of *agency* and its importance in understanding politics and power in MNCs is either neglected or not fully explored. Economic theories of the firm, including the eclectic OLI paradigm, are mainly interested in actors that make efficient decisions in order to minimize transaction costs and increase the economic performance of the international ventures of the MNC (see also Haunschild *et al.* 2009). Evolutionary scholars, including those who study subsidiary entrepreneurship, adopt a managerialist orientation to politics and power. They discuss power and politics in an implicit manner as a function of management: managers need to balance global–local dilemmas and the HQ has to give up power (need for local responsiveness) or centralize its power (need for global integration), if strategy and organizational structures do not fit with economic and task environmental demands. The scholars studying entrepreneurship, drawing largely on resource dependency theory, are mainly interested in how either HQ or subsidiaries gain or lose power, applying rationalistic premises to how top managers either in the HQ or in subsidiaries make decisions and negotiate deals. In these approaches, actors make either rational choices which lead to improved economic performance or they take suboptimal decisions based on irrational assumptions, leading to dysfunctional results that are considered as a sign of inefficient organization and management.

In contrast, both neo-institutionalist and comparative institutionalist studies of the MNC stress that managerial decisions are social context bound. However, both institutionalist approaches are highly focused on the "historical development and structural contextualization" of organizations (Reed 1996: 43) and neglect to reflect on how structures and institutions are locally produced and reproduced "through micro-level practices" (Reed 1996). In short, the focus is on how macro-level institutional logics shape power relations within the MNC, ignoring "interactional processes or 'micro-politics' through which power relationships are temporarily sedimented into relatively permanent and stable authority structures" (Fincham 1992: 742). The emphasis should be put here on "temporarily," meaning that micro-political processes are dialectical, referring to both aspects of social agency which can stabilize but also destabilize established power relation and authority, e.g. of the HQ.

It is here where our volume makes a new contribution, by providing a more bottom-up interactionist view that goes beyond mainstream studies to open up new routes for studying power and politics in the MNC. We build on two new developments in neo-institutionalist and comparative institutionalist research, which see the study of the MNC as a challenge for theory building and call for a more actor-centered approach with power and politics at center stage. We will discuss these new developments next, followed by a section reflecting on how the research in this volume contributes to them, both conceptually and empirically.

The MNC as a challenge for mainstream neo-institutionalist theory: a call to study social agency

The first new development in institutionalist theories about the MNC can be seen in a recent "provocative" essay by Kostova *et al.* (2008) which questions whether basic ideas of neo-institutionalism can be uncritically applied to the study of MNCs. They argue that, despite being subject to institutional influences, "MNCs have a very different institutional story that fits better the conditions of equivocality, ambiguity, and complexity" (Kostova *et al.* 2008: 997). Reflecting critically on neo-institutionalist key ideas, they conclude that a "blended institutional perspective" is needed to study MNCs, leaving space for understanding the role of social agency and power and politics. The main argument is that the MNC as a collective actor has the power to influence transnational and national institution building, and that its subunits and individual key actors are not just responding to a variety of institutional pressures and "pulls," but that MNCs are political arenas where powerful actors "must make sense, manipulate, negotiate, and partially construct their institutional environments" (Kostova *et al.* 2008: 1001). The former view is in line with Morgan's research (2001b), which argues that MNCs do not just respond to regulative institutional pressures but actively influence transnational standard setting, e.g. product standards, "fit and proper person" standards and standards of "fair dealing" (Morgan 2001b: 228–47). This research comes close to the focus of our volume, by showing that MNCs should not be seen as coherent organizations which can be controlled top-down and which mainly respond to external economic and institutional pressures, leaving no "space" for social agency.

In this approach, social agency comes into play for two reasons. First, the agency of individuals becomes important because isomorphic institutional pressures are seen as "limited" in the case of the MNC, which "creates a rich landscape of diverse practices and patterns of activity" (Kostova *et al.* 2008: 999). This "institutional freedom" provides actors with strategic choices (Child 1972), an issue which links this debate to earlier debates conceptualizing MNCs as transnational social spaces, which will be discussed in more detail in our next section. Second, it is assumed that actors' strategies to achieve legitimacy make MNCs not more, but less similar. This argument touches directly on the political dimension of social agency and institution building, because institutions are seen not just as constraining agencies but also as enabling factors, a fact which has political implications. The political implications that Kostova *et al.* (2008) have in mind are twofold. First, they emphasize the "symbolic" aspects of interaction processes in MNCs in which an image or identity is presented to outside stakeholders even though this does not necessarily mean that transferred "best practices" are actually implemented. In addition, they stress that because MNC contexts are less homogenous than originally assumed, actors must increasingly deal with "institutional contradictions," creating room for "praxis" (see also Seo and Creed 2002), i.e. room for political action to challenge existing or established institutional regimes or organizational practices.

This new institutionalist approach argues that the key tools of mainstream neo-institutionalist studies of the MNC (e.g. the role of isomorphism and how legitimacy is achieved across national and intra-organizational borders) need to be revised. A more actor-centered approach is needed to understand the dialectics of institutional stability and change, which brings the role of political processes and power relations in the MNC from the shadows into the limelight. It is acknowledged that collective and individual actors have different identities and interests, creating (transnational) social spaces which are increasingly "contested," especially when MNC strategies narrowly focus on financial control mechanisms and global standardization of organization and work.

The MNC as a challenge for comparative institutionalism: the MNC as a socio-politically contested terrain

The second new institutionalist development introduces ideas about the MNC as a "transnational social space" (Geppert and Williams 2006; Morgan 2001b) and a "contested terrain" (e.g. Edwards and Bélanger 2009; Ferner *et al.* 2006). Similarly to Kostova *et al.* (2008), this approach challenges mainstream studies of the MNC by stressing that these are not unique organizational forms but multi-level and diverse organizations which must socially and societally embed their managerial and organizational practices locally. It is suggested that this is actually a more difficult process in the case of the MNC because the diversity of contextual rationalities of both collective and individual actors is much higher than in a domestic firm. This argument also points to the socio-political dimensions of emerging transnational social spaces within and through the various cross-border activities of the MNC. Here different actors within the MNC, their particular identities and interests, as well as the social constitution of their agency come to the fore (cf. Becker-Ritterspach 2006; Becker-Ritterspach and Dörrenbächer 2009, 2011; Clark and Geppert 2006, 2011; Dörrenbächer 2007; Dörrenbächer and Geppert 2006, 2007, 2009a, 2009b, 2010). From a socio-political perspective the impact of the key actors' career patterns, their professional and career ambitions, their specific resource mobilization strategies and their political sensemaking approaches are highlighted. In short, it is shown that local adaptation of global strategies and "best practices" cannot be reduced to its technical or economic rational and institutional constraining nature, but involves often lively and dynamic political activities of actors, making the MNC a "contested terrain." This also means that the process of political contestation is not just an "effect," following the "logic" of relatively stable and coherent home country or host country institutional features, as mainstream comparative institutionalist scholars believe. MNCs are indeed social constructs enacted by powerful actors which bring diverse and sometimes contradictory "contextual rationalities" into play when contesting and negotiating the methods and degrees of local adaptations. Taking a bottom-up view, the analysis of the MNC as transnational social space focuses on the process and political nature of the internal functioning and structuring of the MNC, which is constituted by a "set of relations between a range of actors with their own powers and interests. Decision processes are characterized by political bargaining and negotiation" (Morgan 2001a: 9–10). Scholars studying the MNC as a "contested terrain" suggest conceptualizing them as a political system, referring to earlier organization studies (e.g. Cyert and March 1992; Mintzberg 1985; Pettigrew 1973), as well as to employment relations studies (Edwards and Bélanger 2009), which have consistently focused on the political nature of management and organizations, in contrast to large parts of organization studies. Accordingly, MNCs are understood as being "coalitions, fragmented not only between competing social forces but across national institutional domains, and along various "horizontal cross-national organizational dimensions, leading to the pervasiveness of a micro-politics with distinct characteristics that reflect the international dimension of MNCs' operations" (Ferner *et al.* 2006: 9). Related to this approach, we would like to highlight three important "distinct characteristics" of the "contested" nature of transnational social spaces in MNCs.

First, it can be argued that the formal authority and power structures of MNCs are not "footloose" but fragmented, bringing together divergent collective and individual actors with different histories and experiences. This is even the case in highly globalized industries and MNCs, as Sorge and Rothe's chapter demonstrates, and is especially important for MNCs that are products of mergers and acquisitions. Therefore, it has been suggested that instead of concentrating on formal authority and power structures, MNCs should be studied as "federations of national companies where expertise and knowledge rested in national contexts" (Morgan and Kristensen 2009) and where the HQ has little ability or interest to exert full control. The HQ's ability to impose hierarchical control and globally standardized organization structures and processes is highly limited, even when they attempt otherwise. Accordingly, Kristensen and Zeitlin (2001), based on an in-depth case study, argue that the "MNC's 'administrative heritage' continues to be diverse and rooted in the experience that local actors had gained from their involvement in the games of diverse regional and national business systems" (Kristensen and Zeitlin 2001: 188). This actually includes not just the subsidiaries but also the HQ, where key actors have had their own experiences when internation-alizing across borders.

Second, the idea of political contestation stresses the importance of local resource-building activities in order to both resist and negotiate the trans-fer and implementation of organizational practices and strategies developed elsewhere. It is shown that local managers and employees in certain local and national contexts have more opportunities to draw on resources and mobil-ize the political support of internal and external stakeholders in processes of political contestation, e.g. with the HQ and governmental bodies about global restructuring and subsidiary mandate development (Geppert and Williams 2006; Kristensen and Zeitlin 2001; Williams and Geppert in this volume). This research has shown that in transnational corporations (which it was assumed are better equipped to deal with the global–local dilemma) local resource-building activities are of utmost importance and require skill-ful political activities (see e.g. Bélanger *et al.* 2003; see also Sorge and Rothe's chapter). For these political activities, local actors draw on distinct societal institutional features, e.g. supportive industrial relations and high-quality skill development systems, which we find in certain regions and manufac-turing sectors of Germany (see e.g. chapters of Williams and Geppert and of Sorge and Rothe in this volume). However, this research also suggests that societal institutional features are only supportive for local actors in certain core sectors of the German economy, and that in other sectors, e.g. food retailing (Wortmann 2004) and fast food (Royle 2002), local actors have fewer opportunities to resist.

This brings us to the third distinct characteristic of contestation that we would like to highlight – the crucial role of social actors in micro-political games played within MNCs. Pioneering research, especially by Kristensen and Zeitlin (2001, 2005) and by authors taking a socio-political perspective (e.g. Becker-Ritterspach and Dörrenbächer 2009; Dörrenbächer and Geppert 2007) has suggested that political contestation can be studied in the various micro-political games found in MNCs. Most studies have focused on the study of micro-political games played between the HQ and its subsidiar-ies to influence budget allocation, mandate change and relocation decisions (Dörrenbächer and Geppert 2009b). Moreover, new micro-political games have emerged around the implementation of benchmarking systems and coercive comparisons in order to meet increasing demands by shareholders and pressures from investors and capital markets (Morgan and Kristensen 2006). The analysis of micro-political game-playing starts from the bottom and asks how different identities and interests of key actors stabilize and destabilize established institutional, cultural and organizational structures, and not the other way around as in mainstream institutionalist approaches. Morgan and Kristensen's (2006) research is a good example of how the role of diverse identities and interests can be analyzed. They distinguish between "Boy Scout" strategists and "subversive" strategists, who respond differently to increased HQ pressures, e.g. to introduce benchmarking systems and coercive comparisons between locations designed to meet increasingly short-term expectations of shareholders. The authors argue that the "Boy Scout" approach of implementing HQ measures can not only lead to the emergence of "transnational battlefields with the MNC in extreme cases, but can also undermine the long and mid-term capabilities of subsidiaries to build resources of entrepreneurship, the basis of being a powerful player in the micro-political games of internationalization. "Subversive" strategies – those based on high resistance, aggressive bargaining and strong local support – might be more suited to maintaining and enhancing local resources to play "the game." Another example of this approach can be seen in recent research on socio-political sensemaking in MNCs operating in post-communist countries, by Clark and Geppert (2011). This research stresses that different identities of subsidiary key actors can be "local patriotic" or "cosmopolitan" strategic orientated, which leads to different approaches of political strategizing when negotiating with HQ managers, who also have their own distinct interests and identities, leading to either ethnocentric or more polycentric strategies in negotiations with local managers. From this perspective, four scenarios or different "political sensemaking" processes are distinguished, which creates either institutionally and politically stable transnational social spaces based on developing mutual interests and shared identities, or more unstable and conflicting transnational social spaces drifting into "disorder."

In summary, in contrast to most mainstream studies that are focused on how MNCs are managed, structured and institutionally constrained, the new approaches reviewed above bring attention to the role of the diverse interests, ideologies and identities of key actors initiating and constituting micro-political games. Power relations are seen as dynamic and relational, interactively created not just by key actors (managers) but also by employees, including international trade unions and their representatives (e.g. Edwards and Bélanger 2009). The latter are often neglected because of the managerialist focus of mainstream IB research, but must be seen as a crucial part of local resource-building activities.

The role of institutions, interests and identities in studying power and politics in the MNC: conceptual ideas and empirical evidence in the contributing chapters

In the previous two sections we have seen that power is not the property of a person (e.g. manager or employee) or an organizational unit (e.g. HQ or subsidiary), but a social relation which is more fragmented and complex, especially in the MNC, than often assumed in functionalist and rationalistic studies that focus on which managers and entities are gaining and losing power. This is because of the diverse contextual identities and interests that constitute the MNC as a contested terrain. Even when power relations are asymmetrical and the HQ or a top manager have some authority to exercise power over other subunits and members of the multinational firm, subsidiaries and lower level managers and employees are not "powerless" and can "gain" influence in decision-making if they actively participate in political processes and micro-political games played in the firm (Bouquet and Birkinshaw 2008). These games are based on formal and informal rules (Crozier and Friedberg 1980), and actors can draw on different resources and skills to influence the setting of these rules. "The rules of the game" developed in the HQ or elsewhere, e.g. by local, national and transnational rule-making bodies, need to be contextualized and interpreted, which opens room for agency and contestation (see e.g. Hardy and Clegg 1996: 634). In comparison to mainstream IB and institutionalist studies, discussed above, we see actors, i.e. managers and employees of the MNC, not just as rule-takers, as often emphasized by institutionalist scholars, or just as rule-makers, often assumed by rationalistic IB approaches (see e.g. Jackson 2010). Organizational rules and practices are often ambiguous and sometimes more contradictory than often assumed (Jackson 2010: 78–9), which makes it difficult for rule-makers to set efficient or clear rules and define best practices transnationally. Moreover, actors might not be able or willing to take (or adapt to) established rules (coercive institutional pressures) and implement best practices (normative institutional pressures), because they are in open or latent conflict with contextual interests and identities of other actors (see also chapter of Blazejewski and Becker-Ritterspach in this volume). In short, actors are interested in achieving legitimacy, when making and taking the rules of the game, both locally and across national borders. This should be seen as political processes, which are mediated by existing power relations. In line with Knights and McCabe (1999), we understand power as "a medium of 'relations' in which subjectivity, as a complex, contradictory, shifting experience, is produced, transformed or reproduced through the social practices within which power is exercised"

(1999: 203). In short, power relations are context-specific (institutional and culturally shaped but not determined) and interactively and discursively constituted by actors with specific identities and interests (subjectivity).

The aim of this volume is to highlight the work of a number of scholars who explore how diverse and ambiguous institutions, interests and identities come into play in terms of MNC power relations and political processes. There are three common threads running through the contributions.

First (in section II), the authors examine the wider national institutional and cultural context, especially how *local embeddedness and societal institutions* both constrain and enable actors to build power resources and mobilize political support. The chapter of **Sorge and Rothe** uses the example of two jet engine manufacturing MNCs – one British and one US – to demonstrate that local subsidiaries situated in Germany do not take local resources for granted as often assumed in the varieties of capitalism literature, but are actively involved in the social construction of these resources. Based on qualitative case studies and historical industry data, the authors show the role of micro-politics in influencing local investment decisions. The authors demonstrate that German sites draw on local resources such as HRM, organizational and technical capacities as well as cooperative relations with important clients, suppliers and partners in micro-political processes and negotiations with the HQ to attract local investment and to develop local resources. In short, local interests and identities are crucial to understanding both investment decisions and political resource mobilization activities. **Williams and Geppert** in their chapter argue in the same direction. Based on their understanding of MNCs as contested terrains, they shed light on how national institutional systems provide resources for local actors to strategize within their MNCs. Their focus is on the German system of employment relations that according to the authors provides plant-level actors in Germany with a particularly robust strategic tool kit to bargain globalization pressures such as intra-firm competition or cross-border standardization policies. It is stressed that the actors' strategic tools look particularly robust when viewed from an Anglo-German comparative angle. Screening the literature on institutional change in Germany, the authors further argue that this will continue into the future, since perceivable disintegration tendencies in the German system of employment relations do not extend to manufacturing core sectors such as the automotive, metalworking and chemical industries. The last chapter of this section, by **Fenton O'Creevy** *et al.*, stresses again the role of social embeddedness but argues that the social skills of actors, especially in bridging roles, are important to understanding local adaptation processes when knowledge is transferred from HQ to subsidiaries. Drawing on data from an ongoing research project and two exploratory case studies of a French and a Norwegian MNC, the authors' research demonstrates that the effectiveness of actors in bridging roles, meaning individual managers which are members of multiple social networks and communities within the MNC, is not so much related to their location in the social network, but to their "cognitive flexibility," "brokering skills" and other social skills. The power position and political strategies of these brokers are linked to their skills in translating meaning between different social, cultural and institutional contexts. They show that some actors in bridging roles act more in the interest of the HQ and others identify more with the local context, leading to the corruption of HQ initiatives.

Second (in section III), the contributors address the role of diverse MNC actors' *interests* in political processes within MNCs. Focusing on subsidiaries and HQ as core MNC actors, *interest formation*, political strategizing and contestation are studied, with conflicts in headquarters–subsidiary relationships being at the center of all contributions. As an introduction, the chapter by **Blazejewski and Becker-Ritterspach** critically reviews theory-bound literature on conflicts in headquarters–subsidiary relations. Overall the chapter identifies 17 contributions that in essence address conflicts in headquarters–subsidiary relations and that show a dedicated interest in using, exploring or developing theories of conflict. These contributions stem from rather diverse theoretical backgrounds, including contingency theory, agency theory, institutional theory, game theory, social identity and role theory. Presenting and analyzing these contributions, Blazejewski and Becker-Ritterspach argue that future theory-bound literature on conflicts in MNCs needs to put a stronger emphasis on three issues: (1) the theoretical link between power and conflict, (2) the role of actors and their structural embeddedness and (3) the process of headquarters–subsidiary conflicts. Focusing on one prominent type of conflict in headquarters–subsidiary relations, i.e. conflicts that emanate from subsidiaries rejecting HQ initiatives, the chapter by **Schotter and Beamish** begins by uncovering when such rejections turn into conflicts. Based on a two-phase quantitative study in US and European MNCs, the authors propose that conflicts on HQ initiative rejections are more likely to occur if communication problems and perception gaps exist between HQs and subsidiaries and if HQs see one or more of their vital interests (global competitiveness of the whole MNC, decision-making authority of the HQ, coordination effectiveness) negatively affected. Next, the chapter takes a closer look at the tactics subsidiaries apply in such conflicts to safeguard their interests. Here the authors distinguish between subsidiaries that showed a stronger sense of belonging to the MNC by displaying a functional task and process orientation in their initiative rejection and others that exhibit different levels of dysfunctional conflict behavior, with the latter encompassing ignoring, redefining, ceremonially adopting, obstructing and attacking the HQ initiative. Finally, "linking power and conflict" (as suggested by Blazejewski and Becker-Ritterspach, see above), the authors maintain that subsidiaries that are relatively more powerful and less dependent on HQ also used more aggressive tactics, including obstructing or attacking HQ initiatives. As the contribution of Schotter and Beamish, the subsequent chapter by **Dörrenbächer and Gammelgaard** looks into a particular hotspot of headquarters–subsidiary relations, namely headquarters-driven charter losses at foreign subsidiaries. Analyzing in depth three episodes of such charter losses at the Hungarian subsidiary of a German MNC over a period of 15 years (1989–2004), the chapter highlights how the particular inner and outer context shaped the interests and behaviors of both the headquarters and the subsidiary in relation to these episodes. Changes in context (from a transition/modernization context to a cross-border rationalization context) translated into changes of interest and behavior (from conciliatory to domination behavior in the case of headquarters and from "Boy Scout" to subversive behavior in the case of the subsidiary). This in turn led to open conflict. The chapter also demonstrates that episodes of headquarters-driven charter loss need to be seen as interrelated events with interests and behaviors at prior episodes having a strong impact on later episodes. The last chapter of this section by **Schmid and Daniel** addresses conflicts in headquarters–subsidiary relationships from a social psychological perspective. Based on Katz and Kahn's open systems approach the authors develop a conceptual framework that explains conflict in headquarters–subsidiary relationships as a consequence of perception gaps between HQ and subsidiary representatives regarding the subsidiary's role. The authors maintain that conflicts emanating from perception gaps might take the form of distribution conflicts, process conflicts or goal conflicts, which is exemplified in detail with regard to perception gaps related to subsidiary capabilities. Finally, the chapter recommends a clear role definition and frequent and open exchange on role perceptions between HQ and subsidiaries as central means to avoid perception gaps and hence related conflicts.

Third (in section IV), the contributions examine the issue of *identity work* and *identity politics* within the local subsidiary itself, which can lead to political conflicts, stereotyping and sometimes misunderstandings, conflicts of interest and political struggle. Here, not only the power and political approaches of local managers and expats are considered but also the role of identities and interests of employees in micro-political game-playing and power struggles. The first contribution of this section can be seen as an attempt to open mainstream culturalist research, which has been criticized for being static and failing to address micro-political processes in the MNC, and introduce a more socio-political perspective. The other three contributions of section IV take an explicit processual view of politics and power by stressing the role of multiple and often contradictory identities dealing with various national cultural and institutional pressures, which leaves room for agency and political strategizing. The chapter of **Williams** studies the impact host country culture has on subsidiary managers' socio-political interaction. Socio-political interaction is captured here by three items: (1) subsidiary managers' knowledge-sharing behavior, (2) his or her proactive behavior, and (3) his or her consent to a set of MNC-wide norms and values (normative integration). Based on a large-scale survey of middle managers located in various subsidiaries of MNCs around the world, the chapter suggests that societal culture matters to MNC internal political phenomena, with notable differences between vertical (with HQ) and horizontal (with peer subsidiaries) interaction. The chapter by **Ybema and Byun** deals with Japanese–Dutch work relations in both Japanese and Dutch MNCs. It is an ethnographic study on how organizational actors talk cultural identities into existence by drawing cultural distinctions between themselves and others, with the purpose of using this sense of identity and cultural distance in political struggles in MNCs. The situated, constructed and strategic nature of cross-cultural identity discourse is demonstrated in a close look at four core issues making up work relations: work ethos, style of communication, superior–subordinate relationship and decision-making. The chapter of **Koveshnikov** shows how national identity construction is linked with power relations within two Russian subsidiaries, a brownfield and a greenfield site, of two Finnish MNCs. It shows especially that national identities are not static and cannot fully be understood without analyzing the subjectivity and political interests of key actors, meaning Russian managers. The study is mainly based on in-depth interviews, providing a rich database to analyze discourses that Russian managers use when constructing their national identities. The research points to two political struggles in which Russian managers engaged when dealing with HQ and globalization pressures. On the one hand, managers tried to present themselves as more "global" than their Finnish counterparts. This is interpreted as a strategic approach to actively resisting attempts of Finns to present western knowledge as universal and superior, and of course as an attempt to improve their power position in the globalization discourse with the Finnish HQ. On the other hand, the discursive struggles of the Russian managers were seen as a strategic approach to preserve their cultural distinctiveness of being Russian as a resource to resist Finnish HQ attempts to impose certain strategic approaches. The author stresses implications of both discursive struggles for power relations within the MNC, especially in terms of Russian managers' attempts to improve subjective and organizational power resources. *Maclean and Hollinshead's* chapter also discusses the role of social identity construction in reference to the "habitus" of not just managers but also of employees of a Serbian subsidary of a Turkish brewery. The authors show that institutional distance is not a sufficient concept to analyze power and politics in MNCs and suggest studying power from an interactionist view as a "relational" construct. Applying this perspective, they found five strategies through which Serbian managers socially constructed their power base: (1) language proficiency, (2) familiarity with western management "tool kits," (3) international experience and fluency in management rhetoric, (4) local knowledge of the Serbian market, and (5) social capital through former employment at the parent company and other western drinks MNCs. However, they also stress the problem of asymmetry of power relations between employees and managers in post-socialist Serbian firms, where workers have fewer opportunities to build power resources (e.g. social capital, social and language skills) as managers in order to escape "their current fate."

Finally, our concluding chapter (in section V) makes a full circle back to the starting point of this chapter, pointing to the need to study politics and power at the micro, meso and macro-level. Moreover, new directions are identified for future research on political issues in the MNC. *Morgan* argues that the micro-politics of multinationals need to be accompanied by a macro-political approach, because MNCs are simultaneously impacted and have an impact on multiple contexts, leading to important questions that have been neglected in traditional institutionalist and culturalist studies, because actors were treated as "cultural dopes." He suggests studying MNCs as transnational social spaces with a diverse set of legitimated practices. With respect to power and politics, the question is which actors' and contexts' legitimacy counts most. Answering this question, Morgan suggests first, that transnational social spaces are pre-structured and therefore need to be studied more carefully, based on detailed empirical analysis in order to show the degree of institutional diversity. In short, the author argues that macro-political and structural differences between MNCs – e.g. whether they originate in small or large countries, operate in manufacturing or service sectors and the degree of investment, sales and employment – matter to understanding the overall logic of micro-political games played in the MNC. Secondly, it is stressed that IB researchers have failed to study MNCs as legal, financial and accounting entities to develop a deeper insight into decisions about investment, disinvestment, closure of sites, mergers and acquisitions etc. Finally, Morgan's chapter points to the urgent need to study global managerial elites, and questions which managers become part of these elites and how and with what effect.

Concluding remarks

The contributions to this volume show that "life is lively" (Ortmann 1988: 7) in multinationals, with power and politics playing an important role. The authors examine how actors with various interests and identities interact across cultural and functional borders, leading to micro-political game-playing when interests or identities conflict. Solving these conflicts requires skillful actors, able to negotiate and develop shared meanings (see also Clark and Geppert 2011; Jackson 2010). Concepts and ideas brought forward in this volume draw heavily on organizational sociology and social psychology, and relevant ideas about power as a social relation which is interactively created in an interplay of social agency with wider societal and intra-organizational structures. We have seen that institutions and structures are not just constraints to social agency but also provide rules and resources (Giddens 1984), enabling actors in the MNC both to resist and to negotiate institutional, social, organizational, technological and economic pressures for change under the banner of globalization. In short, we hope that this volume does more than "fill a gap" in IB research, where power and politics in the MNC has been either completely neglected or addressed in a very limited way. The contributions of our book have not just shown *that* power matters but discuss *how* and *why* power matters, pointing to the political interactions of key power holders and actors within the MNC, both managers and employees. We hope that our book provides insights that will help to overcome a common problem in organization studies – that "power remains the most overused and at least understood concept in organization analysis" (Reed 1996: 40).

Acknowledgement

The authors would like to thank participants of subtheme 5 on the "Politicized MNC: the role of actors and institutions" at the 3rd LAEMOS conference in Buenos Aires in April 2010, especially John Child and Suzanna Rodriguez, and participants of the research seminar at the Nijmegen School of Management in May 2010, especially Max Visser, for their helpful comments on an earlier draft. Moreover, we wish to thank Cly Wallace for her support with comments and the editing of this chapter.

REFERENCES

Almond, P. and A. Ferner 2006. American Multinationals in Europe: Managing Employment Relations across National Borders. Oxford University Press

Andersson, U. and U. Holm 2010. Managing the Contemporary Multinational. Cheltenham: Edward Elgar

Andersson, U., M. Forsgren and U. Holm 2007. "Balancing subsidiary influence in the federative MNC: a business network view," Journal of International Business Studies 38: 802–18

Barner-Rasmussen, W., R. Piekkari, J. Scott-Kennel and C. Welch 2010. "Commander-in-chief or absentee landlord?: key perspectives on headquarters in multinational corporations" in Andersson and Holm (eds.) Managing the Contemporary Multinational. Cheltenham: Edward Elgar, pp. 85–105

Bartlett, C. A. and S. Ghoshal 1989. Managing Across Borders: The Transnational Solution. Boston, MA: Harvard Business School Press

Becker-Ritterspach, F. 2006. "The social constitution of knowledge integration in MNEs: a theoretical framework," Journal of International Management 12: 358–86

Becker-Ritterspach, F. and C. Dörrenbächer 2009. "Intra-firm competition in multinational corporations: towards a political framework," Competition and Change 13: 199–213
    2011. "An organizational politics perspective on intra-firm competition in multinational corporations," Management International Review (in print)

Bélanger, J. and P. Edwards 2006. "Towards a political economy framework: TNCs as national and global players" in Quintanilla and Sánchez-Runde (eds.) Multinationals, Institutions and the Construction of Transnational Practices: Convergence and Diversity in the Global Economy. Basingstoke: Palgrave Macmillan, pp. 24–52

Bélanger, J., A. Giles and J.-N. Grenier 2003. "Patterns of corporate influence in the host country: a study of ABB in Canada," International Journal of Human Resource Management 14: 469–85

Birkinshaw, J. 1996. "How multinational subsidiary mandates are gained and lost," Journal of International Business Studies 27: 467–95
    2000. Entrepreneurship in the Global Firm. London: Sage

Birkinshaw, J. and J. Ridderstråle 1999. "Fighting the corporate immune system: a process study of subsidiary initiatives in multinational corporations," *International Business Review* 8: 149–80

Bluhm, K. 2001. "Exporting or abandoning the 'German Model'?: labour policies of German manufacturing firms in Central Europe," *European Journal of Industrial Relations* 7: 153–73

Bouquet, C. and J. Birkinshaw 2008. "Managing power in the multinational corporation: how low-power actors gain influence," *Journal of Management* 34: 477–508

Child, J. 1972. "Organizational structure, environment and performance: the role of strategic choice," *Sociology* 6: 1–22

Clark, E. and M. Geppert 2006. "Socio-political processes in international management in post-socialist contexts: knowledge, learning and transnational institution building," *Journal of International Management* 12: 340–57

2011. "Subsidiary integration as identity construction and institution building: a political sensemaking approach," *Journal of Management Studies* (in print)

Clegg, S. R., D. Courpasson and N. Phillips 2006. *Power and Organizations*. London: Sage

Collinson, S. and G. Morgan 2009. *Images of the Multinational Firm*. Chichester: Wiley & Sons

Crozier, M. 1964. *The Bureaucratic Phenomenon*. University of Chicago Press

Crozier, M. and E. Friedberg 1980. *Actors and Systems: The Politics of Collective Action*. University of Chicago Press

Cyert, R. M. and J. G. March 1992. *A Behavioral Theory of the Firm*. Cambridge, MA: Blackwell

DiMaggio, P. J. and W. W. Powell 1991. "The iron cage revisited: institutional isomorphism and collective rationality in organizational fields" in Powell and DiMaggio (eds.) *The new Institutionalism in Organizational Analysis*. University of Chicago Press, pp. 63–82

Dörrenbächer, C. 2004. "Fleeing or exporting the German model? The internationalization of German multinationals in the 1990s," *Competition and Change* 8: 443–56

2007. "Inside the transnational social space: cross-border management and owner relationships at a German subsidiary in Hungary," *Journal of East European Management Studies* 4: 318–39

Dörrenbächer C. and F. Becker-Ritterspach 2009. "Introducing socio-political perspectives on intra-firm competition, production relocation and outsourcing," *Competition and Change* 13: 193–8

Dörrenbächer, C. and M. Geppert 2006. "Micro-politics and conflicts in multinational corporations: current debates, reframing, and contributions of this Special Issue," *Journal of International Management* 12: 251–65

2007. "The impact of foreign subsidiary manager's socio-political positioning on career choices and their subsequent strategizing: evidence from German-owned subsidiaries in France" in Ozbilgin and Malach-Pines (eds.) *Career Choice in Management and Entrepreneurship: A Research Companion*. Cheltenham: Edward Elgar, pp. 240–57

2009a. "A micro-political perspective on subsidiary initiative-taking: evidence from German-owned subsidiaries in France," *European Management Journal* 27: 100–12

2009b. "Micro-political games in the multinational corporation: the case of mandate change," *Management Revue* 20: 373–91

2010. "Subsidiary staffing and initiative-taking in multinational corporations: a socio-political perspective," *Personnel Review* (in print)

Doz, Y. L. and C. K. Prahalad 1991. "Managing DMNCs: a search for a new paradigm," *Strategic Management Journal* 12: 145–64

Dunning, J. 2000. "The eclectic paradigm as an envelope for economic and business theories of MNE activity," *International Business Review* 9: 163–90

Dunning J. and S. M. Lundan 2009. "The multinational firm as a creator, fashioner and respondent to institutional change" in Collinson and Morgan (eds.) *Images of the Multinational Firm*. Chichester: Wiley & Sons, pp. 93–115

Dunning, J. and A. Rugman 1985. "The Influence of Hymer's dissertation on the theory of foreign direct investment," *American Economic Review* 75: 228–33

Edwards, P. and J. Bélanger 2009. "The multinational firm as a contested terrain" in Collinson and Morgan (eds.) *Images of the Multinational Firm*. Chichester: Wiley & Sons, pp. 193–216

Ferner, A., J. Quintanilla and C. Sánchez-Runde 2006. "Introduction: multinationals and the multi-level politics of cross-national diffusion" in Ferner, Quintanilla and Sánchez-Runde (eds.) *Multinationals, Institutions and the Construction of Transnational Practices: Convergence and Diversity in the Global Economy*. Basingstoke: Palgrave, pp. 1–23

Fincham, R. 1992. "Perspectives on power: processual, institutional and 'internal' forms of organizational power," *Journal of Management Studies* 40: 641–759

Fischer, F. 2005. "Revisiting organizational politics: the postempiricist challenge," *Policy and Society* June: 1–23

Geppert, M. and K. Williams 2006. "Global, national and local practices in multinational corporations: towards a sociopolitical framework," *International Journal of Human Resource Management* 17: 49–69

Geppert, M., K. Williams and D. Matten 2003. "The social construction of contextual rationalities in MNCs: an Anglo-German comparison of subsidiary choice," *Journal of Management Studies* 40: 617–41

Geppert. M., D. Matten and P. Walgenbach 2006. "Transnational institution building and the multinational corporation: an emerging field of research," *Human Relations* 59: 1451–65

Giddens, A. 1984. *The Constitution of Society: Outline of the Structuration Theory*. Cambridge: Polity Press

Granovetter, M. 1985. "Economic action and social structure: the problem of embeddedness," *American Journal of Sociology* 91: 481–510

Hall, P. A. and D. Soskice 2001. *Varieties of Capitalism: The Institutional Foundations of Comparative Advantage*. Oxford University Press

Hardy, C. and S. Clegg 1996. "Some dare call it power" in Clegg, Hardy and Nord (eds.) *Handbook for Organization Studies*. London: Sage, pp. 622–41

Harzing, A.-W. and A. Sorge 2003. "The relative impact of country of origin and universal contingencies on internationalization strategies and corporate control in multinational enterprises: worldwide and European perspectives," *Organization Studies* 24: 187–214

Haunschild, A., W. Nienhueser and R. Weiskopf 2009. "Power in organizations – power of organizations," *Management Revue* 20: 320–25

Hedlund, G. 1986. "The hypermodern MNC – a heterarchy?," *Human Resource Management* 25: 9–35

Hinings, C. R. and R. Greenwood 2002. "Disconnects and consequences in organization theory?," *Administrative Science Quarterly* 47: 411–21

Hollingsworth, J. R. 1997. "Continuities and changes in social systems of production: the cases of Japan, Germany, and the United States" in Hollingsworth and Boyer (eds.) *Contemporary Capitalism: The Embeddedness of Institutions*. Cambridge and New York: Cambridge University Press, pp. 265–310

Hymer, S. H. 1970. "The multinational corporation and the law of uneven development" in Bhagwati (ed.) *Economics and World Order*. London: Macmillan, pp. 113–140

Jackson, G. 2010. "Actors and institutions" in Morgan, Campbell, Crouch, Pedersen and Whitley (eds.) *Oxford Handbook of Comparative Institutional Analysis*. Oxford University Press, pp. 63–86

Jackson, G. and R. Deeg 2008. "Comparing capitalisms: understanding institutional diversity and its implications for international business," *Journal of International Business Studies* 39: 540–61

Knights, D. and D. McCabe 1999. "Are there limits to authority?: TQM and organizational power," *Organization Studies* 20: 197–224

Kostova, T. 1999. "Transnational transfer of strategic organizational practices: a contextual perspective," *Academy of Management Review* 24: 308–24

Kostova, T. and S. Zaheer 1999. "Organizational legitimacy under conditions of complexity: the case of the multinational enterprise," *Academy of Management Review* 24: 64–81

Kostova, T. and K. Roth 2002. "Adoption of an organizational practice by subsidiaries of multinational corporations: institutional and relational effects," *Academy of Management Journal* 45: 215–33

Kostova, T., K. Roth and M. T. Dacin 2008. "Institutional theory in the study of multinational corporations: a critique and new directions," *Academy of Management Review* 33: 994–1006

Kristensen, P. H. and J. Zeitlin 2001. "The making of a global firm: local pathways to multinational enterprise" in Morgan, Kristensen and Whitley (eds.) *The Multinational Firm: Organizing Across Institutional and National Divides*. Oxford University Press, pp. 172–95

2005. *Local Players in Global Games*. Oxford University Press

Lash, S. and J. Urry 1987. *The End of Organized Capitalism*. Madison, WI: University of Wisconsin Press

Meyer, J. W. 1994. "Rationalized environments" in Scott and Meyer (eds.) *Institutional Environments and Organizations*. Thousand Oaks, CA: Sage, pp. 28–54

2000. "Globalization – sources and effects on national states and societies," *International Sociology* 15: 233–48

Mintzberg, H. 1985. "The organization as political arena," *Journal of Management Studies* 22: 133–54

Morgan, G. 2001a. "The multinational firm: organizing across institutional and national divides" in Morgan, Kristensen and Whitley (eds.) *The Multinational Firm: Organizing Across Institutional and National Divides*. Oxford University Press, pp. 1–24

2001b. "The development of transnational standards and regulations and their impacts on firms" in Morgan, Kristensen and Whitley (eds.) *The Multinational Firm: Organizing Across Institutional and National Divides*. Oxford University Press, pp. 225–52

Morgan, G. and P. H. Kristensen 2006. "The contested social space of multinationals: varieties of institutionalism, varieties of capitalism," *Human Relations* 59: 1467–90

2009. "Multinational firms as societies" in Collinson and Morgan (eds.) *Images of the Multinational Firm*. Chichester: Wiley & Sons, pp. 167–91

Morgan, G. and R. Whitley 2003. "Introduction to the Special Issue: the changing multinational firm," *Journal of Management Studies* 40: 609–16

Nohria, N. and S. Ghoshal 1997. *The Differentiated Network: Organizing Multinational Corporations for Value Creation*. San Francisco: Jossey-Bass Publishers

Ortmann, G. 1988. "Macht, Spiel, Konsens" in Küpper and Ortmann (eds.) *Mikropolitik*. Opladen: Westdeutscher Verlag, pp. 13–26

Perrow, C. 1986. *Complex Organizations: A Critical Essay*, 3rd edn. New York: McGraw-Hill

Pettigrew, A. 1973. *The Politics of Organizational Decision Making*. London: Tavistock

Pfeffer, J. and G. Salancik 1978. *The External Control of Organizations: A Resource Dependence Perspective*. New York: Harper & Row

Redding, G. 2005. "The thick description and comparison of societal systems of capitalism," *Journal of International Business Studies* 36: 123–55

Reed, M. 1996. "Organizational theorizing: a historically contested terrain" in Clegg, Hardy and Nord (eds.) *Handbook of Organization Studies*. London: Sage, pp. 31–56

Royle, T. 2002. "Resistance is useless! The problem of trade union organization in the European fast-food industry: the case of McDonald's" in Geppert, Matten and Williams (eds.) *Challenges for European Management in a Global Context: Experiences from Britain and Germany*. Basingstoke: Palgrave Macmillan, pp. 189–214

Scott, R. W. 2001. *Institutions and Organizations*, 2nd edn. Thousand Oaks, CA: Sage

Seo, M.-G. and W. Creed 2002. "Institutional contradictions, praxis, and institutional change: a dialectical perspective," *Academy of Management Review* 2: 222–47

Sorge, A. and W. Streeck 1988. "Industrial relations and technical change: the case for an extended perspective" in Hyman and Streeck (eds.) *New Technology and Industrial Relations*. Oxford: Blackwell, pp. 19–47

Stopford, J. M. and L. T. Wells 1972. *Managing the Multinational Enterprise: Organization of the Firm and Ownership of Subsidiaries*. New York: Basic Books

Tempel, A. 2002. "Multinational companies, institutional environments and the diffusion of industrial relations practices" in Geppert, Matten and Williams (eds.) *Challenges for European Management in a Global Context: Experiences from Britain and Germany*. Basingstoke: Palgrave Macmillan, pp. 143–64

Tempel, A. and P. Walgenbach 2007. "Global standardization of organizational forms and management practices? What new institutionalism and the business-systems approach can learn from each other," *Journal of Management Studies* 44: 1–24

Vernon, R. 1966. "International investment and international trade in the product cycle," *Quarterly Journal of Economics* 80: 190–207

Vora, D. A., T. Kostova and K. Roth 2007. "Roles of subsidiary managers in multinational corporations: the effect of dual organizational identification," *Management International Review* 47: 595–620

Weber, M. 1947. *The Theory of Social and Economic Organization*. New York: Free Press

Westney, E. D. 1993. "Institutionalization theory and the multinational corporation" in Ghoshal and Westney (eds.) *Organization Theory and the Multinational Corporation*. London: Macmillan, pp. 53–76

    2009. "The multinational firm as an evolutionary system" in Collinson and Morgan (eds.) *Images of the Multinational Firm*. Chichester: Wiley & Sons, pp. 117–44

Whitley, R. 1999. *Divergent Capitalisms: The Social Structuring and Change of Business Systems*. Oxford University Press

    2001. "How and why are international firms different?: the consequences of cross-border managerial coordination for firm characteristics and behavior" in Morgan, Kristensen and Whitley (eds.) *The Multinational Firm: Organizing Across Institutional and National Divides*. Oxford University Press, pp. 27–68

Williamson, O. E. 1985. *The Economic Institutions of Capitalism*. New York: Free Press

Wortmann, M. 2004. "Aldi and the German model: structural change in German grocery retailing and the success of grocery discounters," *Competition and Change* 8: 425–41

Xu, D. and O. Shenkar 2002. "Institutional distance and the multinational enterprise," *Academy of Management Review* 27: 608–18

Part II

Institutions, social embeddedness and knowledge

Resource dependence and construction, and macro- and micro-politics in transnational enterprises and alliances: the case of jet engine manufacturers in Germany

Arndt Sorge and Katja Rothe

Introductory overview

We are concerned with the relative importance of different factors for the internationalization strategy and localization patterns in a highly globalized industry, with non-routine value creation and vertical integration or strong vertical alliances. To take a prime example for this situation, we investigated the evolution of two different multinational corporations (MNCs) developing and manufacturing jet engines in Germany. This study is embedded in an analysis of the jet engine industry and its worldwide development. Germany afforded a unique chance to study a combination of continuity and radical change in a high-technology industry. The business model of the industry is generally not known or appreciated, and it deviates remarkably from what is usually claimed for high-technology industries and for Anglo-American business systems. Furthermore, whilst the product and its supply are truly global, local influences are strong on the resource side, and a combined balance of resources affects localization decisions within the wider strategy of an enterprise. The strength of globalization, together with the interdependency between sites across borders, leverages the importance of local resource endowments, including socio-economic institutions (see also chapter of Maclean and Hollinshead in this volume).

This situation is poorly considered in the international business literature. Also, resource endowments mainly work differently from what the varieties of capitalism and business systems literature suggest. Such approaches seem to misunderstand high-technology industries to an extent which remains to be researched in greater detail, in view of what we know from the literature on national business systems. But a part is also confirmed, concerning the importance of maintenance skills in the industry and their construction in Germany, and in relation to the global business model of the industry. We show that a combination of international business and management research and theory with varieties of capitalism and business systems approaches is useful, although large parts of the latter approaches are disconfirmed. On the other hand, management writings on internationalization strategy are seriously incomplete if they are not complemented by business systemic theories that adequately address the origin of comparative advantage of socio-economic contexts and settings. This is necessary in order to explain localization decisions well.

Conceptual foundations and challenges

Why subsidiaries, with which functions, or headquarters are established or disestablished in which countries sounds like a straightforward question dealt with by the internationalization strategy literature in international business and management (IB&M). This field has performed well in explaining internationalization processes using general and empirically based theories. It is theoretically diverse and its foundations are "eclectic" (Dunning 1988), with more functionalist theories such as those founded on transaction costs theory (such as Anderson and Gatignon 1986; Hennart and Reddy 1997), knowledge and learning (Barkema and Vermeulen 1998; Johanson and Vahlne 1977; Saka 2007), or the strategy and marketing literature on the one hand, and more actor-centric theories stressing the capacities and interests of specific individual and collective actors and the way they make sense of their potential and external opportunities or threats (Aharoni 1966; Cyert and March 1992).

The IB&M literature does mention the comparative advantage of countries in attracting investment and subsidiaries, but it is hardly connected or confronted with a literature that has sought to explain the origins of institutional comparative advantage. On the other hand, there is a substantial literature on comparative institutional advantage which has hardly looked at how policies of multinational enterprises and globally integrated markets affect, or interfere with, comparative advantages of national institutional settings. Although such bodies of theory should be natural complements, they have grown apart. Theories as on "business systems" (Whitley 1992, 1999), "national innovation systems" (Lundvall 1992) and "varieties of capitalism" (VoC) (Hall and Soskice 2001), although the multinational enterprise is not their core concern, do have implications for which types of enterprises or subsidiaries will thrive or suffer in which types of economies and societies, and in which industries, market niches or types of firms that will happen.

VoC theory has suggested that radical innovation will work better in liberal market economies such as the UK and the USA, whereas piecemeal innovation thrives in coordinated market economies such as Germany, Austria, Switzerland and Scandinavian countries. A similar point has been made by Whitley (2006) for what he called business systems. The institutionalist core of this argument and the evidence is that societal institutions in domains such as entrepreneurship and corporate governance, economic contracting between firms, management and organization of enterprises, work and employment relations, and the financial system are not independent of one another but interact and correspond, bringing forth, for example, the association between the type of innovation and VoC or business systemic characteristics mentioned above. And this has implications not only for headquarters of non-multinational companies but also for the management of subsidiaries and functions in the MNC. Ideally, MNCs should locate radical innovation in liberal market economies and piecemeal innovation in coordinated market economies.

But theories and studies are often unconnected, although they look at the same or related aspects of a broad class of phenomena: why it is that multinationals come from which types of countries and go to which others, by setting up subsidiaries or alliances, and how they go about it. We have good accounts of what multinationals in larger populations of organizations do, and on the other hand we have good accounts of the specific and often idiosyncratic behavior of organized and organizing actors. We also have good studies that relate the behavior of firms and subsidiaries to a complex set of contextual settings, both societal (country of origin and host country) and industrial. What we lack are studies of counterfactual cases that are actor-centric without neglecting the influence of a society–economy and how outcomes have come about over time. Organization studies have in general tended to be either more "nomothetic," interested in building general or middle-range theory, or "idiographic," i.e. interested in the specifics of cases (Lammers 1978). The management literature has to be good at explaining the specifics of companies, industries or markets, but much of the international management literature has come to excel in generalization. Our contention is that the competent explanation of the specifics requires combination of theories that have remained unconnected, to examine compatibility and contradictions in addition to empirical proof. Our interest here is in a country case, and two enterprise cases in this country case, that implicate IB&M as well as VoC and business systems theories, and that explore contradictions and links between these bodies of theory.

To obtain this theoretical confrontation and link in the space we have here, we have to look at a particular industrial situation. We opted for a truly globally integrated market and production and service delivery setting, in a high-technology industry, dominated by MNCs, but a market and a setting in which the policies of actors subject to resource dependencies in diverse institutional contexts would count. We wanted an industry in which networking of actors in and across suppliers would be important for strategy and where resources such as knowledge and capabilities (Schmid and Schurig 2003) would add to the power of local actors (Andersson *et al.* 2007; Forsgren *et al.* 2005). This would be an industry with global products but locally embedded subsidiaries, best exemplified by the detailed and suggestive case of Kristensen and Zeitlin (2005), in which interdependent yet also partly competing subsidiaries could manage their power in the MNC through the management of capabilities in networks, in the enterprise, the supply chain and the supportive national or local environment. To obtain a sharp test case, we opted for a situation of MNC subsidiaries that had not become part of an MNC or international alliance by merger or acquisition – which tends to give power to distinct national components – but to a national industry which emerged through foreign direct investment or the importance of an international alliance (by licensed production and maintenance). That loads the dice heavily towards the power of headquarters and the country of origin or of a dominant multinational alliance partner, so that evidence for the power of local actors becomes particularly significant.

This led us to the development, manufacturing and maintenance of jet engines, as a classic case of a high-technology industry that has become firmly dominated by MNCs. What makes it interesting is that overtly it goes against the grain of nomothetic theories in use: the industry is dominated by MNCs from the USA that, contrary to expectations, do not exhibit the characteristics of the country-of-origin business system according to general institutional theories such as those on business systems and varieties of capitalism. Furthermore, the manufacturing of jet engines for aircraft is atypical in both the USA and Germany, following business systems and VoC approaches. It should not be a well-performing industry, neither in the country that dominates (the USA) because short-termism is absent in this industry in the USA, nor in Germany because subsidiaries are not expected to thrive there because it is not a country for high-tech industries. Our treatment therefore has three main analytical levels: the highly internationalized world industry of jet engineering, Germany as a location of that industry, and sites in the industry in Germany.

We do not go into detailed interview results or other sources here, because even crude and indisputable results are poorly known or appreciated. Interestingly, simple evidence runs counter to much that VoC/business systems theories have had to offer, particularly if one looks at the development of technology and the industry over time. At first sight, the IB&M literature on the resource-dependent construction and management of network relations is much more pertinent and seems to render VoC/business systems theory redundant or contradict it sharply. This comes out notably in the historical treatment of the industry, which again leads to the cited IB&M concepts and flies in the face of VoC/business systems. The picture emerging from this analysis might lead to the conclusion that the latter theories are overridden by MNCs in globally integrated industries, with products that are internationally the same and international mobility of highly qualified workers and technical knowledge. But closer analysis and reflection show that resource construction and management interact with specificities of the industry in such a way that some aspects of VoC/business systems are indispensable for the explanation. An eclectic combination of different theories is indeed called for, although an overarching theory is not visible.

Jet engines for aircraft only came into use in the 1940s, at first for military planes and then in the 1950s also for civil passenger planes. The industry began to develop and manufacture more seriously precisely at the moment when Germany was not allowed to make larger aircraft and engines. All the aircraft and aircraft engine industry had been shut down after the end of World War II. The jet engine industry clearly is a high-technology industry and counted as such in comparative studies. It is research and development intensive, and development has a scientific basis insofar as research and theory building on the dynamics of gases, materials, measurement and controls is required. The industry is distinctly knowledge-based and knowledge-creating, employing substantial numbers of engineers with research experience and keeping close contact with university departments through R&D contracts and personnel recruitment and exchange.

In addition, the period in which the industry took off, in the 1940s, was particularly marked by radical innovation destroying conventional aero engine competence; conventional aero engines had been piston driven, rather like car engines. Because of the complex mechanics of moving parts and the use of a propeller, the speed that could be reached with such engines was limited. Jet engines work on thrust rather than on the aerodynamic "pull" of a propeller; their power generation process is simpler and the fuel they need less demanding (kerosene instead of high octane fuel). There have of course also come to be "prop jets," which drive a propeller in addition to the thrust delivered, and recently there are jet engines under development which have a new type of propeller, with many curved blades, which allows speeds higher than with conventional propellers that have straight blades. In jet engines, the thrust is generated through compression of air to a density and heat that ignites fuel injected, and the continuous combustion of the compressed fuel–air mixture drives a turbine which in turn drives the compressor that sucks in and compresses the air needed for the process (Wikipedia: Jet engine). This principle of functioning is radically different from that of piston engines, and its development constituted a radical innovation that made conventional engine knowledge redundant to a large degree. Now, Germany is described by VoC as a country promoting piecemeal innovation rather than radical innovation. Students of business systems, varieties of capitalism and innovation could rightly point to the fact that the aero engine industry came to be dominated by British, US and French manufacturers in the post-WWII period, i.e. in either liberal-capitalist or state-dominated countries promoting fundamental and applied research.

This serves to define the research question: why should Germany have jet engine manufacturing at all, given that its institutional setting was not conducive to the industry, particularly at a time after a radical innovation when it was barred from entering the industry and existing capacities were either wiped out or transferred to foreign engine makers? Should this not have been enough to lay a solid basis for a cumulative disadvantage which would have prevented multinational engine companies from starting a subsidiary or domestic companies from emerging?

Against this research question, built on the essence of the VoC literature, we have a countervailing literature which stresses the micro-political capacities of actors to attract, maintain or further develop enterprise activities. More recent findings (Dörrenbächer 2007; Dörrenbächer and Geppert 2005; Forsgren et al. 2005; Kristensen and Zeitlin 2005; Schmid and Schurig 2003 and others) have shown that micro-politics and local resource construction (in HRM, organizational and technical knowledge, relations with important clients, suppliers or partners) have a decisive role in attracting, developing or reducing direct investment into subsidiaries. Local resources are to some extent given but also constructed by the enterprise; they are both internally and externally generated. They influence the intra-organizational power that organized units have in the decision-making (Astley and Sachdeva 1984). They may consist of available factors of production, finance, subsidies and also social institutions in management, education, human resources and industrial relations. The action of MNCs can be explained as resource based (Wernerfelt 1984) and also as resource seeking and resource constructing. Economically, socio-economic institutions are a type of specific assets, which makes them part of the resource base (Sorge 2006): they enable producers or service providers to do things more easily or more profitably than under a different cultural and institutional context. In this constructed resource dependency perspective, enterprises not only use resources taken as given, but help bring them about. To some extent, socio-economic institutions may be public goods, if enterprises cooperate in their construction on a non-commercial basis, if they are provided by schools, colleges and universities that do not charge a price to the user, or if they are suggested by knowledge shared in professional communities.

In between such concepts and VoC, we also have studies of national innovation systems (Lundvall 1992), which have disconfirmed the relation between radical innovation and liberal market order propagated by VoC, which the latter hardly noticed (Lange 2006: 43f.). The USA became a leader in fundamental technical innovation through the involvement of the state, with development contracts and subsidies to an extent unparalleled not only in liberal market economies but also coordinated market economies; radical innovation in the USA is a post-war phenomenon. This has been the case in atomic energy, jet propulsion and rockets, electronics and also more recently in biotechnology. Where radical innovation is concerned, the USA has excelled through government involvement.

For a local MNC subsidiary, resource balance and construction is crucial for the management of its importance and contribution within the wider MNC. This was intensively demonstrated by Kristensen and Zeitlin (2005). This is also the most clearly and convincingly social interactionist work on MNCs, showing that headquarters and subsidiary policies are always mutually intertwined and constituted. They demonstrated this in a case of an engineering industry MNC with a number of acquired or merged subsidiaries, entities that had therefore originally been constituted independently and whose identities and policies may for this reason weigh more heavily against the identity and policy of the headquarters. One may conjecture that a similar picture is appropriate in any engineering-dominated firm, a firm which sells to producers or sophisticated service providers rather than end consumers, and which develops and produces in small and medium-sized batches. When a product or service spectrum is wide and complex, and contextual differences between national settings motivate an enterprise to develop locally different competence centers, then the situation described by Kristensen and Zeitlin (2005) may conceivably prevail.

Whilst micro-political influences due to the construction and management of capabilities thus go against the influences of varieties of capitalism, it also becomes clear that they are not merely opposites; for the construction and manipulation of resources or assets is tied into existing resource endowments of firms, networks, political authorities and collectivities. And in this way, institutions of capitalism enter the play of forces attracting or repelling the localization of activities and enterprise functions. At least conceptually they have to, because resource construction cannot start from nowhere. It implies learning with regard to knowledge, and also internalization or acquisition of financial or material resources. Resource generation then tends to be either based on power, or it leads to it, or both. This is where micro-politics come in. Whilst ideal-typical micro-politics might lead to an enterprise-specific distribution of activities and functions across societies and economies, only depending on games and players, the fact that players are socio-economically and politically embedded brings in existing and evolving resource distributions, among them institutions (Sorge 2006; see also chapters of Maclean and Hollinshead and Ybema and Byun in this volume).

Such influences may go against "footloose" MNCs (moving headquarters or subsidiaries about geographically, at will), even if their components do not have a strong identity or history of their own. Transnational MNEs will thus develop distributed authority and competence even when they in principle centralize the allocation of authority and competence, making it possible to relocate functions at will, as markets, prices or other economic parameters and strategies change. In the terms of Bartlett and Ghoshal (1989), an MNC may thus become transnational without ever having had a multi-domestic background and, what is more, it may walk this path to a transnational structure although on the product or service market side there is no pull in the direction of regional or national differentiation or adaptation of products or services. That factor prices and transaction costs may attract or prevent the establishment of subsidiaries, and influence the entry or the establishment mode, has been well researched in the literature for some time. But comparative resource endowments and notably institutional landscapes, as a foundation for the micro-politics of subsidiaries, deserve more attention.

In the jet engine industry, product market differences across the world do not exist, or have come to disappear completely. Furthermore, the comparative cost of transporting output to users has come to be negligible. Whilst the engines are heavy and bulky, they do after all finish up in planes that can fly and reduce the importance of distance, at least the distance between the plane manufacturer and its client; the costs of transporting engines to plane manufacturers vary little or do not influence the choice of engines for a plane, compared to other parameters of competition. What comparative advantages or disadvantages may suppliers (subsidiaries) then have in this highly globalized industry dominated by a competitive oligopoly of a few MNCs and multinational alliances? The industry is the best one to explore this, because it has a truly global product and market, where firms are highly globally integrated, knowledge and human resources are globally present and recognized, and enterprises can in principle choose potential locations at will. And in one way Germany is the best place to study it, to find out about the interplay and opposition of micro-politics and resource endowments including institutions, in a place that should not have had a jet engine industry.

The industry in Germany is not large. It employs about 10,000 people in two enterprises, a third of them in Rolls-Royce and the rest in MTU (Motoren- und Turbinenunion) Aero Engines. But the border of the industry is fuzzy, because maintenance of products is offered by both manufacturers and some users; it would be larger if engine maintenance workers in Lufthansa Technik were included. We suggest that it is more significant than its small size indicates, because it exemplifies a particular situation which is conceptually and practically general and important: a non-routine high-tech industry with the most highly globalized product and service conceivable, in which only multinational enterprises and their subsidiaries are of importance, and one which was newly built up from scratch under conditions of high internationalization of business and industrial governance. At the end, we hypothesize for which more general situation the findings could possibly stand.

The empirical foundation of this paper lies first, in generally available records, documents and publications and second, in interviews conducted in the two enterprises in the industry in Germany. In order to cut a long story short, we largely develop our paper in the form of a narrative. The reason for this is that the picture is amazingly clear-cut, undisputed by any information available on the industry. For the jet engine industry and particularly Rolls-Royce Aero Engines, the gist of our findings is also reported in *The Economist* (2009). Whilst IB&M and political economy scholars tend to marvel at the bare and unfamiliar facts of life in this worldwide industry, such facts are hardly understood in the industry and in urgent need of ethnographic discovery by IB&M and comparative political economy students. We only make a first step in this direction here, on the basis of two aero engine enterprises in Germany. Both are multinational enterprises: one company of domestic origin has foreign subsidiaries and is committed to an alliance with a US MNC; the other one, the subsidiary of Rolls-Royce, is the German part of an MNC with Britain as the country of origin.

The fascinatingly atypical world of aero engines

We mainly deal here with the civilian side of the jet engine industry, because this is where freedom of international competition in a global market is strongest. Jet engines have come to be a global product like few others, i.e. their design and operating principles hardly vary from one part of the world to another. The planes that the engines go into have over time increasingly been designed to be compatible with at least two sorts of engines offered by different manufacturers. Engine developers configure their engines to fit the power requirements of the leading aircraft manufacturers, as they come up with new models or extended or shortened versions of available models. Worldwide, there are the following major suppliers of jet engines (including development, production, maintenance/service) for fixed-wing civil passenger and transport aircraft: General Electric (GE), Pratt & Whitney (P&W, both originating from the USA), SNECMA (France) and Rolls-Royce (RR, UK). The CFM alliance consists of GE and SNECMA, and it has developed and marketed some larger engines. It was, however, far from a foregone conclusion when it happened. At first, it was P&W, as the perceived leader in the industry, that SNECMA approached for an alliance, in order to establish a solid position in civil jet engines. P&W declined the offer, which made SNECMA turn to GE (Bonaccorsi and Giuri 2001; Hayward 1986). This alliance subsequently became very successful. P&W appears to have been reluctant to establish proprietary consortia, preferring full integration by acquisition as it did in the case of P&W Canada.

Under this first tier of suppliers, there is a second tier of mostly more national suppliers that do not cover the full range of activities arising around jet engines, concentrating on licensed production of parts or components, licensed service and maintenance or specific development activities. On the other hand, although the first tier of major suppliers does not have many enterprises and these are strongly multinationalized, suppliers often form consortia in order to develop, manufacture and service engines. The most prominent consortium with the most long-standing experience probably is CFM, but others have been formed for specific engine projects. Initially, the forming of consortia and alliances was started in the military field, as governments maneuvered national champions in the industry into position when they commissioned a plane or helicopter project together with other governments. But as civil jet customers ordered bigger planes with heavier and more sophisticated engines, and as the market increasingly asked for a choice of alternative engines, consortia became plausible solutions to combine the concentration of resources in specific engine projects with the independence of distinct firms.

At first sight, the industry might be seen to conform with a VoC (varieties of capitalism) logic: being a high-tech industry, it is dominated by liberal-capitalist countries (the UK and the USA) and one state-dominated economy (France) that has also consistently had a strength in fundamental innovation; all of them have a research and development environment which is said to be loaded towards fundamental research and application of science to engineering in such way that they make radical innovation more likely. The national innovation systems literature has shown this. A severe jolt to VoC thinking, however, is the very long-term perspective common to all the suppliers in the world. To this extent, it is fundamentally opposed to VoC theory. The payback period for R&D and other investment is at least twenty years. Contrary to expectations based on VoC, firms do not make a profit on the development, production and sales of engines, but on their maintenance. Engines have a product life of about twenty to thirty years, during which time maintenance is crucial and frequent. Once an airline has bought an engine, it is compelled to have it maintained and repaired at regular intervals and with substantial costs in terms of personnel, capital and flight operation time foregone.

But locking into a maintenance obligation when buying an engine does not constitute a service monopoly for the supplier. This is because the servicing and maintenance of engines are not firmly in the hands of the manufacturers. A number of reputable airlines have established (licensed) engine maintenance facilities, which they also offer to other airlines. There are, to be sure, "barriers to entry" with regard to maintenance, because it depends on possessing a license based on qualifications certified by the manufacturer, on the basis of conventions drawn up by the International Civil Aviation Organization and the American Federal Aviation Authority regulation. The competition of users and suppliers in maintenance might be less intense than in engine development and production: engine manufacturers earn hardly any profit from the sale of engines, most of the profit coming from their maintenance. Thus, although the industry has an oligopoly of suppliers at the R&D and the production end of the value chain, it is highly competitive in sales prices, and the major revenue-generating function of maintenance is competitively shared with some airlines. This global business model is an uncontested institution in the industry. The development and production of engines are, economically speaking, a means to entice airlines to buy maintenance services in order to obtain the funds for new development and innovation. And it is clear that the maintenance revenues from an engine sale have to be spread out over a minimal product life of twenty years, which is the time it takes to make a product development investment pay back.

It is also understood that, since engines have a product life of decades and maintenance is crucial for safety, such services are preponderant value-adding activities, as is research and development. Services are thus very important for value generation, without disparaging the role of production that is also very knowledge intensive to assure safety of operations. Finance is marked by the pressure to invest into development and expect payback over decades, by maintenance, which denotes a longer time horizon than usual in finance and notably finance doctrines in liberal market economies. Specialized technical staff at all levels and in all functions are an important part of the human resource endowment. It is difficult for readers of the VoC literature to imagine an industry which is all of the following: strongly globalized, high-tech, yet on the other hand focused on long-term planning horizons, with regard to both material and immaterial assets in totally analogous and related ways, and dominated from the USA in addition. VoC would see the industry as high-tech by the prevalence of liberal market economy principles. The complete opposite is true, as we have seen. So-called liberal market economies, which in some industries are exactly the opposite of this because of governmental coordination and subsidies, obviously can do anything that is required to achieve a long-term orientation in specific industries, do this in a high-tech industry and establish the market leaders in this industry.

Subsidiaries and sites of jet engine MNCs are integrated into the larger concerns in highly intricate ways. To map the specific specialization and integration patterns in comparison, the following criteria are used for describing the characteristics of a site and its place in the intra-enterprise division of labor and in the value chain:

(a) Functional

These relate to the classical terminology of functions in the enterprise, i.e. research, development, marketing, sales, production, customer service and maintenance, finance, accounting and controlling. There are more refined subtypes, e.g. machining, welding, painting, assembly and testing in production. Such types vary according the material and technical specificities of an industry.

(b) Class of product

Jet aero engines mainly vary by size and thrust on the one hand, and end-use destination (combat aircraft, helicopters, civil jets, propeller jets). Fuel efficiency and environmental friendliness also differ, but they have evolved over time across the board, rather than being generically different from one type to another.

Engines have become technically much more complex, in order to combine thrust, efficiency and environmental friendliness. Whereas immediately post-WWII engines had a compressor, a turbine and combustion chambers in-between as the main components, the section in front of combustion became increasingly differentiated into a fan, compressor stages at different levels of pressure, and separate air streams, the internal one for fuel injection and combustion and the external (by-pass) one for making thrust aerodynamically efficient and less noisy. For combat aircraft, afterburners were added aft of the turbine, in order to reach higher supersonic speeds. Increasing technical sophistication gives rise to the next characteristic:

(c) (Sub)systemic focus

Types of compressors, fans, turbines and combustion, and associated sections of the engine, alone or in combination, represent foci of sites. Both development and production specialists specialize and acquire comparative advantage in subsystems. Such a systemic focus is developed or rewarded by attribution of a "competence center" which also serves other engine development sites.

In principle, there is medium and long-term exchangeability of subsidiaries, sites or parts of them, in joint ventures and other alliances. Given the international professional community in aero engine engineering, it is clear that although the top tiers in the industry may appear rather stable, it is far from a foregone conclusion which functional, product class or systemic specialization will be allocated by a headquarters for existing or emerging parts of the activity spectrum in the group. Investment into new or existing sites in emerging economies may be closer to some markets and offer cost or "political" advantages such as package deals whereby direct investment and allocation of activities is compensated for by orders for engines from a particular country. But on the whole, most national markets are not large enough to generate substantial orders in return for direct investment or activity localization in a particular country.

The industry is thus marked by intense globalization of products, services and firms, few and concentrated firms, great complexity in products and the value chain, contestable markets but also opportunities for acquiring relatively stable but differentiated comparative advantages in subsidiaries and sites. In line with the long-term time horizon, and the asset specificity of both human resources and invested capital, there is no short-term acquisition or closure of facilities. Respondents in the enterprises visited made statements about the importance of factors in localization decisions which will be discussed further below.

The historical origin

The origins of jet engines are in military requirements, fuelled of course by WWII but dating back to a period in which a war on this scale was not yet imminent. The pioneers in jet engine development and manufacture were mainly in two countries, Britain and Germany, in the second half of the 1930s. Much as the USA and France are often stylized as "mission-oriented" by Ergas (1984) and liberal-capitalist in the case of the USA (Hall and Soskice 2001), countries that facilitate technological break-through and radical innovation (Whitley 2006), nothing of the sort applied to jet engines, one of the most fundamental innovations in the 1930s. The liberal-capitalist country Britain did not have the edge, either. It was Germany that had jet engine powered aeroplanes flying and in service (jet fighters entering military service in 1943) two years before Britain did, and Germany had previously had the first experimental jet (He 178) flying in 1938. This is very much against the myth of a "British first" in jets which is still subtly being extolled (Marr 2007: 11, 30). The development of the jet engine was, to be sure, parallel in mainly Britain and Germany, but Germany was clearly ahead in getting jet-powered planes airborne. This is not an accidental result due to the capacity of a dictatorship to break the laws of VoC. It is not the result of a warmon-gering command economy pooling resources at will and pushing through a fundamental venture. Adolf Hitler even took personal steps, at first, to delay the development of jets and then divert allocation of planes to a purpose for which they were ill-suited (tactical bombing); his belief, initially shared with most air ministry superiors, was that jets were something extravagant for after the war (Galland 1993: 285–95).

Instead, development was instigated by the entrepreneurship of far-sighted engineers such as Ernst Heinkel and Hans Joachim Pabst von Ohain, and their networking in the air ministry and with a competitor (Junkers) that made the first jet engines. The same was true for other fundamental inno-vations in aerospace, such as the rocket-propelled plane (He 176, Me 163) and the ballistic missile (V2) over longer distances, innovations made in Germany that after 1945 provided the initial impetus to both US and Soviet programs. Britain, of course, is the liberal market economy and Germany at that time was more of a "coordinated" economy than it has ever been in its modern history, under Nazi dictatorship needless to say. Such radical inno-vations clearly owed more to corporatism and government control than they did to liberal market economies (Gersdorff *et al.* 1995).

This is the second jolt to VoC and business system concepts, then: the radi-cal innovation of the time in aeronautical engineering was advanced more rapidly in a coordinated economy which allowed break-through entrepre-neurship to happen with greater ease than in the runner-up country. The question could even be generalized further, to ask whether those fundamen-tal innovations in which the USA has excelled over the years since, are not more due to business system characteristics which VoC unduly neglect but the national innovation systems literature did point out: the tendency for fun-damental innovation to be promoted by the government, to an extent which has been far above that for any other country. Lundvall (1992) and colleagues have shown this throughout but it was neglected in the VoC literature. In this respect, the USA has had more governmental coordination of and subsidies for radical innovation, whether this was the building of the atomic bomb and of nuclear reactors, microelectronics or biotechnology, from the 1940s until the present day (Lange 2006: 43f.). The question could also be framed thus: is either the USA or Britain a liberal market economy where research and development are concerned? A provisional answer would be: hardly, and the United States clearly less so than Britain.

On the other hand, there are a number of observations that support sys-temic characteristics advanced by Hall and Soskice (2001) and by Whitley

(2006). In Britain, the jet engine was developed under the leadership of Frank Whittle, in conjunction with Rolls-Royce but also outside it, in a dedicated R&D enterprise started by Whittle. The account of the development emphasizes this "arm's length relationship" between Whittle and Rolls-Royce, as needed to pursue the project but also a source of delays and upsets. Whittle had to set up his own enterprise which was related to Rolls-Royce but formally independent; this was the reason for a number of delays and difficulties. Rolls-Royce, as the eventual manufacturer, had to pass on knowledge to other British and US engine makers, under instruction by the Allied war governments (Wikipedia: Frank Whittle). This became the most important route by which jet engine knowledge was diffused in the world, next to the "head-hunting" of German engineers by the Allies at the end of WWII.

This account is different for Germany. The established piston engine manufacturers (mainly Daimler-Benz and BMW) were at first not involved in the development and production of jet engines. The crucial impetus came from Heinkel and Junkers, two separate enterprises which did build planes but were not aero engine specialists. Heinkel launched itself into a completely new field; the expertise of Junkers who made the engines for the first operational jet fighter (Me 262) was more related to a specialty in their other business, continuous gas combustion. Jet engines are a specific form of gas turbine, and imply a process with which piston engine makers were not familiar. For the aero engine industry of the time it was a competence-destroying innovation, and initial success was helped by involving a firm from outside the piston engine industry. The relationship between Heinkel, Junkers and others in the development of jets was intimate. Furthermore, German firms in the aero engine industry took up the new technology quickly, learning from the initial Junkers engines. Within a year, the jet engines destined for military use were mainly offered by BMW and Daimler-Benz. In short, inter-firm and inter-industrial coordination and transfer of knowledge appeared to be less of a problem, which tallies with what was brought out later by studies on innovation and inter-firm relations that compared the Federal Republic of Germany and Britain (Lane and Bachmann 1996).

The head-start advantage which Germany had was, however, promptly and radically lost in 1945, with unconditional surrender and the annihilation of the defense and aircraft industries. That removed Germany from the jet set in more ways than one and shifted the expertise to British, US, French and Soviet manufacturers. The first sustainable passenger jet aircraft in the 1950s then were British (DeHavilland Comet), Soviet (Tu 104) and French (Caravelle). Contrary to VoC concepts again, the Americans were later to arrive on the scene. The engine first used in the French Caravelle was British (the Rolls-Royce Avon). The pioneers in passenger jets now were Britain, France and the Soviet Union, but they only had short to medium-haul passenger jets, even the four-engined Comet being at the upper end of the medium range and a less fortuitous project because of dramatic crashes due to metal fatigue. In engine development and manufacture, the US manufacturers benefited greatly from the technology transfer from Britain and Germany, as did the Soviet Union, but they were at first reluctant to expand the use of jet engines beyond military planes, unlike the British and the French. At that time, with regard to jets, the USA was a highly successful technology adopter and improver, focused on military jets. US jet engine manufacturers were not the radical innovators but piecemeal innovative adopters, once the major break-throughs had happened in Europe. But in military jets, they accumulated an inestimable advantage which led on to further, more fundamental innovation. This was instrumental in setting major US jet engine manufacturers on their path of long-term success in civil applications.

This development by-passed Germany entirely because the country was at first not allowed to make planes, let alone jets. Thus, although the advantages attributed to liberal market economies in innovation are mostly refuted but confirmed by the Anglo-German contrast between arm's length relations in radical innovation on the one hand and smooth industrial networking on the other, the question why Germany should have a jet engine industry later remains, in view of the destruction of accumulated advantages.

The development of the post-war situation

Anything to do with jet engines was inconceivable in Germany, for a period of at least ten years. In 1955, German armed forces were re-started at the behest of both NATO and the Warsaw Pact. With re-militarization, a new question was how to organize the development, production and maintenance of aeroplanes and their engines. Now, in the sourcing of military procurement, there is a tendency in most developed countries to source activities locally as far as possible, so that domestic industries can benefit from military expenditure. However, in Germany it was also clear that both east and west Germany would have been overburdened with extensive local sourcing. In both countries, involvement in jet engines started with the maintenance of engines acquired from abroad, as part of the jet fighters bought from foreign manufacturers, or used by the powers of occupation.

In East Germany, the Soviet forces sourced maintenance of engines to a facility re-started south of Berlin. In West Germany, the new airforce instigated activities near Munich, first again under the umbrella of BMW, and also helicopter engine maintenance under KHD (Klöckner-Humboldt-Deutz), an enterprise with experience in gas turbines) in Oberursel near Frankfurt am Main. Although experience with jet engines had been interrupted for more than ten years, investment went into sites which had previous experience with either jets or gas turbines. It can be assumed that despite the discontinuity, resource dependency – on human resources and knowledge – must have been significant enough to lead back to sites which were "brownfields" to some extent, and in the case of BMW even connected with an enterprise formerly very active in this field, as the major supplier of jet engines when the war came to an end. It can thus be said that government procurement – political effects – interacted with human resource dependencies, to re-vitalize sites that were shades of brown. Although we do not have any proof for the measure of brownness of sites, one may infer that some capabilities and human resources in the field must have remained, despite the lengthy interruption.

Although this at first "only" concerned maintenance, knowing the importance of maintenance in the industry that emerged in due course, it is clear that a central function was established that might eventually link up with development and manufacturing again. Sourcing policies of governments busy with military procurement certainly could be expected to promote an extension of the range of activities and functions located in the acquiring country. This tendency was more pronounced in West than in East Germany, since Soviet policy was not to let production of military equipment of higher value and of civil aircraft and engines slip out of the territory of the Soviet Union. There were very clear-cut directives on the intra-COMECON division of labor between member countries. Production of civil jet aircraft and engines remained in the Soviet Union; the development of a civil jet aircraft in East Germany had been started but was aborted.

The path towards re-establishing an aero engine industry was, however, far from straight or clear. Let us trace this step by step, first for West Germany. Here, a slow process started when US jets (F 84, F 86) were supplied to the new Luftwaffe. At the time, the Federal Ministry of Economic Affairs was, under the influence of Ludwig Erhard, a solid advocate of developing comparative advantage in international trade, averse to promoting aircraft and jet engine development and manufacture, a business in which the western allies had acquired an advantage which was to be countered by comparative advantages on other terrains, following the liberal doctrine of the ministry that remained its espoused theory for a long time. It was as if Erhard already knew theories about VoC and applied them, although the industry went completely counter to the prevailing statements of this theory from the beginning. The point could be made that Germany had not only lost the war but everything in the aircraft industry, so that its advantage in knowledge was gone and it would have been economically highly inefficient to re-establish domestic suppliers beyond licensed production, service and maintenance. This slow crawl-back was not limited to West Germany but also took place in the east, mainly in the areas around Dresden and south of Berlin.

Germany did, however, have a powerful advocate of rebuilding the aircraft industry, in the person of Franz-Josef Strauss, initially minister of atomic energy development (the germ for the Ministry of Research and Technology), then of defense and, last but not least, prime minister of Bavaria. Strauss became a keen aviator and made a new aircraft industry not only his own project but that of the Bavarian CSU party, not least in order to promote regional development in Bavaria by attracting innovative industries. But in keeping with both the political and economic necessities and opportunities of the time, the project was European and international. The first major stepping-stone towards functions beyond maintenance was the building of F 104G fighters from 1963 onwards, which included the licensed production and maintenance of J79 military jet engines. Something similar is the re-entry into helicopter engine maintenance and manufacture, which also latched onto local assets of experience, in Oberursel in this case. On the fighter jet engine side, it was an off-shoot of BMW, one of the pre-1945 aircraft engine manufacturers, which re-entered the scene. This was to become MTU (Motoren- und Turbinenunion), the first major supplier of jet engine development, production and services in West Germany. MTU also became the major interlocutor for the Ministry of Defense for fighter, military transport and helicopter engines. In military projects, international consortia are usually politically combined national champions in the respective industry. Thus, when engines had to be developed for the German–British–Italian Tornado fighter-bomber, MTU joined Rolls-Royce to develop and produce the RB 199. Likewise, when the Eurofighter Typhoon was developed, MTU joined the jet engine consortium for the new EJ 2000.

For the jet niche targeted here, however, for civil passenger and transport planes, MTU was slower to establish itself. Still, German governments and jet engine companies, all of whom had initially only or mainly been concerned with military aircraft, began to diversify their portfolio and to develop civil jet engines, for civil passenger and freight planes. This followed the diversification of military aircraft makers towards civil aircraft. The Airbus program is crucial in this respect. This also had a political foundation consisting of Franz-Josef Strauss, the emerging tighter Franco-German collaboration under de Gaulle and Adenauer, and the diversification interests of German aircraft and engine manufacturers. Since both industries employ substantial numbers of development staff, a succession of development projects is crucial in order to keep development staff engaged, retain important resources and generate new revenue. Diversification allows smoother change-over from one huge development project to another, which is one of the arts in aerospace management.

MTU did get a share in the General Electric CF 6–50 development and production effort, the first engine for the first (A 300) European Airbus. This initially was a government-sponsored venture, to bring together European manufacturers, in order to compete with the mainly US makers of passenger jets. But this did not mean that a European alliance was viable in jet engines across the board. The absence of nationalism in the choice of engines by aircraft manufacturers or airlines in the civil markets confronted MTU with entry barriers much more severe than for defense, or for the initial Airbus development in the 1960s and 70s when the Airbus was still a hobby-horse of some politicians and industrialists. MTU only got a foothold in development, rather than exclusive competence for a specific engine.

But on the other hand, aero engine manufacturers have been very adept at forming alliances, consortia or subcontracting relationships, literally in all directions. There has never been a rigid exclusion of a potential partner firm for a specific purpose, when an alliance with a different partner for a different purpose was not seen to threaten it. For instance, in the post-war period MTU had already collaborated with major suppliers from the USA (GE), Britain (RR) and France (SNECMA as well as the earlier Turboméca). Apparently, in this international industry, professionalism overrides any enmity between competing suppliers and makes cooperation possible in any venture, as long as it appears advisable under the market, technical and capacity situation prevailing at the time (Bonaccorsi and Giuri 2001).

Where corporate control is concerned, MTU had almost gone through the who's who in German engineering, turning from an off-shoot of BMW (which as we saw had an aero and even jet engine past) via MAN and Daimler-Chrysler to ownership by Kohlberg Kravis Roberts. Corporate control was, however, unrelated to its position in the industry. This has evolved from privileged national participant in defense consortia to increasing activity in civil jet engine markets. MTU however never became an all-round provider of all the services and production activities for a major jet engine. It did, though, enter projects in many places. Not obtaining controlling responsibility for a major civil jet engine development, despite a strong presence in both development and production but in specific roles for a wide range of engines, it developed a different focus. The firm established itself as what it calls "the leading supplier of maintenance services in the world," by founding subsidiaries in other countries. One of the openings for this strategy occurred through an alliance with P&W, notably for sales and service centers. The civil jet engine market has therefore seen the rise and integration of MTU towards a distinctive profile, focused on maintenance, and on the development and production of systems rather than complete engines, as a contractor of other first-tier suppliers in the civil jets market but with a strong presence in maintenance, and definitely as a multinational enterprise. This was one way of coming back onto the jet engine scene in Germany, after its annihilation in 1945. Again, knowing the importance of maintenance in aero engines, it was not a minor come-back, even though it was functionally restricted, because the value-added accruing in maintenance is crucial.

In East Germany, where a "brownfield" site from before the end of WWII had been redeveloped to maintain Russian origin jet engines, something akin to a new industrial district emerged south of Berlin after the unification of Germany in 1990. First, MTU acquired facilities and developed a maintenance center in Ludwigsfelde. At that time, a new joint venture of RR and BMW also invested in the region. In a curious twist, BMW thus came back both to aero engines and the region, having "left" it in this respect after the end of the war, but it came back in a new facility outside MTU, its former subsidiary. The new facility with Rolls-Royce was directed at engines for planes with one hundred seats or business jets. RR, of course, had its traditional and principal aero engine site at Derby, in the English Midlands. RR was looking for a new site outside Derby, and a mixture of governmental subsidies and a regional labor pool attracted it to the area south of Berlin, to build the facility in Dahlewitz. Now, BMW thus allied with RR to do something new, separate from its earlier spin-off MTU. But in this case, too, ownership was not indefinite and BMW later pulled out of the joint venture, leaving the new subsidiary to continue as a wholly owned RR subsidiary. RR had located development, production and maintenance of the BR 700 series of engines on the site, a specialization technically described as in two-shaft engines, whereas the Derby site of RR retained a focus on three-shaft engines. By that token, Dahlewitz became the first site in Germany after the war on which all the activities relating to a particular class of engines were concentrated. Of course, development and production of systems or modules had often been subcontracted elsewhere, in an industrial group or to suppliers. RR had also taken over the aforementioned site for helicopter or mainly military engines in Oberursel.

Although the birthplaces for jet engines had mainly been in Europe, the balance of relative advantages had shifted to the USA, mainly through the impetus of military contracts and the larger size of the market and industrial concentration. A further and decisive shift in this direction was triggered when Boeing, in the USA, developed and offered the first long-distance passenger plane with four engines (the 707) in the 1960s. This was also a commercial and marketing break-through, based, interestingly, on a military project: the 707 was first used by the US Air Force, as a tanker plane for the in-flight refueling of its strategic bomber fleet. Douglas, then the world market leader in long-distance passenger planes, offered its DC 8 more or less at the same time and Convair followed suit, which gave a powerful impetus notably to P&W and GE, firms that had become main suppliers for military jets. As a consequence, jet propulsion became the state of the art in passenger transport planes with more than, roughly, one hundred seats. But for smaller planes, too, piston engines were driven out and replaced by more economical and cleaner prop jets or turbo-props, i.e. jet engines that also drove a propeller rather than providing propulsion through thrust alone.

During this period in the 1960s, the dominant position of the British and particularly the US engine manufacturers was built up. SNECMA was added later to the first tier, mainly by forming a highly successful alliance with GE for engines for wide-bodied ("jumbo") aircraft (the CFM mentioned above). The present constellation of first-tier suppliers was only unstable for a while in the 1970s, when RR was the privileged developer and supplier of the engine for the Lockheed TriStar and seriously overran development deadlines and costs, which jeopardized the competitive position of this plane against the DC 10 as much as the existence of RR. The firm was rescued with government finance and split up into independent aero engine and motor car parts, which then continued on their own. This led RR back to success. It also instilled a lesson for aeroplane makers, not to commit themselves unilaterally to an engine but allow for the mounting of competing engines. The experience was instrumental in safeguarding competition in the industry. There has come to be an established practice whereby aircraft developers collaborate with different engine makers, communicating information on planes in development and helping the engine makers to develop the corresponding engines.

The industry has, however, not become marked by one-sided competition between isolated manufacturers. With the increasing size, sophistication and development capital outlay required, alliances have been formed between enterprises for specific engines. Industrial concentration meant that specific alliances could bring together different partners. This was also the opening for second-tier manufacturers to enter a globalized industry. One of the initial pioneering adopters, the Soviet Union, has, however, hardly played a role in a world market, outside the users of Soviet planes in the former COMECON.

Localization decisions

Why and how a jet engine industry has come back on the scene in Germany is to some extent explained by the politics of rearmament, and the drive of re-established firms to diversify into civilian engine construction. But national politics was not enough to sustain and expand the industry. In the two subsidiaries visited, localization decisions were mainly said to be based on two sorts of factors. One is the resource endowment of a particular context, such as offering existing or constructible ties with research institutes, universities, colleges, schools and other knowledge-producing institutions. Another important resource is logistical accessibility of a site. Notably with regard to the maintenance function, accessibility is crucial because clients do not like engines being away for service for too long, and in the case of an aircraft being grounded, technicians are expected to solve a problem rapidly. It is also in this context that untroubled industrial relations are seen to be an advantage. This fits the industry emphasis on reliability, safety and rapid response to problems. Other locational advantages are the quality of life offered, and the receptiveness of a cosmopolitan milieu (knowledge of English, multilingual schools, sophisticated entertainment). All these advantages were naturally considered more advantageous if they were available at lower prices. RR was, for example, setting up a facility for the maintenance of Trent (three-shaft engines for very large planes) engines in Thüringen; this region has a good supply of craft labor, an advantageous collective agreement for metal industry wages, a regional airport and motorway links to Frankfurt Airport, a convenient distance away. This facility is a joint venture with Lufthansa Technik and therefore also an example of the tendency to either cooperate or compete flexibly with other service providers, depending on capacities and opportunities in specific fields.

Both enterprises, RR and MTU, have cooperated in the provision of training in the little industrial district that had formed south of Berlin, and in the representation of interests to the state government. They have thus helped to maintain an education and training infrastructure around the occupational school and apprenticeship profiles and examinations of aviation mechanics and electronic engineers. This is an infrastructure which they depend on, especially for the more localized segment of human resources. But in other respects they are clearly rivals, for clients and for human resources, although the local sites have come to specialize in very different parts of the three-dimensional range of activities outlined above (Gottschling 2006). Also, their fates in the larger multinational enterprises to which they belong, are largely independent from one another. The rivalry has not prevented MTU and RR from cooperating in more recent international joint ventures or alliances, such as the International Aero Engines Consortium.

Asked whether national or local institutions offer advantages, the most direct and operationally relevant response was that German occupational training was more broadly based and work organization less specific to engine models. This allowed service and maintenance craftsmen to handle different types of engine one after the other, so that engines could be serviced as urgency required, rather than waiting for specialized resources to be available. In this way, locally specific resources may confer a comparative advantage even in a highly globalized and far-flung industry. It is a well-known advantage for Germany established by many studies for non-routine industries, especially investment goods industries. The advantage has clear cost implications. Competitiveness is less affected by the labor costs of service providers; the costs that matter are those of aircraft standing idle (opportunity costs on the part of the buyer). Thus, even when competition on the basis of selling price may be fierce, such that product sales hardly add to profit margins, the direct production costs in maintenance are not under similar pressure because down-time of engines (and the aircraft around them) weighs much more heavily in the users' calculations. However, the existence of profit margins does not mean that competition is felt to be slack; Lufthansa Technik is a powerful competitor that also serves other airlines, and similar facilities of British Airways, Air France and KLM are not far away. But again, the response was that where capacities and opportunities make cooperation plausible, everyone in the industry, in the first tier or subsequent ones, and in the technological services of clients, is also a potential collaborator. Despite the limited number of direct competitors in the industry, competition is both facilitated and limited by a history of project and functionally specific cooperation and competition, and by having learned to change from one to the other without acrimony.

It is clear from the comparison that RR was more willing to delegate responsibility for a new engine class to a completely new, expatriate location, than MTU was able to translate more long-standing proven competence in international consortia into overall product responsibility for a civil jet engine that tied development, production and maintenance together. In this sense, RR created more space for its German subsidiary than did P&W, the main alliance of MTU, apart from the space for service centers. Expansion apparently led RR to Germany more systematically. Derby, the home of RR, was already so large that this appeared to restrict the build-up of further capacities. It is also noteworthy that in RR, a transfer to Derby is considered less coveted than a move to the Berlin area. In interviews, international engineering staff were said to be drawn to regions with both cosmopolitan/school and quality-of-life advantages.

The RR site and enterprise at Dahlewitz has become specialized in the BR 700 class of engines, their development, production and maintenance, as well as expertise in compressors for different types of RR engines. The first specialization was, more or less, there from the start, and deliberately located near Berlin to tap into existing knowledge and infrastructure resources but also governmental subsidies to rebuild industry after East Germany became part of the Federal Republic. These motives had also attracted MTU to the area. However, the basic knowledge and social infrastructure for the industry were already there in a rudimentary form. It was not as if investment went into these subsidiaries *ex nihilo*, in return for lower wages and subsidies. One can also see that the development of the site was contingent not only on calculated or arbitrary top management decision, but on the emergence of demonstrated and acknowledged competence in a technology that mattered to all the RR sites. Both enterprises demonstrate that subsidiaries and sites can and do develop competence, extend their activities and even spawn other sites, at home or abroad. They do this in the way that the subsidiaries described by Kristensen and Zeitlin (2005) went about their business. However, they can also be seen to build their local strengths on the institutional strengths of the societal business system; these enable polyvalent craft skills linking manual labor with intellectual and technical sophistication, and the companies turn them to good use, notably in the maintenance function, which is the main generator of direct revenue in the industry. The micro-politics of localization thus play on competitive strategies in the industry (see also chapter of Williams and Geppert in this volume), they profit from local resource limitations such as those of RR in the case of Derby but also from local resource endowments in the place of localization.

Interpretation and conclusions

The fate of sites and subsidiaries appears, in this comparison, to depend on the continual cultivation of institutional and other local resources. They have to be "sold," not only commercially but also discursively in the enterprise. Professional reputation and experience matter greatly in this discourse, which takes place in a community of practice that exceeds not only a site and subsidiary, but also an enterprise and is worldwide. One may give this process of persuasion the label of "micro-politics." Micro-politics does not mean that the name of the game is to derive any short-term advantage that may quickly turn out to be spurious, in a manipulative way, such that actors regard each other as tools on the way to maximizing the advantage of their own person or party. Engine safety, time of response to problems, durability and the long-term synergetic relationship between equally important functions ensure that demonstrably sustainable solutions are selected with a critical eye.

Important resources are to some extent globally tapped into, when they are mobile, such as east European engine engineers tend to be, or when the enterprise promotes occupational and hierarchical advance through expatriation, as both enterprises do. But there is also a resource segment which is nationally and locally conditioned, rooted in occupational training, work organization and industrial relations. Now, this resource segment is not a residual element in an increasingly internationalized world, although it is totally unrelated to any possible diversity of output markets. Instead, it is precisely the high international interdependency of functions and events in a transnational company, between, say, an engine failure in Thessaloniki and a service center near Berlin, in the very capital-intensive world of international air transport, that puts specific local resources in the limelight.

Based on this resource development, local sites and subsidiaries are to some extent able to manage their fate in the larger enterprise and in the global community of practice, even if they do not have much of a history, identity and inherited resource base of their own, and even if their resource base has partly been constituted by a mother enterprise, or a license-holding or cooperating enterprise. They can do so by exploiting and cultivating local resources, both internal and external ones, company resources and resources of a local or national institutionalized system. The overall strategy of the enterprise, however, also has to create a space in which the resources can be demonstrated to be useful. The contrast between P&W and RR is particularly instructive in this respect: P&W mainly created space in the maintenance function, RR in all the functions in a specific part of the product range and a part of all products. At this level, not only the individual strategy of the enterprise comes into play but also inter-organizational relations, through which the enterprise forms consortia with other manufacturers for the purposes of specific engines, modules or functions.

Across the vicissitudes of enterprises and industries over time, for which Germany in the aircraft industries is an outstanding example, fundamental knowledge resource endowments have a surprising capability to persist, even in a rudimentary form and when a site was abandoned for ten years. This does not apply to all or even most of the locations in which they had come into existence, but new investment characteristically went into an older knowledge habitat in all the cases. Probably in such kinds of industries, any kind of direct investment goes into fields that are various shades of brown. Path dependency coexists with radical path ruptures, by sites being reinvented and re-cast into new molds. Without initial government support for the aircraft industry, it is doubtful what breadth and depth the development of aero engine manufacturing would have gained in Germany. However, that is not only true for Germany but, in the origin of the industry, even more so for the jet engine manufacturers in other countries that imported the technology from Britain and Germany, notably the most prolific country with regard to governmental support for radical innovation, the USA.

In both our cases, government procurement or other policies were important to attract direct investment, localize activities and build up comparative advantage. But none of the advantages would have been sustainable had these not been continuously developed through both cooperation and competition in the international jet engine community of practice, and had this not happened in tune with the building up of a knowledge infrastructure linking public and private facilities.

Theories on varieties of capitalism and innovation in business systems are to some extent disproved, notably in the historical part and in the general setting of the aero engine industry. Its very long-term time horizon contradicts VoC/business systems theory, as does its origin in a coordinated market economy. Furthermore, the industry combines high knowledge intensity and traditional industrialism, which is linked to the importance of maintenance competence for generating a profit and investment resources. This is linked in turn to uniform and industrially idiosyncratic pricing strategies that also put a premium on vertical integration, rather than decomposition of the value chain. To this extent, the industry is not accounted for by VoC and business system concepts, although Whitley (1999) on business systems has allowed for nations to combine types of business systems.

However, even the uniform global strategy in the industry gives particular leverage to national and local institutions, practices and experience. Through the pricing strategy, it is precisely the implementation of knowledge related to the product and production that most directly contributes to profit margin. In this respect, VoC and business system concepts were confirmed; global properties of the industry (the pricing strategy and the importance of maintenance in the value chain) gave German human resource and organizational institutions competitive advantages. We could also see that in the pioneering phase of the industry, the established differences – arm's length relations and company individualism in Britain versus a more integrated industrial space and easier cooperation between firms in Germany – had prevailed. So, after some modification and combination with other theories, VoC/business systems have potential still. They may usefully be combined with the IB&M literature, which highlights actors, their resources and the action they deploy, rather than the institutions and systemic complementarities dear to VoC and business systems. But the overlap or link occurs where resources include institutions. Thus, through the combination one can explain how actors in MNCs build up, mobilize and valorize resources, by locating subsidiaries and in developing local or national capabilities.

Some constellations of the industry are undoubtedly specific. But we would also argue that organization theory and comparative political economy have unduly neglected such specifics. Whilst information technology industries probably confirm the VoC/business system picture better (short-termism, short innovation cycles, vertical disintegration, direct profitability of research and development), there are other industries which are high-tech and would merit closer scrutiny, such as aerospace, pharmaceutics, medical research technology (X-ray and other imaging technologies) or energy generation equipment. There might be further aberrations from the stereotypical VoC picture waiting to be unearthed, in business models, strategies and socio-economic institutions. Both comparative political economy and IB&M have not only increasingly neglected work systems but also, to some extent, history. As we saw, history has both surprising discontinuities and continuities of developmental paths to offer.

If we are to offer a specific statement as an attempt at theory building, it might be one for internationalization strategies of multinational enterprises in globalized industries:

- If these strategies do not imply large batch production but customization, prevalence of quality and responsiveness,
- and if there are barriers to the segmentation of the value chain into independent firms,

then localization decisions are dependent on the embeddedness of locations or subsidiaries in socio-institutional contexts; they are sticky (less reversible) because of the asset specificity of resources.

This is in line with IB&M research, but inputs need to be given more attention than output markets and downstream transactions, the area where such theory and research have looked for explanations more intensively. What Kristensen and Zeitlin showed for an MNC arising from mergers and acquisitions also applies to enterprises that found wholly new sites and subsidiaries. Even a wholly new transnational enterprise would, through the interdependencies between localized competence centers, thus be constrained to cultivate and valorize local resources. In doing so, they exploit, maintain and develop different local or national institutions. In a more representative inquiry comparing industries and firms-in-industries, such propositions could be examined more thoroughly.

Acknowledgements

This chapter has greatly profited from the comments of anonymous reviewers and/or Mark Fenton-O'Creevy at the Amsterdam Colloquium of the European Group for Organization Studies in 2008; in the memory of the first author, these were the best comments ever.

REFERENCES

Aharoni, Y. 1966. *The Foreign Investment Decision Process*. Boston, MA: Harvard University Graduate School of Business Administration, Division of Research

Anderson, E. and H. Gatignon 1986. "Modes of foreign entry: a transaction cost analysis and propositions," *Journal of International Business Studies* 17: 1–26

Andersson, U., M. Forsgren and U. Holm 2007. "Balancing subsidiary influence in the federative MNC: a business network view," *Journal of International Business Studies* 38: 802–18

Astley, W. G. and P. S. Sachdeva 1984. "Structural sources of intraorganizational power. a theoretical synthesis," *Academy of Management Review* 9: 104–13

Barkema, H. G. and F. Vermeulen 1998. "International expansion through start-up or acquisition: a learning perspective," *Academy of Management Journal* 41: 7–26

Bartlett, C. A. and S. Ghoshal 1989. *Managing Across Borders: The Transnational Solution.* London: Century Business

Bonaccorsi, A. and P. Giuri 2001. "Network structure and industrial dynamics. The long-term evolution of the aircraft-engine industry," *Structural Change and Economic Dynamics* 12: 201–33

Cyert, R. M. and J. G. March 1992. *A Behavioral Theory of the Firm.* Cambridge, MA: Blackwell

Dörrenbächer, C. 2007. "The challenges for foreign-owned subsidiaries in FDI-led modernization strategies: the case of Hungary," *Competition and Change* 11: 179–97

Dörrenbächer, C. and M. Geppert 2005. "Micropolitical aspects of mandate development and learning in local subsidiaries of multinational corporations." Discussion Paper SP III 2005–202, Social Science Research Center Berlin

Dunning, J. 1988. "The eclectic paradigm of international production: a re-statement and some possible extensions," http://aib.msu.edu/awards/19_1_88_1.pdf (last accessed 29 October, 2009)

Ergas, H. 1984. "Why do some countries innovate more than others?," http://ssrn.com/abstract=1430184 (last accessed 29 October, 2009)

Forsgren, M., U. Holm and J. Johanson 2005. *Managing the Embedded Multinational: A Business Network View.* Cheltenham: Edward Elgar

Galland, A. 1993. Die Ersten und die Letzten. Deutsche Jagdflieger im 2. Weltkrieg. Munich: Schneekluth

Gersdorff von, K., K. Grasmann and H. Schubert (with Karl Prestel) 1995. Flugmotoren und Strahltriebwerke. Entwicklungsgeschichte der deutschen Luftfahrtantriebe von den Anfängen bis zu den internationalen Gemeinschaftsentwicklungen. Bonn: Bernard & Graefe

Gottschling, D. 2006. "Triebwerke der Region. Die Wachstumsbranche der Luft- und Raumfahrt in der Hauptstadtregion Berlin-Brandenburg kann sich sehen lassen: Millionen-Umsätze, tausende Arbeitskräfte, internationale Anerkennung – und kein Ende," *FORUM – Das Brandenburger Wirtschaftsmagazin* 6: 4–5

Hall, P. A. and D. Soskice (eds.) 2001. *Varieties of Capitalism: The Institutional Foundations of Comparative Advantage.* Oxford University Press

Hayward, K. 1986. *International Collaboration in Civil Aerospace.* London: Frances Pinter

Hennart, J.-F. and S. Reddy 1997. "The impact of culture on the strategy of multinational enterprises: does national origin affect ownership decisions?," *Journal of International Business Studies* 29: 515–38

Johanson, J. and J. E. Vahlne 1977. "The internationalization process of the firm – a model of knowledge development and increasing foreign market commitment," *Journal of International Business Studies* 8: 23–32

Kristensen, P. and J. Zeitlin 2005. *Local Players in Global Games.* Oxford University Press

Lammers, C. J. 1978. "The comparative sociology of organizations," *Annual Review of Sociology* 4: 485–510

Lane, C. and R. Bachmann 1996. "The social constitution of trust: supplier relations in Britain and Germany," *Organization Studies* 17: 365–95

Lange, K. S. G. 2006. "Deutsche Biotech-Unternehmen und ihre Innovationsfähigkeit im internationalen Vergleich – eine institutionentheoretische Analyse." Doctoral thesis, Rijksuniversiteit Groningen

Lundvall, B. A. (ed.) 1992. *National Systems of Innovation*. London: Frances Pinter

Marr, A. 2007. *A History of Modern Britain*. London: Macmillan

Saka, A. 2007. "Unravelling learning within multinational enterprises," *British Journal of Management* 18: 294–310

Schmid, S. and A. Schurig 2003. "The development of critical capabilities in foreign subsidiaries: disentangling the role of the subsidiary's business network," *International Business Review* 12: 755–82

Sorge, A. 2006. "Organizing socially constructed internal and external resources," *Journal of Institutional and Theoretical Economics* 162: 172–93

The Economist 2009. "Rolls-Royce. Making things in a post-industrial society," 8 January

Wernerfelt, B. 1984. "A resource-based view of the firm," *Strategic Management Journal* 5: 171–80

Whitley, R. 1992. *European Business Systems. Firms and Markets in Their National Contexts*. London: Sage

  1999. *Divergent Capitalisms*. Oxford University Press

  2006. "Understanding differences: searching for the social processes that construct and reproduce variety in science and economic organization," *Organization Studies* 27: 1153–77

Wikipedia: Frank Whittle: http://en.wikipedia.org/wiki/Frank_Whittle (last accessed October 29, 2009)

Wikipedia: Jet engine: http://en.wikipedia.org/wiki/Jet engine (last accessed October 29, 2009)

3 Bargained globalization: employment relations providing robust "tool kits" for socio-political strategizing in MNCs in Germany

Karen Williams and Mike Geppert

Germany has somehow managed to create a high-wage, unionized economy without shipping all its jobs abroad or creating a massive trade deficit, or any deficit at all … Why is Germany beating us?

(Geoghegan 2010: 7)

Introduction

The above quote appeared in a recent edition of *Harper's Magazine* in the USA and raises some interesting questions by contrasting distinctive management and employment practices in the German manufacturing sector with current dilemmas faced by firms situated in and originating from liberal market economies in the wake of the recent financial crisis. In this chapter we seek to explain why these distinctive practices remain robust in the face of pressures from globalization, based on a survey of some of the current literature on plant-level employment relations in Germany. Our survey focuses on the important role played by local managers and workers' representatives as socio-political strategists, who are able to draw on critical power resources within multinational companies (MNCs) operating in Germany to safeguard skills and jobs in German plants.

In the first part of the chapter we reflect on ideas that stress the importance of local institutions and the role of local actors for institution building in transnational social spaces, referring to the idea of the MNC as a "contested terrain" (Edwards and Bélanger 2009; see also chapter of Morgan in this volume). We look at emerging opportunities for socio-political strategizing by local actors in Germany and link these to institutional resources provided by the German model of employment relations, which provide local actors with critical resources. However, the mere existence of these local resources is insufficient to generate effective socio-political strategies; for this to occur, local actors need to have the social skills to use these resources. We will argue that culturally and institutionally shaped "tool kits" support key actors in producing "acceptable rationales" within the MNC to secure jobs and skills.

The second part of the chapter investigates the debate about whether the German model is disintegrating under the pressures of globalization, particularly the pressures exerted by the international financial markets and shareholder value orientation. This has had some serious implications for local actor resources and national vocabularies and logics used by key actors in their socio-political strategizing processes within MNCs in Germany.

In the discussion section we look at the emergence of flexible learning processes within "core segments" of the German economy, in particular the manufacturing sector, in which German actors and institutions are engaging with change. We contrast this briefly with features of the Anglo-American liberal market systems, where local actors have far fewer institutional resources to draw upon in promoting their interests in a globalized environment.

In the conclusion we summarize some of the main arguments arising from this review of literature on the German model of employment relations, and propose some answers to three key questions about how the operation of this model in the German manufacturing sector supports the retention of high-skilled manufacturing and R&D capabilities in German plants.

Strategizing opportunities: the importance of societal institutions, particularly employment relations, in Germany

The mainstream of international business (IB) literature has largely neglected the importance of social institutions for the operation of MNCs, being predominantly focused on the question of how MNCs can be more efficiently managed in light of global market and technological pressures. Often headquarters (HQ) managers are still seen in the driver's seat steering the integration of business activities of MNCs across national borders to achieve efficient local adaptation to host country pressures and the implementation of global best practices to improve global integration (e.g. Andersson and Holm 2010; Bartlett and Ghoshal 1989). Other research emphasizes more the role of subsidiary management and entrepreneurship in order to gain mandates and resources from HQ (e.g. Birkinshaw 2000). In summary, the focus of analysis of most IB studies remains one-sidedly on how management and organizational structures combine "business with efficiency, geography with local responsiveness and function with expertise" (Westney 2009: 128). By contrast, a newly emerging literature on "transnational social spaces" focuses on the role of individual and collective actors and their relationship to social institution building (Geppert and Clark 2003; Morgan 2001).

Thus the role of home and host country institutional influences on management of the MNC and, what is more, its socio-political dimensions, have been neglected in mainstream IB. These issues, however, have been recently addressed by comparative institutionalist scholars (see e.g. Ferner *et al.* 2000; Geppert *et al.* 2003; Morgan 2001). Country of origin and its societal institutions have been shown to explain differences in how companies internationalize and structure their operations abroad (e.g. Noorderhaven and Harzing 2003). Newer discussions have also stressed that host country institutional differences are important in understanding local adaptation of global best practices and strategies of MNCs (see also chapter of Sorge and Rothe in this volume). For example, it has been shown that coordinated market economies, such as Germany, provide more critical resources than liberal market economies to negotiate MNC strategies locally (Geppert *et al.* 2003). However, mainstream institutionalist studies have been rightly criticized for downplaying the critical role of social agency and focusing too much on the determining features of national institutions and path dependencies. Local institutional resources are in fact intertwined with agency so that the MNC must be understood as a "contested terrain": "MNCs comprise groups with differing interests, and these groups use their resources to pursue their own ends" (Edwards and Bélanger 2009: 193) and look for opportunities for socio-political strategizing (Dörrenbächer and Geppert 2009). Thus the strategic orientations of managers are not just shaped by institutional features but also by their career interests and aspirations (Dörrenbächer and Geppert 2009). Moreover, the idea of analyzing the MNC as "contested terrain" goes beyond common IB debates, where strategic decision-making is exclusively interpreted as a managerial task in which HQ and subsidiary managers are the key power holders. This mainstream IB approach, however, tells us only one part of the story, failing to address the problem that strategic decisions require legitimacy and that the political role of workers and employee representatives is important in this process.

Starting at the subsidiary level, the concept of MNCs as "contested terrains" means, firstly, and in line with institutional theory, that managers must legitimate their decisions not just to the HQ but also locally to other key stakeholders or actors (Scott 2001), with workers being a core group in manufacturing firms. Secondly, compared to mainstream IB research, the idea of "contested terrains" focuses on the potentially differing interests of managers and workers. The interests of both groups can overlap to a certain extent at certain times but have been described as being more often conflicting (Edwards and Bélanger 2009). How much the interests between managers and workers overlap and whether each of the two groups pursues more short-term or long-term oriented strategies is not just influenced by the HQ strategy but also by the local institutional settings. These settings provide strategic resources and "tools," as we will show, for actors to influence and resist strategies and practices transferred from the HQ to the subsidiary (see also chapters of Fenton-O'Creevy *et al.* and of Schotter and Beamish in this volume).

In this chapter we are interested in the question of how the German model of employment relations influences the social construction of "contested terrains." We concentrate on the question: how does employee voice and involvement help to develop and maintain high-quality production and skilled labor in German plants, compared to plants in Anglo-American capitalist countries? In liberal market economies traditional conflicting relations between managers and workers with weak employment relation systems hinder knowledge sharing between managers and workers, a precondition to maintaining and improving high performance, quality and work systems (Delaney and Godard 2001; Whitley 1999). In contrast to the majority of comparative institutionalist studies (e.g. Hall and Soskice 2001), we focus not only on structural features and subsidiary roles but on social processes, especially how socio-political strategizing is intertwined with local institution building. These processes are emergent and constantly shifting and changing as a result of socio-political interaction based on the exercise of power at all levels within the MNC as well as with groups outside the companies.

There are many studies on the important role that local subsidiaries play in MNCs and how they gain and lose critical resources, gain autonomy for learning, establish local capabilities and influence strategic decision-making in the MNC (see e.g. the review in Geppert and Saka-Helmhout 2007). Studies such as those by Birkinshaw *et al.* (2000) have, however, tended to neglect the institutional context, including employment relations, in which subsidiaries are embedded, preferring to focus on their position within the MNC itself. However, a more recent study by Bouquet and Birkinshaw (2008) investigating the factors leading actors to strategize to gain power includes critical resources. The focus is still predominantly on strategic resources within the MNC itself, but a brief allusion is made to the importance of institutional contexts (Bouquet and Birkinshaw (2008: 490). Geppert and Saka-Helmhout

(2007), on the other hand, emphasize the local embeddedness of subsidiary capabilities and the use of institutions as resources providing opportunities for particular types of action. Oliver and Holzinger (2008), in a recent study of how companies use capabilities to stay innovative, similarly underline the importance of social capital, membership of local social networks, for proactive strategies by companies (Oliver and Holzinger 2008: 510). This is also emphasized by Kristensen and Zeitlin (2005) in relation to local actors in MNCs, who need to develop local capacities for collaborative action. These help them to influence and even resist HQ management decisions to globally standardize and financialize organization and management processes. Work by Bélanger *et al.* (2006) explores the factors influencing the development of organizational capability in order to prevent the spread of the "hollowed-out firm" among Canadian subsidiaries of MNCs (Bélanger *et al.* 2006: 69). They point to the important role played by local institutions, which can provide levers to improve a plant's strategic capabilities. Thus it is argued that "firms better able to develop local networks and use the resources and leverage afforded by their institutional environments are also able to reinforce the depth and nature of their firm-specific capabilities that seem so important in differentiating and reinforcing their role within their worldwide company" (Bélanger *et al.* 2006: 68). The most important influence they found for plants securing investment mandates was the ability of senior national management to make the case for their operations.

Our review of recent studies provides evidence that the German model and, in particular, its employment relations institutions still provide institutional resources, which local plant actors can use to develop and maintain positions of power within MNCs. Our survey of relevant literature, however, is confined to the metalworking and engineering sectors, where the model has had its strongest effects. By German model we are referring to elements of the German business system such as patient capital, a long-term management perspective with high levels of investment in research and development (R&D), a highly developed vocational, education and training system, highly skilled labor, strong internal labor markets with enhanced job security and cooperative management–labor relations (see e.g. Ferner *et al.* 2000; Gospel and Pendleton 2003; Grahl and Teague 2004). The framework of employee relations within the German business system is orientated towards a negotiated approach to change, both at plant and company board levels. This facilitates a "bargained approach" to dealing with global business challenges, which still has strong legal and trade union support in the German manufacturing sector. It enables works councils to represent the "employee voice" (Royle 2004) in global restructuring processes. In contrast to research pointing to the "disorganiza-tion" of the German industrial relations system (Doellgast and Greer 2007), we contend that power relations between local management and works councils in MNCs still "accompany cooperative attitudes" (Frege 2003: 317) and that workplace relations are more stable than it is often assumed (Frege 2002), espe-cially in MNCs committed to high-quality production.

Moreover, we found support for this argumentation in international comparisons of home and host country influences on MNCs. Authors such as Bélanger et al. (1999) use the example of ABB to underline the import-ant role played by institutional factors, since "embeddedness in the local environment sometimes generates additional resources for a local company to develop more autonomy in its relations with corporate management" (Bélanger et al. 1999: 262). Much more extensive job regulation possibilities in both the German and Swedish subsidiaries of ABB offer greater possi-bilities to negotiate and resist global strategic approaches. One of the areas where job regulation is still very supportive for socio-political strategizing is the German car industry. Accordingly, Kädtler and Sperling's study of the German car industry (2002) provides many examples of strategic action by management and works councils. This study argues that increasing global competition actually "accelerates the need and opportunities for strategic choice by management and the need for workers' representation to respond by taking an active part in defining the company's strategy" (2002: 158). Examples given include workforce–management alliance building in General Motors (GM) to resist standardization (2002: 160), in Daimler Benz to resist outsourcing (2002: 163) and local agreements to win investment mandates from the MNCs. In the case of GM, an alliance of management and works council were able to use worker codetermination rights in the supervisory board as well as a production-oriented chairman on the board of directors and the European works council to influence corporate management goals. Their aim was to keep and upgrade the established management approach based on German high-quality engineering expertise, in spite of global standardization and cost-reduction pressures. In Daimler Benz, coalitions of local management, works councils and the heads of distribution centers supported in-house production, arguing in favor of its technological advan-tages, which were important to meet the high quality expectations of cus-tomers. Even in cases where local management had limited influence on HQ decision-making, the strong ties between local and central company works councils, in Volkswagen for example, also promoted successful production upgrading in line with local manager interests (2002: 158).

Strong social networks exist in the car industry between the different levels of works council representation, including European and even world works councils, the IG Metall (metalworkers) union and local management. Studies agree that the power of the workforce is particularly high in the German car industry (Kädtler and Sperling 2002; Pries 1999) and in the heavy manufacturing sector generally. Greer and Hauptmeier's (2008) recent studies of the German car industry underline the important role played by German actors in the development of transnationalism in the European car industry, emphasizing the strategic use of institutional resources, particularly the European Works Council Directive. Blazejewski's (2009) study of three plants of Opel/GM, however, highlights the diversity in the approaches of works councils and local trade union representatives depending on factors such as previous experience of conflicts with management and local actor responses to these. There were different interpretations of what actions by shop floor representatives, central works councils and unions were permitted under German labor law. The latter actors eventually reclaimed shop floor action, including a "wildcat strike," being taken against job cuts and reinstated a negotiated settlement (2009: 23). Blazejewski's study underlines the local actors' use of employment relations resources as political tools in their attempts to influence corporate strategies. Another study by Raess and Burgoon (2006) of eight Siemens plants in Germany points to similar works council strategies in the car industry. Their aims are to lock in capital investment via investment guarantees in return for local labor concessions such as Saturday working without premium payment, working time flexibility and use of temporary employment contracts among other initiatives. Raess and Burgoon argue that FDI is affecting plant bargaining in Germany negatively in terms of the depth of concession bargaining by works councils. However, the type of concessions being granted by works councils would be seen as extremely mild from a British trade union standpoint and underline the amount of bargaining and leeway for local actors to negotiate global strategic approaches in German plants. Greer's recent work (2008) similarly argues that there has been a roll-back in working conditions due in particular to outsourcing of production from the core plant to suppliers. This impacts conditions in both types of plants due to fears of job losses. Employment relations resources are, however, still there and the power of the union should be considerable but has not been used strategically, in Greer's view, to influence outsourcing and the reorganization of the supply chain in MNCs (2008: 194).

The above examples deal with German companies and German plants; what about situations where German companies are taken over by foreign

MNCs? Zeller (2000) investigates the fight of German plants against job cuts when the German pharmaceutical company, Boehringer-Mannheim, was acquired by Hoffmann-La Roche. Here a different, less powerful union than the IG Metall was involved which was "fully embraced by the logic of factual constraints and consensual agreements with the executives of the multinationals" (Zeller 2000: 1554). The former German parent company had a long tradition of trade unionism and workforce mobilization and the works council forged alliances with the city, grass roots organizations and artists to retain jobs and R&D capabilities. However, they lost out to two other German sites, although a non-competition agreement between the plants was agreed. Zeller argues that the works council's narrow parent-company focus and the failure to understand the larger context of the restructuring was a key reason for the failure to shape the MNC agenda in their interests. Our own studies of a German plant taken over by a Finnish MNC was another example of a battleground between works council and local management on the one hand and the MNC headquarters on the other over corporate strategy, which threatened the skills and R&D base of the German plant (Geppert *et al.* 2003). Greer and Hauptmeier (2008) found differences in the strategies adopted by local actors in German-owned and foreign-owned car companies in Germany. Local actors were heavily involved in decision-making and responsibility for restructuring of the German MNCs. The more limited access to the world headquarters in the US MNCs led to the development of greater trade union transnational strategies to influence restructuring across all the European plants led, in many cases, by the German members of the European works councils.

The new agreements between management and works councils in the car industry are described by Kädtler and Sperling (2002: 164) as bargaining in complex relations of production, leading to investment in new product development, production volumes and employment maintenance in Germany. This kind of bargained globalization is discussed, e.g. in Geoghegan's polemic article (2010), as a more robust way to resist current globalization pressures, which are often seen as inevitable especially in the Anglo-American context. Accordingly, he stresses that even when local managers and workers in Germany "can't stop a sale. They can't stop outsourcing. But they can cut deals … If a company wants to start a plant abroad, the workers can pressure the board to plow some money back into the German plant or provide a ten-year employment guarantee. Or they can fight to get a better owner …" (Geoghegan 2010: 8). The wider collaborative networks in which German companies work aid strategic action and proactive strategies on the part of management, as do the wider networks in which many works councils operate, particularly in the manufacturing sector. Bluhm (2003) pointed to their importance in explaining why German MNCs held to a collective-cooperative approach in labor relations in their eastern European subsidiaries. Thus employment relations institutional resources are an integral part of the German model in manufacturing and show mutual interdependencies with such resources in helping to build and maintain a stable, highly skilled workforce. This workforce is capable of sustaining the high-skill production and service models (Streeck 1996), which in turn bolster the role of employees and their representatives.

Strategizing opportunities: the importance of robust strategic "tool kits" of local German plant actors to bargain globalization

In this section we are going to argue that global strategic approaches of MNCs, seen as possible drivers for convergence of the German model of employment relations, do not necessarily lead to the transformation of societal institutions, if social skills of key actors are robust. Social skills and "strategic choices" of powerful key actors are interdependently linked with certain cultural and institutional characteristics of particular societal contexts (see e.g. Child 1997; Sorge 2004). Accordingly, we believe that socio-political strategizing can be related to certain societally shaped "tool kits" (Swidler 1986: 273), which are defined as "habits, skills, and styles" from which key actors construct their "strategies of action" (Swidler 1986). We also assume that these historically grown tool kits differ between countries, industries and regions and, what is more, are more or less robust in terms of their usefulness for bargaining purposes. In this chapter, however, we stress that the robustness of tool kits depends on whether these are supported by societal institutions and cultural values and norms which encourage knowledge sharing and development of mutual interests between various key actors, including local managers and employees. We will demonstrate that the tool kits of key actors in the German industrial core sectors are quite robust because they are more likely to be based on the shared interests of local managers and employee representatives. We provide evidence of institutional support for actors in building robust tool kits in Germany. These provide German MNCs and subsidiaries of foreign-owned MNCs in industrial core sectors in Germany with critical resources to resist and bargain globalization, in comparison to their counterparts in the context of Anglo-American liberal capitalism.

In line with Swidler (1986), we see institutional and cultural change not so much as a voluntary process where the interests and values of new or old powerful elites in the MNC can be directly linked with desired outcomes. Institutional change and its outcomes are instead understood as being influenced by the habits, social skills and capabilities (tool kits) of key actors. These are interdependently linked with the distinct cultural and institutional features of a particular society. In comparison to Anglo-American capitalist societies, key actors' tool kits are rather robust in core industrial sectors of Germany because interests of local key actors (e.g. managers and employee representatives) are rather overlapping than contradictory and therefore have at least the potential to enable local actors to effectively resist, bargain and negotiate global change management strategies. In short, we believe that these robust tool kits enable collective and therefore often more effective forms of resistance to and negotiation of the global strategies of MNCs.

However, we do not share the assumptions of mainstream institutionalist studies. They stress that the institutional logic of national business systems can be explained with reference to the most dominant business model (e.g. Hall and Soskice 2001; Whitley 1999) and that its benefits in the case of Germany are equally relevant across the whole society and all industrial sectors. Instead, we believe that the possibilities for employment relation systems, as a major feature of the national business system, to provide critical resources differ between societal contexts and also between industrial sectors and regions within a country. Thus, for example, research has shown that employment relation institutions are not just weak but also easier to hollow out in industrial sectors with highly standardized and centralized production systems such as the fast food industry. Even here, however, the empirical findings are mixed. On the one hand, a study of employment relations in the global fast food MNC McDonalds provides evidence that local actors, especially workers, lack critical resources to resist, and feel powerless even in coordinated market economies (see e.g. Royle 2002). Moreover, it has been emphasized that the bargaining power of trade unions and works councils differs significantly in the new Bundesländer, in comparison to west Germany, the heartland of the German model of capitalism. On the other hand, there is also research providing evidence that the robustness of core employment relations institutions and interrelated "tools" of key actors support "spill-over effects" into other sectors where these have been traditionally rather weak. Thus, for example, Turner's research (2009) found that new forms of union activism were more successful in the German retail sector, in comparison with the labor movement in the USA (Turner 2009). This was because of the stronger institutional basis of employment relations and stronger institutional support for local actors to build robust tool kits. He provides evidence of the importance of German employment institutions as a viable basis, an anchor and tool kit, on which trade unions and workers can build "to promote innovative strategies" (Turner 2009: 303). Thus his case studies document the successful setting up of works councils at the anti-union German drugstore chain Schlecker, which spread across the retail sector and also led to mobilization of employees and establishment of some works councils, e.g. at another anti-union employer, the European low-budget retailer Lidl.

Thus studies of core industrial sectors in Germany and MNCs from different home countries investing in these industries demonstrate that key features of the German system of employment relations, although under pressure, continue to provide strategic "tools" for both key groups of actors. This is a precondition for more negotiated forms of institution building within globally operating firms. Research points to continued scope for strategic choice for local subsidiary actors in decision-making in MNCs. Edwards *et al.* (2007), for example, point to diversity of practice and the scope for choice in the area of decisions about human resource policies and practices, even in US MNCs, often viewed as highly top-down organizations (Edwards *et al.* 2007: 107). Kädtler and Sperling (2002), as mentioned earlier, found considerable scope for bargaining and strategic choice in the German car industry, even with the pressures of globalization and shareholder value imperatives (Kädtler and Sperling 2002: 165). Management decisions are not just a question of them "applying financial parameters" but "the outcome of complex negotiations, which bring together different economic logics and diverging interests, as well as questions of power and aspects of concrete situations" (Kädtler and Sperling 2002). This opens up opportunities for strategic action. Subsidiary managers and employees in particular can use a very specific "kit" of locally available "tools" enabling active agency.

Shared interests and abilities of both management and workforce representatives in engineering and manufacturing have been linked to strategically entrepreneurial types of behavior when trying to enhance plant mandates within MNCs. Dörrenbächer and Geppert's (2009) investigation of French subsidiaries of German MNCs isolated the following mutually shared interests used as tool kits when socio-politically strategizing: managerial expertise, product portfolios, specialized technologies, internal R&D as well as HQ policies. All the German expatriates interviewed in this study had a strong technical and innovation orientation and engaged in pronounced strategizing to improve plant resources. This included R&D, forming coalitions with the workforce and lobbying the German HQ in order to replicate the high-skill, high-tech model found in German manufacturing within the French context. In their study of US MNCs in Europe, Almond and Ferner (2006) point out that the German managers were seen as having far more critical resources, particularly because of the employment relations system, to preserve their autonomy and fight for their plants' resources in US MNCs. For example, German managers used the argument that the works council would not agree to certain measures to resist MNC decisions. National HR directors were also much stronger in France and Germany for the same institutional reasons. In comparison, British managers in the MNCs have a rather limited "kit of tools" they can employ for socio-political strategizing (see e.g. Geppert and Williams 2006). There has been lower institutional support to build and maintain manufacturing capabilities in the national economy and historically adverse management–employee relations. The very different cultural and educational backgrounds between managers and workers also hinder mutual strategizing and coalition building. Therefore, British managers see themselves often as being on their own without substantive resources to fall back on when confronting the global change strategies of the HQ (Geppert *et al.* 2003).

Research into the role of location for MNC strategizing stresses that subsidiary managers might start to act "subversively," especially when HQ global restructuring strategies threaten to undermine local power resources (Morgan and Kristensen 2006). In contrast to Anglo-Saxon countries, such an approach of local management might be actually more successful in coordinated market economies, where local managers are not necessarily interested in undermining the resistance of unions and local works councils when implementing HQ global restructuring plans. In Germany there is evidence that works councils in particular are often seen as partners of local management in order to build coalitions to resist change, defend local resources, including employment relations, and negotiate the pace and content of planned changes (see also Dörrenbächer and Geppert 2009). Kristensen and Zeitlin (2001) similarly underline the importance of historically grown and robust institutional and cultural tool kits of subsidiary actors, which provide them with opportunities for strategic experimentation and power. HQ decisions, which predominantly focus on global standardization and financialization, can turn MNC operations into "a battlefield among subsidiaries representing and mobilizing their own regional capabilities and national institutional means against the rest" (Kristensen and Zeitlin 2001: 192). In this "contested terrain" German managers and works councils show considerable robustness in their use of strategic tools when bargaining globalization in the MNC, locking in capital investment by engaging in concession bargaining on employment conditions (see Raess and Burgoon 2006).

The ability to build up social networks and coalitions based on shared interest which go beyond individual manufacturing sites seems to be critical for both managerial and works council strategizing. In the same ways as MNCs are seeking to leverage external capabilities from, for example, the political environment to maintain or create value (see Oliver and Holzinger 2008), local actors can also leverage capabilities from their institutional environment, for example, to support networking at local plant, company and corporate levels. This is particularly true in the German car industry. Greer and Hauptmeier (2008) also point to the institutional support in the EU for transnational networking for trade unions and employees, which are lacking in the USA.

There are of course also some examples where globalization rationales undermine the consensual forms constituting the tool kits based on shared interests between local managers and employees. This sort of managerial rationale sometimes severely restricts the scope for strategic negotiations and for the development of subversive socio-political approaches. Thus, for example, Greer and Hauptmeier (2008) argue that works councils in some German car companies adopt "co-management roles" that make them increasingly reliant on HQ management support, which could be avoided if they would instead adopt "mobilization roles" in which they use various forms of leverage independent of HQ management. Frege (2003), however, in her study of the chemical and postal-telecom industries in Germany, found little evidence of subservient co-management attitudes among works councilors.

However, we believe that the German employment relations system in large part still provides critical resources and "tools" which enable local actors, both managers and employee representatives, to develop shared or mutual political interests, enabling them to negotiate and resist HQ global standardization attempts. As research has shown, this often helps German plants to maintain and gain important strategic positions within MNCs in the manufacturing sector. Technical and R&D prowess of subsidiaries then helps them to defend and enlarge their mandates; both are mutually reinforcing. Local actors, however, need to engage in both "selective international learning and skilful mobilization of local resources" (Berggren and Köhler 1999: 215) for their socio-political strategizing to be effective. They have to be able to produce "acceptable rationales" to the MNC HQ (see Blazejewski 2009) to convince those with decision-making power of the virtues of the case. As mentioned earlier, one of the recognized virtues of the German model to build robust tool kits has been its capacity to support high-skill manufacturing operations. Employment relation institutions provide opportunities for socio-political strategizing not just to avoid "charter removals" but also to improve "centrality" of the subsidiaries in the MNC network in the MNC's "interfirm competition" (see e.g. Becker-Ritterspach and Dörrenbächer, 2011; Dörrenbächer and Gammelgaard 2010). Evidence for the latter was found in a German subsidiary we investigated as local actors, managers and the works council joined forces to fight off attempts by the Finnish HQ to standardize production, ending a long history of diversified quality production in the plant (Geppert *et al.* 2003). In short, developing successful political "strategies in actions" (Swidler 1986) in this case meant that local management and workforce representatives were able to build coalitions and formulate a joint case in the right way, at the right time and in the right place to both resist the original strategic approach of the HQ management and to negotiate alternatives.

Our discussion has shown that employment relations entitlements giving extensive employee voice along with other business system elements providing technical and networking resources in the German manufacturing industry provide local key actors with robust tool kits on which an actively strategic role for local actors can be developed. This leads either to the possibility of political battles within MNCs or a more bargained approach to globalization pressures (Kädtler and Sperling 2002: 158) as the different actor groups make use of different vocabularies and rationales to persuade and to shape the emerging MNC organization in their own interests. Both in our own research and Bélanger *et al.*'s work on ABB the German core plants of the MNCs "retained a strong attitude of independence," in comparison to plants operating in societal contexts with weaker employment relations systems, such as, for example, the UK. This, was, however, interpreted by corporate management at the HQ level as inertia due to their opposition to radical change based on the standardization of production (see Berggren and Köhler 1999: 210). This can lead to the emergence of increasing contradictory rationalities and clashes among subsidiaries and between labor and management within MNCs. This is especially the case when the HQ strategy is narrowly focused on short-term returns, rationalizing and optimizing on a global corporate scale, and when local actors narrowly follow only their own logics, restricting opportunities to negotiate and build viable local coalitions. Figure 3.1 below illustrates different levels of social support and robustness of tool kits with the implications for local actor socio-political strategizing.

High

Limited tool kits (from societal bases) but possibilities for socio-political strategizing – we don't give examples but local actors may be able to draw on their intra-MNC position, providing tools for bargaining	**Robust tool kits and successful exploitation of them** – we argue that coalition building between local management and employee representatives is institutionally supported and inter-related with intra-MNC power position, bolstering local actors' bargaining strategies
Limited tool kits available and thus limited exploitation possible – see e.g. our references to examples in Anglo-American contexts	**Robust tool kits but limited room for exploitation of them** – we refer to studies pointing to new forms of activism from trade unions and employee representatives, stressing both the limits of established 'tool kits' and possibilities for their renewal

Low   *Societal support base for local actors*   *High*

Vertical axis = *Impact of tool kits in socio-political strategizing*

Fig. 3.1   Summary of key argumentation

In short, from a comparative perspective we found evidence in our review of literature on plant-level employment relations in MNCs that the tool kits of German key actors (local managers and workers) in core sectors of the German economy are still quite robust to bargain globalization, despite global standardization pressures, outsourcing threats, etc. However, there are mixed views on whether the German model of employment will continue to be supportive and thus whether the robustness of local actors' tool kits is sustainable in the longer term, which we will refer to in the next section.

Strategizing constraints: the disintegration of the German model of employment relations?

Some academic scholars, as well as business practitioners, have recently started to question the capacity of the German model of employment relations to continue furnishing subsidiary-level actors with the strategic resources to keep moving up the value chain by developing new competences and diversity quality production (DQP) models (see e.g. Djelic and Quack 2003; Doellgast and Greer 2007; Höpner 2005a; Lane 2006; Pries 1999). This would point to a weakening of the critical resources, national vocabularies and logics that form part of the tool kits currently being used by local actors in German manufacturing plants in their socio-political strategies. Kitschelt and Streeck (2004), for example, outline the debate about the German model, which emerged in the 1990s, when the German institutional framework began to be seen as a block to successful adjustment to the new global imperatives, and greater liberalization was seen as the solution. Lane (2006) argues that the changes to corporate financing and the rise of shareholder value mentalities in large German companies will lead to an unraveling of features of the societal system such as employment relations and education. Doellgast and Greer (2007) similarly predict an increased "disorganization" of the German industrial relations system. This is where market-based relations in MNCs undermine traditionally strong collective bargaining as more decentralized network structures allow managers to move jobs "from a well-organized core to a poorly organized periphery of firms that have no collective agreements or that are covered by firm-level agreements" (Doellgast and Greer 2007: 56). Moreover, Greer and Hauptmeier (2008) found increasing evidence in German car plants of "transnational in-firm competition," where management increasingly uses benchmark measures to compare company performance "in order to extract concessions from labor" (Greer and Hauptmeier 2008: 77). However, the German MNCs in their study, compared especially to their US counterparts at General Motors, had a greater commitment to social partnership and involvement of employment representatives.

Whilst some scholars share the rather pessimistic view that the core of the German model of employment relations will change significantly because of globalization pressures and the power of key players such as MNCs to facilitate these significant institutional changes, other researchers are more cautious, especially when interpreting the changes in the core industrial sectors. Thus Vitols (2004b), summarizing the findings from a Max Planck Workshop, also points to the German model becoming less homogeneous than previously thought and signs of a shift in some actors' behavior, particularly some large companies and banks. There has been an increase in the influence of the Anglo-Saxon model of business, but traditional attitudes were still widespread. There were some changes in German institutions but still significant continuity. Höpner (2005b) points to the surprising consensus between capital and labor over, for example, the shareholder value reforms in companies. Works councils saw it as a means of increasing transparency and thus the possibilities of their influence inside companies. At the same time, however, the financial sector has been increasing its influence or its place in the hierarchy of institutions from the 1990s and thus its ability to impose its logic on other actors has increased (Höpner 2005b: 58). Schroeder and Weinert (2003), however, point to the hesitancy and slowness of social change in Germany and the widespread support for the continuation of the German model among, for example, management, trade unions and the SPD (Höpner 2005b: 19–20). Although there are changes in the issues being bargained about in the German car industry and in the negotiating arenas, the bargaining process still dominates adjustments to globalization (Kädtler and Sperling 2002). Experimentation is taking place, for example, with outsourcing in the car industry but there has also been retrenchment back to in-house production when quality and competence problems emerged (Jürgens 2004: 420). Recent events are also leading to cuts in outsourcing in the German car industry (*The Times* 2009). There have been some shifts in production to eastern Europe for new investment but Germany is still the main research and product development location (*The Times* 2009; Dörrenbächer 2004: 453). Recent problems with the adoption of elements of the Anglo-American model include the failed merger of Daimler-Chrysler, failed acquisitions as in the BMW-Rover case and the ongoing retrenchment of many SMEs back to Germany after major problems were encountered operating in countries such as China. These experiences are likely to reinforce the more traditional German approach to business management. Similarly, the subprime mortgage debacle impacts negatively on the standing of international financial institutions and on their ability to promote their particular Anglo-American logic for shaping transnational social spaces. Geoghegan's article (2010) reflects this search for ways to reform liberal capitalism.

Thus, although there is evidence to support a measure of pessimism about the future of the German model of employment relations, seen from a comparative, and especially from a UK, perspective, German manufacturing industry still exhibits a strong bargained approach to the resolution of globalization issues. Both management and worker representatives continue to engage in socio-political strategizing and construction within the MNC. The employment relations resources provided by the German model strongly support this strategizing by local actors, who can use works councils to block radical change seen as detrimental to technical capabilities of German plants.

Other elements of the German model, such as the fact that German plants are often the lead manufacturing and R&D plants for the MNCs, are, however, critical to making this strategizing effective. The links between the possession of critical resources and their interrelatedness with robust tool kits of local actors needs to be further explored but we believe there would appear to be a co-evolution of the two, and not a radical dismantling or "disorganization." Changes to the German model in areas such as finance, with the German banks playing a reduced role in large companies, has not in fact led to the end of stakeholder coalitions. Companies have been bringing in new actors to form modified stakeholder coalitions (Vitols 2004a). Shareholder value has been introduced but in a much more moderate form than in Anglo-American companies (Vitols 2004a) and with the support often of workforce representatives (see also Ferner and Quintanilla 1998).

The legal basis of employment relations in Germany prevents the unilateral abolition of a bargained approach to change by companies. Works councils, even when not mandatory, are still powerful players in large foreign-owned and internationally operating German firms (Frege 2002; Höpner 2005a). Codetermination is said to have allowed the restructuring of German companies on relatively peaceful terms (Höpner 2005b) but the issues negotiated and the levels at which they are negotiated have been changing. An example of this is government funding for early retirement of employees affected by structural adjustments, which has helped to smooth the adjustment process negotiation between management and works councils. Government funding has now been replaced by collective agreements to continue to support the adjustment process. Despite evidence of a weakening of the hold of employment institutions in research by Greer and Hauptmeier (2008), Turner shows possibilities for institution building and revitalization of employment relations in Germany (Turner 2009: 305). He gives examples of alternative forms of institution building by the union IG Metall in Nordrhein-Westfalen. Here, a new "active bargaining" approach in regard to MNCs and other local companies has been adopted. This supports "aggressive negotiations at the firm level" leading to "acceptable company agreements" (Turner 2009: 302), where "gains in training rights and employment security made other concessions more palatable" (Turner 2009). The latter are seen as preconditions to maintain and further develop high-quality production systems in Germany (see e.g. Sorge 2005). However, institutional resources do need to be combined with activism from trade unions and members. In short, we believe that globalization opens up new opportunities for socio-political activity if local actors have robust tool kits, enabling them to act strategically in response to them, to bargain and, when necessary, to resist these global pressures.

In summary, there are several signs that the German model of employment relations is changing. Most of the commentators refer to structural shifts, and stress the weakening of traditionally strong collective bargaining agreements and declining union membership and the growth of "new" industrial sectors with weak or even no union and work council influences (e.g. Hassel and Beyer 2001; Streeck 2009). Streeck summarizes these new developments regarding the "German model" of capitalism as a "shrinking core, expanding fringes." However, how far the core will actually shrink and to what extent established employment relations will lose the power to provide critical resources for key actors in local subsidiaries to "bargain globalization," remains disputed. Moreover, as stressed earlier, international comparisons at the company level show that German subsidiaries are in a better position to keep and develop high-quality production and skilled labor than subsidiaries in liberal or emerging market economies. This argument is underlined by the observation of Geoghegan (2010: 9), who in comparison to his home country the USA, finds it quite astonishing that "the private export sector is the most unionized part of the German economy (even more than the public sector). And is understood to be the vanguard, the industry on the front lines of the global economy."

Discussion

Our chapter has argued that institutional resources, particularly employment relations, provide more robust tool kits for actors in German manufacturing firms to collectively resist and negotiate global change management approaches, in comparison to their Anglo-American counterparts. Therefore, German companies tend be in a better power position to occupy strategic technical leadership positions in MNCs (Geppert *et al.* 2003). This can be in the form of independent companies in manufacturing industry or as acquired companies within MNCs, who buy the plants for their technical expertise and use them as lead manufacturing plants and centers for R&D. National and local German management and works councils and unions often form alliances to safeguard and extend this critical position by shaping MNC HQ policy-making and implementation processes. The long-standing strong networks within and between companies and public institutions in Germany and the common technical background of many of the actor groups in the manufacturing sector, together with the social partnership model of employment relations, create strong national allegiances and defense of what is viewed as German national competitive advantage – the high skills base linked to lead manufacturing and a strong R&D focus. The fact that MNC subsidiaries are increasingly being placed in situations of fierce competition both with each other and with providers outside the MNC, as well as the increasing recourse to network organizational forms (Greer and Hauptmeier 2008), may only serve to reinforce strategic socio-political activity within MNCs. The possession of critical resources provides local actor groups in Germany with robust tool kits for shaping institutional changes in the MNC. However, most of the studies of German subsidiaries involve the metalworking and engineering sector, where the German model has had the strongest impact, in particular the automobile industry, which is the world leader. This sector has the strongest trade union, works council and employment relations resources since the decline of the iron, coal and steel industries in Germany. We would therefore not expect this argument to be equally applicable to highly standardized German manufacturing subsidiaries, especially those owned by foreign MNCs and the service industries, where the model has had less impact (Wortmann 2004). It could still, however, act as a reference point for works councils and trade unions in industrial sectors where employment relations have traditionally been weak (see Turner 2009).

The existence of bargained forms of globalization in German subsidiaries and MNCs points to the continuities and extensions of long-standing forms of engagement between capital and labor in the German economy. Sorge (2005: 220) argues that despite the rise of concession bargaining by works councils, the German industrial relations system has not changed fundamentally. Hyman and Ferner (1998) made a similar point back in the 1990s when German employment relations were facing new challenges. New forms of flexibility, new substantive agreements and new workplace actors were emerging. However, the basic processes of resolving issues remained the same – a collaborative approach of capital and labor. This "social partnership" approach is protected by national legislation as well as by collective agreements and provides labor with the possibility of a real voice in the construction of company strategies and their implementation, whilst subjecting them to some constraints such as the obligation to maintain "social peace" in the workplace (Frege 2002). The current neo-liberal pressure to liberalize national institutions often threatens to remove the very resources MNCs rely on when they invest in national economies such as Germany, including skills, stability, social peace etc. In Anglo-American type systems institutional frameworks do not strongly support this process and this is one factor which limits the transfer of German characteristics of employment relations by German MNCs investing abroad. Instead, they often seek to establish equivalencies to reap some of the business benefits enjoyed by the German system of collaborative partnership (see e.g. Bluhm 2003; Tüselmann *et al.* 2003).

The German model of capitalism in studies from the 1970s and 1980s was never a fixed or perfect model for all time. Even in its heyday it posed large structural challenges to German actors and was subject to ongoing shifts and changes (see e.g. Jürgens 2004; Sorge 2005; Streeck 2009). Experimentation, power games and evolution are constantly taking place in institutional construction and maintenance (see Höpner 2005a), as well as in organizations like MNCs. Thus change is continuously taking place in German institutions but there are also deep underlying stabilities, which mean that change is pursued in a cautious and rather incremental manner (Turner 2009: 306). Hyman and Ferner (1998: xxiv) referred to the "flexible rigidities" of the German system of employment relations: the processes of resolving conflict issues stayed largely the same whilst substantive issues changed considerably to meet internationalization pressures. A more recent study by Frege (2003: 319) echoes this point: core components of the German model of employment relations such as the openness to negotiation of managerial decisions and the need to consult works councils remain intact and safeguard a bargained approach to globalization. Since the elements of the German model form the basis of German national competitive advantage in the manufacturing sector, there is likely to be a slow cautious approach in a flexible learning manner even to global standardization pressures.

In this chapter we have *firstly* found some evidence that the German system of employment relations remains relatively robust in its "core." It continues to provide critical resources and thus robust tool kits for local actors, both managers and workers, to engage in socio-political strategizing, to negotiate and find compromises. However, pressures to globally standardize products and organizational structures are also leading to a reduction of core employees benefiting from the established system of employment and to the argument about the "shrinking core" of the traditional "German Model" (Streeck 2009). Such developments will challenge the traditional social partnership approach between managers and workers. Short-term stock market driven global restructuring strategies in particular are leading to increased "contests" in German manufacturing firms. Severe conflicts of interest can lead to "battlefields" between HQ and local companies (Kristensen and Zeitlin 2001). However, employment relations resources do provide various possibilities to negotiate the conditions of implementing standardized financial measures (see e.g. case 2 in Dörrenbächer and Geppert 2009). However, managers and workers must jointly develop alternative concepts in order to save the long-term viability of the enterprise, or workforce representatives and employees need to be able to network beyond the plant, as in the case of national and transnational strategies. There is evidence that, even in situations where local managers join forces with HQ in moving towards increased global standardization of the local production system, resistance is still possible and not "useless." This requires works councils who are strategically aware of their consultation rights, have close contacts with the external unions and use the available "tools" to "force" both local and HQ management to rethink and redesign certain operational measures (see e.g. the Finnish case in Geppert *et al.* 2003).

Secondly, we would like to re-emphasize the significant contrasts between liberal Anglo-Saxon and the more coordinated German models of employment relations, and the remaining institutional advantages of the latter. There are a few studies, such as Edwards *et al.* (2006) and Almond and Ferner (2006), which show some possibilities for local managers and trade unions in societal contexts with weak employment relations to exercise some influence on MNC HQ decisions. However, when assessing the benefits of strong employment relations in Germany, in comparison to liberal market employment relations models, we conclude that Germany still provides more critical resources for local actors to develop robust tool kits, based on supportive employee representation rights and high-quality engineering expertise, which can be used to resist and/or negotiate strategic decisions in MNCs. Our own research (Geppert *et al.* 2003) indicates that subsidiaries in the UK – compared to their counterparts in Germany – were reluctant to mobilize resources and mount resistance to often major changes such as redundancies and the shift of all manufacturing operations overseas. Indeed, one of the big advantages of the UK system according to senior management was the lack of obstacles posed to proposed management changes, especially plant closures, in contrast to the German subsidiaries (Geppert *et al.* 2003). This confirms the findings of Godard (2002) that in Anglo-American countries it is hard to find either managerial commitment to the workforce or joint efforts of managers and workers to develop mutual understanding. There is an absence of robust tool kits which can be applied effectively to negotiate change. In Anglo-American capitalist countries "the employment relation become[s] an asymmetric one once entered, managers are generally by law under a fiduciary obligation to owners ... The result is that capital–labor interest conflicts become internalized within the employment relations as managers seek to manage the firm in accordance with ownership interests, unelected by and with little accountability to employees" (Godard 2002: 269). Many studies have underlined the lack of institutional supports, particularly in the USA, to develop robust tool kits that enable more bargained approaches to global restructuring pressures (see Greer and Hauptmeier 2008; Turner 2009: 303). The shape and robustness of these tool kits are to a large extent dependent on whether local managers and workers representatives are institutionally and culturally encouraged to join forces to bargain globalization. This is a key aspect of German employment relations which is mainly absent in the Anglo-American capitalist societies. In short, from an international comparative perspective German employment relations look more robust and provide more critical resources to bargain globalization. This is not least because of strong regulatory support for works councils, sometimes even in sectors with weak industrial relations as stressed above.

Conclusion

In this chapter we have argued that the MNC is often a "contested terrain." In the German manufacturing sector, we argue that contestations among actors (management and employees) at the local level are more likely to be successfully negotiated in opposition to global standardization strategies because local institutions (e.g. German labor law and works councils) provide more robust tool kits for political resistance and bargaining. With this institutional backing, if the employment conditions suffer, or there are perceived threats to the long-term viability of the firm, workers and local managers, despite having different interests, may be encouraged to work together and build powerful coalitions against HQ policies. We have argued further that there is a greater chance that the interests of both groups of local key actors overlap in coordinated market economies like Germany, especially in comparison to Anglo-Saxon capitalist societies. We have discussed this issue with reference to the absence of robust tool kits based on institutional and cultural support for knowledge sharing and mutual interests in such societies. We have surveyed some of the current literature on plant-level employment relations in Germany and found evidence of joint local socio-political strategizing efforts. These efforts are aimed at either resisting or negotiating short-term oriented globalization strategies in order to maintain and further develop established high-skill systems. We have sought to provide some answers to the following questions:

1. Why are German MNCs and German subsidiaries of foreign MNCs more likely to retain high-level manufacturing and R&D capabilities compared to, for example, subsidiaries in the UK?

Our chapter has shown that societal institutions, particularly the employment relations system in Germany, remain an important critical resource for local actors in the manufacturing industry to make effective use of their institutionally and culturally based tool kits in representing their interests in the MNC. There are strong links between the German production model and the position many German plants occupy in MNCs as highly influential subsidiaries focusing on R&D and high-skill manufacturing activities. Many were formerly independent German companies bought by MNCs for their technical and engineering expertise. Both their position in the MNC and the resources of their national institutional context (which helped them to become what they were in the first place) provide fertile soil for socio-political strategizing by local German actors to defend local interests. The links between the possession of critical resources and the robustness of the tool kits used by local key actors need to be further explored but there would appear to be a co-evolution of the two.

2. Why is "bargained globalization" more likely to be found in Germany than in other countries?

This question has been linked to societal institutional resources, particularly employment relations, which provide tool kits for more negotiated approaches to change management. There are no real indications that these resources are significantly weakening in the manufacturing sector, as employment relations resources are safeguarded by law, and union and works council presence remains strong. Both local management and works councils can form coalitions and draw on these resources to resist HQ pressures to standardize, which are seen as threatening the national competitive advantages of German manufacturing plants.

3. Why, despite considerable pressures to liberalize, is the German model of employment relations still strongly reflected in German manufacturing industry?

We have contended that much of the pressure for liberalization has come from outside the manufacturing sector in Germany, for example, from international financial markets. The German model not only places constraints on certain types of global business activities, but also provides robust tool kits for local managers and workers' representatives to negotiate global change management strategies. The effectiveness of such tool kits can be seen in the world leadership position of the German car industry, despite (or, as we would argue because of) the strong forms of workforce representation and collaborative approaches to globalization challenges. The state of manufacturing in liberal market economies such as the UK and the USA does not reflect similar institutional "benefits" when facing global financial and standardization pressures. There are limited institutional resources, provided by national legal, education and training, and industrial relations systems to enable local actors to build robust tool kits. The opportunities to resist and bargain global change management processes, compared to those of their German counterparts, are restricted.

Changes to the German model of employment relations are therefore expected to be cautious and evolve more incrementally than is often assumed by skeptical scholars questioning the sustainability of the German model of employment relations. Moreover, there are signs that employment relations institutions can be "revitalized," if local key actors develop new strategic and innovative approaches, e.g. to maintain and further develop highly skilled labor practices in the companies instead of just focusing on wage and working time concessions. In short, tool kits cannot be seen as stable entities but must be understood as dynamic capabilities supported by dense societal institutions and accompanying cultural values which actors can draw on. The actual practice in the use of such tool kits will lead to changes in their shape and content, as will changes in the form and operation of the societal institutions underpinning them.

REFERENCES

Almond, P. and A. Ferner (eds.) 2006. *American Multinationals in Europe. Managing Employment Relations in Europe*. Oxford University Press

Andersson, U. and U. Holm (eds.) 2010. *Managing the Contemporary Multinational: The Role of Headquarters*. Cheltenham: Edward Elgar

Bartlett, C. A. and S. Ghoshal (1989). *Managing Across Borders: The Transnational Solution*. London: Century Business

Becker-Ritterspach, F. and C. Dörrenbächer 2011. "An organizational politics perspective on intrafirm competition in multinational corporations," *Management International Review* (in print)

Bélanger, J., C. Berggren, T. Björkman and C. Köhler (eds.) 1999. *Being Local Worldwide – ABB and the Challenge of Global Management*. Ithaca, NY: Cornell University Press

Bélanger, J., P.-A. Harvey, P. Jalette, C. Levesque and G. Murray 2006. *Employment Practices in Multinational Companies in Canada: Building Organizational Capabilities and Institutions for Innovation*. Interuniversity Research Centre on Globalization and Work, University of Montreal.

Berghahn, V. R. and S. Vitols 2006. *Gibt es einen Deutschen Kapitalismus?: Tradition und Globale Perspektiven der Sozialen Marktwirtschaft*. Frankfurt am Main: Campus Verlag

Berggren, C. and C. Köhler 1999. "Global policies and the dynamics of local variation" in Bélanger, Berggren and Björkman (eds.), pp. 198–216

Birkinshaw, J. M. 2000. *Entrepreneurship in the Global Firm*, London, Sage

Blazejewski, S. 2009. "Actors' interests and local contexts in intrafirm conflict: the 2004 GM and Opel crisis," *Competition and Change* 13: 229–50

Bluhm, K. 2003. "Dealing with the regulation gap: labor relations in Polish and Czech subsidiaries of German companies." Paper for the 13th World Congress of the IIRA in Berlin, September

Bouquet, C. and J. Birkinshaw 2008. "Managing power in the multinational corporation: how low-power actors gain influence," *Journal of Management* 34: 477–508

Child, J 1997. "Strategic choice in the analysis of action, structure, organizations and environment: retrospect and prospect," *Organization Studies* 18: 43–76

Delaney, J. T. and J. Godard 2001. "An industrial relations perspective on the high performance paradigm," *Human Resource Management Review* 11: 395–429

Djelic, M.-L. and S. Quack (eds.) 2003. *Globalization and Institutions*. Cheltenham: Edward Elgar

Doellgast, V. and I. Greer 2007. "Vertical disintegration and the disorganization of German industrial relations," *British Journal of Industrial Relations* 45: 55–76

Dörrenbächer, C. 2004. "Fleeing or exporting the German model? The internationalization of German multinationals in the 1990s," *Competition and Change* 8: 443–56

Dörrenbächer, C. and J. Gammelgaard 2010. "Multinational corporations, interorganizational networks and subsidiary charter removals," *Journal of World Business* 45: 206–16

Dörrenbächer, C. and M. Geppert 2009. "A micro-political perspective on subsidiary initiative-taking: evidence from German-owned subsidiaries in France," *European Management Journal* 27: 100–12

Edwards, P. and J. Bélanger 2009. "The multinational firm as a contested space" in Collinson and Morgan (eds.) *Images of the Multinational Firm*. Chichester: Wiley, pp. 193–216

Edwards, T., X. Coller, L. Ortiz, C. Rees and M. Wortmann 2006. "National industrial relations systems and cross-border restructuring: evidence from a merger in the pharmaceuticals sector," *European Journal of Industrial Relations* 12: 69–87

Edwards, P., T. Edwards, A. Ferner, P. Marginson and O. Tregaskis 2007. "Employment practices of MNCs in organisational context: a large-scale survey: report of the main survey." King's College University of London, June

Ferner, A. and J. Quintanilla 1998. "Multinationals, national identity and the management of HRM: 'Anglo-Saxonisation' and its limits," *International Journal of Human Resource Managament* (Special Issue) 9: 710–31

Ferner, A., J. Quintanilla and M. Z. Varul 2000. "Country of origin effects, host country effects and the management of human resources in multinationals: German companies in Britain and Spain," *Journal of World Business* 36: 107–27

Frege, C. M. 2002. "A critical assessment on the theoretical and empirical research on German works councils," *British Journal of Industrial Relations* 40: 221–48

  2003. "Transforming German workplace relations: quo vadis cooperation?," *Economic and Industrial Democracy* 24: 317–47

Geoghegan, T. 2010. "Consider the Germans," *Harper's Magazine*, March, pp. 7–9

Geppert, M. and E. Clark 2003. "Knowledge and learning in transnational ventures: an actor-centred approach," *Management Decision* 41: 433–42

Geppert, M. and A. Saka-Helmhout 2007. "Organisational learning within MNCs: the role of institutions and actors' orientations." Paper for 23rd EGOS Colloquium, Sub-theme 44: Unravelling organisational learning in MNCs, Vienna

Geppert, M. and K. Williams 2006. "Global, national and local practices in multinational corporations: towards a socio-political framework," *International Journal of Human Resource Management* 17: 49–69

Geppert, M., K. Williams and D. Matten 2003. "The social construction of contextual rationalities in MNCs: an Anglo-German comparison of subsidiary choice," *Journal of Management Studies* 40: 617–41

Godard, J. 2002. "Institutional environment, employer practices, and states in liberal market economies," *Industrial Relations* 41: 249–86

Gospel, H. and A. Pendleton 2003. "Finance, corporate governance and the management of labour: a conceptual and comparative analysis," *British Journal of Industrial Relations* 41: 557–82

Grahl, J. and P. Teague 2004. "The German model in danger," *Industrial Relations Journal* 35: 557–73

Greer, I. 2008. "Organised industrial relations in the information economy: the German automotive sector as a test case," *New Technology, Work and Employment* 23: 181–96

Greer, I and M. Hauptmeier 2008. "Political entrepreneurs and co-managers: labour trans-nationalism at four multinational auto companies," *British Journal of Industrial Relations* 45: 76–97

Hall, P. and D. Soskice 2001. *Varieties of Capitalism: The Institutional Foundations of Comparative Advantage*. Oxford University Press

Hassel, A. and J. Beyer 2001. "The effects of convergence: internationalization and the changing distribution of net value added in large German firms." MPfG Discussion Paper, July 1, Max Planck Institut für Gesellschaftsforschung, Cologne

Höpner, M. 2005a. "What connects industrial relations and corporate governance? Explaining institutional complementarity," *Socio-Economic Review* 3: 331–58

  2005b. *What Connects Industrial Relations and Corporate Governance? Explaining Institutional Complementarity*. Cologne: Max-Planck-Institute for the Study of Societies

Hyman, R. and A. Ferner 1998. *Changing Systems of Industrial Relations in Europe*. Oxford: Blackwell Publishers

Jürgens, U. 2004. "An elusive model-diversified quality production and the transformation of the German automobile industry," *Competition and Change* 8: 411–23

Kädtler, J. and H.-J. Sperling 2002. "After globalization and financialisation: logics of bargaining in the German automotive industry," *Competition and Change* 6: 149–68

Kitschelt, H. and W. Streeck 2004. "From stability to stagnation: Germany at the beginning of the 21st century" in Kitschelt and Streeck (eds.) *Germany: Beyond the Stable State.* London: Frank Cass & Co, pp. 1–34

Kristensen, P. H. and G. Morgan 2007. "Multinationals and institutional competitiveness." *Regulation & Governance* 1: 197–212

Kristensen, P. and J. Zeitlin 2005. *Local Players in Global Games.* Oxford University Press

Lane, C. 2006. "Institutional transformation and system change: changes in corporate governance of German corporations" in Morgan, Whitley and Moen (eds.) *Changing Capitalisms? Internationalization, Institutional Change, and Systems of Economic Organization.* Oxford University Press, pp. 78–109

Morgan, G. 2001. "The multinational firm: organizing across institutional and national divides" in Morgan, Kristensen and Whitley (eds.) *The Multinational Firm.* Oxford University Press, pp. 1–24

Morgan, G. and P. H. Kristensen 2006. "The contested space of multinationals: varieties of institutionalism, varieties of capitalism," *Human Relations* 59: 1467–90

Nohria, N. and S. Ghoshal 1997. *The Differentiated Network: Organizing Multinational Corporations for Value Creation.* San Francisco, CA: Jossey-Bass

Noorderhaven, N. G. and A. W. K. Harzing 2003. "The 'country-of-origin effect' in multi-national corporations: sources mechanisms and moderating conditions," *Management International Review* 43: 47–66

Oliver, C. and I. Holzinger 2008. "The effectiveness of strategic political management: a dynamic capabilities framework," *Academy of Management Review* 33: 496–520

Pries, L. 1999. Auf dem Weg zu global operierenden Konzernen? BMW, Daimler-Benz und Volkswagen -Die *Drei Großen* der deutschen Automobilindustrie. München/Mering: Rainer Hampp Verlag

Raess, D. and B. Burgoon 2006. "The dogs that sometimes bark: globalization and works council bargaining in Germany," *European Journal of Industrial Relations* 12: 287–309

Royle, T. 2002. "Resistance is useless! The problem of trade union organization in the European fast-food industry: the case of McDonald's" in Geppert, Matten and Williams (eds.) *Challenges for European Management in a Global Context.* Palgrave: Basingstoke
    2004. "Employment practices of multinationals in the Spanish and German quick food sectors: low road convergence?," *European Journal of Industrial Relations* 10: 51–71

Rugman, A. and R. Hodgetts 2001. "The end of global strategy," *European Management Journal* 19: 333–43

Schroeder, W. and R. Weinert 2003. "Zwischen Verbetrieblichung und Europaisierung. Oder 'Can the German model survive'?," *Industrielle Beziehungen* 10: 97–117

Schultz-Wild, R. 1999. "ABB in Germany: is excellence enough to survive?" in Bélanger, Berggren, Björkman and Köhler (eds.) *Being Local Worldwide – ABB and the Challenge of Global Management.* Ithaca, NY: Cornell University Press, pp. 179–197

Scott, R. 2001. *Institutions and Organizations.* 2nd edn. Thousand Oaks, CA: Sage

Sorge, A. 2004. "Cross-national differences in human resources and organization" in Harzing and Van Ruysseveldt (eds.) *International Human Resource Management.* 2nd edn. Sage: London, pp. 117–140
    2005. *The Global and the Local: Understanding the Dialectics of Business Systems.* Oxford University Press

Streeck, W. 1996. "Lean production in the German automobile industry" in Berger and Dore (eds.) *National Diversity and Global Capitalism*. Ithaca, NY: Cornell University Press, pp. 138–70

2009. *Re-forming Capitalism: Institutional Change in the German Political Economy*. Oxford University Press

Streeck, W. and T. Kathleen (eds.) 2005. *Beyond Continuity: Institutional Change in Advanced Political Economies*. Oxford University Press

Swidler, A. 1986. "Culture in action: symbols and strategies," *American Sociological Review* 51: 273–86

The Times 2009. "Sleek, stylish Karmann Ghia has run into trouble", March 9, 2009

Turner, L. 2009. "Institutions and activism: crisis and opportunity for German labor movement in decline," *Industrial and Labor Relations Review* 62: 292–310

Tüselmann, H.-J., F. McDonald and A. Heise 2003. "Employee relations in German multinationals in an Anglo-Saxon setting: toward a Germanic version of the Anglo-Saxon approach," *European Journal of Industrial Relations* 9: 327–49

Vitols, S. 2004a. "Reforming the German labour market: the case of temporary agency work," *Competition and Change* 8: 375–89

2004b. "Negotiated shareholder value: the German variant of an Anglo-American practice," *Competition and Change* 8: 357–74

Westney, E. D. 2009. "The multinational firm as an evolutionary system" in Collinson and Morgan (eds.) *Images of the Multinational Firm*. Chichester: Wiley, pp. 117–144

Whitley, R. 1999. *Divergent Capitalisms*. Oxford University Press

Wortmann, M. 2004. "Aldi and the German model: structural change in German grocery retailing and the success of grocery discounters," *Competition and Change* 8: 425–41

Zeller, C. 2000. "Rescaling power relations between trade unions and corporate management in a globalizing pharmaceutical industry: the case of the acquisition of Boehringer Mannheim by Hoffman-La Roche," *Environment and Planning* 32: 1545–67

4 Bridging roles, social skill and embedded knowing in multinational organizations

Mark Fenton-O'Creevy, Paul Gooderham, Jean-Luc Cerdin
and Rune Rønning

Introduction

It has been common for MNEs to develop structures that have resembled federative rather than unitary organizations. In these MNEs, subsidiaries have a national focus and substantial latitude to forge locally oriented strategies (Birkinshaw and Hood 2000). Porter (1986) and Prahalad and Doz (1987) referred to this particular generic MNE strategy as the multi-domestic strategy and contrasted it with a second generic strategy, the global strategy. The essence of the multi-domestic strategy is its emphasis on the need to be responsive to each local environment in order to achieve local competitive advantage (Yip 1989). In contrast, a global strategy views competitive advantage as being based on capturing global scale or scope economies through the integration of the activities of the business and focusing on customer demands that are standardized across markets (Roth 1992). Thus in terms of the degree of integration of activities across locations, whereas MNEs pursuing a global strategy seek to exploit cross-national sources of advantage through a high level of intra-firm resources, those pursuing a multi-domestic strategy allow business units to be largely autonomous and to depend more on locally-sourced resources as opposed to inputs from affiliated business units (Prahalad and Doz 1987). This embeddedness in host country networks is potentially a source of strategic power for subsidiaries and thus may constitute a serious challenge to the MNE headquarters' monopoly over strategy (Yamin and Forsgren 2006). However, local embeddedness may also result in knowledge that is so highly integrated in the local context that transfer is not readily achievable even in the absence of political resistance.

Yamin and Sinkovics (2007), among others, have argued that globalization and environmental drivers, including increasing market liberalization and advances in information and communication technologies have enabled multi-domestic or federative MNEs to seek global integration of operational and functional activities (see also Buckley and Ghauri 2004). Yamin and Sinkovics (2007: 329) argue that:

... the demise of the federative MNE is at root a process in which the power and the position of national subsidiaries in the MNE is radically declining.

Indeed Birkinshaw (2001: 281) has claimed:

Most MNCs have now moved towards some variant of the global business unit structure in their international operations and a corresponding dilution in the power and responsibilities of the country manager. *The result is that the national subsidiary no longer exists in most developed countries.* Instead there is a series of discreet value-adding activities (a sales operation, a manufacturing plant, an R&D centre) each of which reports through its own business unit or functional line [Own emphasis].

In this chapter we argue that the demise of the multi-domestic MNE and hegemony of the globally integrated MNE is overstated. Focusing on the transfer of knowledge-based practices we argue that their integration across the MNE confronts both micro-political resistance and local cognitive hurdles. While we readily acknowledge that these two causes may overlap, cognitive hurdles may exist in the absence of significant political resistance. We further argue that overcoming political resistance and cognitive hurdles are both dependent on skilled actors who possess "bridging" social capital (see also chapters of Schmid and Daniel and Williams and Geppert in this volume).

Our article is structured as follows. Initially, we present the theoretical background which comprises a number of building-blocks. First, we present the concepts of "epistemology of practice" and "collective" knowledge and second, four generic knowledge transfer outcomes. In the process, we raise concerns about the utility of the concept of "knowledge transfer" and suggest instead a focus on the travel of practices. Thereafter, we address micro-political resistance and cognitive hurdles to the travel of practices in MNEs. We then introduce the concept of social capital and argue that its bridging variant is highly potent at the micro-level both in regard to political resistance and cognitive hurdles. With these theoretical foundations in place, we present two exploratory case studies. We use these two cases to enquire into the micro-foundations of success and failure in the travel of practices within MNEs. These cases have stimulated much of the theorizing within this chapter in an iterative fashion (not least the importance of bridging roles) as we have moved between the cases and literature. However, we have chosen to organize the chapter conceptually rather than chronologically.

The first case, Scanfood, is an MNE that fails in an attempt to "transfer" collective knowledge, despite substantially overcoming political resistance. The cognitive hurdles remain intractable. The second case, ElecCo, displays a broader range of outcomes than Scanfood, in particular, in certain subsidiaries, ElecCo has managers whose bridging skills and roles enable them to surmount cognitive hurdles and enable an alignment of interests.

Theoretical background

Collective knowledge and epistemology of practice

Can knowledge and management practices really be said to be transferred across national boundaries? Cook and Brown (1999) distinguish between knowledge as something people possess (an "epistemology of possession") and knowing-in-action (an "epistemology of practice"). They argue, for example, that "knowing how to ride a bike" comes into being in the moment of practice and draws on knowledge (tacit and explicit) but also on the affordances of the particular bike and terrain. Learning takes place in the generative interplay between knowledge of bike riding and the knowing-in-action of riding a bike. Similarly, for example, we might consider that knowing how to manage employee performance in one part of an MNE may depend on explicit knowledge of general rules of human behavior and of systems, tools and processes; and on tacit knowledge developed in specific contexts. However, it will also depend on the affordances of those contexts. These affordances may vary according to, for example, legal constraints, local norms and culture, the nature of employees' work or employee relations institutions.

Thus, to continue the example, transferring performance management practices from one context to another is not simply a matter of moving knowledge, or even of successfully codifying and transferring tacit knowledge. It is a generative process of producing new knowledge and new ways of knowing by engaging in the activity of performance management in the new context.

Research on professional expertise also emphasizes the situated nature of knowing. There is now a great deal of evidence that much expert performance rests on complex and situation-specific representations, or schemata, held in long-term memory (Gobet and Simon 1996). Expert knowledge does not though, in general, inhere in highly abstract or strongly generalizable monolithic knowledge structures. Rather, expert knowledge rests on a foundation of very many situational experiences, is strongly domain-specific and requires extensive participation in practice (Ericsson, Krampe and Tesch-Roemer 1993). In other words, expertise is strongly embedded in particular contexts. Many scholars (e.g. DiMaggio and Powell 1983; Lave and Wenger 1991; Vygotsky 1986) emphasize the socially embedded nature of knowledge. Knowing is a social act; the tools we use for thinking and acting, the categories available to us, through which we know, are the products of social action and negotiation. The social institutions in which we partake frame the ways we know. In this view, expertise is a property of social groups and embedded in a social context (e.g. Hakkarainen *et al.* 2004). This view is most often associated with a sociological perspective, but is also represented in psychology, in work on "distributed cognition." The idea of distributed cognition treats thinking as an activity that is located in social groups and their tools, not in individuals: see e.g. Hutchins' work on airline cockpit crew and ship navigation (Hutchins 1990, 1995; Hutchins and Klausen 1996).

This emphasis on the centrality of tools and activity is also a central feature of the work of activity theorists such as Vygotsky (1930) and more recently Engeström (1999). We constantly use tools, ideas and categories created by others, in our thinking. Imagine a surgeon working in an operating theatre: she does not work alone but in constant communication with a team of nurses, an anesthetist, and most likely another surgeon. She uses equipment which embodies knowledge about approaches to treatment. As the operation proceeds, then the understanding of the patient's condition and appropriate action evolves dynamically and across the team and the technologies they employ.

Or consider a scholar sitting at a computer, writing a paper. He is apparently alone, but much of his thinking is "contracted out." He refers to an email from a co-author, or a review from a journal. He re-reads a theory paper and some previous research published on the same topic. He conducts a search on Google Scholar, he employs a diagram or conceptual framework devised by someone else. All these activities tie him into a web of cognitive activity. He is not a thinker alone but part of a thinking system. His identity as a scholar, membership in a community and facility with scholarly discourse provide him access to tools, routines, ideas and knowledge which cannot so easily be accessed by others outside or at the edge of his community of practice. From this perspective, the scholar is not so much an expert because of his internal organization of knowledge structures. Rather his expertise lies in his ability to access and engage with the intellectual resources of a community of which he is part. These resources include the internal mental representations of peers, but also their externalized embodiments such as books, diagrams,

	Individual	*Social*
Explicit	Conscious	Objectified
Implicit	Automatic	Collective

Fig. 4.1   Different types of organizational knowledge

tools, software and so on. Similarly, a computer systems engineer draws on not only the knowledge of his peers but also on the knowledge embodied in his books, tools and equipment. From this perspective, expertise requires learning to be part of a community of expertise and is concerned not only with acquiring knowledge but with engaging with a culture and developing an identity within a community which has its own particular regime of competence.

In his attempt to develop a knowledge-based theory of the firm, Spender (1996) proposed that in addition to distinguishing explicit and tacit or implicit knowledge one should distinguish individual from social knowledge. This results in four generic knowledge types (Figure 4.1).

Conscious knowledge is held by individuals and comprises established standards of practice that are a product of their technical training. Automatic knowledge is also held by individuals but is more psychological in the sense that it comprises the hunches, intuition and automatic skills of individuals. The objectified knowledge of a firm comprises its intellectual property such as its patents and registered designs, as well as its canonical knowledge embodied in forms, manuals, databases and IT systems. Finally, the collective knowledge of a firm comprises key aspects of its organizational culture that involve distinct, firm-specific, processes of knowledge production underpinned by emergent idiosyncratic practices and rules. Such knowledge may be relatively unknown to individual actors but is accessible and sustained through their interaction (Spender 1994).

For a given firm these four elements collectively constitute its intellectual capital. While these four elements are interdependent, Nahapiet and Ghoshal (1998) distinguish the two types of social knowledge in their analysis of what constitutes a firm's organizational advantage. Further, they argue that it is the two types of social knowledge that distinguish individuals working within an organization from individuals working at arm's length across a hypothetical market. Spender (1996: 52) himself is even more precise in terms of organizational advantage, suggesting that "it is collective knowledge [that] is the most secure and strategically significant kind of organizational knowledge." Its strategic significance lies in that it influences individual learning to such an extent that individuals can only be proficient once they are "socialized" into the organization and "have acquired much of the collective knowledge that underpins 'the way things are done around here'" (Spender (1996: 54).

In other words the "travel of ideas" (Czarniawska and Joerges 1996) within a firm is dependent on sustained exposure to collective knowledge. Not only does this imply that without that exposure cognitive hurdles will prevent knowledge exchange, but it also implies that parties must be politically motivated to engage in that process of exposure. We will present four possible outcomes of knowledge transfer attempts.

Outcomes of transfer attempts

We draw attention to two key dimensions of variation in the travel of practices from one context to another. First, as Lozeau et al. (2002) have noted, in any transfer there is always some degree of customization necessary to the local context. Czarniawska and Joerges (1996) remind us that ideas are transformed as they are transferred. Given any significant degree of difference in context, transfer requires not just the encoding and movement of knowledge about practices, but making use of this knowledge and local knowledge to construct new practices which function in the context of local affordances.

As we will argue later, it is not only institutional and cultural distance that prevents adoption. Tensions between the interests of key groups and individuals may also play an important role. For example, Lozeau et al. (2002) carried out a case study of the transfer of private-sector strategic management practices into a public hospital setting. A key feature of their findings was the corruption of these practices by powerful groups to serve their own purposes. Practices were customized not to serve their original intention, but rather to reinforce the status quo.

Second, as Kostova and Roth (2002) have noted, the extent to which practices are fully internalized locally versus only superficially adopted, varies considerably – high internalization being more likely where the local institutional and cultural context is receptive to what is being transferred. Coercive pressures to adopt transferred knowledge and practice, in the absence of a receptive local context lead most often to purely ceremonial adoption. This is perhaps akin to Whitehead's (1967) notion of inert knowledge: knowledge

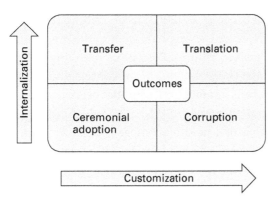

Fig. 4.2   Outcomes of knowledge transfer

which is separated from or plays no part in practice since it is represented in ways which do not align well with contexts of application.

This suggests a categorization of outcomes of transfer attempts as we see in Figure 4.2. Where the original context and the context of transfer are highly similar in salient features, where there is considerable exposure to shared cognitive social processes and shared goals, we might expect that transfer of knowledge and practices could be achieved with little customization. While we would argue that there is always some reconstruction of practices in relation to local affordances, in practice two contexts may share such similarities and common assumptions that this work is quite small. Thus for this case we retain the term "transfer."

However, given that there is recognition that significant local customization of knowing and practice is required, shared goals and effective engagement between contexts may result in significant effort being made to translate knowing and practice into the local context. We refer to this as "translation"; as what is implied is new meanings consistent with the original purpose of transfer. New practices are constructed with similar goals, drawing on both local knowledge and knowledge carried from the original context.

Either a lack of exposure to shared cognitive social processes or the absence of shared goals may lead to low internalization. This may lead to a purely "ceremonial adoption," in a "box ticking" approach characterized by no real identification with or understanding of the knowledge or practice.

The low internalization case may also be marked by significant efforts at customization, but in this case local efforts are largely directed at co-option of knowing and practice to secure the status quo or reinforce purely local objectives. We follow Lozeau *et al.* (2002) in describing this as "corruption" of the original practice, since the original intent of the practice is corrupted.

Although the emphasis in Figure 4.2 is on the receiving unit, we acknowledge that the role of the transferor may be of consequence. This will be the case when the transferor is not identical with that of corporate headquarters. Thus, in the case of a multi-domestic MNC, the role of corporate headquarters may be akin to that of a holding company. In such cases, in pursuing knowledge integration corporate headquarters is dependent on motivating a knowledge-rich subsidiary to engage in knowledge sharing. Thus the outcomes in Figure 4.2 may have their primary genesis in the transferor rather than the recipient, in which case the concept of "ceremonial transfer" replaces that of "ceremonial adoption."

In the next sections we elucidate the role of the absence of shared goals and shared cognitive social processes.

Political resistance

Morgan and Kristensen (2006: 1473) contend that the MNE as a totality "may be seen as a highly complex configuration of ongoing micro-political power conflicts at different levels in which strategizing social actors/groups inside and outside the firm interact with each other and create temporary balances of power that shape how formal organizational relationships and processes actually work in practice." We believe that this characterization of MNEs is particularly apposite for the multi-domestic MNE. That is, in line with business network theory, we view the multi-domestic MNE as a set of business actors whose corporate embeddedness is limited but whose external embeddedness, in the sense of connections to host country networks, is substantial (cf. Bouquet and Birkinshaw 2008). Thus multi-domestic MNEs should not be viewed as just comprising one business actor, the legal entity, but several more or less loosely coupled business actors, i.e. the subsidiaries. As each of these is embedded in specific local networks of business relationships it can be assumed that each is driven by self-interest that is shaped by the subsidiary's particular business network. Thus "each subsidiary will identify problems and opportunities in its own business network, it will strive either for autonomy in relation to the rest of the company, or for power to influence the development of other parts of the multinational firm in a way that supports the development of its own business network" (Forsgren 2008: 108). The power of the subsidiary is derived from its knowledge of its business networks, meaning that top management may be more dependent on the subsidiary than the reverse. In this conception of the multi-domestic, political resistance from subsidiaries may take various forms. As discussed above, one is that recipient subsidiaries may fail to internalize the knowledge or practices that corporate headquarters wishes to see adopted, because of a lack of shared goals. What is perceived by corporate headquarters as being of benefit to the MNE as a whole may not be perceived as beneficial by local managers who are accustomed to autonomy and who may question the relevance and appropriateness of the corporate initiative. Thus subsidiaries can:

choose to behave in a 'boy scout' way and implement … (what) the head office recommends or treat the MNE as just one, albeit important arena in which to participate … and evoke special circumstances inherent to their local contexts to interpret corporate directions in ways that best fit their interests." (Bouquet and Birkinshaw 2008: 493)

However, we would also point to another form of resistance to knowledge integration within multi-domestic MNEs. Corporate headquarters may identify a subsidiary as possessing superior knowledge and practices that it wishes to have transferred to other subsidiaries. However, this subsidiary may resist transferring its knowledge and practices because of a lack of perceived incentives to do so.

Cognitive hurdles

A second factor that hinders global integration is that of cognitive barriers that prevent locally embedded collective knowledge being readily transferred across the MNE. These hurdles are a product of the complexity and the embeddedness of collective local practices and knowledge. While knowledge transfer makes immediate sense within an epistemology of possession, it is more problematic from the standpoint of an epistemology of practice; knowing-in-action is less easily transferred. Yet it is precisely this epistemology of practice with which MNEs have to wrestle if economic value is to be built from knowledge transfer. Economic value is created not by "knowing things" but by "doing things."

Nahapiet (2008) argues that the dominant tradition in the knowledge sharing/transfer literature is to view knowledge as packets of information passing through the "pipes" of structural linkages. Within the pipes perspective on knowledge sharing, the assumption is that knowledge is an entity that can be sent or transferred from a sender to a receiver. When knowledge is not shared this is ascribed to a lack of willingness to transfer or to receive, often referred to as not-invented-here (NIH).

Using the "practice metaphor," Nahapiet points to a second perspective on knowledge sharing where knowledge is perceived as shared through interaction where relationships co-evolve in situated and embedded communities of practice. In contrast to the pipes perspective the practice perspective does not focus to the same extent on the flow between a sender and a receiver, but rather on formal and informal relationships based on trust and opportunities to meet and exchange experiences, thoughts and ideas. Knowledge is not necessarily transferred from one person/unit/division to another, but rather generated and shared among several parties. Moreover, in the practice perspective, the key aspects to knowledge are precisely the collective aspects we discussed above; such social and implicit knowledge cannot be readily articulated.

Social capital

The extant literature related to the transfer of practices from the headquarters to subsidiaries of multinational corporations focuses mainly on structural explanations (e.g. Fenton-O'Creevy et al. 2008; Fenton-O'Creevy and Wood 2007; Kostova and Roth 2002; Taylor et al. 1996). One important structural perspective, neo-institutional theory, has been frequently used by scholars in the international business field as a lens to examine transfer. In this paradigm the adoption of practices is an outcome of institutional pressures such as a country's culture and legal system or pressures from the headquarters (itself embedded in a national institutional context). Researchers have discussed institutional complexity at the level of MNEs (e.g. Ghoshal and Bartlett 1988; Grant 1996) and at the level of MNCs' subsidiaries (Kostova and Roth 2002).

Drawing on Oliver (1991), Kostova and Roth (2002) also employ an active agency perspective, suggesting that subsidiaries will differ in their adoption of a headquarters' practices. This agency perspective refers to both senior subsidiary managers and non-managerial employees. While not rejecting the neo-institutional structural perspective, we seek to enrich it through attention to local agency and the micro-processes which play out as firms seek to transfer practices across national borders.

Another structural approach which has been frequently deployed to understand knowledge transfer within multinational firms is social capital theory. Social capital theory has provided a particularly compelling account of mechanisms for knowledge transfer. In this chapter we draw key ideas from this literature and pay particular attention to the distinction between bridging versus bonding forms of capital and the role of key role holders in bridging structural holes. Although there is no unanimity as to how social capital should be precisely defined (Nahapiet 2008), there is broad consensus in regard to its essential properties. Thus Adler and Kwon (2002: 17) define it as "the good-will that is engendered by the fabric of social relations that can be mobilized to facilitate (knowledge-sharing)." In other words, networks of social relations can engender resources that enable individuals and social groupings to share and generate new iterations of knowledge-based practices that they could not otherwise accomplish.

Nahapiet and Ghoshal (1998) argue that social capital theory provides a sound basis for identifying the capabilities organizations are uniquely equipped to develop for the sharing of knowledge. Social capital, they contend, increases the efficiency of knowledge transfer because it encourages cooperative behavior in the form of exchange and combination of intellectual capital. They propose that differences between firms in terms of knowledge transfer may represent differences in their ability to create and exploit social capital. They distinguish three dimensions of social capital: the relational, the cognitive and the structural. The relational dimension of social capital refers to such facets of networks and links as trust, obligations, respect, identification and even friendship, which together increase the motivation to engage in knowledge exchange and teamwork. The cognitive dimension refers to shared interpretations and systems of meaning, and shared language and codes that provide the foundation for communication. The structural dimension of social capital refers to the presence or absence of specific network links or social interaction ties between units of the MNC and the overall configuration of these ties. The core intuition at the heart of accounts of the role of social capital is of appropriability; relationships and networks formed for one purpose may be used for others.

The development of social capital theory has provided a new tool for analyzing the diffusion of knowledge in organizations. Consequently it seems likely to bring useful insights to understanding the transfer of management practices within multinational organizations from one national location to another.

However, social capital theory has a number of deficits in supporting a coherent micro-level account of practice transfer. First, much of the social capital literature concerned with knowledge sharing/transfer has adopted what Nahapiet (2008) has described as the "pipes" metaphor. Social networks are treated as pipes through which knowledge flows. This approach has tended to treat knowledge as a commodity which can be moved unproblematically from location to location. We argue that rather than the movement of canonical, universally applicable knowledge, firms are often concerned with the translation of highly situated practices between different contexts. However, in addition, social capital theory lacks a good account of power relationships and organizational politics. This is particularly apparent in the context of multi-domestic MNEs as the "goodwill" of subsidiary managers towards integration may be highly problematic. Thus we question whether knowledge is a commodity which can be simply moved from one context to another.

Bridging roles

Within the social capital literature there is awareness that the bonding that is a prerequisite for the formation of social capital excludes those who are not perceived as members of the social community (Burt 1992). Without individual agents with multiple social community memberships within the MNE and networks which bridge "structural holes" in social networks, the transfer of practices and thereby the integration of the MNE will be undermined. At the heart of this use of social capital theory to understand knowledge diffusion lies a key insight, memorably expressed by Burt "[people who live in the intersection of social worlds are at] higher risk of having good ideas" (Burt 2004: 349).[1] People who bridge social groups are able to bring knowledge and ways of thinking from one domain into another, thus contributing to the emergence of new ideas.

More recent accounts (e.g. Adler and Kwon 2002; Edelman *et al.* 2004) make a crucial distinction between bonding and bridging aspects of social capital. Bonding social capital concerns the internal ties within a group which gives that group cohesiveness and facilitates the pursuit of collective goals. This foregrounds the importance of shared goals, shared cognitive representations of the world, and shared discourse. In network terms, bonding social capital arises most strongly in "closed" networks with multiple redundant ties. In contrast, bridging social capital concerns the "external," between-group, social ties of focal actors which bridge social networks.

If we return to our earlier discussion of knowledge, new ideas and information are most likely to be mediated through bridging roles; bonding social capital is largely concerned with what is shared and "taken for granted." Yet

---

[1] The words in brackets are a quote from a pre-publication version of the manuscript.

there is a paradox: actors with bridging social capital are likely to bridge between fairly closed groups with significant (internal) bonding social capital. Within those groups strong ties and social closure may be associated with a degree of resistance to ideas and practices originating elsewhere. In Lave and Wenger's (1991) terms, bridging roles span the boundaries of different communities of practice. In the context of multinational firms and human resource practices, for example, we can speculate that it will be common to find bonding social capital within geographically bounded operations such as a subsidiary or HQ location, but bridging social capital between such locations. In these circumstances, local groups will not only have dense local ties and sparse bridging ties, but are embedded in broader, within-country social networks (or institutions) which imply taken-for-granted local cognitive, normative and regulatory frames. Further, as we noted earlier, individual managers may experience that expertise built up in one context does not easily translate to another.

As Powell and Smith-Doerr put it "the ties that bind may turn into the ties that blind" (1994: 393, cited in Adler *et al.* 2002). To return to Burt's notion that people in bridging roles are at higher risk of good ideas, they may be more likely to have the ideas, but will often find it hard to get them accepted.

An epistemology of possession allows us to consider focal actors in networks simply as nodes though which information flows. However, an epistemology of practice points to a more complex role, requiring an active local engagement in constructing new knowing-in-action, in the context of local affordances, values and interests. Thus we argue that the effectiveness of individuals in bridging roles is a function of more than network position: individual skills and biographies are an important part of the picture. We further argue that these individual bridging skills also have micro-political aspects to them. As we explore later in the ElecCo case, individuals who bridge (skillfully) between different parts of an MNE are not only able to draw on the socio-cognitive resources of both social worlds, but are also likely to construe their individual interests more broadly in consequence. Interests are also socially constructed and multi-membership affects their construction.

The implication is that multi-domestic MNEs that lack such bridging linkages and individuals will experience considerable difficulty in integrating and brokering collective knowledge. As we will show in the context of our first case, Scanfood, brokering political deals that align the interests of subsidiaries with those of corporate headquarters is cumbersome and even when these have been achieved there remain substantial cognitive hurdles. Our second case, ElecCo, is one of variation across operations. In some subsidiaries we observe individuals playing effective bridging roles, while in others there is an absence of skilled individuals in bridging roles. This is associated with a variety of transfer outcomes.

The cases

As Yin (2003: 13) notes, case study research is particularly appropriate to the investigation of contemporary phenomena within their real life contexts; especially when the boundaries between phenomenon and context are not clearly evident. Our intent with these two case studies has not been to test propositions but rather to focus "on understanding the dynamics present within (each of the two) single settings" (Eisenhardt 1989: 534). However, we have had a clear focus for our explorations guided by prior theory and our own prior work in this field.

While committed to an understanding of human action as socially embedded, we also suspected that the agency of key actors in MNEs would be an important element in the success or failure of attempts to "transfer" practices across national boundaries within MNEs. Our chosen focus was on the travel of practices across national boundaries. Our chosen level of analysis was the actions, discourse and interactions of key actors in these "transfer" processes.

Thus in our selection of cases we needed to identify MNEs in which: active attempts to transfer practices were going on; access to data on relevant actors was available; and there was a range of different transfer contexts available to study. We also wished to achieve some variation in the kinds of practices we studied and some variation in the perceived "success" of transfer. We were fortunate in being able to identify two organizations which met these criteria and with which we had existing relationships. As is often the case, our selection of cases had an element of convenience – access was available and they fitted our criteria. However, the two cases are particularly useful in terms of covering attempts to transfer a range of practices. In terms of Scanfood there is a focus on production practices, while in ElecCo the focus is on "strategic HRM" practices.

Our data collection primarily involved interviews and collection of key documents. In both cases data collection was an iterative process with theorizing and data collection working in parallel. In both cases we discussed emerging findings and ideas with key actors in those organizations, using these discussions to collect further data; and modified our thinking in consequence of their feedback.

Interviews have been (where appropriate) transcribed both verbatim and in translation. Close reading and classification of data, memo writing and iteration between data and literature have all been used in the process of analysis. An important feature of this work has been the multinational composition of the team (English, Anglo-Norwegian, French and Norwegian). Dialogue within this team has helped us surface and work with our own embeddedness in national systems. Thus, as a team, we have been able to challenge emerging interpretations to ensure robust results.

We give further detail of the data collection process in our discussion below of each case.

Scanfood[2]

Scanfood is a Norwegian multinational food company with dried foods as a particular specialization. It currently has 4,000 employees of whom 3,000 are located outside Norway. For the purposes of this research we concentrate on Scanfood Corporate Headquarters and its Norwegian, Polish and Czech business units, Norfood, Polefood and Czechfood respectively. From September 2007 to June 2009 two of the authors were given substantial access to operations in these units in order to assist the company to reflect on their attempts to move from a federative to an integrated structure. Thirty informants, both at corporate headquarters and in the various business units, were interviewed, some of whom were interviewed on more than one occasion. At Scanfood we interviewed four erstwhile CEOs as well as the current CEO, the chair of the board of directors, the director of human resources, the supply chain director and the manager of the current purchasing integration project. At Norfood we interviewed the managing director and three senior purchasing managers. At Polefood we interviewed the managing director, a senior purchasing manager and a marketing manager. At Czechfood we interviewed the managing director, its senior product development engineer, its purchasing director and a senior purchasing manager. With one exception (a Czech national), all interviews at Scanfood and Norfood were conducted in Norwegian and all other interviews in English. Interviews were conducted by two of the authors on the basis of a semi-structured interview guide and recorded. The interviews were then analyzed. Additionally, Scanfood made

---

[2] The names Scanfood and ElecCo are pseudonyms to protect the identity of the firms concerned.

available key strategy documents and invited one of the researchers to attend a top manager meeting which included the Scanfood CEO and director of human resources and the managing directors of Norfood, Polefood and Czechfood.

History and culture

Scanfood has a 170-year history, mainly as a conglomerate. For most of its existence Scanfood comprised divisions spread across unrelated businesses including food, stone, asphalt and paper. These divisions competed for the goodwill of a small and "hands-off" conglomerate top management. This mechanism of internal competition for resources remained a feature of Scanfood even after it departed, in 2001, from the conglomerate model to focus entirely on food. It remained a feature despite attempts at coordination and integration post-2001.

As a consequence, its traditions, organizational culture and governance systems have been very much oriented towards individual business units, partly enforcing and partly supporting independence and individual responsibility.

In its earliest days Scanfood was a merchant and trading company in which diluting risk through "not putting all one's eggs into the same basket" and "having more than one sound leg to stand on" was a central tenet of the owners. As Scanfood started to expand through acquisitions its philosophy was that of "being a good parent." This notion remains very explicit as a premise for decision-making and governance; acquired companies are to be allowed opportunities and freedom to develop through taking advantage of business opportunities as they emerge, providing this is done, from the parental point of view, in a prudent and responsible manner. Thus from Scanfood's inception, independence and dilution of risk, as well as autonomy and sober responsibility, have been core values. Each new product line and each new area of business in Scanfood is expected to contribute independently to the company's overall results. This has been reflected in a control and incentives structure that is highly focused on the individual accountability of units.

After the successful acquisition of the dried food company Czechfood in Czechoslovakia in 1992, in 1996 Scanfood acquired Polefood, a Polish company that also spanned dried foods. Further foreign acquisitions were made in the Czech Republic and Poland in 1997 and 1998 respectively and in subsequent years in Russia, Denmark, the Netherlands, Sweden and Germany. To date, Scanfood's two most significant foreign acquisitions remain Czechfood and Polefood. In contrast to Scanfood's Norwegian business unit, Norfood, neither has ever been particularly profitable. As a result, Norfood dominates the company in terms of both financial contributions and also in terms of perceived strategically important competencies.

Strategy and vision

With the launch and implementation of a company-wide leadership development program in 2000, when the company focused on food, work started on formulating a common strategy and some degree of integration. In 2006/7 a company-wide appraisal system for managers was developed and implemented and several horizontal networks came into existence within the areas of purchasing, production, product development, marketing and sales. The vision of Scanfood as an international foodstuffs company has been to become the "local taste champion" in each of its national markets; a key facet to the Scanfood strategy has been to meet local consumer preferences. Given this focus on local responsiveness, acquired companies have had a large degree of autonomy. This autonomy was not only strategically acceptable, but also, given Scanfood's history as a conglomerate where autonomy and independence were highly prioritized, culturally acceptable. Norfood is renowned in Norway for its branding, marketing and product development competencies, while these competencies are not as pronounced in Czechfood and Polefood. The resources made available to these subsidiaries are also far smaller than Norfood's. In terms of the inter-unit integration of production the achievements during 2004–07 were relatively sparse. By 2007 Czechfood had increased its inter-unit production as a proportion of its total production from 0 percent to 7 percent, while Polefood had achieved 4 percent. In other words, Scanfood remained very much a multi-domestic company with not only locally evolved products but also local purchasing and production.

The focus at Scanfood has predominantly been one of transferring knowledge from Norfood to the foreign business units. Indeed, the idea was quite explicitly to replicate the Norfood success abroad. At Scanfood knowledge has been primarily viewed as something to be transferred and not so much described as something to be developed jointly or shared. Thus Scanfood has had a "pipes" perspective towards knowledge sharing. Cognitive barriers in recipient business units have been evident. Polish and Czech managers and employees tended to perceive the Norwegian management style as indecisive and confusing, and therefore frustrating and ineffective. In their view Norfood, which has always been closely entwined with Scanfood's top management, has held a dominating rather than cooperative mindset. Indeed,

Norfood managers readily concede that they believe there is relatively little to learn from Scanfood's foreign business units. For example, when a study conducted by leading consultants concluded that Czechfood's sales systems constituted Scanfood's best practice, this was either ignored by Norfood managers or even actively repudiated.

At least since 2002 corporate headquarters at Scanfood has been conscious of the lack of synergies between the main business units, Norfood, Czechfood and Polefood. During 2004–07 a number of activities were implemented, under the so-called PRO 07 project.

This project included the harmonization of raw materials in food production across the company. However, a feature of the project was also that no business unit was to be obliged to go against its business judgment. In other words, it remained up to each business unit whether they cooperated or not. Nevertheless, in terms of reducing the range of raw materials used across Scanfood, the project reached significant results. However, as we will now observe, in terms of production practices involving substantially greater "collective" knowledge, significantly less was achieved.

Interviews

In an interview with the managing director of Norfood, he reflected on Norfood's experiences with attempts to transfer production to Polefood and Czechfood. He reflected: "Our attitude to the issue of quality is different to that of eastern (sic) Europe." He then recounted that nearly 70 percent of Norwegian customer complaints Norfood receives involve products emanating from the business units in Central Europe, although these account for no more than 10 percent of the products Norfood delivers to the Norwegian market. Likewise, attempts to get Polefood to produce cake mixes on behalf of Norfood have constantly had to cope with quality problems whose causes were impossible to determine. "Therefore" he commented, "we are skeptical as to 'their' ability to deliver quality over time." Equally, given Norfood's long-term quality criticisms "they are browned-off with us."

The Norfood MD speculated that the quality problem stemmed from the "shop-floor," i.e. from insufficiently motivated production employees who feared sanctions if mistakes were exposed, rather than any lack of goodwill from top management at Czechfood and Polefood. However, regardless of the cause of variable quality, he emphasized that common standards had to apply across Scanfood if any further production was to be transferred from Norfood to Czechfood or Polefood. Apparent savings because of cheaper labor were simply insufficient. Employees and managers at Norfood described their lack of interest, incentives and rewards for sharing their knowledge with other business units. While there had been considerable goodwill on the part of Norfood's managers in terms of supporting other parts of the company, efforts at "knowledge transfer" had required investments in time and resources which could otherwise be used in value-creating activities for Norfood. This had represented a cost for Norfood, and Norfood employees observed that they risked being "punished" for spending their time transferring knowledge to other subsidiaries instead of generating results within Norfood.

Given Norfood's lack of incentives for knowledge sharing and its general lack of trust in the ability of Czechfood and Polefood to deliver sufficiently reliable quality, the failure to follow up on the ambitions of the time-limited PRO 07 project was understandable. Moreover, our interviews with managers at Czechfood and Polefood exposed a lack of trust on their part in regard to Norfood. As one Czech manager remarked, the view of managers at Norfood was that anything that originates from the Czech Republic was by definition substandard. Added to that was a feeling, on the part of the Czech and Polish managers, of Norfood not wanting to enable them to acquire key knowledge of production practices and that this could be explained as an outcome of micro-political processes, in particular in terms of the perceived disincentives to engagement for Norfood.

Given these micro-political processes, not least Norfood's perceived disincentives to engage in knowledge sharing, in combination with Scanfood's "pipes" perspective towards knowledge sharing, the outcome was one of a failure to achieve the successful internalization of Norfood's production practices in Czechfood or Polefood. In terms of Figure 4.2, given also that there were no obvious attempts to engage in local customization on the part of Czechfood or Polefood, it would be reasonable to characterize this outcome as one of "ceremonial transfer."

Since 2008, with the appointment of a new CEO, a more comprehensive and decisive integration of Scanfood's value chains has become an explicit ambition. A new integration project, "Program Future" has been launched in which knowledge sharing is "mandatory." Key aims of Program Future were the integration of production, necessitating the development and sharing of knowledge and competencies across units. Because Norfood, Czechfood and Polefood constitute a dried foods triangle of companies it was an explicit requirement of Program Future that these three business units should re-engage in the task of production integration and knowledge sharing. It should be noted that this was to take place against a backdrop of virtually no common knowledge or common communities of practice. Program Future is aimed at rectifying this. Additionally, efforts were made to address the politics of knowledge sharing by addressing the disincentives for knowledge sharing. In 2008 a new bonus system was introduced that primarily rewards the managing directors on the basis of the overall performance of Scanfood. This constituted a dramatic change from the previous system in which the emphasis had been on business unit performance. By aligning the bonuses of senior managers with overall corporate performance rather than their own business units arguably a key political barrier to knowledge sharing was removed.

We have noted the lack of trust across Scanfood. In part this is due to the fact that up until 2001 managers of the various business units had scarcely met. Program Future represents a further attempt towards developing and implementing integration.

While there is now greater alignment between managers' self-interest and the goals of knowledge sharing across Scanfood we found only scattered evidence of attempts to share collective knowledge through a "practices" perspective on knowledge sharing. Only a small number of managers had worked for any substantial amount of time (i.e. three months or more) in units in other countries and that was mainly within marketing. As Program Future was initiated recently it would be premature to draw firm conclusions but there appears to be a trend towards greater awareness of the need to develop a practices perspective for knowledge sharing. However, this has not informed the continuing attempt to get Polefood to succeed in producing cake mixes that are acceptable to Norfood. A recent interview with a Scanfood manager indicates that despite a realignment of the incentives system and an enthusiastic response by Norfood to Program Future little or no progress has been made. Despite a series of attempts to transfer the production knowledge and practices from Norfood to Polefood the resultant mix continues to dissatisfy Norwegian consumers. Complaints have now risen to alarming levels. Notwithstanding continuous efforts to identify the source of the problem it has proved impossible to isolate its causes. Scanfood management accepts that production will probably have to be moved back to Norfood in order to save a very popular product. The Norfood managing director commented:

We simply do not understand why these cake mixtures do not work in Poland. We have looked at everything. But we just can't make it work.

Various explanations of this continuing "ceremonial adoption" of Norfood practices by Polefood are feasible including the common Norfood claim of "*lack of quality consciousness*" in Poland. However, we suggest that the inability of Norfood to transfer successful production practices to Polefood may serve to illustrate that while significant political issues had been resolved, considerable cognitive hurdles remained. This case involves the travel of practices that are a product of collective knowledge entailing interdependence and interaction. Because production practices involve substantial elements of tacit knowing and interdependent interaction they are inherently difficult to describe exhaustively and therefore to transfer. This is the case even when political resistance is negligible. For example, Norfood assumptions about appropriate production processes are founded in experience of a well trained and well paid Norwegian workforce with a well developed understanding of the Norfood approach to quality. These assumptions do no not easily transfer into the emerging economy context. Arguably what Scanfood lacks are managers who possess the necessary bridging skills who can facilitate and act as catalysts in the negotiated development of practices which meet Norfood quality objectives within the affordances of the Polefood context.

ElecCo

Our second case study considers a French-headquartered MNC (ElecCo), in the process of establishing a global approach to talent management: their "Organization and Staffing Review" (OSR). ElecCo is a large, global, manufacturer of electrical products which serves both consumer and business-to-business markets. They have around 30,000 employees across 70 countries. After a year of negotiations, through a personal contact of one of the authors in the ElecCo headquarters HR department, we were given access to multiple sources of information. In January 2007 ElecCo placed all their files related to the OSR at the researchers' disposal. These files included a forty-page manual for the OSR process implementation, an internal report on progress with implementation of OSR and slides presented at an international human resources seminar. In March 2007 we conducted four semi-structured interviews at ElecCo's corporate headquarters in France. Each interview lasted about three hours and was conducted with the corporate HR personnel in charge of transferring the OSR into the foreign subsidiaries. Between them, these four senior HRM personnel had participated in the implementation of the OSR process in every one of the MNC's subsidiaries, making multiple visits to the subsidiaries. The same questions were asked in each interview. They focused on four basic issues: (1) the OSR's objectives and design, (2) the method used by corporate HR personnel to transfer the practice to each subsidiary, (3) the outcomes of transfer, and (4) the influences on outcomes. Since the four HR managers between them had responsibility for OSR transfer to all of the subsidiaries involved in the roll-out to date, we were able to review outcomes for the majority of subsidiaries during these interviews.

The researchers sent a preliminary report to the interviewees in July 2007. This report presented our understanding, so far, of the OSR process and our analysis of its transfer to the subsidiaries. In September 2007 two of the researchers went to the headquarters in order to present their analysis and results. The four interviewees (one of whom has been promoted to HR corporate director since January 2008) and five other corporate HR personnel attended the meeting. This four-hour meeting was an opportunity to get feedback on our analysis and deepen our understanding of the transfer of the OSR within ElecCo. We also revisited our classification of subsidiary outcomes with the corporate HR team in this meeting and revised our analysis in the light of the discussion this triggered.

Until 2002 ElecCo's approach to human resource management (HRM) was polycentric: decentralization, with each national unit having its own particular HRM system. ElecCo has since deliberately departed from its polycentric approach to HRM to a "geocentric" approach to HRM. This has been driven by multiple factors, including exposure to a different approach to HRM via a prospective merger partner, the arrival of a new CEO, ownership changes and a reorganization of the group into five globally integrated divisions. Fundamental to this new approach is the ambition to achieve a common, group-wide system for the identification and development of talent, the Organizational Staffing Review (OSR). ElecCo is seeking to globalize its talent management pool through the application of OSR.

The annual OSR has been designed with a view to identifying and documenting employees' behavioral skills rather than their current professional performance; and involves employees being assessed in relation to three categories, that of *new talents, potentials* or *high potentials*. Employees who are identified as belonging to one of these groups will participate in common group-wide training and development programs. Additionally those assessed as high potentials will be specifically developed for group-wide careers. A version of this process has been in place in France since 1997.

It is the subsidiary general managers who are charged with implementing the OSR. Thus, although the ElecCo group HRM department in France is the driving force behind the development and transfer of OSR, they believe that the long-term success of the implementation of OSR depends on each subsidiary being motivated to adopt and apply the OSR in accordance with its original intentions.

One measure that was taken to anchor OSR at the subsidiary level was to organize a group-wide seminar on OSR for subsidiary HR managers in September 2004 in order to explain its workings and its purpose. Prior to this, another measure was to work on its development with the two largest subsidiaries, the US and the Italian subsidiaries. This was, in part, a desire to get subsidiary feedback on the process before moving to global roll-out. However, it also represented a recognition of the power of these subsidiaries within ElecCo. Finally, prior to implementation, meetings were held with subsidiary managers to persuade them of the benefits of OSR and to provide them with a simulation of its workings. This was followed by a review meeting about six months later. Work on embedding OSR in subsidiaries has taken place during 2005 and 2006, with follow-up work continuing.

Outcomes to date of transfer attempts

We introduced the notion of classifying outcomes of "transfer" efforts in terms of customization and internalization in our later discussions with the HR team. In discussion, the team expressed the view that this framework made intuitive sense to them in terms of their own experiences. They felt comfortable classifying outcomes in these terms. We drew up a classification of outcomes of the OSR roll-out on the basis of discussions with HR managers responsible for the transfer process to individual countries. We then shared this classification with them in a later meeting and revised it based on their feedback. They found the framework a useful vehicle for discussing the implementation process but felt it important to emphasize the dynamic nature of the process; for example, in some countries they felt that there was a process of drift as the OSR implementation began to take second place to other priorities. Figure 4.3 shows the results of this classification process.

As we discuss below, a strong emergent theme was the role played by the general managers and HR managers in each subsidiary in enabling or resisting implementation of the OSR process. Table 4.1 describes the basis of classification of "transfer" outcomes and gives brief details of the role and background of key actors in the implementation process.

The ElecCo approach to the global roll-out of the OSR process was in many ways quite sophisticated and broadly successful. There was an acceptance from the outset that the OSR would need adaptation to local circumstances. One HR manager described this as each subsidiary making OSR "in their own sauce" (*à leur sauce*). The initial piloting process in Italy and the USA

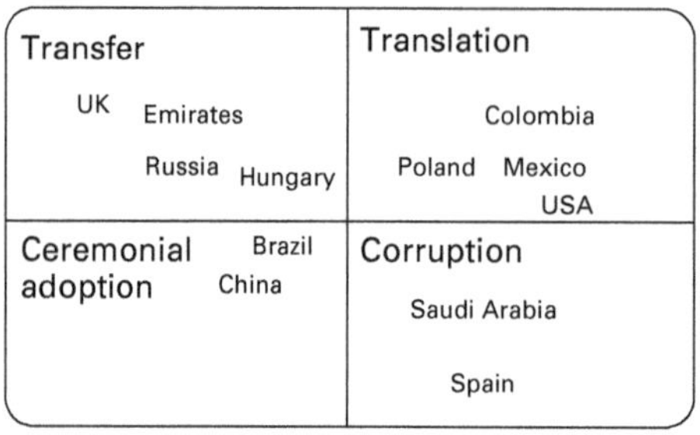

Fig. 4.3   Outcomes of OSR transfer attempts

was designed to allow for learning about the problems of implementation in other countries. The corporate HR team traveled to each subsidiary and spent time with local managers exploring what adaptations might need to be made and seeking to get buy-in from local senior managers. Nonetheless, there was considerable variation in the outcomes achieved in each subsidiary.

It was clear that cultural distance did have some impact on "transfer" outcomes. For example, the two corporate HR managers responsible for China did feel that there were difficulties in transferring a European approach to HR management into a very different cultural setting:

China is a special case for human resource management and one sees that we have a model which is above all, very western. The culture is very paternalist and it is not common in China to have the kind of movement between jobs which we see in France.

Culture, though, was by no means dominant, in the view of the HR team; more idiosyncratic local factors, driven by local institutions, often dominated. To return to the Chinese example, the principal difficulty in transferring the OSR approach into China was the nature of the highly competitive local labor market for trained managers. As one HR manager explained:

In China we are dealing with a very fast moving context, we are growing fast and need to retain key people ... we are dealing with local managers, whether they are Chinese or not, who are reticent to send their talent on corporate training schemes because they say this is just a way of speeding up the departure of these people to other companies once they have enriched their CV and their credentials by some high-class training in Europe or the US.

To give another example of local factors; in the USA, the nature of local legislation in relation to age discrimination meant the version of the OSR used in France which had a "young potentials" category had to be adapted to include all age groups.

Table 4.1 "Transfer" outcomes and roles of key actors

Outcome	Subsidiary	
Transfer	UK	The adoption of the OSR in the UK was fairly unproblematic. It was a good fit with existing HR approaches and the general manager had a close working relationship with the corporate center. He was a local national but his mother was French and he had spent much time working in France including time at the corporate center.
	Emirates	The subsidiary was faced with existing difficulties in retaining talent. The OSR was welcomed as a process which would support identification and retention of talent. The OSR was also integrated with an initiative to benchmark local pay. The general manager was a French expatriate from a North African background with a good understanding of local language and culture. (Note the contrast with Saudi Arabia– facing similar challenges and in a similar institutional and cultural setting but a very locally focused manager).
	Russia	The Russian subsidiary faced a highly competitive labor market and was experiencing problems with high labor turnover, especially among more talented employees. This meant they were very receptive to the OSR which they saw as a tool for retaining key people. This acceptance and the subsequent implementation were aided significantly by the support and skills of the general manager and HR manager. The general manager was a French expatriate who had long experience of working in Russia and "considerable sympathy" for the local culture. The HR manager (another French expatriate) had less depth of experience in Russia but had prior experience of implementing the OSR in France.
	Hungary	While the local general manager in the Hungarian subsidiary is indigenous he has spent a substantial period of time at ElecCo's group headquarters. This has resulted in a strong identification with ElecCo at the group level and an interest in career development internationally within the group. His enthusiastic approach to implementing HQ policies has led to adoption with little customization (*transfer*). The OSR process has been adopted broadly as specified and seems to be addressing the goals of identifying and developing a cadre of high-potential and internationally mobile employees. However, more recently there are indications that the local general manager is attempting to use OSR as means of raising the profile of the subsidiary by exporting a significant number of Hungarian employees to HQ and other parts of the group. This has resulted in a list of potentials that was too long to be credible. In that sense (in the view of the corporate HR team) there is a potential for a shift from *transfer to corruption*.

Table 4.1 (cont.)

Outcome	Subsidiary	
Translation	Colombia	The Colombian subsidiary is a relatively small operation headed by an Italian manager (with significant South American experience and experience of working in the French parent) who had been charged with reinvigorating the operation. The general manager is keen to raise the profile of the subsidiary (and hence his own profile) within the group. He sees this as opening up the possibility of more investment. The OSR process provides an opportunity to engage with the headquarters in a meaningful way on a high-profile project. In practice he treated the OSR project as a vehicle for adoption of a wide range of systematic HR processes. (He provided 700 pages worth of OSR documentation for twenty people.) Moreover, he has sought to adapt OSR to local conditions.
	Poland	The initial process in Poland was a procedural implementation without any real attention to the underlying goals of the OSR process. This was driven by the local HR manager who had little experience of such initiatives. However, over time, the Polish subsidiary has, through its new Italian general manager (formerly based in France) engaged in a much more thoughtful adoption of the OSR process.
	Mexico	In Mexico the OSR process was fairly rapidly implemented and adapted to local needs. The general manager was an expatriate supported by a Mexican HR manager who had significant experience of working in US firms.
	USA	The US subsidiary had considerable power and autonomy within the group. Management was entirely local. However, corporate HR invested significant time and effort in engaging with this subsidiary and in involving them in piloting and modifying OSR. In consequence the Group OSR approach was modified significantly to meet US needs. For example, the "young potentials" category was changed to "potentials" to avoid problems with age discrimination legislation. However, concern grew over time within corporate HR that the US subsidiary was increasingly following its own path with talent management and coming out of step with corporate policy. In particular they were able to use claims concerning the high level of professionalization of HRM in the USA and their own expertise as a power base in negotiating with the corporate center.
Ceremonial adoption	China	Initial indications in China were of a completely implemented OSR system with little deviation from parent company processes, in large part due to the support of the three French expatriate senior managers. However, the initial enthusiasm of these expatriate managers waned as they came to realize the consequences of the OSR in the local context. First there is the difficulty in retaining local talent because of the high degree of competition for talent in the Chinese employment market. Employees identified for inclusion in the scheme typically used this to seek a higher salary in the highly competitive local labor market where MNEs were

seen as an important training ground for the development of domestic talent. This pressure has already given rise to an erosion of the principles underlying OSR. Care is taken to avoid formal communication of status on the program to employees thought to be at risk of leaving the organization. An additional factor in the Chinese operation is the difficulty in providing objective evaluations to employees in the context of a culture in which face saving is critical. This has led to a customization of OSR (less explicit approach). There have also been difficulties in sending Chinese employees who speak no English or French on global training programs. Thus there has been drift over time in the direction of *ceremonial adoption*. The paperwork is completed but there is little impact on employees.

Brazil	The Brazilian operation was headed by a French expatriate who was mostly focused on the challenges of moving the production location and little interested in HR issues. Unlike in Mexico, the local HR manager had no experience outside Brazil and had a very local focus. Initial implementation was very "box ticking" in nature. Later work by the HR team in the corporate center was successful in getting greater engagement from the general manager, and at the time of data collection showed some signs of leading to a more successful implementation which would take account of local conditions.
Corruption	
Saudi Arabia	In Saudi Arabia, by contrast to the (culturally similar) Emirates, the OSR process met significant resistance and problems of understanding. There was suspicion of the HQ motives in introducing the process. The subsidiary was headed by a local national who does not speak French or English. There was a perception on the part of headquarters' HR managers that the process had been co-opted to serve purely local goals.
Spain	In Spain the OSR process was seen as a tool to get rid of employees they did not want by placing them in the high potential list. Employees they wished to retain were kept off the lists. The (Spanish) general manager had considerable power to resist pressure from corporate HR – founded in the size and strategic importance of the subsidiary.

However, the strongest theme emerging from the case was the role of individual general managers and HR managers in the subsidiaries. There was significant variation between these individuals in both the motivation to adopt the OSR processes and their skills in successfully adapting the OSR process to the local context.

Bridging roles, interests and career trajectories

It was clear that the interests and power resources of managers in bridging roles played a crucial role in how transfer attempts played out. Career trajectory of these managers seemed an important influence on their interests; in particular on whether they saw their own interests as tied narrowly to the subsidiary or they identified more closely with the group as a whole. At the same time the role and size of the subsidiary had an important impact on the power resources they could draw on. Where the general manager had an international career trajectory, it was often the case that they offered significant support for this initiative from the corporate center. By contrast, those managers with career experience entirely within one country seemed to see their interests more narrowly and to have greater suspicion about the goals of the OSR program; a common suspicion was that the OSR would lead to the group bleeding away the best talent from the subsidiary.

For example, in Spain the local subsidiary manager had a career history entirely within that country and seemed to understand his role narrowly in relation to the local success of the subsidiary he managed. At the same time this (fairly large) subsidiary was highly important to the company and had the power to demand a good deal of autonomy. As one of the parent company managers responsible for the OSR rollout told us:

In Spain they actually use the OSR for their own means rather than try and actually follow the [ElecCo] approach. They use it for what they want. The general manager is now very independent from the corporate. He doesn't care about the corporate. He's like a big boss in Spain, he can do business without the corporate.

A particular concern about the OSR implementation in Spain seemed to be the distortion of the assessment process to retain key talent within the subsidiary while using the process to get rid of those who were less valued.

It was, of course, not always the case that expatriate general managers saw their interests as aligned with implementing the OSR initiative:

... for example one of our other Chinese subsidiaries whose general manager who is someone with a very strong personality with a need for autonomy, for decision-making initiative and an appetite for power which probably contributes to the fact that probably makes him not spontaneously a transmitter of whole group processes. (HQ senior HR manager)

Beyond social capital: the role of social skill

Subsidiary managers who were identified as effective in enabling the translation of HQ (France) policies into the local context often had characteristics which located them in multiple national contexts. For example, the Hungarian manager of the Hungarian subsidiary had previously spent several years working in the French HQ and has many years' international experience. The British manager of the UK subsidiary had a French mother and much experience of working in France, including time at the ElecCo corporate center. The Italian manager of the Polish subsidiary had a career history which included multiple countries and a spell at the corporate center. The French manager of the Russian subsidiary had international experience, a history of close working with the corporate center, but also deep experience of and commitment to the Russian context.

In contrast, other individuals played less successful bridging roles. For example, while the OSR process eventually began to take root successfully in Poland under a new (Italian) general manager with close ties to the center, initial attempts to implement the process by the HR manager were seen less positively from the center:

The local HR manager was very keen to satisfy the demands the group was making of her, was discharging her function in too much of a procedural fashion, basically seeing everything as a question of forms to be filled out, squares to be filled in, boxes to be ticked rather than giving a genuine meaning to what all this was about or seeing in terms of possible benefit to the managers within her subsidiary. The process of identifying the most adept people in their department, she didn't actually develop the idea of the possible benefits at subsidiary level and the same goes for the way she approaches the training plan that is drawn up for training requirements within her subsidiary and other similar exercises. (HR manager at HQ responsible for roll-out)

To give another example, the Saudi general manager lacked both experience of management outside Saudi Arabia and spoke neither French nor English. There was little sign in the subsidiary he managed of successful implementation and there seemed (in the view of corporate HR managers) to be considerable suspicion of the parent company's motives.

It is clear from the comparisons between different subsidiaries, that there were not only differences in the extent to which local managers saw OSR as serving their interests. There were also important differences in the skill with which the OSR process was adapted successfully to the local context. This adaptation happened most readily where the experience of the senior management team in the subsidiary spanned multiple countries and where they had strong relationships both within the parent company and within the subsidiary.

Conclusions

The exploratory case studies we report in this chapter suffer some important limitations. Unlike the Scanfood case, in the ElecCo case we rely on documents and interviews with managers at the corporate center. We lack the direct perspective of the subsidiary managers. For example, it is likely that subsidiaries we categorized as falling in the "transfer" box might turn out to be more properly classified as having engaged in translation once we had detailed accounts from subsidiaries themselves about the nature of the local practices (see also chapter of Schmid and Daniel this in volume). Nonetheless, the interviews were with managers who had spent a significant amount of time in each of the subsidiaries they reported. In the Scanfood case we have data from both "transferor" and "transferee" but lack the range of subsidiaries in the ElecCo case. We have also examined only a limited range of practices. Furthermore, comparability between cases is limited by the differences in practices we examine; production practices in the Scanfood case and talent management in the ElecCo case. However, there is nothing in the cases which suggests the difficulties of "transfer" to be highly specific to the nature of the practices we examined.

While we should be cautious about our conclusions on the basis of the case studies, they have provided an important basis for theorizing about the nature of the micro-processes inherent in cross-national practice "transfer" within MNEs.

Despite recent obituaries (Birkenshaw 2001; Yamin and Sinkovics 2007), the demise of the multi-domestic MNC and hegemony of the globally integrated MNC is overstated. Paying attention to the micro-foundations of practice transfer processes in MNCs makes it clear that transnational standardization of management practices is beset with difficulty. In other words, we suggest that any "retreat from federative multinationality" (Yamin and Sinkovics 2007: 325) in terms of transferring and integrating "collective" knowledge is far from being a foregone conclusion. This is in part due to "political sense-making" on the part of business units that leads to perceptions of interest non-compatibility (Clark and Geppert 2011). However, it may also in part be because of the complexity inherent in ensuring processes that lead to the internalization of such knowledge.

The social capital metaphor has value in helping us understand how ideas and practices travel. It draws attention to the role played by social networks and by actors who occupy roles which bridge structural holes in those networks. However, the tendency in the social capital literature to characterize social capital as pipes though which knowledge travels obscures important features of the travel of ideas and practices and obscures the skilled and partisan agency of actors in bridging roles. In this chapter we have paid particular attention to the role of these actors, their skills and motivation.

In the ElecCo case we saw that the greatest success in translating the talent management process into new settings was achieved where the managers responsible for implementation had identities which spanned local subsidiary and the wider organization. This was sometimes because they were expatriates with a deep understanding of the local context. In other cases they were third-country nationals who had spent time at head office with highly internationally mobile career histories. This implied an understanding of the affordances of the local setting and sympathy with local concerns but also identification with the purposes of the parent company. It also often implied an international career trajectory within ElecCo, which led to a greater alignment of their personal interests and parent-company policies. By contrast, local managers with a local career history and identification were often less successful in translating parent practices into the local context.

It seems likely that the managers who are able to play bridging roles effectively do so not just because of their location in networks, but also because of their cognitive flexibility (Spiro et al. 1987), brokering skills (Wenger 1998) and other social skills (Fligstein 1997, 2001). Further, it seems likely that the work of translating ideas across community boundaries requires the capacity to negotiate multiple identities in different communities and to reframe ideas in the currency of local mindsets and aspirations. It may be insufficient to bridge the different social groups. Rather it is necessary to partake of the cognitive social capital of both groups while possessing the skill to translate meaning between contexts. Creed et al. (2002) have drawn on accounts of social activism to suggest some of the strategies that are useful in mobilizing ideas and meanings. They suggest that institutional entrepreneurs: (1) work with multiple contradictory cultural accounts and create narratives about what available institutional logics and cultural accounts "really mean" (see also chapters by Koveshnikov and Ybema and Byun in this volume); (2) work with key constituents' sense of identity and the meaning for their identity of adopting ways of knowing.

However, it is also clear from the case study that network position is important in terms of identification with values and interests. For some actors in bridging roles, loyalty seemed more aligned with HQ priorities, while for others identification with local interests led to the use of network location to block or corrupt HQ initiatives. Those with cross-national career trajectories seem not only more likely to be skilled in bridging between the two contexts, they were also more likely to construct their own interests broadly in relation to the whole MNC rather than purely locally.

The ElecCo case raises important questions about the interplay between social capital, knowledge and practices. While from this case we can see the value of the focus social capital theory gives us on network position and bridging roles in particular, we have argued that an account of the role of social capital in the travel of ideas and practices within MNCs needs to draw on an epistemology of practice, to engage with the skilled agency of individuals in bridging roles and to consider the interaction between network position and prior experience, values and interests.

The Scanfood case illustrates that attempts to integrate federative MNEs may be thwarted by the localized nature of knowledge. This remains a hurdle even when political resistance to its transfer has been addressed. In part the inability of Scanfood to transfer knowledge is due to its "pipes" perspective on knowledge transfer. In part it is because Scanfood lacks those individuals with bridging skills and social capital. Encounters between Norfood, Polefood and Czechfood managers involved them meeting at boundaries rather than bridging across them. As a consequence, despite efforts by management it would appear that Scanfood finds it very difficult to move beyond its federative structure.

Seo and Creed (2002) have developed a dialectical model for understanding the mutually constitutive nature of agency and institutions. They describe praxis (political action embedded in a historical system of interconnected yet incompatible institutional arrangements) as arising out of the contradictions which develop over time in any process of institutionalization. In their view, such contradictions are inevitable as competing institutions arise and interact. It is these contradictions which make agency both possible and necessary.

Their account is of such contradictions evolving over time. However, in our account of bridging roles in MNCs, we can see that the institutional contradictions span geographical space rather than time. The managers in bridging roles who have been most effective in bringing about change have developed identities which span multiple national settings (see also chapter of Maclean and Hollinshead in this volume). They live the contradictions between the different national institutions within which their identities are constituted. To return to Burt's claim, about people at the intersection of social worlds: the position of these boundary creatures is powerful, not just because they act as a conduit for the flow of ideas through a network; they also experience directly the contradiction between different national institutional settings and the tension between different goals and interests.

An important question for MNEs concerns whether such bridging skills can be developed. The ElecCo case would suggest these skills develop across the course of a career. Thus they can be fostered and their development supported over time not least by attention to supported international work assignments. However, it would seem naive to imagine they might be developed through a few days on a course for "global leaders."

REFERENCES

Adler, P. S. and S. W. Kwon 2002. "Social capital: prospects for a new concept" *Academy of Management Review* 27: 17–40

Birkinshaw, J. 2001. "Strategy and management in MNE subsidiaries" in Rugman and Brewer (eds.) *The Oxford Handbook of International Business*. Oxford University Press, pp. 380–401

Birkinshaw, J. and N. Hood 2000. "Characteristics of foreign subsidiaries in industry clusters," *Journal of International Business Studies* 31: 141–154

Bouquet, C. and J. Birkinshaw 2008. "Managing power in the multinational corporation: how low-power actors gain influence," *Journal of Management* 34: 477–508

Buckley, P. J. and P. N. Ghauri 2004. "Globalisation, economic geography and the strategy of multinational enterprises," *Journal of International Business Studies* 35: 81–98

Burt, R. 1992. *Structural Holes: The Structure of Social Capital Competition*. Cambridge, MA: Harvard University Press

Burt, R. S. 2004. "Structural holes and good ideas," *American Journal of Sociology* 110: 349–99

Clark, E. and M. Geppert 2011. "Subsidiary integration as identity construction and institution building: a political sensemaking approach," *Journal of Management Studies* (in print)

Cook, S. D. N. and J. S. Brown 1999. "Bridging epistemologies: the generative dance between organizational knowledge and organizational knowing," *Organization Science* 10: 381–400

Creed, W. E. D., M. A. Scully and J. R. Austin 2002. "Clothes make the person? The tailoring of legitimating accounts and the social construction of identity," *Organization Science* 13: 475–96

Czarniawska, B. and B. Joerges 1996. "The travel of ideas" in Czarniawska and Sevon (eds.) *Translating the Organizational Change*. New York: Walter de Gruyter, pp. 13–48

DiMaggio, P. J. and W. W. Powell 1983. "The iron cage revisited – institutional isomorphism and collective rationality in organizational fields," *American Sociological Review* 48: 147–60

Edelman, L. F., M. Bresnen, S. Newell, H. Scarbrough and J. Swan 2004. "The benefits and pitfalls of social capital: empirical evidence from two organizations in the United Kingdom," *British Journal of Management* 15: 59–69

Eisenhardt, K. 1989. "Building theories from case study research," *Academy of Management Review* 14: 532–50

Engeström, Y. 1999. "Activity theory and individual and social transformation" in Engeström, Mietinen and Punamäki (eds.) *Perspectives on Activity Theory*. Cambridge University Press, pp. 19–38

Ericsson, K. A., R. T. Krampe and C. Tesch-Roemer 1993. "The role of deliberate practice in the acquisition of expert performance," *Psychological Review* 100: 363–406

Fenton-O'Creevy, M. and S. Wood 2007. "Diffusion of human resource management systems in UK headquartered multinational enterprises: integrating institutional and strategic choice explanations," *European Journal of International Management* 1: 329–49

Fenton-O'Creevy, M., P. Gooderham and O. Nordhaug 2008. "Human resource management in US subsidiaries in Europe and Australia: centralisation or autonomy?," *Journal of International Business Studies* 39: 151–66

Fligstein, N. 1997. "Social skill and institutional theory," *American Behavioral Scientist* 40: 397

    2001. "Social skill and the theory of fields," *Sociological Theory* 19: 105–25

Forsgren, M. 2008. *Theories of the Multinational Firm: A Multidimensional Creature in the Global Economy*. Cheltenham: Edward Elgar

Gobet, F. and H. A. Simon 1996. "Templates in chess memory: a mechanism for recalling several boards," *Cognitive Psychology* 31: 1–40

Ghoshal, S. and C. Bartlett 1988. "Creation, adoption, and diffusion of innovations by subsidiaries of multinational corporations," *Journal of International Business Studies* 19: 365–88

Grant, R. 1996. "Toward a knowledge-based theory of the firm," *Strategic Management Journal* 17: 109–22

Hakkarainen, K., T. Palonen, S. Paavola and E. Lehtinen 2004. *Communities of Networked Expertise: Professional and Educational Perspectives*. 1st edn. London: Elsevier

Hutchins, E. 1990. "The technology of team navigation" in Galegher, Kraut and Egido (eds.) *Intellectual Teamwork: Social and Technical Bases of Collaborative Work*. Hillsdale, NJ: Lawrence Erlbaum, pp. 191–220

    1995. *Cognition in the Wild*. Cambridge, MA: MIT Press

Hutchins, E. and T. Klausen 1996. "Distributed cognition in an airline cockpit" in Engeström and Middleton (eds.) *Cognition and Communication at Work*. Cambridge University Press, pp. 15–34

Kostova, T. and K. Roth 2002. "Adoption of an organizational practice by subsidiaries of multinational corporations: institutional and relational effects," *Academy of Management Journal* 45: 215–33

Lave, J. and E. Wenger 1991. *Situated Learning: Legitimate Peripheral Participation.* Cambridge University Press

Lozeau, D., A. Langley and J. L. Denis 2002. "The corruption of managerial techniques by organizations," *Human Relations* 55: 537–64

Morgan, G. and P. H. Kristensen 2006. "The contested space of multinationals: varieties of institutionalism, varieties of capitalism," *Human Relations* 59: 1467–90

Nahapiet, J. 2008. "Social capital and knowledge: pipes, prisms and practices," *Presentation at Second Annual Workshop on Enactment and Development of Social Capital*, NHH, Bergen, November 10–11

Nahapiet, J. and S. Ghoshal 1998. "Social capital, intellectual capital, and the organizational advantage," *Academy of Management Review* 23: 242–66

Oliver, C. 1991. "Strategic responses to institutional processes," *Academy of Management Review*, 16(1): 145–179

Porter, M. E. 1986. "Changing patterns of international competition," *California Management Review* 28: 9–40

Powell, W. and L. Smith-Doerr 1994. "Networks and economic life" in Smelser and Swedberg (eds.) *The Handbook of Economic Sociology.* Princeton University Press, pp. 379–402

Prahalad, C. K. and Y. Doz 1987. *The Multinational Mission: Balancing Local Demands and Global Vision.* New York: Free Press

Roth, K. 1992. "Implementing international strategy at the business unit level: the role of managerial decision-making characteristics," *Journal of Management* 18: 769–89

Seo, M. and W. Creed 2002. "Institutional contradictions, praxis, and institutional change: a dialectical perspective," *Academy of Management Review* 27: 222–47.

Spender, J.-C. 1994. "Organizational knowledge, collective practice, and Penrosian rents," *International Business Review* 3: 353–67

  1996. "Making knowledge the basis of a dynamic theory of the firm," *Strategic Management Journal* 17: 45–62

Spiro, R. J., W. P. Visipoel, J. P. Schmitz and J. Samarapungavan 1987. "Knowledge acquisition for application: cognitive flexibility and transfer in complex content domains" in Britton and Glynn (eds.) *Executive Control Processes in Reading.* Hillsdale, NJ: Lawrence Erlbaum, pp. 177–99

Taylor, S., S. Beechler and N. Napier 1996. "Toward an integrative model of strategic international human resource management," *Academy of Management Review*, 21: 959–85

Vygotsky, L. S. 1930. *Mind in Society.* Cambridge, MA: Harvard University Press

  1986. *Thought and Language.* Cambridge, MA: MIT Press

Wenger, E. 1998. *Communities of Practice: Learning, Meaning and Identity.* Cambridge University Press

Whitehead, A. N. 1967. *The Aims of Education and Other Essays.* New York: Free Press

Yamin, M. and M. Forsgren 2006. "Hymer's analysis of the multinational organization: power retention and the demise of the federative MNE," *International Business Review* 15: 166–79

Yamin, M. and R. R. Sinkovics 2007. "ICT and MNE reorganisation: the paradox of control," *Critical Perspectives on International Business* 3: 322–36

Yin, R. K. 2003. *Case Study Research: Design and Methods*. London: Sage

Yip, G. 1989. "Global strategy – in a world of nations?," *Sloan Management Review* 31: 29–41

Part III

Headquarters–subsidiary relations

5 Conflict in headquarters–subsidiary relations: a critical literature review and new directions

Susanne Blazejewski and Florian Becker-Ritterspach

Introduction

The objective of this chapter is to provide a critical overview over recent theory-based research on multinational corporations (MNC) conflict. In particular, we seek to understand and explicate the contributions of the various theoretical approaches and perspectives applied in international business (IB) research towards the analysis of conflictual situations and processes in MNC contexts. In modeling conflict in MNC international business, authors draw on diverse theoretical traditions, including psychology, sociology and economics as well as organizational conflict theory. We wish to critically fathom their respective potential for the description and explanation of MNC conflict and, in addition, provide some insights into the theoretical lacunae remaining within the IB conflict research: where and how can we better integrate and extend conflict research in the IB field in order to fully capitalize on the theoretical advancements in conflict research at large? And where do we need to adjust concepts and constructs drawn from related fields to better account for the complex context of MNC conflicts? For reasons expounded upon below, the critical review concentrates on conflicts arising in the MNC headquarters–subsidiary relationship.

Since the MNC as an organization has become an object of study in its own right, it has been characterized as an inherently conflictual arena (Bartlett and Ghoshal 1989; Doz and Prahalad 1991; Gladwin and Walter 1980; Pahl and Roth 1993; Prahalad and Doz 1987). Alternately, authors have discussed different causes of conflict: the heterogeneity of cultures (Ayoko *et al.* 2002; Graham 1985; Roth and Nigh 1992; Tjosvold 1999), stakeholder interests (Gladwin and Walter 1980; Zietsma and Winn 2008) or institutional contexts (Kostova *et al.* 2008; Morgan 2003), the contested allocation of limited resources to multiple MNC subunits and strategic dilemmas resulting from the innate contradiction between local responsiveness and global integration

Table 5.1 Levels of conflict in MNC

Conflict level	Research object in IB (ex.)	Primary research field
Intra-personal	Expats (intra-role conflict, problems of adjustment, psychological coping with foreign context)	Psychology
Inter-personal	Expat–local relationship	Social-psychology
Intra-group	Conflict in multicultural and/or geographically distributed teams	Social-psychology, sociology
Intra-organizational/ inter-group	Headquarters–subsidiary, peer subsidiaries	Organizational studies, international business
Inter-organizational	MNC competitor or strategic partner, MNC–government relationships	Organizational studies, international business, sociology
International	Trade conflict between countries	Political science, economics

(Bartlett and Ghoshal 1989; Prahalad and Doz 1987). Conflict in MNC has been investigated on multiple levels of analysis (Table 5.1), although more recently work on intra-group and inter-personal conflicts is most prevalent. In particular, empirical studies based on psychological models demonstrate that cultural diversity in MNC working teams leads to higher levels of and more intense inter-personal conflict (Alper *et al.* 2000; Ayoko *et al.* 2002; Earley and Laubach 2002; Jehn *et al.* 1999) and increases the likelihood of conflicts becoming manifest (Armstrong and Cole 1996; Joshi *et al.* 2002). Compared to culturally homogeneous groups, international working teams "suffer more conflict, higher turnover and more communication difficulties" (Ayoko *et al.* 2002), as well as more emotional conflict (Von Glinow *et al.* 2004). Geographical distance has been shown to increase the likelihood of protracted and dysfunctional conflict (Armstrong and Cole 1996).

Studies investigating conflicts between MNC and their multiple external stakeholders (e.g. alliance partners, host country governments, NGOs) form a second focal point of MNC conflict research (Bennett 2002; Danskin *et al.* 2005; Gladwin and Walter 1980; Schepers 2006; Whiteman 2009) in IB. Here, the incompatible interests of different stakeholders are considered the main causes of conflict, and conflict management is primarily concerned with the better integration of multiple interests.

This chapter, in turn, focuses on intra-organizational conflict, in particular the relationship between MNC headquarters and its international subsidiaries.[1] Birkinshaw and Hood (1998) argue that the headquarters–subsidiary relationship is still the most important intra-MNC relationship. In addition, it is clearly a focus of research, producing numerous papers using highly different theoretical angles (see Table 5.2). Research on conflict in the headquarters–subsidiary relationship hence provides a broad spectrum of theoretical lenses although with a shared phenomenon of interest, i.e. conflictual situations and processes. It thus presents a particularly suitable field for comparative review. Vertical conflicts between peer subsidiaries have recently become a focus of attention (Birkinshaw and Lingblad 2005), but so far without making conflict a central construct or interest. As a further argument, Rössing maintains that the current "level of maturity of research into conflicts between headquarters and subsidiary within the MNC is low" (2005: 90). This chapter, therefore, aims at a systematic investigation of research approaches and their respective contributions in order to provide a sound theoretical foundation as well as several starting points for the further advancement of the field. The objective is in line with recent demands by several leading scholars (Kostova *et al.* 2008; Tsui 2007) who urge the IB field to use the MNC context more critically to challenge and eventually extend the manifold theories and models borrowed from other disciplines.

The multiplicity of levels of research and theoretical foundations in conflict research (see Table 5.1) reflects a similar variety in definitions of the key term "conflict." While most authors in the field agree that conflict always entails some kind of opposition, tension or incompatibility, their respective definitions espouse, depending on their research interests, highly different foci and definitional elements. Whereas Deutsch (1973) emphasizes the behavioral dimension of conflict ("A conflict exists whenever incompatible *activities* occur," our emphasis), many other authors concentrate on the incompatibility of goals or interests (Jameson 1999; Rössing 2005). Others, in turn, employ a definition focusing on opponent "strategies" (Crozier and Friedberg 1981; Easton and Araujo 1992), thereby connecting interests to behavior and context in conflict situations. The definition by Thomas (1992) introduces yet another two dimensions to the definition of conflict: perceptions and process. Similar to Pondy (1967), Thomas' (1992) definition of conflict as process leads him to develop his seminal stage model of conflict (see below). Putting perceptions center stage, in turn, enables Thomas (1992) to bridge the gap between interests and actions: incompatible interests only produce

---

[1] We also refer to literature investigating other levels of analysis but only if the conflict of interest is explicitly linked to the inter-organizational level, i.e. the headquarters–subsidiary relationship.

Table 5.2 Conflict perspectives on headquarters–subsidiary relations

Theory	Centrality of conflict (explanans/ explanandum)	Conflict process (antecedents, causes, episodes, outcomes)	Actors and their behavioral orientation in conflict	Influences/ context (structural model)	Power	Authors (ex.)
Contingency theory	Explanans & explanandum	Conflict generation: Conflicting pressures of global integration and local differentiation as central conflict source. Conflict outcome: Negative impact of conflict on performance, requiring different structure and strategy contingent conflict resolution mechanisms	Collective and individual actors considered. Behavioral assumptions and determinants: Organization determined through structure, systems, processes and control, coordination and socialization	Mutinational strategy, structure, paradigm; different market and task environments and corresponding organizational contexts. Conflict design options to prevent conflict generation	Implicit "power over" as one conflict source (power-dependency perspective) and "power to" as means to avoid or resolve conflict	Doz et al. (1981) Roth and Nigh (1992) Pahl and Roth (1993) Gupta and Cao (2005)
Agency theory	Explanandum	Conflict generation: Information asymmetry and deviant perceptions of subunit competencies	Collective or individual actors. Behavioral assumptions and determinants: Opportunism, asymmetrical information and bounded rationality	Conflict design options to prevent conflict generation	Implicit "power over" concept tied to hierarchical position of principal, power as delegated at will to agent	Tasoluk, et al. (2006) Mudambi and Pedersen (2007)
Game theory	Explanandum	Conflict generation: Conflicting interests of headquarters and subsidiary in an	Collective or individual actors. Behavioral assumptions and determinants:	Conflict design options to prevent conflict generation	Implicitly assumed to be symmetrical	Rössing (2005) Kaufmann and Rössing (2005)

Perspective		Conflict generation and outcomes	Actor perspective / behavioral assumptions and determinants	Institutional context	Power	References
		interdependent technology transfer situation with incomplete information	Rational choice model (individual utility maximization) Determined by available strategies, rules of the game, expected decision/ behavior of opponent	inside the game (i.e. both actors have the same, given alternatives for action)		
Institutional (new institutionalism)	Explanans	Conflict outcomes: Conflicting institutional pressures impact transfer/ innovation outcomes in subsidiaries	Collective or individual actors Behavioral assumptions and determinants: Combination of organization and host institutional context pressures determine actor response	Institutional duality mainly involving organizational and host institutional context	Marginal to no consideration of power	Westney (1993) Kostova (1999) and Kostova and Roth (2002)
Institutional (comparative historical and micro-political)	Explanans & explanandum	Conflict generation: Caused by different actor interest leading to functional and dysfunctional outcomes Conflict outcomes: e.g. Unintended restructuring or transfer results	Differentiated individual actor perspective Behavioral assumptions and determinants: Differentiated institutional embeddedness of actors' structure but do not determine behavior	Different institutional contexts and levels, inside and outside the organization	Implicit "power over" and some explicit "power to" linked to its structuration by institutional conditions	Edwards et al. (2006) Dörrenbächer and Geppert (2006) Morgan and Kristensen (2006)
Postcolonial perspective	Explanandum	Conflict generation: Rooted in geopolitical power relations or power asymmetries between first- and third-world states Conflict outcome: Knowledge transfer, emergence of hybrid cultures	Differentiated individual actor perspective Behavioral assumptions and determinants: Differentiated geopolitical embeddedness of actors' structure but do not determine behavior	Colonial encounter; geopolitical context and relations	Explicit concern with "power over," i.e. power asymmetries as source of conflict. Implicit concern with "power to" focusing on cultural repertoires as means to influence conflict	Mir and Sharpe (2004), Frenkel (2008), Mir and Sharpe (2009)

Table 5.2 (cont.)

Theory	Centrality of conflict (explanans/ explanandum)	Conflict process (antecedents, causes, episodes, outcomes)	Actors and their behavioral orientation in conflict	Influences/ context (structural model)	Power	Authors (ex.)
Social identity and role theory – intra-personal	Explanandum	Conflict generation: Rooted in different forms of dual identification of subsidiary managers with headquarters and subsidiary. Conflict outcome: Personal and organizational consequences	Individual actor perspective. Behavioral assumptions and determinants: Conflict experience determined by type of MNC embeddedness and exposure to national context difference	Cultural, institutional distance and corporate strategy impact kinds of dual identity and thereby intra-personal conflict levels	Not considered	Vora and Kostova, (2007), Vora et al. (2007)
Role theory – intra-organizational	Explanandum	Conflict generation: Rooted in perception gaps about subsidiary role. Conflict outcome: Negative impact of conflict requiring conflict avoidance through negotiation and communication	Individual actor perspective. Behavioral assumptions and determinants: Role sets expectations and individual ideas on role.	Contradicting expectations from internal and external role sets, plus individual ideas based on biography	"Power to" and implicit "power over"	Schmid and Daniel (2007)

conflict handling behavior when the incompatibility is perceived as frustrating and acted upon by at least one of the actors involved. Especially in the MNC context, it is easily conceivable that many conflicts (due to incompatible interests) remain latent because the potentially opposing actor does not even notice (due to geographic, cultural or hierarchical distance) or deliberately suppresses that his/her interests are colliding with those, for instance, of actors in another subsidiary.

Paying attention to definitional choices and nuances opens up more sound paths to a better understanding of conflicts in general (Barki and Hartwick 2001) and MNC conflict in particular. Definitions also set the ground for the development of conflict management and resolution alternatives. Where they draw attention to conflicts of interests, conflict design alternatives are likely to focus on re-setting or satisfying actors' interests (e.g. through incentive systems); where they entail a processual element, conflict management and prevention are plotted against each one of the different conflict phases. Against this background it remains conspicuous that most articles reviewed in this chapter fail to provide a definition of their core construct at all.[2] Still, we can often delineate the key implicit elements of the respective conflict construct from the theoretical approach selected and/or the variables traced in the analysis. In any case, the variety of (implicit) definitions and constructions of conflict in our review mirrors the variety of theoretical approaches and research foci in the conflict field at large and precludes any attempt at unifying the definitional strands.

Paper selection and methodology

The selection of papers included in the critical review is informed by three aspects: (1) a focus on headquarters–subsidiary relationships, (2) conflict as the central concern or construct, and (3) an identifiable interest in using, exploring or developing theory (or theories) of conflict.

Corresponding key words have been used to search for relevant articles in bibliographical databases such as Ebsco, Web of Science and Google Scholar to ensure a maximum capture for both published and manuscript papers from journals as well as books or conference proceedings across disciplines. We also conducted archival and journal-by-journal searches in a broad array of prominent journals from all related fields, i.e. international business

---

[2] Exceptions include Rössing (2005), Pahl and Roth (1993) and Gupta and Cao (2005) who explicitly provide a definition of conflict in their respective articles.

and management (*Journal of International Business Studies, Management International Review, Journal of International Management, Journal of World Business, International Business Review, Critical Perspectives on International Business*), conflict, communication and negotiation (*International Journal of Conflict Management, Journal of Conflict Resolution, International Journal of Cross Cultural Communication*), as well as general management and organizational studies (*Academy of Management Journal, Academy of Management Review, Strategic Management Journal, Journal of Management, Organization Studies*). The search generated 17 articles applying different theoretical lenses on the headquarters–subsidiary conflict phenomenon. Table 5.2 provides an overview of the papers included in our critical review, grouped according to the dominant theoretical perspective used in each paper. It contains both empirical studies and conceptual papers. Our aim was to include as wide a variety of approaches, methods and theories as possible in order to represent the actual development and heterogeneity of MNC conflict research without, however, any claim or intention of exhaustiveness.

In order to structure the critical analysis and assess the comparative contribution of each approach we apply a set of criteria comprising (1) the respective definition and conceptualization of conflict, (2) the centrality of the conflict construct (whether it is used as explanans, i.e. an independent variable, or explanandum, i.e. the dependent variable), (3) conceptualization of constructs linked to the conflict phenomenon, in particular power, and (4) a focus on structural or processual dimensions of conflict based on the reference framework by Thomas (1992). In view of the overall theme of this book, the analysis takes particular account of how power is understood and modeled in each approach. Power is closely linked to conflict in at least three ways: as an object of conflict in interdependent relationships (i.e. conflicts *about* power and its distribution in MNC), as a source of conflict handling means (e.g. personal power bases such as charisma are required to solve conflict through strategies of persuasion or identification; sanctioning and reward power form the basis for bargaining or dominating conflict handling strategies), and as structuring the conflict situation (e.g. by defining the actors' position in hierarchies) (Cheldelin *et al.* 2003; Coleman 2006; Frost 1987; Hardy 1996; Hayward and Boeker 1998; Lukes 1986; Pfeffer 1992).

The Thomas-framework (1976, 1992) analytically distinguishes between two dimensions[3] of conflict research. The process model of conflict focuses

---

[3] Glasl (2010) convincingly argues that both dimensions need to be integrated in conflict research and management. We still consider the distinction useful for analytical purposes. As the critical review

on "the temporal sequence of events which occur as the system operates – e.g. the mental and behavioral activities of the conflicting parties" (Thomas 1992: 267). The conflict process comprises the phases of conflict generation (frustration), conflict conceptualization (perception and framing), conflict handling (behavior) and conflict outcomes (side-effects, escalation) (Pondy 1967; Thomas 1992). The processual approach is concerned with what happens over the course of a conflictual process and takes the structural and situational context of this process as given. Conflict management strategies in the processual model concentrate on the modification of actors' perceptions, motivation and behavior in conflict situations. In turn, the structural model focuses on "the more or less stable (slow-changing) conditions which shape or control the system's process" (Thomas 1992: 267). It directs attention towards the structure and the context in which the conflict occurs. Whereas Thomas (1992) concentrates on the organizational context as affecting conflict processes (incentive systems, organizational procedures and norms), we extend the concept to cover also the larger MNC environment including host/home country institutions, socio-cultural, economic as well as political influences on the conflict situation. From this perspective, conflict management and prevention requires the adjustment of structural and contextual constraints impacting the conflict situation. In the 1992 review of his first seminal contribution developing the conflict reference framework Thomas deplores the "modest impact" (Thomas 1992: 272) that the structural perspective has had on conflict research while – at that time – studies on the conflict process proliferated. As we will demonstrate below, in the area of MNC headquarters–subsidiary relationships, the focus has clearly shifted in favor of the structural model.

Conflict perspectives on headquarters–subsidiary relationships: a critical review

Contingency theory

One of the first and most prominent perspectives that has considered conflict in MNCs and in headquarters–subsidiary relations is the contingency theory. Within this context it was the differentiation–integration framework

reveals, there is in fact a lack of integrated approaches, with structural conflict research clearly dominating the field.

that proved to be central to understanding conflicts. The framework was originally introduced by Prahalad (1975) and subsequently taken up by a number of scholars. It rests on the contingency theory as presented by Lawrence and Lorsch (1967), on the idea, that is, that firms face two fundamental environmental forces, i.e. pressures for differentiation and pressures for integration. Translated to the MNC, these pressures were labeled by Prahalad and Doz (1987) "pressure for global integration" and "pressure for local responsiveness" and similarly by Bartlett and Ghoshal (1989) "forces for global integration" and "forces for national differentiation." It is also these different pressures that have been discussed as sources of "conflict" and "tension" within the MNCs, leading frequently to "strained and adversarial" headquarters–subsidiary relationships (Bartlett and Ghoshal 1986; Doz *et al.* 1981; Doz and Prahalad 1981, 1984). Doz *et al.* (1981: 65) argue, for example, that the conflict between "host country demands and competitive forces turns strategic decision-making in MNC into an advocacy process between two competing perspectives" resulting in frequent conflicts about major decisions. They go on to argue that such tension between "national and global views" needs to be properly managed in different organizational forms to avoid an organizationally dysfunctional bias towards either side. To solve the tension they suggest a "flexible decision process" that relies on different administrative solutions.

In terms of conflict actors, these are mainly seen to be represented by headquarters executives and subsidiary managers as "[n]eeds for responsiveness typically enter the MNC via subsidiary managers, whereas needs for integration are usually more acutely perceived by headquarters executives" (Doz and Prahalad 1984: 56). Given these conflicting perspectives, the MNC faces the challenge of finding the right trade-off in every single decision while maintaining the overall balance between the two forces. The authors suggest a range of management tools to handle the conflicting forces including "data management," the "management of managers' perceptions" and "conflict resolution" mechanisms. The latter include formal organizational solutions such as "planning procedures," "the creation of specialized coordinator's roles, the clear assignment of responsibilities in the decision processes, and the provision of specific channels for preparing decisions such as committees, task forces, study groups, business teams, and so forth" (Doz and Prahalad 1984: 61, see also Doz and Prahalad 1981).

Bartlett and Ghoshal (1989) argue along similar lines. Extending the integration–differentiation framework, they suggest that MNCs face not only the often conflicting forces of global integration and local differentiation but additionally the need for worldwide innovation. However, MNCs that respond

to these forces are simultaneously exposed to enormous forces of fragmentation and conflict. They contend that without a strong source of unification,
such a company risks deterioration into organizational anarchy or, worse,
an "international network of fiefdoms" (Bartlett and Ghoshal 1989: 204).
To resolve conflict, that is to reconcile antagonistic perspectives and resolve
opposing interest, they suggest, similar to Doz and Prahalad (1981), a whole
range of mechanisms, including structures, systems, processes and coordination mechanisms. Most important, however, they hail the coordination
mechanism of normative integration through socialization. In view of MNC
complexity, Bartlett and Ghoshal (1989) stress that coordination cannot rest
on formal mechanisms alone but must consider the mindset of the individual
manager. Managers need to be socialized in such a way that shared understandings of, identification with and commitment to the company's broader
purpose, values and goals is achieved. In their view, integrating managerial
mindsets are the "global glue" that keeps in check the centrifugal forces in
the transnational corporation (Bartlett and Ghoshal 1989).

While the integration–differentiation framework lays the basis for understanding conflict from a contingency perspective, it has also had a strong
influence on more sophisticated contingency perspectives on conflict in IB as
presented by Roth and Nigh (1992) and Pahl and Roth (1993). Roth and Nigh
(1992) seek to understand how the perceived effectiveness of headquarters–
subsidiary relationships is influenced by coordination, control and conflict
between the headquarters and the subsidiary. While conflict here is an independent variable rather than a dependent variable as presented in the early
work above, Roth and Nigh (1992) are intimately concerned with conflicts
and their emergence in headquarters–subsidiary relationships. Drawing on
the integration–differentiation framework, they reason:

Foreign subsidiaries must be responsive to integration demands inherent in being interdependent with or part of a multinational organization; only through such integration
are market imperfections exploited, thereby allowing the corporation to effectively
compete with the domestic firm (Hymer 1976). However, a foreign subsidiary must
also respond to the local context (Hamel and Prahalad 1983). Thus the headquarters–
subsidiary relationship often becomes "strained or even adversarial" (Bartlett and
Ghoshal 1986: 88) as the subsidiary attempts to respond to both independent and
interdependent interests. Consequently, some degree of conflict inevitably accompan-
ies the headquarters–subsidiary relationship. (Roth and Nigh 1992: 285)

In contrast with much work on intra-unit conflict in IB, they clearly define
conflicts and their manifestations. Based on Anderson and Narus (1990: 285),

conflicts are defined as *"the level of disagreement between two social units –* in the case at hand, between the headquarters and the subsidiary." And, citing Walton and Dutton (1969), manifestations of inter-unit conflicts are seen to include "competitive orientation, bargaining and restrictions on information, circumscribed interaction patterns, and antagonistic feelings" (Anderson and Narus 1990: 285). While Roth and Nigh (1992) acknowledge that conflict theory sees conflicts as having both functional and dysfunctional outcomes, they hypothesize and empirically confirm that in the case of headquarters–subsidiary conflicts, outcomes will be more dysfunctional for the headquarters–subsidiary effectiveness. This is based on the reasoning that the separation in time and space between headquarters and subsidiaries impedes communication and interaction required for functional conflict outcomes, which is aggravated by the additional potential for cross-cultural misunderstandings.

The work on headquarters–subsidiary conflict by Pahl and Roth (1993) points into a similar direction. Pahl and Roth (1993) develop and test an extensive model to understand headquarters–subsidiary effectiveness. They investigate "how conflict between the headquarters and the subsidiary of an MNC, and the styles used to manage conflict, vary depending on the international strategy of the MNC" (Pahl and Roth 1993: 140). Specifically, their model tests, on the one hand, how the MNCs international strategy, conflict management style (based on Rahim's (1983) Organizational Conflict Inventory) and integration mechanisms are related to inter-unit conflict and, on the other hand, how conflict management styles and inter-unit conflicts are related to headquarters–subsidiary effectiveness. The starting point to understand inter-unit conflict is once more the differentiation–integration framework. Similar to Roth and Nigh (1992), they define inter-unit conflict "as conflict which exists between two social units" (Pahl and Roth 1993: 140). They also refer to Thomas's (1976) definition of conflict as a process "which begins 'when one party perceives that the other party has frustrated, or is about to frustrate some concern of his'" (Pahl and Roth 1993: 140). Adding to this, they cite a wide range of factors that can give rise to inter-unit conflict such as "goal incompatibility," "activity interdependence," "drives for autonomy," "shared resources," "jurisdictional ambiguity," "communication barriers" related to time, space and physical distance, "ignorance of other party," "dependence," "conflict of interest" or "heterogeneity of organizational member background." As such conditions apply to a large degree to headquarters–subsidiary relationships, they see these as a "fertile ground for conflict." Further, they suggest that different international strategies reflect to different degrees the responsiveness and/ or integration, implying different propensities for headquarters–subsidiary conflicts. Hence, as each of these strategies involves different types and levels of interdependency between headquarters and subsidiaries, they assume that international strategies have an impact on inter-unit conflicts. Along similar lines, they hypothesize that the influence of conflict management styles and integration mechanisms on inter-unit conflict depends on the international strategy. Finally, they suggest that conflict management styles influence relationship effectiveness and the level of inter-unit conflict. For example, an "avoiding management style" is seen to be generally negatively related to the effectiveness of the headquarters–subsidiary relationship. And, while "integrating conflict management" is hypothesized to be negatively related to headquarters–subsidiary conflicts in global integration and multifocal MNCs, a "dominating conflict style" is assumed to increase headquarters–subsidiary conflicts. Regarding the influence of headquarters–subsidiary conflicts on conflict outcomes, i.e. the perceived headquarters–subsidiary effectiveness, Pahl and Roth (1993) are in line with the reasoning of Roth and Nigh (1992) and posit a negative relationship between conflict and effectiveness. However, putting their framework to an empirical test, Pahl and Roth (1993) find only partial confirmation of their hypotheses. Although Pahl and Roth's (1993) framework builds crucially on the responsiveness–differentiation framework, they do not find a direct influence between international strategy and the degree of inter-unit conflict in the headquarters–subsidiary relationship. They find, however, that subsidiary managers following global integration strategies employ personal integration mechanisms to diffuse conflicts with headquarters, which could indicate that proper conflict style styles offset higher conflict propensities of certain strategy types. At the same time, they cannot confirm that the dominating conflict style reduces inter-group conflict in locally responsive MNCs and that the integrating conflict style reduces inter-group conflict in multifocal MNCs. With regard to headquarters–subsidiary effectiveness they find that an avoiding conflict management style in inter-unit conflict reduces the perceived headquarters–subsidiary effectiveness.

A last contribution that needs to be discussed here is the recent work by Gupta and Cao (2005). Combining contingency theory and the theory of intra-group conflict developed by Jehn (1995), Gupta and Cao (2005) have recently taken up the issue of parent–subsidiary conflict. They are interested in both antecedents and performance-related consequences of conflict. Their argument is that the geographical and cultural differentiation implies potentially conflicting cognitive maps. However, reaching beyond the inte-gration–differentiation framework, they take a closer look at how different subsidiary-level conditions moderate the antecedents and consequences of parent–subsidiary conflict. They hypothesize that the greater the geograph-ical and/or cultural distance between parent and subsidiary, the higher the magnitude of the conflict over strategic and organizational decisions (see also chapter by Williams in this volume). This relationship is seen to be moder-ated by the "strategic orientation" of the subsidiary. Here they argue that the more the subsidiary's mandate involves exploration, the weaker the impact will be of distance on the conflict. Building on March's exploration–exploi-tation framework, the basic rationale is:

As seems clear organizational units whose strategic mission is orientated towards greater exploration would, *by design*, be expected to engage in greater search for *novel* information and cognitive lenses. Accordingly, we should expect that the extent of a subsidiary's exploration orientation would moderate the impact of cogni-tive diversity on the emergence of decision conflict between managers at the parent and the subsidiary levels. (Gupta and Cao 2005: 6)

Regarding the consequences, they suggest that parent–subsidiary conflict is likely to have a negative influence on the performance of the subsidiary and the organizational commitment of subsidiary general managers. They also look here at the moderating effect of conflict resolution, which is again related to a subsidiary-level variable, namely entry mode. The line of rea-soning is that greenfield sites, as compared to acquisition, involve stronger network ties and trust between subsidiary and headquarters actors and will, therefore, be positively related to conflict resolution, implying that conflict will have less adverse effects on subsidiary performance and managers' com-mitment. Gupta and Cao (2005) proceed to test their hypotheses and find them, with the exception of the moderating effect of geographical distance, confirmed.

Looking at contingency theory within the context of IB it is fair to say that headquarters–subsidiary conflict is a central concern. In the work of Roth and Nigh (1992), Pahl and Roth (1993) and Gupta and Cao (2005) conflict particularly takes center stage, is clearly defined and closely related to organ-izational conflict theory. Studies in this stream are concerned with anteced-ents, consequences and resolution mechanisms of conflict. Depending on the study, conflict becomes both a dependent and independent variable. This literature highlights how firm-specific context, such as structure, strategy and strategic roles, potentially influence conflict. In terms of the underlying structural causes for conflict, the differentiation–responsiveness framework and the strategic role focus, both of which are embedded in contingency theory's environment–strategy–structure paradigm, form the core explanatory constructs. While consequences or outcomes of conflicts in organizations are not always seen as dysfunctional, the particular properties of the MNCs and their headquarters–subsidiary relationships are seen to lead to dysfunctional effects in headquarters–subsidiary conflicts. At the same time, most contributions in this stream are not only intimately concerned with conflict avoidance and resolution but also rather optimistic about the possibility of managing conflicts, be it through different structural, coordination and control mechanisms, processes or conflict resolution mechanisms and management styles.

Despite the fact that all of these contributions introduce the notion of conflict in the MNCs, there remains, particularly in the early contributions, some fundamental question mark as to whether conflicting forces (global–local) actually lead to a material conflict among actors. Conversely, it remains unclear whether the conflict-resolution mechanisms actually solve extant material conflicts among actors or just serve to avoid such conflicts appearing in the first place, or else simply help to come to a decision under conditions of conflicting pressures, irrespective of the underlying conflict levels among actors. Another problem is the weak conceptualization of actors and their behavioral rationale. If individual actors are considered (departing from headquarters and subsidiaries as organization-level collective actors), their behavioral orientation is largely organizationally determined, for example, by their structural location in the MNC. We may question, however, if headquarters and subsidiary managers' orientation vis-à-vis the global or local orientation can be simply equated with their location in headquarters and subsidiaries (see Becker-Ritterspach and Dörrenbächer 2011). Moreover, as in most work on conflict in headquarters–subsidiary relationships, there is neither a strong process perspective in this stream, nor is there a systematic theorization of the relationship between the concepts of conflict, power or politics. Pahl and Roth (1993), who explicitly refer to the power-dependence perspective, are a notable exception here. For the most part the power and conflict relationship remains implicit. It reflects the concept of "power over" as a source of conflict and "power to" as a means to manage or avoid conflict. Nevertheless, although these are serious questions to be raised, the integration–responsiveness framework emphasizes important sources of conflict in headquarters–subsidiary relations that derive from different strategic environments and the corresponding structural embeddedness of actors in MNCs.

Agency theory

In agency theory, conflicts are subsumed under the label of "agency problems." Only rarely do authors actually employ the term "conflict" (Mudambi and Pedersen 2007; Tasoluk *et al.* 2006), though, without providing a definition or clearly differentiating it from the more general label of "agency problems." Agency problems arise when actors in an interdependent principal–agent relationship have different goals, information and risk preferences and it is difficult or too costly for the principal to verify what the agent is actually doing (Eisenhardt 1989; Jensen and Meckling 1976). Agents might take advantage of information asymmetries and pursue their own interests to the detriment of the principal's goals. Apart from a clear-cut typology of conflicts/agency problems, including moral hazard and adverse selection, agency theory develops a number of conflict prevention devices focusing on monitoring (in order to reduce information asymmetry and prevent opportunistic behavior) and contract design (in order to create incentives for the agent to act in accordance with the principal's interests) (Eisenhardt 1989).

Agency theory has been widely applied to the analysis of corporate governance and motivation problems in organizations in general, but research on headquarters–subsidiary relationships using agency theory remains scarce (Tasoluk *et al.* 2006). After the pioneering work by Hennart (1991), who first systematically applied new institutional economics to the MNC, research is currently concentrated in three areas: selection, compensation and contract design for expatriates (Björkman and Furu 2000; Gong 2003; Roth and O'Donnell 1996; Sanders and Carpenter 1998), relationships between the MNC and external stakeholders (Chen 2004; Peng 2000), and headquarters–subsidiary coordination and conflict (Mudambi and Pedersen 2007; Nohria and Ghoshal 1994; Tasoluk *et al.* 2006). This broad spectrum of research applying agency theory is reflective of its applicability to micro, meso as well as macro phenomena (Jensen and Meckling 1976).

Prima facie headquarters–subsidiary relationships in an MNC are a particularly rich field for agency-theory-based conflict research: subsidiaries (as agents) might make use of their local market knowledge and resources to pursue idiosyncratic interests which are not necessarily in line with the headquarters' global strategy. Cultural and geographical distance increases information asymmetries so that in an MNC context it is even more difficult for the principal (headquarters) to observe and assess the agent's intentions and actual behavior, creating space for opportunistic maneuvers. Using this typical principal–agent situation as a starting point, Tasoluk, *et al.* (2006) investigate conflicts between an MNC headquarters and its Turkish subsidiary in product roll-out processes. According to Tasoluk *et al.* (2006) conflict arises because subsidiary and headquarters hold diverging information and perceptions about each other's level of competencies in managing the roll-out. For instance, when headquarters perceive the subsidiary's competences, e.g. regarding brand management, as being insufficient, they will actively interfere in the local product roll-out and re-centralize decisions. The subsidiary, perceiving itself as being up to the task, feels frustrated by this attempt to reduce its autonomy and reacts by resisting and subverting headquarters' initiatives (Tasoluk *et al.* 2006: 340). Similarly, when the subsidiary perceives headquarters' local market knowledge as inadequate, it may pursue roll-out strategies aligned to the local context irrespective of their compatibility with headquarters' marketing objectives. Still, Tasoluk *et al.* (2006: 335) assume that the overall goals of the MNC are shared by headquarters and subsidiary; conflict only arises regarding the means considered useful to achieve these goals. In so far, their paper offers an interesting variation of "classical" agency theory.

In order to counter conflict generation, the authors discuss the implementation of various context-enhancing mechanisms such as regular and frequent information meetings, two-way dialogue (e.g. using evidence-based information about local market knowledge), active signaling of competence levels by both headquarters and subsidiary to reduce information asymmetries and the establishment of a culture of trust (Tasoluk *et al.* 2006). They maintain that the increased provision of resources to the subsidiary by headquarters (in order to close a perceived competence gap) would be detrimental to the conflict situation because a competent subsidiary might consider this an affront. In addition, increased monitoring by headquarters would only prolong and escalate the conflict when the subsidiary considers itself to be sufficiently knowledgeable about local market conditions to act on its own (Tasoluk *et al.* 2006: 344).

The strength of the agency approach for understanding headquarters–subsidiary relationships lies in the clear conceptualization of causes of conflict (diverging interests of principals and agents, information asymmetry; cf. Mudambi and Pedersen 2007) and of potential remedies aimed at redesigning the conflict situation to prevent future conflicts; the conflict process itself – similar to game theory (see below) – is not the center of interest. Regarding conflict handling devices it is, however, interesting to note that the standard mechanisms advocated by agency theory – monitoring and incentives – are rejected by Tasoluk and his co-authors (2006) as well as other authors applying agency theory to the MNC context (Ghoshal and Moran 1996; O'Donnell 2000). Contrary to Chang and Taylor (1999), O'Donnell (2000: 531), for instance, maintains that excessive monitoring is counterproductive because enforceable bureaucratic norms restrict the flexibility, information and resource exchange required in MNCs. Ghoshal and Moran (1996) suggest that hierarchical control increases negative feelings, leading to opportunism and conflict escalation. Similarly, the use of incentives to realign headquarters and subsidiary goals is judged to be unsuitable to the MNC context. Whereas Tasoluk *et al.* (2006) argue that the additional provision of resources to the subsidiary could be interpreted as an indication of perceived need, O'Donnell (2000) points to the complexity of the MNC context and the correspondingly low measurability of outcome variables required for the allocation of rewards. Instead, authors working on the basis of agency theory frequently discuss conflict prevention mechanisms derived from socialization theory, such as increased communication and interaction, trust and clan building (Björkman *et al.* 2004; O'Donnell 2000; Roth and O'Donnell 1996; Tasoluk *et al.* 2006), thereby acknowledging, more or less explicitly, the limited contribution agency theory makes to the understanding of efficient conflict handling in MNC. In line with this observation, empirical research testing hypotheses derived from agency theory against alternative approaches (Björkman *et al.* 2004; O'Donnell 2000) indicates that its explanatory power is "not particularly strong" in MNC contexts (O'Donnell 2000: 541).

The inherently hierarchical concept of the principal–agent relationship is a second caveat against its more extensive application in headquarters–subsidiary conflict research. The concept of the conflict situation in agency theory is clearly dyadic and hierarchical, with the principal assigning (and revoking at will) tasks, resources and power to the agent. Both aspects, the uni-directional "power over" concept and the hierarchical structure of the firm in agency theory, have been put to critique. Mudambi and Pedersen (2007) argue based on resource dependence theory that subsidiaries are not only at the receiving end relying on power delegated by headquarters. They might just as well develop their own power bases locally or through their idiosyncratic business network and put them to use in bargaining conflicts with headquarters. Other authors emphasize that subsidiaries have been evolving out of their traditional role of being the subservient executors of headquarters' commands and research needs to pay closer attention to conflicts arising in multilateral interdependent networks of MNC subunits

(Birkinshaw and Hood 1998; Mudambi and Pedersen 2007; O'Donnell 2000; Shapiro 2005). Here, sociological approaches to agency theory (Kiser 1999; Shapiro 2005) go beyond simplifying assumptions about dyads and offer helpful insights into the wider embeddedness of the principal–agent relationship.

Game theory

Game theory has been characterized as a quintessential conflict theory (Axelrod 1970; Jost 1998; Murninghan 1994; Schelling 1958, 1960). According to Schelling (1960) game theory is, in fact, nothing but a theory of conflict. It has been used to model conflicts in all kinds of fields, ranging from political science and international relations (Scharf 2006; Schelling 1960) to economics and business (Brandenburger and Nalebuff 1996; Dixit and Skeath 1999). The primary advantages of game theory are its maturity, deriving from more than five decades of accumulated empirical and theoretical research, and its use of established standards for formal mathematical modeling. Game theory defines three archetypal types of conflict: (1) zero-sum games in which all interests and preferences of the players are incompatible (Jost 1998), associated with fierce, intractable conflict, (2) cooperative games where the players' shared interests preclude conflict, and (3) mixed motive games where both competing and cooperative interests exist (Schelling 1960). The third type of conflict corresponds most adequately to the situation of subsidiaries and headquarters in MNC where subunits are assumed to pursue idiosyncratic, e.g. local interests, while at the same time sharing an interest in overall MNC efficiency and survival, the protection and development of strong global brands, or the maintenance of a joint corporate identity. Contrary to the principal–agent approach, game theory, thus, does not assume that diverging interests automatically lead to conflict (cf. Dörrenbächer and Gammelgaard in this volume). Instead, the level of conflict depends on the players' expectations and weighting of pay-offs associated with alternative decisions (Jost 1998). Still, according to Rössing (2005: 20), "game theory has found little to no application in the context of International Management" and even less so in the analysis of headquarters–subsidiary relationships. Our critical review is thus limited to the work by Rössing (2005) and Kaufmann and Rössing (2005).

In their study (Kaufmann and Rössing 2005; Rössing 2005) conflict arises in a situation of technology transfer by headquarters to a Chinese subsidiary where headquarters is insecure about the trustworthiness of the subsidiary and the risk of expropriation of the technology. Here, conflict is defined by three conditions: (1) two or more parties interacting (2) in an interdependent relationships (3) where their goals are perceived as being incompatible (Rössing 2005: 29). The focus of the analysis is on the structure and characteristics of the conflict situation (e.g. regarding the vulnerability and competitive importance of the technology transferred) and on the development of design options aimed at conflict prevention. The deliberate concentration on the structure of the conflict and conflict design is reflective of game theory at large where the actual processes, behaviors, perceptions, identities of "real" actors are excluded from view in favor of abstract "players" characterized by their set of preferences and predefined decision alternatives (Binmore 1987). Dynamics are introduced through repeated games as a design option (see below) but the actual conflict process – What happens when the technology is transferred and then expropriated? How does the subsidiary react when important technology is withheld? – is not discussed.

The methodology employed by Rössing (2005) and Kaufmann and Rössing (2005) for conflict analysis is also characteristic of game theory and brings to light another key advantage of this approach, i.e. its well-developed, highly systematic way of increasing the analytical complexity in a stepwise manner. They start out by investigating the conflict situation in a highly reduced form (in order to keep it "manageable," Rössing 2005: 65) and then step-by-step relax the rather stringent assumptions common to traditional game theoretical modeling such as complete information and finiteness of the game (Rössing 2005: 63). At each step the authors assess the respective expected outcomes of the conflict situation, such as pay-offs for each player, level of conflict and organizational efficiency.

The results include a game theoretical framework for headquarters–subsidiary conflict on technology transfer (Kaufmann and Rössing 2005) and an empirical case-study-based test of the model's key hypotheses (Rössing 2005). The authors develop a typology of conflict situations along the two dimensions of vulnerability (ease of expropriation) and competitive advantage (importance of resource protection). They also present a number of design alternatives for conflict prevention, systematically derived from the game theoretic analysis of the conflict structure and established, often empirically sound results on standard games such as "tit-for-tat," the "shadow of the future" or "credible commitment" (Axelrod 1984; Mailath and Samuelson 2006; Parkhe 1993; Schelling 1960). "The information game" (Rössing 2005: 80) involving threats or screening mechanism to elicit information from the subsidiary regarding its trustworthiness is considered a suitable device to prevent conflict in one-round games (single incident of technology transfer). Much more realistic are repeated games where over time multiple incidents of technology transfer occur and thus the concern for the future development of the headquarters–subsidiary relationship gains in importance. In "cooperation games" (Rössing 2005: 84), headquarters can design the transfer situation over time in a way that the risk associated with each transfer is gradually increased when the subsidiary proves to be trustworthy. Alternatively, it may instill a sense of prolonged interaction among subsidiary managers (e.g. through detailing future career prospects or shared corporate values) to create a "shadow of the future" which then prevents players to focus on short-term interests.

This systematic development of conflict design options on the basis of the broad and empirically sound stock of knowledge accumulated in game theory is the core benefit of applying game theoretical thinking to conflict analysis. It comes at the costs of a high level of abstraction (even though Rössing and Kaufmann refrain from mathematical modeling), limiting actors' behavioral alternatives to either cooperation or non-cooperation and retaining the dyadic structure of the conflict already familiar from principal–agent theory. Also, contrary to institutionalism, game theory tends to isolate (dis-embed) the conflict from its wider social, institutional and historical environment. The potential influence of the socio-cultural and institutional context (e.g. the legal system, power relations) on the conflict process is deliberately severed to allow for a purely structural "solution" – at the risk of losing practical relevance for understanding and managing conflicts with "real" actors (Binmore 1987).

Still, game theory deserves further consideration as a theory of conflict beyond the current application in Kaufmann and Rössing's (2005) work. In fact, recent developments regarding multilateral, psychological and evolutionary game theory (Chatterjee 1996; Coleman 2003; Skyrms 2004) promise remedies for many weaknesses associated with traditional game theoretical modeling. Evolutionary game theory, for instance, allows the players' strategies to change over time, adopting their behavior to previous outcomes or a changing environment (e.g. institutional changes affecting the perceived expropriation risk in China), thus taking better account of the contextual embeddedness of conflict processes.

Institutionalism and micro-politics

Two other theoretical streams that have been concerned to varying degrees with conflicts as a result of or in headquarters–subsidiary relationships are institutionalist and micro-political perspectives. While some institutionalist and micro-political contributions provide distinct perspectives on the issue, many contributions combine institutionalist and micro-political perspectives emphasizing one or the other.

In regards to institutionalist perspectives on headquarters–subsidiary conflicts, it makes sense to follow the common distinction between new institutionalist (e.g. DiMaggio and Powell 1983; Scott 1995) and comparative or historical institutionalist approaches (e.g. Whitley 1999). Relevant research from a new institutionalist tradition touching upon headquarters–subsidiary conflicts in an MNC has mainly framed the issue as the occurrence of conflicting institutional pressures. Facing the institutional pressure of the MNC and, at the same time, the institutional pressure of the host environment, the subsidiary is at the epicenter of conflicting pressures and demands from the parent and the host context. In this respect, the perspective is similar to the contingency perspective on conflicts.

It is worth noting, however, that while new institutionalist perspectives do emphasize conflicting institutional pressures, there is with the exception of Oliver's (1991) work, which is not addressing MNCs, little interest in conflicts and conflict processes as such. Rather the conflicting institutional contexts and headquarters–subsidiary relationships set the scene to understand (more of an explanans) the emergence of innovation (Westney 1993) or success of knowledge transfer in MNCs (Kostova 1999; Kostova and Roth 2002). Kostova (1999) argues, for example, that if a practice is perceived by the employees at a recipient unit to be in conflict with the regulatory, cognitive and normative institutions of the host context, the implementation and internalization will be difficult. Hence, while institutional distance (Kostova 1999) or exposition to "institutional duality" (Kostova and Roth 2002) define crucial causes or antecedents of conflicting pressures in the subsidiary and different degrees of knowledge implementation and internalization of the outcomes, there is only limited concern for the process and actors on the ground that constitute the conflict and its development over time (for an exception see Blazejewski (2005) who extends Kostova's model to include a dynamic dimension). It is a neglect that is, on one the hand, related to the limited conceptualization of conflict in much of the institutionalists' work and, on the other hand, to the prevalence of cross-sectional survey studies that are not well suited to explore micro-level interaction over time.

This contrasts with comparative and historical institutionalist approaches on headquarters–subsidiary conflicts. Not only have these approaches focused more on understanding conflicts as such (as explanandum) but they have also paid close attention to the micro-politics and actors that are involved and constitute such conflicts. This makes it also difficult to draw a clear line between institutional and micro-political approaches on headquarters–subsidiary conflicts in this stream. There are, nevertheless, some fine differences in emphasis that can be identified. At the one end of the spectrum we find comparative and historical institutionalists who see the national institutional embeddedness of the actors involved as strongly structuring relations and conflicts among actors. A case in point is the work by Morgan (2003), Kristensen and Zeitlin (2001, 2005) and Morgan and Kristensen (2006) who view MNCs and headquarters–subsidiary relations alternatively as "sites of conflict and contradiction," "battlefields," "war-games" and "contested spaces." Similar to new institutionalists, Morgan and Kristensen (2006) hold that "institutional diversity" is the root cause for "conflicts and micro-political struggles over the nature of manage-ment and work in subsidiaries, divisions and headquarters" (2006: 1468). However, authors crucially differ in their adoption of a differentiated actor and politics perspective. For example, Morgan and Kristensen (2006: 1473) state "MNC as a totality may be seen as a highly complex configuration of ongoing micro-political power conflicts at different levels in which strategiz-ing social actors/groups inside and outside the firm interact with each other and create temporary balances of power that shape how formal organiza-tional relationships and processes actually work in practice." These micro-political power conflicts that revolve around transfer of processes, people and resources are seen as deeply embedded in institutional conditions. That is: "Institutions enter into these processes, firstly as co-constitutors of the set of actors/groupings and their mutual roles and identities, secondly as forms of restriction on the choices actors make, thirdly as resources that empower actors and finally as rule-givers for the games that emerge" (Morgan and Kristensen 2006: 1473). Although Morgan and Kristensen (2006) emphasize that actors are not determined by institutional requirements and have, par-ticularly under conditions of institutional duality, "a range of manoeuvre" given that they can mobilize a variety of institutional resources from the home and host context, the regional or national institutional embeddedness is generally seen as strongly structuring actor behavior. Clearly, to under-stand micro-politics and conflicts in the headquarters–subsidiary rela-tionship the focus remains here on the regional and national institutional embeddedness of actors, even if the institution–actors nexus implies that actors can actively select, mobilize and interpret institutional arrangements (cf. Kristensen and Zeitlin 2001, 2005).

At the other end, we find approaches which adopt strong actor and micro-politics perspectives, taking a more voluntaristic vantage point. These approaches also see conflicts and micro-politics between headquarters and subsidiary as influenced by institutional embeddedness in organizational and societal contexts; nevertheless, there is a stronger emphasis on the ability of actors to follow interests that are not simply reflective of macro-societal embeddedness. The work by Geppert, Dörrenbächer and colleagues is a case in point revolving empirically around issues of subsidiary role development (Dörrenbächer and Gammelgaard 2006), charter changes (Dörrenbächer and Geppert 2009) and best practices transfer (Geppert and Williams 2006), knowledge acquisition and learning (Clark and Geppert 2006; see chapter by Fenton O'Creevy *et al.* in this volume) and production relocation (Becker-Ritterspach and Dörrenbächer 2009; Blazejewski 2009). Dörrenbächer and Geppert (2006) see, for instance, micro-politics and conflicts as "everyday occurrences" in MNCs. Conflicts "emerge when powerful actors with different goals, interests and identities interact with each other locally and across national and functional borders" (2006: 255). In terms of outcomes, conflicts are not seen as useful or harmful per se; rather, they are seen as a "fundamental mechanism of social interactions" (2006: 256). The starting point of the analysis tends to be the identification of powerful or relevant actors and their differing interests, orientations, behavioral rationales or strategies in the conflict. While this stream also considers the structuring influence of national institutional contexts, it also includes the micro-institutional or situatedness of actors. Clark and Geppert (2006), for example, look at "historical and contemporaneous experience" of local managers, implying different biographical backgrounds of actors to understand headquarters–subsidiary conflicts over knowledge transfer. Fenton-O'Creevy *et al.* (this volume) contend that actors' idiosyncratic interests, life paths and personal career outlooks, as well as their ability to act as boundary spanners (i.e. translators of practices) rather than the institutional/cultural context as such determine the outcomes of conflictual practices transfer processes (transfer, translation, ceremonial adoption or corruption). Becker-Ritterspach (2006) looks at the actors' social-systemic positioning and their related affectedness, interests and resources to pursue their objectives in conflicts resulting from knowledge transfer processes. Similarly, Blazejewski (2009) shows that regional, local, organizational and even departmental situatedness plays an important role in understanding multiple lines of conflicts in MNC (see also chapter by Dörrenbächer and Gammelgaard in this volume). Hence, exploring conflicts in MNCs, this stream focuses on actors, their differing rationales, resources, orientations and strategies, and relates these not only to the macro-institutional embeddedness of actors but also to their micro-institutional and even personal biographical position and paths. This perspective essentially gives the actors more room to act in idiosyncratic voluntaristic ways that may be quite emancipated of broader macro-institutional pressures at national and regional levels.

The middle ground between these poles is probably taken by the work of Ferner, Edwards and colleagues (Edwards *et al.* 2006, 2007; Ferner 2000; Ferner and Edwards 1995). These contributions have treated political/power and institutional perspectives as equally important, complementary and even interdependent (e.g. Edwards *et al.* 2006, 2007; Edwards and Kuruvilla 2005; Ferner *et al.* 2005). While conflicts have, for the most part, not been the main focus of investigation, this work has very much touched upon conflicts that revolve around headquarters–subsidiary relations, be they "struggles for control and autonomy" between headquarters and subsidiaries or "resistance" in restructuring processes or transfer of employment policies, "revolts" and "rebellions" in corporate policy development and "micro-political struggles" in reverse transfer processes, or "disputes and battles" resulting global–local pressures or MNCs as a "contested terrain" (Edwards *et al.* 2006, 2007; Edwards and Bélanger 2009; Edwards and Kuruvilla 2005; Ferner 2000; Ferner *et al.* 2005).

For instance, within the context of cross-border restructurings and centralizing pressures in MNCs Edwards *et al.* (2006) touch upon resistance on the part of subsidiaries. "Active resistance" by subsidiaries is one source of variation to understand different restructuring outcomes. The resistance potential of subsidiary actors, in turn, is strongly informed by institutional conditions in the host context (including its distance to the home context). "Institutions set constraints within which political activity within firms can operate, shaping the preference of actors and the feasibility of certain courses of action, but they do not determine outcomes on their own" (Edwards *et al.* 2006: 72; see also Edwards *et al.* 2007; Edwards and Kuruvilla 2005). Headquarters actors, in turn, "often control sufficient resources to override host-country effects" (Edwards *et al.* 2006: 84). Hence, while much of the actors' strategic maneuvering is derived from institutional embeddedness and constraints, actors are not seen as being determined by their institutional context. Other aspects of contextual embeddedness come into play here, such as organizational embeddedness in the corporate division of labor (Edwards and Kuruvilla 2005), being at the headquarters with particular resource endowments or being a subsidiary (Edwards *et al.* 2006, 2007) and structurally sharing the interests with other subsidiaries to resist the headquarters' centralizing pressures (cf. Ferner 2000). Edwards *et al.* (2006: 84) argue that an institutional explanation needs to be complemented by a perspective that focuses on "the material interest of organizational actors and the resources available to advance their interests." Yet, similar to the work of Morgan and Kristensen (2006), the contextual emphasis in institutional terms tends to be more on national level institutions and less at the micro-institutional embeddedness of actors. At the same time, there is some consideration for the relevance of differing organizational situatedness of actors in micro-political struggles in MNCs (Edwards *et al.* 2007).

Despite all differences between new and comparative institutionalism, a common strength is that they both focus on the wider societal constitution of conflict. Apart from this common strength, however, it is the comparative institutionalism that has been much more intimately concerned with power, politics and conflicts in multinationals, including headquarters–subsidiary relations. Depending on approaches, some have been concerned with both conflict generation and conflict consequences. Importantly, these approaches have adopted differentiated micro-level actor perspectives and have related the behavioral orientation of actors in conflicts to complex institutional influences. This involves different levels of institutional embeddedness inside and outside the organization. Moreover, actors are seen to have diverging interests which often depart from the overall organizational goals or rationality. While these are structured by their organizational and environmental embeddedness, they are not uni-directionally determined by them. Specifically, some approaches see actors as proactive agents in conflict that are not merely determined by institutional conditions in their conflict behavior but can actively interpret, draw on or even shape institutional conditions in their interest. Also, contrasting with, for example, the contingency perspective, conflicts are not seen as functional or dysfunctional per se, but rather as a central and fundamental constant of organizational life. This stance may also explain why this literature is not much concerned with the manageability of conflict or (normative) conflict resolution mechanisms.

Although a range of comparative and historical institutionalist approaches are intimately concerned with micro-politics and conflicts in headquarters–subsidiary relationships, these approaches fail to adopt a clear conflict perspective. We rarely find explicit definitions of conflicts or explicit reference to extant conflict theory. By the same token, although politics, power and conflict are frequently mentioned terms, their conceptual relationship is hardly ever theorized. Even though the relationship of power and conflict is recognized, it is rarely critically and explicitly discussed. Similarly, the concepts of "power over" and "power to" remain for the most part implicit. Lastly, conflict processes as sequences of events, i.e. the temporal dimension of conflict, is so far not at the center of attention (see work by Blazejewski 2009 and chapter by Dörrenbächer and Gammelgaard in this volume as notable exceptions).

Postcolonialist perspective

Postcolonial perspectives in IB center on the question of how asymmetric power relations between the first- and the third-world countries shape management discourses and practices. Focusing on geopolitical power relations or power asymmetries between states – particularly between developed and developing countries – the approach also touches upon headquarters–subsidiary conflict in MNCs (Frenkel 2008; Mir and Mir 2009; Mir and Sharpe 2004, 2009). In this perspective, headquarters–subsidiary conflicts are mainly a result of the geopolitical dominance of the colonizers over the colonized. Frenkel (2008) serves as a nice example here. Focusing on processes of knowledge transfer in MNCs, Frenkel is interested in how first world–third world geopolitical power relations shape the process of knowledge transfer. Drawing on the postcolonialist Homi Bhabha, she starts with the assumption that power relations between colonizer and colonized cannot be simply captured by looking at the resources and structural conditions that force the behavior. Instead, she argues power has to be seen "as relational, emerging out of the mutual process of identity construction in both participants" (Frenkel 2008: 926). The focal points of conflicts are for Frenkel (2008: 928) colonial encounters that are seen "as a space of contradiction, repetition, ambiguity, and disavowal of colonial authority." They are encounters between the colonizers and the colonized that are "conflict-laden" and can involve the active resistance of the colonized. The outcomes of such struggles are hybrid cultures that emerge through processes of interpretation and reinterpretation (Frenkel 2008).

In the postcolonial perspective, MNCs, and particularly their subsidiaries, are contested and power-laden places in which colonizers and colonized encounter and struggle with each other. They involve, for example, encounters where subsidiary actors contest the headquarters' claimed superiority of the transferred knowledge (cf. Mir and Mir 2009). Frenkel (2008) provides the example of knowledge transfer within an Israeli MNC in Jordan, where knowledge was rejected because it was identified with the firm's Israeli background. At their very core, such conflicts are manifested in identity struggles, involving attributions of identities by colonizers through dominant discourses and local contestations of such attributions. They are struggles that are structured by the differing geopolitical embeddedness of actors and asymmetric power relations.

It is important to note that Frenkel (2008: 935) sees these colonial encounters as defined by "hierarchical power relations" in which "all actors in the MNC can strategically draw on different cultural repertoires available to them both inside and outside the firm." While the colonized are not powerless and may use active resistance as a deliberate strategy, the colonizers may have a potential advantage as they have wider cultural repertoires and symbolic systems at their disposal.

Postcolonial perspectives strongly focus on conflict generation and, to a weaker extent, on conflict outcome. Conflict generation is mainly rooted in power asymmetries between first and third world countries. Specifically, the postcolonial perspective discusses headquarters–subsidiary conflicts that result from the "hierarchical power relations" between organizational units and their actors that are related to their different geopolitical embeddedness. An interesting addition to the headquarters–subsidiary conflict perspective is that it does not primarily focus on interests and resources as causes, objects or means of conflict but on identities and hidden power structures that are embedded in discourses. Conflicts arise to protect or reconstitute identities that are threatened by the colonizers' dominant discourses. Hence, the postcolonial perspective clearly links power and conflict. The main focus is the concept of "power over" as the central cause of conflict. At the same time, the concept of "power to" is also implicitly adopted as colonizers and colonized can draw on different cultural repertoires to influence the colonial encounter in their interest. A clear strength of postcolonial perspectives is their micro-level and differentiated actor focus, considering their ability to act strategically. This entails that actors have degrees of freedom to use different repertoires of culture or signification, while being enabled and constrained in their use by geopolitical embeddedness.

Like in most work discussed, the postcolonial perspective offers no immediate concern with conflict processes and escalation. Furthermore, conflict generation in headquarters–subsidiary relations is mainly related to geopolitical asymmetries. Although Mir and Mir (2009) have recently pointed out that conflicts related to the dominance of the colonizer over the colonized need not be restricted to headquarters–subsidiary relation that are embedded in the developed–developing country difference (see Dörrenbächer 2007), the essence of the postcolonial perspective is seeing conflicts in MNCs as rooted in geopolitical power relations or power asymmetries between first and third world states. This, however, neglects a whole range of other causes of conflict in headquarters–subsidiary relations.

Social identity and role theory

A final perspective that we wish to discuss is a conflict perspective that derives from social identity and role theory (Ashforth and Mael 1989; Katz and Kahn 1978; Tajfel and Turner 1986). These theories have been applied in two different ways to headquarters–subsidiary conflicts. In particular, while a first stream looks at intra-personal role conflict related to the exposure of subsidiary managers to headquarters–subsidiary pressures, the second emergent stream focuses on intra-organizational conflict rooted in role perception gaps between headquarters and subsidiaries (see chapter by Schmid and Daniel in this volume).

The first stream centers on intra-personal conflict. It is related to the exposure of subsidiary managers to headquarters–subsidiary pressures and to more or less distant home and host contexts in the MNC (Dalton and Chrobot-Mason 2007; Earley and Laubach 2002; Vora *et al.* 2007). The conflicts that are examined are rooted in different degrees of competing or integrated organizational identifications. The work of Vora and Kostova (2007) and Vora *et al.* (2007) on the dual identification of subsidiary managers in an MNC supports this recent stream of research (see also Black and Gregersen's 1992 early contribution and Reade's (2001) work on dual organizational identification in MNCs). Drawing on social identity theory (e.g. Ashforth and Mael 1989; Dutton *et al.* 1994) and role theory (e.g. Katz and Kahn 1978), Vora and Kostova (2007: 328) explore how "dual organizational identification" (DOI) and role conflict of subsidiary managers occur. They ask "how managers can relate to both the MNE and subsidiary and be effective despite the potential conflicts." Vora and Kostova (2007) see subsidiary managers as exposed to complex role structures as they are facing multiple, and often conflicting, requirements and expectations from headquarters and the subsidiary context. Drawing on IB's contingency, culturalist as well as new institutionalist theory, they propose that different international strategies of MNCs and different cultural and institutional distances give rise to the emergence of different types of "dual organizational identification" among subsidiary managers. Vora and Kostova (2007), however, not only consider the antecedents, but also the consequences of "dual organizational identification."

Regarding consequences, they are interested in how the dual organizational identification of subsidiary managers impacts their role fulfillment, subsidiary–parent cooperation, knowledge transfer and role conflict (see also Mohr and Puck 2007). Vora and Kostova (2007) and Vora *et al.* (2007) specify, for instance, that the role conflict experienced by a subsidiary manager depends on the form and magnitude of "dual organizational identification." They define role conflict with Miles and Perrault (1976: 22) as "the degree of incongruity or incompatibility of expectations associated with a role" which is particularly prevalent among boundary spanners such as subsidiary managers. Additionally, they define dual organizational identity as the "individual's sense of identification with two organizational entities, which could be at various levels, such as department, division, subsidiary, or overall organization" (Vora and Kostova 2007: 331) and distinguish the distinct, compound and nested form of dual identification. Connecting the two constructs, they propose that subsidiary manager role conflict will be highest for the distinct form, moderate for the compound and lowest for the nested form. They base this on the following reasoning:

As discussed earlier, managers with distinct DOI sense a separation between their identifications with the subsidiary and MNE and may find it difficult or impossible to reconcile the two. They are thus likely to "switch" their attachments depending on the situation. However, because they have a sense of identification with both entities, they would like both to succeed. This becomes difficult because at times the goals and values of these entities may be so different that pursuing the objectives of one may hinder those of the other. Hence, the manager who has distinct identification is likely to experience role conflict. With compound or nested identification, such conflict is less likely, since there are more perceived similarities. Because of such a perceived alignment in values and goals, the advancement of one entity's objectives could be viewed as advancing the other entity's objectives as well, reducing the role conflict felt by the manager. This convergence will be highest in nested DOI. (Vora and Kostova 2007: 343)

In a similar paper, Vora *et al.* (2007) not only hypothesize but also test the effect of dual organizational identification on a subsidiary manager's roles and role conflict. Their findings show that a high identification with both subsidiary and parent is related to a high fulfillment of roles, and that similarity in organizational identity has a direct negative effect on role conflict. They find contrary to their expectation that "although dual identification was shown to be negatively related to role conflict, there were no significant differences between different levels of dual identification and role conflict" (Vora *et al.* 2007: 613).

The dual organizational identification approach looks at intra-personal role conflict. The strength of this stream is that it adds a whole new theory perspective and analytical level to the context of headquarters–subsidiary conflicts. The approach focuses on both conflict generation and outcome. However, while there is some discussion about the personal and organizational outcomes of role conflict, the approach mainly looks at conflict generation related to the degree and kind of subsidiary manager's organizational identification with both the subsidiary and the parent organization. The actors considered are subsidiary managers in MNCs. The kind and degree of their dual identification is, in turn, related to their organizational-strategic (MNC strategy) and cultural–institutional (home–host distance) embeddedness (see also chapter by Williams in this volume regarding culture as a source of managerial identity and cultural distance as a predictor for headquarters–subsidiary socio-political interaction). The role conflict experience of subsidiary managers is, therefore, indirectly structured by their embeddedness in the MNC type and the national contextual difference that it is exposed to. Although the approach offers a differentiated view of contextual embeddedness of actors by looking at both organizational and environmental embeddedness, it implies a rather deterministic view on how such conditions structure actor rationales and conflict perceptions. Similar to most approaches, we again find no process perspective on conflict in this stream. This may not be surprising, however, as the conflict focused on here is at the intra-personal level. Lastly, whereas role conflict is a central variable, neither conflict, power nor their relationship are strongly theorized in this stream.

The second emerging stream we wish to discuss has been introduced by Schmid and Daniel in their chapter in this volume (see also Schmid and Daniel 2007) who transfer the role concept to an inter-unit level. Drawing on Katz and Kahn's (1978) role theory, Schmid and Daniel (this volume) see headquarters–subsidiary conflict as rooted in perception gaps, where its role as perceived by the subsidiary differs from the role as expected/assigned by headquarters. Schmid and Daniel argue that such perception gaps cause conflict. They define conflict with Katz and Kahn (1978) "as behavior of one party that tends to prevent or compel some outcome against the resistance of the other party." Connecting inconsistent role expectations to the emergence of conflict they reason:

Behavior that is inconsistent with the other side's expectations may be interpreted as interference or blocking by the other party. Empirical research confirms that behavior that is considered as interference, blocking or otherwise conflictful will evoke conflictual behavior in response. (Katz/Kahn 1978: 635; see also Schmid and Daniel in this volume)

With regard to the contextual conditions that influence the emergence of perception gaps, the authors put forward that potentially contradicting sets of expectations are rooted in the subsidiary managers' embeddedness in three different contexts. The first is the internal MNC network, understood as the "internal role set." The second is the external network of the subsidiary, understood as the "external role set," and the third is the individual actor's own understanding of the subsidiary role. The latter may differ substantially based on individual interests, motives and experience. In a further step, Schmid and Daniel illustrate how perception gaps between the subsidiary and the headquarters regarding subsidiary capabilities can lead to three types of conflict, namely input conflict (resource distribution), throughput conflict (conflict about practices and processes) and output conflict (objectives pursued). For instance, output conflict arises when subsidiary managers who perceive their unit as highly capable try to pursue their own goals beyond the role assigned by headquarters.

In summary, Schmid and Daniel focus on conflict generation. In addition they discuss options for conflict prevention, in particular through negotiation processes that lead to an unambiguous and consensual definition of subsidiary roles. Although their conceptualization of role conflict in headquarters–subsidiary relationships is, similar to Vora *et al.* (2007), limited to a static, single-phase model, it contains some interesting starting-points for further research. More specifically, it offers the opportunity to integrate the established IB research on subsidiary roles, role evolution and multiple roles into MNC conflict research (e.g. Birkinshaw and Hood 1998). While Schmid and Daniel's approach includes theory-derived definition of conflict, the approach only weakly explores the link to power. The authors mention, for example, that MNCs have the "power to" unilaterally impose certain roles onto a subsidiary. The discussion of the power–conflict link ends at this point, however. This limited exploration of the role of power is a lost opportunity, because the empirical case study presented by Schmid and Daniel seems to suggest that power and politics are the crucial link to explain how and why subsidiaries can resist role expectations and even successfully change headquarters' role expectations. Regarding their take on actors, Schmid and Daniels focus on the individual actor such as subsidiary managers. They suggest that the actor's individual ideas also play an important role in understanding conflict, but don't explore in much detail how these ideas are contextually constituted. A shortcoming that their approach shares with all other perspectives discussed so far is the absence of a process lens on conflict. It should be noted, finally, that the work of Vora *et al.* (2007) and Schmid and Daniel complement each other. While actors in the former stream internalize the conflicting expectations, potentially leading to intra-personal conflict, they remain external in the latter stream, leading to the rejection, disappointment, or change of certain external expectations.

Conclusion and new directions

Discussion

In this chapter we identified major contributions that apply a conflict perspective to the headquarters–subsidiary relationship. These approaches differed substantially with regard to how central conflict is, whether conflict is seen as a dependent or independent variable and what kind of contextual factors are seen to influence or structure conflicts. We saw that this can range from organizational strategic and structural embeddedness to cultural, institutional and even geopolitical embeddedness. The approaches presented also differed markedly in whether they interpret conflict more as an aberration to the normalcy of cooperative relations or a common *sine qua non* of organizational life and whether they considered the need for conflict resolution mechanisms, their application and their effectiveness. The review also showed that there is a major difference in the level of analysis of conflict and the type of actors looked at. While some approaches focus on headquarters and subsidiaries as conflicting units, others looked at conflicts between individual actors or the intra-personal level of conflict (see Table 5.3).

Despite the variety presented, there are also some common traits that are worth discussing and which may point to limitations in the current contributions. Overall, we suggest that theory-bound conflict research in the IB field needs to pay more attention to (1) the conflict construct itself, (2) the complex interaction between actors in conflict and conflict embedding contexts, (3) the dynamics of conflict processes, (4) the relationship between power and conflict, (5) the integration of literature from related fields such as organizational/socio-psychological conflict research, and (6) a more thorough putting-to-use of theories and models selected for conflict analysis.

In fact, with only some exceptions, most contributions do not even define conflict. As suggested above, a clearly defined construct, however, serves

Table 5.3 Summary of strengths and weaknesses

	Strengths	Weakness
Contingency theory	Concern with strategic and structural antecedents, consequences and resolution of conflict in MNCs Explicit reference to organizational conflict theory	Conflicting environmental forces implicitly equated with emergence of material conflict Reductionist view of actors as organizationally determined No sense of conflict process and weak theorization of power–conflict link
Agency theory	Information asymmetry as cause of conflict in MNC (increased by cultural and geographical distance) Established theoretical foundation providing empirically sound concepts for conflict generation and conflict design (monitoring, incentives)	Lack of empirical evidence for agency approach in MNCs Negative concept of conflict Limited to dyadic, hierarchical conflict No sense of conflict process (focus on conflict generation through information asymmetry)
Game theory	Maturity, empirical evidence and methodology (formalization) of game theory in general; allows for development of conflict design alternatives on the basis of established concepts such as tit-for-tat, shadow of the future, credible commitment	High level of abstraction (dyadic conflict, behavioral options, a-historicity) No sense of conflict process (focus on characteristics of the conflict situation)
Institutional (new institutionalism)	Institutional duality as cause of conflict in MNCs	Overall weak concern with power, politics and conflict Reductionist actor and agency perspectives No sense of conflict process and weak theorization of power–conflict link No focus on conflict resolution

Approach	Strengths	Limitations
Institutional (comparative historical and micro-political)	Interplay of different analytical levels (variety of institutional levels, organization and individual interests) to understand causes and consequences of conflict Clear focus on power, (micro-)politics and conflict Differentiated and complex actor and agency perspectives	Weak reference to organizational conflict theory Weak theorization of power–conflict link No sense of conflict process and no focus on conflict prevention and management
Postcolonial perspective	Geopolitical power asymmetries as cause of conflict in MNCs Considers the relations between discourse and identity in the constitution of conflict Establishes power and conflict link Differentiated and complex actor and agency perspectives	Restriction to first-world/third-world power relations Weak reference to organizational conflict theory No sense of conflict process and no focus on conflict management
Social identity and role theory	Conflicting role expectations as cause of conflict situations: perceptions, expectations, identity Focus on cognitive processes in conflict Theory-derived definition of conflict Established research on subsidiary roles and role development in IB field Focus on conflict prevention and management	Limited conceptualization of role construct Reductionist actor and agency perspectives No sense of conflict process and weak theorization of power–conflict link

to focus and steer the analysis of conflict and prepares the ground for the development of suitable alternatives for conflict prevention and management. This lack of conceptual clarity is, on the one hand, related to the missing integration of literature from the wider field of conflict research, in particular organizational conflict research, where the debate around "conflict" as term and construct is much more advanced and fine-grained than what it seems from the contributions discussed in this chapter alone. With the exception of Pahl and Roth (1993; using Rahim's organizational conflict inventory), Gupta and Cao (2005; based on Jehn's 1997 work on group conflict) and Schotter and Beamish (this volume, using the task, process and relationship conflict categorization well established in group-psychology research), barely any of the authors introduced above refers to models, journals, studies or researchers from the field of organizational conflict research. Instead, it seems as if by basing their research in a well-established theoretical tradition such as the game, agency, role or institutional perspective, authors feel confident in largely ignoring other approaches relevant to their area of study. As a result, conflict research in the IB field currently develops largely independent of the advancement of other, often more mature fields of conflict research such as political, organizational or group conflict. This criticism also holds true the other way around, with other fields or disciplines of conflict research essentially ignoring developments in IB research and, in particular, the peculiar phenomenon of conflict in an MNC.

The concentration on an established theory of choice in IB conflict research has a number of advantages: it provides a clear direction for (empirical) research, possibly including established measures, frameworks and empirical results which can then be adapted to and tested on conflicts in an MNC. According to Kostova and colleagues (2008), the application of established theories from other disciplines and fields to the MNC context offers an ideal opportunity to test their potential and advance theory development at large. In their view, IB research should concentrate more on theory development in this sense than on mere application (Kostova *et al.* 2008). As a necessary requirement, however, authors would need to actually apply their theories of choice more thoroughly and fully to the study of MNC conflict. Currently, some authors contend with a limited, selective and sometimes simplifying usage of the focused theory ("cherry picking"), for instance by introducing some key terms ("game," "role," "identity") and hypotheses but without providing a fully fledged explanation, integration and/or transposition of the concepts to the MNC context.

Regarding the important link between conflict and power, none of the contributions reviewed above makes and explicitly conceptualizes the arguably intimate connection. Furthermore, while a wide range of contextual conditions impacting conflict are considered, few approaches combine or integrate these contextual factors into a coherent framework. Instead, a rather static perspective is adopted that sees actors' conflict-related perception and behavior as more or less determined by specific contextual circumstances. How conflict leads to a change of circumstances or how actors can make differentiated use of their circumstances to further their own objectives still remains a black box. In our view, this is largely due to the fact that very few approaches take a concrete conflict situation or a definite case of conflicting actors as a starting point and try to understand from the bottom up which kind of context actually matters in understanding the antecedents, manifestations and consequences of conflict, and if and how the relevance of this context may change dynamically over the course of a conflict. This brings us to our final point that very few approaches look at the processual dimension of conflict, which would not only help to understand subsequent conflicts but also potential intervention points for conflict management and prevention. We examine these points more closely in the following paragraphs.

Linking power and conflict

Power and conflict have been viewed as intimately related in conflict theory (Clegg *et al.* 2007). Power and its asymmetrical distribution (including its maintenance or change) in social systems is often seen as an antecedent, cause or object of conflict (e.g. Coleman 2006; Collins 1975, 1993; Dahrendorf 1959, 1968; Pondy 1967). In this view, power and its unequal distribution structure different interests that potentially conflict with each other. While this power–conflict nexus basically springs from "power over" conceptualization of power, we also find in the literature the link that is more in line with the "power to" conceptualization (e.g. Clegg *et al.* 2007; Hardy 1996). In this latter view, power is a means, medium, or instrument that actors can or need to employ to wage a conflict (Hardy 1996; Hayward and Boeker 1998; Collins 1975 and 1993). Coleman (2006: 120) states, for example, that "[c]onflict is often a means of seeking or maintaining the balance or imbalance of power in relationships." Hence, the unequal distribution of power in social systems, not only causes and structures issues and lines of conflict, but it simultaneously structures the means or strategies that parties can employ in the conflict (Coleman 2006).

By the same token, the unequal distribution of power is seen to impact the outcome of conflict (e.g. Hayward and Boeker 1998). Coleman (2006: 121) argues that "the powerful also largely determine what is considered to be important, fair and just in most settings and thus shape and control many methods of resolution." In fact, power may function to prevent conflict from surfacing in the first place (Hayward and Boeker 1998). Drawing on Bachrach and Baratz (1962), Lukes (1974) and Foucault (1979; 1980; 1982), Hardy (1996) argues that power, be it deliberately employed by actors or systemically constituted and taken for granted, can function to control decision-making processes (agenda setting), perceptions, cognitions and preferences that prevent conflict issues from becoming manifest or even perceived (see also Thomas 1992). It is important to note, however, that the conceptual hierarchy of power vis-à-vis conflict implied so far can easily be reversed. Drawing on Stern and Gorman (1969), Gaski (1984: 12; see also Coleman 2006) argues that "the causal sequence between power and conflict can, and does, proceed in either direction." Clearly, conflict can change the balance of power and can redistribute power (within and between the conflicting parties) which is, after all, often viewed as a prime goal of conflict (Blalock 1989). This, in turn, feeds into ever new causes of conflict (cf. Coser 1956; Dahrendorf 1959, 1968). Indeed, conflict has the potential to change the distribution of power, leaving some actors with more and others with less power in the aftermath of the conflict. Turning the conceptual hierarchy of power vis-à-vis conflict on its head, some even suggest that power relations result or only come into existence through conflict (Bachrach and Baratz 1969; Dahl 1963; cf. Gaski 1984). In this view, the use of power becomes a "conflict response" (Stern and Gorman 1969).

To introduce the nexus between power and conflict to IB research in general, and headquarters–subsidiary relations in particular, we advocate, as a starting point, an analysis of the (unequal) distribution of power among different organizational actors located in different kinds of MNCs, as well as different organizational and geographical positions within MNCs. Such an analysis can provide us with crucial leads where, why, between whom and on what issues conflict lines potentially emerge. It simultaneously gives us hints about what kind of power is mobilized or available and what power or resource mobilization strategies actors can and will employ to wage the conflict in their interest (Becker-Ritterspach and Dörrenbächer 2011; Dörrenbächer and Geppert 2009; see also chapter by Geppert and Dörrenbächer in this volume). Particularly in the context of the MNC, the analysis of the power distribution, i.e. not only of an organizational system (say between headquarters and subsidiaries) but also between and within the different institutional or geo-political settings in which the MNC operates (see also Hardy 1996), can further our understanding of conflict sources and strategies of different actors (Blazejewski 2009). Finally, to understand the outcomes of conflict, we may want to explore if and in what way conflict has changed the MNC's distribution of power. Specifically, which actors have gained, maintained or lost which kind of power as a result of the conflict. This also raises the question of how past conflicts and their effect on the power distribution condition influence new and ongoing conflict processes in MNCs. Such a power outcome focused conflict analysis could provide us with new insights with regard to organizational change and power in MNCs (see Buchanan and Badham 1999). The chapter presented by Williams in this volume also gives us some leads in this direction. Williams shows, for example, how power shifts between headquarters and subsidiaries are linked to subsidiary manager change initiatives. As the review of the literature above has demonstrated, however, sophisticated discussions of power, taking into account the recent development of the power concept (e.g. by Clegg *et al.* 2007), are largely missing from the IB literature on headquarters–subsidiary conflicts.

Taking actors seriously in the structural perspective: a bottom-up situation-positioning approach

In organization conflict theory, the context conditions play a crucial role in understanding causes and outcomes of conflict. This perspective is exemplified by the structural model of Thomas (1992) who discusses context variables such as behavioral predisposition of conflict parties, social pressure or normative forces, incentive structures and rules and procedures. Reflective of an organizational physiological perspective, however, there is little consideration how this micro-organizational context and behavioral predispositions are influenced or related to the wider societal context. Organization sociologists, in turn, have often tended to focus on wider societal influences without adopting a fine-grained perspective on how these macro-contexts interact with micro-level organizational conditions, let alone with the psychological predispositions of individuals. This is also reflected in some of the institutionalist conflict literature on headquarters–subsidiary relations, which has seen actors as being strongly structured, if not determined by their societal embeddedness.

Addressing these shortcomings, we opt for a conflict approach that starts from the bottom up by identifying actors in situations of conflict. This involves, first, understanding the stage of the conflict situation that the actor is in. Second, reconstructing the organizational and wider societal structural conditions, which influence both the actors' interests and his or her cognitive and behavioral repertoire referred to in the conflict situation. This implies that all of the structural contexts discussed – organizational, cultural, and national or regional institutional, geopolitical, etc. – may affect the occurrence of conflict and may be relevant and referred to by actors in different situations over time. Yet, it is above all an empirical question which context is relevant and how it is interpreted in a given situation. Here, we very much agree with approaches that adopt a strong micro-political perspective or with the postcolonialists who see actors as able to strategically draw on different repertoires inside and outside the firm (Blazejewski 2009; Frenkel 2008; see also chapter by Dörrenbächer and Gammelgaard in this volume).

What is crucial for such a conflict approach is to understand the actors' situation and position in context. Blazejewski (2009: 234) argues, for example, with Schütz (1972) that a situation "defines an actor's position with respect to their contextual conditions." More specifically:

The situational constitution opens up (and simultaneously delimits) the actor's access to resources and determines their positions in networks and coalitions by literally "situating" them inside their perceived environment. Depending on the actor's situational positioning, institutions enable or constrain individual action (Giddens 1984) by either providing or denying access to the required power bases. (Blazejewski 2009: 234)

We advocate a situational conflict approach that takes as a vantage point actors and their interest in conflict analysis. In line with Blazejewski (2009: 232), this involves an exploration into a second step, how "institutions function as repertoires (Clemens and Cook 1999; Whittington 1992) from which actors select meanings and behavioral patterns, which, based on their interest, they perceive as relevant, legitimate and possible in a specific situation (Child 1997; Karnoe and Nygaard 1999)." While in this view, structural conditions inform situational interests that may give rise to conflict and the cognitive and behavioral options that may be referred to in the conflict, they do not "supersede the actors' 'reflexive capacity' in interpreting and applying them, consistent with their personal experiences, positions and concerns" (Karnoe and Nygaard 1999: 232).

A similar approach is suggested by Becker-Ritterspach (2006), who draws on Giddens' (1984) structuration theory. The approach suggests that the positioning of actors in the organization and society at large may indicate: how actors differ in their interest in the first place, explaining causes of conflict; what kind of rules (normative and cognitive, we could also say identities) and resources (allocative and authoritative) are at stake for the differently positioned actors involved in the conflict; and, in turn, how such a positioning structures the rules and resources referred to by differently positioned conflicting actors. Within the context of conflicts related to knowledge transfer he explicates his perspective as follows:

When knowledge enters a new social arena of an MNE's subsystem its translation will be more or less contested depending on the different affectedness and the corresponding conflicting interests between actors that are differently positioned. Under such conditions translations will therefore be the result of more or less conflictual negotiations in which differently positioned actors have different rules as cognitive means for translation and different resources (cf. Crozier and Friedberg 1981) as means of power available to render their translations valid. These different position-related referabilities constitute the unequal opportunities of actors to see their preferred translation gain systemic meaningfulness, legitimacy and enactment. Finally, to understand the outcome of translations as a collective process, it is important to inquire which actors are similarly affected by the knowledge transfer, come to shared translations and are likely to form coalitions to pool their resources to render their preferred translations socially meaningful, legitimate and put into practice. (Becker-Ritterspach 2006: 372)

Hence, a position perspective also helps to understand why individual actors come to share interests in conflicts and form coalitions. This last point also suggests that an actor-centered situation or positioning conflict approach needs to look at sets of actors in relationships, be they the relationships of opponents or partners in conflict, rather than looking at atomistic actors. It signals the need to consider the level of relationships between actors, the nature of their interdependence (Sheppard 1992) and how these relationships are structurally informed by the actor's situation and position in context. We, therefore, share with Sheppard (1992) the contention that individual, relational and institutional levels of analysis are required to obtain a complete picture in organizational conflict analysis.

Taking a processes perspective seriously

Research on headquarters–subsidiary conflict is currently dominated by the structural approach (Thomas 1992) to the detriment of processual, dynamic conflict aspects. On the one hand, this one-sidedness might be related to methodological constraints – it is often much easier to gather and handle data on single conflicts or crises than on several, perhaps drawn out conflictual processes over time (Blazejewski 2010; Diehl 2006). On the other hand, it is connected to the theoretical perspectives selected for conflict analysis. Theories such as game theory, agency theory, institutionalism, and contingency theory per se are more concerned with contextual influences and the design of conflict situations than with processes and conflict action. Where elements of the processual model (Thomas 1992) are investigated, they are limited to single phases, for instance conflict generation (Kaufmann and Rössing 2005; Tasoluk *et al.* 2006) or conflict behavior (Pahl and Roth 1993). In none of the contributions reviewed do authors pay attention to all of the conflict phases of the Thomas-model (Thomas 1992). Where two phases are (often implicitly) included, they remain unconnected. According to Diehl (2006: 199), this kind of "single phase analysis" disregards the fact that "what happens in one stage of conflict has downstream consequences in a later stage." The perceived reasons for conflict generation, for instance, influence actors' choices of conflict handling devices which, in turn, affect conflict outcomes. How a headquarters–subsidiary conflict about resource allocation or knowledge transfer is framed (conflict conceptualization) and handled by each party (conflict behavior: open dialogue or suppression or threat) largely determines the outcomes (functional or dysfunctional) of this conflict process. The interdependence between the different phases in each conflict episode so far is missing from MNC conflict research. The contribution by Schotter and Beamish (this volume) is a first laudable attempt at tackling this task. While they do include several elements of the conflict process, including conflict generation/sources of conflict, conflict tactics and conflict outcomes, the relationship between the different process elements as well as the connection between the different concepts employed towards its analysis (type of conflict, conflict tactics, conflict outcomes) still remains in part hazy. As Pearson d'Estrée (2003: 80) emphasizes, however, "only by understanding the dynamics and processes of conflict can we hope to understand the processes of reversing and reorienting such momentum for constructive results." In addition, Diehl (2006) stresses that understanding the interconnectedness of conflict phases is crucial for effective conflict management as well as theoretical integration and advancement.

Taking process in conflict research seriously requires a workable conceptualization of the term itself. Process is generally defined as a sequence of events unfolding over time (Huber and Van de Ven 1995; Pettigrew *et al.* 2001). According to Scheffer (2007), the two core elements of the definition are "events" and "time," the "fourth dimension" of conflict research (Pearson d'Estrée 2003). In his view, a process perspective necessarily needs to emphasize "the temporal stretch" (Scheffer 2007: 173) of conflict. It also needs to recognize that events do matter, that is what actually happens over the course of a conflictual process is important in itself (Scheffer 2007) and cannot be collapsed (and thereby eradicated) into the final stage of conflict outcome.

A process perspective on conflict can account for two temporal dimensions: Thomas (1992) provides a concept to understand the multiple, interconnected stages inside each conflict episode, i.e. frustration, conceptualization, behavior and outcomes. In addition, it takes into view the conflict dynamics beyond the single episode, in particular the escalation of conflict into multiple rounds (Deutsch 1973, 1980, 1982; Glasl 2010; Rubin *et al.* 1994) as well as the history of conflict and identity formation leading up to and impacting the current conflict episodes (Diehl 2006; Jones and Khanna 2006; Mahoney 2000). Both aspects require longitudinal research approaches – as opposed to the cross-sectional designs dominating the international business field (Blazejewski 2010) – which explicitly account for the temporal dimension of conflict.

Escalation is elaborately discussed in conflict research outside of the IB field. The "conflict spiral" developed by Rubin *et al.* (1994) maintains that in escalation processes conflict tactics transform from light to heavy, from persuasion to violence; the number of conflict issues increases; the number of participants grows; goals switch from achieving specific objectives and change to winning and outdoing the other party. Escalation processes not only trigger retaliating activities by conflict parties and provoke yet another round of conflict, they also may eventually produce structural changes, including negative stereotypes and interpretative schemas which then make resistance, retribution and reduced empathy more and more acceptable (Pearson d'Estrée 2003). In his seminal work, Deutsch (1973, 1980, 1982) also draws attention to this self-enforcing nature of conflict interaction. The processes and effects of a competitive stance in conflict processes induces further competition. In turn, cooperative conflict behavior in one round encourages cooperative behavior in ensuing rounds. The cooperative strategy recommended by Rössing and Kaufman (Kaufmann and Rössing 2005; Rössing 2005) for conflict prevention in repeated headquarters–subsidiary games on technology processes follows a similar logic. Still, in restricting their perspective on structural design options, they refrain from investigating potential escalation dynamics over time.

The historical perspective on conflict has received much less attention, although past conflicts can safely be assumed to impact future conflicts

through learning effects, processes of identity formation and coalition building as well as patterns of conflict perception, conceptualization and behavior
evolving over time. A recent paper on conflict processes at Opel (Blazejewski
2009), in fact, demonstrates that past conflict episodes strongly affect the perception, interpretation and preferred handling strategies in ongoing conflictual processes. Diehl (2006) and Mahoney (2000) suggest that past conflicts
can even lead to path-dependencies where the choice about adequate conflict
handling strategies to be employed in a current conflict situation is severely
constrained through lock-in effects, self-reinforcing processes and routines.

In any case, a process perspective on conflict in headquarters–subsidiary
relationships has implications regarding the adequate selection of underlying
theoretical perspectives as well as research methodology. Regarding theoretical approaches, a process view requires a shift of focus towards or integration
of more dynamic theories such as systems or complexity theory or evolutionary game theory as yet underemployed in conflict research. Regarding
methodology, conflict processes research needs to acknowledge time itself
as a crucial dimension: "time must be an essential part of investigation [...]
if processes are to be uncovered" (Pettigrew *et al.* 2001: 697). Here, longitudinal research designs are suitable to identify the temporal interrelatedness
of different conflict episodes and the temporal, not just the structural embeddedness of current conflict situations. So far, they are not only missing from
MNC conflict research but from international business research in general
(see also Blazejewski 2010; Jones and Khanna 2006). A first effort to address
this gap is provided by the chapter of Dörrenbächer and Gammelgaard in this
volume who observe the development of conflict at a German–Hungarian
company over a period of fifteen years. They show how different levels of
conflict found in three episodes of charter loss are interrelated with changing
situational contexts and their interpretation by headquarters and subsidiary
actors over time.

REFERENCES

Alper, S., D. Tjosvold and K. S. Law 2000. "Conflict management, efficacy, and performance
in organizational teams," *Personnel Psychology* 53: 625–42
Anderson, M. and J. A. Narus 1990. "A model of distribution firm and manufacturing firm
working partnership," *Journal of Marketing* 54: 42–58
Armstrong, D. and P. Cole 1996. "Managing distances and differences in geographically
distributed work groups" in Jackson and Ruderman (eds.) *Diversity in Work Teams.*
Washington DC: American Psychological Association, pp. 185–215

Ashforth, B. E. and F. Mael 1989. "Social identity theory and the organization," *Academy of Management Review* 14: 20–39

Axelrod, R. M. 1970. *Conflict of Interest. A Theory of Divergent Goals with Application to Politics*. Chicago, IL: Markham

1984. *The Evolution of Cooperation*. New York: Basic Books

Ayoko, O. B., C. E. J. Härtel and V. J. Callan 2002. "Resolving the puzzle of productive and destructive conflict in culturally heterogenous workgroups: a communication accommodation theory approach," *International Journal of Conflict Management* 13: 165–95

Bachrach, P. and M. S. Baratz 1962. "Two faces of power," *The American Political Science Review*, 56(4): 947–52

1969. "Decisions and non-decisions: an analytical framework" in Bell, Edwards and Wagner (eds.) *Political Power: A Reader in Theory and Research*. New York: Free Press, pp. 100–9

Barki, H. and J. Hartwick 2001. "Conceptualizing the construct of interpersonal conflict," *The International Journal of Conflict Management* 15: 216–44

Bartlett, C.A. and S. Ghoshal 1986. "Tap your subsidiaries for global reach," *Harvard Business Review* 64: 87–94

1989. *Managing Across Borders: The Transnational Solution*. Cambridge, MA: Harvard Business School Press

Becker-Ritterspach, F. 2006. "The social constitution of knowledge integration in MNEs: a theoretical framework," *Journal of International Management* 12: 358–77

Becker-Ritterspach, F. and C. Dörrenbächer 2009. "Intra-firm competition in multinational corporations: towards a political framework," *Competition and Change* 13: 199–213

2011. "An organizational politics perspective on intra-firm competition in multinational corporations," *Management International Review* (in print)

Bennett, J. 2002. "Multinational corporations, social responsibility and conflict," *Journal of International Affairs* 55: 393–410

Binmore, K. G. 1987. "Why game theory 'doesn't work'" in Bennett (ed.) *Analysing Conflict and its Resolution*. Oxford: Clarendon Press, pp. 23–42

Birkinshaw, J. M. and N. Hood 1998. "Multinational subsidiary evolution: capability and charter change in foreign-owned subsidiary companies," *Academy of Management Review* 23: 773–95

Birkinshaw, J. and M. Lingblad 2005. "Intrafirm competition and charter evolution in the multibusiness firm," *Organization Science* 16: 674–86

Björkman, I. and P. Furu 2000. "Determinants of variable pay for top managers of foreign subsidiaries in Finland," *International Journal of Human Resource Management* 11: 698–713

Björkman, I., W. Barner-Rasmussen and L. Li 2004. "Managing knowledge transfer in MNCs: the impact of headquarters control mechanisms," *Journal of International Business Studies* 35: 443–54

Black, J. S. and H. B. Gregersen 1992. "Serving two masters: managing the dual allegiance of expatriate employees," *Sloan Management Review* 33: 61–71

Blalock, H. M. 1989. *Power and Conflict: Towards a General Theory*. Newbury Park: Sage

Blazejewski, S. 2005. "Transferring value-infused organizational practices in MNCs: a conflict perspective" in Geppert and Mayer (eds.) *Global, Local and National Practices in Multinational Companies.*, Basingstoke: Palgrave, pp. 63–104

2009. "Actors' interests and local contexts in intrafirm conflict: the 2004 GM and Opel crisis," *Competition & Change* 13: 229–50

2010. "When truth is the daughter of time: longitudinal case studies in international business research" in Piekkari and Welch (eds.) *Rethinking the Case Study in International Business and Management Research: Towards Greater Pluralism*. Cheltenham: Edward Elgar (in print)

Brandenburger, A. and B. Nalebuff 1996. *Co-opetition*. New York: Doubleday

Buchanan, D. and R. Badham 1999. "Politics and organizational change: the lived experience," *Human Relations* 52: 609–29

Chang, E. and M. S. Taylor 1999. "Control in multinational corporations (MNCs): the case of Korean manufacturing subsidiaries," *Journal of Management* 25: 541–65

Chatterjee, K. 1996. "Game theory and the practice of bargaining," *Group Decision and Negotiation* 5: 355–69.

Cheldelin, S., D. Druckman and L. Fast (eds.) 2003. *Conflict*. 1st ed. London: Continuum

Chen, Y.-R. R. 2004. "Effective public affairs in China: MNC – government bargaining power and corporate strategies for influencing foreign business policy formulation," *Journal of Communication Management* 8: 395–413

Child, J. 1997. "Strategic choice in the analysis of action, structure, organizations, and environment: retrospect and prospect," *Organization Studies* 18: 43–76

Clark, E and M. Geppert 2006. "Socio-political processes in international management in post-socialist contexts: knowledge, learning and transnational institution building," *Journal of International Management* 12: 340–57

Clegg, S. R., D. Courpasson and N. Phillips 2007. *Power and Organizations*. London: Sage

Clemens, E. S. and J. Cook 1999. "Politics and institutionalism: explaining durability and change," *Annual Review of Sociology* 25: 441–66

Coleman, A. M. 2003. "Cooperation, psychological game theory, and limitations of rationality in social interaction," *Behavioral and Brain Science* 26: 139–53

Coleman, P. T. 2006. "Power and conflict" in Deutsch, Coleman and Marcus (eds.) *The Handbook of Conflict Resolution: Theory and Practice*. San Francisco: Jossey-Bass, pp. 120–43

Collins, R. 1975. *Conflict Sociology: Toward an Explanatory Science*. New York: Academic
1993. "What does conflict theory predict about America's future? 1993 presidential address," *Sociological Perspectives* 36: 289–313

Coser, L. 1956. *The Functions of Social Conflict*. New York: Free Press

Crozier, M. and E. Friedberg 1981. *Actors and Systems*. Chicago University Press

Dahl, R. A. 1963. *Modern Political Analysis*. Englewood Cliffs, NJ: Prentice-Hall

Dahrendorf, R. 1959. *Class and Class Conflict in Industrial Society*. Stanford, CA: Stanford University Press
1968. *Essays in the Theory of Society*. Stanford, CA: Stanford University Press

Dalton, M. and D. Chrobot-Mason 2007. "A theoretical exploration of manager and employee social identity, cultural values and identity conflict management," *International Journal of Cross Cultural Management* 7: 169–83

Danskin, P., C. Dibrell and B. L. Kedia 2005. "The evolving role of cooperation among multinational corporations and indigenous organizations in transition economies: a migration away from confrontation," *Journal of World Business* 40: 223–34

Deutsch, M. 1973. *The Resolution of Conflict*. New Haven: Yale University Press

1980. "Fifty years of conflict" in Festinger (ed.) *Restropections on Social Psychology*. New York: Oxford University Press, pp. 46–72

1982. "Conflict resolution: theory and practice," *Political Psychology* 4: 431–52

Diehl, P. F. 2006. "Just a phase? Integrating conflict dynamics over time," *Conflict Management and Peace Science* 23: 199–210

DiMaggio, P. J. and W. W. Powell 1983. "The iron cage revisited: institutional isomorphism and collective rationality in organizational fields," *American Sociological Review* 48: 147–60

Dixit, A. K. and S. Skeath 1999. *Games of Strategy*. New York: Norton

Dörrenbächer, C. 2007. "Inside the transnational social space: cross-border management and owner relationships at a German-subsidiary in Hungary," *Journal of East European Management Studies* 13: 318–39

Dörrenbächer, C. and J. Gammelgaard 2006. "Subsidiary role development: the effect of micropolitical headquarters–subsidiary negotiations on the product, market, and value-added scope of foreign owned subsidiaries," *Journal of International Management* 12: 266–83

Dörrenbächer, C. and M. Geppert 2006. "Micro-politics and conflicts in multinational corporations: current debates, re-framing, and contributions of this Special Issue," *Journal of International Management* 12: 251–65

2009. "A micro-political perspective on subsidiary initiative-taking: evidence from German-owned subsidiaries in France," *European Management Journal* 27: 100–12

Doz, Y. L. and C. K. Prahalad 1981. "Headquarters influence and strategic control in MNCs," *Sloan Management Review* 23: 15–29

1984. "Patterns of strategic control within multinational corporations," *Journal of International Business Studies* 15: 55–72

1991. "Managing DMNCs: a search for a new paradigm," *Strategic Management Journal* 12: 145–64

Doz, Y. L., C. A. Bartlett and C. K. Prahalad 1981. "Global competitive pressures and host country demands, managing tensions in MNCs," *California Management Review* 23: 63–73

Dutton, J., J. Dukerich and C. Harquail 1994. "Organizational images and member identification," *Administrative Science Quarterly* 39: 293–363

Earley, P. C. and M. Laubach 2002. "Structural identity theory and the dynamics of cross-cultural work groups" in Gannon and Newman (eds.) *The Blackwell Handbook of Cross-Cultural Management*. Oxford: Blackwell, pp. 256–82

Easton, G. and L. Araujo 1992. "Non-economic exchange in industrial networks" in Axelsson and Easton (eds.) *Industrial Networks: A New View of Reality*. London: Routledge, pp. 62–84

Edwards, P. K. and J. Bélanger 2009. "The MNC as a contested terrain" in Collinson and Morgan (eds.) *Images of the Multinational*. Oxford: Wiley, pp. 193–216

Edwards, T. and S. Kuruvilla 2005. "International HRM: national business systems, organisational politics and the international division of labour in global value chains," *International Journal of Human Resource Management* 16: 1–21

Edwards, T., X. Coller, L. Ortiz, C. Rees and M. Wortmann 2006. "How important are national industrial relations systems in shaping restructuring in MNCs?," *European Journal of Industrial Relations* 12: 69–88

Edwards, T., T. Colling and A. Ferner 2007. "The transfer of employment practices in multi-national companies: towards an integrated conceptual approach," *Human Resource Management Journal* 17: 201–17

Eisenhardt, K. 1989. "Agency theory: an assessment and review," *Academy of Management Review* 14: 57–74

Ferner, A. 2000. "The underpinnings of 'bureaucratic' control systems: HRM in European multinationals," *Journal of Management Studies* 37: 521–40

Ferner, A. and P. Edwards 1995. "Power and diffusion of organizational change within multi-national enterprises," *European Journal of Industrial Relations* 37: 229–57

Ferner, A, P. Almond, T. Colling and T. Edwards 2005. "Policies on union representation in US multinationals in the UK: between micro-politics and macro-institutions," *British Journal of Industrial Relations* 43: 703–28

Foucault, M. 1979. *Discipline and Punish: The Birth of the Prison*. New York: Vintage Books
  1980. *Power/Knowledge: Selected Interviews and Other Writings 1972–1977*. Edited by C. Gordon. Brighton: Harvester Press.
  1982. "The subject and power" in Dreyfus and Rabinow (eds.) *Michel Foucault: Beyond Structuralism and Hermeneutics*. Brighton: Harvester Press, pp. 208–26

Frenkel, M. 2008. "The multinational corporation as a third space: rethinking international management discourse on knowledge transfer through Homi Bhabha," *Academy of Management Review* 33: 924–42

Frost, P. J. 1987. "Power, politics and influence" in Jablin (ed.) *Handbook of Organizational Communication: An Interdisciplinary Perspective*. Newbury Park: Sage, pp. 503–48

Gaski, J. F. 1984. "The theory of power and conflict in channels of distribution," *Journal of Marketing* 48: 9–29

Geppert, M. and E. Clark 2003. "Knowledge and learning in transnational ventures: an actor-centred approach," *Management Decision* 41: 433–42

Geppert, M. and C. Williams 2006. "Global, national and local practices in multinational corporations: towards a sociopolitical framework," *International Journal of Human Resource Management* 17: 49–69

Ghoshal, S. and P. Moran 1996. "Bad for practice: a critique of the transaction cost theory," *Academy of Management Review* 21: 13–47

Giddens, A. 1984. *The Constitution of Society, Outline of the Structuration Theory*. Berkeley, Los Angeles: University of California Press

Gladwin, T. N. and I. Walter 1980. *Multinationals under Fire: Lessons in the Management of Conflict*. New York: John Wiley & Sons

Glasl, F. 2010. *Konfliktmanagement*. 9th edn. Bern: Haupt

Gong, Y. 2003. "Toward a dynamic process model of staffing composition and subsidiary outcomes in multinational corporations," *Journal of Management* 29: 259–80

Graham, J. L. 1985. "The influence of culture on the process of business negotiations: an exploratory study," *Journal of International Business Studies* 16: 81–96

Gupta, A. K. and Q. Cao 2005. "Parent-subsidiary conflict within multinational enterprises" Working Paper presented at Academy of Management Conference 2005: Honolulu, HI.

Hardy, C. 1996. "Understanding power: bringing about strategic change," *British Journal of Management* 7: 3–16

Hayward, M. L. A. and W. Boeker 1998. "Power and conflicts of interest in professional firms: evidence from investment banking," *Administrative Science Quarterly* 43: 1–22

Hennart, J. F. 1991. "Control in multinational firms: the role of price and hierarchy," *Management International Review* 31: 71–96

Huber, G. P. and A. H. Van de Ven 1995. *Longitudinal Field Research.* Thousand Oaks, CA: Sage

Jameson, J. 1999. "Toward a comprehensive model for the assessment and management of intraorganizational conflict: developing the framework," *International Journal of Conflict Management* 10: 268–94

Jehn, K. A. 1995. "A multimethod examination of the benefits and detriments of intragroup conflict," *Administrative Science Quarterly* 40: 256–82

Jehn, K. A., G. B. Northcraft and M. A. Neale 1999. "Why differences make a difference: a field study of diversity, conflict and performance in workgroups," *Administrative Science Quarterly* 44: 741–63

Jensen, M. and W. Meckling 1976. "Theory of the firm: managerial behavior, agency costs and ownership structure," *Journal of Financial Economics* 3: 305–60

Jones, G. and T. Khanna 2006. "Bringing history (back) into international business," *Journal of International Business Studies* 37: 453–68

Joshi, A., G. Labianca and P. M. Caligiuri 2002. "Getting along long distance: understanding conflict in a multinational team through network analysis," *Journal of World Business* 37: 277–84

Jost, P.-J. 1998. *Strategisches Konfliktmanagement in Organisationen. Eine spieltheoretische Einführung.* 1st edn. Wiesbaden: Gabler

Karnoe, P. and C. Nygaard 1999. "Bringing social action and situated rationality back in," *International Studies of Management & Organisation* 29: 78–93

Katz, D. and R. L. Kahn 1978. *The Social Psychology of Organizations.* 2nd edn. New York: John Wiley & Sons

Kaufmann, L. and S. Rössing 2005. "Managing conflicts of interests between headquarters and their subsidiaries regarding technology transfer to emerging markets – a framework," *Journal of World Business* 40: 235–53

Kiser, E. 1999. "Comparing varieties of agency theory in economics, political science, and sociology: an illustration from state policy implementation," *Sociological Theory* 17: 146–70

Kostova, T. 1999. "Transnational transfer of strategic organisational practices: a contextual perspective," *Academy of Management Review* 24: 308–24

Kostova, T. and K. Roth 2002. "Adoption of an organizational practice by subsidiaries of multinational corporations: institutional and relational effects," *Academy of Management Journal* 45: 215–33

Kostova, T., K. Roth and M. T. Dacin 2008. "Institutional theory in the study of multinational corporations: a critique and new directions," *Academy of Management Review* 33: 994–1006

Kristensen, P. H. and J. Zeitlin 2001. "The making of a global firm: local pathways to multinational enterprise" in Morgan, Kristensen and Whitley (eds.) *The Multinational Firm. Organizing Across Institutional and National Divides.* Oxford University Press, pp. 172–95

2005. *Local Players in Global Games: The Strategic Constitution of a Multinational Corporation.* Oxford University Press

Lawrence, P. and J. Lorsch 1967. "Differentiation and integration," *Administrative Science Quarterly* 12: 1–30

Lukes, S. 1974. *Power: A Radical View.* London and New York: Macmillan
1986. *Power: A Radical View.* New York University Press

Mahoney, J. 2000. "Path dependency in historical sociology," *Theory and Society* 29: 507–48

Mailath, G. J. and L. Samuelson. 2006. *Repeated Games and Reputations: Long-Run Relationships.* Oxford University Press

Miles, R. H. and W. D. Perrault 1976. "Organizational role conflict: its antecedents and Consequences," *Organizational Behavior and Human Performance* 17: 19–44

Mir, R. and A. Mir 2009. "From the Colony to the corporation: studying knowledge transfer across international boundaries," *Group and Organization Management* 34: 90–113

Mir, R. and D. R. Sharpe 2004. "Transferring managerial practices within multinationals: control, resistance and empowerment," *Academy of Management Proceedings* 2004: E1–E6
2009. "The multinational firm as an instrument of exploitation and domination" in Collinson and Morgan (eds.) *Images of the Multinational Firm.* Chichester: Wiley, pp. 247–65

Mohr, A. T. and J. F. Puck 2007. "Inter-sender role conflicts, general manager satisfaction and joint venture performance in Indian-German joint ventures," *European Management Journal*, 25(1): 25–35.

Morgan, G. 2003. "International business and multinationals: a critical management approach." Paper read at Best Paper Proceedings, Academy of Management Conference 2003: Seattle, WA

Morgan, G. and P. H. Kristensen 2006. "The contested space of multinationals: varieties of institutionalism, varieties of capitalism," *Human Relations* 59: 1467–90

Mudambi, R., and T. Pedersen 2007 "Agency theory and resource dependence theory: complementary explanations for subsidiary power in multinational corporations." SMG Working Paper, Copenhagen Business School, http://uk.cbs.dk/content/download/60978/ 840515/ file/SMG%20WP%202007_5.pdf (last accessed October 13, 2010)

Murninghan, J. K. 1994. "Game theory and organizational behavior" *Research in Organizational Behavior* 16: 83–125

Nohria, N. and S. Ghoshal 1994. "Differentiated fit and shared values: alternatives for managing headquarters–subsidiary relations," *Strategic Management Journal* 15: 491–502

O'Donnell, S. 2000. "Managing foreign subsidiaries: agents of headquarters, or an interdependent network?," *Strategic Management Journal* 21: 525–48

Oliver, C. 1991. "Strategic responses to institutional processes," *Strategic Management Review* 16: 145–79

Pahl, J. M. and K. Roth 1993. "Managing the headquarters–foreign subsidiary relationship: the roles of strategy, conflict, and integration," *The International Journal of Conflict Management* 4: 139–65

Parkhe, A. 1993. "Strategic alliance structuring: a game theoretic and transaction cost examination of interfirm cooperation," *Academy of Management Journal* 36: 794–829

Pearson d'Estrée, T. 2003. "Dynamics" in Cheldelin, Druckman and Fast (eds.) *Conflict.* London: Continuum, pp. 68–87

Peng, M. W. 2000. "Controlling the foreign agent: how governments deal with multinationals in a transition economy," *Management International Review* 40: 141–65

Pettigrew, A. M., R. W. Woodman and K. S. Cameron 2001. "Studying organizational change and development: challenges for future research," *Academy of Management Journal* 44: 697–713

Pfeffer, J. 1992. *Managing with Power: Politics and Influence in Organizations.* Boston, MA: Harvard Business School Press

Pondy, L. R. 1967. "Organizational conflict: concepts and models," *Administrative Science Quarterly* 12: 296–320

Prahalad, C. K. 1975. "The strategic process in a multinational corporation." Unpublished doctoral dissertation, School of Business Administration, Harvard University

Prahalad, C. K. and Y. L. Doz 1987. *The Multinational Mission: Balancing Local Demands and Global Vision.* New York: Free Press

Rahim, M. A. 1983. "A measure of styles of handling interpersonal conflict," *Academy of Management Journal* 26: 368–76

Reade, C. 2001. "Dual identification in multinational corporations: local managers and their psychological attachment to the subsidiary versus the global organization," *International Journal of Human Resource Management* 12: 405–24

Rössing, S. M. 2005. *Technology Transfer to China.* Frankfurt am Main: European Management Publications

Roth, K. and D. Nigh 1992. "The effectiveness of headquarters–subsidiary relationships: the role of coordination, control, and conflict," *Journal of Business Research* 25: 277–301

Roth, K. and S. O'Donnell 1996. "Foreign subsidiary compensation strategy: an agency theory perspective," *Academy of Management Journal* 39: 687–703

Rubin, J. Z., D. G. Pruitt and S. H. Kim 1994. "*Social Conflict: Escalation, Stalemate, and Settlement.* 2nd edn. New York: McGraw-Hill

Sanders, W. G. and M. A. Carpenter 1998. "Internationalization and firm governance: the roles of CEO compensation, top team composition, and board structure," *Academy of Management Journal* 41: 158–78

Scharf, F. W. 2006. *Interaktionsformen. Akteurszentrierter Institutionalismus in der Politikforschung.* 2nd edn. Wiesbaden: VS Verlag für Sozialwissenschaften

Scheffer, T. 2007. "Event and process: an exercise in analytical ethnography," *Human Studies* 30: 167–97

Schelling, T. C. 1958. "The strategy of conflict: prospectus for a reorientation of game theory," *Journal of Conflict Resolution* 2: 203–64
1960. *The Strategy of Conflict.* Cambridge, MA: Harvard University Press

Schepers, D. H. 2006. "The impact of NGO network conflict on the corporate social responsibility strategies of multinational corporations," *Business & Society* 45: 282–99

Schmid, S. and A. Daniel 2007. "Are subsidiary roles a matter of perception? A review of the literature and avenues for future research." Working Paper No. 30, ESCP-EAP European School of Management, Berlin

Schütz, A. 1972. *Collected Papers. Volume 1.* Edited by M. A. Natanson and H. L. Van Breda. Berlin: Springer.

Scott, W. R. 1995. *Institutions and Organizations.* Thousand Oaks, CA: Sage

Shapiro, S. P. 2005. "Agency theory," *Annual Review of Sociology* 31: 263–84

Sheppard, B. H. 1992. "Conflict research as schizophrenia: the many faces of organizational conflict," *Journal of Organizational Behavior* 13: 325–34

Skyrms, B. 2004. *The Stag Hunt and the Evolution of Social Structure*. Cambridge University Press

Stern, L. W. and R. H. Gorman 1969. "Conflict in distribution channels: an exploration" in Stern (ed.) *Distribution Channels: Behavioral Dimensions*. Boston, MA: Houghton Mifflin Company, pp. 156–175

Tajfel, H. and J. C. Turner 1986. "The social identity theory of intergroup behavior" in Worchel and Austin (eds.) *Psychology of Intergroup Relations*. Chicago, IL: Burnham Inc Pub, pp. 7–24.

Tasoluk, B., A. Yaprak and R. J. Calantone 2006. "Conflict and collaboration in headquarters–subsidiary relationships. An agency-theory perspective on product roll-outs in an emerging market," *International Journal of Conflict Management* 17: 332–51

Thomas, K. 1976. "Conflict and conflict management" in Dunnette (ed.) *Handbook of Industrial and Organizational Psychology*. Chicago, IL: Rand McNally College Publishing Company, pp. 889–935

Thomas, K. W. 1992. "Conflict and conflict management: reflections and update," *Journal of Organizational Behavior* 13: 265–74

Tjosvold, D. 1999. "Bridging east and west to develop new products and trust: interdependence and interaction between a Hong Kong parent and north American subsidiary," *International Journal of Innovation Management* 3: 233–52

Tsui, A. 2007. "From homogenization to pluralism: international management research in the Academy and beyond," *Academy of Management Journal* 50: 1353–64

Von Glinow, M. A., D. L. Shapiro and J. M. Brett 2004. "Can we talk. And should we? Managing emotional conflict in multicultural teams," *Academy of Management Review* 29: 578–92

Vora, D. T. and T. Kostova 2007. "A model of dual organizational identification in the context of the multinational enterprise," *Journal of Organizational Behavior* 28: 327–50

Vora, D., T. Kostova and K. Roth 2007. "Roles of subsidiary managers in multinational corporations: the effect of dual organizational identification," *Management International Review* 47: 595–620

Walton, R. E. and J. M. Dutton 1969. "The management of international conflict: a model and review," *Administrative Science Quarterly* 14: 73–84

Westney, D. E. 1993. "Institutionalization theory and the multinational corporation" in Ghoshal and Westney (eds.) *Organization Theory and the Multinational Corporation*. New York: St. Martin's Press, pp. 53–76

Whiteman, G. 2009. "All my relations: understanding perceptions of justice and conflict between companies and indigenous peoples," *Organization Studies* 30: 101–20

Whitley, R. 1999. *Divergent Capitalisms: The Social Structuring and Change of Business Systems*. Oxford University Press

Whittington, R. 1992. "Putting Giddens into action: social systems and managerial agency," *Journal of Management Studies*, 29(6): 693–712

Zietsma, C. and M. I. Winn 2008. "Building chains and directing flows: strategies and tactics of mutual influence in stakeholder conflicts," *Business & Society* 47: 68–101

6 | Intra-organizational turbulences in multinational corporations

Andreas Schotter and Paul W. Beamish

Introduction

Scholars have recently pointed out that intra-organizational conflict in multinational corporations (MNCs) between headquarters (HQ) and their foreign subsidiaries is not necessarily dysfunctional (Dörrenbächer and Geppert 2006; see also chapter by Blazejewski and Becker-Ritterspach in this volume) or a sign of unsuccessful global integration (Bouquet and Birkinshaw 2008; Tasoluk *et al.* 2006), as often stressed in previous management research. Instead, the growing importance of foreign subsidiaries, especially from large emerging markets, requires a different approach when managing headquarters–subsidiary relationships. This includes a departure from the traditional antagonistic view of the global integration versus local responsiveness quandary. This chapter aims to advance the literature on MNC headquarters–subsidiary relationships by adding new insights to the global versus local discussion (Bartlett 1986; Bartlett and Ghoshal 1989; Ghemawat 2007; Prahalad and Doz 1987; Roth and Morrison 1990).

Global integration refers to strategic and organizational activities that seek to reduce organizational and operational dissimilarities between different MNC subunits (Prahalad and Doz 1987). The objectives of global integration include efficiency improvements through aggregation, the exploitation of scope and scale economies, and the transfer of knowledge and practices across the MNC network. Local responsiveness refers to subsidiary decision-making autonomy while responding to local customer needs and specific host market competitive demands (Bartlett 1986; Doz and Prahalad 1991). Local responsiveness activities usually increase intra-organizational heterogeneity in MNCs. Coordination in the context of this chapter is defined as the efficient management of the headquarters–subsidiary link while generating value over and above the sum of the individual organizational units (Burgelman and Doz 1996). It is at the intersection of these tasks that a multitude of factors at the headquarters or the subsidiary level can trigger conflict. These factors include differing market and customer preferences, global and local competitors' strategies, host country and home country regulatory requirements, managerial characteristics and managerial preferences at headquarters and the subsidiaries, strategic misalignments, and asymmetries between the local and global industry levels (see also chapter by Dörrenbächer and Gammelgaard in this volume).

HQ initiative rejection

The research underlying this chapter focused on rejection of HQ initiatives by foreign subsidiaries, a phenomenon that has been mainly overlooked by previous management research. We took an organizational evolution perspective (Birkinshaw and Hood 1998; see also chapter by Schmid and Daniel in this volume), which is especially relevant for emerging market subsidiaries. As these foreign subsidiaries mature, the initial high level of knowledge and capability transfer from headquarters slows, more decisions are being made locally, and HQ-imposed initiatives often face more scrutiny (Birkinshaw 1995), while at the same time a sense of independence develops. In addition, with growing levels of independence, subsidiary managers gain more power and more confrontational organizational politicking becomes a viable option for negotiating with headquarters. Therefore, we argue that when HQ initiatives affect subsidiary independence they are more likely to face rejection. We illustrate the phenomenon with the following example:

A global integration initiative by an MNC, "MNC A," is intended to reduce the number of individual manufacturing plants worldwide for a specific global product in order to achieve better economies of scale. "Subsidiary X" is therefore requested to close its plant for this product and to source from a sister subsidiary ("Subsidiary Y") in another country. Now, while Subsidiary X might benefit from reduced manufacturing cost by sourcing from the new global facility, Subsidiary X rejects the HQ initiative to close its plant. The local subsidiary manager argues that, because of additional tariffs and transportation costs, global sourcing provides only a marginally better price, but as a downside, longer delivery times, and an increased foreign exchange rate risk threatens Subsidiary X's local competitiveness. In addition, there are more subtle reasons for the rejection: because headquarters reduces the mandate of Subsidiary X, the subsidiary's intra-MNC importance and power position are likely to be negatively affected. However, from the HQ perspective, a global facility makes sense since it reduces redundancies across all countries, which more than offset the negative effect on one individual subsidiary.

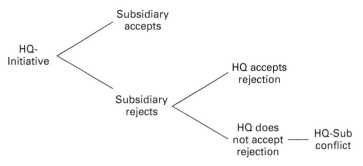

Fig. 6.1   Phenomenon positioning

One can see that the problem is complex and involves multiple levels, including the subsidiary, the headquarters, the managerial, and the headquarters–
subsidiary relationship level. Figure 6.1 illustrates the HQ initiative rejection
and conflict logic that underlies this research.

During the initial exploratory fieldwork, we found support for the supposition that HQ initiative rejection by foreign subsidiaries is a far more common
phenomenon than suggested by the amount of existing research on headquarters–subsidiary relationships. In addition, the majority of practitioners
with whom we talked confirmed the relevance of the topic and their interest
in better understanding headquarters–subsidiary conflict. Most interviewees mentioned that while conflict does not always lead to negative outcomes,
or a clear winner or loser, the conflict process usually results in operational
and organizational disruptions that demand additional resource allocation,
including valuable managerial time. There was one theme mentioned repeatedly, which is best depicted by the following statement:

To me, the most interesting question is: When subsidiaries resist HQ initiatives,
how do we know if this is good or bad for the business? Some level of disagreement
is almost certainly a good thing but we have seen examples both ways. (A chief technology officer)

To date, scholars have not systematically answered this question. This is
partly due to the one-dimensional approaches used, which have been mainly
based on the analysis of inter-personal conflict situations, and, in addition,
partly due to the conceptual pre-dispositions of most studies that label conflict either good or bad, or functional or dysfunctional, right from the beginning of the investigation (Eisenhardt and Zbaracki 1992; Menon *et al.* 1996).
The goal of this research was to rectify this situation from an academic perspective, keeping practitioner relevance in mind.

While we chose not to explicitly adopt a micro-political perspective that focuses solely on inter-personal relationships between managers, we did not regard MNCs as monolithic and we acknowledged that different managers and organizational subunits within the MNC have their own individual aspirations, which often lead to conflicting interests. However, the level of analysis was predominantly organizational. The purpose was to reduce the gap between existing organizational theories that are mainly based on very simplified models of international firms, and the mostly data-driven investigations that follow structuralism.

We used a qualitative, iterative, multiphase research approach to develop new theory pertaining to the phenomenon of interest. For the purposes of presentation, we adopted the convention, set by the post-positivist research paradigm, of presenting literature up front, followed by methods and then findings (Suddaby 2006). It is, nevertheless, important to stress that this choice was made foremost to provide clarity to the reader, rather than to reflect the chronological unfolding conduct of the research. The primary research questions to be addressed were:

1) What are the antecedents to HQ initiative rejection by foreign subsidiaries that lead to intra-organizational conflicts?
2) How are these conflicts managed at headquarters and the subsidiaries?

Defining conflict

During the preliminary phase of the fieldwork it became evident that the term "conflict" carries a more negative connotation than a positive connotation, which cannot be eradicated by theoretical approaches based on stylized organizational configurations like the transnational solution (Bartlett 1986; Bartlett and Ghoshal 1989) or the metanational firm (Doz *et al.* 2001). Pondy (1992), while reflecting on his influential article on organizational conflict (Pondy 1967), stated that conflict is not always negative. Instead, he argued that conflict is a normal consequence of managing and that firms should internalize conflict rather than attempt to eliminate it. Later, Menon *et al.* (1996) investigated conflict by dividing it into two types, dysfunctional and functional. They showed that dysfunctional conflict in the decision-making process has generally negative effects on performance, while functional conflict can lead to improved firm performance.

More recent research (Amason and Sapienza 1997; Jehn 1994, 1995; Jehn and Shah 1997; Pahl and Roth 1993; Pelled 1996; Pinkley 1990) divided organizational conflict into three distinct but intertwined categories, including task, process and relationship conflict (Jehn and Mannix 2001). Task conflict refers to differences in viewpoints and opinions regarding a group or joint undertaking (Amason and Sapienza 1997). It is fact-oriented and involves animated discussions and personal excitement but without intense negative emotions (Jehn and Mannix 2001). Process conflict (Jehn et al. 1999) involves disagreement concerning how specific goals should be achieved. Process conflict concerns issues such as resource allocation, task responsibility, and task execution. Relationship conflict (Jehn and Mannix 2001) is characterized by inter-personal incompatibilities and emotional components involving tension and friction. Relationship conflict includes personal issues such as dislike among different individuals and feelings such as annoyance, frustration and irritation. All three types of conflict appear simultaneously in a conflict situation, but with varying levels of individual strength during the conflict process. Jehn and Mannix (2001) called this phenomenon the "dynamic nature of conflict."

Functional conflict behavior, which is characterized by high levels of task and process orientation and low levels of relational conflict orientation (Jehn and Mannix 2001), can be encouraged by enhancing organizational characteristics such as formalization, interdepartmental interconnectedness, low communication barriers and team spirit. In contrast, centralization, physical distance and high communication barriers increase the potential for dysfunctional conflict (Menon et al. 1996).

The definition of conflict adopted in this chapter reflects the general understanding of conflict in the existing international management literature, with additional arguments derived from relevant sociological literature on intra-organizational relationships. We specifically conceptualized conflict as a process. The focus of the inquiry was on organizational conflict, but acknowledges that inter-personal and organizational conflicts are often intertwined (Jehn and Mannix 2001).

Definition: Conflict is awareness on the part of the parties involved of discrepancies, goal incompatibility, or irreconcilable desires (Boulding 1962). Conflict is based on interest divergence (Axelrod 1970), information asymmetry between actors (Deutsch 1973), or perception gaps (Birkinshaw et al. 2000) of more than one party (Kriesberg 1973) with an interdependent relationship (Thompson 1967).

Managing the integration versus local responsiveness quandary

The complexities of managing across borders and the divergent objectives of MNC headquarters and foreign subsidiaries frequently prevent the adoption of simple organizational arrangements. Therefore, international management research often suggests that some form of matrix arrangement, like the transnational (Bartlett and Ghoshal 1989), which recognizes the need for local responsiveness and global integration simultaneously, would be ideal. However, successfully implementing a matrix structure requires a change in the attitude of managers toward a more participatory decision-making culture (Prahalad and Doz 1987). Bartlett and Ghoshal (1989) recognized that advances in MNC strategies have developed faster than organizational and managerial capabilities. As a result, MNCs now regularly develop complex strategies that are extremely difficult to implement. For example, if the capabilities required to implement a matrix structure do not exist, and cannot be developed or acquired within a realistic timeframe, new strategies that rely on those structures may actually fail. This, then, may lead to headquarters–subsidiary conflict and suboptimal MNC performance. Naylor (1985) takes a different position by arguing that the matrix organization is not the cause of organizational complexities, but the reflection of complexity inherent in large MNCs.

Goold (1996) stated that the purpose of headquarters should be to add value to the MNC so that the individual subsidiaries perform better together than they would as independent businesses. The benefits of having headquarters should outweigh its cost (Ghoshal and Nohria 1993). Hence, if integration efforts do not create a competitive advantage, they destroy rather than create value (Birnik 2007). Jemison and Sitkin (1986) argued that arrogant and defensive behavior from HQ managers and heavy-handed imposition of HQ initiatives on the subsidiary might eliminate subsidiary-level capabilities as well as the interest of subsidiary managers to respond to local demands.

On the other hand, HQ management often considers the bigger picture and while some HQ integration initiatives might limit a subsidiary's ability to react to external responsiveness needs, those initiatives could benefit the MNC as a whole (Birkinshaw and Morrison 1995). In addition, in industries where global integration is a key success factor, poor integration and the reliance on the success of individual subsidiaries may prove detrimental in the long run. So far, we have not identified empirical studies that investigate the net effects of global integration initiatives.

Ghoshal and Westney (1993) argued that organizational theories represent the most appropriate starting point for MNC research that is concerned with structure and control issues. Interestingly, previous investigations have implicitly assumed that HQ initiatives do not face resistance to the extent that they have serious consequences for individual organizational subunits or the MNC as a whole. It appears that in this stream of research the effectiveness of managerial fiat (Williamson 1981) and structure and control configuring is a widely accepted assumption and therefore HQ initiatives are not expected to cause organizational conflict. As this study unfolded, we found that some theories are more relevant than others. The findings connected especially well with the concepts underlying resource dependency theory (Pfeffer and Salancik 1978). In the following section we briefly describe the underlying logics of resource dependency theory and how the theory connects with our research.

The resource dependency perspective

The basic premise of resource dependency theory is that power derives from the control of specific resources that are critical for coping with the demands of the external environment (Pfeffer and Salancik 1978). Pfeffer (1981) defined organizational success from a resource dependency perspective as the maximization of power over other interconnected organizations, based on the exchange of resources. Organizations that lack critical resources will seek relationships with other organizations in order to obtain needed resources. Organizations make efforts to adjust their dependency relationships by minimizing their own dependence, or by increasing the dependence of other organizations on them (Pfeffer and Salancik 1978).

Resource dependency theory rests on three assumptions (Pfeffer and Salancik 1978). First, organizations are understood to comprise internal and external coalitions, which emerge from social exchanges that are formed to influence and control individual behaviors. Second, the operating environment is assumed to contain scarce and valuable resources that are critical for organizational survival. Third, organizations are assumed to work toward the acquisition and control over resources that minimize their own dependence on other organizations and maximize the dependence of other organizations on themselves. Achieving control over resources that either minimize or maximize dependency is considered to positively affect the outcomes from exchange among organizations and to increase an organization's power (Pfeffer 1981; Pfeffer and Salancik 1978).

While Pfeffer and Salancik (1978) initially framed resource dependency theory to explain relationships between independent organizations, the theory is also applicable to relationships among units within organizations (Bouquet and Birkinshaw 2008; Mudambi and Pedersen 2007). Although there are hierarchical dependencies between foreign subsidiaries and MNC headquarters that are derived from structure rather than the control of tangible resources, the powers that arise from being the focal interface in the host environment provides foreign subsidiaries with specific, often tacit, local knowledge, which creates bargaining power (Osborne and Rubinstein 1990) when negotiating with corporate headquarters (see also chapter by Williams and Geppert in this volume). In an effort to integrate the literature on power and influence in MNCs, Bouquet and Birkinshaw (2008) identified that organizational actors within MNC networks share some interdependencies that cannot be explained with hierarchical relationships alone. The general notion is that while subsidiaries evolve, the relationships between MNC headquarters and subsidiaries change in such a way that hierarchical dependencies become undermined by increased interdependencies due to increased stocks of specific strategic resources that are predominantly related to the subsidiaries' growing connections within the host country environment. To date, these arguments lack empirical validation (Mudambi and Pedersen 2007), which we aimed to correct with our research.

Methodology

We followed a multiphase research approach as suggested by Parkhe (1993) (Figure 6.2). The advantage of a multiphase approach is that each phase builds on the findings of the preceding phase, which leads to a better understanding of the phenomenon and to steady increases in the level of generalizability (Parkhe 1993). Further, an iterative theory-building approach is suitable for investigating phenomena that are not well understood (Glaser and Strauss 1967), and when the researcher aims to develop new conceptual insights. This is especially the case when the phenomenon under investigation is a process (Eisenhardt 1989) and the phenomenon is being studied as it occurs naturally (Yin 2003).

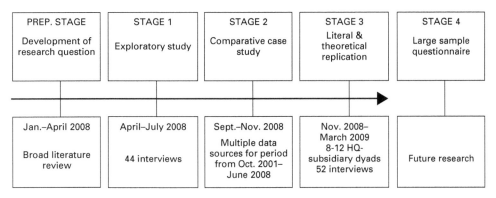

Fig. 6.2   Research schedule

One could argue that a survey or questionnaire may also be suitable for addressing some of the proposed questions. However, managerial post-hoc rationalization, or what Weick (1995) described as post-hoc sensemaking, limits the validity of descriptions of already completed events. For example, after the fact, conflicts are often not regarded as such, especially when the outcomes were positive. This is even true for cases with significant real disruptions to regular business activities during the actual conflict process. Another reason why we chose this empirical approach was that prior studies showed that for phenomena that involve substantial rather than incremental variations of theory, survey methodology would be constrained by a lack of awareness regarding what questions to ask (Yin 2003).

Exploratory study (phase 1)

The objective of the exploratory phase was to identify the phenomenon in the field in a variety of industries based on informants from both MNC headquarters and foreign subsidiaries. Between April and July 2008, 44 interviews were conducted with executives whom we knew personally. We recorded 127 HQ initiatives, of which 67 were rejected (Table 6.1). It became clear that HQ initiative rejection that involves conflict is a far more common phenomenon in MNCs than the existing amount of research on the topic indicates. Changes in the subsidiary mandate, specifically the geographical responsibilities, and changes to the product/service autonomy created the highest number of rejections, followed by new product and/or service introductions. In 56 of all cases, headquarters–subsidiary conflicts were reported.

Table 6.1 HQ Initiatives directed toward subsidiaries

Type	Initiatives	Rejection	Conflicts
1) New management practice	22	7	5
2) New compensation system	5	3	3
3) Corporate-wide ERP system	4	2	2
4) Downsizing	8	7	5
5) Upsizing (e.g. new management	2	1	2
structure)	9	4	4
6) New reporting procedure	7	4	3
7) Supplier change	12	8	7
8) New product/service introduction	9	4	2
9) Changes in legal structure of subsidiary			
10) Mandate change			
(a) Geographical market	15	10	9
(b) Product/service autonomy	16	8	6
(c) Production vs no production	3	1	1
(d) Changes to the R&D mandate	5	2	1
(e) Reduce local market autonomy	10	6	6

Comparative case study (phase 2)

During the process of analyzing the exploratory data, we discovered that we had access to multiple sources of longitudinal data for one specific HQ initiative at two independent subsidiaries for the entire duration of the conflicts. We therefore decided to follow a comparative case study design. This approach provided us with the same level of in-depth contextual understanding as for a single case study (Parkhe 1993), but with the added benefits of comparing the same initiative in two different settings. However, it is important to point out that the comparative power of this analysis was based on a sample of only one MNC in only two countries. For future research, it would be desirable to increase the number of countries and subsidiaries. Nevertheless, we benefited from the comparative approach by identifying important differences regarding conflict processes over time.

While we were not personally involved in the conflict situations, we had complete access throughout and after the actual active conflicts to the subsidiaries, to the corporate headquarters and to all managers involved, including those who had in the meantime left the company. One of the main investigators was present during most corporate meetings, or he was informed by internal memos or first-hand reports by subsidiary managers and HQ managers. Later, we were able to go back to conduct further clarification interviews and to collect additional secondary data, including internal communication documentations such as e-mails. We were also able to inquire about the relational conflict situations, which were not explicitly visible in the official documents.

The specific conflict at Z-Corp[1] involved a so called "value-added product initiative" that represented a new product category aimed at forward-integration in order to generate higher overall margins. The situation was very similar to the hypothetical example that we described in the introductory section. The reason behind the Z-Corp initiative was that the company's products faced more and more price pressure due to a commoditization trend in the component market. Z-Corp's top management felt that the company had enough expertise and the necessary capabilities to compete in specific segments of the system market. Z-Corp's management was aware of the potential hostile reaction from their customers and therefore was careful to only enter a segment where market fragmentation was high and no large and powerful component customers would be affected.

Z-Corp was a European-based company that conducted 85 percent of its sales and 50 percent of its manufacturing outside of the home country. The company was among the top three worldwide in its industry in terms of gross sales. Z-Corp was known as a high-quality manufacturer with a flexible multi-domestic strategy, but a strong, globally unified product portfolio. The subsidiaries under investigation were located in China and the USA. Both subsidiaries were mature and wholly owned by the holding company in Europe. Both subsidiaries had mandates that included sales, service, manufacturing and all other functions that stand-alone companies would have had. Strategically, both were equally important to the MNC. The North American market represented the largest market for the type of industrial equipment that the company manufactured and was home to the ten top global target customers. However, China had the strongest growth and was expected to equal, or surpass, the market volume in the USA during the coming five to ten years. The difference between the company's positions in each of the two markets was that in North America, due to competition, Z-Corp had a

---

[1] Name and company specifics were disguised to guarantee confidentiality.

relatively smaller market share compared to other markets like Europe, Asia, or South America. In China, in contrast, the company was doing extremely well and was essentially on an equal footing with or ahead of its main competitor, a US-based MNC.

The HQ initiative was categorized under new product/service introduction (see Table 6.1), an initiative that is more frequent according to the data. Both subsidiaries were somewhat successful in rejecting the initiative but not without dramatic effects. In both cases, subsidiary general managers (GMs) were replaced during the course of the rejection process. Although the dismissals could not be directly related to the actual rejections there seemed to be some sort of correlation. In addition, in China, while the local subsidiary was able to reject the initiative, headquarters established a separate system solution company that operated independently from Z-Corp China.

Literal and theoretical replication (phase 3)

The results from the exploratory fieldwork showed that HQ initiatives are very diverse and that the complexity of individual company environments might limit the generalizability of results that are based on single-company case studies. We therefore followed Parkhe's (1993) recommendation to conduct a "literal" replication study. The goal was to identify research sites that were as similar as possible to the comparative case study in the expectation that they would yield similar results (Parkhe 1993).

We selected global corporations that included those with significant operations in terms of size and number, ideally on all major continents, and which pursued a global strategy (Porter 1998) in gaining competitive advantage by operating internationally (Kobrin 1991). We followed Birkinshaw's (1996) logic that larger and established subsidiaries are more important to MNCs than smaller subsidiaries with limited mandates. The reason was that the exploratory phase of our research showed that younger and smaller subsidiaries tend to be more reliant on HQ support than larger and well-established subsidiaries. In addition, HQ initiatives were usually not as frequent or diverse here, because smaller subsidiaries often only have limited scope. Those subsidiaries were typically concerned with market penetration, not profitability (Birkinshaw 1995). Also, smaller subsidiaries appeared to have only limited internal and external power compared to larger subsidiaries.

We conducted 52 interviews with 38 individual managers during the replication stage of this research (see appendix 1 for details on the companies and individuals). The average company tenure of HQ managers was more than

17 years. The average company tenure for subsidiary GMs was 12 years. In most cases, we were able to speak to either an HQ CEO or business unit vice president and, additionally, to some functional department managers who could provide information about the individual initiative rejection process under investigation.

One imperative of this study was an emphasis on data reliability and integrity (Jick 1979; Miles and Huberman 1994). We therefore made sure that we had access to data from multiple sources for the main research sites. This allowed triangulation, an important step to enhance data reliability and integrity (Eisenhardt 1989). Overall, the design of the study, the data collection process and the subsequent analysis and interpretation aimed to meet the five criteria of credibility, transferability, dependability, conformability and authenticity, as laid out by Guba and Lincoln (1989) for this type of research.

Data analyses

First, we looked at the antecedents to rejection, then at the conflict processes, and finally at the outcomes. What became clear was that we had to account for asymmetries in the perceptions of HQ managers and subsidiary managers. One problem encountered was that the objective goals of the HQ initiatives were often not aligned with the subsidiaries' perceptions of HQ initiative intentions. On the other hand, the reasons for initiative rejections by subsidiaries were often not understood by headquarters. At first we struggled with this issue, but later it became clear that these perception asymmetries are a central construct. In addition, we found support for the supposition that HQ initiative rejection is a far more common phenomenon than suggested by the amount of existing research on the headquarters–subsidiary relationship.

One of the primary goals of this study was to build theory in the context of MNC headquarters–subsidiary conflict. We therefore looked for parallels across cases, especially during the final coding rounds. We looked for words, patterns and themes, and collected quotes in coding sheets, to identify similarities between cases and to evaluate relationships, their relevance and strength. We sorted the data by their sequential occurrence during the HQ initiative rejection process. We collected quotes in coding sheets manually and later used NVivo 8, a software program for qualitative data analysis, to connect the emerging constructs and to evaluate relationships, their relevance and strength. During the different rounds of the iterative data analyses and literature reviews, we gradually refined our coding. Two different sets of overarching reasons emerged, suggesting why HQ product or service introductions faced subsidiary rejection. The first is related to local competitiveness and implementation limitations and were explicitly mentioned by the interviewees. Arguments here appeared to be fact based and not so much built on individual opinions or emotions. The second category was less explicit, but still clearly observable and included perceived negative effects of HQ initiatives on the decision-making autonomy of subsidiaries.

Engaging in conflict

One condition set for the case selections was that the initiative rejection processes had to involve organizational conflicts. Comments like, "there is conflict all the time," or "conflict is a reality," or "when you want to push ahead, you often step on someone's toes," were recorded during most of the interviews. Interestingly, when we referred to conflict between headquarters and subsidiaries, none of the interviewees showed signs of personal discomfort. This supports Dörrenbächer and Geppert's (2006) argument that headquarters–subsidiary conflict is indeed a normal consequence of organizing across borders.

Threat to global competitiveness

Research on managerial goal expectation divergence in MNCs found considerable differences between functions, between different actors of individual departments, and between different organizational subunits, including headquarters and foreign subsidiaries (Brockhoff 1998). While foreign subsidiaries are mainly concerned with their own performance assessment, subsidiary performance is ultimately evaluated by HQ management. However, local constraints, including different laws or differences in market characteristics, require a different set of performance goals than those headquarters can incorporate during the goal formation process (Doz and Prahalad 1984).

Another potential source for divergent interests is differences in planning horizons (Kaufmann and Rössing 2005). Subsidiary management has an incentive to maximize profit and sales in the short run at the subsidiary level, and to re-invest some of these short-term profits in order to improve long-term local competitiveness. HQ management is more interested in achieving overall MNC performance and in extracting subsidiary profits, in transferring them back to the corporate level, and ultimately in distributing them according to its own discretion.

Additional problems arise, especially when expectations with regard to strategic goals are not easily quantifiable in a manner acceptable to both the subsidiary and headquarters (Prahalad and Doz 1987), or when they are not made explicit. It is therefore common that headquarters and foreign subsidiaries set their own diverging expectations, especially in situations where headquarters–subsidiary relationships are already somewhat tense (Taggart 1999). Prahalad and Doz (1987) found that in these situations, even if differences in expectations are detected, communication is usually limited or inefficient. The latter might be particularly true in the case where sources of divergent expectations are amplified by conflicting demands for global integration and local responsiveness (Taggart 1999).

Goal incompatibility

Our fieldwork supported the notion that conflicts between MNC headquarters and their foreign subsidiaries most often arise when the global integration tasks of the MNC as a whole are incompatible with the local goals of the subsidiary (Bartlett and Ghoshal 1989; Kaufmann and Rössing 2005).

In the case of B-Corp, for example, headquarters pushed strongly for the adoption of the new technology through a new product line. It was expected that all subsidiaries would immediately roll out the new products. However, B-Corp Japan rejected the initiative successfully, though at the expense of a lengthy conflict. B-Corp headquarters was not happy with the pushback and decided to force B-Corp Japan to implement the new product. Over a period of 48 months, a series of meetings took place, both in Japan and at the corporate headquarters in the USA, but neither side wanted to give in. Evidence of conflict included heightened levels of frustration, including comments about the long negotiation process and the ongoing rejection by the B-Corp Japan management. The process was complicated and distracting. Ultimately the product has never been sold in the Japanese market.

Perception gaps

Aside from differences in expectations, headquarters–subsidiary conflict also arises because of perception gaps between the two (Birkinshaw *et al.* 2000; Bouquet and Birkinshaw 2008). Birkinshaw *et al.* (2000) argued that three sets of factors seem to create perception gaps between MNC headquarters and their foreign subsidiaries. These factors include differences in the level of information provided and differences in the level of perception regarding variations in the dependence of subsidiaries on headquarters (Birkinshaw *et al.*, 2000). Recent research showed that perception gaps often lead to dysfunctional conflict (Asakawa 2001; Birkinshaw *et al.* 2000; Holm *et al.* 1995). Chini *et al.* (2005) pointed out that identifying perception gaps might be the most critical HQ coordination task involved in improving and sustaining overall MNC performance.

The fieldwork suggested that perception gaps are common and handling them appears to be complex due to the ongoing evolution of the individual subsidiaries, the changes in the external environments, and the transformation of the MNC as a whole. For example, at A-Corp headquarters management at first did not understand why the subsidiary did not want to implement the new product. While carrying a strong global brand identity, A-Corp operated more as a network, instead of a top-down hierarchical organization.

In the case of Z-Corp USA, headquarters assumed that the subsidiary managers should be favorable to the value-added product initiative since the subsidiary already manufactured systems. What headquarters did not understand was that Z-Corp USA was not ready to build or sell standardized systems in volume for the North American market. This part of the market was a completely different business compared to the system solutions Z-Corp USA was building at the time.

Threat to decision-making authority

Another reason headquarters engaged in conflict was that the subsidiary pushback was perceived as a threat to HQ decision-making authority. This was especially the case for more hierarchically organized firms. In the case of I-Corp and Z-Corp China, the perceived threat to decision-making authority was personal. Here, the corporate CEOs saw the pushback as a threat to their individual decision-making authority. Interestingly, in both cases, the corporate CEOs were either 100 percent owners, or the largest individual shareholders. Personal reasons were relatively easy to identify in the case of Z-Corp China, since the CEO made this very explicit.

In the I-Corp case, the signs were subtler. In fact, the interview with the corporate CEO at first did not provide much insight at all. Only after we repeatedly revisited the issue and later checked other data sources, including internal e-mails and interviews with other managers at I-Corp, could we identify that there was reason to believe that the corporate CEO saw his decision-making authority threatened.

Communication problems

The data also provided evidence that communication problems create head-quarters–subsidiary conflicts. This hardly seems surprising, but effective inter-unit communication is one of the most often cited conditions required for MNCs to achieve satisfactory performance (Ghoshal *et al.* 1994). Even though scholars, practitioners and consultants focus on improving communication and provide ready-made and custom solutions, these problems are still very common. During the fieldwork, we found that communication problems that caused headquarters–subsidiary conflict were not structural. All organizations had somewhat efficient reporting and communication procedures and tools. Communication problems seemed to be generated at the individual managerial level by either senders or recipients.

The fieldwork showed that in some cases initiatives were not communicated in a way that made sense to the subsidiaries. Also, when intermediaries were involved in the communication process critical issues would get misinterpreted. For example, in the case of E-Corp, the corporate CEO was not involved in the execution of the initiative or the day-to-day coordination, but insisted that critical decisions must be presented to him before they would be decided. The problem was that the HQ-based product managers who were to coordinate the implementation did not have the authority to force the subsidiary to follow their instructions. In the end, everything had to be referred back to the corporate CEO, who did not want to deal with operational issues directly. This situation was frustrating for the subsidiary GM.

Negative effects on HQ control and coordination ability

In two of the cases, we could find evidence that headquarters did not accept the initiative rejection because the rejection would have had negative effects on the ability of headquarters to coordinate the exploitation of products or services across borders. In the case of F-Corp, the main objective for introducing the new insurance products was improving the firm's global presence in the insurance market. The regional office was put in charge of reducing the number of product groups across the Asian markets. F-Corp's HQ management argued that the portfolio was too diverse and that some of the subsidiaries were not focusing on the insurance business because they were distracted by other, non-core business activities, as was the case with F-Corp Japan's retirement investment business. Headquarters felt that if they allowed F-Corp Japan to resist the new insurance products, their ability to coordinate their global products would be compromised. We argue that if subsidiaries reject HQ initiatives that have the goal to improve HQ coordination effectiveness, HQ managers will likely not consent to the rejection, even if the process creates conflict between headquarters and the subsidiaries. The following propositions were developed:

> **Proposition 1**: Headquarters are more likely to engage in intra-organizational conflict if HQ product/service initiative rejections by foreign subsidiaries are perceived to negatively affect one or more of the following variables: (a) global competitiveness of the MNC as a whole, (b) HQ decision-making authority, and (c) HQ coordination effectiveness.

> **Proposition 2**: HQ initiative rejections by foreign subsidiaries are more likely to cause conflict when one of the following is true: (a) perception gaps between headquarters and subsidiaries exist about the reasons for and/or implications of the initiatives, and (b) communication problems between headquarters and their foreign subsidiaries exist.

During the fieldwork, it became evident that conflict outcomes depended on the dominant characteristics of specific conflict processes. As a response to the question by the executive cited in the introduction of this research, we suggest that positive and negative rejection/conflict outcomes depend not so much on context, but primarily on the process of initiative rejection and how conflict is managed.

Conflict types

At the start of the fieldwork, no signs were found that a specific headquarters–subsidiary relationship was dysfunctional when the individual initiatives were introduced. The same could be confirmed for the individual managerial relationships on both sides, though it would be naive to assume that the sample possessed similar corporate structure, managerial characteristics and relationships.

However, in situations where MNCs possess coordination mechanisms that allow pushback by subsidiaries, and where headquarters allow consultation of subsidiary management, the initiative rejection processes can be positive, without the disruptive effects of conflict (Rahim 2000). Here, conflict can potentially lead to significantly improved solutions that may or may not end up with initiative implementation. This, for example, was the case in some of the companies whose managers were interviewed during the exploratory stage of the research (phase 1). In the following section we look more closely at the different conflict types including task, process and relational conflict following Jehn and Mannix's (2001) logic.

Task conflict

It was evident in all cases that the initial rejections and the conflict initiation points were based on task or process-related arguments. All interviewees unanimously agreed that some level of discourse was beneficial for the effective operation of the MNCs. All interviewees reported examples when decisions were revised or products improved based on task conflict. We argue that task conflict improves performance through a synthesis of diverse perspectives and an increased bilateral understanding. The vice president of financial control at F-Corp, for example, stated:

We take great pride in having a very diverse company culture. This is somewhat unique, but everybody accepts that there are other opinions. Don't get me wrong, not everything here gets sugarcoated and we do not always agree. In fact, our culture allows for disagreement. What makes a difference is that at the end we focus on the task on hand and not on personal bickering.

At A-Corp similar evidence was found. The head of global HR stated:

I guess A-Corp attracts people that enjoy discourse. We do not see it necessarily as bad. Those individuals who add little value to a specific issue and only play politics usually are weeded out quickly.

This evidence also supported the findings from conflict research in other fields that certain levels of task conflict improve organizational performance (Amason and Schweiger 1994; Jehn and Mannix 2001). We therefore argue that when headquarters and subsidiaries engage in task conflict, higher-quality outcomes can be expected, while conflict avoidance lacks this process and consequently leads to suboptimal outcomes.

Relational conflict

During the fieldwork, it was possible to identify certain events that triggered relational conflict. For example, in the case of Z-Corp China, when the subsidiary GM eliminated the project manager from the invitation list at a trade show, the conflict became relational. The relational aspects were not isolated to certain individual managers. Sides formed quickly. For example, the project manager immediately began to seek support from the chief sales officer at headquarters and from some of the more senior engineers. He stated:

I was blown away that Mr. X would do this. After all who is he to decide who attends a trade show that is important for Z-Corp International? Others have always told me that I have to be careful and that X has the ear of the CEO. I tried to find support here at HQ but WE really despised this cheap shot.

From the moment that coalitions started to form and communication was reduced, the subsidiary GM used his relationship with the CEO to discredit the pro-initiative coalition. This was a somewhat risky move, since the CEO was the one who had initiated the project. The conflict dragged on for six years, and despite the fact that headquarters–subsidiary project meetings often began with a task or process-oriented agenda, relational issues were always present.

   In the case of D-Corp, the regional VP pushed the relational issues. While he had personal reasons to improve his own legitimacy at headquarters, he used dysfunctional measures to achieve this. For example, the subsidiary GM was no longer allowed to discuss strategic issues, as well as most operational issues, directly with headquarters. This included issues that were not connected with the initiative. The regional VP also started to interfere in day-to-day operations of the subsidiary. In addition, he often summoned the subsidiary GM for meetings on Friday afternoons at the regional office in Singapore, even though the meetings were either not relevant for the China operation or only lasted 45 minutes and could have easily been handled by a conference call. These meetings easily took a day out of the subsidiary GM's schedule and he often would not be able to fly back until the next day. The subsidiary GM stated:

He (the regional VP) made things really difficult for me. I tried to get along but there was this spitefulness. I resented it. Whenever possible I tried to avoid the guy. I hoped that I could use my contacts at HQ to get him off our backs but I guess his contacts were even better. The whole thing still did not make sense from a business perspective.

In all cases where relational conflict was evident, it quickly escalated and an individual manager was affected. It appears that MNC headquarters–subsidiary relationships are more vulnerable when relational conflict emerges, as compared to settings where the conflict parties are more inter-connected and/or co-located and have to sort things out in order to work on a day-to-day basis. In the case of I-Corp, managerial change came quickly. In fact, the corporate CEO was fired shortly after the final interview was conducted (although not because of it). The firing was the result of a poorly prepared tradeshow and the fact that the majority shareholders of the company had lost trust in him. The subsidiary GM took over as corporate CEO. He stated:

The CEO and I had a history from the old days. I was prepared to put things aside for the good of the company, but I could not have him push this project through. I used some underground tactics. I tried to discredit him a little, just a little. I mean I never said anything that was not true! It surprised me though that they would kick him out. I just wanted him to let us do our thing. In the end, it was the CEO's own fault I guess. He always had those 30,000 feet high ideas, which were great. He was really bad at executing though. He did not have any key account lined up for meetings with our VCs [venture capital firms] during the show. My guys had 50 meetings in 3 days. That says it all!

Overall, we found evidence that relational conflict increases the duration of the conflict process, and reduces both focus and resources from task or process issues.

Interestingly, management changes took place in the six cases with the highest levels of relational conflict. The management changes altered the overall conflict orientation in most cases, except for the Z-Corp China and the G-Corp cases, where the new subsidiary GMs picked up where their predecessors left off. Both of these managers were outsiders to the firm, without any HQ experience. This was different in the D-Corp, E-Corp, and Z-Corp USA cases. Here, the new managers had either extensive previous experience at the corporate headquarters of their respective parent companies, or at headquarters of their previous employers.

Process conflict

Process conflict seemed to increase when both conflict parties had accepted that the other conflict party had valid task-oriented arguments. Process conflict appeared to be part of the conflict resolution process. For example, in the case of A-Corp, the new bandage product was rejected right from the beginning. Later, both headquarters and the subsidiary agreed on the middle ground. The initiative was put on hold, and a joint task force was formed that ultimately led to a repositioning of the product for the Canadian market. During that process, discussions were intense and at times seemed to lead nowhere as one A-Corp marketing manager recalled:

When we put the task force together we still had intensive discussion and tempers were flying high. Our goal was still to reject the product. Once we got a break from HQ we somewhat worked more towards a way to make it happen. Still HQ had to understand that the market here in Canada was different.

In the case of F-Corp, the subsidiary GM recognized early that he had to find a way to satisfy HQ's goals. Instead of focusing on building a rejection strategy around product–market fit arguments and subsidiary independence, he complied with the new reporting tool before focusing on the specific product rejection. Once they were in place and the subsidiary showed compliance, the subsidiary used the reporting tools to build their case. The subsidiary GM stated:

I knew that HQ was concerned with all the different local subsidiary strategies globally. Also, our finance VP here at the subsidiary, who just recently joined us from HQ, confirmed that they are really focused on streamlining things. The product change still did not make sense for Japan. We tried to get around it by beating them with their own weapon. We used the reporting tool, showed compliance, but also built a strong case for our product mix. Although it required some tough negotiating, in the end we had a great win–win situation.

In organizations that perform well, process conflict at an early stage allows work norms and interaction procedures to be agreed upon and to improve inter-organizational understanding. The focus is on responsibilities and deadlines, the pacing of tasks, and planning to meet resource requirements (Jehn and Mannix 2001). Experienced managers seem to understand this and build their rejection arguments on those issues. For example, the Z-Corp USA GM stated:

Often there is no point in arguing with the individual department managers at HQ. They have their mandates. The bigger issues have to be battled out with the big boss. However, if we can agree on processes with the department managers we might be able to come to a mutual agreement. Don't get me wrong, we still have to fight for our position. Often it is more the "how" question that must be answered rather than the "if" question.

The underlying notion here is that once conflicting parties agree on how and when tasks will be completed, positive outcomes can be expected. If the parties do not agree to those responsibilities, process conflict has the potential to delay conflict resolution. For example, in the case of I-Corp, the corporate CEO and the subsidiary GM could not agree on how to implement the project. The subsidiary CEO was not against the initiative in general, he simply did not want to start working on it right away, because other platform tools had to be finished first, and the subsidiary's developers were completely occupied with other tasks. In contrast, the corporate CEO wanted to start right away:

I believe our platform tool is phenomenal and we should try to push it out for all platforms right from the beginning. I do not understand why he (the subsidiary GM) does not want to allocate resources to it. He should be able to hire more developers easily.

At I-Corp, process conflict led to negative conflict effects. We further argue that while task conflict is beneficial, and relational conflict is generally negative, process conflict has the potential to be either positive or negative. Based on the previous discussion, the following proposition was developed:

> **Proposition 3**: Positive or negative conflict outcomes depend on the levels of task, process and relationship orientation during the conflict process. Any kind of relational conflict between MNC headquarters and their subsidiary likely leads to negative outcomes. Positive outcomes are most likely if task conflict dominates the conflict process.

Conflict tactics

One of the primary goals of this study was to build theory in the context of MNC headquarters–subsidiary conflict. We therefore looked for general patterns across cases, especially during the final coding rounds. We specifically looked for words, patterns, and themes and collected quotes in coding sheets, to identify similarities between cases and to evaluate relationships, their relevance and strength. Several overarching themes emerged, which significantly affected the conflict processes. These themes were not always explicitly observable but became transparent during the data coding process.

We summarized these themes under the term "tactics," which refers to subsidiary behaviors that arise during headquarters–subsidiary conflicts and are most closely related to organizational politics and the organizational power concept (Pfeffer 1981) that underlies resource dependency theory (Pfeffer and Salancik 1978). Tactics, as the name suggests, are practices that subsidiaries deploy to negotiate the rejection with headquarters. The final set of tactics included "ignoring," "distracting," "shifting emphasis," "ceremonial adoption," "obstructing" and "attack."

The development of these second-order themes was whenever possible based on existing literature, like in the case of ceremonial adoption (Meyer and Rowan 1977). In other more implicit cases we used labels that best described the underlying conflict behaviors. Independent coders were used in all cases to verify our initial labeling. Whenever there were discrepancies between the different coders, we brought both groups together to agree on the best matching label. For example, ignoring was at first labeled "staying under the radar," but the iterative coding process led to the term "ignoring," which captures better the passive characteristics of the behaviors grouped under this label. The term "obstructing," which replaced the term "stonewalling," was later adopted based on reviewer feedback. Whenever necessary we went back to the data sources on both sides to confirm whether or not we captured the essence of the actual process with our labeling. In our final report, we only included those tactics that were confirmed on both sides of the headquarters–subsidiary dyads.

During the fieldwork, it became evident that different types of subsidiaries behaved differently in the deployment of tactics during HQ initiative rejection processes. The first type could be characterized as functional task and process-oriented subsidiaries with a stronger sense of belonging to the MNC as a whole. Here, HQ initiatives were not regarded as threats to the organizational subunit or their individual managers. Both initiative rejection and conflict were task and process-oriented and seemed to lead to above average organizational effectiveness. Other subsidiaries exhibited different levels of dysfunctional conflict behaviors. These included what we call "ignoring," "shifting emphasis," "ceremonial adoption," "obstructing" and "attacking." Table 6.2 summarizes the characteristics of the dysfunctional tactics.

Ignoring

Some of the subsidiaries in the sample ignored HQ initiatives. They conducted business as usual, as though the initiatives were not relevant to them. Typically, they avoided discussions concerning the initiatives, and when someone from headquarters inquired, they would not respond. These subsidiaries did not rely extensively on HQ support for their day-to-day business, and were not at the center of HQ attention. In these cases, headquarters were busy dealing with other, larger, or strategically more important subsidiaries. While some subsidiaries continued using the ignoring tactic for a long time,

Table 6.2 Characteristics of dysfunctional rejection tactics

	Ignoring	Ceremonial adoption	Shifting emphasis	Obstructing	Attacking
Rejection behavior	Ignoring instructions or enquiries Otherwise business as usual No active push back No initiative implementation	Pretending to follow up on all HQ instructions Report some progress Prepare some brochures Some production preparation	Subsidiary launches other, unrelated initiative Raise other ongoing issues Report unrelated product successes	No follow-up on initiative Holding back of requested information Blocking access to subsidiary and/or local market for HQ managers	Active dismissing of initiative Very explicit rejection often paired with personal attacking of key HQ personnel Threat of negative consequences
HQ reaction	No response, no active follow-up on rejection	Routine enquiries as part of global implementation efforts No visits	Active follow-up Regular HQ manager visits	Active follow-up Regular HQ manager visits	Active follow-up Attempts to convince subsidiary Early involvement of top management in conflict process
Relational conflict	Low	Low	Low to medium	Medium to high	High
MNC structure/	Hierarchical	Hierarchical	Hierarchical or network	Hierarchical or network	Hierarchical or network
HQ–subsidiary relationship	Medium to high sub. autonomy	Medium to high sub. autonomy	Medium sub. autonomy	Medium to high sub. autonomy	High sub. autonomy
Relative subsidiary importance	Low	Medium	Medium to high	Medium to high	Medium to high
Level of integration	Low	Low	Low to medium	Low to high	Low to high
Contribution to MNC revenue	Low to medium	Low to medium	Low to high	Medium to high	High
Subsidiary growth potential	Low to medium	Low to medium	Low to medium	Medium to high	High
Relative subsidiary power	Low to medium	Low to medium	Low to high	Medium to high	High
Sub. GM power	Low to medium	Low to medium	Low to high	High	High

it was mostly used during the early stages of HQ initiative rejection processes. A marketing manager at B-Corp's headquarters recalled:

We totally forgot about Japan at the beginning. They did not raise the issue and we were so busy with China, Germany and the rest of Europe that we did not notice that they kind of disappeared on us.

Similar behaviors could be observed at C-Corp. Here the subsidiary GM stated:

I knew that HQ was so busy with the global launch, especially in all the large markets like the US and Europe that they would not get to us right away. I wanted to buy time. I had to! If we had been more active, it would have cost us badly I believe. I tried to avoid running into the project manager whenever I was at HQ. I expected that I would have to answer their questions one day but that day was hopefully much later.

Most subsidiaries that ignored an HQ initiative found they could not do so indefinitely. Headquarters would eventually become aware of the ignoring tactic and would then push harder for initiative implementation. However, as in the case of C-Corp, the initiative faced so much resistance from other subsidiaries that the ignoring tactic worked until headquarters finally canceled the initiative. When HQ pressured subsidiaries to implement initiatives, and ignoring was no longer an option, subsidiaries used other tactics including shifting emphasis.

Shifting emphasis

Once the rejection process manifested, some subsidiaries used distraction tactics to avoid initiative implementation. For example, in the case of Z-Corp China, the subsidiary urged headquarters to develop a new component for transport cooling, completely unrelated to the system solution initiative launched by headquarters. The subsidiary GM advocated the market potential for such a component to the corporate CEO, and engaged HQ engineers to encourage enthusiasm. The subsidiary GM even made sure that the HQ engineers, when they travelled to China, would meet with customers for transport-cooling equipment instead of customers and engineers who would be relevant for the system solutions initiative. However, the transport-cooling component was a major R&D activity that would require substantial resources, and would take years to materialize.

At G-Corp, the subsidiary GM also used shifting emphasis as a rejection tactic. Instead of a product diversion, the G-Corp subsidiary GM made facility relocation a top priority. For a period of six months, every time the product initiative came up during meetings with HQ managers, he would quickly raise the relocation issue. As one HQ executive stated:

At first I did not know where the relocation issue came from. All of a sudden, we were negotiating with banks about financing and our architects got involved. Some people started to rewrite marketing materials and mission statements. Nobody was focusing on products anymore. The board got all excited about having a building in California that would show features of our new HQ facility here in Germany.

Shifting emphasis created less explicit relational conflict, as compared to obstructing. Nonetheless, shifting emphasis engaged more individuals in managing issues unrelated to the actual initiative. This tactic resulted in inefficiency and, at various junctures, caused frustration for HQ managers. One of Z-Corp's HQ product managers recalled a meeting with the subsidiary GM, the corporate CEO and the R&D director at headquarters. This meeting was originally scheduled to discuss the value-added product initiative:

I was prepared to finally go through the system solution project and to come to an implementation agreement when I arrived that morning. But by the time we wrapped up for lunch everybody was talking about transport cooling again. All in a sudden we were talking about manufacturing products in China that we hadn't even developed. I was pissed off to say the least.

Ceremonial adoption

Ceremonial adoption refers to practices that appeared to, but in actuality did not, produce direct organizational improvements (Meyer and Rowan 1977). Ceremonial adoption had similar effects to non-adoption, with the added feature of having wasted implementation resources. It could, however, be considered more effective if its negative effects were lower than a more explicit rejection tactic such as obstructing, or attacking, which is discussed later. Ceremonial adoption was an option for those subsidiaries that had relatively low levels of power, but relatively high levels of autonomy. Ceremonial adoption might be chosen in a cultural context where an inclination toward conflict avoidance is high, as in the case of many Asian cultures.

Ceremonial adoption is a controversial method of dealing with conflict, as it attempts to avoid directly confronting the issue at hand. Ceremonial adoption can be used as a temporary measure to buy time, or as a permanent means of sidestepping an issue. The latter may be indistinguishable from simple compliance to the extent that the party avoiding the conflict subordinates its own wishes to the other conflict party.

Ceremonial adoption was observed at B-Corp and C-Corp. In both cases, the tactic was used after the initial tactics that included ignoring and obstructing were no longer successful. At B-Corp, ceremonial adoption included the preparation of Japanese language sales brochures and technical materials needed for the approval process with local authorities. The approval process, however, was not initiated, as one of B-Corp's HQ managers noted after visiting Japan:

We [HQ] were under the impression our colleagues in Japan were finally in the midst of the initiative implementation. After the initial lack of response, we finally received some of the Japanese brochures as samples. When I visited Japan six months later, I was also pleased to see that there were pictures of our promotional material from the US hung in the lobby. It looked good. The big surprise came when we met for our annual subsidiary meeting at HQ and all the subsidiaries had to provide a report about the implementation of the new elevator technology. The Japanese wrote a lot about their brochures and about how well they prepared the technical approval process, but real projects were not mentioned. During my next trip to Japan I was surprised to see all these brochures and manuals untouched. It looked like the project never really got off the ground. My Japanese colleagues assured me that this was not the case but that they were in fact just waiting for the approval of the authorities. Later I learned that the approval process was never actively pursued. It was all smoke and mirrors!

At C-Corp, the subsidiary appeared to obey HQ instructions. A delivery of promotional materials and a small batch of Z-line products were accepted. However, both the materials and the products never made it into the company's stores. The subsidiary's marketing manager stated:

We know that the Z-line was not right for us and I heard through the grapevine that the initial sales figures from Europe and the US were disappointing. We were hoping that the Z-line would just die before we had to act. However, at one point we had to comply – HQ was getting pushy. It was late in the season and we did not use the marketing materials at all. Although, I have to say the Z-line promotional materials were a nice touch when we finally dumped the product at our local factory outlet store.

Obstructing

Obstructing differed from ignoring in that it created intense relational conflicts. Obstructing involved ignoring an initiative, despite substantial retaliatory pressure from headquarters. Here subsidiary and HQ management clashed over the HQ initiative rejection. Conflict became less task or process-oriented. Obstructing was only possible at those subsidiaries that had a greater level of independence from headquarters. Obstructing included non-response behavior, as one HQ director of G-Corp stated:

It is extremely difficult to get hold of our GM over there. It appears that all e-mail related to the new products ends in his spam folder. I also can't reach him by phone. This is frustrating to say the least. I also can't talk to anybody else over there. They all say that it is the GM who handles the initiative.

The case of B-Corp Japan showed similar behaviors, as one HQ marketing executive recalled:

They were just not answering anything about the new product. We did not get an implementation schedule, just some marketing figures that referred to some customers having no interest in the product.

Z-Corp China was also obstructing the HQ initiative by not allowing HQ managers access to the local market or to, for example, local subsidiary engineers who would be important for initiative implementation. Similar to the ignoring tactic, obstructing was used at the early stages of the rejection process.

Attacking

Attacking is essentially the opposite of ceremonial adoption. Some of the cases had high levels of relational conflict originating from the subsidiaries. Z-Corp China, I-Corp and D-Corp were most prominent. All three of these cases were characterized by relational conflict that was more intense and inter-personal than in the other cases. Here, powerful subsidiary GMs attempted to derail the initiative by attacking and discrediting HQ and/or project managers.

In the Z-Corp and the I-Corp cases, this was a dangerous tactic, since the initiatives were priority projects of the respective corporate CEOs. At D-Corp, the regional manager took personal ownership over the project, and the considerable power he possessed made the case very similar to Z-Corp China and I-Corp.

The subsidiary GM at Z-Corp targeted a GM at another subsidiary who was very supportive of the HQ initiative. Owing to his expertise, this GM was part of the global initiative development and implementation team. The attack on this other GM was not direct at first, but the Z-Corp China GM was blackmailing this particular manager during his daily telephone briefings with the CEO. The Z-Corp China GM was also trying to seek alliances with other HQ managers who were skeptical about the initiative. For example, the vice president R&D was known to be critical with regard to the system solution initiative. He also enjoyed trips to China, and subsequently received and accepted many invitations by the Z-Corp China GM. During these visits, the Z-Corp China GM would vigorously attempt to discredit the initiative and the individual members of the project team. At I-Corp, the subsidiary GM used a similar tactic. He lobbied against the issue to some of the major non-managing shareholders of the company. He stated:

Sure, I use everything possible to make this stupid idea go away. It is critical that I have to get the shareholders on my side. We will see what happens at the next board meeting, but I'm sure it won't be pretty.

The D-Corp subsidiary GM employed a less aggressive approach. He used forecasts, market statistics and arguments based on implementation impediments caused by local regulations to discredit the project. The GM made an effort to minimize explicit relational conflict. However, he was aware that his strategy was aimed at hurting the regional manager's credibility:

I just wanted him to get off my back. This initiative was not right. I tried first to explain this in a more cooperative way, by going through the regional office. Ultimately I felt I had to go straight to HQ. I had to do it.

In all three cases, the conflict ended when one of the key actors was dismissed. In the case of Z-Corp China, the subsidiary GM had alienated so many HQ managers that a functional headquarters–subsidiary relationship was no longer possible. When, a year later, the subsidiary's performance showed signs of weakness, he was dismissed. At D-Corp, the subsidiary GM was also dismissed, thereby ending the conflict. In the case of I-Corp, events unfolded differently. The corporate CEO was fired during a board meeting following a poorly prepared trade show. The subsidiary GM was then promoted to corporate CEO. Interestingly, in all cases, the subsidiary management was united behind the respective subsidiary GM. This provides evidence that powerful individuals within organizations should be explicitly included in the analysis of strategic decision-making (Eisenhardt and Zbaracki 1992). The various tactics also reflected differences in organizational power, consistent with resource dependency theory (Pfeffer 1981). Figure 6.3 illustrates how the relative level of power of a subsidiary relates to the likelihood of the use of different tactics.

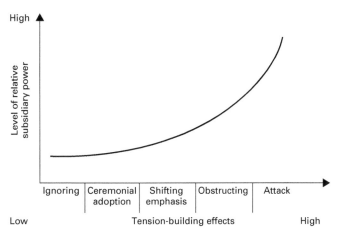

Fig. 6.3   Relationship between subsidiary power and the use of tactics

The relationship is depicted as curvilinear due to the requirement for increasing tension building or relational tactics in order for the subsidiary to defend its position against headquarters. The probability of using right-hand-side tactics increases with subsidiary power. Thus, in quantitative terms, the graph depicts a probability density function, not a direct relationship.

Conclusion, contributions and future research

Our research contributes to theory and practice in several ways. By focusing on the headquarters–subsidiary dyad, it avoided a bias toward one perspective, which is a common limitation of prior MNC headquarters–subsidiary conflict research. For management theory and international business research, new insights were developed by extending resource dependency theory. Data gathered during the fieldwork allowed for multiple theoretical interpretations, each explaining different parts of the phenomenon.

The investigation into conflict antecedents showed that despite their subordinate position in the MNC hierarchy, foreign subsidiaries regularly create conflict by rejecting HQ initiatives. We found empirical support for the relevance of resource dependency theory (Pfeffer and Salancik 1978) to explain headquarters–subsidiary conflict as suggested by Mudambi and Pedersen (2007). Global integration initiatives are typically the result of managerial decisions related to the aggregated cross-border value-creation mandate of headquarters (Bartlett and Ghoshal 1989), or they are attempts to reduce organizational complexity in order to boost efficiency. Changes in resource dependency positions at the organizational subunit level are thus an unintended by-product of HQ initiatives, which in turn, increases the likelihood of rejection by subsidiaries. The results from the data analysis suggest that MNC headquarters do not intentionally launch initiatives with the goal to increase foreign subsidiaries' dependencies on headquarters, as often perceived by subsidiary management (see also Schmid and Daniel in this volume).

Several other important organizational insights emerged from the research. Less confrontational tactics, such as ignoring or ceremonial adoption were used by subsidiaries that had relatively higher levels of HQ dependency or in cases where headquarters were not dependent on those subsidiaries. Subsidiaries that were relatively more powerful and less dependent on HQ resources used more aggressive tactics, including obstructing or attacking.

Beyond the conclusions of prior research (Jehn and Mannix 2001; Menon et al. 1996), we found that relational conflict between MNC headquarters and foreign subsidiaries had deleterious consequences. When present, solving relational conflict was almost impossible. Relational conflict was often followed by the dismissal of the subsidiary GM. We argue that in the case of the MNC, while some organizational design characteristics such as formalization, functional and departmental interconnectedness, and cross-border organizational identity reduce the likelihood of relational conflict, the uniqueness of non-co-location in environmentally distinct contexts carries intrinsic coordination impediments that are seemingly impossible to overcome. Here, communication and cultural barriers rank highest. These two factors appeared to make it exceptionally difficult to solve relational conflict (see also Schmid and Daniel in this volume).

Our distinction between confrontational and non-confrontational tactics brings individual managerial actors more prominently into the picture. One could argue that the ways in which actors get involved politically is related to their personal interests and identities. For example, prior research (Dörrenbächer and Geppert 2009) has shown that some managers are more interested in an international career within the MNC, which leads to different approaches of socio-political strategizing, as compared to managers who are mainly interested in building their local careers and legitimacy in a specific host country. Therefore, one could argue that the reason behind why some managers seem not to fear being dismissed as a consequence of their active political behavior is the fact that these managers are highly sought-after experts or professionals, who can easily find jobs in other companies. Another explanation could be that managers differ in their political skills when bargaining with headquarters. Some are more diplomatic than others (see also chapter by Fenton-O'Creevy *et al.* in this volume).

While some of our propositions would also hold in a domestic setting, the international context in which this research is grounded creates a unique set of characteristics that make the MNC different from a domestic firm. In addition to cross-border effects such as currency and political risks, MNCs also have to deal with international differences in institutional and cultural settings. Further, MNCs must deal with international variations in the levels of host country development, social values, trust and ethics, and customer and employee characteristics and preferences. In a domestic setting where the different actors are co-located, these international problems do not typically emerge.

This research uncovered a substantial number of avenues for a wide stream of future research on headquarters–subsidiary conflict. The rich data that were gathered during the fieldwork, and the theoretical linkages developed during the data analysis, provide a foundation for this future research. First, we suggest that the validity and generalizability of the findings presented can be improved by using a (possibly longitudinal) survey approach on a larger sample. In addition, some of the more broadly developed themes, such as initiative rejection tactics, should be researched in more detail. Here, combining concepts from social network theory (Granovetter 1983) and structuration theory (Giddens 1984) at the organizational level, and micro foundations aspects at the managerial level (Felin and Foss 2005; Gavetti 2005; Salvato 2009) could increase our understanding of the dynamic nature of the global integration versus local responsiveness quandary. This study also provides some initial evidence for Blazejewski and Becker-Ritterspach's (see chapter in this volume) argument that longitudinal approaches lead to substantial advances in MNC headquarters–subsidiary conflict research. We agree with Blazejewski and Becker-Ritterspach that it is necessary to include both alternative theoretical and methodological orientations in future studies. Conflicts should be understood as multiphase processes and sequential relationships of the occurrences and effects of the different conflict phases. For example, the perceived reasons for conflict initiation influence actors' choices of conflict tactics, which, in turn, affect conflict outcomes at multiple levels (Blazejewki and Becker-Ritterspach), including the organizational, sub-organizational and actor level. We found some evidence for these sequential interdependencies when we analyzed the data from the comparative case study.

Further, a large sample analysis should have the goal of providing a managerial toolkit to help predict HQ initiative rejections by foreign subsidiaries. These could then be incorporated into an MNC management framework. Finally, future research should attempt to analyze the rejection phenomenon by comparing different home and host country configurations. While phase 2 of this research has an explicit comparative objective, a broader set of countries and an increase in the number of cases would be certainly desirable and should be the goal of subsequent research.

This research implicitly controlled for home and host country effects by investigating conflict based on US-headquartered or European-headquartered MNCs. However, it would be interesting to investigate how the cultural differences between different home and host countries would affect the result if this condition were relaxed. For example, during the fieldwork for this study we found initial support for the idea that non-USA-based MNC headquarters have to overcome a much higher legitimacy barrier with their USA-based subsidiaries than with subsidiaries located in other countries. This might be caused by the relative power positions, given the relative market size of the US subsidiaries compared to their non-USA headquarters. Future research should consider this idea.

Acknowledgement

This research was supported by the Engaging Emerging Markets Research Center at the Richard Ivey School of Business, University of Western Ontario.

REFERENCES

Amason, A. and H. Sapienza 1997. "The effects of top management team size and interaction norms on cognitive and affective conflict," *Journal of Management* 23: 496–516

Amason, A. and D. M. Schweiger 1994. "Resolving the paradox of conflict, strategic decision making, and organizational performance," *International Journal of Conflict Management* 5: 239–53

Asakawa, K. 2001. "Organizational tension in international R&D management – the case of Japanese firms," *Research Policy* 30: 735–57

Axelrod, R. 1970. *Conflict of Interest: A Theory of Divergent Goals with Applications to Politics.* Chicago, IL: Markham

Bartlett, C. A. 1986. "Building and managing the transnational: the new organizational challenge" in Porter (ed.) *Competition in Global Industries.* Boston, MA: Harvard Business School Press, pp. 367–99

Bartlett, C. A. and S. Ghoshal 1989. *Managing Across Borders: The Transnational Solution*. Boston, MA: Harvard Business School Press

Birkinshaw, J. M. 1995. "Entrepreneurship in multinational corporations: the initiative process in Canadian subsidiaries." Unpublished doctoral research, University of Western Ontario, London, Canada

1996. "How multinational subsidiary mandates are gained and lost," *Journal of International Business Studies* 27: 467–95

Birkinshaw, J. M. and N. Hood 1998. "Multinational subsidiary evolution: capability and charter change in foreign owned subsidiary companies," *Academy of Management Review* 23: 773–95

Birkinshaw, J. M. and A. J. Morrison 1995. "Configurations of strategy and structure in subsidiaries of multinational corporations," *Journal of International Business Studies* 26: 729–53

Birkinshaw, J. M., U. Holm, P. Thilenius and N. Arvidsson 2000. "Consequences of perception gaps in the headquarters–subsidiary relationship," *International Business Review* 9: 321–44

Birnik, A. 2007. "Cross-border integration in the multinational corporation: the subsidiary management perspective." Unpublished doctoral research, Cranfield University, Bedfordshire, UK

Boulding, E. K. 1962. *Conflict and Defense: A General Theory*. New York: Harper & Row

Bouquet, C. and J. M. Birkinshaw 2008. "Managing power in the multinational corporation: how low-power actors gain influence," *Journal of Management* 34: 477–508

Brock, D. M. and J. M. Birkinshaw 2004. "Multinational strategy and structure: a review and research agenda," *Management International Review* 44: 5–14

Brockhoff, K. 1998. *Internationalization of Research and Development*. Berlin: Springer

Burgelman, R. A. and Y. L. Doz 1996. "Complex strategic integration in the lean multi-business corporation." Unpublished Research Paper Series, INSEAD

Chini, T., B. Ambos and K. Wehle 2005. "The headquarters–subsidiaries trench: tracing perception gaps within the multinational corporation," *European Management Journal* 23: 145–53

Deutsch, M. 1973. *The Resolution of Conflict: Constructive and Destructive Processes*. New Haven, CT: Yale University Press

Dörrenbächer, C. and M. Geppert 2006. "Micro-politics and conflicts in multinational corporations: current debates, re-framing, and contributions of this Special Issue," *Journal of International Management* 12: 251–65

2009. "Micro-political games in the multinational corporation: the case of mandate change," *Management Revue* 20: 373–91

Doz, Y. L. and C. K. Prahalad 1984. "Patterns of strategic control within multinational corporations," *Journal of International Business Studies* 15: 55–72

1991. "Managing DMNCs: a search for a new paradigm," *Strategic Management Journal* 12: 145–64

Doz, Y. L., J. Santos and P. J. Williamson 2001. *From Global to Metanational: How Companies Win in the Knowledge Economy*. Boston, MA: Harvard Business School Press

Eisenhardt, K. M. 1989. "Building theory from case study research," *Academy of Management Review* 14: 532–50

Eisenhardt, K. M. and M. J. Zbaracki 1992. "Strategic decision making," *Strategic Management Journal* 13: 17–37

Felin, T. and N. J. Foss 2005. "Strategic organization: a field in search of micro-foundations," *Strategic Organization* 3: 441–55

Gavetti, G. 2005. "Cognition and hierarchy: rethinking the microfoundations of capabilities' development," *Organization Science* 16: 599–617

Ghemawat, P. 2007. "Managing differences: the central challenge of global strategy," *Harvard Business Review* 25: 1–12

Ghoshal, S. and N. Nohria 1993. "Horses for courses: organizational forms for multinational corporations," *Sloan Management Review* 34: 23–35

Ghoshal, S. and E. Westney 1993. *Organization Theory and the Multinational Corporation.* New York: St. Martin's Press

Ghoshal, S., H. Korine and G. Szulanski 1994. "Inter-unit communication in multinational corporations," *Management Science* 40: 96–110

Giddens, A. 1984. *The Constitution of Society.* Berkeley, CA: University of California Press

Glaser, B. G. and A. L. Strauss 1967. *The Discovery of Grounded Theory: Strategies for Qualitative Research.* New York: Aldine

Goold, M. 1996. "Parenting strategies for the mature business," *Long Range Planning* 29: 358–69

Granovetter, M. 1983. "The strength of weak ties: a network theory revisited," *Sociological Theory* 1: 201–33

Guba, E. and Y. Lincoln 1989. *Fourth Generation Evaluation.* Beverly Hills, CA: Sage

Holm, U., J. Johanson and P. Thilenius 1995. "Headquarters' knowledge of subsidiary network contexts in the multinational corporation," *International Studies of Management and Organization* 25: 97–119

Jehn, K. A. 1994. "Enhancing effectiveness: an investigation of advantages and disadvantages of value-based intra-group conflict," *International Journal of Conflict Management* 5: 223–38

1995. "A multi-method examination of the benefits and detriments of intra-group conflict," *Administrative Science Quarterly* 40: 256–82

Jehn, K. A. and E. A. Mannix 2001. "The dynamic nature of conflict: a longitudinal study of intra-group conflict and group performance," *Academy of Management Journal* 44: 238–51

Jehn, K. A. and P. Shah 1997. "Interpersonal relationships and task performance: an examination of mediating processes in friendship and acquaintance groups," *Journal of Personality and Social Psychology* 72: 775–90

Jehn, K. A., G. B. Northcraft and M. A. Neale 1999. "Why differences make a difference: a field study of diversity, conflict, and performance in workgroups," *Administrative Science Quarterly* 44: 741–63

Jemison, D. E. and S. B. Sitkin 1986. "Corporate acquisitions: a process perspective," *Academy of Management Review* 11: 145–63

Jick, T. D. 1979. "Mixing qualitative and quantitative methods: triangulation in action," *Administrative Science Quarterly* 24: 602–11

Kaufmann, L. and S. Rössing 2005. "Managing conflict of interests between headquarters and their subsidiaries regarding technology transfer to emerging markets: a framework," *Journal of World Business* 40: 235–53

Kobrin, S. J. 1991. "An empirical analysis of the determinants of global integration," *Strategic Management Journal* 12: 17–31

Kriesberg, L. 1973. *The Sociology of Social Conflict*. Engelwood Cliffs, NJ: Prentice Hall

Menon, A., S. G. Bharadwaj and R. Howell 1996. "The quality and effectiveness of marketing strategy: effects of functional and dysfunctional conflict in intraorganizational relationships," *Journal of the Academy of Marketing Science* 24: 299–313

Meyer, J. W. and B. Rowan 1977. "Institutionalized organizations: formal structure as myth and ceremony," *American Journal of Sociology* 82: 340–63

Miles, M. and A. M. Huberman 1994. *Qualitative Data Analysis: An Expanded Sourcebook*. Thousand Oaks, CA: Sage

Mudambi, R. and T. Pedersen 2007. "Agency theory and resource dependency theory: complementary explanations for subsidiary power in multinational corporations" in Pedersen and Volberda (eds.) *Bridging IB Theories, Constructs, and Methods Across Cultures and Social Science*. Basingstoke: Palgave-Macmillan

Naylor, T. H. 1985. "The international strategy matrix," *Columbia Journal of World Business* 20: 11–9

Osborne, M. J. and A. Rubinstein 1990. *Bargaining and Markets*. San Diego, CA: Academic Press Inc

Pahl, J. M. and K. Roth 1993. "Managing the headquarters–foreign subsidiary relationship: the roles of strategy, conflict, and integration," *International Journal of Conflict Management* 4: 139–65

Parkhe, A. 1993. "'Messy' research, methodological predispositions, and theory development in international joint ventures," *Academy of Management Review* 18: 227–68

Pelled, L. H. 1996. "Demographic diversity, conflict, and work group outcomes: an intervening process theory," *Organization Science* 7: 615–31

Pfeffer, J. 1981. *Power in Organizations*, Marshfield, MA: Pitman Publications

Pfeffer, J. and G. R. Salancik 1978. *The External Control of Organizations: A Resource Dependence Perspective*. New York, NY: Harper & Row

Pinkley, R. 1990. "Dimensions of the conflict frame: disputant interpretations of conflict," *Journal of Applied Psychology* 75: 117–28

Pondy, L. R. 1967. "Organizational conflict: concepts and models," *Administrative Science Quarterly* 12: 296–320
  1992. "Reflections on organizational conflict," *Journal of Organizational Behavior* 13: 257–61

Porter, M. E. 1998. "Competing across locations: enhancing competitive advantage through a global strategy" in Porter (ed.) *On Competition*. Boston, MA: Harvard Business School Press

Prahalad, C. K. and Y. L. Doz 1987. *The Multinational Mission: Balancing Local Demands and Global Vision*. New York, NY: Free Press

Rahim, M. A. 2000. *Managing Conflict in Organizations*. 3rd edn. Westport, CT: Quorum Books

Roth, K. and A. J. Morrison 1990. "An empirical analysis of the integration-responsiveness framework in global industries," *Journal of International Business Studies* 21: 541–64

Salvato, C. 2009. "Capabilities unveiled: the role of ordinary activities in the evolution of product development processes," *Organization Science* 20: 384–409

Suddaby, R. 2006. "From the editors: what grounded theory is not," *Academy of Management Journal* 49: 633–42

Taggart, J. H. 1999. "MNC subsidiary performance, risk, and corporate expectations," *International Business Review* 8: 233–55

Tasoluk, B., A. Yaprak and R. J. Calantone 2006. "Conflict and collaboration in headquarters–subsidiary relationships," *International Journal of Conflict Management* 17: 332–51

Thompson, J. D. 1967. *Organizations in Action*. New York, NY: Mc Graw-Hill

Weick, K. E. 1995. *Sensemaking in Organizations*. London: Sage

Williamson, O. E. 1981. "The modern corporation: origins, evolution, attributes," *Journal of Economic Literature* 19: 1537–68

Yin, R. K. 2003. *Case Study Research: Design and Methods*. 3rd edn. London: Sage

Appendix 1: Summary of main research sites (Phase 3)

Company	A-Corp	B-Corp	C-Corp	D-Corp	E-Corp	F-Corp	G-Corp	H-Corp	I-Corp
Industry	Healthcare	Industrial	Sporting goods	Logistica	Chemical prod.	Bank/insurance	Electronic	Healthcare	Software
Home region	North America	North America	North America	Europe	Europe	Europe	Europe	Europe	North America
No. of foreign subsidiaries	60	70	45	130	18	55	10	36	2
Size (revenue in USD)	25 billion	128 billion	18.6 billion	13.2 billion	1.8 billion	1.300 billion	1 billion	700 million	N/A
Size (staff)	78,000	64,000	30,000	91,000	6,000	125,000	2,500	3,700	175
Industry position	No. 1	No. 1	Top 3	Top 5	No. 1	Top 10	No. 1	No. 1	Top 3
Interviewee 1									
Position	Global Dep. VP	Global VP	Global Dep. VP	Regional VP	Fin. Exec.	Global BU CEO	VP Fin. Control.	Fin. Exec.	CEO
Nationality	Foreign	Home	Home	Home	Foreign	Home	Home	Home	Home
Tenure with MNC (years)	15	25	21	21	12	35	13	8	5
Position tenure (years)	3	14	9	2	6	15	3	5	5
Interviewee 2									
Position	R&D Manager	Mark. Executive				VP Finan. Contr.	Director	Tech. Sales Exec.	
Nationality	Host	Foreign				Home	Home	Foreign	
Tenure with MNC (years)	12	18				15	28	9	
Position tenure (years)	12	2				2	28	6	
Subsidiary									
Location	North America	Asia	Asia	Asia	Asia	Asia	North America	Asia	Asia
Age (years)	58	82	8	43	6	19	9	10	3

(cont.)

Company	A-Corp	B-Corp	C-Corp	D-Corp	E-Corp	F-Corp	G-Corp	H-Corp	I-Corp
Local mandate	Sales, marketing, R&D	Sales, marketing, R&D	Sales	Sales	Sales, marketing	Sales	Sales (future marketing)	Sales (limited marketing)	Sales, marketing
Global mandate	No	No	Yes/No	No	No	No	No	No	Yes
Size (revenue)	1.1 billion	approx. 800 million	N/A	approx. 900 million	approx. 200 million	950 million	50 million	50 million	N/A
Size (staff)	1,840	1,000	approx. 400	4,300	550	8,900		240	130
Local industry position	No. 1	Top 3	Top 3	Top 3	Top 2	Top 2	Top 2	Top 2	Top 3
Interviewee 1									
Position	National BU VP	Sub. GM	Mark. Exec.	Sub. GM	Sub. GM	Sub. GM	Sub. GM	Sub. GM	Sub. GM
Nationality	Host	Foreign	Host	Home	Home	Home	Home	Foreign	Home
Tenure with sub. (years)	12	28	11	27	3	8	2	3	1
Tenure with MNC (years)	15	30	11	27	11	30	2	10	2
Position tenure (years)	3	11	6	10	3	7	2	3	1
Interviewee 2									
Position	Mark. Manager			Mark. Manager	Sub. VP	Department VP			R&D Director
Nationality	Host			Home	Foreign	Dutch			Foreign
Tenure with sub. (years)	15			4	1	5			3
Tenure with MNC (years)	15			7	9	15			3

7 Conflicts in headquarters–subsidiary relationships: headquarters-driven charter losses in foreign subsidiaries

Christoph Dörrenbächer and Jens Gammelgaard

Introduction

Headquarters and subsidiaries are the two generic organizational units that form multinational corporations (MNCs). Their specific relationship is of central importance, as conflicts in these relationships threaten the effectiveness, or even the operations, of MNCs. Reasons for conflicts in headquarters–subsidiary relationships are manifold.[1] They range from differing perceptions of business opportunities (see e.g. Schmid and Daniel in this volume) to the introduction of corporate-wide standards (see e.g. Fenton-O'Creevy et al. in this volume). In particular, conflict potential can be linked to headquarters-driven charter losses, i.e. an active move by headquarters to withdraw a charter from a particular subsidiary.

Headquarters-driven charter losses in subsidiaries are typically an outcome of headquarters redefining the strategic mission of the MNC. One example is the implementation of a rationalization strategy, in which some production plants are to be closed and production capacities are reallocated to other subsidiaries. Another occurs when a subsidiary loses its charter because the parent company downgrades the importance of the host country market. These charter reallocations are likely to increase competition among subsidiaries and, for the "losers," a conflicting relationship with the parent company is likely to arise (e.g. Blazejewski 2009; Dörrenbächer and Becker-Ritterspach 2009). However, little is known about what causes conflicting interests in charter losses between headquarters and subsidiaries to turn into an open conflict, nor is much known about the role of headquarters' and subsidiaries' agency.

---

[1] We use the rather imprecise term "headquarters–subsidiary relationships" as it is commonly used in international business and management literature to describe the relationships between parent companies and their foreign subsidiaries (e.g. Johnston 2005; Otterbeck 1981).

This chapter addresses this research gap using the case of a German MNC in the telecommunications equipment industry (Siemens). The chapter analyses three episodes of headquarters-driven charter losses at Siemens' Hungarian subsidiary (Telefongyár) and the different levels of conflict that were associated with each event.

According to Pettigrew's structure-agency approach (Pettigrew 1987; Pettigrew *et al.* 2001), headquarters-driven charter losses (along with organizational change in general) are shaped by the inner and outer contexts of the charter loss. This involves the underlying interests and commitments of stakeholders, most notably those of headquarters and subsidiaries. As is outlined in greater detail below, both headquarters and subsidiaries have a certain behavioral repertoire they can draw on in such cases, with the specific context and the history of the relationship influencing the actions taken and the resulting conflicts.

The chapter aims to make several contributions. In focusing on the conflicts that emerge from headquarters-driven charter losses, it is one of the first attempts to go beyond the broad generalities that characterize most analyses of headquarters–subsidiary relationships. Furthermore, the chapter contributes through its historical case study approach. It covers three significant episodes of headquarters-driven charter losses, occurring between 1989 and 2004 in one particular MNC, and allows for the study of conflict interrelatedness (Pettigrew *et al.* 2001). Finally, the chapter considers headquarters–subsidiary relationships in the fast-changing central and east European context, where the complete demise of the command economy turned the region into a laboratory for radical change on all levels of social, economic and political life, with important implications for headquarters–subsidiary relationships (Soulsby and Clark 2007). This is a clear differentiation from previous surveys, which have studied headquarters–subsidiary relationships and associated conflicts in more stable contexts (e.g. Johnston 2005; Pahl and Roth 1993; see also Blazejewski and Becker-Ritterspach in this volume).

The next section provides a brief overview of the existing literature on charter reallocation processes in MNCs. It is followed by an examination of literature on headquarters–subsidiary relationships, while the following section deals with conflicts in such relationships. The two main research questions are then set out, and some associated theoretical and methodological issues are discussed. The chapter then moves on to an empirical analysis, which includes an in-depth discussion of three episodes of charter losses. This is followed by a discussion and conclusion section that focuses on the contextual situation, the role of agency and conflict in headquarters-driven charter losses.

Charter reallocation and subsidiary evolution in MNCs

An MNC is a corporation that owns or controls production or service facilities located outside the country in which it is based. Therefore, the MNC's headquarters organizes the organization's activities by delegating business areas and strategic responsibilities to its subsidiaries. In the terminology of Galunic and Eisenhardt (1996: 256), various subsidiaries are thereby "chartered" to look after certain business areas or take on specific responsibilities. Following Galunic and Eisenhardt, a charter encompasses a subsidiary's product or service line, and the markets on which these products or services are to be sold.[2] Newer research has added the value-chain activities delegated to the subsidiary to this definition, including sales, production, logistics and R&D (Dörrenbächer and Gammelgaard 2006), as well as the strategic mission of the unit, which has been negotiated with its stakeholders (Birkinshaw and Lingblad 2005).

Charters are likely to change over time, as highlighted by several surveys (Birkinshaw and Hood 1997; Birkinshaw and Lingblad 2005; Cantwell and Mudambi 2005; Delany 1998; Dörrenbächer and Gammelgaard 2006; Egelhoff *et al.* 1998; Gammelgaard 2008; Hood *et al.* 1994; Pearce 1999; Walsh *et al.* 2002; Williams 1998). Reasons for charter changes are manifold, though Birkinshaw and Hood (1997) categorize them into parent-company-driven, subsidiary-driven, and host-country-driven development processes (for similar classifications, see Crookell and Morrison 1990; Rugman and Verbeke 2001).

This chapter focuses on the reallocation of subsidiary charters in an MNC as an outcome of parent-company-driven developments. Basically, headquarters (representing the parent company) drives subsidiary development through direct investments. Therefore, headquarters can either strengthen the position of a subsidiary through investments or weaken it through sanctions (Birkinshaw and Hood 1997). However, headquarters-driven subsidiary charter reallocations often create a situation in which some subsidiaries

---

[2] Galunic and Eisenhardt (1996: 256) define a charter as: "the businesses (i.e., product and market arenas) in which a division actively participates and for which it is responsible within the corporation". In this definition, Galunic and Eisenhardt's level of analysis is the division of an MNC. In this chapter, however, the concept of a charter is applied to the subsidiary level.

gain charters and others lose them. For example, a decision made by head-quarters to execute a rationalization strategy can lead to a plant closure and a corresponding shift of production capacity to another plant (Delany 1998). In relation to such an incident, Birkinshaw and Hood (1997: 340) find that "it is recognized, that in differential subsidiary development (i.e. between units in a network) and/or between different host countries, there will inevitably be winners and losers."

The concept of headquarters-driven charter reallocations, including charter losses and charter gains, departs from the strategic management perspective on corporate decision-making in multidivisional firms. In the latter perspective, subsidiaries are managed as a portfolio of assets that is continuously reviewed with regard to financial and strategic considerations (Gammelgaard 2009; Luostarinen and Marschan-Piekkari 2001; Morgan and Kristensen 2006). Such continual reviews, such as budgetary reviews, are not only of high importance to headquarters but also for subsidiaries, as poor performance might imply unwanted subsidiary charter losses, which are likely to lower the importance of the subsidiary in the MNC, or even lead to the closure or divestiture of the subsidiary (Benito 2005). Overall, this turns headquarters-driven charter losses in a subsidiary into a particularly critical event in headquarters–subsidiary relationships, which harbors significant potential for conflict.

Headquarters–subsidiary relationships

Otterbeck (1981: 1) describes headquarters–subsidiary relationships as "what goes on inside the corporation between the home country firm (parent company or headquarters) and the local firm (subsidiary or affiliated company)." Research on headquarters–subsidiary relationships explores the ways in which these two entities, as the two generic organizational units that constitute an MNC, are connected to each other.[3]

Early research on headquarters–subsidiary relationships essentially took a headquarters perspective by focusing on such aspects as the level and type of control (Baliga and Jäger 1984; Doz and Prahalad 1981) or on the centralization of decision-making (Gates and Egelhoff 1986; Van den Bulcke 1984). Later research, spurred by new meta-concepts, such as the MNC as a

[3] Other important relationships are inter-subsidiary relationships (O'Donnell 2000; Schmid and Maurer 2008) and external relationships with business partners in the home and host countries (Forsgren et al. 2005).

heterarchy (Hedlund 1986) and the MNC as an inter-organizational network (Ghoshal and Bartlett 1990), increasingly mirrored a subsidiary perspective. Recent research has further emphasized this angle by focusing on such factors as issue selling or attention-attraction strategies within headquarters–subsidiary relationships (Bouquet and Birkinshaw 2008; Gammelgaard 2009; Ling *et al.* 2005).

Despite this shift in perspective, limited progress has been made with respect to gaining an understanding of headquarters–subsidiary relationships. According to a recent overview: "The current and previous literatures have begun the process of mapping the detailed inner working of MNCs but with only very few exceptions the headquarters–subsidiary link still remains a 'black box'" (Johnston 2005: 4). This is viewed as a fundamental research gap, for "… the subsidiary's most critical relationship was, and still is, with its corporate headquarters" (Birkinshaw and Hood 1998: 6). Moreover, the importance of headquarters–subsidiary relationships has grown in recent decades, a trend that is summarized by Roth and Nigh (1992) as follows: first, industry globalization no longer allows for management of MNCs as portfolios of independent subsidiaries; second, subsidiaries that have grown in size and capabilities are increasingly assigned strategic responsibilities, which require more effective headquarters–subsidiary relationships (as described, for example, in the center of excellence concept developed by Holm and Pedersen [2000]); third, headquarters–subsidiary relationships have been the subject of heightened scrutiny from host country governments, which burdens these relationships with legitimacy issues (Kostova and Zaheer 1999).

Most existing studies on headquarters–subsidiary relationships propose ideal relationships, usually defined as relationships that support MNC performance. According to Bartlett and Ghoshal (1986), Asakawa (2001) and Kim *et al.* (2005), headquarters–subsidiary relationships need to be optimized according to the specific charters that subsidiaries maintain in the MNC. Furthermore, Nohria and Ghoshal (1997) argue that headquarters–subsidiary relationships will have a differentiated fit in terms of degrees of centralization, formalization and normative integration. Kim and Mauborgne (1993) claim that sticking to procedural justice is a key facet of effective headquarters–subsidiary relationships. Going beyond that, Kristensen and Zeitlin (2005: 264) propose to partly dissolve headquarters–subsidiary relationships and replace them with a new "multinational public" as the best way of developing mutually beneficial relationships among different actors in and around MNCs. Finally, an opposing best practice is suggested by a number of authors, who view the introduction of intra-firm competition as a key structural element of effective headquarters–subsidiary relationships (e.g. Birkenshaw 2001; Cerrato 2006; Luo 2005).

Despite the many differences that characterize the ideal type approaches, many of them take a broad view as to what headquarters–subsidiary relationships encapsulate and, therefore, they often lack conceptual precision. Others operate with highly specific measurements created for empirical analytical purposes, which are of little relevance. Furthermore, all of these studies fail to capture conflicts in headquarters–subsidiary relationships in greater detail.

Conflicts in headquarters–subsidiary relationships

According to Rothman and Friedman (2001), conflicts between groups are a natural outcome of competition over scarce resources and disagreements regarding interests. As an example of inter-unit conflicts in organizations, Pahl and Roth (1993: 140–42) suggest that headquarters–subsidiary conflicts essentially center on three issues: (1) the goals and priorities of the subsidiary, (2) the specific way in which the subsidiary is doing its job, and (3) the terms of the headquarters–subsidiary relationship. These conflicts may be influenced by a multitude of factors, including goal incompatibility, activity interdependence, drives for autonomy, shared resources, jurisdictional ambiguity, communication barriers, space and time distance, ignorance of the other party, and dependence (see Kaufmann and Rössing 2005; Pahl and Roth 1993; Tasoluk *et al.* 2006).

This leads to the issue of why and when conflicts in headquarters–subsidiary relationships actually occur, an issue that has often been investigated from a principal–agent point of view. Mudambi and Navarra (2004), for instance, argue that subsidiary managers are likely to seek and appropriate rents generated by their subsidiary in the local market. Furthermore, subsidiary managers will attempt to maximize their share of rents generated by the MNC. Therefore, headquarters should either control or use incentives in order to regulate subsidiary rent-seeking behavior. Along the same lines, Sölvell and Zander (1998), and Bartlett and Ghoshal (1986) stress that the subsidiary's desire to become as autonomous as possible is always in latent opposition to headquarters' desire to maintain control. A study by Johnson and Medcof (2007) indicates that this might be a result of the different risk profiles of principals (headquarters) and agents (subsidiaries). Kim *et al.* (2005) take a more in-depth approach and describe different types of agency problems in headquarters–subsidiary relationships, which are dependent on the individual charter or role maintained by a subsidiary (such as "world mandate," "specialized contributor" or "local implementer"; see Birkinshaw and Morrison 1995). Subsequently, they propose a set of tailor-made governance structures to control these problems.

Principal–agent approaches to headquarters–subsidiary relationships suggest behaviors that are typical of subsidiaries and headquarters, behaviors that inevitably lead to problems and conflicts. However, the interaction of headquarters and subsidiaries does not always lead to conflict, as some empirical studies have demonstrated (see also Schotter and Beamish in this volume). Using the case of MNCs active in post-socialist countries, Clark and Geppert (2006) develop a taxonomy of the different shapes that headquarters–subsidiary relationships might take depending on the particular behaviors chosen by headquarters (polycentric versus ethnocentric orientation; exploration versus exploitation) and subsidiaries (different forms of opposition or conformity). These choices might result in relatively conflict-free, trust-based forms of relationships, as would be the case when headquarters takes a polycentric–exploration oriented approach and is actively supported by the subsidiary. However, these choices might also lead to conflict-ridden forms of headquarters–subsidiary relationships, such as when an ethnocentric-exploitation oriented headquarters faces active opposition from a subsidiary. This research, therefore, implies that conflicts in headquarters–subsidiary relationships depend on the particular behaviors that headquarters and subsidiaries chose from their repertoires for action.[4]

Headquarters' repertoire for action

Sui generis, the MNC is a hierarchy, and headquarters will always be able to enforce its will, regardless of what that will is. This type of behavior has been labeled "domination" by Mir and Sharpe (2009: 247) in reference to a case in which headquarters – in the name of cross-border standardization – destroyed subsidiary-level knowledge. Another aspect of headquarters' domination that Yamin and Sinkovics (2007) believe occurs more often is evident when local subsidiary practices are devalued by the MNC. For example, Dörrenbächer and Geppert (2009) present a case in which a clash between the short-term, shareholder-value orientation of a German headquarters and the longer-term, technological orientation of its French subsidiary ends with

---

[4] The repertoires for action are derived from existing literature. They represent bi-polar, ideal, behaviors that might, in reality, come in different shades.

the headquarters deciding not to use the technological achievements of the French subsidiary, despite the effort that the subsidiary had put into them.

However, the headquarters does not necessarily always apply a domination strategy. To different degrees, headquarters might show conciliatory behavior and make concessions to the will of the subsidiaries. In relation to charter losses, such concessions might come as compensations or as delays in implementation of charter removals. Headquarters might even completely back away from an original decision to withdraw a charter. Headquarters might grant such concessions on the basis of two rationales. First, headquarters might feel attached to corporate-wide norms, values and standards of procedural justice (Kim and Mauborgne 1993), which prevent or limit a domination strategy. In such cases, the headquarters prioritizes long-term, intra-organizational co-operation and stability over the short-term gains it might derive from enforcing its immediate will. Second, a domination strategy might be hampered by the intra-organizational power that subsidiaries can derive from their resource position (Forsgren *et al.* 2005). In this case, the headquarters might be subject to resource dependency situations (Pfeffer and Salancik 1978), i.e. situations in which the headquarters (or the MNC as a whole) depends on a particular resource that a subsidiary controls. Newer studies demonstrate that, in addition to resource dependency power, subsidiaries can possess systemic power, which arises from functional interdependencies in the MNC value chain (Astley and Zajac 1991). However, this type of power, as well as power derived from the locational advantages of the host country (e.g. Egelhoff *et al.* 1998; Holm *et al.* 2003; Walsh *et al.* 2002) is less sustainable because headquarters can bypass these resources with relatively short notice. In such cases, the limiting effects on the headquarters' domination strategy are always threatened and can vanish quickly.

Subsidiaries' repertoire for action

The headquarters is not the only actor that can choose among different strategies – subsidiaries can also draw on a certain repertoire for action. The ideal type taxonomy presented by Morgan and Kristensen (2006: 1479) indicates that subsidiaries can either behave as "Boy Scouts" or as "subversive strategists." Boy Scout subsidiaries follow the demands of the headquarters without resistance. Charter losses that are the result of headquarters' decisions are implemented fully, despite the will of a particular subsidiary's stakeholders (such as the labor force of the subsidiary), by managers that have a clear orientation towards headquarters. Boy Scout behavior is equivalent to a policy of conflict avoidance (Bacharach and Lawler 1984) and, therefore, might lead to generally conflict-free headquarters–subsidiary relationships.

However, subsidiaries might also behave as "subversive strategists." Such subsidiaries constantly search for an extension or renewal of their own charter, and headquarters' goals, strategies and rules are viewed as secondary. Unwanted charter losses that are driven by headquarters are resisted by such subsidiaries. Subsidiaries that follow the subversive approach are typically managed by locally embedded, entrepreneurial-oriented managers, who prioritize coalitions within the subsidiary and with external stakeholders (mainly in their local environment) over coalitions with headquarters. While this behavior stimulates entrepreneurship, it easily leads to conflicts with headquarters, especially if such strategies turn out to be unsuccessful (Bouquet and Birkinshaw 2008). In such situations, these managers are often stereotyped as "loose cannons" or "empire builders" (Taplin 2006), and headquarters treats their initiatives with caution (see Koveshnikov in this volume).

Research questions, theoretical and methodological issues

Given the fact that both headquarters and subsidiaries can draw on a repertoire of different actions, a crucial question arises as to when headquarters and subsidiaries engage in behaviors that breed conflicts. This leads to the two core research questions that guide this chapter:

(1) What behavioral patterns do headquarters and subsidiaries display with regard to headquarters-driven charter losses?

(2) What leads headquarters and subsidiaries to choose behaviors that lead to conflicts in cases of headquarters-driven charter losses?

Given the scarcity of existing knowledge on these subjects, a case study approach was chosen to provide more insight. The case study was designed to be both descriptive and explanatory (Yin 2003). It is descriptive, as it aims to provide missing insights into the behavioral patterns of headquarters and subsidiaries in cases of subsidiary charter losses (research question 1). As discussed above, headquarters behaviors might range from domination to the granting of some concessions, while subsidiaries might show Boy Scout or subversive behaviors to varying degrees.

The case study is explanatory in that it tries to explain the driving forces behind headquarters' and subsidiaries' behavioral choices that lead to conflicts in cases of headquarters-driven charter losses (research question 2). In this respect, we assume, in line with Pettigrew (1987) and some recent work that applies structuration theory to the MNC (Becker-Ritterspach 2006; Blazejewski 2009), that the situational context exerts a strong influence on the behavioral patterns of headquarters and subsidiaries in cases of head-quarters-driven charter losses. Pettigrew (1987) states that the situational context is made up of the outer context, which refers to the social, economic, political and competitive environment of the MNC, and the inner context, which refers to the structure, corporate culture and political context within the firm. Both the inner and outer contexts are understood as mutually influencing each other and evolving over time. However, in contrast to simple contingency approaches, these contexts are not seen as mechanistically influencing the behaviors of actors. Pettigrew *et al.* (2001) state that context is "… a nested arrangement of structures and processes in which the subjective interpretations of actors perceiving, learning and remembering help shape process" (Pettigrew *et al.* 2001: 699). In line with this understanding, which draws on Weick's sensemaking approach (Weick 1995), the case study aims to demonstrate that it is the interpretation of the evolving outer and inner contexts through the idiosyncratic lenses of the actors that constitutes head-quarters' and subsidiaries' interests and behaviors. This, in turn, determines the level of conflict in headquarters–subsidiary relationships. When combined with the specific history of the headquarters–subsidiary relationship in question, this allows for an explanation of why some headquarters-driven charter losses are generally void of conflict while others trigger conflicts between headquarters and subsidiaries.

Methodological rigor was enhanced in this study through the use of three episodes of subsidiary charter losses in the same organizational setting over a period of fifteen years (1989–2004). We rely on the multiple-case-study logic of replication and extension (Eisenhardt 1991; Gibbert and Ruigrok 2010; Gibbert *et al.* 2008). Case study data was collected in 26 in-depth interviews carried out between 1998 and 2004 at different Siemens units in Germany, Austria and Hungary. Therefore, the case time and research time partially overlap, which combines the real time and retrospective approaches (Blazejewski 2010). In-depth interviews were particularly suitable for this research because they not only allowed for the mapping of actors' behaviors but also for a reconstruction of their associated interpretations of the inner and outer contexts, which constituted their standpoints and behaviors. The semi-structured interviews, which were based on an interview questionnaire, dealt with the development of the Hungarian subsidiary (Telefongyár) from the beginning of its transition in 1989 until 2004. The three episodes of charter loss were unanimously considered by all interview partners to be the most important charter losses during this period of time.

All interviews lasted about ninety minutes. Most of them were conducted at the interviewees' offices. Although no interview partner is mentioned by name because of confidentiality obligations, an anonymous list of the interview partners is given in the appendix. Access to interview partners was eased by the involvement of a sponsor at headquarters. After conducting several interviews, we adopted a snowball approach in which interviewees were asked to provide the names of other potentially relevant interview partners (Welch *et al.* 2002). This ensured a multi-faceted view of the sometimes rather conflict-burdened issue of headquarters-driven charter losses and enhanced the internal validity of the actions described and standpoints assumed for headquarters and subsidiaries. All interviews, with the exception of one, were taped and transcribed verbatim. After the interviews were triangulated with document data, a summary report was produced and sent to the interviewees for approval and to eliminate mistakes, misunderstandings and analytical errors. In addition, two intense feedback meetings were held with interview partners to improve data interpretation.

Case study: three headquarters-driven[5] charter losses in Siemens Telefongyár, Hungary

Strategic background and history

The acquisition of the Hungarian telecommunication equipment supplier Telefongyár was one of many acquisitions that Siemens undertook in central and eastern Europe immediately after fall of the Berlin Wall. At the time, the low volumes in the central and east European markets for electronic products and services suggested tremendous growth potential when compared to volumes in the west European market. Siemens expected market opportunities in infrastructure businesses, such as telecommunications, energy and transportation. In addition, low wages and the skilled workforce, which were now available in close geographic proximity to Siemens' home market, supported the build-up of major manufacturing facilities in central and eastern Europe (Mirow 1996; see also Maclean and Hollinshead in this volume).

---

[5] If not otherwise stated, "headquarters" refers to the divisional headquarters of the Siemens telecommunications switching division (based in Bruchsal, Germany).

Prior to the fall of the Iron Curtain, Budapest-based Telefongyár was one of three leading telecommunication equipment suppliers in Hungary. As Hungary was a major supplier of telecommunications equipment in the Comecon (Müller 1998), a notable part of Telefongyár's production was exported. Russia alone accounted for about 75 percent of production in 1988 (Neumann *et al.* 1993). Other exports went to other Comecon countries and to some Arab countries.

In June 1989, Siemens and Telefongyár engaged in close discussions about a cooperative agreement regarding public switching technology. These discussions led to a joint Siemens–Telefongyár bid in the 1990 tender for the switching technology offered by MATAV, the main Hungarian Telecom operator. When the success of the Siemens–Telefongyár bid was announced by MATAV at the end of 1990, discussions about the friendly takeover of Telefongyár by Siemens gained momentum. This was, in particular, a result of the formal obligation in the tender that the contractor had to maintain a local production unit in Hungary to serve the contract. This obligation was restated in the 1995 follow-up tender, which imposed a local production clause on Siemens that was valid until 2001.

Managers from Siemens Austria were designated to handle the takeover and modernization of Telefongyár. They began working at Telefongyár in the first months of 1991, although the formal acquisition did not take place before September 1991. Several important changes were prepared or implemented during this phase, such as the dismantling of some operations, the screening of the stock of orders and an assessment of Telefongyár's top management.

A complete reorganization of Telefongyár began almost immediately after the formal acquisition was finalized. It was based on the insights gained in the pre-takeover phase, and it affected all functional areas and hierarchical levels. Under the guidance of Austrian expatriates, the first years were used to downsize the subsidiary, to refocus production, to find and train new middle management, and to implement Siemens' standards throughout Telefongyár. By the mid-1990s, the initial transition process at Telefongyár had come to an end, and a period of positive business development and high dividends followed. For about five years, the profitability of Telefongyár clearly exceeded that of other Siemens' subsidiaries in Hungary as well as the profitability of Siemens' switching subsidiaries elsewhere in Europe. However, this situation changed at the turn of the century. A downturn in the Hungarian market as well as a defeat of the subsidiary's attempt to become the European center of competence for switching production led to the closure of production at Telefongyár in early 2003.

Three episodes of headquarters-driven charter losses, 1989–2004

The brief history of the venture reveals three crucial episodes of partial or total charter losses at Telefongyár between 1989 and 2004.

The first episode was the partial loss of production resources and market areas, which took place in 1991 before Siemens had even acquired Telefongyár. While management personnel from Siemens Austria undertook due diligence at Telefongyár, the dismantling (sale and closure) of Telefongyár's peripheral manufacturing units, as well as a notable downsizing of its central plant in Budapest, were decided upon by the Hungarian privatization authority in order to make it a more attractive takeover target. In total, these changes reduced employment at Telefongyár from approximately 4,000 to 1,200. Moreover, following the screening of existing orders, the overwhelming majority of orders, mainly coming from Russia and the Arabic region, were canceled, which resulted in a sharp reduction in Telefongyár's market scope.

The second episode of partial charter losses occurred around the mid-1990s when Siemens decided to sell the production line at Telefongyár (analogue switching system production), which had initially been kept to serve several pre-transition contracts. This decision was spurred by the fact that the Hungarian government decided to curb export credits to central and east European markets. The loss of the production charter, however, was only partial, as a new production line for digital switching technology was put into place. Operation of this new production line, however, required fewer staff members.

Simultaneously, Telefongyár lost large parts of its R&D charter. As early as 1991–1993, a large number of software engineers from Telefongyár began working for Siemens Programm- und Systementwicklung (Siemens PSE), the Vienna-based subsidiary responsible for the overall development of communications software at Siemens. They were either transferred to Vienna or they worked in PSE projects from Budapest. In 1994, most expatriated software engineers were transferred back to Hungary and pooled with those that had stayed at Telefongyár in a newly founded software subsidiary of PSE called Sysdata. Subsequently, Sysdata was allocated a charter to develop a notable part of the overall communications software for Siemens. Only a few R&D tasks remained at Telefongyár, such as the adaptation of some communication software to the specifications of the Hungarian and other eastern European markets. Together, charter losses in the mid-1990s and cuts in the administration meant that the number of people employed at Telefongyár fell to about 400 in 1998.

The third episode of charter loss took place in early 2003 when the digital switching production, which had been built up only seven years previously, was closed. Several factors led to headquarters' decision to close production at Telefongyár. One was the uneven investment policy pursued by MATAV, Telefongyár's main customer. In 2000/2001, MATAV made a significant effort to finalize the digitalization of its fixed telephone network, which led to an excess of orders for digital switching systems and to a great deal of overtime at the Telefongyár plant. However, after completion, the Hungarian market collapsed, since there were no orders for next-generation equipment, such as broadband applications or voice-over-IP.

In addition to the temporary breakdown of the Hungarian market, there were several long-standing structural changes that resulted in the closure of the plant. Spurred by an increasing overall orientation of Siemens towards shareholder value (Bluhm and Dörrenbächer 2003) and pressured by the increasingly competition-oriented sourcing strategy of its customers,[6] headquarters issued a division-wide rationalization program in 1996. This program basically indicated the future elimination of many of the small plants that were producing switching equipment for national markets (such as Telefongyár). In light of this strategic reorganization plan, which clearly endangered the existence of the production site at Telefongyár in the longer term, the Hungarian subsidiary tried to make better use of Telefongyár's favorable tax regime (which was basically designed for cost-driven investments) starting in the mid-1990s. However, attempts to acquire a critical amount of additional orders[7] from other Siemens divisions and from external customers were not successful enough to enlarge the plant in a way that it could compete with plants managed by external contract manufacturers or with larger Siemens plants. Although there were some investments in more efficient machinery, which were strongly pushed for by the Hungarian management, a real enlargement of the plant was not possible, as headquarters refused to agree with Telefongyár's proposal to turn the Budapest plant into the European center for switching production. Instead, the plant located at

---

[6] Under pressure from alternative carriers, most of the telecom operators around the world abandoned their former policy to require local production. "Squeezed" by competition, they put more pressure on prices for network equipment, which led to a dramatic fall of the price per subscriber line (from $200 in 1995 to about $50 in 2001). For equipment manufacturers, such as Siemens, these changes translated into a strong rationalisation potential: once there was no longer a political requirement for local production, small plants, such as the one at Telefongyár, were recognized as relatively inefficient compared to larger plants, such as the one located at Siemens' divisional headquarters in Germany.

[7] These orders mainly related to the fitting of printed circuit boards with components.

the headquarters in Bruchsal, Germany was given that role as a result of its larger, more elaborate R&D capabilities (for a detailed account of this decision, see Dörrenbächer and Gammelgaard 2010).

Finally, the breakdown of the Hungarian market at the end of 2001 meant that volumes fell below the threshold for using the tax alleviation provision and, more generally, at the same time, the contractual end of tax alleviation was in sight (December 2003). A decision was made to shut down production at Telefongyár in early 2003. As a result, the subsidiary was downsized to approximately 250 employees.

The impact of charter losses on headquarters–subsidiary relationships

All three episodes of charter loss at Telefongyár implied a significant loss of resources for Telefongyár, including resources in production, R&D and marketing. However, the level of conflict associated with these charter losses varied considerably. While the first two episodes (in 1991 and the mid-1990s, respectively) hardly created any conflict, the third charter loss, implemented by headquarters in early 2003, led to severe conflicts between headquarters and Telefongyár.

Given our theoretical assumptions, the different levels of conflict associated with the three episodes of charter losses can be attributed to the different situational contexts, and their interpretations by headquarters and the subsidiary. The context relevant to the charter losses in 1991 and the mid-1990s can be labeled as a transition/modernization context. In both cases, the divisional headquarters imposed charter losses on Telefongyár. However, headquarters' domination strategy was accompanied by significant compensation. Siemens invested heavily in technology transfers and human resource development at Telefongyár with the aim of achieving a good reputation and broad, sustainable market access to the growing central and east European market. At Telefongyár, the advent of Siemens as an investor in 1991 was, first and foremost, interpreted as an opportunity to escape transition turmoil, survive transition and adapt to new world market standards. For Telefongyár, this meant the 1991 charter loss was a necessary evil and it was not resisted.

A similar Boy Scout attitude was evident a few years later in the mid-1990s. At that time, headquarters' offer to produce digital switching products as a compensation for the loss of the analogue production and some R&D responsibilities silenced concerns of the subsidiary. These concerns mainly referred to the loss of R&D responsibilities, which were considered as a sacrifice due to the strategic importance of R&D activities for the future development of Telefonygár and due to the fact that they were seen as a pre-transition achievement of Telefongyár. Nevertheless, the combination of relatively conciliatory headquarters' behavior and the subsidiary's adoption of a Boy Scout behavior led to a rather peaceful headquarters–subsidiary relationship from 1991 to 1995.

However, the situation changed with the release of the division-wide rationalization program in 1996, which occurred in a significantly different context. The headquarters, now "pressured" by shareholder value expectations and somewhat "relieved" from previous market access rationales, turned towards a more clear-cut domination strategy by indicating that the production of Telefongyár might be closed in the long run without concessions. As a result, Telefongyár abandoned its Boy Scout behavior and adopted a subversive strategy. This strategy aimed to prevent the announced charter loss, regardless of the cost, by finding new internal and external customers, and by lobbying to become the new European center for switching production. Telefongyár's shift towards a pronounced subversive strategy was, in particular, spurred by the interpretation of the new rationalization context and the related headquarters' policy as something that threatened not only Telefongyár's charter but also its identity. First, the subsidiary was frustrated that it could suffer a charter loss despite many years of excellent performance. Second, losing the production charter for digital switches was seen as an ex-post violation of an agreement made in conjunction with a previous charter loss (as the digital production line was given as compensation for the sale of the analogue production line in the mid-1990s). Third, the loss of the production charter obscured the "production pride" prevalent in the subsidiary as well as the pride of having developed state-of-the-art capabilities during transition.

Over the course of several years, the conflict associated with the closure of Telefongyár's production was mainly evident in the dispute over investments, with the demands of Telefongyár only reluctantly and, at best, partially met by headquarters. After several years of following a half-hearted investment policy, headquarters finally made the decision to close the plant at Telefongyár. With that move, the conflict came to an end. However, the decision burdened the future relationship between Telefongyár and headquarters not only because the decision strongly affected the identity of Telefongyár, but also because of the way in which the decision was conveyed. The decision was communicated by telephone, even though high-ranking managers from headquarters had visited Telefongyár almost weekly in the months leading up to the decision. In addition, the decision was communicated immediately after Siemens had failed to win a tender for military communication

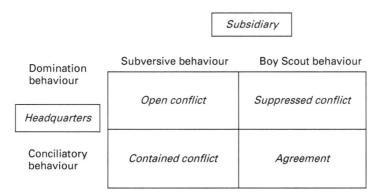

Fig. 7.1   Headquarters–subsidiary interaction in cases of headquarters-driven charter losses

equipment in Hungary. Many Telefongyár managers perceived this as a sign of disrespect for local actors in a global company. Headquarters managers, however, saw it as an end to a long story of concessions made to the local subsidiary for the sake of organizational justice. From headquarters' perspective, there was nothing left to negotiate.

Discussion and conclusions

One basic finding of this study is that while headquarters-driven charter losses at subsidiaries are critical events in headquarters–subsidiary relationships, they do not necessarily lead to conflict. The charter loss that occurred in 1991 and the charter loss that occurred in the mid-1990s did not lead to open conflict between Telefongyár and its headquarters. This indicates the need to study the inner and outer contexts, as well as the resulting behaviors and interactions of headquarters and subsidiaries in cases of headquarters-driven charter losses. With regard to the former, our case study found a notable difference between the modernization/transition context prevalent in the early 1990s and the cross-border rationalization context that began to unfold in the second half of the 1990s. With regard to the latter, our case study confirms our theoretical assumptions that headquarters can show a domination or a conciliatory behavior to varying degrees, whereas subsidiaries might behave as Boy Scouts or as subversive strategists to varying degrees.

This leads to the following interaction patterns and associated shapes of headquarters–subsidiary relationships (see Figure 7.1).

Open conflict emerges when headquarters' domination strategy meets or breeds subversive behavior in the subsidiary. This was clearly the case with the loss of the production charter at Telefongyár, which was announced in the second half of the 1990s and implemented in early 2003.

A *contained conflict* occurs if headquarters' conciliatory behavior meets subversive behavior in the subsidiary. This was the case when Siemens' headquarters allowed Telefongyár to make some investments in more efficient machinery, starting in the mid-1990s. Through these investments, Telefongyár intended to improve its position within the switching division in order to have a better chance of becoming the European center for switching production.

A *suppressed conflict* occurs if headquarters' domination strategy enforces Boy Scout behavior in the subsidiary. Such a situation was evident following the charter loss that occurred at Telefongyár in the mid-1990s. Headquarters vigorously asserted its will to spin off Telefongyár's R&D activities, and this was not resisted even though the move was strongly disliked and viewed as a major sacrifice by Telefongyár. The suppressed conflict over the R&D spin-off did not move into the open until the loss of the production charter was implied by the announcement of a division-wide rationalization program. By that point, Telefongyár no longer felt that its sacrifice was paying off (which had been the basic reason for its original adoption of a Boy Scout strategy).

Finally, if a conciliatory behavior adopted by headquarters meets a Boy Scout behavior in the subsidiary, then headquarters-driven charter losses are implemented in *agreement*. This situation can be associated with the charter loss at Telefongyár in 1991, when an overriding win–win constellation was created, with Telefongyár trading its market access for headquarters' support in the transition turmoil.

In terms of confirming and elucidating the different shapes headquarters–subsidiary relationships might take in cases of headquarters-driven charter losses, the empirical findings also allow us to make a few remarks on current literature and future research.

First, our case study of three subsequent episodes of charter losses in one subsidiary over a period of fifteen years has demonstrated that charter losses might be closely interrelated. Even if this finding might be accidental (or a side-effect of a fast-changing transition context, in which headquarters-driven charter losses might occur more frequently), the impact of the historical headquarters–subsidiary relationship on the behavior of headquarters and subsidiaries in actual cases of charter loss is not. Coping with such influences, however, requires use of a longitudinal approach, or evaluation of the former headquarters–subsidiaries relationship and its impact. Most previous studies on headquarters–subsidiary relationships have failed to do this. Principal–agent approaches, for instance, reflect an Anglo-Saxon governance perspective and simply assume that headquarters–subsidiary relationships are generally characterized by antagonism. This excludes the possibility of institutionally underpinned, trust-based relationships between headquarters and subsidiaries that have a long-term orientation (see Williams and Geppert in this volume). Such long-term-oriented relationships might, for example, allow a subsidiary to accept a harmful charter loss or enable headquarters to abandon the implementation of a planned charter removal. Game theory might be fruitful in the explanation of such phenomena, as game theory is concerned with the prediction of outcomes of iterated "games" – social situations involving two or more actors (players) whose interests are interconnected or interdependent (Zagare 1984).

Second, our case study has demonstrated that it is not only the historical headquarters–subsidiary relationship that might matter for the actors' behavior but also the contextual situation related to a charter loss. What is viewed as a necessary evil in one context might be welcomed or fiercely objected to in another context. Therefore, contextual influences can only be objectified to a limited extent, not only because they are complex but also because it is their specific perception and interpretation by the actors that is translated into the actors' standpoints and behaviors (see Schmid and Daniel in this volume). Such processes of sensemaking (Weick 1995), however, are hard for quantitative studies or studies that aim to develop a best practice for headquarters–subsidiary relationships to grasp. To do so requires more in-depth ethnographic and socio-political studies (for an example, see Clark and Geppert 2011).

Third, our model of headquarters–subsidiary interaction raises the question of whether subsidiary behavior in situations of headquarters-driven charter losses is an outcome of headquarters' behavior or vice versa. This mutual influence has not been widely addressed in the existing literature. Given the hierarchical setting, a subsidiary might await headquarters' behavior before deciding on its response in respect to the inner and outer contexts. However, more research is needed to explore and substantiate this assumption.

Appendix – Interview partners

- One top manager at the divisional headquarters in Bruchsal, Germany
- One middle manager at the divisional headquarters in Bruchsal, Germany

- One middle manager at Siemens' headquarters in Munich, Germany
- One representative of the general works council (Konzernbetriebsrat) and member of the supervisory board of Siemens AG in Munich, Germany
- One middle manager for corporate personnel at Siemens AG in Berlin, Germany
- Four middle managers at Siemens Österreich AG in Vienna, Austria, working as expatriates at Telefongyár
- Three top managers at Telefongyár in Budapest, Hungary
- Seven middle managers at Telefongyár in Budapest, Hungary
- One middle manager at Sysdata in Budapest, Hungary, a software spin-off of Telefongyár
- Two staff representatives at Telefongyár in Budapest, Hungary
- One representative of the Hungarian Investment Promotion Agency (ITD) in Budapest, Hungary
- One representative of the Hungarian Ministry of Economics dealing with foreign direct investments in Budapest, Hungary

Note: Some of the interviews were group interviews; some interviewees were interviewed several times during this study.

REFERENCES

Asakawa, K. 2001. "Evolving headquarters–subsidiary dynamics in international R&D: the case of Japanese multinationals," *R&D Management* 31: 1–14

Astley, W. G. and E. J. Zajac 1991. "Intraorganizational power and organizational design: reconciling rational and coalitional models of organization," *Organization Science* 2: 399–411

Bacharach, S. and E. J. Lawler 1984. *Power and Politics in Organizations. The Social Psychology of Conflict, Coalitions and Bargaining.* New York: Wiley

Baliga, B. R., and A. M. Jäger 1984. "Multinational corporations: control systems and delegation issues," *Journal of International Business Studies* 15: 25–40

Bartlett, C. and S. Ghoshal 1986. "Tap your subsidiaries for global reach," *Harvard Business Review* 64: 88–94

Becker-Ritterspach, F. 2006. "The social constitution of knowledge integration in MNEs: a theoretical framework," *Journal of International Management* 12: 358–77

Benito, G. R. G. 2005. "Divestment and international business strategy," *Journal of Economic Geography* 5: 235–51

Birkinshaw, J. 2001. "Strategies for managing internal competition," *California Management Review* 44: 21–38

Birkinshaw, J. and N. Hood 1997. "An empirical study of development processes in foreign-owned subsidiaries in Canada and Scotland," *Management International Review* 37: 339–64

1998. "Introduction and overview" in Birkinshaw and Hood (eds.) *Multinational Corporate Evolution and Subsidiary Development*. Basingstoke: Macmillan, pp. 1–19

Birkinshaw, J. and M. Lingblad 2005. "Intrafirm competition and charter evolution in the multibusiness firm," *Organization Science* 16: 674–86

Birkinshaw, J. and A. J. Morrison 1995. "Configurations of strategy and structure in subsidiaries of multinational corporations," *Journal of International Business Studies* 26: 729–53

Blazejewski, S. 2009. "Actors' interests and local contexts in intrafirm conflict: the 2004 GM/Opel crisis," *Competition & Change* 13: 229–50

2010. "When truth is the daughter of time: longitudinal case studies in international business research" in Piekkari and Welch (eds.) *Rethinking the Case Study in International Business and Management Research: Towards Greater Pluralism*. Cheltenham: Edward Elgar

Bluhm, K. and C. Dörrenbächer 2003. "Systematischer Modelltransfer oder emergenter Wandel? Standortentwicklung und Arbeitspolitik des Siemenskonzerns in Mittel- und Osteuropa" in Dörrenbächer (ed.) *Modelltransfer in Multinationalen Unternehmen. Strategien und Probleme Grenzüberschreitender Konzernintegration*. Berlin: Edition Sigma, pp. 77–112

Bouquet, C. and J. Birkinshaw 2008. "Managing power in the multinational corporation: how low-power actors gain influence," *Journal of Management* 34: 477–508

Cantwell, J. and R. Mudambi 2005. "MNE competence-creating subsidiary mandate," *Strategic Management Journal* 26: 1109–28

Cerrato, D. 2006. "The multinational enterprise as an internal market system," *International Business Review* 15: 253–77

Clark, E. and M. Geppert 2006. "Socio-political processes in international management in post-socialist contexts: knowledge, learning and transnational institution building," *Journal of International Management* 12: 340–57

2011. "Subsidiary integration as identity construction and institution building: a political sensemaking approach," *Journal of Management Studies* (in print)

Crookell H. and A. Morrison 1990. "Subsidiary strategy in a free trade environment," *Business Quarterly* 55: 33–9

Delany, E. 1998. "Strategic development of multinational subsidiaries in Ireland" in Birkinshaw and Hood (eds.) *Multinational Corporate Evolution and Subsidiary Development*. Basingstoke: Macmillan, pp. 239–67

Dörrenbächer C. and F. Becker-Ritterspach 2009. "Introducing socio-political perspectives on intra-firm competition, production relocation and outsourcing," *Competition and Change* 13: 193–98

Dörrenbächer, C. and J. Gammelgaard 2006. "Subsidiary role development: the effect of micro-political headquarters–subsidiary negotiations on the product, market and value-added scope of foreign owned subsidiaries," *Journal of International Management* 12: 266–83

2010. "Multinational corporations, inter-organizational networks and subsidiary charter removals," *Journal of World Business* 44: 206–216

Dörrenbächer, C. and M. Geppert 2009. "A micro-political perspective on subsidiary initiative-taking: evidence from German-owned subsidiaries in France," *European Management Journal* 27: 100–12

Doz, Y. and C. K. Prahalad 1981. "Headquarters influence and strategic control in MNCs," *Sloan Management Review* 23: 15–29

Egelhoff, W. G., L. Gorman and S. McCormick 1998. "Using technology as a path to subsidiary development" in Birkinshaw and Hood (eds.) *Multinational Corporate Evolution and Subsidiary Development*. Basingstoke: Macmillan, pp. 213–38

Eisenhardt, K. M. 1991. "Better stories and better constructs: the case for rigor and comparative logic," *Academy of Management Review* 16: 620–27

Forsgren, M., U. Holm and J. Johanson 2005. *Managing the Embedded Multinational: A Business Network View*. Cheltenham: Edward Elgar

Galunic, D. C. and K. M. Eisenhardt 1996. "The evolution of intracorporate domains: divisional charter losses in high-technology multidivisonal corporations," *Organization Science* 7: 255–82

Gammelgaard, J. 2008. "Subsidiary influence and its impact on role development: three cases from the coatings industry in China" in Worm (ed.) *China: Business Opportunities in a Globalizing Economy*. Copenhagen: Copenhagen Business School Press, pp. 91–112

   2009. "Issue selling and bargaining power in intrafirm competition: the differentiating impact of the subsidiary management composition," *Competition and Change* 13: 214–28

Gates, S. and W. Egelhoff 1986. "Centralization in headquarters–subsidiary relations," *Journal of International Business Studies* 17: 71–92

Ghoshal, S. and C. Bartlett 1990. "The multinational corporation as an interorganizational network," *The Academy of Management Review* 15: 603–25

Gibbert, M. and W. Ruigrok 2010. "The 'What' and 'How' of case study rigor, three strategies based on published work," *Organizational Research Methods* 13(4): 710–37

Gibbert, M., W. Ruigrok and B. Wicki 2008. "What passes as a rigorous case study?," *Strategic Management Journal* 29: 1465–74

Hedlund, G. 1986. "The hypermodern MNC – a heterarchy?," *Human Resource Management* 25: 9–35

Holm, U., and T. Pedersen (eds.) 2000. *The Emergence and Impact of MNC Centres of Excellence – A Subsidiary Perspective*. Basingstoke: Macmillan

Holm, U., Malmberg, A., and Sölvell, O. (2003). Subsidiary impact on host country economies: The case of foreign-owned subsidiaries attracting investment into Sweden. Journal of Economic Geography, 3(4): 389–408

Hood, N., S. Young and D. Lal 1994. "Strategic evolution within Japanese manufacturing plants in Europe: UK evidence," *International Business Review* 3: 97–122

Johnson, W. H. A. and J. W. Medcof 2007. "Motivating proactive subsidiary innovation: agent-based theory and socialization models in global R&D," *Journal of International Management* 13: 472–87

Johnston, S. 2005. *Headquarters and Subsidiaries in Multinational Corporations. Strategies, Tasks and Coordination*. Basingstoke: Palgave Macmillan

Kaufmann, L. and S. Rössing 2005. "Managing conflict of interests between headquarters and their subsidiaries regarding technology transfer to emerging markets – a framework," *Journal of World Business* 40: 235–53

Kim, W. C. and R. Mauborgne 1993. "Procedural justice theory and the multinational corporation" in Ghoshal and Westney (eds.) *Organization Theory and the Multinational Corporation*. New York: St. Martin's Press, pp. 237–55

Kim, B., J. E. Prescott and S. M. Kim 2005. "Differentiated governance of foreign subsidiaries in transnational corporations: an agency theory perspective," *Journal of International Management* 11: 43–66

Kostova, T. and S. Zaheer 1999. "Organizational legitimacy under conditions of complexity: the case of the multinational enterprise," *Academy of Management Review* 24: 64–81

Kristensen, P. H. and J. Zeitlin 2005. *Local Players in Global Games: The Strategic Constitution of A Multinational Corporation*. Oxford University Press

Ling, Y., S. W. Floyd and D. C. Baldrigge 2005. "Toward a model of issue-selling by subsidiary managers in multinational organizations," *Journal of International Business Studies* 36: 637–54

Luo, Y. 2005. "Toward coopetition within a multinational enterprise: a perspective from foreign subsidiaries," *Journal of World Business* 40: 71–90

Luostarinen, R. and R. Marschan-Piekkari 2001. "Strategic evolution of foreign-owned subsidiaries in a host country: a conceptual framework" in Taggart, Berry and McDermott (eds.) *Multinationals in a New Area*. Basingstoke: Palgrave, pp. 180–93

Mir, R. and D. R. Sharpe 2009. "The multinational firm as an instrument of exploitation and domination" in Collinson and Morgan (eds.) *Images of the Multinational Firm*. Chichester: John Wiley & Sons, pp. 247–66

Mirow, M. 1996. "Kooperations- und Akquisitionsstrategie in Osteuropa am Beispiel der Elektroindustrie," *Zeitschrift für betriebswirtschaftliche Forschung* 10: 934–46

Morgan, G. and P. H. Kristensen 2006. "The contested space of multinationals: varieties of institutionalism, varieties of capitalism," *Human Relations* 59: 1467–90

Mudambi, R. and P. Navarra 2004. "Is knowledge power? Knowledge flows, subsidiary power and rent-seeking within MNCs," *Journal of International Business Studies* 35: 385–406

Müller, J. 1998. "Restructuring of the telecommunications sector in the west and the east and the role of science and technology," Final Summary Paper (mimeo). Berlin

Neumann, L., A. Tóth and L. Berkó 1993. *Management/Labour Relations at Hungarian Affiliates of Multinational Enterprises*. Budapest OECD – Ministry of Labour

Nohria, N. and S. Ghoshal 1997. *The Differentiated Network – Organizing Multinational Corporations for Value Creation*. San Francisco: Jossey-Bass

O'Donnell, S. W. 2000. "Managing foreign subsidiaries: agents of headquarters, or an independent network?," *Strategic Management Journal* 21: 525–48

Otterbeck, L. (ed.) 1981. *The Management of Headquarters–Subsidiary Relationships in Multinational Corporations*. Aldershot: Gower

Pahl, J. M. and K. Roth 1993. "Managing the headquarters–foreign subsidiary relationship: the roles of strategy, conflict and integration," *The International Journal of Conflict Management* 4: 139–65

Pearce, R. 1999. "The evolution of technology in multinational enterprises: the role of creative subsidiaries," *International Business Review* 8: 125–48

Pettigrew, A. M. 1987. "Context and action in the transformation of the firm," *Journal of Management Studies* 24: 649–70

Pettigrew, A. M., R. W. Woodman and K. S. Cameron 2001. "Studying organizational change and development: challenges for future research," *Academy of Management Journal* 44: 697–713

Pfeffer, J. and G. R. Salancik 1978. *The External Controls of Organizations – A Resource Dependence Perspective.* New York: Harper & Row

Roth, K. and D. Nigh 1992. "The effectiveness of headquarters–subsidiary relationships: the role of coordination, control and conflict," *Journal of Business Research* 25: 277–301

Rothman, J. and V. J. Friedman 2001. "Identity, conflict, and organizational learning" in Dierkes, Berthoin-Antal, Child and Nonaka (eds.) *Handbook of Organizational Learning and Knowledge.* Oxford University Press, pp. 582–97

Rugman, A. M. and A. Verbeke 2001. "Subsidiary-specific advantages in multinational enterprises," *Strategic Management Journal* 22: 237–50

Schmid, S. and J. Maurer 2008. "Relationships between subsidiaries – towards a classification scheme." Working Paper No. 35 (mimeo) ESCP-EAP, Berlin

Sölvell, Ö. and I. Zander 1998. "International diffusion of knowledge: isolating mechanisms and the role of the MNE" in Chandler, Hagström and Sölvell (eds.) *The Dynamic Firm: The Role of Technology, Strategy, Organization and Regions.* Oxford University Press, pp. 402–16

Soulsby, A. and E. Clark 2007. "Organizational theory and the post socialist transformation: contributions to organizational knowledge," *Human Relations* 60: 1419–42

Taplin, I. M. 2006. "Strategic change and organisational restructuring: how managers negotiate change initiatives," *Journal of International Management* 12: 284–301

Tasoluk, B., A. Yaprak and R. J. Calantone 2006. "Conflict and collaboration in headquarters–subsidiary relationships," *International Journal of Conflict Management* 17: 332–51

Van den Bulcke, D. 1984. "Decision-making in multinational enterprises and the information and consultation of employees: the proposed Vredeling directive of the EC Commission," *International Studies of Management and Organization* 14: 26–60

Walsh, S., J. Linton, R. Boylan and C. Sylla 2002. "The evolution of technology management practice in developing economies: findings from northern China," *International Journal of Technology Management* 24: 311–29

Weick, K. E. 1995. *Sensemaking in Organizations.* London: Sage

Welch, C., R. Marschan-Piekkari, H. Penttinen and M. Tahvanainen 2002. "Corporate elites as informants in qualitative international business research," *International Business Review* 11: 611–28

Williams, D. 1998. "The development of foreign-owned manufacturing subsidiaries: some empirical evidence," *European Business Review* 98: 282–86

Yamin, M. and R. R. Sinkovics, 2007. "ICT and MNE reorganisation: the paradox of control," *Critical Perspectives on International Business* 3: 322–36

Yin, R. K. 2003. *Case Study Research Design and Methods.* 3rd edn. Newbury Park/London/New Delhi: Sage

Zagare, F. C. 1984. *Game Theory.* London: Sage

8 Headquarters–subsidiary relationships from a social psychological perspective: how perception gaps concerning the subsidiary's role may lead to conflict

Stefan Schmid and Andrea Daniel

Introduction

In the international business (IB) literature, headquarters–subsidiary relationships are one of the central research topics (Johnston 2005; Paterson and Brock 2002). The question of how to manage relationships between headquarters and subsidiaries is also of practical relevance (Doz and Prahalad 1981; 1984). In this context, perception gaps between headquarters and subsidiary managers are a common phenomenon in multinational companies (MNCs) that is, however, still under-researched (Schmid and Daniel 2007). To illustrate the character and the implications of perception gaps, we will start this chapter with a brief case study. Research for the case was conducted in 2008, and comprised interviews with headquarters and subsidiary managers of a German MNC (for more details on the empirical case see Daniel 2010: 170–81).

In 1999, Autocomp – a German automotive supplier – acquired a Turkish firm to become one of several foreign subsidiaries of Autocomp. In its former group, the subsidiary had enjoyed considerable autonomy in its decision-making and operations. At the time of the acquisition, however, Autocomp's management aimed at integrating the new subsidiary into its network to the same extent as its other subsidiaries. From the perspective of the headquarters, this integration implied significant cuts in the subsidiary's autonomy in such areas as purchasing and sales, which were highly centralized at Autocomp. However, the Turkish subsidiary's management did not consider any potential impact of a change in ownership on the subsidiary's autonomy. This difference of perception led to serious conflict between headquarters and the Turkish subsidiary on a number of occasions.

The Turkish subsidiary management had, for instance, many personal relationships and contacts with suppliers that it did not intend to give up.

The managing director of the Turkish subsidiary was convinced that he could achieve the best results when he negotiated with his suppliers by himself, not involving headquarters representatives. Headquarters management, however, assumed that all purchasing negotiations were to be led by headquarters representatives. Assuming that it could still act autonomously, the subsidiary repeatedly ordered raw materials without the central purchasing department in Germany being aware of it. This not only undermined the central purchasing department's authority, but was also problematic because it concerned transactions requiring consent from the headquarters' supervisory board. "When your subsidiary signs contracts without you knowing, while your board needs to agree on such transactions beforehand, you have a serious problem," was mentioned by one headquarters representative. After a period of conflict, with intense discussions and arguments, a solution was found that was deemed acceptable by both parties: the subsidiary received permission to source specific materials locally that were available in the region around Turkey (and that were even available at lower prices), while most other materials were purchased centrally. One headquarters representative admitted that "it is true that they can get much better conditions locally. By giving them the mandate to buy certain materials, they get more freedom and the entire group can benefit from the good price."

In terms of sales, the Turkish subsidiary also continued its relationships with local customers. This led to problems, as the same customers were approached by central key account managers from Germany and by the subsidiary in Turkey – sometimes quoting different prices. From the headquarters' perspective, the subsidiary's behavior generated a conflict as the subsidiary acted quite differently from its expected role. A similar agreement as described above was finally found for the sales function in order to resolve the conflict: subsidiary management accepted that key account customers were handled by the central sales department at headquarters. The subsidiary, in turn, received sales responsibility for local customers in the sales areas of Turkey, India, the Middle East and Africa. First, this allowed the subsidiary to maintain at least some of its business relationships. Second, headquarters management realized that the subsidiary's sales qualities offered considerable potential benefits and could be used as a resource for Autocomp. Nevertheless, it was agreed that all contracts had to be approved by the headquarters before being signed by the Turkish subsidiary management.

Examples such as this can be found in numerous cases where MNCs face the challenge of coordinating their subsidiaries around the world in the most effective way. This short case illustrates the relevance of the major theme of this volume – politics, conflict and power in MNCs – for the relationship between headquarters and foreign subsidiaries in MNCs. On the one hand, German headquarters would have had the formal power to define a specific role for the subsidiary of Autocomp and force that role upon the subsidiary without going into dialogue with the subsidiary (such an imbalance of power is a general characteristic of headquarters–subsidiary relationships and poses a challenge for network models of MNCs, which will be mentioned below). On the other hand, the decision to grant the Turkish subsidiary a certain degree of autonomy in the purchasing and sales functions can be considered the result of a highly political process including questions of colliding interests, negotiating identities, resolving conflicts and approaching solutions (Dörrenbächer and Geppert 2006).

Traditionally, the IB literature conceived MNCs as strictly hierarchical organizations. Headquarters were considered the center, foreign subsidiaries the periphery. However, network models of the MNC that imply a different understanding of the relationship between headquarters and subsidiaries have become more popular over the last two decades (Hedlund and Kogut 1993; Schmid 2003: 274). While many contributions focus on inter-organizational and local networks (e.g. Andersson et al. 2002; McEvily and Zaheer 1999; Powell et al. 1996), this chapter concentrates on intra-organizational networks (Bartlett and Ghoshal 1991; Hedlund 1986; Prahalad and Doz 1987; Schmid et al. 2002). One important assumption of MNC network models is that subsidiaries can take highly differentiated roles and can fulfill different functions for the entire MNC or for parts of the MNC (Bartlett and Ghoshal 1986: 88; Birkinshaw and Hood 1998a: 6; Ghoshal and Nohria 1989: 323; Paterson and Brock 2002: 142).[1] The notion of differentiated subsidiary roles has inspired a considerable amount of conceptual work as well as empirical research (e.g. Gupta and Govindarajan 1994; Jarillo and Martinez 1990; White and Poynter 1984; Young et al. 1988; for an overview see Schmid et al. 1998; Schmid and Kutschker 2003).

---

[1] Network models assume that resources and competencies are distributed among different units of the MNC and that headquarters and subsidiaries cooperate with each other at the same level. Nevertheless, the exchange between different units needs to be organized and coordinated (Birkinshaw et al. 2000: 321–2; O'Donnell 2000: 543; Johnston 2005: 3); in order to fulfil this coordinating task, headquarters are required to play a strong central role in network MNCs (Ensign 1999: 301; Lipparini and Fratocchi 1999: 663). Implicitly, this (still) gives the headquarters a certain degree of power over the subsidiaries. However, in the network MNC power is not only residing at headquarters level; power is also shifted to (some or many) subsidiaries, for instance to subsidiaries that are centres of excellence or centres of competence (Schmid 2000; Moore 2001; Schmid 2003).

So far, the question of whether headquarters and subsidiary managers perceive a certain subsidiary's role in the same way has been largely neglected in IB research, despite its empirical relevance, as outlined at the beginning of this chapter by the case of Autocomp (for some exceptions, see Arvidsson 1999; Asakawa 2001; Birkinshaw *et al.* 2000; Chini *et al.* 2005; Denrell *et al.* 2004; for an overview see Schmid and Daniel 2007). A number of factors, such as different experiences of headquarters and subsidiary managers, imperfect flow of information within the MNC and decreasing dependence of subsidiaries on headquarters, might be expected to lead to differing perceptions of the subsidiary's role on both sides (Birkinshaw *et al.* 2000: 328; Chini *et al.* 2005: 146; Schmid and Daniel 2007: 14–16). Not only the introductory example of Autocomp and its Turkish subsidiary, but also various other examples (such as the perceptions of General Motors and General Motors' German subsidiary Opel about Opel's role, which recently received considerable public attention) highlight the practical relevance of the phenomenon (see also chapters of Koveshnikov and of Ybema and Byun in this volume). However, the theoretical foundation that the IB literature in general, and the subsidiary role research stream in particular, offer to study this issue seems limited. Many role typologies that we find in the IB literature have been established without a clear theoretical underpinning.

Setting out from this starting point, the present contribution has two major objectives. First, it aims at analyzing the possible implications of perception gaps between headquarters and subsidiary representatives – regarding the subsidiary's role[2] – on the headquarters–subsidiary relationship. Second, in order to reach the first objective, a role theoretical framework will be proposed that can be helpful for the analysis of the subsidiary role concept, and perception gaps between headquarters and subsidiaries with respect to subsidiary roles. The suggested framework is based on the open system approach proposed by Katz and Kahn (1978) in their "Social Psychology of Organizations." The role theoretical framework provides grounds for the general proposition that perception gaps are likely to lead to headquarters–subsidiary conflict. We can differentiate among three types of conflict: (1) distribution conflict, (2) process conflict and (3) goal conflict. Finally, we not only discuss possible ways to avoid the emergence of perception gaps, but we also reflect on the management of conflicts (see also Schmid and Daniel 2009).

[2] As will be shown later on, the role a subsidiary has can be determined along various dimensions (see, for instance, Schmid *et al.* 1998). We will focus on capabilities as one potential dimension.

Subsidiary roles in the international business literature

In the IB literature, the term "subsidiary role" is commonly used in relation to the differentiation of subsidiaries in a specific type of MNC – the network MNC. Network MNCs are the dominant type of MNCs in transnational industries in which forces of globalization and localization exist simultaneously (Bartlett and Ghoshal 1991). However, what is conceived as a subsidiary role in the IB literature? While Young and Tavares (2004: 224) interpret subsidiary roles in terms of a subsidiary's scope of responsibility, most authors do not reveal their general understanding of subsidiary roles. Instead, they typically consider two or three specific characteristics according to which they differentiate subsidiary roles without providing a definition of the subsidiary role concept. The number of dimensions that have been associated with the notion of a subsidiary's role is large. The range includes, for instance, "market scope," "product scope," "value added scope" (Birkinshaw and Morrison 1995; White and Poynter 1984), "decision-making autonomy" (D'Cruz 1986; Taggart 1997a), "strategic importance of the local environment," "subsidiary capabilities" (Bartlett and Ghoshal 1986, 1991; Hoffman 1994), "inflow of knowledge to the subsidiary," "outflow of knowledge from the subsidiary" (Gupta and Govindarajan 1991, 1994) or the subsidiary's "degree of localization and integration" (Jarillo and Martinez 1990; Taggart 1997b).

Although the literature generally assumes that subsidiaries possess a specific role, it may well be the case that multiple roles co-exist in a subsidiary (Schmid 2004: 247; Schmid and Kutschker 2003: 174; Tavares and Young 2006: 596). This may be due to the fact that subsidiaries frequently include distinct business units, have different products and therefore "may exhibit clear traits of one role in a certain business unit, but a distinct strategy concerning another business line" (Tavares and Young 2006: 596; see also Pearce and Tavares 2002). Furthermore, it can be argued that subsidiaries play different roles in different contexts, in different situations and at different points in time. For instance, a subsidiary may fulfill a particular role within the network of the MNC while playing another role in the context of its local business network (Johanson *et al.* 1996: 253; Miles and Perreault 1980: 138). Whereas this may instigate discussions of whether it is justified to refer to one specific subsidiary role, empirical research seems to confirm that a subsidiary can be associated with one predominant (overall) role within the MNC – at least at first sight (e.g. Birkinshaw and Morrison 1995; Furu 2001; Gupta and Govindarajan 1994; Harzing and Noorderhaven 2006; Jarillo and Martinez 1990; Young *et al.* 1988).

In the headquarters–subsidiary relationship, subsidiary roles are usually not explicitly determined, but develop in the interaction of several actors and are shaped by complex processes (Birkinshaw and Hood 1998b: 775; Dörrenbächer and Geppert 2006: 259; Hood and Taggart 1999: 515). First, a subsidiary's role is influenced by headquarters (for instance, via the assignment of a particular role to a subsidiary) as well as by the subsidiary itself (for instance, by efforts to increase its capabilities and to acquire new responsibilities) (Birkinshaw et al. 2000: 324; Young and Tavares 2004: 224). In addition, various stakeholders in the local environment – for instance, suppliers and customers – have an impact on a subsidiary's role, by exerting pressure on the subsidiary to adjust to their expectations (regarding the influence of the local environment see, for example, Benito et al. 2003; Eckert and Rossmeissl 2007; Schmid and Schurig 2003; see also chapters of Sorge and Rothe and of Williams and Geppert in this volume).

Furthermore, subsidiary roles are not static categories, but can evolve over time (see, for instance, the contributions in Birkinshaw and Hood 1998c). Subsidiaries can develop new capabilities, be granted more autonomy or gain responsibility for a larger market. However, subsidiaries' capabilities can also deteriorate or fall behind market requirements, so that responsibilities can consequently be lost (Birkinshaw 1996; Galunic and Eisenhardt 1996; see also Dörrenbächer and Gammelgaard in this volume). The process through which a subsidiary's role develops can also vary according to several characteristics (Schmid et al. 1998: 97). First of all, a role can be deliberately designed in order to fulfill a certain purpose or it may develop rather randomly due to emergent circumstances (Brock and Barry 2003: 552; Schmid 2003: 284–85). Second, a subsidiary's role can be more or less explicitly defined (Birkinshaw et al. 2000: 324). Third, the role may have evolved incrementally over a long-term process, or revolutionary changes may have led to the present situation (Pahlberg 1996: 22; Tavares and Young 2006: 596).

These various influences and development paths make it difficult to clearly determine a subsidiary's role at a certain point in time. Additionally, these factors increase the likelihood of perception gaps regarding the subsidiary's role. Despite the large number of contributions on subsidiary roles in the IB literature, the theoretical basis of this research is limited. Thus one objective of the present contribution is to develop a theoretical framework that can be used to study subsidiary roles. In the following section, we will build on the open system approach developed by Katz and Kahn (1978) so as to analyze the implications of perception gaps. To this end, we first argue that network MNCs can be viewed as open systems. We continue by outlining Katz and Kahn's approach. Next, we apply Katz and Kahn's approach to network MNCs and describe that subsidiaries can be considered as role takers within network MNCs. From this basis, we use Katz and Kahn's approach to derive that conflict can be expected as an implication of perception gaps between headquarters and subsidiary managers. We first outline the general relationship between perception gaps regarding subsidiary roles and conflict and then illustrate this relationship along the dimension of "subsidiary capabilities."

Theoretical development

Network MNCs as open systems

Although Katz and Kahn's "Social Psychology of the Organization" has been frequently cited referring to issues of organizational behavior (Katz and Kahn 1978), it has hardly been drawn on in empirical research (Miner 2003: 258). Katz and Kahn view organizations from an open system perspective, according to which the organization receives energetic input from its environment that is transformed in order to produce a certain output. The present contribution will adopt an open system approach to the network MNC. While this decision has various implications, the differentiation of roles according to the open system approach is most relevant in this context. From an open system perspective, social systems, such as organizations, lack a structure apart from their functioning and are held together by psychological forces, such as attitudes, perceptions, beliefs and motivations. They are based on the role behavior of their members, the norms that prescribe these behaviors and the values underlying these norms. Consequently, the internal differentiation of roles is as central for the open system approach as for the MNC network model approach. As roles constitute an essential element that is necessary for the social organization's functioning, a role theoretical framework is presented by Katz and Kahn as an integrated part of their open system approach. Katz and Kahn's role theoretical framework will be briefly outlined below, before it is applied to subsidiary roles in network MNCs.

Katz and Kahn's role theoretical approach

Role theory has long been a popular approach in sociology and social psychology (Biddle 1986: 67). In general, role theory attempts to explain individual behavior in the context of groups or the society at large (Jones and Deckro

1993: 218; Sarbin and Allen 1968: 490). The central idea within role theory is the role concept. Katz and Kahn (1978: 187) define social organizations as systems of roles. In their terminology, an individual's location within the total set of actions and interactions taking place in the organization is termed the individual's "office," "position," or also his or her "job" (Kahn and Quinn 1970: 52; Katz and Kahn 1978: 188). Each position within the organization is seen as associated with a set of behaviors expected of any person occupying that position. The behaviors that are expected in connection with a certain social position are considered the "role" (Kahn and Quinn 1970: 52; Katz and Kahn 1978: 188), while the behavioral demands made of a person in relation to a role are termed "role expectations" (Kahn and Quinn 1970: 53; Katz and Kahn 1978: 190). Since the role of the conduct of individuals is always interdependent with the behavior of individuals in complementary positions, the roles are generally defined in relation to other positions in the social structure (Katz and Kahn 1978: 189).

The set of people in an organization who are in some way dependent upon the behavior of an individual occupying a particular role, and who consequently have specific expectations regarding his or her behavior, are defined as the "role set" (Katz and Kahn 1978: 189). In addition to individuals inside the organization, persons outside the organization can also be members of the role set. The expectations held by members of the role set for a certain person will reflect their conception of the occupied office and its requirements, modified by their impression of the abilities and the personality of the holder of the position (Katz and Kahn 1978: 190). The role expectations, according to which the members of the role set evaluate the role occupant's performance, tend to be communicated or "sent" to the focal person (Katz and Kahn 1978: 190). Expectations of the role set can be communicated directly or indirectly and more or less completely or ambiguously (Kahn and Quinn 1970: 53). Behaviors by which members of the role set convey their role expectations could include explicit descriptions of their expectations, more subtle attempts to influence the main role occupant's behavior or positive or negative reinforcement (Katz and Kahn 1978: 190–92).

These influences, which are directly associated with the focal person's formal position within the organization, however, are not the only factors affecting the role occupant's understanding of his or her role (Katz and Kahn 1978: 192–94). Objective, impersonal properties of the situation itself can also influence role taking. In addition, internal motivation, motives, interests, personality traits, cognitive or social abilities, as well as an individual's understanding of his or her identity can have an impact on the individual's understanding of his or her role. For instance, when a person is highly moti-vated to reach a certain goal, he or she might be inclined to selectively per-ceive information that is in line with that goal (on the concept of selective perception in organizations see e.g. Beyer *et al.* 1997 or Dearborn and Simon 1958).

Subsidiary roles from Katz and Kahn's theoretical perspective

A network MNC represents a social organization that can be defined as a sys-tem of roles, according to Katz and Kahn (1978). Although Katz and Kahn do not explicitly outline the transfer of the role concept to organizational units, it seems legitimate to interpret subsidiaries as role bearers.[3] Corresponding to Katz and Kahn, subsidiary roles can be understood as patterns of behavior that are related to a specific position in the MNC and that fulfill a particu-lar function for the MNC. It may be argued that the subsidiary consists of a group of individuals who collectively behave in a certain way and thereby constitute the subsidiary's behavior. As with roles of individuals, subsidiary roles have to be defined in relation to other interdependent or complemen-tary positions in the social structure (Ensign 1999: 303–5; Katz and Kahn 1978: 189; Malnight 1996: 43; White and Poynter 1989: 58). The subsidiary's role set may be seen as comprising, for instance, headquarters, subsidiaries or other organizational units. Representatives of these units have certain expec-tations concerning the subsidiary's enactment of the role (Kahn and Quinn 1970: 52). In the present context the focus will be exclusively on headquar-ters–subsidiary relationships and the role of a focal subsidiary.

Role theory researchers generally assume that a role occupant can play more than one role (Katz and Kahn 1978: 53; Witte 1994: 31). As was out-lined above, this supposition is shared by researchers in the IB literature (Schmid 2004: 247; Schmid and Kutschker 2003: 174; Tavares and Young 2006: 585). However, when defining subsidiary roles according to Katz and Kahn's organizational role theoretical framework, this conceptualization does not fully correspond to the usage of the term subsidiary roles in the IB literature. While some subsidiary role dimensions, such as "outflow of knowledge" (Gupta and Govindarajan 1991, 1994), "outflow of resources"

---

[3] It is common practice in the business literature to define organizational units or entire organizations as "actors." For instance, agency theory in the context of headquarters–subsidiary relationships may be considered: both headquarters and the subsidiary are viewed as actors who behave in a specific way and who have certain cognitions (e.g. Kim *et al.* 2005; O'Donnell 2000; Yu *et al.* 2006). Role theory as well is applied to organizations within the context of business networks (Knight and Harland 2005).

(Randøy and Li 1998) or "extent of technical activities" (Ferdows 1989, 1997), represent attributes that can be interpreted as "behavior" shown by the subsidiary, other dimensions describe aspects of a different nature: "strategic importance of the local environment" (Bartlett and Ghoshal 1986, 1991), for instance, refers to the market in which a subsidiary is active, rather than the subsidiary itself; "inflow of knowledge" (Gupta and Govindarajan 1991, 1994) and "inflow of resources" (Randøy and Li 1998) consider activities that are executed by other organizational units than the subsidiary itself. "Procedural justice" addresses the "extent to which the dynamics of an MNC's strategy-making process are judged to be fair by the top managers of its subsidiaries" (Kim and Mauborgne 1993: 503), but does not imply any clear behavioral consequences for the subsidiary following from the respective judgment.[4] The literature on subsidiary roles not only lacks a clear definition of the subsidiary role concept, but it also generally lacks a theoretical basis. This often leads to an arbitrary selection of subsidiary role dimensions that differ in focus as well as level.

As role theory concedes, the role occupant and members of the role set may have different perceptions of the role occupant's role and consequently differing expectations regarding the related role behaviors (Kahn and Quinn 1970: 73). The diverse influences and expectations that affect the role occupant's role perception are primarily responsible for the emergence of these gaps (Kahn and Quinn 1970: 70–75). In the case of subsidiary roles within the MNC, the subsidiary representatives' perception of the subsidiary's role is mainly influenced by three sources of role expectations: (1) members of the subsidiary's internal role set – such as headquarters – who communicate expectations to the subsidiary more or less clearly (Birkinshaw and Hood 1998b: 775; Dörrenbächer and Geppert 2006: 259; Hood and Taggart 1999: 515); (2) members of the subsidiary's external role set, who may have totally different expectations than internal members (Johanson et al. 1996: 253; Miles and Perreault 1980: 138); and (3) the subsidiary managers have their own ideas regarding the subsidiary's role, which are influenced by their experiences, motives, interests and ambitions (Birkinshaw et al. 2000: 328; Chini et al. 2005: 146; Kahn and Quinn 1970: 73). Consequently, the subsidiary representatives develop a perception of the subsidiary's role that may differ from the expectations held by representatives of its network

---

[4] Judging the strategy-making process, fair or unfair does not determine the behavior that will follow; this behavior can take many different forms.

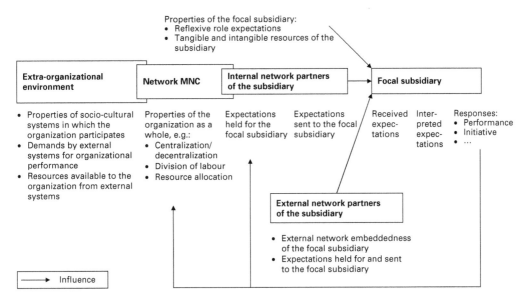

Fig. 8.1   Organizational role theoretical framework

partners (Kahn and Quinn 1970: 73; Katz and Kahn 1978: 203). For instance, a subsidiary manager might be interested in increasing and emphasizing a subsidiary's power within the MNC, as his own power is directly linked to the subsidiary's power. This personal motivation might bias his perception of the subsidiary's role. As an example, a subsidiary manager might be inclined to overestimate the subsidiary's capabilities in specific areas. Bouquet and Birkinshaw outline that controlling valuable resources (including specific capabilities or leading to specific capabilities) is one possibility for low-power actors in MNCs to increase their influence within the MNC (Bouquet and Birkinshaw 2008: 479).

Finally, the subsidiary as the role occupant enacts its role according to the role perception prevailing among its top managers (Ammeter *et al.* 2004: 55; Sarbin and Allen 1968: 140). This role enactment is met by the expectations of representatives of the subsidiary's network partners and may or may not satisfy these expectations. A schematic overview of the described application of the role theoretical framework to subsidiaries is provided in Figure 8.1. In the following, the implications of perception gaps will be analyzed on the basis of the role theoretical framework.

When interpreting Autocomp's Turkish subsidiary as a role occupant, the role set consists of Autocomp's headquarters and other Autocomp subsidiaries. The example shows that the role perception of the role bearer may differ significantly from the perception of members of the role set. Headquarters envisioned the subsidiary's function within the MNC mainly as a production location with no involvement in purchasing and sales activities. Although headquarters may have communicated these expectations, subsidiary managers did not agree and therefore, did not adjust their role perceptions. According to subsidiary managers, their former business partners in the region (members of the subsidiary's external role set) expected to continue to do business with them. As the management of the Turkish subsidiary also considered the headquarters management's ideas as disadvantageous, it did not stop acting according to its own role perception – and this behavior did not match the expectations of the managers at the headquarters.

Implications of perception gaps

Conflict as a general consequence of perception gaps

In the following, the focus will be on situations in which headquarters and subsidiary managers perceive the subsidiary's role differently (see also chapter of Blazejewski and Becker-Ritterspach in this volume). Role theory provides arguments for why a perception gap concerning a subsidiary's role is bound to result in conflict between headquarters and subsidiary. When the role occupant and members of the role set perceive the occupant's role differently, this situation can be referred to as "role dissensus" (e.g. Floyd and Lane 2000: 164; Toffler 1981: 401). It was argued that such inconsistencies within a role system decrease the efficiency of the interaction between role occupant and members of the role set (Solomon *et al.* 1985: 105). In particular, role theory proposes that role dissensus will lead to conflict:

Role theory is clear in its implications regarding the consequences of role dissensus. If it is not removed, the interaction is unlikely to proceed smoothly and satisfactorily. If there are important differences in the participants' roles, their behaviors will not mesh and cooperative action will be difficult to achieve. What actor views as the correct response to his behavior will not be the behavior suggested to other by his role definition. In addition, a mutual dislike is likely to develop because each will feel that the other is not behaving properly. In fact, just the knowledge that one's interaction partner sees things differently may be sufficient to cause a significant degree of enmity. (Heiss 1981: 120–21)

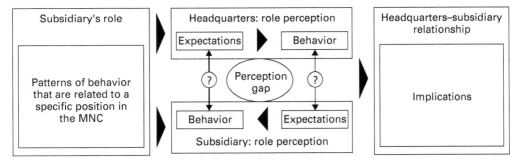

Fig. 8.2   Proposed conceptual framework

Role dissensus is first of all a perceptual or cognitive concept. However, perceptions and cognitions are central triggers of human actions and as such are also the bases of role behavior (Deutsch 1969: 14; Fisher 1990: 6; Grinyer and Spender 1979: 130; Mantere 2008: 294; March and Simon 1958: 127–29). In the case of the subsidiary's role, a certain role perception will entail corresponding role expectations. When headquarters and subsidiary managers develop differing role expectations, the behavior of one party will not match the expectations of the other party (Bartlett and Ghoshal 1986: 88). Katz and Kahn define conflict as behavior of one party that tends to prevent or compel some outcome against the resistance of the other party (Katz and Kahn 1978: 613). Behavior that is inconsistent with the other side's expectations may be interpreted as interference or blocking by the other party. Empirical research confirms that behavior that is considered as interference, blocking or otherwise conflicting will evoke conflicting behavior in response (Katz and Kahn 1978: 635). It should be emphasized, however, that conflict is not assumed to be necessarily negative. Rather, it may just as well lead to positive consequences, such as changes or innovation (Alter 1990: 482; Berkel 2003: 402; Litterer 1966: 179–80; Rahim 2002: 211).[5] Figure 8.2 summarizes the arguments presented above. Katz and Kahn outline that overt conflict does not necessarily occur

> … at the point of the essential incompatibility … The locus of the overt conflict might presumably be chosen for reasons of strategy, left to chance, or might develop out of competitive activities in the area of incompatibility. (Katz and Kahn 1978: 623–24)

---

[5] Similar reasoning can, for instance, be found in the literature on international joint ventures, where the fact that perceptual differences often result in conflict is discussed as well (see, for instance, Fey and Beamish 2000: 143), and in the literature on headquarters–subsidiary relationships in general, where Bartlett and Ghoshal (1986: 88) find empirical evidence that differing perceptions and expectations of headquarters and subsidiary representatives lead to conflict.

While this statement cautions us to keep in mind that the connection between a perception gap and overt conflict is probably not always straightforward, it is not assumed that both issues are entirely unrelated. Consequently, in the following paragraphs, we will present our arguments regarding pathways along which perception gaps concerning a subsidiary's role might affect the headquarters–subsidiary relationship. The dimension "subsidiary capabilities" will be taken into account as an example for three reasons: first, this dimension is frequently considered in IB research on subsidiary roles (e.g. Bartlett and Ghoshal 1986; 1991; Harzing 2000; Harzing and Noorderhaven 2006). Second, in contrast to many other subsidiary role dimensions, it can be directly associated with the definition of subsidiary roles as patterns of behavior. Third, specific capabilities can be a source of power for a subsidiary (Bouquet and Birkinshaw 2008). In the following, we will draw on Bartlett and Ghoshal's role typology, in which "subsidiary capabilities" constitute one dimension besides "market importance" (Bartlett and Ghoshal 1986; 1991).

It is not intended to provide a comprehensive list of the consequences that perception gaps concerning a subsidiary's capabilities may have. Rather, the intent is to show how Katz and Kahn's framework can be combined with contributions from the IB literature in order to suggest potential effects of perception gaps. The basic idea can be described as follows: the IB literature states various assumptions concerning characteristics of the headquarters–subsidiary relationship, depending on the subsidiary role or individual subsidiary role dimensions. These relationships between a subsidiary's role and the headquarters–subsidiary relationship are conceptually derived or empirically established. The framework presented above brings in an additional dimension. According to the framework, the subsidiary's role is associated with specific behaviors and specific expectations of both headquarters and the subsidiary. Consequently, when differing perceptions of the subsidiary's role exist among headquarters and subsidiary managers, it can be assumed that the behavior of one party will probably not match the expectations of the other party. In the following paragraphs, the nature of expectations associated with the role dimension "subsidiary capabilities" will be discussed, as well as the consequences of perception gaps regarding this dimension. The consequences of perception gaps will be structured into three conflict types, according to the system's theoretical categories: input, throughput and output. In terms of input, the distribution of resources to the subsidiary will be taken into account; regarding throughput, we consider the processes carried out at the subsidiary; and when it comes to output, the goals of the subsidiary are examined. For this reason, we differentiate between (1) distribution conflicts, (2) process conflicts and (3) goal conflicts in the next subsection.

Conflict in the case of perception gaps concerning subsidiary capabilities

The capabilities of a subsidiary can be expected to influence the unit's processes, as well as its results and the amount of resources it receives. In general, two situations may emerge that can be referred to as perception gaps. On the one hand, subsidiary managers may perceive a subsidiary as more capable than headquarters managers. On the other hand, the reverse situation is conceivable (Arvidsson 1999: 102–3; Birkinshaw *et al.* 2000: 326). In order to be able to present a clear argument, the following rationale will be based on the simplifying assumption that either subsidiary managers perceive high capabilities and headquarters managers perceive low capabilities, or vice versa. While our argument concentrates on the extreme cases, it is acknowledged, however, that in reality, many constellations in between can occur.

(1) Distribution conflict: first of all, input into the subsidiary in the form of resources is taken into account. In accordance with other authors in the IB literature, Bartlett and Ghoshal (1991: 105–11) assume that an MNC's investment in a subsidiary should increase with increasing capabilities, as well as with increasing market importance. Despite the expected interaction effect between subsidiary capabilities and market importance, a trend can be predicted for each individual dimension. For subsidiary capabilities this implies that a higher degree of capabilities tends to be associated with a higher degree of investment (Lusk 1972: 567). Such a relationship has been empirically confirmed for financial and non-financial investments (Furu 2001: 143). According to the proposed conceptual framework, it may be assumed that differing perceptions of the subsidiary's position in terms of capabilities may be associated with differing expectations concerning the distribution of resources. Subsidiary managers who perceive their subsidiary as more capable than headquarters managers may feel deprived of due recognition from headquarters, in the form of various types of resources that would allow for the utilization of the subsidiary's capabilities to their fullest extent. This situation may result in distribution conflict. In the reverse situation, however, when headquarters managers regard a subsidiary as more capable than subsidiary managers, subsidiary managers

will not expect to obtain more resources from headquarters than they receive. Therefore, distribution conflict is less likely when headquarters managers perceive a subsidiary as more capable than subsidiary managers do.

(2) Process conflict: empirical research shows that headquarters managers who perceive a subsidiary as insufficiently capable are likely to interfere with the subsidiary's processes (Tasoluk et al. 2007: 337). Headquarters managers may attempt to change processes at the subsidiary or interfere with the subsidiary's practices in its market. When subsidiary managers, at the same time, rate their subsidiary's capabilities rather high, they will attempt to resist headquarters' interference, so that process conflict arises. As subsidiary capabilities can be observed in relation to processes in various functional areas, i.e. R&D, production, marketing, logistics and so on (Benito *et al.* 2003: 450; Moore 2000: 161, 2001: 285; Porter 1986: 20–1), conflict is expected to emerge in the functional area in which the perception gap exists, or even in the organization as such. In contrast, when headquarters managers perceive a subsidiary as more capable of a particular function than subsidiary managers, this is probably associated with the judgment that the related processes at the subsidiary are satisfactory. Headquarters managers are supposed to be less inclined to change the subsidiary's processes. This proposition is backed by the finding that more capable subsidiaries are likely to enjoy higher autonomy than less capable subsidiaries (Young and Tavares 2004: 217). As the transfer of best practices is costly and difficult, due to the "stickiness" of knowledge (Davenport *et al.* 1998: 46; Szulanski 1996: 29–30; Teece 1977: 242), the probability that headquarters managers will attempt to introduce new processes to a capable subsidiary, in the face of subsidiary managers' resistance, is rather low. A reason for conflict regarding processes at the subsidiary is consequently not detected.

(3) Goal conflict: finally, attention is directed to the subsidiary's goals. Depending on its perceived capabilities, certain goals will be regarded as realistic for a subsidiary (Delios and Beamish 2001: 1029). When subsidiary managers judge their subsidiary more capable than headquarters managers, it might be assumed that subsidiary managers will consider the goals set by headquarters as easy to reach (Luo 2002: 194). However, at the same time, it is possible that subsidiary managers who perceive their subsidiary as very capable might try to pursue their own

goals, which may not be fully aligned with the headquarters' goals, thereby paving the way for goal conflict. If headquarters managers perceive higher capabilities than subsidiary managers, they will aim at higher goals and will expect better results than subsidiary managers. Therefore, subsidiary managers who do not consider their subsidiary as capable as headquarters managers do, will judge the goals of the headquarters managers as too ambitious. Consequently, goal conflict may follow.

The case of Autocomp's Turkish subsidiary, as described in the introduction, can be interpreted as a case of process conflict regarding the subsidiary's autonomy in the areas of purchasing and sales. Headquarters managers perceived the subsidiary as less autonomous than the subsidiary managers did. Subsidiary managers assumed that they could operate autonomously in the areas of purchasing and sales without involving headquarters in the process. Headquarters managers envisioned a much less independent role for the subsidiary. This perception gap led to process conflict, which was finally resolved by a compromise between the two extreme positions.

Conclusions

The present contribution suggests a role theoretical framework which can serve as a basis for analyzing subsidiary roles in network MNCs. In particular, the framework may be used in order to study headquarters and subsidiary representatives' perceptions and expectations regarding subsidiary roles. The role theoretical framework offers insights into factors that influence the development of specific role perceptions. It is argued that the role occupant's perception of the role is affected by role expectations of internal and external members of the role set (that are communicated to the role occupant, as well as the role occupant's own ideas of the role). Consequently, theoretical reasoning is presented for the emergence of perception gaps between the subsidiary as role occupant and headquarters as internal network partner. At the same time, propositions are developed regarding the implications of differing perceptions. In general, the role theoretical framework assumes that perception gaps between headquarters and subsidiary representatives regarding the subsidiary's role will lead to headquarters–subsidiary conflict. It is illustrated how perception gaps concerning the subsidiary role dimension "capabilities" may result in distribution, process and goal conflicts. This highlights the fact that perceptions of subsidiary roles are not only interesting from a theoretical perspective, but also for the management of MNCs.

While differing perceptions of the subsidiary's role as such cannot be considered positive or negative, their consequences for the MNC are decisive. The presented approach emphasizes headquarters–subsidiary conflict as an implication of perception gaps regarding a subsidiary's role. Although the general conflict literature asserts that functional and dysfunctional implications of conflict are conceivable (Jehn and Mannix 2001; Litterer 1966: 179–80; Rahim 2002: 211), most authors emphasize the dysfunctional consequences of headquarters–subsidiary conflict (Johanson et al. 1996: 254; Roth and Nigh 1992: 286). In terms of negative implications, headquarters–subsidiary conflict may, for instance, result in the reduction of overall effectiveness, impede the achievement of the firm's goals and lead to frustration (Johanson et al. 1996; Roth and Nigh 1992). From this point of view, it seems desirable to avoid the emergence of perception gaps and subsequent conflict whenever possible. At the same time, it is frequently assumed that the consequences of conflict can be shaped by appropriate conflict management (Pahl and Roth 1993: 148; Tasoluk et al. 2007: 341). This means that effective conflict management strategies have to be identified to reduce the negative effects of conflict and to stimulate functional outcomes, such as increased creativity, innovation and change. In the following, we will briefly reflect on both perspectives: first, we will review some possibilities to prevent perception gaps and second, we will take a look at conflict management strategies.

Whereas some factors that may affect perception gaps, such as cultural differences, geographical distance and characteristics of the persons involved, cannot be deliberately manipulated, other influencing factors are within management's grip. A clear role definition that unambiguously determines rights and responsibilities may contribute to the prevention of perception gaps (Hulbert et al. 1980: 13). However, it seems advisable that headquarters does not dictate such a definition. Headquarters in (strictly) hierarchical MNCs generally can be assumed to have (or assume to have) the power to unilaterally assign a certain role to a subsidiary (Bartlett and Ghoshal 1986: 93; Ferdows 1997: 78); this is the reason why such exercise of power can still be frequently observed in traditional headquarters–subsidiary relationships (Schmid et al. 1998: 97–8). However, in the network MNC, we have to depart from the assumption and practice of unilateral power. In the network MNC, there is a clear advantage to developing consent that is acceptable to both sides. Communication appears to be a central means to avoiding perception gaps between headquarters and subsidiary managers. Frequent and open exchange, as well as the discussion of ideas and perspectives emerging on each side, may establish a common understanding of the subsidiary's role. Even if gaps appear, they can be bridged through frank interaction. Admittedly, political reasons may sometimes cause the interacting parties to hide their true motives and interests and thereby inhibit such frank interaction. While regular and open communication may positively influence the quality of a headquarters–subsidiary relationship, personal contact in the form of visits to each other's locations might even enhance this effect.[6] Particular attention regarding the perceptions of subsidiary roles may be necessary for headquarters–subsidiary relationships that involve acquired subsidiaries with developed structures and "identities." While some acquisitions require a high degree of adjustment on the side of the newly acquired unit (Haspeslagh and Jemison 1991: 145–66), the subsidiary managers may possess a predetermined idea of the subsidiary's role that may not be easily altered (Garnier 1982: 900).[7] The case of Autocomp and its Turkish subsidiary illustrates such a situation.

It is frequently assumed that the question of whether the functional or dysfunctional implications of conflict prevail mainly depends on the way in which conflict is managed (Alper *et al.* 2000: 625; Hignite *et al.* 2002: 316; Kelly 2006: 27; Thomas 1976: 891–92). Therefore, the second option that managers have in dealing with perception gaps is to try to manage the resulting role-related conflict in a constructive way. A considerable number of researchers promote collaboration as the most beneficial conflict management strategy, when the goal is to optimize the welfare of both parties or a larger system of which the parties are members (e.g. Blake and Mouton 1964; Brown 1983; Eiseman 1978; Fisher *et al.* 1991; Likert and Likert 1976; Rubin *et al.* 1994). Not only theoretical contributions, but also empirical findings support this assumption. The results indicate that collaboration can lead to superior outcomes for the involved individuals (e.g. satisfaction and self-esteem), for their relationship (e.g. trust and respect) and for the entire organization (e.g. more open exchange of information and more integrative decisions) (Thomas 1992a: 682–90, 1992b: 271). The compromise found by Autocomp's

---

[6] For a more differentiated discussion on sociopolitical approaches, see Geppert and Williams (2006).
[7] The IB literature confirms a positive relationship between subsidiaries that were established through acquisition (versus greenfield establishments) and the subsidiary's autonomy (Young and Tavares 2004: 217). However, it should be kept in mind that there are various alternatives for integrating acquired subsidiaries that imply differing requirements for the adjustment of the subsidiary's role (see, for instance, Haspeslagh and Jemison 1991: 145–66).

headquarters and the Turkish subsidiary presents an instance where collaboration led to a superior solution for the parties involved. Despite the fact that headquarters could have exerted its formal power over the Turkish subsidiary and forced it into compliance with the less autonomous perception of the subsidiary's role, a collaborative solution was chosen. For Autocomp, the decision to concede part of the overall purchasing responsibility to its Turkish subsidiary, based on the subsidiary's specific competence in this area, represents a step from a more hierarchical towards a more network-type of MNC. Similarly, the sales mandate that the Turkish subsidiary received for local customers in the areas of Turkey, India, the Middle East and Africa was another step in this direction, even if final approval for major contracts is still required from headquarters.

However, although collaboration may be the most functional solution for the entire system in the long term, the individual actors may find other modes, such as competition, more attractive in the short term. It is therefore crucial to organize structural variables of the headquarters–subsidiary relationship in a way that provides incentives for collaboration (Katz and Kahn 1978: 644; Thomas 1992b: 271). MNCs have not only to find the right structural prerequisites; they also need to have an organizational culture that emphasizes collaboration (and not just competition). This includes fostering human resource practices, leadership styles and management systems that are appropriate for the network MNC.

REFERENCES

Alper, S., D. Tjosvold and K. S. Law 2000. "Conflict management, efficacy, and performance in organizational teams," *Personnel Psychology* 53: 625–42

Alter, C. 1990. "An exploratory study of conflicts and coordination in interorganizational service delivery system," *Academy of Management Journal* 33: 478–502

Ammeter, A. P., C. Douglas, G. R. Ferris and H. Goka 2004. "A social relationship conceptualization of trust and accountability in organizations," *Human Resource Management Review* 14: 47–65

Andersson, U., M. Forsgren and U. Holm 2002. "The strategic impact of external networks: subsidiary performance and competence development in the multinational corporation," *Strategic Management Journal* 23: 979–96

Arvidsson, N. 1999. *The Ignorant MNE. The Role of Perception Gaps in Knowledge Management*. Stockholm School of Economics

Asakawa, K. 2001. "Organizational tension in international R&D management: the case of Japanese firms," *Research Policy* 30: 735–57

Bartlett, C. A. and S. Ghoshal 1986. "Tap your subsidiaries for global reach," *Harvard Business Review* 64: 87–94

Bartlett, C. A. and S. Ghoshal 1991. *Managing Across Borders: The Transnational Solution*. Boston, MA: Harvard Business School Press

Benito, G. R. G., B. Grøgaard and R. Narula 2003. "Environmental influences on MNE subsidiary roles: economic integration and the Nordic Countries," *Journal of International Business Studies* 34: 443–56

Berkel, K. 2003. "Konflikte in und zwischen Gruppen" in von Rosenstiel, Regnet and Domsch (eds.) *Führung von Mitarbeitern*. 5th edn. Stuttgart: Schäffer-Poeschel, pp. 397–414

Beyer, J. M., P. Chattopadhyay, W. H. Glick, D. Ogilvie and D. Pugliese 1997. "The selective perception of managers revisited," *Academy of Management Journal* 49: 716–37

Biddle, B. J. 1986. "Recent developments in role theory," *Annual Review of Sociology* 12: 67–92

Birkinshaw, J. 1996. "How multinational subsidiary mandates are gained and lost," *Journal of International Business Studies* 27: 467–95

Birkinshaw, J. and N. Hood 1998a. "Introduction and overview" in Birkinshaw and Hood (eds.) *Multinational Corporate Evolution and Subsidiary Development*. Basingstoke: Macmillan, pp. 1–19

1998b. "Multinational subsidiary evolution: capability and charter change in foreign-owned subsidiary companies," *Academy of Management Review* 23: 773–95

1998c. *Multinational Corporate Evolution and Subsidiary Development*. Basingstoke: Macmillan

Birkinshaw, J. and A. J. Morrison 1995. "Configurations of strategy and structure in subsidiaries of multinational subsidiaries," *Journal of International Business Studies* 26: 729–53

Birkinshaw, J., U. Holm, P. Thilenius, and N. Arvidsson 2000. "Consequences of perception gaps in the headquarters–subsidiary relationship," *International Business Review* 9: 321–44

Blake, R. R. and J. S. Mouton 1964. *The Managerial Grid*. Houston: Gulf

Bouquet, C. and J. Birkinshaw 2008. "Managing power in the multinational corporation: how low-power actors gain influence," *Journal of Management* 34: 477–508

Brock, D. M. and D. Barry 2003. "What if planning were really strategic? Exploring the strategy-planning relationship in multinationals," *International Business Review* 12: 543–61

Brown, L. D. 1983. *Managing Conflict at Organizational Interfaces*. Reading: Addison-Wesley

Chini, T., B. Ambos and K. Wehle 2005. "The headquarters–subsidiaries trench: tracing perception gaps within the multinational corporation," *European Management Journal* 23: 145–53.

D'Cruz, J. 1986. "Strategic management of subsidiaries" in Etemad and Séguin (eds.) *Managing the Multinational Subsidiary: Response to Environmental Changes and to Host Nation R&D Policies*. London: Croom Helm, pp. 75–89

Daniel, A. 2010. *Perception Gaps between Headquarters and Subsidiary Managers: Differing Perspectives on Subsidiary Roles and Their Implications*. Wiesbaden: Gabler

Davenport, T. H., D. W. De Long and M. C. Beers 1998. "Successful knowledge management projects," *Sloan Management Review* 39: 43–57

Dearborn, D. and H. Simon 1958. "Selective perception: a note on the departmental identifications of executives," *Sociometry* 21: 140–4

Delios, A. and P. W. Beamish 2001. "Survival and profitability: the roles of experience and intangible assets in foreign subsidiary performance," *Academy of Management Journal* 44: 1028–38

Denrell, J., N. Arvidsson and U. Zander 2004. "Managing knowledge in the dark: an empirical study of the reliability of capability evaluations," *Management Science* 50: 1491–503

Deutsch, M. 1969. "Conflicts: productive and destructive," *Journal of Social Issues* 25: 7–41

Dörrenbächer, C. and M. Geppert 2006. "Micro-politics and conflicts in multinational corporations: current debates, re-framing, and contributions of this Special Issue," *Journal of International Management* 12: 251–65

Doz, Y. and C. K. Prahalad 1981. "Headquarters influence and strategic control in MNCs," *Sloan Management Review* 23: 15–30

  1984. "Patterns of strategic control within multinational corporations," *Journal of International Business Studies* 15: 55–72

Eckert, S. and F. Rossmeissl 2007. "Local heroes, regional champions or global mandates? Empirical evidence on the dynamics of German MNC subsidiary roles in central Europe," *Journal of East-West Business* 13: 191–218

Eiseman, J. W. 1978. "Reconciling 'incompatible' positions," *Journal of Applied Behavioural Science* 14: 133–50

Ensign, P. C. 1999. "The multinational corporation as a coordinated network: organizing and managing differently," *Thunderbird International Business Review* 41: 291–322

Ferdows, K. 1989. "Mapping international factory networks" in Ferdows (ed.) *Managing International Manufacturing*. Amsterdam: North-Holland/Elsevier, pp. 3–21

  1997. "Making the most of foreign factories," *Harvard Business Review* 75: 73–86

Fey, C. F. and P. W. Beamish 2000. "Joint venture conflict: the case of Russian international joint ventures," *International Business Review* 9: 139–62

Fisher, R. J. 1990. *The Social Psychology of Intergroup and International Conflict Resolution*. New York: Springer

Fisher, R., W. Ury and B. Patton 1991. *Getting to YES: Negotiating Agreement without Giving In*. 2nd edn. Boston, MA: Houghton Mifflin

Floyd, S. W. and P. J. Lane 2000. "Strategizing throughout the organization: managing role conflict in strategic renewal," *Academy of Management Review* 25: 154–77

Furu, P. 2001. "Drivers of competence development in different types of multinational R&D subsidiaries," *Scandinavian Journal of Management* 17: 133–49

Galunic, D. C. and K. M. Eisenhardt 1996. "The evolution of intracorporate domains: divisional charter losses in high-technology, multidivisional corporations," *Organization Science* 7: 255–82

Garnier, G. H. 1982. "Context and decision making autonomy in the foreign affiliates of US multinational corporations," *Academy of Management Journal* 25: 893–908

Geppert, M. and K. Williams 2006. "Global, national and local practices in multinational corporations: towards a sociopolitical framework," *International Journal of Human Resource Management* 17: 49–69

Ghoshal, S. and N. Nohria 1989. "Internal differentiation within multinational corporations," *Strategic Management Journal* 10: 323–37

Grinyer, P. H. and J. C. Spender 1979. "Recipes, crises, and adaptation in mature business," *International Studies of Management & Organization* 9: 113–33

Gupta, A. K. and V. Govindarajan 1991. "Knowledge flows and the structure of control within multinational corporations," *Academy of Management Review* 16: 768–92

1994. "Organizing for knowledge flows within MNCs," *International Business Review* 3: 443–57

Harzing, A.-W. 2000. "An empirical analysis and extension of the Bartlett and Ghoshal typology of multinational companies," *Journal of International Business Studies* 31: 101–19

Harzing, A.-W. and N. Noorderhaven 2006. "Knowledge flows in MNCs: an empirical test and extension of Gupta and Govindarajan's typology of subsidiary roles," *International Business Review* 15: 195–214

Haspeslagh, P. C. and D. B. Jemison 1991. *Managing Acquisitions.* New York: Free Press

Hedlund, G. 1986. "The hypermodern MNC – a heterarchy?," *Human Resource Management* 25: 9–35

Hedlund, G. and B. Kogut 1993. "Managing the MNC: the end of the missionary era" in Hedlund (ed.) *Organization of Transnational Corporations.* London, New York: United Nations Library on Transnational Corporations, pp. 343–58

Heiss, J. 1981. "Social roles" in Rosenberg and Turner (eds.) *Social Psychology. Social Perspectives.* New York: Basic Books, pp. 94–129

Hignite, M. A., T. M. Margavio and J. M. Chin 2002. "Assessing the conflict resolution profiles of emerging information systems professionals," *Journal of Information Systems Education* 13: 315–24

Hoffman, R. C. 1994. "Generic strategies for subsidiaries of multinational corporations," *Journal of Managerial Issues* 6: 69–87

Hood, N. and J. H. Taggart 1999. "Subsidiary development in German and Japanese manufacturing subsidiaries in the British isles," *Regional Studies* 33: 513–28

Hulbert, J. M., W. K. Brandt and R. Richers 1980. "Marketing planning in the multinational subsidiary: practices and problems," *Journal of Marketing* 44: 7–15

Jarillo, J. C. and J. I. Martinez 1990. "Different roles for subsidiaries: the case of multinational corporations in Spain," *Strategic Management Journal* 11: 501–12

Jehn, K. A. and E. A. Mannix 2001. "The dynamic nature of conflict: a longitudinal study of intragroup conflict and group performance," *Academy of Management Journal* 44: 238–51

Johanson, J., C. Pahlberg and P. Thilenius 1996. "Conflict and control in MNC new product introduction," *Journal of Market Focused Management* 1: 249–65

Johnston, S. 2005. *Headquarters and Subsidiaries in Multinational Corporations: Strategies, Tasks and Coordination.* Basingstoke: Palgrave Macmillan

Jones, R. E. and R. F. Deckro 1993. "The social psychology of project management conflict," *European Journal of Operational Research* 64: 216–28

Kahn, R. L. and R. P. Quinn 1970. "Role stress: a framework for analysis" in McLean (ed.) *Mental Health and Work Organizations.* Chicago, IL: Rand McNally, pp. 50–115

Katz, D. and R. L. Kahn 1978. *The Social Psychology of Organizations.* 2nd edn. New York: Wiley

Kelly, J. 2006. "An overview of conflict," *Dimensions of Critical Care Nursing* 25: 22–8

Kim, W. C. and R. A. Mauborgne 1993. "Procedural justice, attitudes, and subsidiary top management compliance with multinationals' corporate strategic decisions," *Academy of Management Journal* 36: 502–26

Knight, L. and C. Harland 2005. "Managing supply networks: organizational roles in net-work management," *European Management Journal* 23: 281–92

Likert, R. and J. Likert 1976. *New Ways of Managing Conflict.* New York: McGraw-Hill

Lipparini, A. and L. Fratocchi 1999. "The capabilities of the transnational firm: accessing knowledge and leveraging inter-firm relationships," *European Management Journal* 17: 655–67

Litterer, J. A. 1966. "Conflict in organization: a re-examination," *Academy of Management Journal* 9: 178–86

Luo, Y. 2002. "Organizational dynamics and global integration: a perspective from subsidiary managers," *Journal of International Management* 8: 189–215

Lusk, E. J. 1972. "Discriminant analysis as applied to the resource allocation decision," *Accounting Review* 47: 567–75

Malnight, T. W. 1996. "The transition from decentralized to network-based MNC structures: an evolutionary perspective," *Journal of International Business Studies* 27: 43–65

Mantere, S. 2008. "Role expectations and middle manager strategic agency," *Journal of Management Studies* 45: 294–316

March, J. G. and H. A. Simon 1958. *Organizations.* New York: Wiley

McEvily, B. and A. Zaheer 1999. "Bridging ties: a source of firm heterogeneity in competitive capabilities," *Strategic Management Journal* 20: 1133–56

Miles, R. H. and W. D. Perreault Jr. 1980. "Organizational role conflict: its antecedents and consequences" in Katz, Kahn and Adams (eds.) *The Study of Organizations.* San Francisco: Jossey-Bass, pp. 136–56

Miner, J. B. 2003. "The rated importance, scientific validity, and practical usefulness of organizational behavior theories: a quantitative review," *Academy of Management Learning & Education* 2: 250–68

Moore, K. J. 2000. "The competence of formally appointed centres of excellence in the UK" in Holm and Pedersen (eds.) *The Emergence and Impact of MNC Centres of Excellence: A Subsidiary Perspective.* London: Macmillan, pp. 154–66

    2001. "A strategy for subsidiaries: centres of excellences to build subsidiary specific advantages," *Management International Review* 41: 275–90

O'Donnell, S. W. 2000. "Managing foreign subsidiaries: agents of headquarters, or an interdependent network?," *Strategic Management Journal* 21: 525–48

Pahl, J. M. and K. Roth 1993. "Managing the headquarters–foreign subsidiary relationship: the roles of strategy, conflict, and integration," *The International Journal of Conflict Management* 4: 139–65

Pahlberg, C. 1996. "MNCs differ – and so do subsidiaries," Department of Business Studies, Uppsala University

Paterson, S. L. and D. M. Brock 2002. "The development of subsidiary–management research: review and theoretical analysis," *International Business Review* 11: 139–63

Pearce, R. and A. T. Tavares 2002. "On the dynamics and coexistence of multiple subsidiary roles: an investigation of multinational operations in the UK" in Lundan (ed.) *Network Knowledge in International Business.* Cheltenham: Edward Elgar, pp. 73–90

Porter, M. E. 1986. "Competition in global industries: a conceptual framework" in Porter (ed.) *Competition in Global Industries.* Boston, MA: Harvard Business School Press, pp. 15–60

Powell, W. W., K. W. Koput and L. Smith-Doerr 1996. "Interorganizational collaboration and the locus of innovation: networks of learning in biotechnology," *Administrative Science Quarterly* 41: 116–45

Prahalad, C. K. and Y. L. Doz 1987. *The Multinational Mission. Balancing Local Demands and Global Vision.* New York: Free Press

Rahim, M. A. 2002. "Toward a theory of managing organizational conflict," *International Journal of Conflict Management* 13: 206–35

Randøy, T. and J. Li 1998. "Global resource flow and MNE network integration" in Birkinshaw and Hood (eds.) *Multinational Corporate Evolution and Subsidiary Development.* Basingstoke: Macmillan, pp. 76–101

Roth, K. and D. Nigh 1992. "The effectiveness of headquarters–subsidiary relationships: the role of coordination, control, and conflict," *Journal of Business Research* 25: 277–301

Rubin, J. Z., D. G. Pruitt and S. H. Kim 1994. *Social Conflict: Escalation, Stalemate, and Settlement.* 2nd edn. New York: McGraw-Hill

Sarbin, T. R. and V. L. Allen 1968. "Role theory" in Gardner and Aronson (eds.) *The Handbook of Social Psychology.* 2nd edn. vol. I. Reading: Addison-Wesley, pp. 488–567

Schmid, S. 2000. "Foreign subsidiaries as centres of competence – empirical evidence from Japanese multinationals" in Larimo and Kock (eds.) *Recent Studies in Interorganizational and International Business Research.* Vaasa: Vaasan Yliopiston Julkaisuja, pp. 182–204

   2003. "How multinational corporations can upgrade foreign subsidiaries: a case study from central and eastern Europe" in Stüting, Dorow, Claassen and Blazejewski (eds.) *Change Management in Transition Economies: Integrating Corporate Strategy, Structure and Culture.* Basingstoke: Palgrave Macmillan, pp. 273–90

   2004. "The roles of foreign subsidiaries in network MNCs – a critical review of the literature and some directions for future research" in Larimo (ed.) *European Research on Foreign Direct Investment and International Human Resource Management.* Vaasa: Vaasan Yliopiston Julkaisuja, pp. 237–55

Schmid, S. and A. Daniel 2007. "Are subsidiary roles a matter of perception? A review of the literature and avenues for future research." Working Paper No. 30, ESCP-EAP European School of Management, Berlin

   2009. "Subsidiary roles, perception gaps and conflict – A social psychological approach" in Schmid (ed.) *Management der Internationalisierung.* Wiesbaden: Gabler, pp. 183–202

Schmid, S. and M. Kutschker 2003. "Rollentypologien für ausländische Tochtergesellschaften in Multinationalen Unternehmungen" in Holtbrügge (ed.) *Management Multinationaler Unternehmungen.* Heidelberg: Physika/Springer, pp. 161–82

Schmid, S. and A. Schurig 2003. "The development of critical capabilities in foreign subsidiaries: disentangling the role of the subsidiary's business network," *International Business Review* 12: 755–82

Schmid, S., I. Bäurle and M. Kutschker 1998. "Tochtergesellschaften in international tätigen Unternehmungen – Ein "State-of-the-Art" unterschiedlicher Rollentypologien." Discussion Paper No. 104, Wirtschaftswissenschaftliche Fakultät Ingolstadt

Schmid, S., A. Schurig and M. Kutschker 2002. "The MNC as a network: a closer look at intraorganizational flows" in Lundan (ed.) *Network Knowledge in International Business.* Cheltenham: Edward Elgar, pp. 45–72

Solomon, M. R., C. Surprenant, J. A. Czepiel and E. G. Gutman 1985. "A role theory perspective on dyadic interactions: the service encounter," *Journal of Marketing* 49: 99–111

Szulanski, G. 1996. "Exploring internal stickiness: impediments to the transfer of best practice within the firm," *Strategic Management Journal* (Special Issue) 17: 27–43

Taggart, J. H. 1997a. "Autonomy and procedural justice: a framework for evaluating subsidiary strategy," *Journal of International Business Studies* 28: 51–76

1997b. "An evaluation of the integration-responsiveness framework: MNC manufacturing subsidiaries in the UK," *Management International Review* 37: 295–318

Tasoluk, B., A. Yaprak and R. J. Calantone 2007. "Conflict and collaboration in headquarters–subsidiary relationships: an agency theory perspective on product rollouts in an emerging market," *International Journal of Conflict Management* 17: 332–51

Tavares, A. T. and S. Young 2006. "Sourcing patterns of foreign-owned multinational subsidiaries in Europe," *Regional Studies* 40: 583–99

Teece, D. J. 1977. "Technology transfer by multinational firms: the resource cost of transferring technological know-how," *Economic Journal* 87: 242–61

Thomas, K. W. 1976. "Conflict and conflict management" in Dunnette (ed.) *Handbook of Industrial and Organizational Psychology*. Chicago, IL: Rand McNally, pp. 889–935

1992a. "Conflict and negotiation processes in organizations" in Dunnette and Hough (eds.) *Handbook of Industrial and Organizational Psychology*. 3rd edn. Palo Alto, CA: Consulting Psychologists Press, pp. 651–717

1992b. "Conflict and conflict management: reflections and update," *Journal of Organizational Behavior* 13: 265–74

Toffler, B. L. 1981. "Occupational role development: the changing determinants of outcomes for the individual," *Administrative Science Quarterly* 26: 396–418

White, R. E. and T. A. Poynter 1984. "Strategies for foreign-owned subsidiaries in Canada," *Business Quarterly* 49: 59–69

1989. "Achieving worldwide advantage with the horizontal organization," *Business Quarterly* 54: 55–60

Witte, E. H. 1994. *Lehrbuch Sozialpsychologie*. 2nd edn. Weinheim, Beltz: Psychologie-Verlags-Union

Young, S., N. Hood and S. Dunlop 1988. "Global strategies, multinational subsidiary roles and economic impact in Scotland," *Regional Studies* 22: 487–97

Young, S. and A. T. Tavares 2004. "Centralization and autonomy: back to the future," *International Business Review* 13: 215–37

Yu, C.-M. J., H.-C. Wong and Y.-C. Chiao 2006. "Local linkages and their effects on headquarters' use of process controls," *Journal of Business Research* 59: 1239–47

Part IV

Role of national identities and identity work

9 Subsidiary manager socio-political interaction: the impact of host country culture

Christopher Williams

Introduction

As a firm internationalizes, it builds a network of operations that creates value by exploiting markets and seeking resources and sources of knowledge that are themselves internationally distributed. This network of operations develops over time. Subsidiaries contribute to the overall MNC through their initial charter and set of capabilities handed to them by the corporation during the establishment phase. Over time, subsidiaries may subsequently attempt to extend their charter and capabilities and develop their influence and power within the MNC. Prior research has shown that subsidiary power enhancement may happen in a variety of ways, for example, as a result of embedment in host country business networks (Andersson *et al.* 2007), through internally driven capability development and local initiatives (Birkinshaw 2000), or seeking control over resources and gaining centrality in strategic networks (Bouquet and Birkinshaw 2008; see also chapters of Sorge and Rothe and Williams and Geppert in this volume). Recent research has highlighted micro-political negotiations between subsidiary and headquarters as an important determinant of subsidiary role development (Dörrenbächer and Gammelgaard 2006), placing a spotlight on the actual interests and goals of key subsidiary managers (Dörrenbächer and Geppert 2009). These explanations of subsidiary power development draw on a behavioral logic: it is ultimately individual subsidiary manager interactions with other actors within the MNC that cause power to ebb and flow.

As the firm internationalizes, however, it also builds a network of operations that is not just geographically and functionally dispersed, but one that is also culturally distant from the country of origin. Every overseas subsidiary is characterized by a psychic distance to its headquarters in addition to its charter, set of capabilities and local environment complexity. Psychic distance incorporates aspects of both cultural difference (e.g. derived from

Hofstede's (1980, 1991) dimensions of national culture), and business difference (economic, legal and political, business practices, market structure and language differences) (Evans and Mavondo 2002). The widely cited ramification of psychic distance is its ability to disrupt the flow of information between market and firm (Johanson and Vahlne 1977). There exists a vast literature examining issues of conducting business in culturally diverse environments, most notably in terms of international strategy (e.g. Kogut and Singh 1988; Hitt *et al.* 2006). Erramilli (1996) argued that beliefs and attitudes of managers, and consequently the patterns of decision-making, are shaped by national cultures. The argument follows that firms are better able to manage employees in culturally similar countries (Hitt *et al.* 2006). This literature also draws on behavioral logic to explain the international strategic choices made by the firm. The core thrust is that national cultural identity shapes how a manager responds to external stimuli and this in turn influences the effectiveness of international strategy.

When we consider these two streams of literature in conjunction, an interesting gap arises. On the one hand, power development in a subsidiary hinges on individual manager behavior, and on the other hand national cultural identity impacts manager behavior. Despite this, our understanding of how national culture influences power relations and political interactions during ongoing operations within the MNC remains weak. Recent syntheses of literature on MNC power development have all but omitted national culture as a potential explanation for power dynamics within the MNC (e.g. Bouquet and Birkinshaw 2008; Verbeke *et al.* 2007). This chapter seeks to address this gap by integrating recent work on internal power dynamics within MNCs and more established work on the influence of national culture on manager behavior. Our central argument is that national culture of the host country in which the subsidiary is located has a direct influence on the propensity of managers in the subsidiary to engage in interactions that have both social and political components, i.e. that are socio-political in nature. We define socio-political interaction as *mechanisms by which managers of subsidiaries relate to other managers within the MNC in order to exert or develop power for themselves*. Examples are as follows: becoming actively involved in budgeting with a headquarters, building alliances with managers in other subsidiaries, starting local entrepreneurial initiatives, attempting to resolve conflicts elsewhere within the MNC, withholding information about changes in the local environment. In all of these cases, the subsidiary manager is attempting to exert or extend the subsidiary's sphere of influence within the MNC. Such interactions can then lead to situations of internal conflict. In this sense, they represent behaviors that can obstruct, or irritate, organizational members outside of the subsidiary, giving rise to conflict (Van de Vliert *et al.* 1999). Furthermore, these interactions and resulting conflicts may occur vertically (with headquarters), horizontally (with peer subsidiaries) or with both simultaneously.

The core argument of this chapter is that subsidiary manager socio-political behaviors are shaped in large part by host country national culture; subsidiary employees' patterns of behavior, including their responses to the situations and issues facing them, are reinforced by their national identity and cultural characteristics (Schneider and De Meyer 1991; Smircich 1983). This perspective is under-researched, yet provides an important explanation for socio-political interaction within the MNC.

This chapter is structured as follows. The next section gives a background to organizational politics and conflict in the MNC, using the definition of socio-political interaction given above. Three important sets of factors that capture *manifestations* of socio-political interaction within the MNC are given. These are knowledge sharing, proactive behavior and normative integration. The first manifestation, knowledge sharing, refers to the inclinations of subsidiary managers to provide useful knowledge to other units of the MNC, and likewise to learn from other units. Second, proactive subsidiary managers are those with an action orientation towards the issues confronting them, and a willingness to exert their influence over other units of the MNC. Third, normative integration occurs when subsidiary managers share the same values and standards of behavior as managers from other units of the MNC, and are willing to socialize within the MNC. We argue that these three manifestations of socio-political interaction can apply in both vertical and horizontal relations. Following this we give a background to the influence of national culture on organizational behavior, highlighting the usefulness of Hofstede's (1980, 1991) dimensions of national culture. A model for empirical exploration is proposed showing how host country culture has the potential to influence knowledge flows, proactive behaviors and normative integration in both vertical and horizontal interactions. In the Methods and findings section we describe the questionnaire survey data used to explore this model, along with the results. Finally, we provide a discussion with implications for theory and practice, as well as recommendations for future research.

Organizational politics in the MNC

The conventional view of power in organizations is as a "capacity of individuals to exert their will over others" (Buchanan and Badham 1999: 611). Scholars have long recognized this capacity for individual influence in organizations, i.e. of workplace politics (e.g. Ferris and Kacmar 1992; Gandz and Murray 1980; Pfeffer 1994; Van de Vliert *et al.* 1999). Organizational politics is seen as "simply a fact of life" (Ferris and Kacmar 1992: 93) and "omnipresent" (Van de Vliert *et al.* 1999: 475). For some, organizational politics is necessary, especially when used by change agents to bring about change in the organization (Buchanan 2008; Buchanan and Badham 1999).

According to Mintzberg (1985), managers use politics to "ease the path for the execution of decisions" (Mintzberg 1985: 150). Politics is seen as a system of influence which can be used to challenge existing systems of influence (authority, ideology and expertise) and overcome sources of resistance to change. Politics can thus be used to promote new power bases and bring about change. Pfeffer (1981, 1994) described organizational power in terms of being in "the right place": having control over resources or budgets, having control or access to key information, and having formal authority. Morgan (1986) defined power in terms of control over decision processes, control over boundaries and even the ability to cope with uncertainty.

Whilst some scholars refer to the negative impact of organization and politics (e.g. Parker *et al.* 1995; Stone 1997), others have argued that organizational politics can actually serve the organization (Buchanan and Badham 1999; Mintzberg 1985; Pfeffer 1981; Williams and Lee 2009). Others have reported mixed findings on managers' perceptions of whether organizational politics is detrimental (Gandz and Murray 1980). This is echoed by the work of Van de Vliert *et al.* (1999), who showed how constructive and destructive ways of handling conflicts can be pursued in organizations, and that an optimum outcome for the organization and for relationships between actors occurs when both modes are pursued.

Mintzberg (1985) described a number of political "games" that organizational members may use in order to exert or develop power. Mintzberg (1985) was one of the first scholars to argue that different games can be used for different purposes. According to Mintzberg, games played to build a power base include sponsorship (an individual attaching to someone else with a higher status or power base with the intention of gaining more power), alliance building (carefully constructed contracts intending to support within peer groups for mutual benefit), empire building (building a power base by relying on subordinates), budgeting (gaining resources in an overt manner and pitting line manager against line manager), expertise (using knowledge in a specialist and non-replaceable way or alternatively refusing to use knowledge) and lording (using "legitimate power in illegitimate ways" such as a technical expert over someone who is not skilled in the specific area).

Within the MNC, subsidiary managers may engage in political games to increase the power base of their subsidiary. The more developed the sources of power in a subsidiary, the more effective its bargaining position is likely to be. Subsidiary managers can develop new competences through political arena, i.e. using social interaction with internal actors in order to develop power for themselves. One example of this is when entrepreneurial initiatives start in a subsidiary (Birkinshaw and Ridderstråle 1999). Entrepreneurial subsidiary initiatives can face significant resistance from a "corporate immune system" – a set of forces in the MNC that attempt to preserve the status quo and "suppress the advancement of creation-oriented activities" (Birkinshaw 2000: 39). The corporate immune system comes about because of "interpreted predispositions" of headquarters managers. Corporate managers act in a way to counter any unplanned opportunism. These headquarters managers may be suspicious and highly skeptical of any new initiative put forward by subsidiary managers. Headquarters managers can also act in an ethnocentric way (Perlmutter 1969) because they have developed strongly embedded world views that reflect the historic success of the corporation, not the current business reality (Birkinshaw 2000: 36).

Headquarters managers may also resist change through parochial self-interest (they perceive a threat to their own status) or lack of trust (the initiative is seen as an "intrusion into their jurisdiction" [Birkinshaw 2000: 42]). This results in delay, rejection or requests for greater justification for the initiative, managing a lobbying process between competing or rival initiatives, and/or an ongoing misalignment and lack of legitimacy (incompatibility with the corporate norms) across units.

Entrepreneurial subsidiary initiatives, however, are not the only reason for the emergence of political arena within the MNC. Williams and Lee (2009) argued that other internal factors within the international management context of the MNC have the potential to encourage internal politics. For example, when change agents fail to appreciate differences in requirements across subsidiaries this can lead to frustration in subsidiaries and provide impetus into an internal political arena. In addition, when individuals put up barriers to knowledge flows because they lack intrinsic motivation, an internal political arena can arise (Williams and Lee 2009). These examples are not necessarily connected to subsidiary initiative and serve to illustrate the precarious nature of the MNC when seen from a micro-political standpoint (Morgan and Kristensen 2006).

In sum, politics can be used by subsidiary managers within the MNC as a way to provide impetus for initiative and competence development, attract resources and new mandates, or even to prevent other subsidiaries from gaining these resources and mandates. The subsidiary resorts to power games in order to overcome perceived problems with its headquarters, or with peer subsidiaries. Confrontation within the MNC is likely to manifest itself in political game-playing where individual subsidiary managers attempt to increase their power base in order to become more influential or otherwise affect organizational change (see also chapters of Dörrenbächer and Gammelgaard as well as of Schotter and Beamish in this volume). In this respect, Mintzberg's insights are particularly interesting as they imply that socio-political interactions within the MNC are a key mechanism by which organizational change is brought about. This is also reflected in detailed inductive research on change processes in organizations (e.g. Buchanan 2008; Buchanan and Badham 1999).

The foregoing indicates that socio-political interaction between individual managers lies at the heart of power diffusion within the MNC. In this chapter we examine different *manifestations* and different *directions* of socio-political interaction involving MNC subsidiary managers. Firstly, we focus on three important manifestations of socio-political interaction involving subsidiary managers within the MNC. Following the definition provided above, the three mechanisms we consider are all ways by which managers of subsidiaries relate to other MNC managers in order to exert or develop power for themselves. These are: (1) the degree to which managers in a focal subsidiary engage in inter-unit knowledge flows – strongly influenced by knowledge-sharing hostility; (2) the degree to which managers in a focal subsidiary engage in proactive behavior as a way of exerting their power; and (3) the extent to which normative integration is embraced by managers within a subsidiary. Secondly, we examine these manifestations of socio-political interactions in both vertical (subsidiary–headquarters) and horizontal (subsidiary–subsidiary) relationships.

Knowledge sharing

The sharing of knowledge within an organization ultimately entails an "exchange … between a source and a recipient" (Szulanski 1996: 28). This process is problematic because of the socially complex and often tacit nature of knowledge (Polanyi 1966). Explicit knowledge can be coded in writing or symbols, but much is tacit (Polanyi 1966). This distinction between the two types of knowledge is important because explicit knowledge is more easily transferable – and can be more easily appropriated (Foss 1996). However, transferred explicit knowledge can still become tacit following the transfer because the receiver may transform the knowledge into tacit form through an internalization process (Nonaka 1994). Tacit knowledge is ultimately acquired by – and stored within – individuals; it cannot be easily transferred or traded as a separate entity. Thus tacit knowledge requires strong social ties and interactions between individuals before it can be transferred (Nobel and Birkinshaw 1998).

In the case of the MNC, individuals engaged in knowledge sharing are dispersed in various geographic locations. Scholars have shown how, due to its internationally dispersed nature, tacit knowledge residing within MNCs is "sticky" (Szulanski 1996). In the MNC, the success of knowledge transfer depends on its context; the greater the contextual gaps between sender and receiver, the greater the risk of knowledge transfer failure (Gammelgaard and Ritter 2008). Thus, as institutional distance between countries increases, so does the problem of knowledge stickiness (Jensen and Szulanski 2004). According to Kostova (1999), some countries are more favorable to the successful transfer of practices than others; success of transfer is contingent on the specific practice–institution fit. Kostova (1999) also argued that, as transfers are organizationally embedded, the corporate context matters. In particular, the culture of the receiving subsidiary, including its inclination to learn, will affect whether a practice is successfully transferred and internalized.

Knowledge flowing in and out of subsidiaries of the MNC represents an important socio-political interaction. Husted and Michailova (2002) argued that individuals are "inherently hostile to knowledge sharing" (Husted and Michailova 2002: 61). Whilst knowledge-sharing hostility may be partly overcome by systematizing flows through knowledge management (IT) solutions, Husted and Michailova (2002) highlighted the importance of tacit knowledge utilization and of diagnosing and stimulating knowledge sharing. Some scholars have also questioned the degree to which IT solutions can be used to transfer knowledge effectively (Hislop 2002). The problem of knowledge sharing consists of both hoarding (by a potential transmitter of knowledge) and rejection (by a potential receiver of knowledge). The root cause of this problem is political in nature. For instance, Husted and Michailova (2002) argued how knowledge hoarding is associated with the perceived threat of loss of bargaining power and individual competitive advantage. Analogous arguments are made for rejecting knowledge of others (e.g. through not-invented-here syndrome, group affiliation and group think).

Lee and Williams (2007) used the concept of knowledge sharing within an entrepreneurial community to explain dispersed entrepreneurship in the

MNC. The MNC provides a basis for which communities of entrepreneur-ship form across national boundaries in order to share knowledge. Lee and Williams (2007) argued that, with the right boundary porosity conditions in place, employees from dispersed practices (i.e. the established functions of the MNC from different geographic locations) interact within emerging social communities in order to create and share tacit knowledge. To some extent, such knowledge communities overcome the problems of knowledge hoarding and rejecting described by Husted and Michailova, although they tend to revolve around a specific focal point (i.e. a new entrepreneurial ini-tiative). If successful, such knowledge communities are able to exert consid-erable power as they develop potential to destroy practices and create new ones.

This line of reasoning is based on the underlying assumption of a motiv-ation to share knowledge, i.e. motivation of individual subsidiary employees to traverse traditional boundaries in order to transmit or receive knowledge. Gupta and Govindarajan (1991) highlighted motivation as an important fac-tor in the sending and receiving of knowledge within the MNC. Furthermore, at a relational level, the motivation, perceived reliability of the source and the degree to which arduous relationships exist between sender and receiver can all contribute to transfer failure (Kostova 1999). Scholars have pointed out that a subsidiary's ability to learn (absorptive capacity), its willingness to share (motivational disposition) and the nature of inter-unit relationships (corporate socialization) can all act as impediments to knowledge trans-fer (Björkman et al. 2004; Gupta and Govindarajan 2000; Minbaeva et al. 2003).

Pfeffer (1994) highlighted gaining and exploiting knowledge of the firm's social system as a potent source of power. Thus subsidiary managers who withhold knowledge may do so in an attempt to avoid their own power erosion or at least to deny a shift of power to those on the receiving end. Withholding knowledge from headquarters managers will restrict the abil-ity of headquarters decision-makers to make well-informed decisions. Withholding knowledge from peer subsidiaries will restrict the ability of the peer subsidiary managers to outplay the focal subsidiary during budgeting and resource requests.

Proactive behaviors

The second manifestation of socio-political interaction in our framework is proactive behavior involving subsidiary managers. Crant (2000) pinpointed four factors that constitute the proactive character of individuals in organizations: (1) *proactive personality* (the inclination to influence the environment in reaction to external conditions – such as control constraints from a headquarters); (2) *personal initiative* (the behavioral pattern to go beyond formally declared role or job description whilst being consistent with the organization's mission); (3) *role breadth self-efficacy* (possessing the interpersonal and integrative skills required to take on a broader role than that defined by "prescribed technical requirements" [Crant 2000: 442]); (4) *taking charge* ("constructive efforts by employees to effect functional change with respect to how work is executed" [Crant 2000: 442]).

Crant highlighted a number of contextual factors that determine proactive behavior. Socialization is used by newcomers to learn behaviors necessary for effective participation in the organization. Modes of socialization include: interactionist, in which the newcomer becomes more proactive over time (Jones 1983), symbolic, where the same meaning to events is ascribed (Reichers 1987) and proactive tactics during the early stages of a new role (Miller and Jabin 1991). Proactive feedback seeking has been positively associated with the learning orientation of the individual, i.e. his or her willingness to learn from negative as well as positive feedback. MNC subsidiary managers engage in a form of self-regulation by adopting these behaviors in relations with their headquarters (Gupta *et al.* 1999). Proactive behaviors have also been seen to have an important change function. For example, with issue selling, middle managers voluntarily attempt to influence decision-making processes, particularly those related to strategy formulation. Previous research (e.g. Kanter 1988) has shown that the innovation process requires proactive involvement by individuals at each stage: transformational leadership, risk-taking behaviors and having more ways to influence others.

Proactive behaviors by subsidiary managers within the internal context of the MNC (with headquarters, and with peer subsidiaries) may be interpreted in a socio-political sense. Behaviors such as feedback seeking and involvement in budgeting and planning with a headquarters imply a direct interaction between subsidiary and headquarters' managers. Involvement in budgeting is a way to extend the power base of the subsidiary through negotiation over resources and expectations (Mintzberg 1985; Morgan 1986). Subsidiary managers are likely to engage in negotiation during budgeting interaction in order to influence headquarter expectations of subsidiary performance. Similarly, proactive feedback seeking with headquarters managers is a way for subsidiary managers to understand headquarters managers' views on subsidiary operations. Subsidiary managers may also behave proactively with peer subsidiaries, resolving problems for the wider corporation, and starting initiatives that may end up being implemented in other subsidiaries (Birkinshaw 2000). Such subsidiary initiatives challenge the status quo within the organization, acting as a counter-force to the headquarters (Bouquet and Birkinshaw 2008). Consequently, proactive behaviors can result in a shift in power within the MNC and even new types of power being endowed to the subsidiary.

Normative integration

The third manifestation of socio-political interaction we consider falls under the banner of normative integration. This relates to the extent to which overseas subsidiary managers share a common set of values with respect to corporate goals. Normative integration enables subsidiaries to use their knowledge "to pursue the interests of the MNC as a whole and not just their partisan interests" (Nohria and Ghoshal 1994: 494). Normative integration has a unifying function within the MNC: shared values can legitimize local decision-making without dispensing with any form of centralization or formalization. Ways of actually implementing shared values are based on socialization: rotation and transfer of managers (Edström and Galbraith 1977), and extensive and open communication among the dispersed units of the MNC (Martinez and Jarillo 1989). Such extensive socialization and communication is aimed at building common behavioral norms and trust between headquarters and subsidiary managers, ultimately increasing social capital within the MNC (Kostova and Roth 2003).

Subsidiaries may be controlled in various ways: through centralization, formal rules and procedures or an emphasis on shared objectives, values and norms (normative integration). Instilling shared values as a control mechanism (Nohria and Ghoshal 1994), developing a strong culture (Deal and Kennedy 1982) and allowing organizational goals to be internalized (Eisenhardt 1985) are possible ways in which internal conflict situations are overcome. Prahalad and Doz (1981) described how headquarters initiatives may lead to resistance and resentment from subsidiaries and a subsequent lack of progress. Birkinshaw (1997), on the other hand, showed how headquarters managers can have a predisposition to resisting initiatives originating in subsidiaries. Bartlett and Ghoshal (1989) identified the unique administrative heritage of the MNC as a potential constraint on strategic renewal and change. Clearly, if internal barriers exist that prevent the allocation of resources to new opportunities, the MNC will not be able to fully (if at all) exploit those opportunities.

Implementation of normative integration within the MNC involves a socio-political interaction between subsidiary managers and headquarters managers. Subsidiary managers that do not accept headquarters requests to implement normative integration, or who are reluctant to contribute to requests to build trust using socialization are likely to adopt a confrontational stance with both headquarters managers and managers from other subsidiaries that *are* implementing shared values. Subsidiary managers may fear that the subsidiary will lose control over the firm's informal organization (Mintzberg 1985) by instilling values set by the headquarters: the subsidiary becomes more dependent on an "outside actor" (the headquarters) for the rules of social engagement and the scope of legitimate behavior. This perception is born out of a fear of loss of power (Pfeffer 1981) and may eventually lead to conflict (see chapter of Blazejewski and Becker-Ritterspach in this volume). In essence, the social capital that is built as a result of socialization and normative integration reduces the need for socio-political interaction between subsidiary managers and headquarters/peer subsidiary managers.

National culture and subsidiary socio-political interaction

Following Smircich (1983), there are two principal types of culture that may influence subsidiary managers' engagement in socio-political interaction in attempts to increase the power base of a subsidiary of the MNC. These relate to internally developed corporate culture, and externally imported national culture. Corporate culture may be seen as an internally developed variable that captures the socio-ideological context of the organization (Smircich 1983). Corporate culture may shape managers' behavior and decision-making, including the choice of control systems. Corporate culture matters to organization decision-making because it represents the system of ideals and beliefs in the organization; it is the "normative glue" that holds the organization together (Smircich 1983).

National culture, however, is also extremely relevant as managers' interpretation of and responses to strategic issues differ according to their cultural characteristics (Schneider and De Meyer 1991). Importantly, national character is enduring as well as distinctive (Clark 1990). Thus a second way of interpreting the role of culture on socio-political interaction within the MNC is in terms of the importing of the external cultural context into the organization through its members. In this sense, culture "is revealed in the patterns of attitudes and actions of individual organization members" (Smircich

1983: 343). National culture is embodied in organizational members as "mental programming" that has been learned by the individual throughout his or her lifetime (Hofstede 1991).

Empirical studies have supported the argument that national culture influences the choices made by individuals within organizations. Schneider and De Meyer (1991), for example, identified how managers from different national cultures respond to strategic issues in different ways. Thomas and Mueller (2000) showed how entrepreneurial traits of individuals vary by national culture; the greater the cultural distance from the United States, the less frequent the internal locus of control, risk-taking propensity and high energy level. Kanungo and Wright (1983) reported evidence that managerial attitudes to rewards and job expectations vary by national culture. Newman and Nollen (1996) showed that it is the fit between management practices and national culture that impacts the performance of overseas work units of the MNC. Salk and Brannen (2000) showed how national culture impacts patterns of relationships within multinational joint-venture teams; the Japanese being more likely to form socio-emotional bonds than the Germans.

There have also been a number of important theoretical studies on the relationship between national culture and internal organization. Clark (1990), for example, argued that national character has an impact on organizational decision-makers in marketing departments of firms, as well as on end consumers in the market. Chen *et al.* (1998) theorized that culture influences the mechanism by which behavioral cooperation within the organization takes place, for instance, that more individualistic cultures require goal interdependence between actors, rather than goal sharing. Similarly, Kirkman and Shapiro (1997) argued that cultural values influence resistance to self-managed (empowered) work teams in overseas subsidiaries, power distance being among the variables that may lead to resistance to self-management, and individualism hypothesized to impact resistance to working in teams.

The dimensions of national culture specified by Hofstede (1980; 1991) have been widely used in both empirical and theoretical studies of international management and organization. Hofstede's (1980) four cultural dimensions are power distance, individualism, masculinity and uncertainty avoidance. These dimensions were derived from a factor analysis of survey data gained from 88,000 employees of IBM worldwide. Whilst these dimensions have been criticized (Baskerville-Morley 2005), they have been validated and continue to be used in the field of international business (Chow *et al.* 1999: 443; Drogendijk and Slangen 2006). Power distance (PDI) refers to the way in which the society handles inequality. According to Hofstede (1991: 27): "in small power distance countries there is limited dependence of subordinates on bosses, and a preference for consultation." Thus in large power distance countries, employees respect hierarchy and centralization; they are comfortable with being dependent on superiors. Individualism (IDV) refers to societies in which the interest of the individual prevails over the interests of a group (or a "collective"). Ties between individuals are loose in individualist cultures. In the workplace, employees within individualistic cultures are expected to focus on their own self-interest and needs, and employees are managed (monitored, motivated, etc.) as individuals. Masculinity (MAS) refers to societies in which achievement, assertiveness and competitiveness are emphasized. Dominant values in such cultures include material success and progress. Fighting is more likely to be accepted as a mechanism for resolving conflict. In feminine cultures, on the other hand, compromise and negotiation are preferred for handling conflict situations. Feminine cultures are more likely to emphasize social harmony, mutual support and caring for others. Uncertainty avoidance (UAV) refers to the degree to which uncertainty causes anxiety in individuals and groups, i.e. the extent to which people feel threatened by unknown situations. This should not be confused with risk avoidance, which refers to the probability of a known event occurring. In high uncertainty avoiding countries there are more formal and informal rules to specify how to deal with unpredictable situations than in lower uncertainty avoiding countries. In the latter case, people tend to be more afraid of such rules (Hofstede 1991).

Figure 9.1 depicts host country culture as a critical context – a wrapper around the subsidiary – through which socio-political interaction with subsidiary managers must be conducted. In other words, the central proposition is that vertical socio-political interactions (with headquarters) and horizontal socio-political interactions (with peer subsidiaries) are influenced by the external cultural context in which the subsidiary resides. Subsidiaries differ from each other in terms of their levels of power distance, individualism, masculinity, and uncertainty avoidance because subsidiary employees diffuse – into the subsidiary organization – cultural traits from the wider society in which they grew up and to which they identify. In this sense, cultural characteristics influence the degree to which individuals interpret and respond to issues facing the subsidiary (Schneider and De Meyer 1991). The types of subsidiary manager socio-political interaction discussed above (knowledge sharing, proactive behaviors, normative integration) are therefore all subject to determination by the cultural context of the subsidiary.

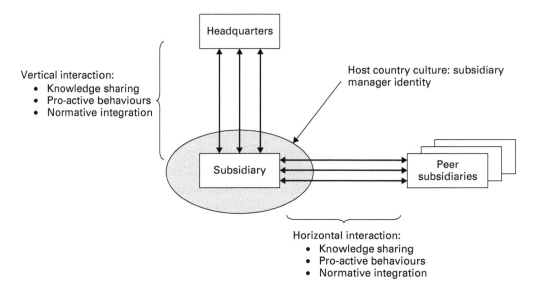

Fig. 9.1   Host country culture, vertical and horizontal socio-political interaction

The proposed model for exploratory analysis is shown in Figure 9.2. The suggested control variables shown here are explained below.

Methods and findings

Data collection

The model was explored using data from a survey of middle managers located in various subsidiaries of MNCs around the world (n = 150). Actors at very high and very low levels in the organizational hierarchy are not as perceptive towards organizational politics as middle-ranking levels (Parker *et al.* 1995). Therefore, middle managers were selected in preference to top management team (TMT) members or operating-level production staff. This type of respondent is also able to combine "strategic macro (context-free) information and hands-on micro (context-specific) information" (Nonaka 1988: 15). The survey instrument is a valid way to assess political phenomena in an organization and has been used to demonstrate the association of actual influence tactics with perceptions of politics in the work environment (Vigoda and Cohen 2002). We executed the survey by a postal pilot and by purposive networking. We used networking in order to screen participants and validate their ability in English, gauge their education level (the vast majority were university educated), and confirm that they had exposure to the concepts captured on

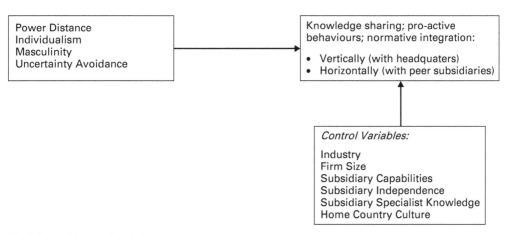

Fig. 9.2   Proposed model

the questionnaire as middle managers of MNC subsidiaries (e.g. Venaik *et al.* 2005). In total, 154 questionnaires were returned, 8 from the pilot and 146 from the purposive phase; 4 had to be omitted from analysis due to incompleteness. This sample of n = 150 covered 18 countries of origin, 21 host countries and 16 distinct industries. Due to missing values on certain questionnaire items and secondary data, the final sample used in regression modeling ranged from 126 to 131 subsidiary managers. This sample consisted both of well-known, diversified MNCs as well as lesser known, more specialized MNCs. At the time of the questionnaire response, 14 percent of the MNCs had more than 100,000 employees, and 19 percent had fewer than 5,000 employees. Some 51 percent of the respondents indicated that they had more than five years' tenure within their MNC, and 35 percent of the respondents indicated that they had experienced an international placement within their MNC lasting more than three months. Respondent functions included country managers, sales directors, marketing directors, engineering and project managers, internal strategy consultants, and training managers.

Dependent variables: We tested six models relating to subsidiary–headquarters interaction (vertical), and six corresponding models relating to focal subsidiary interaction with peer subsidiaries (horizontal). We used two models to capture each of the manifestations of socio-political interaction described above (i.e. knowledge sharing, proactive behaviors, normative integration). Original Likert style statements were used, against which managers indicated agreement on a five-point scale (1 = disagree strongly, 5 = agree strongly). We also tested two scale models in order to compare overall effects of host country culture on vertical and horizontal interaction. The variable VERTICAL was calculated as the arithmetic mean of the six single indicators of vertical interactions, and likewise with the variable HORIZONTAL. We note acceptable reliability of the scales: VERTICAL, $\alpha = 0.71$; HORIZONTAL, $\alpha = 0.72$. All models were tested using linear regression. For each model the set of independent and control variables remained the same. Table 9.1 summarizes the focal constructs for analysis and shows the single questionnaire items used.

Independent variables: The measures for national culture of home and host country were taken as a secondary data measure from the Hofstede index (1980, 1991) for each of the cases. Despite criticism (e.g. Ailon 2008; see also chapter of Ybema and Byun in this volume), Hofstede's measures continue to be used in the field of international business study. Many large-scale studies have supported, rather than contradicted the original conclusions; however, there have been calls for exploring new dimensions of culture (Kirkman *et al.* 2006). An alternative would have been to use indices from the GLOBE study (e.g. Reus and Lamont 2009). The GLOBE data is indeed more recent than Hofstede's, but it has also faced criticism – including interpretation of negative association between values and practices. Another alternative would have been to use Schwartz-based measures (Schwartz 1994), which are based on more recent data and obtained through a purposefully chosen research design. Drogendijk and Slangen (2006) concluded that the explanatory power of the Hofstede and Swartz-based measures are comparable. We use Hofstede's (1980) dimensions of power distance (PDI), individualism (IDV), masculinity (MAS), and uncertainty avoidance (UAV) as the underlying components of national culture. Recent empirical MNC research has testified to the utility of Hofstede dimensions in understanding subsidiary-level phenomenon (e.g. Williams and Van Triest 2009).

Control variables: Firstly, as the largest industry subgroup in the sample were MNCs involved in services (42 percent), a dichotomous variable was used to control for industry (services = 1, non-services = 0). Secondly, we controlled for MNC size. The natural log of employees (sourced from company files) was used for this. Thirdly, we controlled for three organizational factors at the level of the subsidiary that have the potential to influence sociopolitical interaction of subsidiary managers. Björkman *et al.* (2004) highlighted the possibility of a range of subsidiary functions impacting knowledge flows. Gupta and Govindarajan (2000) found support for a link between knowledge stocks and outward flows of knowledge from a subsidiary. The resource dependency of a subsidiary on its headquarters represents a power relation and may influence the degree to which subsidiary managers engage

Table 9.1 Subsidiary manager socio-political interaction: focal constructs and questionnaire items

Direction of interaction	Focus of analysis	Questionnaire items [LABEL FOR ANALYSIS] (1 = disagree strongly, 5 = agree strongly)
Vertical	Knowledge sharing with headquarters	This subsidiary provides information about changes in the local environment to the corporation on a regular basis [VERT-PROVIDE-INFO]
		Managers in this subsidiary monitor a regional or global headquarters for information on how well the subsidiary is doing [VERT-SEEK-FEEDBACK]
	Proactivity with headquarters	Managers in this subsidiary are actively involved in budgeting with a regional or global HQ [VERT-BUDGETING]
		This subsidiary starts initiatives which tend to be adopted by a regional or global HQ [VERT-INITIATIVES]
	Normative integration with headquarters	This subsidiary emphasizes corporate values on internal induction and training courses [VERT-VALUES]
		Managers in this subsidiary use the same standards of behavior as HQ colleagues [VERT-BEHAVIOR]
Horizontal	Knowledge sharing with other subsidiaries	Managers in this subsidiary …
		… are strongly inclined to share their knowledge with managers in other subsidiaries [HORIZ-K-SHARING]
		… accept new knowledge from other subsidiaries without putting up any barriers [HORIZ-K-ACCEPTING]
	Proactivity with other subsidiaries	This subsidiary gets involved in resolving conflicts elsewhere in the corporation, e.g. between other subsidiaries [HORIZ-CONFLICTS]
		This subsidiary starts initiatives which tend to be adopted by other subsidiaries [HORIZ-INITIATIVES]
	Normative integration with other subsidiaries	This subsidiary encourages its managers to have face-to-face meetings with managers in other subsidiaries [HORIZ-F2F]
		Managers in this subsidiary build alliances with managers from other subsidiaries [HORIZ-ALLIANCES]

in socio-political interaction. Single five-point items were used to control for subsidiary range of capabilities ("this subsidiary possesses broad capabilities, e.g. design, production, marketing and sales, customer service"), resource independence from headquarters ("this subsidiary is dependent on a foreign HQ for access to critical resources") [this item was inverted] and level of specialist knowledge in the subsidiary ("this subsidiary possesses a high level of specialist knowledge"). Finally, we controlled for home country culture using Hofstede's four dimensions for the home country of the MNC.

Findings

Table 9.2 shows the descriptive statistics for the main dependent and independent variables. Variables were normally distributed and did not require transformation. Importantly, there was adequate variance in the Hofstede dimensions for home country (controls) as well as for host country.

Overall, the regression models show a stronger impact of host country culture on vertical socio-political interactions than on horizontal interactions. We note from the scale models (Table 9.3) that this is driven by host country UAV.

Table 9.4 shows the linear regression models for the single indicators of vertical socio-political interaction. The results for vertical feedback seeking and budgeting show little influence of host country culture (no significant coefficient). Host country PDI is negatively related to vertical initiatives, i.e. the subsidiary starting initiatives that are adopted by the headquarters ($p < 0.01$). Host country PDI is positively related to subsidiary managers adopting common standards of behavior (although this is just outside the $p < 0.1$ level). Host country IDV appears to be negatively related to the subsidiary starting initiatives that are adopted by the headquarters ($p < 0.01$). Host country MAS is seen to positively impact vertical knowledge outflows, operationalized here as the subsidiary providing information about the local environment to the headquarters ($p < 0.1$) and to vertical initiatives ($p < 0.1$). Host country UAV has significant and positive relationships with vertical knowledge outflows ($p < 0.05$), emphasizing corporate values on subsidiary induction courses ($p < 0.1$) and sharing standards of behavior with headquarter colleagues ($p < 0.1$). Host country UAV is positively related to feedback seeking from headquarters and active involvement in budgeting with headquarters, although these are not unequivocal.

Table 9.5 shows the linear regression models for the single indicators of horizontal socio-political interaction. The results for horizontal knowledge accepting, conflict resolution and face-to-face interaction with managers in other subsidiaries show little host country culture influence (coefficients are not significant). Host country PDI is negatively related to horizontal initiatives ($p < 0.1$) reflecting the finding in the vertical models regarding vertical initiatives. Host country IDV is positively related to horizontal knowledge sharing ($p < 0.1$), but not knowledge accepting. There are no significant relationships between host country MAS or UAV and horizontal interactions.

Table 9.2 Descriptive statistics of main variables (n = 135–150)

Variable	Mean	Standard deviation
Controls:		
Industry (Services = 1)	0.62	0.49
Ln (employees)	9.71	2.17
Subsidiary range of capabilities	3.74	1.15
Subsidiary resource independence	3.02	1.26
Subsidiary specialist knowledge	3.70	1.08
Home country PDI	45.41	13.57
Home country IDV	73.91	24.08
Home country MAS	57.43	16.25
Home country UAV	53.36	19.38
Host country culture:		
Host country PDI	46.26	17.19
Host country IDV	70.22	20.37
Host country MAS	55.63	15.66
Host country UAV	49.35	20.69
Dependent variables:		
VERT-PROVIDE-INFO	3.57	1.04
VERT-SEEK-FEEDBACK	3.30	1.12
VERT-BUDGETING	3.53	1.19
VERT-INITIATIVES	3.17	1.03
VERT-VALUES	3.48	1.19
VERT-BEHAVIOR	3.38	1.06
VERTICAL (scale)	3.41	0.70
HORIZ-K-SHARING	3.18	1.05
HORIZ-K-ACCEPTING	3.43	0.89
HORIZ-CONFLICTS	1.95	0.99
HORIZ-INITIATIVES	3.00	1.11
HORIZ-F2F	2.92	1.14
HORIZ-ALLIANCES	3.13	1.09
HORIZONTAL (scale)	2.94	0.68

Discussion

This chapter addresses power and politics in the MNC by exploring how sub-sidiary manager identities influence their socio-political interaction with managers in other units of the MNC. In this analysis, we assume subsidiary manager identity as being shaped by national culture of the host country. After controlling for firm and subsidiary factors that have the potential to explain subsidiary manager socio-political interaction, the results suggest

Table 9.3 Linear regression models – vertical vs horizontal interaction scales

	Direction of socio-political interaction			
	VERTICAL		HORIZONTAL	
	1	2	3	4
Services	−0.19*	−0.18*	−0.07	−0.07
Ln (employees)	0.24**	0.22**	0.11	0.10
Capabilities	0.05	0.04	0.14	0.13
Independence	−0.08	−0.03	0.09	0.12
Specialist	0.46**	0.45***	0.29***	0.28**
Home-PDI		0.08		0.04
Home-IDV		−0.23+		0.00
Home-MAS		−0.05		−0.15
Home-UAV		−0.20+		−0.07
Host-PDI		0.02		−0.03
Host-IDV		0.01		−0.00
Host-MAS		0.10		0.10
Host-UAV		0.20*		0.03
F	8.97***	4.70**	4.56***	2.36**
Adj. R2	0.24	0.28	0.12	0.12
N	130	127	129	126

***$p < 0.001$ **$p < 0.01$ *$p < 0.05$ +$p < 0.10$

that individual identity does matter to the dynamics of power development within the MNC. However, the results portray a somewhat complex
picture. Firstly, different *manifestations* of subsidiary manager socio-political interaction are affected in different ways by host country culture, and
secondly, dimensions of national culture impact the different *directions* of
socio-political interaction in markedly different ways (vertical impact being
stronger than horizontal impact). These findings enable us to refine our definition of socio-political interaction amongst managers of the MNC. We now
say: socio-political interaction within the MNC comprises *mechanisms by
which identities of subsidiary managers influence how they exert or develop
power for themselves through vertical and horizontal relations*.

Some agreement may therefore be drawn from these findings with the
body of literature on cultural explanations of managerial behavior (Hofstede
1980, 1991). We concur in a broad sense with the argument that national
culture affects manager response and patterns of actions (Schneider and De
Meyer 1991; Smircich 1983). A contribution of our analysis is to show how,
in the specific case of the MNC, host country culture matters to the types

Table 9.4 Linear regression models – vertical socio-political interaction

	Knowledge sharing				Proactive behaviors				Normative integration			
	VERT-PROVIDE-INFO		VERT-SEEK-FEEDBACK		VERT-BUDGETING		VERT-INITIATIVES		VERT-VALUES		VERT-BEHAVIOR	
	1	2	3	4	5	6	7	8	9	10	11	12
Services	−0.06	−0.08	−0.01	0.03	−0.10	−0.05	−0.08	−0.03	−0.31***	−0.29***	−0.17*	−0.23**
Ln (employees)	0.05	−0.02	0.23**	0.23*	0.06	0.08	0.15+	0.17+	0.16+	0.14	0.28***	0.24**
Capabilities	0.08	0.11	−0.10	−0.08	0.01	0.01	0.06	0.05	0.04	−0.00	0.10	0.07
Independence	−0.08	−0.06	−0.06	−0.03	−0.08	−0.06	0.06	0.12	−0.06	−0.01	−0.06	−0.06
Specialist	0.43***	0.40***	0.35***	0.35***	0.24**	0.22**	0.25**	0.25**	0.19**	0.18+	0.29***	0.27**
Home-PDI		0.21*		−0.07		−0.06		−0.00		0.02		0.21**
Home-IDV		−0.10		−0.25+		−0.16		−0.10		−0.19		−0.03
Home-MAS		−0.00		0.02		0.11		−0.70		−0.09		−0.18**
Home-UAV		0.10		−0.13		−0.18		−0.70		−0.26*		−0.19+
Host-PDI		0.06		−0.02		−0.05		−0.27**		0.14		0.20
Host-IDV		−0.01		−0.02		0.12		−0.32**		0.08		0.13
Host-MAS		0.17+		0.00		−0.03		0.19+		−0.04		0.13
Host-UAV		0.18*		0.14		0.13		−0.08		0.17+		0.16+
F	5.81***	4.08***	4.09**	1.91*	1.61	0.94	2.85**	2.14**	4.14*	2.65**	5.49***	4.37***
Adj. R2	0.16	0.24	0.11	0.09	0.02	−0.01	0.07	0.10	0.11	0.14	0.15	0.26
N	130	127	130	127	131	128	131	128	131	128	130	127

***$p < 0.001$ **$p < 0.01$ *$p < 0.05$ +$p < 0.10$

Table 9.5 Linear regression models – horizontal socio-political interaction

	Knowledge sharing				Proactive behaviors				Normative integration			
	HORIZ-K-SHARING		HORIZ-K-ACCEPTING		HORIZ-CONFLICTS		HORIZ-INITIATIVES		HORIZ-F2F		HORIZ-ALLIANCES	
	13	14	15	16	17	18	19	20	21	22	23	24
Services	−0.07	−0.06	−0.13	−0.13	0.13	0.17+	−0.02	−0.05	−0.09	−0.08	−0.10	−0.11
Ln (employees)	0.09	0.06	0.19*	0.16+	−0.04	−0.03	0.07	0.10	0.05	0.04	0.09	0.08
Capabilities	0.05	0.03	0.07	0.05	−0.00	0.02	0.13	0.12	0.10	0.09	0.17+	0.16
Independence	0.09	0.10	0.06	0.11	0.10	0.10	0.02	0.01	0.16+	0.21*	−0.04	−0.04
Specialist	0.27**	0.16	0.26**	0.24**	0.25**	0.27**	0.28***	0.31**	0.02	0.07	0.08	0.06
Home-PDI		0.07		0.07		−0.15		0.10		0.02		0.04
Home-IDV		−0.19		−0.13		0.09		0.13		0.06		0.04
Home-MAS		−0.13		−0.18+		0.10		−0.19+		−0.04		−0.14
Home-UAV		−0.29**		−0.03		0.12		0.00		0.04		−0.09
Host-PDI		0.14		−0.03		0.01		−0.24+		−0.04		0.06
Host-IDV		0.26+		−0.20		0.12		−0.19		−0.09		0.08
Host-MAS		0.02		−0.02		−0.01		0.12		0.13		0.12
Host-UAV		0.10		0.02		0.01		−0.07		0.07		−0.01
F	2.81**	2.55**	3.68**	2.34**	2.92*	1.99*	3.59**	2.24**	1.69	0.95	1.44	1.08
Adj. R2	0.07	0.14	0.09	0.12	0.07	0.09	0.09	0.11	0.03	−0.01	0.02	0.01
N	131	128	131	128	129	126	131	128	131	128	131	128

***$p < 0.001$ **$p < 0.01$ *$p < 0.05$ +$p < 0.10$

of subsidiary manager behaviors that underpin power development. Given that subsidiary managers are central actors in the phenomenon of political arena arising within the MNC (Williams and Lee 2009), understanding the determinants of these behaviors from the point of view of manager identity appears to have merit. Recent work on internal politics and power development within the MNC has neglected to take this view (e.g. Bouquet and Birkinshaw 2008), despite the copious literature on cultural effects in international business, and an enormous amount of anecdotal evidence from practising managers of international firms.

One key implication of our findings and refined definition of socio-political interaction concerns the functionalist view of internal organizational politics. This becomes more culturally complex when the organizational context moves from domestic to international network. Whilst some argue it is not necessarily dysfunctional, internal politics in the MNC is shaped, in part at least, by the cultural programming of the individuals involved. Thus differences in national culture, often treated as a problem in international business, as a source of risk and uncertainty, and as a barrier to be overcome, may actually be central to functional internal politics. Whether a particular type of socio-political interaction is healthy for the wider MNC depends on the specific nature of the interaction and the business issue at stake. What this suggests is that a highly internationalized MNC with operations in many different cultures will contain a broad variety of individuals with varying degrees of latent inclination towards socio-political interaction. Where there are situations in which such interaction is actually beneficial to the MNC (e.g. to improve innovation or production efficiency) the MNC should be sensitive to culture as a determinant of vertical and horizontal integration. In this scenario, cultural competence (Johnson *et al*. 2006) becomes important for managing, not suppressing, cultural differences between nationals from different cultures.

A number of interesting relationships emerge from our empirical test. Firstly, we find that subsidiary managers' exertion of power over headquarters by generating initiatives that are eventually accepted by the headquarters is strongly associated with host country culture. Indeed, three out of the four Hofstede dimensions appear to influence vertical initiatives (Model 8, Table 9.4), the highest of any of the models tested. The possibility that host country culture can affect genesis and promulgation of subsidiary initiatives within the MNC has been largely absent in prior studies (e.g., Verbeke *et al*. 2007). The body of literature on MNC transnational management and subsidiary initiatives does examine local context, but treats this in broad industry terms

through concepts such as local environment turbulence and strategic importance of the host country (Bartlett and Ghoshal 1989; Verbeke *et al.* 2007). The
current study suggests that the role of national culture has been underplayed
in literature to date. We find that the greater the power distance within the
host country culture, the less likely it will be that subsidiary managers will
attempt to exert power over their headquarters in the form of vertical initiative diffusion. In large power distance countries, employees' latent respect for
hierarchy and centralization, and their acceptance of dependence on headquarters managers, will mean that vertical initiatives are less likely. Host
country individualism also has a negative impact in this respect. Subsidiary
managers are likely to be too concerned with their own operations and application of entrepreneurial initiative to worry about diffusion to other nodes of
the MNC. Masculinity, on the other hand, appears to have a positive impact
on vertical initiatives. The emphasis on material success and progress found
in masculine cultures means that subsidiary managers from these cultures
will find it second nature to embark on entrepreneurial initiatives that are
sanctioned by headquarters. For such managers, this will be a potent symbol
of their progress and success within the MNC. Where a corporate immune
system exists to stifle subsidiary initiatives, subsidiary managers from masculine countries will not worry about internal fighting as a mechanism for
resolving conflict. Thus our findings provide viable explanations for this particular manifestation and direction of socio-political interaction within the
MNC.

Secondly, we find interesting differences between the dimensions of
national culture in terms of their influence on socio-political interaction. The
findings suggest that power distance may impact the extent to which subsidiary managers choose to share the same corporate values and standards of
behavior as those from headquarters. We note the coefficients here are positive but just outside the 10 percent level of significance (Models 10 and 12,
Table 9.4). In contrast, power distance has little influence on horizontal normative integration (Models 22 and 24, Table 9.5). Subsidiary managers from
societies with high power distance are more likely to respect those in formal
authority within the MNC, i.e. headquarters' managers. Host country power
distance appears to mould subsidiary manager response here, discriminating
between their vertical and horizontal interactions.

In terms of the relationship between individualism and initiative diffusion, we find that national culture does not discriminate between vertical
and horizontal effects. Here, there is a negative association between host
country individualism and initiatives started in the subsidiary becoming

adopted by (1) a headquarters (Model 8, Table 9.4) *and* (2) other subsidiaries (Model 20, Table 9.5). The cultural explanation is that individualistic subsidiary managers consider it in their own self-interest to avoid initiatives that need sanctioning by headquarters or, for that matter, peer subsidiaries. We know from extant literature that the process of approval seeking is likely to be confrontational in nature. Perhaps managers in individualistic cultures focus more on local-for-local initiatives, avoiding the costs of confrontation. Another possible explanation here is that headquarters' managers are more likely to approve initiatives that can be exploited in a wider range of subsidiaries. Those that arise from individualistic cultures might be more narrow and self-focused on the originating subsidiary, neglecting the needs of other subsidiaries. There is a suggestion that individualism is positively related to subsidiary managers sharing their knowledge with other units (Model 14, Table 9.5), but negatively related to accepting knowledge from other units (Model 16, Table 9.5). Again, it is plausible that the degree to which self-interest is promoted over common interest has a direct bearing on subsidiary manager hostility to knowledge inflows but not to knowledge outflows.

Masculinity appears to positively impact initiatives becoming adopted by the headquarters (Model 8, Table 9.4), as well as subsidiary managers socializing and building alliances with managers in peer subsidiaries (Models 22 and 24, Table 9.5). We note the significance for the latter is just outside the 10 percent level. However, the combination of these associations does make sense. We know that alliance and coalition building amongst subsidiaries assists in overcoming MNC headquarter resistance (Birkinshaw and Ridderstråle 1999; Bouquet and Birkinshaw 2008); alliance building can contribute to the power base underpinning the initiative, as well as allowing the initiative to be annotated such that it may be exploited beyond the focal subsidiary. Thus masculinity is beneficial here. The achievement, assertiveness and progress orientation found in masculine societies helps subsidiary managers influence their headquarters – in part at least – as a result of the power they amass through horizontal normative integration. Interestingly, we also see that subsidiary managers in more masculine societies are more likely to provide information on changes in the local environment on a regular basis. Building alliances and power bases around subsidiary initiatives is therefore only one side of the masculinity coin. Maintaining good communications with headquarters, and reducing information asymmetry between headquarters and subsidiaries, appears to be the other.

That uncertainty avoidance is related to aspects of vertical knowledge flows and normative integration also makes sense (Models 2, 10 and 12,

Table 9.4); the subsidiary manager seeks to cope with perceived uncertainty in the environment by close cooperation and alignment with the headquarters, as opposed to peer subsidiaries (Models 14, 22 and 24, Table 9.5). Whilst prior literature places an emphasis on complexity and turbulence in the local environment as a determinant of innovative and entrepreneurial behavior in subsidiaries (Bartlett and Ghoshal 1989; Verbeke *et al.* 2007), our finding suggests that it is not some absolute measure of uncertainty that matters, rather the individual's perception and interpretation of uncertainty that is embedded within their national identity (see also chapters of Koveshnikov, and Ybema and Byun in this volume).

There have been calls for extending beyond Hofstede and exploring new dimensions of culture (e.g. Kirkman *et al.* 2006). The question arises: do the findings of the present study enable us to refine Hofstede's view of national culture? We uncover a disparity in explanatory power of Hofstede dimensions when we consider vertical versus horizontal interactions. As shown in Table 9.3, uncertainty avoidance is the only Hofstede dimension influencing overall vertical interaction. The individual indicator models show Hofstede dimensions account for greater variance in a vertical as opposed to horizontal direction for what are essentially similar types of interaction. This begs the question: what other aspects of national culture not captured by Hofstede dimensions explain horizontal socio-political interaction within the international context of an organization? Perhaps there exists a latent "heterarchical orientation" in societies at large (rather than in organizations) that has become more prominent since Hofstede's work was conducted, as a result of globalization. Such an as yet undetected component of national culture could influence how individual managers interact horizontally across national borders. To date, heterarchy has been discussed mainly in organizational terms (Hedlund 1986, 1993; Hedlund and Rolander 1990). Future work could consider this a possibly powerful feature of culture in wider society and investigate whether this becomes internalized into manager identity and, consequently, into behavior.

The current analysis has limitations that can be addressed in future work. Variable and construct selection in this study have been based around the central argument that host country national culture influences the way in which subsidiary managers engage in socio-political interaction with managers from headquarters and other subsidiaries. There are likely to be additional insights pertinent to this relationship. By extending the model presented here to include other aspects of national culture and institutional distance, aspects of organizational culture, and aspects of individual managers, the model may be evaluated in a more complete way. For instance, the cultural contexts of peer subsidiaries should be taken into account in future study. We find uncertainty avoidance to be less salient in horizontal interactions, but we did not control for national culture of specific peer subsidiaries. It may be that our finding can be explained by subsidiary managers not needing to cope with uncertainty through internal lateral networks when peer subsidiaries have similar reactions to uncertainty. Our findings may also be explained by differences in national culture between a focal subsidiary and the range of other subsidiaries with which it has interdependencies. In other words, diversity in cultural contexts becomes more of an issue in horizontal relationships than in the vertical relationship, and this diversity may have a role to play. Kostova and Roth (2002) highlight the importance of institutional profile of the host country on the adoption of practices within the MNC. Regulative and cognitive dimensions of the institutional environment of subsidiary and headquarters could be included in an extended analysis. Likewise, other operationalizations of culture, such as GLOBE or Schwartz-based measures, and the more recent of Hofstede's dimensions, long-term orientation (not included here due to restricted country coverage), may provide additional insight into the influence of national culture on socio-political interactions involving subsidiary managers. Future work could extend this to look at the dual impact of the national and organization culture of both MNC and MNC subsidiary. In addition, trust and procedural justice (e.g. Kim and Mauborgne 1991; Taggart 1997) have received attention in recent years and may have an important role to play in the types of socio-political interactions conducted by subsidiary managers. Also, other variables at the individual level (such as interests and goals, career advancement opportunity, age and gender) have the potential to influence socio-political behavior (Dörrenbächer and Geppert 2009; Ferris and Kacmar 1992; Gandz and Murray 1980) and these were not included in the conceptualization in the present study.

From the viewpoint of empirical fieldwork, this study has limitations in terms of operationalization and sample size, and these limitations should also be addressed in future work. Overall, causality cannot be claimed and no generalizations to the wider population can be made. As an exploratory investigation into the influence of host country culture on subsidiary manager socio-political interaction, the sample can be considered adequate. Future research in this line of enquiry could modify the operationalization of the different dependent variables. Inductive study and mixed methods could extend the current analysis to explore contingencies between culture, specific interests and goals of managers, and political phenomena. In particular, active interviews with subsidiary managers from different cultures could be held to elicit biographical details and examples of socio-political interaction and influence (Holstein and Gubrium 1997) under different circumstances. These would enable the model to be developed further.

Concluding remarks

This chapter has explored the idea that host country national culture influences subsidiary manager socio-political interaction within the MNC. The findings appear to echo the main argument: host country national culture does have a role to play in socio-political interaction as operationalized through knowledge flows, proactive behavior and normative integration within the MNC. Socio-political interaction is a way of influencing the distribution of power within the MNC and can be applied in vertical and horizontal relationships. Such interaction manifests itself in various ways and our empirical tests show a complex pattern in which vertical and horizontal interactions are influenced in different ways by different aspects of host country culture. This extends the functionalist view of internal organizational politics by suggesting that, in the case of the MNC, external societal culture matters to internal political phenomena. Future research should develop this further with additional data collection and refinement of the core model. If this perspective is found to have merit, host country national culture may need to be re-evaluated with the same degree of importance as organizational attributes have had in the literature in terms of impact on evolution and distribution of power within the MNC.

REFERENCES

Ailon, G. 2008. "Mirror, mirror on the wall: culture's consequences in a value test of its own design," *Academy of Management Review* 33: 885–904

Andersson, U., M. Forsgren and U. Holm 2007. "Balancing subsidiary influence in the federative MNC: a business network view," *Journal of International Business Studies* 38: 802–18

Bartlett, C. and S. Ghoshal 1989. *Managing Across Borders: The Transnational Solution.* Boston, MA: Harvard Business School Press

Baskerville-Morley, R.F. 2005. "A research note: the unfinished business of culture," *Accounting, Organizations and Society* 30: 389–91

Birkinshaw, J. 1997. "Entrepreneurship in multinational corporations: the characteristics of subsidiary initiatives," *Strategic Management Journal* 18: 207–29

2000. *Entrepreneurship in the Global Firm*. London: Sage

Birkinshaw, J. and J. Ridderstråle 1999. "Fighting the corporate immune system: a process study of subsidiary initiatives in multinational corporations," *International Business Review* 8: 149–80

Björkman, I., W. Barner-Rasmussen and L. Li 2004. "Managing knowledge transfer in MNCs: the impact of headquarters control mechanisms," *Journal of International Business Studies* 35: 443–55

Bouquet, C. and J. Birkinshaw 2008. "Managing power in the multinational corporation: how low-power actors gain influence," *Journal of Management* 34: 477–508

Buchanan, D. A. 2008. "You stab my back, I'll stab yours: management experience and perceptions of organization political behaviour," *British Journal of Management* 19: 49–64

Buchanan, D. A. and R. Badham 1999. "Politics and organizational change: the lived experience," *Human Relations* 52: 609–29

Chen, C. C., X.-P. Chen and J. R. Meindl 1998. "How can cooperation be fostered? The cultural effects of individualism-collectivism," *Academy of Management Review* 23: 285–304

Chow, C. W., M. D. Shields and A. Wu 1999. "The importance of national culture in the design of and preference for management controls for multi-national operations," *Accounting, Organizations and Society* 24: 441–61

Clark, T. 1990. "International marketing and national character: a review and proposal for an integrative theory," *Journal of Marketing* 54: 66–79

Crant, M. J. 2000. "Proactive behaviour in organizations," *Journal of Management* 26: 435–62

Deal, T. E. and A. A. Kennedy 1982. *Corporate Cultures: The Rites and Rituals of Corporate Life*. Reading, MA: Addison Wesley

Dörrenbächer, C. and J. Gammelgaard 2006. "Subsidiary role development: the effect of micro-political headquarters–subsidiary negotiations on the product, market and value-added scope of foreign-owned subsidiaries," *Journal of International Management* 12: 266–83

Dörrenbächer, C. and M. Geppert 2009. "A micro-political perspective on subsidiary initiative-taking: evidence from German-owned subsidiaries in France," *European Management Journal* 27: 100–12

Drogendijk, R. and A. Slangen 2006. "Hofstede, Schwartz, or managerial perceptions? The effects of different cultural distance measures on establishment mode choices by multinational enterprises," *International Business Review* 15: 361–80

Edström, A. and J. R. Galbraith 1977. "Transfer of managers as a coordination and control strategy in multinational organizations," *Administrative Science Quarterly* 22: 248–63

Eisenhardt, K. M. 1985. "Control: organizational and economic approaches," *Management Science* 31: 134–49

Erramilli, K. M. 1996. "Nationality and subsidiary ownership patterns in multinational corporations," *Journal of International Business Studies* 27: 225–48

Evans, J. and F. T. Mavondo 2002. "Psychic distance and organizational performance: an empirical examination of international retailing operations," *Journal of International Business Studies* 33: 515–32

Ferris, G. R. and K. M. Kacmar 1992. "Perceptions of organizational politics," *Journal of Management* 18: 93–116

Foss, N. J. 1996. "Knowledge-based approaches to the theory of the firm: some critical comments," *Organization Science* 17: 470–76

Gammelgaard, J. and T. Ritter 2008. "Virtual communities of practice: a mechanism for efficient knowledge retrieval in MNCs," *International Journal of Knowledge Management* 4: 46–61

Gandz, J. and V. V. Murray 1980. "The experience of workplace politics," *Academy of Management Journal* 23: 237–51

Gupta, A. K. and V. Govindarajan 1991. "Knowledge flows and the structure of control within multinational corporations," *Academy of Management Review* 16: 768–92
  2000. "Knowledge flows within multinational corporations," *Strategic Management Journal* 21: 473–96

Gupta, A. K., V. Govindarajan and A. Malhotra 1999. "Feedback-seeking behaviour within multinational corporations," *Strategic Management Journal* 20: 205–22

Hedlund, G. 1986. "The hypermodern MNC – a heterarchy?" in Ghauri and Prasad (eds.) *International Management: A Reader.* Chicago, IL: The Dryden Press, pp. 64–84
  1993. "Assumptions of hierarchy and heterarchy, with applications to the management of the multinational corporation" in Ghoshal and Westney (eds.) *Organization Theory and the Multinational Corporation.* London: Macmillan, pp. 211–36

Hedlund, G. and D. Rolander 1990. "Action in heterarchies – new approaches to managing the MNC" in Bartlett, Doz and Hedlund (eds.) *Managing the Global Firm.* London: Routledge, pp. 15–45

Hislop, D. 2002. "Mission impossible? Communicating and sharing knowledge via information technology," *Journal of Information Technology* 17: 165–77

Hitt, M. A., V. Franklin and H. Zhu 2006. "Culture, institutions and international strategy," *Journal of International Management* 12: 222–34

Hofstede, G. 1980. *Culture's Consequences: International Differences in Work-Related Values.* London: Sage
  1991. *Cultures and Organizations: Software of the Mind.* Berkshire: McGraw-Hill

Holstein, J. A. and J. F. Gubrium 1997. "Active interviewing" in Silverman (ed.) *Qualitative Research: Theory, Method and Practice.* London: Sage, pp. 113–29

Husted, K. and S. Michailova 2002. "Diagnosing and fighting knowledge-sharing hostility," *Organizational Dynamics* 31: 60–73

Jensen, R. and G. Szulanski 2004 "Stickiness and the adaptation of organizational practices in cross-border knowledge transfers," *Journal of International Business Studies* 35: 508–23

Johanson, J. and J.-E. Vahlne 1977. "The internationalization process of the firm – a model of knowledge development and increasing foreign market commitments," *Journal of International Business Studies* 8: 305–22

Johnson, J. P., T. Lenartowicz and S. Apud 2006. "Cross-cultural competence in international business: toward a definition and a model," *Journal of International Business* 37: 525–43

Jones, G. R. 1983. "Psychological orientation and the process of organizational socialization: an interactionist perspective," *Academy of Management Review* 8: 464–74

Kanter, R. M. 1988. "When a thousand flowers bloom: structural, collective, and social conditions for innovation in organizations" in Staw and Cummings (eds.) *Research in Organizational Behavior.* Greenwich, CT: JAI Press Inc, pp. 169–211

Kanungo, R. N. and R. W. Wright 1983. "A cross-cultural comparative study of managerial job attitudes," *Journal of International Business Studies* 14: 115–29

Kim, W. C. and R. A. Mauborgne 1991. "Implementing global strategies: the role of procedural justice," *Strategic Management Journal* (Special Issue: Global Strategy) 12: 125–43

Kirkman, B. L. and D. L. Shapiro 1997. "The impact of cultural values on employee resistance to teams: toward a model of globalized self-managing work team effectiveness," *Academy of Management Review* 22: 730–57

Kirkman, B. L., K. B. Lowe and C. B. Gibson 2006. "A quarter century of Culture's Consequences: a review of empirical research incorporating Hofstede's cultural values framework," *Journal of International Business Studies* 37: 285–320

Kogut, B. and H. Singh 1988. "The effect of national culture on choice of entry mode," *Journal of International Business Studies* 19: 411–32

Kostova, T. 1999. "Transnational transfer of strategic organizational practices: a contextual perspective," *Academy of Management Review* 24: 308–24

Kostova, T. and K. Roth 2002. "Adoption of an organizational practice by subsidiaries of multinational corporations: institutional and relational effects," *Academy of Management Journal* 45: 215–33

2003. "Social capital in multinational corporations and a micro-macro model of its formation," *Academy of Management Review* 28: 297–317

Lee, S. H. and C. Williams 2007. "Dispersed entrepreneurship within multinational corporations: a community perspective," *Journal of World Business* 42: 505–19

Martinez, J. I. and J. C. Jarillo 1989. "The evolution of research on coordination mechanisms in multinational corporations," *Journal of International Business Studies* 20: 489–514

Miller, V. D. and F. M. Jablin 1991. "Information seeking during organizational entry: influences, tactics, and a model of the process," *Academy of Management Review* 16: 92–120

Minbaeva, D., T. Pedersen, I. Björkman, C. F. Fey and H. J. Park 2003. "MNC knowledge transfer, subsidiary absorptive capacity, and HRM," *Journal of International Business Studies* 34: 586–99

Mintzberg, H. 1985. "The organization as political arena," *Journal of Management Studies* 22: 133–54

Morgan, G. 1986. *Images of Organization*. London: Sage

Morgan, G. and P. H. Kristensen 2006. "The contested space of multinationals: varieties of institutionalism, varieties of capitalism," *Human Relations* 59: 1467–90

Newman, K. L. and S. D. Nollen 1996. "Culture and congruence: the fit between management practices and national culture," *Journal of International Business Studies* 27: 753–79

Nobel, R. and J. Birkinshaw 1998. "Innovation in multinational corporations: control and communication patterns in international R&D operations," *Strategic Management Journal* 19: 479–96

Nohria, N. and S. Ghoshal 1994. "Differentiated fit and shared values: alternatives for managing headquarters–subsidiary relations," *Strategic Management Journal* 15: 491–502

Nonaka, I. 1988. "Toward middle-up-down management: accelerating information creation," *Sloan Management Review* 29: 9–18

1994. "A dynamic theory of organizational knowledge creation," *Organization Science* 5: 14–37

Parker, C. P., R. L. Dipboye and S. L. Jackson 1995. "Perceptions of organizational politics: an investigation of antecedents and consequences," *Journal of Management* 21: 891–912

Perlmutter, H. V. 1969. "The tortuous evolution of the multinational corporation," *Columbia Journal of World Business* 4: 9–18

Pfeffer, J. 1981. *Power in Organizations*. Marshfield, MA: Pitman Publishing
    1994. *Managing with Power: Politics and Influence in Organization*. Boston, MA: Harvard
    Business School Press
Polanyi, M. 1966. *The Tacit Dimension*, London: Routledge and Kegan Paul
Prahalad, C. K. and Y. L. Doz 1981. "Strategic control – the dilemma in headquarters–
    subsidiary relationships" in Otterbeck (ed.) *The Management of Headquarters–subsidiary
    Relationships in Multinational Corporations*. Aldershot: Gower, pp. 187–203
Reichers, A. E. 1987. "An interactionist perspective on newcomer socialization rates,"
    Academy of Management Review 12: 278–87
Reus, T. H. and B. T. Lamont 2009. "The double-edged sword of cultural distance in inter-
    national acquisitions," *Journal of International Business Studies* 40: 1298–316
Salk, J. E. and M. Y. Brannen 2000. "National culture, networks, and individual influence in
    a multinational management team," *Academy of Management Journal* 43: 191–202
Schneider, S. C. and De Meyer, A. 1991 "Interpreting and responding to strategic issues: the
    impact of national culture," *Strategic Management Journal* 12: 307–20
Schwartz, S. H. 1994. "Beyond individualism/collectivism: new cultural dimensions
    of values" in Kim, Triandis, Kagitcibasi, Choi and Yoon (eds.) *Individualism and
    Collectivism: Theory, Methods, and Applications*. Thousand Oaks, CA: Sage, pp. 85–119
Smircich, L. 1983 "Concepts of culture and organizational analysis," *Administrative Science
    Quarterly* 28: 339–58
Stone, B. 1997. *Confronting Company Politics*. Basingstoke: Macmillan
Szulanski, G. 1996. "Exploring internal stickiness: impediments to the transfer of best prac-
    tice within the firm," *Strategic Management Journal* 17: 27–43
Taggart, J. H. 1997. "Autonomy and procedural justice: a framework for evaluating subsid-
    iary strategy," *Journal of International Business Studies* 28: 51–76
Thomas, A. S. and S. L. Mueller 2000. "A case for comparative entrepreneurship: assessing
    the relevance of culture," *Journal of International Business Studies* 31: 287–301
Van de Vliert, E., A. Nauta, E. Giebels and O. Janssen 1999. "Constructive conflict at work,"
    Journal of Organizational Behavior 20: 475–91
Venaik, S., D. F. Midgley and T. M. Devinney 2005. "Dual paths to performance: the
    impact of global pressures on MNC subsidiary conduct and performance," *Journal of
    International Business Studies* 36: 655–75
Verbeke, A., J. J. Chrisman and W. Yuan 2007. "A note on strategic renewal and corpor-
    ate venturing in the subsidiaries of multinational enterprises," *Entrepreneurship Theory
    and Practice* 31: 585–600
Vigoda, E. and A. Cohen 2002. "Influence tactics and perceptions of organizational polit-
    ics: a longitudinal study," *Journal of Business Research* 55: 311–24
Williams, C. and S. H. Lee 2009. "International management, political arena, and dispersed
    entrepreneurship in the MNC," *Journal of World Business* 44: 287–99
Williams, C. and S. P. Van Triest 2009. "The impact of corporate and national cultures
    on decentralization in multinational corporations," *International Business Review*
    18: 156–67

10 Unequal power relations, identity discourse, and cultural distinction drawing in MNCs

Sierk Ybema and Hyunghae Byun

Introduction

While organizational scholars have shown a sustained interest in cultural processes in transnational contexts, the dominant approach in cross-cultural research has overlooked processes of culture construction and distinction drawing, and offers an a-contextual and a-political understanding of cultural encounters. Cultural identity, as it is usually conceptualized, starts from the assumption that national identity imprints a value-based, mental program or collective "software" in peoples' minds (Hofstede 1991). These cognitive models are represented through a small set of continua – individualism–collectivism, masculinity–femininity, power distance, anxiety reduction, long-term or short-term orientation (for similar approaches, see e.g. House *et al.* 2004) – which are claimed to manifest themselves in organizations through stubbornly distinctive patterns of thinking, feeling and acting located in the nationally constituted actors. Despite the appealing simplicity of a description in terms of dimension scores and the useful grip it promises to provide on a complex phenomenon, such a description gives a rather minimal, static and monolithic sketch of national cultures (for a critical discussion of Hofstede's work, see e.g. Ailon 2008). A few general characteristics are considered to be deep-rooted determinants of behavior that are assumed to constitute a true and timeless cultural essence. This type of cross-cultural organization research ignores identity and ethnicity theorists, who have put emphasis on the situational and relational character of social identification processes (e.g. Barth 1969; Jenkins 2004) by treating national identity as "merely the passive embodiment of a predetermined cultural template" (Ailon-Souday and Kunda 2003: 1074) and restricting respondents to answering predefined questions without any reference to a specific situation or intercultural relation. So, even if the variance that is measured in survey research does capture some "real" or experienced cultural essence, it does not represent the actualities of everyday work situations. Consequently, the question of how organizational actors draw on and deploy these presumed cultural differences in specific intercultural contexts remains unanswered.

An emerging tradition of interpretive research in the field of cross-cultural management is more sensitive to situated sensemaking practices; that is to how organizational actors make sense of their experiences within particular social contexts and infuse the social worlds they inhabit (and the identities of the actors involved) with meaning. This research shows the significance of power relations between cultural partners in transnational enterprises for cultural processes of identification (e.g. Ailon-Souday and Kunda 2003; Byun and Ybema 2005; Dahler-Larssen 1997; Koot 1997). In multinational companies, management often remains firmly rooted in the parent country's culture (Schneider and Barsoux 1997). Being subordinated under foreign rule, the nationals of the host culture tend to challenge the management of the parent country's culture (see e.g. Brannen and Salk 2000; Van Marrewijk 2004; Wong 1999). In this political process, organizational actors draw on culture as a rich symbolic resource and strategic weapon in their meaning-making efforts, deploying cultural differences to promote their own interests and identity. Noorderhaven *et al.* (2007) show, for instance, how Japanese and Dutch managers alike see their own decision-making style as less hierarchical than the other's.

In this chapter, we build on these insights, drawing on data derived from interviews and ethnographic case studies of Japanese–Dutch work relations in multinational corporations in Japan and the Netherlands. Focusing on the ways in which various organizational actors talk cultural identities into existence by drawing cultural distinctions between themselves and others, we analyze differences in actors' cultural identity talk in two different power contexts: Japanese management–Dutch staff and Dutch management–Japanese staff. The chapter makes two contributions. First, the research offers evidence in support of the claim that a national culture – that is its ascribed qualities and characteristics – constitutes a symbolic resource that is actively and creatively used by organizational actors to create a sense of identity and cultural distance in political struggles in multinational corporations. Second, we further underscore the constructed and context-dependent nature of culture and cultural distance in intercultural encounters by describing instances of cultural identity talk in two different social contexts, showing how use of cultural discourse is dependent on the specific power constellation within each organizational setting. The study reveals small, but meaningful differences in organizational actors' cultural identity talk that are intimately related to the specific power asymmetries (unequal distribution of rewards, status and control over decisions and resources) within multinational corporations (see also chapter of Maclean and Hollinshead in this volume). While case studies of intercultural communication have illustrated the relevance of a power-sensitive understanding of culture in multinational corporations, none have shown how culture is differently constructed in different power contexts.

The argument proceeds as follows. To foreground the relationship between cultural discourse and social context, and to lay a foundation for the analysis of the empirical material, the first theoretical section discusses the role of power and politics in processes of cultural identity formation. After explaining the research methodology, we then present the research findings in detail and discuss the implications of our study for theorizing and studying culture in multicultural corporations.

Power and identity in cross-cultural encounters

In order to sensitize culture research in the field of cross-cultural management to organizational actors' situated sensemaking practices, there is a need to critically re-think current theorizing of cultural encounters in international business (Jack *et al.* 2008) and explore new perspectives and new methodologies (Primecz *et al.* 2009). Particularly promising in this respect is the increasing interest in micro-political processes in multinational corporations, a largely neglected and marginalized topic in the field of international business (Dörrenbächer and Geppert 2006; see also introduction to this volume). A focus on micro-politics is, as Dörrenbächer and Geppert (2006: 255) note, about "bringing back the actors and examining the conflicts that emerge when powerful actors with different goals, interests and identities interact with each other locally and across national and functional borders." A discursive approach to culture and identity may help to bring into view the micro-processes of power and politics in everyday interactions and negotiations in MNCs (see also chapter of Maclean and Hollinshead in this volume). Such an approach shifts attention away from studying culture per se, to exploring culture and cultural boundaries as being constituted in organizational actors' "self–other identity talk" (Søderberg and Holden 2002; Ybema *et al.* 2009a), conceptualizing "culture" as "mutable, negotiated, and infused with contestation and power relations" (Jack *et al.* 2008: 875).

From a discursive perspective, identity can be viewed as enacted through the situated practices of talking and writing. An intrinsic part of the discursive enactment of an "identity" involves the discursive separation of "self" from the "other" by establishing and signifying "sameness" and "otherness" (Ybema *et al.* 2009a), usually through invoking stark contrasts – good versus bad, management versus staff, the West versus the Orient, Dutch versus Japanese. And, as Ainsworth and Hardy (2004: 155) remind us, such discursive positioning is often utilized to establish or maintain a sense of "moral uprightness" of the "self" (Watson 2009) and to position the other not merely as different, but also as less acceptable, less respectable and, sometimes, less powerful (Hall 1997). Identity construction may thus be a far from neutral process, colored by emotions, moral judgments, and political or economic interests. Identity discourse appears to be instrumental in attempts to establish, legitimate, secure, or challenge the prevailing relationships of power and status. It implicates social maneuvering and power games.

Seen from this theoretical vantage point, studying cross-cultural communications essentially means shedding light on symbolic classifications, which are generally built on putative differences in national or ethnic culture. Sociological and anthropological studies of collective identity have already shown processes of appropriation and mobilization of culture for the purpose of constructing collective "selfhood" and distinctiveness through cultivating a discourse of common culture and, simultaneously, casting the "other" as "strange" (e.g. Cohen 1985; Elias and Scotson 1965). Instead of treating culture as a historically based "given," these studies focus on processes of social categorization and distinction drawing (Barth 1969) and the symbolic construction of community (Cohen 1985). It is assumed that culture, within the bounds of institutional conditions and constraints, can be invented or invoked by culture members in order to present an identity, establish a truth, enhance status and self-esteem, or defend an interest (Eriksen 1993). Cultural identities should thus not be understood as coherent, stable entities, but as shifting social constructs that are dependent on specific interests that are at stake at a certain moment in a certain situation. In a similar, albeit more critical vein, postcolonial studies, drawing inspiration from the work from Said, Spivak, Bhabha and others, highlight the exercise of imperial power through representational strategies that build binary oppositions between self and other to denigrate and diminish "the other" whilst empowering the self (e.g. Jack *et al.* 2008; Prasad 2003; Westwood 2006). Rather than understanding or allowing others to construct themselves in terms of their own codes and categories, the other is abstracted and reified in negative terms. Ultimately seeking to produce and perpetuate power asymmetries (Westwood 2006), members signal how they like to see themselves while, at the same time, disciplining newcomers and excluding "deviants" (Bhabha 1989).

In this chapter we analyze talk of cultural differences in dominant group–marginal group dynamics and draw attention to the role of power and politics in cross-cultural relations. Taking account of context as well as agency (Bate 1997), we conceive of cultural identities as talked into being in a specific power figuration, shaped by, and shaping, social processes. In addition to a cultural explanation, a social-political reading can draw attention to ongoing negotiations and power dynamics in intercultural relations in organizational settings. Power and politics are inherent to organizational processes (Hardy and Clegg 1996) and culture (Alvesson 1996) and, more specifically, to the social construction of cultural boundaries and identities (Elias and Scotson 1965; Eriksen 1993). A power perspective lays emphasis on strategic agency in processes of ethnicization (see e.g. Van Marrewijk 2004) while simultaneously acknowledging the embeddedness of interactions and interpretations within historical processes, long-standing traditions, and organizational structures that constitute the "unacknowledged conditions" and "unintended consequences" of human action (Berger and Luckmann 1991; Giddens 1979; see also chapter of Fenton-O'Creevy *et al.* in this volume).

Various in-depth case studies of multinational corporations highlight the situational and strategic use of national culture differences or ethnicity (e.g. Dahler-Larssen 1997; Olie 1994). An ironic illustration of this is given by Koot (1997), who describes how employees of a Shell oil refinery on the Dutch Caribbean island of Curaçao were keen to express their affinity with Latino culture when in the 1960s and 1970s the management of the Shell plant was Dutch, while the same Curaçaoan workers started to dissociate themselves from Latino culture when the refinery was rented out to a Venezuelan company in the 1980s, instead calling upon their Dutch roots and praising the old Shell culture. Such instances of cultural identity talk testify to the importance of socially situated use of culture, illustrating the significance of power asymmetries for intercultural relations. Organizational hierarchy is a crucial factor influencing how people perceive and present themselves and others. In line with this idea, Watanabe and Yamaguchi (1995) found that locals with higher ranks from British subsidiaries of Japanese firms were likely to perceive Japanese expatriates more negatively than locals with lower ranks, due to greater frustration generated by the lack of promotion and authority (see also Byun and Ybema 2005; Hong and Snell 2008). As an inequality in terms of political influence, rewards, and advancement opportunities is often a structural characteristic of cross-cultural cooperation in multinational corporations, it is important to further investigate the relationship among power and culture in MNCs and explore how cultural identity discourse is specific to particular power asymmetries in multinational corporations.

To conclude, our review of the literature shows the relevance of a perspective on cross-cultural relations in multinational corporations that acknowledges the situated, constructed and strategic nature of cultural identity discourse (see also chapter of Koveshnikov in this volume). Cross-cultural relations in multinational firms are marked, not by cultural differences per se, but by cultural identity formation within contexts of specific power-constellations. We are interested in seeing whether and how culture is situationally and strategically used in Japanese–Dutch relations in both Dutch and Japanese multinational organizations, and how specific power asymmetries between parent country and host country nationals impact on the ways in which cultural differences are constructed.

Research design and methods

Exploring members' subjective perception and presentation of intercultural encounters calls for an analysis of the situated knowledge held by members of the setting under study (Geertz 1973) and seeing culture through their eyes (Bate 1997). Therefore, it was essential to conduct the research with methods that could provide depth and detail and remain sensitive to situation and context (Ybema *et al.* 2009b), such as in-depth interviews, participant observations and documentary analysis. The fieldwork consisted of two phases.

Phase 1

The first part of the research was conducted in subsidiaries of Japanese corporations in the Netherlands. To get a first idea of the possible cultural issues relevant to Dutch–Japanese interactions, we analyzed in-depth studies of Japanese and Dutch culture (e.g. Befu 1986; Moeran 1986; Vossestein 1997) and earlier research of graduate students in Japanese organizations in the Netherlands. In addition, the second author, who carried out all fieldwork, conducted nine interviews with selected informants (five Dutch and four Japanese) from the European head offices in the Netherlands of Nissan, Fuji Film and Mitsubishi (before it was taken over) and one interview with an expert from an intercultural training center. The fieldworker, a woman born and raised in Korea and living in the Netherlands

Table 10.1 Nationality and positions of interviewees

		Top management	Middle management	Employee	Total
In the Netherlands	Japanese	3	10	1	14
	Dutch	—	6	9	15
In Japan	Japanese	3	13	5	21
	Dutch	11	5	1	17
Total		17	34	16	67

since 1987, then conducted three months of ethnographic research at the European head office of Rajio Corporation (a pseudonym), a Japanese firm in consumer electronics, introducing her research interest broadly as being about "cross-cultural communication." Fieldwork consisted of formal interviews, field observations, informal conversations and document analysis.

In keeping with Sackmann's (1991) advice, we decided to focus on concrete issues in studying culture within the focal firm. On the basis of the in-depth studies of Japanese and Dutch culture, the graduate students' research in Japanese organizations in the Netherlands, and the nine interviews, we selected seven issues that seemed relevant to Japanese–Dutch encounters. We then distributed a questionnaire among organizational members at Rajio to check whether they found the selected topics relevant to the situation at Rajio (we dropped two issues: "problem-solving process" and "flexibility"). The remaining issues were then used as topics for conversation in interviews: work ethos, communication style, decision-making, the superior–subordinate relationship and language (although as cultural differences were sometimes framed as "language problems," we focus on the first four, culturally sensitive issues in this chapter). In observations and interviews organizational members frequently raised these issues themselves, drawing upon them as interpretive repertoires to describe cultural differences. Standardized, open-ended interviews were conducted with ten Japanese expatriates (all three directors, six middle managers and one shop-floor technician) and ten Dutch staff members (three middle managers and seven shop-floor employees) (see Table 10.1).

Interview transcriptions were coded and categorized, using the five topics selected in the preliminary research, focusing our analysis on the construction of national cultural differences in organizational discourse. To get a sense of the everyday talk and "lived experience" of organizational members, the fieldworker observed daily work activities and participated in the monthly management team meeting, as well as in informal settings, such as lunchtime in the company cafeteria, coffee breaks, the after-work drinks on Fridays, farewell parties, the Easter lunch and the family day on board two tall ships on a Dutch lake. The time spent in the field was crucial for establishing close rapport with participants, which improved the informational yield from interviews with Japanese participants in particular. Her position as, at the same time, insider (being familiar with Asian and Dutch culture) and outsider (being non-Japanese and non-Dutch) helped her to empathize while simultaneously maintaining analytic distance.

Phase 2

The analysis of the Rajio case suggested the significance of social context for cross-cultural communications and, in particular, the relative power positions of the Japanese and the Dutch within the organizational hierarchy (Byun and Ybema 2005). For this reason, we decided to extend the study to Dutch multinationals in Japan in order to be able to compare the cultural identity talk of research participants at Nissan, Mitsubishi, Fuji Film and, especially, Rajio, with cross-cultural experiences in a context that constitutes, metaphorically speaking, the Dutch–Japanese power asymmetry in reverse: Dutch management and Japanese staff within Dutch multinationals operating in Japan. In this second part of the research, the second author spent a period of three months and a subsequent period of nine months in Japan to conduct an ethnographic case study of a Dutch subsidiary. In the same period, she also conducted interviews with Dutch managers and Japanese staff working for other Dutch multinationals.

An inequality in terms of political influence, rewards and advancement opportunities is often characteristic of the structure of many Japanese multinationals, where subsidiaries tend to be tightly integrated into the head office strategy (Whitley *et al.* 2003) and strong central controls remain a dominant feature of the management model (Bartlett and Ghoshal 2002; Gong 2003). In the last decade or so, a more moderate type of management is claimed to be gaining popularity in Japanese firms (Clegg and Kono 2002), but within Rajio the Dutch staff were formally and informally subordinated to a rather autocratic Japanese management. In contrast with the tendency in Japanese MNCs "to have strong centralized capabilities and a headquarters-based decision-making process" (Bartlett and Ghoshal 2002: 17, 59) and

323   Power, identity discourse, and cultural distinction

to employ parent country nationals in overseas subsidiaries (Gong 2003; Wong 1999), Dutch multinationals commonly practice a more decentralized organizational structure, giving "substantial strategic freedom and organizational autonomy," and building a "strong local presence" in foreign subsidiaries (Bartlett and Ghoshal 2002: 17), following a "multinational" strategy or "polycentric approach" (Fung 1995) of localization. As a consequence, Dutch multinationals operating in Japan dispatched a very limited number of expatriates (and they were not necessarily from the Netherlands). In order to enlarge the number of Dutch participants and to ensure our Japanese participants worked together with Dutch managers, we decided to involve different subsidiaries of Dutch multinationals (and Dutch managers of one British multinational) in Japan: Akzo Nobel, ASM, DSM, KLM, KPN Mobile, Nippon Lever (Unilever), Philips, Rabo Bank, Shell and Vodafone. These organizations varied significantly in size (from 6 employees to more than 1000 employees), types of operation (sales office, production, research, services, etc.), industry, market and local organizations' history in Japan (chosen strategy for, and time period of, entrance in the Japanese market). Rather than compare these various settings, we wanted to collect a broad set of data on organizational members' perceptions and presentation of cultural differences within Dutch multinational corporations in Japan.

All interviews were conducted in English (one Japanese interviewee needed the assistance of an interpreter). Seventeen Dutch expatriates and twenty-one Japanese staff members were interviewed. As shown in Table 10.1, all Dutch interviewees were in managerial positions except for one technician. The majority of Japanese interviewees held positions at middle management level. It was natural for Dutch expatriates to have daily interactions with their Japanese colleagues, but, since not all Japanese staff members had daily interactions with their expatriate colleagues, we only used the interview material of twenty-one Japanese who had day-to-day experience in intercultural communication with the Dutch expatriates or Dutch colleagues from the head office.

Data analysis

All interviews were tape-recorded and transcribed and subsequently analyzed by coding and categorizing statements about national culture differences, using the same topics as in our earlier study in the Netherlands. Again, analysis consisted of multiple readings and iterations of the data as well as member-checking to see if we did a good job capturing *their* understandings

(Schwartz-Shea and Yanow 2009), a process of analysis that is not designed to make generalizable claims, but to strengthen assertions made about actors' interpretations. In this way, we were able to identify cultural "identity talk" (Snow and Anderson 1987) or "identity narratives" (Brown 2006), analyze the patterns of similarity and variation, and recognize traces of contextual influences. We focused specifically on how references to national culture and cultural difference functioned in accounts and explanations used to explain, justify, or construct particular versions of reality and identity. Practices of talking and writing do not create a "reality" of identities in an "institutional, socio-economic or political vacuum" (Keenoy et al. 1997: 154) and therefore we try to understand the content of identity talk within its particular social context. Focusing our analysis on participants' "self–other identity talk" (Ybema et al. 2009a), we systematically compared the ways in which Japanese and Dutch research participants in Japan presented cultural differences with the study of Dutch–Japanese interrelations in the Netherlands. In order to get a focused and sufficiently detailed empirical illustration of the theoretical argument, we concentrate on four issues, which we describe in the subsequent section of this chapter: work ethos, style of communication, superior–subordinate relationship and decision-making.

Work ethos

A first difference between Japanese and Dutch culture that research participants repeatedly constructed in their cultural identity talk concerns the work ethos. We first present cultural identity talk of research participants in Japanese firms in the Netherlands, and then turn to the identity talk of those working for Dutch firms in Japan.

Japanese firms in the Netherlands

Although the Dutch working for Dutch subsidiaries of Japanese firms respect the hard-working attitude of the Japanese in general, they have a hard time understanding the utmost priority that is given to work by their Japanese colleagues. "The Japanese live to work instead of working to live," is a common remark among the Dutch, who also cherish the idea that the Japanese have to put in extra hours because of their presumed inefficiency (see Table 10.2). To explain the working attitude of the Japanese to new employees, the Dutch at Rajio like to recall an incident where a Japanese employee fell asleep at his

Table 10.2 Talk of "cultural difference" in relation to work ethos

Japanese firms in the Netherlands	Dutch firms in Japan
Japanese senior manager: "[The Dutch] always have excuses about family and private things. That's why we, Japanese, always have to work till late."	**Dutch senior manager**: "I like that people are working really hard. I really prefer to work with Japanese rather than with Dutch."
Dutch staff member: "The Japanese live to work, but do not work to live."	**Japanese staff member**: "[The Dutch] don't do much overtime. In Japanese companies, overtime is our culture."

desk and was found by security the next morning. Since then a new regulation has been established that gives the security officer the authority to send people home after midnight (most Japanese leave the office between 8 and 10 P.M.).

Most Dutch employees do not feel any pressure or expectation from the Japanese management to adopt the same working attitude. A Dutch manager maintains that "they [the Japanese managers] just cannot expect us to show such commitment when so little responsibility is given to us locals." According to a shop-floor worker it is plain logic: "Their salaries are much higher and they get much more benefits – *of course* they have to put in more hours and take less holidays." So, the Dutch tend to deny any formal or moral obligations to work harder by referring to cultural differences and the unequal distribution of power and rewards. Ironically, they defend themselves as having a *joie de vivre*, whereas their fellow countrymen usually think of themselves as having a protestant work ethic.

To legitimate their own work ethos, the Japanese point to the intrinsic value of work: "We understand that it is Dutch culture to enjoy life, but for us it is more important to accomplish something that will give meaning to life *through* our work." Commenting on the Dutch work ethic they stress the importance of moral commitment: "we don't fail in our duty to our company and our colleagues … no matter how much overtime we have to do." The "nine-to-five mentality" of the Dutch is thus not much appreciated. A Japanese technician from an IT department:

I cannot understand the Dutch attitude. They can just leave undone work on their desk and go home. They always have excuses about family and private things. That's why we, the Japanese, always have to work till late.

Japanese irritation within Rajio is aroused by Dutch colleagues chatting loudly in the middle of the corridor, preferably about off-the-job rather than work-related issues. A disgruntled Japanese manager noticed that the summer holiday schedules are already on the agenda in January and February, while the company's Christmas party "becomes a topic already in August." These are taken as instances of Dutch indolence and self-centered individualism.

The Dutch complaint about a lack of responsibilities and opportunities at Rajio Europe is met with ambivalence. Some Japanese argue that the Dutch are nagging about this, while at the same time they are not willing to do extracurricular work that could earn them new responsibilities. One Japanese manager asserts that the Dutch do not work on something if it is not included in the job description, even if it is important for the success of the company. Yet, despite Japanese irritations about the level of commitment and the lack of initiative on the part of the Dutch employees, most Japanese admit that the Dutch are disadvantaged within the company: "Most of the important positions are taken by Japanese and less responsibility is given to the locals." Being in a privileged position, the Japanese feel compelled to live up to high standards and to always work hard, also because career opportunities at Rajio depend on the evaluation of their work as an expat. The Japanese therefore also assume that both cultural habits and inequalities underlie a typical difference in work ethos.

Dutch firms in Japan

In contrast to the Dutch staff working for Japanese subsidiaries in the Netherlands, Dutch expatriates in Japan – working long hours themselves – praise the devotion Japanese show to their work. The Japanese take fewer days off per year than the twenty days they are entitled to (working for a Dutch firm) and usually work ten to twelve hours a day, willing to sacrifice evenings and weekends if necessary. "They don't even ask for compensation," a Dutch manager said in surprise. The Dutch do not understand why the Japanese "don't care about private life," and several Dutch companies in Japan either informally encouraged or issued a formal regulation for the timely departure from the office to avoid long working hours. Managers in particular are encouraged to leave on time, a Dutch executive explains, because subordinates "are waiting for the bosses to go home here in Japan. This is exactly opposite to the Netherlands. In the Netherlands, bosses often find out their subordinates are already gone. Ha! Ha!"

Although some Dutch interviewees occasionally evince some doubts about the efficiency of Japanese employees and presume that they have to work long hours to compensate for that, they generally admire their hard-working attitude. Arguably, the Dutch interviewees' managerial position explains their appreciation of Japanese staff, as a Dutch managing director readily admits:

> I like it that the people are working very hard. If you have to run an organization and you have hard-working people you can only like it. I really prefer to work with Japanese rather than with Dutch.

Sometimes, Dutch managers' admiration for the Japanese even goes together with complaints about the Dutch work ethos, that, according to one manager, is built on the belief that "weekdays are terrible and on Friday evenings – or Friday afternoon! – life starts."

Unlike their compatriots in the Netherlands, Japanese employees from the subsidiaries of Dutch multinationals in Japan were not annoyed by the Dutch working style. Some of the Japanese interviewees appreciated the incitement of the head offices and their Dutch managers to seek a better balance between work and private life; others experienced it as rather incompatible with increasing workloads or asserted it was "unrealistic" to adopt the Dutch style in a Japanese context. Japanese customers or partners could still try to reach the office at 8 or 9 P.M. and colleagues would interpret punctual leaving of the office and insisting on your rights to holidays as "inconsiderate," "individualistic" behavior and as evidence of "a lack of collegiality." Nevertheless, the majority of Japanese interviewees believed and appreciated that their working hours were better balanced than those of their compatriots working in traditional Japanese companies. We may thus conclude that there is a striking difference in the appreciation of the differences in work ethos between the Japanese and the Dutch that is closely linked to the social context that they work in and the position they hold in the organizational hierarchy.

Analysis

Consistent with literature on the subject (see e.g. Befu 1986; Hofstede 1991; Moeran 1986), Japanese and Dutch research participants alike report that Japanese culture demands loyalty and devotion to work, group, organization and superiors, and imposes a moral imperative to subordinate personal interests to group goals. Curiously, however, the hard-working attitude of the Japanese is appreciated quite differently by those working in Dutch companies in Japan and those working in Dutch subsidiaries of Japanese firms in the Netherlands. Japanese managers at Rajio Europe, as well as their compatriots at Fuji Film, Mitsubishi and Nissan, are easily annoyed by Dutch unwillingness to stay overtime or do extra work, "selfishly" prioritizing their private lives. Japanese employees working under a Dutch managerial regime in Japan, on the other hand, do not complain about the working attitude of their expatriate colleagues and show some appreciation for the Dutch style of balance seeking between professional and private life. Among the Dutch we find the opposite pattern. For Dutch staff members of Japanese subsidiaries the Japanese "over-devotion" to their work is proof of an inefficient working style that they find hard to understand. They like to point out that, rather than demanding full dedication to the group, it is accepted and appreciated in Dutch society that the individual's private life and a family orientation are highly valued (cf. Vossestein 1997). In contrast, however, Dutch expatriate managers praise and appreciate the hard-working attitude of their Japanese subordinates. So, although the difference in work ethos is generally acknowledged, the appreciation (or "depreciation") of this difference depends on a person's political interests and specific position in the organizational hierarchy. The next section further clarifies this point.

Communication

A second cultural difference between Japanese and Dutch culture that was frequently constructed in research participants' cultural identity talk concerns the style of communication.

Japanese firms in the Netherlands

Dutch staff members of Dutch subsidiaries of Japanese corporations maintain that Japanese communication circuits are closed and hard to penetrate, excluding foreigners. Contacts with the head office, for instance, are controlled completely by Japanese managers, probably, the Dutch think, to preserve their power base (see Table 10.2). A Dutch manager who maintained good relationships with Japanese top managers heard through the grapevine about a meeting meant only for the Japanese managers to discuss the company's strategies. It had been scheduled in the evening to be sure that all Dutch personnel would have left the office. What annoyed the Dutch manager most was that they did not even bother to inform the Dutch personnel about the results of the meeting.

The Japanese interviewees agree that the Dutch have a more direct and open communication style that can improve clarity. One Japanese manager, for instance, said that, initially, he found it difficult to deal with Dutch people who did not accept his elaborate "maybe" or "probably" as an answer, but he came to realize that clear "yes" or "no" answers make life at the office easier for everybody, including himself. There are, however, several Japanese managers (not always the older ones) who believe that the openness and directness of the Dutch demonstrates a lack of political sensitivity, too little consideration for others, and an incapacity for deep thinking, expressed in remarks like "they [the Dutch] would not bother even if it embarrasses somebody, they will just say it very, very directly." Moreover, the Dutch make promises as easily as they break them. One Japanese manager told that he was pleasantly surprised with the immediate "yes" from his Dutch colleague when, for the first time, he asked for a favor in the Netherlands. A few days later he was surprised again when he found out that this Dutch colleague could not even remember the request. Japanese people, he claimed, prefer to give a negative answer in words, but try to come up with positive results in action.

Dutch firms in Japan

Dutch expatriates in Japan also think Japanese employees do not express their thoughts and opinions openly or directly and "obscure" rather than clarify their position in discussions. For Dutch managers, it is hard and time-consuming to find out about disagreements or objections of Japanese employees. Just as a Dutch "yes" is unreliable in the eyes of Japanese managers, Dutch managers complain about the untrustworthiness of a Japanese "yes," not because a promise is easily broken (the Japanese managers' complaint about the Dutch), but because the Japanese are assumed to be too polite to say no. The way they handled client relations make the presence in Japan of Dutch expatriates in their own eyes "absolutely necessary," because the Japanese would wait endlessly without informing clients about problems, only making things worse. The observation by the Dutch of Japanese "indirectness" was thus widely shared, although a Dutch controller had been involved in negotiations with the unions and suggested the Japanese are "indirect" only with outsiders, not with insiders.

Although the majority of all Dutch interviewees were in favor of the Dutch style of communication, Dutch top managers were more positive about the Japanese style. One Dutch managing director muttered about the blunt directness of his compatriots.

I think that it is more difficult for me to go back and get used to the Dutch culture. When I am back in the Netherlands for my vacation, I get so irritated. Sometimes people are so insensitive about other people's feelings. They believe that it is their right to say what is in their mind, even if it can be rude or hurt someone's feelings. In that respect I am more Japanese.

Japanese interviewees affirmed that their communication style was indirect and not always as open, clear and sharp as the style of Dutch expatriates and members of the head office. According to a Japanese manager, the Dutch create clarity through expressions like "I want this" or "I don't want that." Indeed, despite occasional miscommunications, alienation from the information flow (experienced by Dutch employees in Japanese firms) was not mentioned. However, the Japanese cautiously point out that being "very clear" can be "rather rude" at the same time, hurting, for instance, a Japanese customer's feelings. Building a good business relationship in Japan requires a more subtle approach and "proper" communication, built on mutual trust and personal relationships and the exercise of prudence, to avoid breaking promises or falling short of others' expectations. The Dutch, on the other hand, make easy promises and, during meetings, express "strong and honest opinions" and like to start "hot discussions," "as if they are afraid of not saying anything." A Japanese interviewee:

For a Dutch[man] or an American, no plan is the worst thing. Even if you are not sure about accomplishing them, you just have to say: "Yes we can." No direct response means that you are incapable. Whether you can accomplish the plan or not is a separate issue for later …

"In Japan," another Japanese manager said, "listening is as important as speaking out. We prefer to wait until the chairman or leader asks you to speak out. I do both to survive in this company."

Analysis

Participants point out that Japanese culture members are expected to show courtesy and cautiousness in communication and to pick up the unspoken wishes of others, while clarity in communication, a certain degree of directness and constructive criticism are said to be valued in Dutch society. However, the variety of ways in which this difference is presented in research participants' identity talk shows culture is actively and strategically used to construct a good/bad contrast. Japanese management and staff create cultural distance and sustain social barriers by depicting their Dutch colleagues as (rather) inconsiderate, imprudent and unreliable, lamenting their lack of "listening skills" and "political sensitivity." In contrast,

Dutch research participants pride themselves for being "clear," "open" and "constructive" in their communications, claiming that, in contrast, their Japanese colleagues tend to be vague and secretive, hiding their true political intentions and keeping information, contacts and decision power to themselves.

In addition, our findings also suggest that the experience of cultural differences depends on each organizational actor's position within the organizational hierarchy. Superiors, whether Dutch or Japanese, are more likely to paint a more positive picture of their subordinates' culture (occasionally sounding complaints about not being assured of their support), while both Dutch and Japanese subordinates are more likely to paint a darker picture of their superiors' cultural idiosyncrasies. It can please a Dutch managing director, for instance, to be treated with courtesy by Japanese employees, but Dutch shop-floor workers and middle managers become frustrated with courteously being locked out of formal and informal communication circuits. Rather than recounting instances of Japanese prudence or politeness, they point at a strong insider–outsider awareness of Japanese that creates barriers for them. So, in sum (and in line with our findings described in the section on work ethos): while a cultural difference between Dutch and Japanese communication styles is generally acknowledged, the positive or negative reception of this difference depends on the speaker's perspective and political interests and his or her position within the organizational hierarchy. Participants' talk of Dutch–Japanese differences in dealing with organizational hierarchy and decision-making styles, discussed in the subsequent sections, offers perhaps even stronger examples of the situatedness of culture discourse.

The superior–subordinate relationship

A third sensitive issue in Dutch–Japanese encounters concerns the hierarchy in work relations, which tends to evoke divergent images of cultural differences in research participants' identity talk.

Japanese firms in the Netherlands

In day-to-day operations the relationship between Japanese managers and their local subordinates in Japanese firms in the Netherlands is usually rather smooth, but Dutch irritation is often aroused by the subservient attitude of Japanese managers towards their superiors. According to the Dutch their

Table 10.3 Talk of "cultural difference" in relation to communication style

Japanese firms in the Netherlands	Dutch firms in Japan
Japanese senior manager: "They have so little political sense. That's why we have to handle communications with the head office." **Dutch staff member**: "They just exclude the locals from the communication channel with the head office."	**Dutch senior manager**: "The Japanese said yes to our suggestions. Later you find out they have not implemented a single thing." **Japanese staff member**: "A European answers easily: we will do [it]. But they often do not keep promises. But Japanese need time to give [an] answer and will strive to meet the promise."

Japanese bosses are submissive, not willing to speak out to the Japanese directors or representatives of the head office in Japan. When a (Dutch) subordinate disagrees, his Japanese boss will first try to persuade the local employee to accept the ideas of his superior and, if that does not work, he will ignore the ideas and comments. Dutch staff members contrast Japanese culture with their own "egalitarian" attitude. A young engineer recounts a conflict during a one-month training period at the Japanese head office he had with the newly appointed Japanese vice president.

Mr. S. has lived and worked for Rajio in several countries in Europe for fifteen years. One would expect that he would be more westernized and open and flexible after his experiences in all these countries but he acted like a dictator instead. He gave me orders in a very unpleasant manner and expected me to react like a robot. I am rather open to the Japanese culture and flexible enough to accept cultural differences, but this was the limit.

An interruption by the Japanese managing director smoothed the situation and the vice president altered his attitude toward the Dutch subordinates afterwards.

It is basic etiquette in Japanese culture to show respect for seniors and superiors, and the promotion system in Japanese companies is often based on one's seniority, which, research participants maintain, is also the case within their firm. Even though the Japanese expatriates understand and accept the egalitarian attitude of their local subordinates as a distinct characteristic of Dutch culture, they find it difficult to get used to (especially the three directors, the most senior members of the Japanese enclave, at Rajio) (see Table 10.3). One Japanese manager explained how surprised and offended the former managing director had been when the receptionist just walked into his office without any notice: "This would never happen in Japan." His successor found a way to avoid possible objections from Dutch managers. Since he did not feel comfortable having to explain the urgency or necessity of a decision, he preferred to give an order directly to a Japanese subordinate who would never argue with his superior.

Dutch firms in Japan

When Dutch expatriates in Japan comment on the attitude of their Japanese colleagues they too point out that a strong respect for hierarchy is a prominent characteristic of Japanese culture. A Dutch senior manager: "For Japanese, the boss is the boss. Whenever the boss says: right, it is right. And if he says: left, it's left." In contrast to the Dutch within Japanese firms this is said, however, as a plain observation, without anger or frustration. One senior manager did have somewhat mixed feelings about "being treated like a king" by Japanese people: "It's a nice feeling but I don't want that and I feel a bit awkward in such situations." Others also stressed that the hierarchic attitude slowed down decision-making and hampered a free exchange of ideas and opinions. Japanese subordinates would ask permission of superiors even for trivial matters, which is strange from a Dutch point of view: "We don't go to our boss easily, because then it looks like you cannot solve a problem [on] your own, which means that you are incapable."

A large majority of the Japanese interviewees also believed that Dutch firms were less hierarchic than traditional (native) Japanese companies. A Japanese manager recounts how all personnel in a large Japanese corporation he worked for wore uniforms with an affixed nametag, each in a different color, "so everybody could immediately see what your position was in the company." While the hierarchic distance in traditional Japanese firms would make it practically impossible to have direct contact with top management for those in lower positions, Dutch top management is more approachable. Several of the Japanese mentioned the visits of Dutch CEOs from the head office who left an impression of being "open and easygoing" towards all organizational members. Some young Japanese interviewees working under Dutch superiors also appreciate the "less hierarchic" attitude of their bosses to whom they can tell their "honest opinion": "Japanese bosses usually don't listen to the opinion of subordinates because they don't want to lose face." Some indicate they would strategically use the cultural difference, such as a junior manager who explained that the meetings with the expatriate president were the best opportunity to express his opinion to his Japanese superior who would hardly listen to it otherwise. Many others experienced mixed feelings, though, feeling pressured to speak out.

Analysis

The talk of differences in styles of coping with organizational hierarchy shows how culture may be actively deployed and even creatively constructed in organizational actors' identity talk in order to defend or oppose established practices and power relations. Japanese managers in Dutch subsidiaries of Japanese firms, for instance, defend their dominant position with the corporation by bearing out that Japanese values prescribe that people should act in accordance with their relative position within the group and maintain consensus if they want to become an accepted member of a group. The way they talk about "the Dutch" shows their indignation with their subordinates' "rudeness" and "improper" behavior towards a senior or a superior. Dutch subordinates of Japanese management, on the other hand, challenge what they see as "highly hierarchical" relations by criticizing both the "submissive" attitude of their Japanese bosses towards their superiors, and their sometimes "dictatorial" attitude towards subordinates. Annoyed at being excluded by their Japanese bosses, they accentuate their own "Dutch" egalitarian values to oppose the Japanese regime, and claim that Japanese management tries to preserve the status quo by emphasizing Japanese values of hierarchy and consensus. Dutch managers in Japan, however, hardly mention the supposed egalitarianism of Dutch culture and do not present the hierarchic attitude of their Japanese subordinates as a hindrance for their work or their functioning. Japanese employees acknowledge that they are being encouraged by their "approachable" Dutch superiors to be more assertive, but they experience the Dutch way of decision-making as being "top-down," rather than egalitarian, as will become clear in the subsequent section. So, we find again a general pattern of self-appreciation and other-deprecation that is intimately connected with participants' national background and hierarchic position. And, interestingly, we also find participants have divergent views on whether Dutch culture is egalitarian or not, an issue that we will explore further in the subsequent section.

Decision-making

The contrast between Japanese and Dutch decision-making style was the fourth issue that was central in research participants' cultural identity talk.

Table 10.4 Talk of "cultural difference" in relation to the superior–subordinate relationship

Japanese firms in the Netherlands	Dutch firms in Japan
Japanese senior manager: "In the Netherlands, everybody is the same; it does not matter what your position in the hierarchy is. I think it can be a good point but, when you have to run the organization, we need respect and authority for the higher position."	**Dutch senior manager**: "I feel like I am being treated as a king by my Japanese people. It's a nice feeling, but I don't want that."
Dutch staff member: "I have seen many excellent [Dutch] people leave this company, because they didn't get enough room to discuss or participate."	**Japanese staff member**: "My direct boss is Dutch and I can tell him my honest opinion and I sometimes have a fight with him and it is okay when it is over. I can't do that with Japanese managers. You should not openly disagree with [a] Japanese boss."

Japanese firms in the Netherlands

The Dutch believe that the Japanese style of decision-making is *not* a "consensus-based" process (see Table 10.4). It is considered as a time-consuming practice of asking permission of one's superior, who has to ask his superior, and, when the highest in rank finally has decided, "the rest just agrees to share the responsibility." This practice stands in the way of a quick response to threats and opportunities. The Dutch often tell stories about slow decision-making or bad decisions made, recounting how Japanese managers go back to the head office in Japan to discuss and decide policies concerning the European market. Clearly, the underlying frustration of Dutch employees is that the Japanese managers and the head office leave little room for the Dutch to participate in, or to influence, the decision-making process. The consequence, according to the Dutch, is widespread discontent:

I have seen many excellent people leave this company, because they didn't get enough room to discuss or participate. They left because of a conflict and not because of cultural differences. As far as I can see, the remarks or opinions of the local staff are valued less than remarks made by the Japanese.

This issue is one of the most important problems that the Dutch experience in their working relationship with Japanese management.

Most Japanese acknowledge that their style of decision-making is time-consuming and one of them even called it "a waste of time" that "is even worse at the head office," but most of them also emphasize the necessity to take time to reach a decision in order to "be prepared," and to document decisions made in order to be able to report to superiors in full detail. The Japanese managers acknowledge the tension in Japanese decision-making between the consensus orientation and its top-down character. "A consensus-based decision in a Japanese company is the ideal situation, but the reality is very different here" (see also Table 10.4). Japanese consensus seeking is aimed at sharing the responsibilities for a decision made rather than making decisions bottom-up, through open discussions. Some Japanese managers prefer the Dutch style of decision-making: "Dutch people make decisions after open discussions and I also think that that is a fair way to do it." Yet, although the Japanese see the imperfections of the Japanese style of decision-making, they also tend to think that the Dutch are too short-term-oriented, base their decisions on "very little information," easily back off when faced with problems, being physically strong, but mentally weak, while "we Japanese will consider all possibilities" beforehand and "don't just give up when we are confronted with difficulties": "Compared to us, they [the Dutch] lack the endurance to pull through in difficult times."

Dutch firms in Japan

Dutch decision-making power makes two differences in decision-making styles, highly salient for both parties. Firstly, both the Dutch and the Japanese research participants in Japan mention the careful and detailed preparation regarding all possible impediments as a distinctive cultural characteristic of the Japanese way of decision-making in comparison to the Dutch "quick" style that prefers to solve problems when they are encountered in the process of implementation. The Japanese thorough preparation and attention to details is described rather neutrally by some Dutch as "just different," while others either praise the Japanese style or even disparage the hasty, unprepared style of the Dutch, or comment that the Japanese style is time-consuming and decelerates the process of reaching final decisions and starting implementation. A Dutch technician, tired of his Japanese colleagues trying to control all risks and never taking responsibility by themselves, even arrives at the conclusion that working with Japanese necessitates centralization.

Secondly, informal negotiations and networks, rather than formal meetings and open discussions, are also mentioned as an inherent part of Japanese-style decision-making. Some expats are acutely aware of the absence of open discussions among the Japanese and the backstage politics involved in

Japanese frontstage obedience. A Dutch shop-floor technician draws a clear cultural contrast:

In the Netherlands the decision-making process is much clearer and more structured, and therefore, it is easier for the people involved to give their opinion and to discuss the issue. But here, there are all kinds of cliques and networks inside the company and they influence decisions. You can say that it is very closed and it is not clear where or how decisions are made.

The influence of informal decision-making channels poses problems for Dutch expatriates, especially for those in lower, more dependent positions in the organizational hierarchy who have a hard time figuring out the informal networks and the sensitivities surrounding these networks. They tend to interpret the Japanese' thorough preparation and informal networks as "backstage politicking."

Japanese employees of Dutch firms in Japan acknowledged that the Dutch way of decision-making is a quicker process than their own, but were annoyed by easy shifts made by the Dutch (particularly by the head office) during the implementation of plans and decisions. Although two of them praised this as "flexibility," the majority thought that quick changes in plans were signs of poor preparation and of a lack of endurance to pull through, which, in turn, made them doubt the quality of the decision and the decision-maker. It certainly did not strike them as a style that aims at bottom-up participation. A senior Japanese manager:

In the Dutch style, the boss will say: *I* made a decision, so please implement it. Of course he will give some explanation why such a decision was necessary. But in Japan, the boss will talk to everybody in order to get their opinion about the decision before he makes it. And he will explain in details why the decision had to be made in a certain way. Plus he will never present it as: *I* made a decision; but he will say: *We* made a decision.

Many Japanese interviewees regard the Japanese way of decision-making as a participatory, consensus-seeking style in comparison with the Dutch style. Apparently, when hierarchic positions between the Dutch and the Japanese are reversed, both parties interpret cultural differences quite differently. Rather than depicting Dutch culture as egalitarian and respect for hierarchy as typically Japanese, Japanese subordinates explain the Dutch inclination to change plans during implementation as a top-down process and maintain that Japanese decision-making is contrary to the Dutch style and involves consensus-seeking consultation (see Table 10.5).

Table 10.5 Talk of "cultural difference" in relation to decision-making styles

Japanese firms in the Netherlands	Dutch firms in Japan
Japanese senior manager: "Even if top management makes an illogical decision you just have to follow it." **Dutch staff member**: "Japanese decision-making is not consensus-based. It is asking permission and the highest in rank will finally make a decision and the rest just agrees to share the responsibility."	**Dutch senior manager**: "Thorough preparation [that Japanese claim is typical of their way of working] is in fact a very closed and secretive process." **Japanese staff member**: "The most important thing is negotiation in Japanese culture and the boss normally has [a] stronger position in [the] negotiation. But in Dutch culture, the opinion of the boss is the most important and the boss is responsible for the decision. The decision-making style of the [Dutch] HO [Head Office] is the same. They usually do not consult the OPCOs [local subsidiary] about the local situation when they make strategic decisions. Only after a decision is made they just order us to implement it."

Analysis

Identity talk about Japanese and Dutch decision-making shows how the meaning of culture is mutable and negotiated, infused with power and contestation. Both Japanese and Dutch claim their own culture to be consensus-oriented, but what is seen to represent consensual decision-making and whether or not "the other" can make a rightful claim to this cultural characteristic is being contested (for more detail about actual practices of decision-making in Japanese–Dutch collaboration, see Noorderhaven *et al.* 2007). Dutch employees working under a Japanese regime in the Netherlands depict Japanese decision-making as highly inefficient and inflexible, and not aimed at reaching consensus at all. Japanese management counters Dutch criticism by asserting that the Dutch are short-term focused and not well prepared and shy away from problems. Within Dutch firms in Japan, neither the Dutch nor the Japanese see differences in decision-making styles as a major obstacle in their intercultural cooperation (contrary to the negativism and agitation observed at Rajio and, to a lesser degree, within other Dutch subsidiaries of Japanese firms). Yet, mutual depictions of decision-making practices also reveal underlying discontentment. Like their compatriots in the Netherlands, the Dutch in Japan who hold middle or lower hierarchical positions within the organization complain about the obscurity of Japanese informal decision-making that, they claim, is not consensus-based or harmony heeding.

Japanese subordinates, on the other hand, criticize the Dutch decision-making style, claiming decisions are being made "top-down." Clearly, this view runs counter to the Dutch self-image of egalitarianism being typical of Dutch culture. Culture, as a discursive construct in organizational members' ongoing identity talk, is actively and creatively being created and contested in ways that are intimately connected to the specific power constellation in which organizational actors are positioned.

Cultivating differences and power inequalities

The research presented in this chapter shows how parent country and host country nationals in Dutch–Japanese multinational corporations cultivate cultural differences. They actively draw on "culture" to discursively erect symbolic boundaries between "self" and "other," promoting or challenging power and status inequalities. They do so by creatively reproducing cultural differences in their identity talk, modifying or manipulating the meanings of not unfamiliar characterizations of Dutch and Japanese culture. The Japanese are keen to underline Japanese virtues, such as loyalty and devotion, perseverance and a long-term orientation, respect and tactfulness. Despite occasional praise, they also like to point to the imprudence and impoliteness of the Dutch, or to their poor working attitude, which they see as proof of their ineptitude. Not only do they derive social status from these favorable comparisons; they also use these images to justify the fact that Japanese hold all important positions (which they see as a reward for being dedicated or working hard) or, in the case of Japanese working under a Dutch regime, to explain why they should play a pivotal role in client relations or should be consulted in decision-making processes. To prevent the Dutch from undermining their position within the firm they keep a distance while engaging in identity talk that commends their own culture and denigrates the "other." The Dutch on their part also like to make self-praising comparisons, emphasizing their cultural distinctiveness vis-à-vis the Japanese by portraying themselves as efficient workers, clear communicators, or flexible decision-makers. Although the Dutch (Dutch managers in Japan in particular) admit to admiring certain cultural traits of the Japanese, such as their politeness, the major issues they bring up are, for instance, Japanese inefficiency in decision-making and filtering of information, and, from their viewpoint as subordinates in a Japanese firm, an overly hierarchic attitude and lack of interest.

Analyzing small but significant differences between management and staff members of the same nationality helps to illustrate the constructed, context-specific and legitimizing nature of cultural identity talk in more detail. Dutch staff working under Japanese rule claim to find their efforts to build closer contacts with the Japanese unreciprocated, which fosters feelings of relative deprivation and resentment about "unfair" treatment and an inclination to resist rather than reciprocate Japanese efforts. From this position, they like to portray egalitarianism and a consensus orientation as "typically Dutch" while describing top-down, inefficient and inflexible decision-making and a sub-missive attitude towards superiors as typical of Japanese culture. Ironically, however, Dutch top managers "ruling over" Japanese do not mention Dutch egalitarianism, nor do they criticize Japanese submissiveness. In a similar vein, Japanese managers acknowledge that their culture is "hierarchic" in comparison to "Dutch egalitarianism," while Japanese subordinates instead criticize their Dutch managers' decision-making style for being "top-down." The Japanese subordinates' complaint echoes Dutch subordinates' claim that top-down decision-making is typical of *their* bosses' (Japanese) culture. So, in unequal relations, subordinates (whether Dutch or Japanese) mark cultural distance by claiming that the national culture of their superiors (whether Japanese or Dutch) is hierarchical or top-down-oriented. Apparently, the political context is crucially important for what people find culturally salient in a specific situation. By presenting particular cultural distinctions rather than others they attempt to legitimize or de-legitimize the existing distribution of power, status and resources.

To summarize the research contributions: the analysis shows the signifi-cance of "context" – the unequal power relation between national groups – and "strategic agency" – the use of cultural characteristics to discursively legitimate or oppose the power asymmetry – for the analysis of cross-cultural communication in multinational corporations. Apparently, culture is not only a code for, or a mode of, communication; it also serves as a discursive resource or an interpretive reservoir drawn on to articulate cultural iden-tities that serve to sustain or resist power and authority relations. Within the politicized context of a multinational cooperation, organizational actors may play up or play down, praise or dispraise, or even ignore or invent culture and cultural differences as part of organizational actors' political game-play-ing. As attempts to buttress or break down the social boundary, organiza-tional actors' cultural identity talk may thus become infused with power and contestation when a structural inequality in terms of power, income and advancement opportunities defines the relations between parent country and host country nationals (see also chapter of Maclean and Hollinshead in this volume).

Limitations and implications

To illustrate this chapter's challenge to studies of cross-cultural communication that insist on measuring and dimensionalizing culture, it is interesting to note that Hofstede's classifications of Japanese and Dutch culture in terms of, for instance, "masculine" versus "feminine" or "collectivist" versus "individualist" (Hofstede 1991), are taken up by participants in our research as issues that are relatively open to subjective construction and political contestation. Cultural characteristics like "consensus-orientation" or "hierarchy" are interpreted quite differently by Japanese and Dutch (see also Noorderhaven *et al.* 2007) and Dutch participants claim, for instance, that Japanese decision-making is not consensus-oriented at all. And, while variance on the "power distance" dimension between Japan and the Netherlands in Hofstede's research was rather small, this very issue constitutes one of the most salient resources for drawing cultural distinctions for both Dutch and Japanese research participants (both usually claiming their own culture is consensus-oriented or egalitarian while depicting the cultural other as hierarchic or top-down oriented). Working together within a context of unbalanced power relations turns "power distance" into a significant and disputed identity-defining cultural characteristic, which further testifies to the importance of a context-sensitive and power-informed perspective on cultural identities.

So, integrating findings from different intercultural contexts and comparing how organizational actors engage in "distinction drawing" discourse within these contexts offered us an interesting opportunity to explore the variety of ways in which cultural differences were constructed in identity talk. Yet, as always, this study is not without its limitations. The focus on the politics of identity making opened up challenging new ways of viewing intercultural relations, but inevitably blinded us to alternative interpretations of the same data at the same time, leaving underexplored more conventional readings (e.g. interpreting some of the cultural differences reported by Japanese and Dutch participants in terms of Hofstede's dimensional scores) and, perhaps, more critical readings of participants' culture talk (exploring in more detail, for instance, how participants' cultural identity talk serves specific political interests). And, naturally, the evidence from various Dutch and

Japanese subsidiaries is unlikely to be representative of all Dutch or Japanese subsidiaries, and in its presentation we could not always avoid stereotyping the identity talk of "the Dutch" and "the Japanese," which illustrates the need for context sensitivity in culture research. Furthermore, for reasons of argumentation we also simplified the power relations in terms of "Dutch dominance in Japan" versus "Japanese dominance in the Netherlands," as if the two social settings studied are a clear mirror image of each other, constituting a reverse division of hierarchic roles. The dynamics of power configurations are more complicated, fluctuating and constantly negotiated (see also chapter of Koveshnikov in this volume). As noted in the methodology section, one difference between the two settings is that centralized control is typical of Japanese MNCs while Dutch MNCs follow more localized management strategies, employing a considerably smaller number of expatriates than Japanese MNCs in the Netherlands. Possibly as a result of that, relations between Dutch and Japanese in Japanese firms in the Netherlands (and certainly at Rajio Europe) were more polarized and antagonistic than in Dutch firms in Japan. Future culture research should thus incorporate a focus on managerial strategies in its exploration of power issues in multinational corporations.

Since this is an exploratory study, more research is clearly in order. As a means of appreciating more fully the role of situated action in constructing cultural identities in transnational organizations, there is a need to complement the kind of research presented in this chapter with studies of cross-cultural relations within other social contexts. More specifically, there is a need for research that explores the use and impact of culture in both unbalanced and balanced power relations. Questions that arise directly from this research are, for example, whether similar or dissimilar processes can be found in a situation where the distribution of power and resources among the Japanese and the Dutch constitutes a more equal relationship, such as in mergers or joint ventures. If the experience of cultural differences is indeed situationally bound, it seems relevant to find out the conditions under which particular cultural characteristics become emotionally charged and politically laden in intercultural collaboration. Such context-sensitive analyses should make cross-cultural researchers more susceptible to the subtleties of intergroup dynamics, taking the role of power and politics more seriously. Rather than pressing a template on cross-cultural communications of, for instance, an imperialist west marginalizing and othering the Orient/Orientals, we suggest focusing research attention on representational strategies of abstracting and reifying "the other" and promoting one's own identity as deployed by both dominant and marginal groups. A discursive approach to cultural identity, with its focus on the negotiated and political dimensions of intercultural relations, can be a valuable aid for analyzing the interconnections between power and culture within multinational corporations.

REFERENCES

Ailon, G. 2008. "Mirror, mirror on the wall: 'culture's consequences' in a value test of its own design," *Academy of Management Review* 33: 885–904

Ailon-Souday, G. and G. Kunda 2003. "The local selves of global workers: the social construction of national identity in the face of organizational globalization," *Organization Studies* 24: 1073–1196

Ainsworth, S. and C. Hardy 2004. "Discourse and identities" in Grant, Hardy, Oswick and Putnam (eds.) *Handbook of Organizational Discourse*. London: Sage, pp. 153–73

Alvesson, M. 1996. *Communication, Power and Organization*. Berlin: Walter de Gruyter

Barth, F. 1969. *Ethnic Groups and Boundaries: The Social Organization of Cultural Difference*. London: Allen and Unwin

Bartlett, C. A. and S. Ghoshal 2002. *Managing Across Borders: The Transnational Solution*. Boston, MA: Harvard Business School Press

Bate, S. P. 1997. "Whatever happened to organizational anthropology? A review of the field of organizational ethnography and anthropological studies," *Human Relations* 50: 1147–71

Befu, H. 1986. "An ethnography of dinner entertainment in Japan" in Lebra, Lebra (eds.) *Japanese Culture and Behavior: Selected Readings*. Honolulu: University of Hawaii Press, pp. 158–70

Berger, P. and T. Luckmann 1991. *The Social Construction of Reality: A Treatise in the Sociology of Knowledge*. New York: Penguin Books

Bhabha, H. K. 1989. *Nation and Narration*. London: Routledge

Brannen, M. Y. and J. E. Salk 2000. "Partnering across borders: negotiating organizational culture in a German-Japanese joint venture," *Human Relations* 53: 451–87

Brown, A. D. 2006. "A narrative approach to collective identities," *Journal of Management Studies* 43: 731–53

Byun, H. and S. Ybema 2005. "Japanese business in the Dutch polder: the experience of cultural differences in asymmetric power relations," *Asia Pacific Business Review* 11: 535–52

Clegg, S. T. and T. Kono 2002. "Trends in Japanese management: an overview of embedded continuities and disembedded discontinuities," *Asia Pacific Journal of Management* 19: 269–85

Cohen, A. P. 1985. *The Symbolic Construction of Community*. London: Ellis Harwood/Tavistock

Dahler-Larsen, P. 1997. "Organizational identity as a crowded category: a case of multiple and quickly shifting 'we' typifications" in Sackmann (ed.) *Cultural Complexity in Organizations: Inherent Contrasts and Contradictions*. London: Sage, pp. 367–89

Dörrenbächer, C. and M. Geppert 2006. "Micro-politics and conflicts in multinational corporations: current debates, re-framing, and contributions of this Special Issue," *Journal of International Management* 12: 251–65

Elias, N. and J. L. Scotson 1965. *The Established and the Outsiders: A Sociological Inquiry into Community Problems.* London: Frank Cass

Eriksen, T. H. 1993. *Ethnicity & Nationalism: Anthropological Perspectives.* London: Pluto

Fung, R. J. 1995. *Organizational Strategies for Cross-Cultural Cooperation.* Delft: Eburon

Geertz, C. 1973. *The Interpretation of Cultures.* New York: Basic Books

Giddens, A. 1979. *Central Problems in Social Theory.* London: Macmillan

Gong, Y. 2003. "Subsidiary staffing in multinational enterprises: agency, resources, and performance," *Academy of Management Journal* 46: 728–39

Hall, S. 1997. *Representation: Cultural Representations and Signifying Practices.* London: Sage/ Open University

Hardy, C. and S. R. Clegg 1996. "Some dare call it power" in Clegg, Hardy and Nord (eds.) *Handbook for Organization Studies.* London: Sage, pp. 622–41

Hofstede, G. 1991. *Culture's Consequences: International Differences in Work-related Values.* Newbury Park: Sage

Hong, J. F. L. and R. S. Snell 2008. "Power inequality in cross-cultural learning: the case of Japanese transplants in China," *Asia Pacific Business Review* 14: 253–73

House, R. J., P. J. Hanges, M. Javidan, P. W. Dorfman and V. Gupta 2004. *Culture, Leadership and Organizations: The GLOBE Study of 62 Societies.* Thousand Oaks, CA: Sage

Jack, G. A., M. B. Calás, S. M. Nkomo and T. Peltonen 2008. "Critique and international management: an uneasy relationship?," *Academy of Management Review* 33: 870–84

Jenkins, R. 2004. *Social Identity.* 2nd edn. London/New York: Routledge

Keenoy, T., C. Oswick and D. Grant 1997. "Organizational discourses: text and context," *Organization* 4: 147–57

Koot, W. C. J. 1997. "Strategic utilization of ethnicity in contemporary organizations" in Sackmann (ed.) *Cultural Complexity: Inherent Contrasts and Contradictions.* London: Sage, pp. 315–39

Moeran, H. 1986. "Individual, group and seishin: Japan's internal cultural debate" in Lebra and Lebra (eds.) *Japanese Culture and Behavior: Selected Readings.* Honolulu: University of Hawaii Press, pp. 62–79

Noorderhaven, N., J. Benders, and A. Keizer 2007. "Comprehensiveness versus pragmatism: consensus at the Dutch-Japanese interface," *Journal of Management Studies* 44: 1349–70

Olie, R. 1994. "Shades of culture and institutions in international mergers," *Organization Studies* 15: 381–406

Prasad, A. 2003. *Postcolonial Theory and Organizational Analysis: A Critical Engagement.* New York: Palgrave Macmillan

Primecz, H., L. Romani, S. A. Sackmann and K. Topcu 2009. "Introduction to Special Issue: multiple views for enhanced understandings in cross-cultural management," *International Journal of Cross-Cultural Management* 9: 267–74

Sackmann, S. A. 1991. *Cultural Knowledge in Organizations: Exploring the Collective Mind.* London: Sage

Schneider, S. C. and J. L. Barsoux 1997. *Managing Across Cultures.* London: Prentice-Hall

Schwartz-Shea, P. and D. Yanow 2009. "Reading and writing as method: in search of trustworthy texts" in Ybema, Yanow, Wels and Kamsteeg (eds.), pp. 56–82

Snow, D. A. and L. Anderson 1987. "Identity work among the homeless: the verbal construction and avowal of personal identities," *American Journal of Sociology* 92: 1336–71

Søderberg, A.-M. and N. Holden 2002. "Rethinking cross cultural management in a globalizing business world," *International Journal of Cross Cultural Management* 2: 103–21

Vossestein, J. 1997. *Dealing with the Dutch*, Amsterdam: Royal Tropical Institute

Van Marrewijk, A. 2004. "The management of strategic alliances: cultural resistance. Comparing the cases of a Dutch telecom operator in the Netherlands Antilles and Indonesia," *Culture and Organization* 10: 303–14

Watanabe, S. and R. Yamaguchi 1995. "Intercultural perceptions at the workplace: the case of the British subsidiaries of Japanese firms," *Human Relations* 48: 581–607

Watson, T. 2009. "Narrative, life story and manager identity: a case study in autobiographical identity work," *Human Relations* 62: 425–52

Westwood, R. 2006. "International business and management studies as an orientalist discourse: a postcolonial critique," *Critical Perspectives on International Business* 2: 91–113

Whitley, R., G. Morgan, W. Kelly and D. Sharpe 2003. "The changing Japanese multinational: application, adaptation and learning in car manufacturing and financial services," *Journal of Management Studies* 40: 643–72

Wong, H. W. 1999. *Japanese Bosses, Chinese Workers: Power and Control in a Hong Kong Megastore*. Honolulu: University of Hawaii Press

Ybema, S., T. Keenoy, C. Oswick, A. Beverungen, N. Ellis and I. Sabelis 2009a. "Articulating identities," *Human Relations* 62: 299–322

Ybema, S., D. Yanow, H. Wels and F. Kamsteeg 2009b. "Studying everyday organizational life" in Ybema, Yanow, Wels and Kamsteeg (eds.) *Organizational Ethnography: Studying the Complexities of Everyday Life*. London: Sage, pp. 1–20

11 National identities in times of organizational globalization: a case study of Russian managers in two Finnish–Russian organizations

Alexei Koveshnikov

Introduction

While there is quite an extensive literature addressing the issue of individual and organizational identity construction (Alvesson 1994; Phillips and Hardy 1997; Sveningsson and Alvesson 2003; Thomas and Linstead 2002), we still know relatively little about the process of how organizational actors construct their national identities in the MNC context. The dominant view presents national identity as the collective programming of people's minds (Hofstede 1980, 1991). Lacking an agreement as to how to define "culture" (Roberts and Boyacigiller 1984), this view tends to categorize the behavioral patterns of individuals based on a limited set of continuums, e.g. collectivism–individualism, high context–low context, masculinity–femininity, etc. Such conceptualizations represent very static (Tayeb 1994), minimal (McSweeney 2002) and essentialist (Ailon-Souday and Kunda 2003; Barinaga 2007) views on national identity that try to fit it into the predetermined categorizations and fail to take into account the subjectivity and agency of organizational actors in choosing and defining "who they are" (see also chapter of Blazejewski and Becker-Ritterspach in this volume).

This chapter posits that nationalism and national identity provide an important set of discourses that are used to make sense of, to legitimize and to normalize various important issues in MNCs. The national identity construction process is far from being an objective and rational one and national identity per se cannot be viewed as static, given or taken-for-granted (Ailon-Souday and Kunda 2003; Barinaga 2007). Rather it is informed by the motivation of organizational actors in different parts of an MNC to define the "self" identity in a more beneficial manner vis-à-vis the "other." This motivation is often interlinked with conflicts of interest in the organization, such as struggles for scarce resources, career advancements, or strategy formulation and agenda-setting participation. The construction of national identities (re)creates a certain net of power relations among organizational actors, which inevitably are more beneficial for some than for other actors (see also chapter of Williams and Geppert in this volume). The possible power effects may be related to the constructed superior–inferior, ethnocentric–polycentric, global–local, developed–undeveloped and other relationships between different organizational actors. Hence, the process of national identity construction cannot be detached from the socio-political setting in which it takes place.

To illustrate it empirically, I examine the process of national identity construction among Russian managers in two Finnish–Russian MNCs. Recently, a relatively large stream of literature has been published which claims that there is a new generation of managers coming to the fore in Russia, which through the processes of socialization into the western "managerial community of practice" embraces western managerial values (Alexashin and Blenkinsopp 2005; Elenkov 1997, 1998; Puffer and McCarthy 1995). Nevertheless, not much has been written to try to explicate the various subtleties and complications of this process. Bearing that in mind, the questions that this chapter tries to shed some light on can be formulated as follows:

(1) What are the consequences and the impact of globalization on self-perception and self-identification of local managers in their locality?
(2) What kind of discourses does the national identity work entail?
(3) What implications does the process of national identity construction have for power and politics in MNCs?

In their illustrative account of national identity construction in an Israeli–American merger, Ailon-Souday and Kunda (2003) stress the need for similar studies but of "other times and places." They argue for the need to study the meanings attributed to national identity in later and more advanced stages of organizational change than they have done. Hence, in this chapter I study the identity construction process among Russian managers in two Finnish–Russian organizations: the first one is the result of an acquisition that took place in 1997 when one Finland-based MNC acquired a prior existing organization in Russia, and the second one is an organization that was established as a greenfield operation in Russia by another Finland-based MNC in 2005.

The analysis is based on the data that was collected from these two Russian organizations which have been subjected to the globalization forces after they have become parts of Finland-based MNCs. The setting of Finnish–Russian organizations is particularly interesting for studying the national identity construction process because it comprises characteristics that can easily be extended into many other contexts that are of great interest to business scholars. Some of these characteristics are: (a) Russia is one of the world's economies in transition with strong societal and organizational inheritance of its communist past, traces of which can still be found in relations between organizational actors within organizations (Holt *et al.* 1994; McCarthy *et al.* 2005; Puffer *et al.* 1997); (b) nationalistic ideas have been prospering in Russia since the 1990s as a base for people's identity construction, which has caused waves of xenophobia and an overall negative attitude towards foreigners, especially in the business sphere (Ayios 2004; Kets de Vries 2001); and (c) relations between Russia and the western countries can be viewed through a postcolonial lens, as western countries and thus western managers are perceived by many as a primary source of knowledge that can foster development in Russia. Together these factors create a social complexity that influences how Russian managers construct their national identities and perceive themselves in relation to the "other" in the context of Finnish–Russian MNCs.

The rest of the chapter is structured as follows. The next section outlines the discursive perspective on national identity and nationalism. Then, the description of the study context is provided, followed by the methodology that was utilized to analyze the data. Finally, the empirical evidence is presented and some conclusions are drawn in the end.

On national identity, organizational power and the discourse of nationalism

There are various ways to conceptualize nationalism (see e.g. Anderson 1983; Billig 1995; Hobsbawm 1990; Wodak *et al.* 1999). For instance, it can be viewed as an ideology or a social movement. For the purposes of this chapter, I use a conceptualization of nationalism as a discourse constructed on the basis of shared understanding of history and continuity. Following Billig's (1995) idea of "banal nationalism," I view "nation" as a construct, which is often accepted and reproduced mindlessly, and uncritically rendered possible by mundane habits of language, thought and symbolism in everyday life creating a sense of national solidarity in the citizenry. In his influential book *Banal Nationalism*, Michael Billig (1995) discusses examples of banal nationalism, such as the use of flags in everyday context, sporting events, national songs, symbols on bank notes, popular expressions and others.

Having stated that I see nationalism as a discourse, now I turn to discussing what I mean by discourse in general and identity work in the discursive context in particular. By discourse I refer to a more or less integrated, pre-fabricated line of using language and reasoning in which the phenomenon is constructed rather than revealed or mirrored (Fairclough 1995; Knights and Willmott 1989; Sveningsson and Alvesson 2003). Furthermore, one cannot understand specific discourses without considering the social context within which they operate (Laine and Vaara 2007; Thomas 2003). Ways of talking, or ideological discourses, do not develop in social vacuums, but are related to forms of life. Therefore it follows that identity can be understood not only as language and ideological discourses, but also as social practices, which constitute what could be called "national identities."

Following a poststructuralist view, I posit that in the turbulent and multi-faceted world of today, identities, including national identities, are in a constant flux. Stuart Hall (2000: 17), one of the leading theoreticians of the notion of "identity," has put it as follows:

> Identities are *never unified* and, in late modern times, increasingly *fragmented* and *fractured*; never singular but *multiply constructed* across different, often intersecting and antagonistic, discourse, practices and positions. They are subject to a *radical historicization*, and are constantly in the process of *change* and *transformation* … Though they seem to invoke an origin in a historical past with which they continue to correspond, actually identities are about questions of using the resources of history, language and culture in the process of becoming rather than being: not *"who we are"* or *"where we came from,"* so much as *what we might become, how we have been represented* and how that bears on *how we might represent ourselves* … [emphasis added]

Hence, identities arise from the narrativization or self-categorization (using humor and other types of storytelling) of the self, i.e. they are discursive constructs and are tied to discourse offering a short-hand description for ways of talking about the self and community (Shotter and Gergen 1989). Social identity theorists (Tajfel 1978; Turner 1985, 1999) claim that individuals in social groups construct their social reality though dividing the world into "us" and "them," giving way to various processes of inclusion and exclusion. Interestingly, this entails the recognition that it is only through the relation to the "other," the relation to what it is not, to precisely what it lacks, to what has been called its constitutive outside, that the "positive" meaning of any term – and thus its "identity" – can be constructed (Derrida 1981; Laclau 1990). Identities can function as points of identification and attachment only because of their capacity to exclude, to leave out, and to render "outside" (for instance, dichotomies of man and woman, manager and worker). Laclau (1990) argues that "the constitution of a social identity is an act of power" rooted in processes of subjugation and resistance within the organization that are contingent and perpetually shifting.

Hence, the process of national identity construction is closely linked to power. I view power as a "relational effect" emerging from the political constitution of the organization rather than a property of certain structures or individuals. More specifically, from a discursive view power is constituted and reproduced through the structures of organizational communication and interaction between organizational actors at different levels of the organization and is conditioned by actors' political interests, agency and subject positions. Power manifests itself both as hierarchy, i.e. as differences among organizational actors' access to specific meanings, and as establishment and maintenance of organization-specific values, symbols and practices. Which practices, norms and values are considered relevant and legitimate to be maintained and reproduced is likely to relate directly to the groups "in power," to their interests and to their influence on organizational attention-setting practices (Iedema and Wodak 1999).

To sum up, in this chapter I build on a poststructuralist view of national identity as an alternative to a widely used essentialist conceptualization of national identity that has previously dominated the literature. In these studies researchers tried to capture the notion of national identity as statically located along the limited set of continuums used to categorize "culture," i.e. collectivism–individualism, high context–low context, high power distance–low power distance, etc. (Hofstede 1980, 1991). The notion of national identity has been treated as "the passive embodiment of a predetermined cultural template" (Ailon-Souday and Kunda 2003: 1074). In turn, this chapter argues that such conceptualization fails to take into account the agency of organizational actors in (re)constructing and making sense of their national identities (Newton 1998). Meanwhile, in the MNC context, national identity might potentially represent a powerful discursive resource available to organizational members, so the agency of organizational actors needs to be considered seriously. Hence, I view national identity as a discourse that can be mobilized and used in specific contexts of an MNC as a strategic resource in a struggle for power (Hardy *et al.* 2000; Hardy and Phillips 1999; Phillips and Hardy 1997).

National identity in Russian organizations

If Russians *hope* to be able to operate successfully in a *global* economy, as their societal transformations suggest that they do, they *must* identify and adopt forms of management and organization *appropriate* to that goal. (Kets de Vries 2001: 586)

> [W]e cannot … merely *teach* (or *preach*) a doctrine of free enterprise development [to Russians]. That would not have greater impact than *trying to explain a sunrise to a blind person.* (Holt *et al.* 1994: 136) [emphasis added]

A lot of literature has been published recently discussing the processes of transformation at both political and societal levels in Russia since the collapse of the Soviet Union. In particular, some studies have focused on changes that took place in managerial practices and mental frameworks of Russian managers in the newly forming capitalist settings. For instance, several studies have stressed the gradual change in managerial behavior in Russia towards western ways of behaving (Alexashin and Blenkinsopp 2005; Elenkov 1997, 1998; Puffer and McCarthy 1995). It was suggested by researchers that being and being viewed as "westernized" has become equivalent to being perceived as professional and knowledgeable among Russian managers (Puffer *et al.* 1997). The "west" in general became seen as the source of knowledge and competence that Russian managers needed to acquire in order to be able to cope with globalization and its consequences and gain legitimate access into the "western managerial community of practice" (Clark and Geppert 2006).

However, to my best knowledge there are no studies that have focused on how Russian managers view themselves and construct their national identities while coping with these globalization forces and trying to make sense of their organizational reality in the Russian setting. We seem to know little about the discursive resources that they draw on to narrate/categorize themselves within the boundaries of "local" versus "global," "us" versus "them," or "HQ" versus "subsidiary" rhetoric. The setting of Russian companies is very interesting, too, in light of a recent debate in the neo-institutional literature concerning the process of institution building in ventures between western MNCs and so called post-socialist organizations (Child and Czegledy 1996; Clark and Geppert 2006; Clark and Soulsby 1999). This literature stream posits that international MNC operations may be more typically characterized by degrees of conflict and disagreement between western knowledge (and its carriers) and local practices (and their practitioners). It is argued that relations between western and local agents can be characterized as "asymmetrical relationships" (Clark and Geppert 2006: 341), in which the balance of power is structurally weighted in favor of the western HQs. The relational asymmetry between western and post-socialist organizations stems from inequalities, which are intrinsic to the initial contract or bargain, e.g. the weak initial capital and technological position of local organizations, imbalance of senior management, and the rights of the partners in strategic control and decision-making (Inkpen and Beamish 1997).

Clark and Geppert (2006) claim that these inequalities become reproduced in asymmetries in management discourse and reputation. In the global management sphere, post-socialist managers have weak claims to legitimacy and one of their aims in international collaboration is to seek the legitimacy of full membership of the "western managerial community of practice." While they remain "peripheral participants," they have a strong incentive to "learn" enough to become accepted as peers. Using the metaphor of Holt *et al.* (1994) quoted at the beginning of this section, Russian managers do want to cease being blind and to be able finally to see the sunrise. This requires gaining knowledge about how to speak "modern management," a problem not faced by their western colleagues.

It is assumed that managers in the former Soviet bloc need to acquire the same set of competencies as managers from the west that would permit them to operate within the market system (Kets de Vries 2001; *The Economist* 1994). As the argument goes, general western management practices and norms should be preferred to specific eastern European ones because the former ones are of greater value since they have been systematized and are already widely applied. Also, from the postcolonial perspective, western management practices are often regarded as a universal norm representing the essence of effectiveness and efficiency, and non-western management is usually judged against this norm (Banerjee and Linstead 2001; Frenkel 2008; Prasad 2003). Building on ideas of pioneering postcolonial theoreticians, like Edward Said (1978), Ashis Nandy (1983) and others, a postcolonial perspective posits that in international settings most of western-driven analyses around national characteristics and differences involve problematic assumptions concerning normality, morality, legitimacy, progress, development, etc. These assumptions are often based on "a system of hierarchical binary oppositions such as active/passive, center/periphery, civilized/savage, developed/undeveloped, masculine/feminine, modern/archaic, scientific/superstitious, and so on" (Prasad 2003: 12) where the west represents the former part of every dichotomous relationship and the non-west the latter.

However, in their critique of such views, Child and Czegledy already in 1996, in a special issue of *Organization Studies* dedicated to "Managerial Learning in the Transformation of Eastern Europe," argued that some skills which western organizations have in recent years come to recognize as crucial for purposes of conducting international business successfully are actually the ones in which eastern European managers are already better versed than their western colleagues. They provide two examples: (1) capability to develop personal business networks, and (2) familiarity with the specific cultural and institutional environment of their own country. As a conclusion, Child and Czegledy (1996: 174) suggest that "Eastern European managers should unlearn less than might be assumed either by western advisors or the members of foreign companies which have located in Eastern Europe."

Western managers and economists often regard the transformation of eastern Europe as a modernist project of a worldwide post-communist convergence onto a liberal and democratic system based on the open market system. At the same time, on the personal level, it creates certain tensions when what westerners perceive as a "learning" opportunity for eastern managers may be interpreted by easterners as unwelcome intrusion. Hence, it is very interesting how Russian managers see themselves in the globalizing environment in which they hold roles defined within the power structures of their organizations, which are foreign-owned, as well as other roles framed for them as members of their national and local communities.

Research context: the Russian–Finnish relations

The case of Finnish–Russian companies examined here is an interesting setting in which to study the process of national identification due to the historical and cultural background that undoubtedly has an impact on which discourses organizational actors draw on and how the power dynamics are played out within the relationship. There is a long history that at different points in time has connected Russia and Finland. Finland was part of the Kingdom of Sweden for about 800 years and adopted its judicial and governmental systems and its political structure from Sweden. Then, in 1809, Sweden lost Finland to Russia, and Finland for more than 100 years became a Great Duchy of the Russian Empire. During that time there were several attempts to "russify" (i.e. to force the adoption of the Russian language) the new territory. After the Russian October Revolution in 1917 Finland declared its independence.

In 1939–40 Finland and Russia were involved in the so called Winter War, which was declared as one of the parts of World War II. Both sides endured heavy losses and the war ended with large parts of eastern Finland being annexed to the Soviet Union, though Finland preserved its independence. Also, the Soviet Union demanded extensive war reparations from Finland. Even today, there is a movement in Finland defending the right of ceded eastern regions (i.e. Karelia) to return to Finland.

In 1948 Finland committed itself to a Treaty of Cooperation, Friendship and Mutual Assistance with the Soviet Union and this became the basis for political and economic relations between the two countries for years to come. This treaty has made Finland appear as a Soviet satellite in the eyes of many western and US observers. However, Finland has deliberately tried to limit the influence of the Soviet Union to economic issues only, resisting any attempts to impose ideological demands.

The strong dependency of the Finnish economy on its trade relations with the Soviet Union caused the deepest recession in the history of Finland when the Soviet Union broke up in 1991. The recession lasted until the mid 1990s and served as the main incentive for investing in new technologies and for the subsequent ascendance of the electronics and telecommunications industry into one of the main foreign trades.

The joint history between the two countries is also reflected in the everyday language that Finns and Russians use. For instance, there are nicknames that both Russians and Finns have adopted for naming each other. Finns use "ryssä" which is often somewhat pejoratively applied to all Russian-speaking people in Finland, including people from the Commonwealth of Independent States (CIS) countries and children from mixed Finnish–Russian marriages. Similarly, Russians use "tsuhna" to name Finns. It has also acquired some pejorative connotations lately. Also, Russians often talk ironically about Finns as being "hot Finnish guys" alluding to the quietness and emotional reservation of Finns.

Research design and methodology

This chapter focuses on managerial identity work and studies the interface between, on the one hand, the organizational/globalization issues and processes and role expectations, and on the other hand, more individual efforts to navigate between and reconcile the discourses within the frameworks of power relations. Special emphasis is given to the discourses that organizational actors use to construct their national identities in the MNC context.

To do that, I studied the social construction of national identity by Russian managers in the setting of two Finnish–Russian organizations. One – RusFood – was acquired by the Finland-based MNC FinFood in 1997 in the food industry, and the other – RusTyres – was established in 2005 as a greenfield operation of another Finland-based MNC, FinTyres, in Russia in the manufacturing industry. In this study I draw on extensive data that was collected from a longitudinal study within an international two-year project on competence management across borders. The data was collected during the period of March 2006–November 2007 using various techniques. First, a total of 37 semi-structured interviews were conducted with managers in both Russian organizations (21 interviews at RusFood and 16 interviews at RusTyres) in order to acquire an appreciation of globalization as an everyday, lived experience and of the ways in which managers socially and culturally managed and reacted to it. The interviews lasted between 45 and 100 minutes and were recorded and transcribed verbatim afterwards. As far as possible, during interviews I followed a "story-telling" approach, that is interviewees were encouraged to tell their own experiences with minimum interference on the part of the interviewers (Czarniawska 2004). Most of the interviews were conducted in Russian, i.e. in the respondent's preferred language. The following topics were discussed: how the respondent perceives the company's organizational competence globally; how the respondent perceives the relations between the HQ and the subsidiary; what role does the language play in these relations; and what are the cultural stereotypes and differences that exist between organizational members and what is their impact on everyday activities.

Second, the author and his colleagues have participated in several managerial meetings within both companies and have taken part in discussions concerning the companies' operations in Russia and the numerous challenges involved. These meetings have provided a good understanding of the process of developing a shared corporate identity and challenges related to it in both companies. Both companies have relatively recently started their internationalization activities and hence the corporate management has been facing the challenge of transforming the mentality of the firm from "being a local player" into "becoming a global company." Finally, I had access to ample secondary sources of information such as company presentations, internal reports, learning diaries, etc. These sources were used to deepen my knowledge of both companies and improve my understanding of relevant issues within and without both organizations.

In the analysis I have focused on distinctive articulated ways of representing organizational reality, that is "discourses" in the organization. These "discourses" can be seen as both alternative and competing ways of socially constructing organizational reality around national identities. I assumed that the ways organizational actors talk about certain organizational events facilitates their own identity construction process. In other words, I have treated discourses as "the principal means by which organization members create a coherent social reality that frames their sense of who they are" (Mumby and Chair 1997: 181, cited in Thomas and Linstead 2002: 75). The identities that emerge through these processes are not value-neutral and have important implications for the organization, leading to particular outcomes and power implications. For instance, studies have shown that organizational actors use a wide range of discursive resources to promote certain views and ideas within organizations but not others (see e.g. Garcia and Hardy 2007; Hardy *et al.* 2000; Hardy and Phillips 1999; Hodge and Coronado 2006; Phillips and Hardy 1997).

The interview material has provided me with an extensive discursive database for examining various discourses around national identity construction. I applied what is called an "abductive" approach to the data analysis, meaning that the theoretical ideas were constantly refined as I was progressing through the data analysis (Van Maanen *et al.* 2007). In the beginning of the analysis, I synthesized the interview transcripts into individual case accounts. In these accounts, I focused on various general narratives in managerial discourses on national identity. I tried to focus on the manifest content of the data (see e.g. Suddaby and Greenwood 2005) by mapping these narratives, focusing on specific textual elements like repeating concepts, metaphors or the signifiers "us" and "them." In doing this, I extensively used participant observation (i.e. my field notes that I was actively taking during the interviews) and numerous secondary sources as recommended by e.g. Lincoln and Guba (1985). This has helped a lot in the task of placing specific narratives in their wider social and intertextual contexts. Then, I tried to extract the discursive struggles over national identities that I was able to identify in the data, thus focusing on the latent content of the data (e.g. Suddaby and Greenwood 2005). The identified narratives/themes were used to generate hypothetical interpretive frames concerning the meaning of national identity. Finally, these interpretive frames were validated, refuted or changed through continuous reading and rereading of the data in search of examples, counterexamples, supporting and refuting evidence. I also have attempted to validate my tentative interpretations by feeding back to the interviewees the findings as I made progress with the analysis in the form of the company reports. In these I have listed the main findings and asked the interviewees to provide me with feedback on my interpretations. Such practice has allowed for the fine-tuning and the validating of my conclusions.

The construction of national identity in Finnish–Russian organizations: "who are we?" and "where do we come from?"

The analysis of the data has showed that national identity was employed by managers of both Russian organizations for two main purposes, which can be described as discursive struggles. The first struggle reflected the desire of Russian managers to position themselves as more "global," professional, superior and knowledgeable than their Finnish counterparts. In so doing, Russian managers tried to establish themselves as being better versed in the dominant western managerial approach than their Finnish counterparts. The main discursive resources that they drew on in this struggle were rooted in their professional experiences, knowledge and skills embedded in the current national and institutional environment of modern Russia.

The second struggle reflected the inherent need and desire of Russian managers to preserve their cultural distinctiveness of being Russians, which was portrayed as a valuable resource in the Russian organizational context. In so doing, Russian managers resisted Finnish management discourses infused with softer values of what can be termed the Nordic approach to capitalism, such as job security and egalitarianism. The main discursive resources that Russian managers utilized in this struggle were their cultural and national characteristics, together with closely related humorous stories and metaphors.

Of course, the author acknowledges the contested nature of these struggles and the difficulty or impossibility of being fully comprehended. Both struggles were not total or ubiquitous in any sense. Still, it is argued that they provide a good basis for discussing the national identity construction process and the discourses that it draws on as strategic resources in the struggle for power in the organizational context (see also chapter of Ybema and Byun in this volume). The following two sections describe these struggles in more detail.

The struggle for global status: "we are more global"

The first type of struggle that I was able to identify in the data is related to the desire of a certain social group – in this case Russian managers who were interviewed for this study – to be established into the position of power in relation to the "other" – Finnish managers – within the organization. It was established by means of subjugation and exclusion of "others" from the category of who can be considered "global" in the global environment. This struggle also reflected the well-documented process of dividing between "us" and "them" that takes place in organizations undergoing various organizational changes, e.g. mergers and acquisitions (see, for instance, Larsson and Finkelstein 1999; Olie 1994). I found that national identity served as a symbolic resource that was invoked by Russian managers to differentiate them from their Finnish colleagues as being more "global".

From the outset, the Russian managers in both organizations felt the need to position themselves as equal partners to their Finnish colleagues. To do that they had to overcome certain stereotypes that existed in the minds of the Finnish managers, which depicted Russians as lagging behind and not well versed in the western managerial approach of doing business. These stereotypes were seen by the Finnish managers as an essential part of their Russian colleagues, as something which is given and cannot be changed but rather has to be dealt with. In turn, the Russian managers viewed the existence of these stereotypes among their Finnish counterparts as a sign of Finnish ethnocentrism and backwardness. These stereotypes were described as being obstacles for Finnish companies' development in Russia. One Russian manager has put it as follows:

I understand that FinFood is afraid of Russia because really even though FinFood is here for more than nine years, even in that case they do not know the Russian market, they do not know the Russian management style and that's why they are afraid.

For the Russian managers interviewed, the existence of these stereotypes served as a proof of Finnish "localness" and non-"globalness." In turn, the Russian managers depicted themselves as possessing a global mentality and hence as more globally oriented than their Finnish colleagues. Note the following extract from the interview with one of the managers:

INTERVIEWER: Is FinTyres MNC in its mentality?
RUSSIAN MANAGER: No. But RusTyres is an MNC in its mentality. FinTyres Corporation is multinational in theory but not in practice.
INTERVIEWER: What needs to be changed then?
RUSSIAN MANAGER: You answered yourself in your question – [the] mentality needs to be changed, habits need to be changed, localization should be avoided, they need to think not only about themselves ... but about the company.

Trying to position themselves as being more "global," the Russian managers have alluded to the general differences in terms of geography and size between Russia and Finland. Note these types of allusions in the following passage narrated by one Russian manager:

[G]enerally about Finns ... it is nothing personal, it is like an observation, what I think ... because I work with Finns since 1993 and that means that I generally like it ... but what is the obstacle for more dynamic and faster development? I think that it is a feeling [among Finns] that Finland is a small country, only 4.5 millions, [and] it is in the corner of Europe …

Another stereotype that, according to the Russian managers, Finns had about their Russian colleagues and that also impeded the successfulness of the Finnish companies' businesses in Russia was related to the Finns' views on the hierarchical nature of Russian organizations. The Russian managers claimed that such views emerged from a somewhat static view of Finns on modern Russia and their reluctance to acknowledge the changes that are taking place in Russia as the business environment becomes more and more international and competitive. Indeed, the hierarchical nature of Soviet organizations, that were the predominant kind of organization in Russia throughout the 1990s, is well documented in the literature (see, for instance, Bollinger 1994). To some extent this fact has become ingrained in the minds of the Finnish managers, supported by various consulting reports and the experiences of western managers in Russia in the 1990s.

It appeared that the existence and persistence of a hierarchical structure had negative connotations in interviews with both Finnish and Russian managers, being seen as a sign of lagging in development. Such views can be attributed to a postcolonial perspective. Within this perspective, "hierarchy" is seen as an antipode of what is considered to be nowadays a universal neo-liberal ideal of an organizational "open" structure – a flat matrix structure – which is perceived as representing progressive and developed aspects of modern western organizations. Hence, in the modern "developed" world, hierarchy is considered to be "non-developed" and an undesirable organizational structure. Along the same lines, Finnish managers often referred to the excessive hierarchical structure of Russian organizations, linking it both with the communist legacy of Russia and with the non-democratic leadership styles and paternalistic relations in Russian organizations, "inherited" from the Soviet times (Fey et al. 2001; Kets de Vries 2001). The Russian respondents have resisted such views by calling them stereotypical and claiming that in reality the Finnish organizations are more hierarchical than Russian ones, thus once again reproducing the "us" versus "them" opposition.

The Finnish stereotype is that here in Russia the structure is highly hierarchical, and everything is done only when the boss says okay, do it. This is not really true. Really not true …

I don't know why, but Finns consider our structures more hierarchical, but I wouldn't say it is so. This is more a clear division of responsibilities. So this is not hierarchy, this is just, I would say, clearer structure.

[O]f course, formally at FinFood it is very democratic but in reality it is only [a] formality. At RusFood ... of course it is not so democratic, only one or two managers can make decisions. But here we really discuss decisions before decisions are made. For example ... if I make some decision, I ask ... opinions [of my subordinates] and if it is some important decision then I ask all the people who can help me to make the best decision. And I am really interested in their opinion because of course nobody knows everything ... In FinFood everyone is responsible only for one service ... And they have different specialists, very good specialists, but if these people do not have [a] wide view, some systematic minds, in that case it is impossible to make good decisions.

The struggle of being recognized as more democratic and less hierarchical than the "other" potentially had very important implications for both organizations in terms of how power relations played out between the HQs and the subsidiaries. Acknowledging that both Russian organizations are less democratic might have implied that the Finnish HQs would be able to legitimately impose means of control on the Russian managers' activities. Such an attempt might be then justified by referring to the inability of the Russian managers to work effectively within a matrix system or to the excessive concentration of decisional power in hands of one person, which is seen as an inefficient way to function. On the other hand, actively rejecting such a view on Russian organizations might have allowed the Russian subsidiaries to acquire more legitimacy for autonomy in pursuing business opportunities in their environments and to resist practices and initiatives imposed on them from the HQ's side. Hence, the struggle around the notion of being democratic/non-democratic can theoretically be seen as a latent conflict aimed at producing a certain social order with differentiated power positions in it.

In drawing a borderline between "us" being more "global" than "them," the Russian respondents used not only the analogies but also involved a third element – a third party – which to some extent served as a measurement scale in a competition for the "global" status among managers. This third party was what the Russian managers labeled as "true global companies" referring to the US multinationals, for instance Coca-Cola. Having been employed by these companies, as many Russian managers have been, the Russian managers claimed to possess truly a global vision of how to run global businesses, which the Finnish managers lacked. For instance, when discussing the HR function that was implemented in one of the organizations in Russia, the Russian manager made the following statements:

The performance appraisal system that we have here ... has not been really transferred [from Finland]. It has been transferred and adopted from the leading multinational companies operating in Russia and other countries.

> Our compensation system was adopted from the experience of multinational companies.
>
> Having that kind of school [a leading US multinational] in my background … helped us to organize [an HR function in the Russian unit] on another level, not as in FinTyres.
>
> We simply try to take the best that they have there [in Finland] and transfer it here [to Russia] and what we do not like, we leave in Finland.

Another characteristic that was drawn on in the struggle between the Finnish and the Russian managers for being more "global" was the ethnocentrism of Finns and their "anti-Russian-ness." For the Russian managers these views served as one more indication of a "local" and not "global" mindset among their Finnish colleagues. The Finnish managers were blamed for holding very simplistic and somewhat narrow-minded views about Russians that only exemplified their "local" mentality and mindsets. Also, willingness and the ability to learn were portrayed as signs of global orientation ("to pick the best from everywhere") and the Finnish managers were depicted as not willing to learn. Finns in general were portrayed as not very knowledgeable about Russia in the first place. Again, by narrating such stories the Russian managers were trying to position themselves as more "global." At the same time, for instance in RusTyres, these kinds of narratives were also used by Russian managers as rhetorical tools to renegotiate the allocation of responsibility between the HQs and the Russian subsidiary. By referring to the situation as "trust crisis" and "imbalance between responsibility and authority given to local management," they were able to shift the balance of authority allocation more in their favor.

> Deeply in their [Finnish] souls there are anti-Russian feelings …
>
> I do not think that Finns do not want to learn from Russians, but I do not see a strong desire. To say more, I see a desire to show us how they work, and have us start working the same way in Russia.
>
> Finns, surprisingly enough, don't know really anything about Russians. I think that is the problem. And those who don't know, they can develop whatever views …
>
> Finns have a certain perception of what a Russian person is – a Russian is either belonging to the mafia or being very, very rich and arrogant. It's not really true of course.

Interrelated with the previous point, there was some evidence that indeed the struggle for "global" status was occurring on both sides. The Russian respondents have justified the need for positioning themselves as more "global" and thus different from the Finns in order to counter the tendency among

Finnish managers to downgrade the competence of their Russian counterparts. That's how one of the Russian respondents symbolically expressed his frustration concerning this matter:

Actually, in the beginning when people do not trust other people, sometimes there is a feeling that Finns perceive you as an idiot, some kind of a bear with *balalaika*, who does not understand anything. So when you say something, Finns reply: "How can you say so, don't you know anything?" Although later you understand that these people just do not understand the rules of the game in Russia.

The competition for "global" status in both organizations also involved references to the historical relationship between Russia and Finland. Some respondents referred to the period of the Winter War and the region of Karelia, which was annexed to the Soviet Union in the aftermath of the war, when discussing the relations between Finns and Russians and the differences between them in the organizational setting. Consider the following extract from one of the interviews:

RUSSIAN MANAGER: In my view, cultural differences do exist. These differences could be not so vivid, but considering events of the Winter War, Karelia and so on … I even bought a book about that …

INTERVIEWER: Book about what?

RUSSIAN MANAGER: About Karelia, whose territory was it, originally Slavic in 1326, there was no even smell of Finns there. Slavs were fighting with Swedes. First one side was conquering it, then the other. And in the end, Swedes brought there a small population of Finns, left them to live there so that these people could protect their own land … so it is possible to argue for a long time, but when a Finn cheers for Mannerheim [the commander-in-chief of the Finnish Army during the Winter War], Russians sitting at the table feel uncomfortable … Just happened recently …

The fact that the Russian environment is more challenging to operate in due to more dynamic social and economic conditions was seen as promoting courageousness and effectiveness among the Russian managers. Living in modern Russia, the Russian managers portrayed themselves as more equipped to face the challenges of the global business environment where efficient decision-making and adaptability to changes are crucial. Also, their ability to sacrifice their own personal interests in favor of organizational goals was seen as underlining their global orientation. On the contrary, the Finnish managers were depicted as badly equipped for global challenges because they were coming from "a warm place" and were prioritizing their own interests over organizational goals. Therefore, they were depicted as being unable to make "big" decisions that are seen as a must in a global business environment to succeed.

Finns never take serious decisions, because the punishment – and the worst punishment – is to lose the job in the company … because it is a warm place, in Finland particularly.

Being an employee in a Finnish firm I should be happy that I will not be fired and they will always find some place for me. But from the point of view of a man who has targets to fulfill, I am not happy, I do not need such stability … If I was picking my nose sitting here, I would still be getting money … It is not like that here – Russia now is a different country. Dynamics here is such that if you sit and pick your nose, you are less than nothing from the societal point of view and so on. It is only possible if you are a son or some cousin of Hodorkovsky or Abramovich, but a simple man has to move …

Generally working with Finnish companies, it is very, very difficult to encourage them to do big things, i.e. to take risks, extremely difficult …

To sum up, this struggle had crucial implications for strategizing and decision-making in both organizations. In fact, in RusFood it produced a concrete outcome leading to the situation when the Russian subsidiary was separated into a stand-alone business unit, granting Russian managers more decision-making responsibility and autonomy. By claiming that the Finnish managers are not easily adaptable to the current global situation worldwide and lack the desire to learn and comprehend new cultures and markets, the Russian managers hinted at the necessity to allocate more decisional power to them and, at least partially, achieved it. It illustrates the situation in which national differences are presented as structural impediments to successful development while the actual political considerations, e.g. gaining more decision-making power or more autonomy, are silenced. It highlights the political nature of the national identity construction process (see also Ailon-Souday and Kunda 2003) and underscores its importance as one of the contributing elements to organizational sensemaking and to strategy debates in organizations.

The struggle for distinct status: national identity is a valuable and distinctive resource

At the same time as the struggle for the recognition of being more "global" than the "other," there were instances of another struggle taking place in both organizations: the struggle to be established as a distinct collective from the counterparty, based on national separateness and distinctiveness. In line with the previous research, our data confirmed that the commitment to the national collective tends to intensify in the global setting (Vaara *et al.* 2003). The Russian respondents drew on discourses related to their national identity to indicate the borderline within the organizational boundaries between two distinct groups – the Russian and the Finnish managers. The Russian national identity was used as a powerful symbol that served as a "natural" and hence "objective" differentiator between two groups (e.g. being Russian and non-Finnish) and in doing so proved to be a potent counterforce to the converging force of the globalization processes.

The struggle was expressed in the attempts of our interviewees to explain various daily work situations in terms of cultural differences, clearly differentiating what can be labeled as "Finnish" or "Russian." Often, what was labeled as being "Russian" was described as a valuable and beneficial resource to possess in an organizational setting. Often Russian managers during interviews utilized humor to indirectly communicate their views about Finnish managers and Finnish culture in general, and to express detachment from their Finnish counterparts. In so doing, they resisted the Finnish management approach and its values from being internalized in the Russian subsidiaries. It concurs with the literature that suggests that humor is widely used by organizational actors as one of the coping strategies to express resistance and the intention to de-legitimize (Grugulis 2002; Hatch 1997; Hatch and Ehrlich 1993).

There are numerous anecdotal stories in Russia that depict Finns as being slow, calm and inexpressive. One can often hear how Russian people imitate the Nordic accent and slow tempo in their speech. Also, Finns are often grouped together with other nations from the Baltic countries, mainly Estonians, who used to be a part of the Soviet Union. It can also be viewed as a patronizing act in light of the fact that Finland itself used to be part of the Russian Empire from 1809 until 1917. In our data there were many examples when the Russian managers tried to employ humor when describing certain situations that they encountered while working with Finns. By so doing, they aimed at indirectly expressing their reluctance to accept the Finnish management approach and its values. Here is one anecdote told during the interview with one Russian manager:

I remember one anecdote about an Estonian guy, but … it can also be applied to a Finnish guy … Man on the road outside of the city is trying to stop a car. He stops it. It is in Estonia. He asks the driver: "To Tallinn, is it far or near?" Driver says: "Near." "Would you take me?" Driver says: "Yes." He sits in a car, car goes, goes, goes. One hour, two hours. Passenger asks: "Sorry, is it now far or near Tallinn?" Driver says: "Now, faaaar." So this is about our neighbors [Estonians and Finns].

Another way of expressing detachment from the Finnish colleagues was the use of metaphors by Russian managers. Metaphors are symbolic resources that are able to communicate more than they literally express. Consider the following narrative from the interview with one of the Russian managers. Note how in this narrative Russians are depicted as being more flexible and open-minded while Finns are portrayed as somewhat narrow-minded and inflexible.

I am often asked about the general difference between Russia and Finland. I even prepared a joke about it. If you take a fly and put it in a can or a bottle it will just move around randomly here and there but it will finally find the way out, so the problem is solved. And I say that this is the way Russians work. Trying lots of things, you fail but you do not care and you try something else and then, here you are. Sometimes I can compare Finns with a bee. If you put a bee in the same situation, you know it is considered to be much more intelligent (laughs), it flies only in one direction and then, after dozens of attempts [hitting the glass wall], it just falls down and dies. So this is the way I see that people in the west often are operating.

Furthermore, the Russian culture was depicted in interviews as a valuable resource that serves the organizational goals well and is better prepared to face the challenges of globalization. For instance, when questioned about the cultural differences that exist between Russians and Finns, one interviewee responded by distinguishing between how Russians are better able to cope with uncertainty than Finns:

I already – based on my experience during these two years – understand that the same word even in English has two different meanings for us and for Finns. For example, "How are you?"; "Good, but there is one problem." So this word "problem" for Finns is a complete collapse, something completely amazing. But for Russians "problem" is just a question that needs to be solved.

The Russian managers' active use of humor and various metaphors to describe their relations with their Finnish colleagues underscores their attempts to downplay the abilities and achievements of their Finnish colleagues within both organizations, as well as to resist the Finnish management discourses that were transferred from the HQs promoting a more egalitarian and less competitive approach to management. It can be seen as an attempt to overturn, de-legitimate and, subsequently, change the existing asymmetrical relations between Russian and Finnish managers (see Clark and Geppert 2006) in favor of the relations that would provide the Russian managers with better access to resources and financial rewards. In both of our case organizations, the existing relations were challenged by referring to the ability of the Russian managers to be more effective when dealing with scarce resources, uncertain and complex environments, and ambiguous social interactions. To some extent it concurs with the arguments found in the literature that eastern European managers are indeed better able to cope with uncertainties and ambiguities due to the socially complex nature of the environment where they come from (see also Child and Czegledy 1996; Stark 1996).

Another positive feature that the Russian managers have associated in their interviews with their Russian identity was their hard-working nature and workaholic attitude towards work. As such, it was claimed to be distinct from the attitude of Finns towards work. The fact that the Finnish managerial approach tends to promote more attention to work–life balance issues was portrayed as a sign of weak organizational commitment and prioritization of personal interests. The Russians, in contrast, were described as very committed and enthusiastic ("crazy") towards their work and organizations. The fact that in Russia people often are forced to work substantially more than they want was not voiced very eagerly by our Russian interviewees. Instead, it was often turned on its head and presented as a distinct feature of "being Russian" that helps people achieve good results and makes them responsible and work-oriented.

[P]eople have to work actively here [in Russia]. If you would come here [to the Russian organization] at 7 o'clock in the evening then this place resembles a trade floor, it is completely crazy.

Another topic which is totally unclear for us [is that] when in Finland people finish their working hours, they leave everything as it is and go home. We do not go [home], we do everything until the end.

So there [in Finland] is an understanding that people here [in Russia] live differently, that they have different perceptions, different mentality … And we would like to be like [Finns] also, staying here [at work] from 9:00 till 17:00, so that in the same way we could close our computers at 17:00 or 17:30 and just go home and then in the morning come back and start again. So we can only envy Finns and try to behave like that also to have some kind of work–life balance. If it is something like 50–50 there, here it is 90–10. And if you are young, I always ask young people here, are you married? They answer no. And I say if you will be working here, you will never get married … For example, my kid goes to sleep at 21:00, so I do not see him at all – I come home he sleeps; I leave he still sleeps …

Another expression of merits embedded in the Russian national identity was associated with the fact that Russian managers were more people-oriented, in contrast to process-oriented and discipline-oriented Finnish managers.

What I really appreciate in our previous general director was that even though he was the biggest shareholder here … he was very, very close to people … And people really trusted him. And they knew that whatever he said it would be really implemented.

Also, Russians were depicted as more caring and even passionate for the ultimate result in both individual and collective work. Such self-portrayal depicted Russian managers as more humanistic and at the same time more dedicated to and responsible for their work, thus questioning the irresponsibility and the lack of a "psychology of self worth" among Russian managers that the extant literature has claimed to be somewhat typical for post-Soviet managers (Holt *et al.* 1994).

I would not be hiding that I and my people got an offer from Company X to double our salaries. It was very simple: come to our side and let's conquer the whole country. It is possible but not interesting to work in a company-loser. Not everything can be measured in money, especially when you do this work already for many years. I know perfectly that I will not be without work, I know my own price, but what we do here is … I do not know but we get high from it … that we killed a competitor here, there, there … so in every issue we are the first ones, everywhere and in everything … So what we are not getting in money, we are getting this way by working in such a company.

The Russian managers quite often stressed the fact that Russia is nowadays a completely different country that has managed to overcome a large number of difficulties that it was facing after the collapse of the Soviet Union. They actually took a lot of pride in highlighting the changes in the social as well as business environment in Russia. In a way, by depicting themselves as some kind of heroes who managed to overcome a great number of problems and challenges during the post-Soviet years, the Russian managers tried to point out their legitimate right to be repositioned as equal partners of their western colleagues. Such attitudes were expressed to undermine the general contribution of the Finnish side in developing the Russian organizations. Consider the following extracts from the interviews:

This industry is now different. I do not want to say that Russia maybe has passed the way which other countries need 50 years to go through, we made it in 10. But this is close to reality because the way the companies are managed, everybody knows that they need financial analysis, they need marketing, they need HR if they want to have good people so on and so forth. So it is kind of standard. I do not think that FinFood in case of RusFood brought a lot.

Honestly, I think that what they [Finns] think [about their contribution] is clearly overestimated …

They [Finns] try to change us [Russians] but I think if they want to work in Russia, they must change themselves because, please do not understand me like some nationalist but in any case, small 5 million people Finland trying to change Russia … (laughs) … it is really funny … it is the same also in China where Finnish people try to change the nation of Chinese people, I do not think that it is possible … If they want to make business here, they must be more flexible …

Hence, by referring to various national characteristics that in the minds of the Russian managers make them better equipped to deal with limited resources and escalating complexity of the environment, the Russian managers aimed at resisting the more egalitarian Finnish managerial approach thus renegotiating the balance of interests between control and autonomy within both MNCs. Such micro-political renegotiation activities were also documented previously in the literature (see also Ferner *et al.* 2004; Martin and Beaumont 1999). This analysis shows that the degree of control imposed on the subsidiary by the headquarters emerges out of a process of negotiation between the two, and the national identity construction processes play an important role in these negotiation activities, constituting one of the main driving forces of the organizational actors' political behavior within MNCs.

Summary

To summarize, the findings of this study indicate that there were two main discursive struggles that the Russian managers were engaged in as they were subjected to the forces of globalization (see Table 11.1). Both struggles involved the (re)construction of specific kinds of managerial subject positions. The first one reflected the struggle to position oneself as more "global," with certain connotations of being more superior and knowledgeable than one's counterparts. Being more "global" was associated with some sort of empowerment and self-realization that the notion of "being a global manager" brings with it. The data suggests that the involvement of the Russian managers into this discursive struggle was intentional and conscious and aimed at actively resisting the hegemonic postcolonial discourse depicting westerners (in this case Finnish managers) as carriers and a source of seemingly "universal" knowledge for non-westerners. The Russian managers tried

Table 11.1 Struggles: types, main characteristics, main discourses and power implications

Type of struggle	Main characteristics	Main discourses used by Russian managers	Power implications
Struggle for being global	Aims at positioning the "self" as more global, open-minded, adaptable and polycentric than the "other," thus positioning itself as better versed in the western managerial approach of "true" multinationals	Russians are more adaptable to the global and dynamic environment Russians are less ethnocentric than Finns Russia is a geographically larger country than Finland Finns are only formally more democratic and less hierarchical than Russians Russians possess more extensive experience from large global "third country" MNCs Russians have the willingness to learn from others which is lacking in Finns Russians are able and willing to make "big" scale and efficient decisions	Redistribution of decision-making power Granting more autonomy to Russian subsidiaries More active participation in agenda setting and strategizing
Struggle for being distinct	Aims at positioning the "self" as possessing more valuable, distinct and beneficial features than the "other" derived from national identification, thus downplaying and resisting the Finnish management approach and managerial discourses	Russians are more flexible and open-minded as opposed to Finns who are slow and inflexible Russians are better able to cope with uncertainty Russians are more enthusiastic about and dedicated to their organizations Russians are more workaholic and "crazy" about work Russians are more people-oriented as opposed to the more process-oriented and discipline-oriented Finns Russians are more passionate for the ultimate result Russians have overcome and achieved a lot since the Soviet Union ceased to exist	Downplaying of Finnish contributions, achievements and capabilities Granting more autonomy to Russian subsidiaries More career promotions and advancements for Russian managers

to reposition themselves as being better versed in the dominant western management discourses than their Finnish colleagues.

The second discursive struggle reflected the inherent need and desire of the Russian managers to preserve their cultural distinctiveness of being Russians, which was portrayed as a valuable resource in the Finnish–Russian organizational context and was used to resist the Finnish managerial approach imposed on them by the HQs. To do that, they drew on the discursive strategy aimed at the construction of national differences. Additionally, this discursive struggle included elements of the heroification discourse, as the Russian managers took a lot of pride in the fact that they belonged to the generation of Russian people who were able to achieve a tremendous and fast-paced social change in Russia following the collapse of the Soviet Union.

Discussion and conclusions

This chapter has attempted to shed some light on the following questions: (1) *What are the consequences and the impact of globalization on self-perception and self-identification of local managers in their locality?*; (2) *What kind of discourses does the national identity work entail?*; and (3) *What implications does the process of national identity construction have for power and politics in MNCs?* To tackle these questions, it examined the process of social construction of national identity among Russian managers of Finland-based organizations in Russia. More specifically, it tried to illustrate how national identity is being built in the face of globalization forces and to challenge some of the existing views on national identity that have dominated the literature, with, however, a few important exemptions (see, for instance, Ailon-Souday and Kunda 2003; Barinaga 2007). The dominant view entails an essentialist and static perspective on national identity construction and denies organizational actors of any subjectivity and agency in this process. This chapter, on the contrary, has attempted to show that the national identity provides organizational actors with an important set of discourses that can be utilized as symbolic resources to resist the hegemonic influence of the globalization meta-discourse and to acquire power within the organizational setting. It argues that the phenomenon of national identity is too complex to be theoretically captured by means of strict and static sets of continuums (e.g. Hofstede 1980, 1991). Rather the national identity can be described as a symbolic discursive resource that organizational actors draw upon in the symbolic production of difference in cross-national organizations, e.g. MNCs. It is often used to marginalize the "other" based on some collective characteristics or features (e.g. stereotypes) which are applied to all members of the "other" "imagined community" (Anderson 1983). For instance, this analysis shows how by juxtaposing themselves to Finnish managers, who were portrayed as "local" in their mentality, coming from a "small" and secure place, and thus not able to cope with the global dynamics and pace, the Russian managers aimed at producing an image of a Finnish manager being poorly equipped to manage global companies adequately, thus trying to shift the power balance in the relationship. Therefore, national identity is an important element of the organizational actors' sensemaking processes (re)producing power relations between organizational actors in the MNC setting.

Following the quest of Ailon-Souday and Kunda (2003) to provide more accounts of how local managers construct their national identities in the face of globalization, this chapter has presented the case of Russian managers in the context of Finnish–Russian organizations. Such setting is a very peculiar one due to several reasons, thus complementing and adding to the generalizability of Ailon-Souday and Kunda's (2003) findings. First, Russia is one of the emerging markets as opposed to the developed Finnish market. Second, historically Finland was part of the Russian Empire from 1809 till 1917. The former aspect has resulted – as illustrated here – in the internal struggle that local managers from the emerging markets have to deal with when faced with the forces of globalization. These managers feel the need to be included into the "western managerial community of practice" and it facilitates their strong intention to be portrayed as "global" managers. It leads to a very aggressive attitude on their part towards the "other" in the organization – the Finnish managers in our case companies. At the same time, the latter point provides a counterforce to the need to adapt and to change for Russian managers. Instead, being Russian creates a sense of pride and self-esteem in particular relationships with Finnish managers. So the final outcome is a complicated intertwined struggle between (a) the desire to become acknowledged as a legitimate member of the western managerial community of practice, and (b) the desire to differentiate from the western affiliation, i.e. the Finnish management approach, preserving the Russian identity precisely as a means for "non-westernization," keeping the borderline between "us" and "them."

Complementing Ailon-Souday and Kunda (2003), who examined the process of national identity construction in a merger between companies from two developed economies (i.e. an Israeli–USA merger), this analysis illustrates a similar process but in a western–Russian setting. It also more explicitly discusses the power implications of national identity construction for organizational decision-making processes. It shows what kind of wider societal, managerial and institutional discourses are drawn upon by organizational actors and underscores the prominent role that cultural stereotypes play in this process. Additionally, it illustrates the existence of a non-organizational global social hierarchy of national identities which renders some national identities to be superior to others. For instance, the analysis showed how the Russian managers resisted the influence of their Finnish colleagues by claiming that they are in fact more knowledgeable than Finns due to the possession of experience from US MNCs, which indeed some of the Russian managers had.

The analysis shows that global and national identities are closely interlinked in the case of Russian managers. Such a finding challenges the dominant view in the literature, which stresses the inevitable convergence of managerial values of Russian managers with "global" western values. Supporting the argument of Child and Czegledy (1996), who state that eastern European managers might need to unlearn less than it is often claimed in the western business community, this chapter provides an indication that Russian managers seem to be of the same opinion and that they see western managers as carriers of knowledge only to a limited extent. The most likely scenario, then, for the future is the one in which Russian managerial values will combine parts from western business practices and some of the existing local ones. This line of argumentation complies with the idea of global "crossvergence" of managerial values, which was coined by Ralston et al. (1993). "Crossvergence" is seen as a continuum between the polar extremes of convergence and divergence. It provides an integrative alternative that might be characterized as the "melting pot" philosophy of managerial values formation (Ralston et al. 2008). When applied to the Russian context, "crossvergence" suggests that there will be an integration of cultural and ideological influences from both within and without Russia that will result in a unique value system that will borrow from both national culture and economic ideology (Ralston et al. 1993).

It should be noted that contrary to initial expectations, no significant differences were found in the types of discursive struggles that were taking place in the two organizations (i.e. one greenfield and one brownfield operation). Both struggles were present in both cases. The only difference was that the struggle for being more global was slightly more salient at RusTyres, i.e. a greenfield operation, and the struggle for being more distinct at RusFood, i.e. a brownfield operation. Russian managers at RusTyres were more inclined to establish themselves as better versed in the western management approach by claiming that they are more global in their mentality, less hierarchical, and possess more international experience from the "true" MNCs. Russian managers at RusFood were more persistent in underlining various differences between Russians and Finns, claiming that Russians are more result-oriented, people-oriented and responsible. However, the fact that both struggles were found in both cases illustrates that the nature of the national identity construction process is, at least to some extent, universal in being linked to power relations and does not depend on the nature of operations that much. The struggle for power seems to be ubiquitous in MNCs.

The findings support the conceptualization of an MNC as a "transnational space" (Geppert *et al.* 2006; Morgan 2001; Pries 2001) and the neo-institutionalist perspective on shared organizational identity and locally indifferent, global attachments. This chapter posits that it is precisely because of globalization that people tend to stress their national identities as a way of differentiating from "others" and as a source of advantage in the organizational context. It illustrates the "precarious nature" of the "transnational space" of the MNC: the emergence of transnational identities is constantly threatened by social relations in and around the MNC, which are to a large extent predetermined by national identities of organizational actors (see also Dörrenbächer 2007; Dörrenbächer and Geppert 2006). Also, national identity provides organizational actors with an important set of discursive resources that can be used in legitimating/de-legitimating and normalizing various organizational practices. For instance, it challenges the idea of "best practices" that – according to the literature – are continuously identified and transferred within MNCs (Szulanski 1996). It follows that what is considered "best practice" within organizations largely depends on organizational actors' power dispositions, in which national identity discourses play a crucial role. In a similar vein, the findings illustrate the subjective nature of such notions as "culture" and "cultural differences" in the MNC context. If the national identity can be utilized as a discursive resource then the notions of "culture" and "cultural differences" as well are powerful tools in political and power games within cross-national organizations.

The extant literature has not been very active in recognizing that cultures and national identities are always embedded in particular political settings. Extant studies tended to view various organizational problems as cultural confrontations or incompatibilities where people representing two different cultural or national collectives do not converge on a common understanding of things. However, it is important to distinguish cultural from political affiliations and to recognize that not all conflicts that occur in cross-national organizations are the result of cultural differences. In fact, this analysis indicates that there are other types of conflicts that emerge due to power dispositions and personal interests of organizational actors, which often are self-centered, self-serving and aimed at gaining power and authority within an MNC through decision-making participation, access to resources and other means (see also chapter of Blazejewski and Becker-Ritterspach in this volume). These interests often become promoted or resisted through various discourses around national identity and cultural differences. Such discourses can be used to either support certain decisions and initiatives or reject them (Holden 2002). Hence, it is important to go beyond traditional theorizations of cultural differences (Hofstede 1980, 1991) and national identities within MNCs and to examine the process of national identity construction from a cognitive or a discursive perspective (see, for instance, Wodak *et al.* 1999). In fact, language and discourses used by organizational actors seem to have the "generative" power to create new meanings and understandings by bringing together different existing meanings from different social domains, thus connecting cognition and action (Vaara *et al.* 2003). These discursive aspects of power should be taken seriously and need to be examined.

The analysis presented here has implications for MNCs. Since nationalism is an important element embedded in the relationships between managers of different nationalities, it impacts the daily decision-making and managerial sensemaking processes in MNCs. It has certain implications for who participates in decision-making processes, and what decisions are made or rejected in the organization. In practical terms it means that organizational members might resist certain initiatives emanating from other parts of the organization, based on nationalistic motives. Such initiatives as transfer of knowledge, diffusion of practices and dissemination of shared corporate cultures might fail because of these motives. Hence, they should be paid attention to and taken seriously.

While these findings can be seen as analytical generalizations (Tsoukas, 1989) that shed some light on the politicized nature of the national identity construction processes in modern MNCs, it is important to contextualize the findings. The Russian–Finnish setting offers an interesting set-up to study the national identity construction processes, but it is also a very unique one considering the joint history these two countries have had. For instance, the applicability of the postcolonial lens is complex in this setting due to the fact that Finland was under the rule of the Russian Empire for more than 100 years and, as our findings show, memories of those times still live on in the minds of both Russians and Finns. Also, national identity is a context-bound resource and some contexts are more fertile in providing various discourses around national identity than others. In this sense, the Russian–Finnish context has a very "rich" historical, cultural and societal content, from which a large number of discourses can be mobilized and utilized by organizational actors as strategic resources in their struggle for organizational power. At the same time, other contexts might not be as "rich" in this respect. However, one might speculate that the main mechanism through which national identity functions or is utilized as a strategic resource in the struggle for organizational power remains the same in other contexts as well. Nonetheless, it would still be important to compare this analysis with cases from other industries and other national settings. It would be especially interesting to study other kinds of post- or neo-colonial settings where specific conceptions of superiority and inferiority could be reflected in sensemaking around national identities (e.g. Frenkel 2008; Prasad 2003). Researchers need to investigate more thoroughly how organizational actors use various metaphors, analogies, humor or irony in the national identity construction processes. Also, future research may examine how the process of national identity construction varies depending on the social position and background of managers in terms of education, age, gender, etc. or on their position in the organizational hierarchy. Then, it could try to identify various measures that MNCs could utilize to minimize the effects of nationalism on daily organizational processes.

REFERENCES

Ailon-Souday, G. and G. Kunda 2003. "The local selves of global workers: the social construction of national identity in the face of organizational globalization," *Organization Studies* 24: 1073–96

Alexashin, Y. and J. Blenkinsopp 2005. "Changes in Russian managerial values: a test of the convergence hypothesis?," *International Journal of Human Resource Management* 16: 427–44

Alvesson, M. 1994. "Talking in organizations: managing identity and impressions in an advertising agency," *Organization Studies* 15: 535–63

Anderson, B. 1983. *Imagined Communities: Reflections on the Origin and Spread of Nationalism.* London: Verso Editions and NLB

Ayois, A. 2004. *Trust and Western-Russian Business Relationships.* Aldershot: Ashgate

Banerjee, B. and S. Linstead 2001. "Globalization, multiculturalism and other fictions: colonialism for the new millennium?," *Organization* 8: 683–722

Barinaga, E. 2007. "Cultural diversity at work: national culture as a discourse organizing an international project group," *Human Relations* 60: 315–40

Billig, M. 1995. *Banal Nationalism*. London: Sage

Bollinger, D. 1994. "The four cornerstones and three pillars in the house of Russia," *Journal of Management Development* 2: 49–54

Child, J. and J.P. Czegledy 1996. "Managerial learning in the transformation of Eastern Europe: some key issues," *Organization Studies* 17: 167–79

Clark, E. and M. Geppert 2006. "Socio-political processes in international management in post-socialist contexts: knowledge, learning and transnational institution building," *Journal of International Management* 12: 340–57

Clark, E. and A. Soulsby 1999. "The adoption of the multi-divisional form in large Czech enterprises: the role of economic, institutional and strategic factors," *Journal of Management Studies* 36: 535–59

Czarniawska, B. 2004. *Narratives in Social Science Research*. London: Sage

Derrida, J. 1981. *Positions*. University of Chicago Press

Dörrenbächer, C. 2007. "Inside the transnational social space: cross-border management and owner relationship in a German subsidiary in Hungary," *Journal of East European Management Studies* 4: 318–39

Dörrenbächer, C and M. Geppert 2006. "Micro-politics and conflicts in multinational corporations: current debates, re-framing, and contributions of this Special Issue," *Journal of International Management* 12: 251–65

Elenkov, D. S. 1997. "Differences and similarities in managerial values between US and Russian managers," *International Studies of Management and Organization* 28: 85–106

1998. "Can American management concepts work in Russia: a cross-cultural comparative study," *California Management Review* 40: 133–56

Fairclough, N. 1995. *Critical Discourse Analysis*. Boston, MA: Addison Wesley

Ferner, A., P. Almond, I. Clark, T. Colling, T. Edwards, L. Holden and M. Muller-Camen 2004. "The dynamics of central control and subsidiary autonomy in the management of human resources: case-study evidence from US MNCs in the UK," *Organization Studies* 25: 363–91

Fey, C. F., M. Adaeva and A. Vitkovskaia 2001. "Developing a model of leadership styles: what works best in Russia?" *International Business Review* 10: 615–43

Frenkel, M. 2008. "The multinational corporation as a third space: rethinking international management discourse on knowledge transfer through Homi Bhabha," *Academy of Management Review* 33: 924–42

Garcia, P. and C. Hardy 2007. "Positioning, similarity and difference: narratives of individual and organizational identities in an Australian university," *Scandinavian Journal of Management* 23: 363–83

Geppert, M., D. Matten and P. Walgenbach 2006. "Transnational institution building and the multinational corporation: an emerging field of research," *Human Relations* 59: 1451–65

Grugulis, I. 2002. "Nothing serious? Candidates' use of humor in management training," *Human Relations* 55: 387–406

Hall, S. 2000. "Who needs 'identity'?" in Gay, Evans and Redman (eds.) *Identity: A Reader*. London: Sage, pp.15–38

Hardy, C. and N. Phillips 1999. "No joking matter: discursive struggle in the Canadian refugee system," *Organization Studies* 20: 1–24

Hardy, C., I. Palmer and N. Phillips 2000. "Discourse as a strategic resource," *Human Relations* 53: 1227–48

Hatch, M. J. 1997. "Irony and the social construction of contradiction," *Organization Science* 8: 275–88

Hatch, M. J. and S.B. Ehrlich 1993. "Spontaneous humor and an indicator of paradox and ambiguity in organizations," *Organization Studies* 14: 505–26

Hobsbawm, E. 1990. *Nations and Nationalism since 1780.* Cambridge University Press

Hodge, B. and G. Coronado 2006. "Mexico Inc.? Discourse analysis and the triumph of managerialism," *Organization* 13: 529–47

Hofstede, G. 1980. *Culture's Consequence: International Differences in Work-related Values.* London: Sage
  1991. *Cultures and Organizations: Software of the Mind.* London: McGraw-Hill

Holden, N. J. 2002. *Cross-cultural Management: A Knowledge Management Perspective.* Pearson Education.

Holt, D. H., D. A. Ralston and R. H. Terpstra 1994. "Constraints on capitalism in Russia: the managerial psyche, social infrastructure, and ideology," *California Management Review* 36: 124–41

Iedema, R. and R. Wodak 1999. "Introduction: organizational discourses and practices," *Discourse & Society* 10: 5–19

Inkpen, A. and P. Beamish 1997. "Knowledge, bargaining power, and the instability of international joint ventures," *Academy of Management Review* 22: 177–202

Kets de Vries, M. F. R. 2001. "The anarchist within: clinical reflections on Russian character and leadership style," *Human Relations* 54: 585–627

Knights, D. and H. Willmott 1989. "Power and subjectivity at work," *Sociology* 23: 535–58

Laclau, E. 1990. *New Reflections on the Revolution of our Time.* London: Verso

Laine, P. and E. Vaara 2007. "Struggling over subjectivity: a discursive analysis of strategic development in an engineering group," *Human Relations* 60: 29–58

Larsson, R. and S. Finkelstein 1999. "Integrating strategic, organizational, and human resource perspectives on mergers and acquisitions: a case survey of synergy realization," *Organization Science* 10: 1–26

Lincoln, Y. S. and E. G. Guba 1985. *Naturalistic Inquiry.* London: Sage

Martin, G. and P. Beaumont 1999. "Co-ordination and control of human resource management in multinational firms: the case of CASHCO," *International Journal of Human Resource Management* 10: 21–42

McCarthy, D. J., S. M. Puffer, O.S. Vikhanski and A. L. Naumov 2005. "Russian managers in the New Europe: need for a new management style," *Organizational Dynamics* 34: 231–46

McSweeney, B. 2002. "Hofstede's model of national cultural differences and their consequences: a triumph of faith – a failure of analysis," *Human Relations* 55: 89–118

Morgan, G. 2001. "Transnational communities and business systems," *Global Networks* 1: 113–30

Mumby, D. K. and R. Chair 1997. "Organizational discourse" in Van Dijk (ed.) *Discourse as Social Interaction.* London: Sage, pp. 181–205

Nandy, A. 1983. *The Intimate Enemy: Loss and Recovery of Self under Colonialism.* Delhi: Oxford University Press

Newton, T. 1998. "Theorizing subjectivity in organizations: the failure of Foucauldian studies?," *Organization Studies* 19: 415–47

Olie, R. 1994. "Shades of culture and institutions in international mergers," *Organization Studies* 15: 381–405

Phillips, N. and C. Hardy 1997. "Managing multiple identities: discourse, legitimacy and resources in the UK refugee system," *Organization* 4: 159–86

Prasad, A. 2003. "The gaze of the other: postcolonial theory and organizational analysis" in Prasad (ed.) *Postcolonial Theory and Organizational Analysis: A Critical Engagement.* New York: Palgrave Macmillan, pp. 3–43

Pries, L. 2001. *New Transnational Social Spaces: International Migration and Transnational Companies in the Early Twenty-First Century.* Routledge: London

Puffer, S. M. and D. J. McCarthy 1995. "Finding the common ground in Russian and American business ethics," *California Management Review* 37: 29–46

Puffer, S. M., D. J. McCarthy and A. L. Naumov 1997. "Russian managers' beliefs about work: beyond the stereotypes," *Journal of World Business* 32: 258–76

Ralston, D. A., D. J. Gustafson, F. Cheung and R. H. Terpstra 1993. "Differences in managerial values: a study of US, Hong Kong and PRC managers," *Journal of International Business Studies* 24: 249–75

Ralston, D. A., D. H. Holt, R.H. Terpstra and Y. Kai-Cheng 2008. "The impact of national culture and economic ideology on managerial values: a study of the United States, Russia, Japan, and China," *Journal of International Business Studies* 39: 8–26

Roberts, K., H. and N. A. Boyacigiller 1984. "Cross-national organizational research: the grasp of the blind man" in Cummings and Staw (eds.) *Research in Organizational Behavior,* vol. 6, Greenwich, CT: JAI Press, pp. 455–488

Said, E. 1978. *Orientalism.* New York: Vintage Books

Shotter, J. and K. J. Gergen 1989. *Texts of Identity.* London: Sage

Stark, D. 1996. "Recombinant property in Eastern European capitalism," *American Journal of Sociology* 101: 993–1027

Suddaby, R. and R. Greenwood 2005. "Rhetorical strategies of legitimacy," *Administrative Science Quarterly* 50: 35–67

Sveningsson, S. and M. Alvesson 2003. "Managing managerial identities: organizational fragmentation, discourse and identity struggle," *Human Relations* 56: 1163–93

Szulanski, G. 1996. "Exploring internal stickiness: impediments to the transfer of best practice within the firm," *Strategic Management Journal* 17: 27–43

Tajfel, H. 1978. "Inter-individual behavior and inter-group behavior" in Tajfel (ed.) *Differentiation between Social Groups: Studies in the Social Psychology of Inter-group Relations.* London: Academic Press, pp. 27–60

Tayeb, M. 1994. "Organizations and national culture: methodology considered," *Organization Studies* 15: 429–45

The Economist 1994. "After communism: counter-revolution." December 3: 23–7

Thomas, P. 2003. "The recontextualization of management: a discourse-based approach analyzing the development of management thinking," *Journal of Management Studies* 40: 775–801

Thomas, R. and A. Linstead 2002. "Losing the plot? Middle managers and identity," *Organization* 9: 71–93

Tsoukas, H. 1989. "The validity of idiographic research explanations," *Academy of Management Review* 14: 551–61

Turner, J. C. 1985. "Social categorization and the self-concept: a social cognitive theory of group behavior" in Lawler (ed.) *Advances in Group Processes: Theory and Research*, Vol. 2. Greenwich, CT: JAI Press, pp. 77–122

Turner J. C. 1999. "Some current issues in research on social identity and self-categorization theories" in Ellemers, Spears and Doosje (eds.) *Social Identity: Content, Commitment, Context*. Oxford: Blackwell, pp. 6–34

Vaara, E., J. Tienari and R. Säntti 2003. "The international match: metaphors as vehicles of social identity-building in cross-border mergers," *Human Relations* 56: 419–51

Van Maanen, J., J. Sodersen and T. R. Mitchell 2007. "The interplay between theory and method," *Academy of Management Review* 32: 1145–54

Wodak, R., R. de Cillia, M. Reisigl and K. Liebhart 1999. *The Discursive Construction of National Identity*. Edinburgh University Press

12 Contesting social space in the Balkan region: the social dimensions of a "red" joint venture

Mairi Maclean and Graham Hollinshead

Introduction

This chapter sheds light on the MNC as a contested transnational social space in the Balkan region of south-east Europe by "deconstructing" a recent "red" joint venture from the perspectives of key stakeholders, "red" referring to the location of the MNC in question in countries belonging to the former communist bloc. The organizational focus of our analysis is the Serbian brewery Weisser,[1] the oldest brewery in the Balkans, situated near Belgrade, and recently acquired by the Turkish-owned MNC Eden; the merger having taken place in an unstable and volatile environment, compared to a "tinderbox" ready to ignite (Lee 2006a). Through examining the merger from the grounded positions of key social actors – indigenous employees, union officials, local Serbian and "westernized" managers, exposed to new market-oriented logics emanating from the west, fuelled by globalization – we discern both conflicting and consonant interests and rationalities relating to the establishment and early operations of the cross-border joint venture.

Our study is informed by the work of Zgymunt Bauman (2000; 2007; Bauman and Vecchi 2004) on identity and Pierre Bourdieu (1984; 1990a; 1990b) on the notion of "habitus." Habitus is conceived by Bourdieu as the ingrained, socially constituted dispositions of social classes that lead actors to make choices and decisions that reproduce existing social structures and status distinctions, orienting their actions and inclinations without precisely determining them. We suggest that the habitus of subsidiary managers and employees is at once *shared*, an extension of long-standing, traditional arrangements dating back to the socialist era, and at the same time *dichotomous*, with a new hiatus having opened up in the status of managers and workers which did not exist before, introducing new frictions to the relationship.

---

[1] The names of case companies and individuals have been changed to preserve anonymity.

This chapter turns the spotlight on conflictual micro-political issues within the newly acquired Serbian subsidiary, examining the diverse rationales and identities of key actors, whose interests are shaped and informed by the contexts in which they operate (Child and Rodrigues 1996; Dörrenbächer and Geppert 2006; Morgan and Kristensen 2006). In this way, the chapter seeks to contribute to the further understanding of MNCs as complex micro-political systems spanning national, cultural, institutional, political and ethnic divides, and dominated by the interplay of power and politics (Clegg *et al.* 2006).

Much of the intrinsic interest of the present chapter derives from the fact that it is not concerned with a western or North American MNC. The fact that Eden, the acquiring company, is Turkish is important. Turkey has enjoyed close historical links with the Balkans, stretching back for centuries. As a host nation, it eschews identification with the vast colonial projects of the nineteenth and early twentieth centuries in which western countries engaged. It therefore taps into the notion of multiple modernities, free from association with the "all too common unidirectional managerial crusade from the west to the east" (Kostera 2002: 115), while allowing for the emergence of other models (Kaya 2004; Lee 2006b). Some commentators have tended to present MNCs as footloose and stateless (Ohmae 1990, 1995), possessing an "internal market of mobile managers" (Mueller 1994: 414). Many of the world's biggest economic entities in terms of turnover are not in fact nation states but MNCs (Sklair 2002). Globalization arguably calls into question the viability of divergent types of capitalism (Crouch 2005), the expectation being that a US style of management might become diffused around the globe as the dominant paradigm. Other observers, however, lay greater emphasis on the *differences* between MNCs, arguing on the contrary that MNCs and the organizational processes they favor are heavily influenced by host country institutions, including industrial relations, education and financial systems (Djelic and Quack 2003; Dörrenbächer and Geppert 2009; Geppert *et al.* 2003; Harzing and Sorge 2003; Tüselmann *et al.* 2009; Whitley 1999). Viewed in this light, organizations and societies may be seen to mirror one another structurally, and markets are inseparable from their social contexts (Maclean and Harvey 2008; Mueller 1994; Quack *et al.* 2000). This argument stresses the embeddedness of organizations in the societal fabric in which they have been constructed (Clark and Soulsby 1998; Hollingsworth and Boyer 1997). Different countries of origin, as Ferner (2000) insists, lead to different patterns of control within MNCs. Harzing and Sorge (2003), indeed, suggest that divergence between MNCs of different countries of origin may actually be greater than assumed.

Mahmed Kari, president and CEO of Eden, appears to support this argument, observing that for Turkish companies the Balkans represent a natural terrain in which to do business, offering cultural consonance, proximity to the west and (one day perhaps) entry to the European Union (EU): "An environment which might seem impossible to a Luxembourg company is business as usual to us" (cited in Barrett 2002: 21). For the Serbian subsidiary, Weisser, meanwhile, the cultural or "institutional distance" between the home and host country is arguably reduced with a Turkish parent than had the merger concerned a western MNC (Morgan and Kristensen 2006: 1470). All of Eden's subsidiaries at the time of the merger were in central and eastern Europe. A so-called "red" multinational, Eden therefore afforded more latitude for the Serbian subsidiary (Birkinshaw 1997), as well as an implicit cultural understanding and sensitivity, arguably conferring quasi-insider status on Eden's Turkish managers, and promoting, in a notoriously low-trust environment, a far higher level of trust (Clark and Michailova 2004; Nojonen 2004).

At the same time, the politically volatile Balkan region has received relatively scant attention in the field of international management (Barrett 2002; Gould and Sickner 2008; Hollinshead 2006; Hollinshead and Maclean 2007). Harzing and Sorge (2003) have highlighted the need for more empirical research on previously neglected multinationals operating in Europe, while Michailova and Clark (2004: 9) have called for more "sensitizing, inductive, bottom-up" research to investigate organization in post-socialist transforming societies. Our study seeks to address these gaps, casting light on issues of transnational and cultural idiosyncrasy in international business activity.

In examining the diverse interests, identities and habitus of key actors involved in the strategic joint venture, this chapter addresses two principal research questions. First, what is the nature of the power base of local, indigenous managers in the Serbian subsidiary? And second, what is the nature of the relationship between subsidiary managers and workers, and to what extent might this be viewed as asymmetrical, founded on a habitus which is no longer shared but dichotomous?

Context

The small state of Serbia provides a compelling context to study. In some respects it emerges as something of a special case within European post-socialist societies, at the forefront of reform until the late 1980s, yet thereafter experiencing economic and social devastation as a result of civil war, western-imposed sanctions and the fragmentation of the former Yugoslavia. Separated from the Republic of Montenegro following the Montenegrin referendum on independence in May 2006, it forms a small, landlocked country bordered by eight neighboring states. Its population of just over 7 million is heterogeneous, comprising a majority of Serbs, in addition to, *inter alia*, Hungarians, Bosnians, Romany, Croats, Albanians and Slovaks. The declaration of independence by the southern province of Kosovo in February 2008 was endorsed by western powers, but incited anti-western sentiment amongst politicians and nationalistic-leaning members of the Serbian population. Kosovo contains a majority Albanian population, yet is regarded by many Serbians as their "ancestral home." Relations between the two remain tense, exacerbated by allegations of human trafficking and drug smuggling, with Serbia stubbornly refusing to recognize the fledgling state, even if this should become a condition of EU membership (Economist Intelligence Unit 2008; Emerging Europe Monitor 2009).

The delivery of indicted war criminals to stand trial in The Hague was stipulated as a condition for opening the doors to EU accession. In April 2008, Serbia signed the Stabilization and Association Agreement (SAA), paving the way for the harmonization of legislation and standards with the EU. The arrest of Radovan Karadzic in July 2008 after 13 years on the run was hailed as a "milestone" by EU Enlargement Commissioner Ollie Rehn; although Ratko Mladic, the principal perpetrator of the 1995 massacre in Srebrenica, a designated UN "Safe Area," at the time of writing remains at large (Obradovic-Wochnik 2009). For Serbia, as for other Balkan states, EU membership is seen as critical to future prosperity. The EU, however, exhausted from enlargement and constitutional reform, and ravaged by recession, may drag its feet. As Lee (2006a: 11–12) insists, "the European Union needs to understand quickly it is solely the promise of membership that provides the impetus in these countries for change." A coalition of democratic, pro-European parties, For a European Serbia (ZES), led by Boris Tadic, took power in July 2008; though the ultra-nationalist Serbian Radical Party continues to enjoy the electoral support of around one third of the population. As Vujadinović (2004: 4) argues, Serbia stands today at a critical crossroads, "either to turn towards a future, modern, state in Europe, or to be pushed backwards to become an ever more traditionalist, xenophobic, isolated and prospectless entity."

In the years following the merger of Eden and Weisser in 2003, the macroeconomic environment remained poor. As Serbia embarked on a program of rapid privatization, including oil, electric power, mining, telecommunications and agriculture, injections of foreign capital were badly needed to propel economic generation. Yet continued political instability in the region, epitomized by the assassination in 2003 of Prime Minister Zoran Djindjić, who had sought to stamp out organized crime, served as a disincentive to potential investors (Hadžić 2002; Ristić 2004). At the time of writing, privatization remains ongoing, with Telekom Serbia, Belgrade Airport Nikola Tesla, and the pharmaceutical firm Galenika all expected to be put up for sale when the financial crisis abates (US Commercial Service Serbia 2009). Privatization has been facilitated by a joint-venture or "flexible" model, signifying privatization through a strategic partnership, offering modernization, new investment, and a boost to jobs and exports. The joint venture of Eden-Weisser (EW) with which we are concerned here was founded on this model of strategic relationship. Arguably, however, privatization recipients have been denied the fundamental institutions of market democracy in an illiberal regime (Gould and Sickner 2008). Corruption levels have remained high, organized crime rife, and tax evasion and financial fraud commonplace (Gordy 2004). Strikes and social unrest are forecast as industrial output slows, and the Serbian government makes stringent budget cuts – the price of having received IMF funds (Emerging Europe Monitor 2009).

Despite the faltering approach to reform taken by post-Milosević governments, some optimism has been generated through GDP growth of around 6 percent in recent years, and the provision of tax concessions to attract inward investment (US Commercial Service Serbia 2009). Serbia benefits from its geopolitical location as a "bridge" between east and west, its highly skilled workforce, its central position in the Central Europe Free Trade Agreement (CEFTA), and its economic relations with the Russian Federation. Nevertheless, the World Bank estimated Serbia's overall rank as a place in which to do business at just 86th in the world (out of 178 countries) in 2008. This compares relatively unfavorably with many other countries from central and eastern Europe, including Estonia (17th), Latvia (22nd), Lithuania (26th), Slovakia (32nd), Slovenia (55th) and the Czech Republic (56th) (World Bank 2008).

This chapter is concerned with issues of power and politics in MNCs, more specifically within the parent–subsidiary relationship between the Turkish parent Eden and the Serbian subsidiary Weisser in the strategic joint venture established in 2003. Organizations are socially constituted, and social relationships in MNCs are institutionally embedded. Power, as Allen (2003: 2, cited in Clegg *et al.* 2006: 223) points out, is not a property but "a relational effect of social interaction." It is a means of coordinating trans-organizational relationships. As such, power may be decentered, crossing transnational social spaces through "mediated relationships or through the establishment of a simultaneous presence" (Allen 2003). Interdependent subunits within trans-organizational systems have a distribution of power often founded on the division of labor (Hickson *et al.* 1971). On its own, however, power is arguably insufficient, requiring the presence of trust to work more effectively, reducing risk and enabling business relationships to rise above the state of *homo homini lupus* articulated by Hobbes (Bachmann 2001). Politics, meanwhile, as Hardy and Clegg assert (1996), is the process of mobilizing power, and is a term not without negative connotations (Pettigrew 1973). Conflicts commonly display as resource-driven, interest-driven or identity-driven (Dörrenbächer and Geppert 2006; Rothman and Friedman 2001; see also chapter of Dörrenbächer and Gammelgaard in this volume). The particular conflict with which we are concerned here, triggered when a "technological surplus agreement" was implemented in the Serbian brewery, leading to a reduction in the workforce from 368 to 235 employees, is primarily resource-driven; but it also spills over on to issues of identity and habitus, as different fates are seen to befall different types of actor, unequally empowered, in the Serbian subsidiary.

Identity and habitus in an uncertain world

Identity, Bauman argues, was once largely determined by employment (Bauman and Vecchi 2004), as the high incidence of surnames relating to occupation, such as "Smith" (Schmidt, Forgeron) or "Miller" (Müller, Meunier), across different societies reflects. This was arguably especially so in the former communist bloc, where individuals were assigned roles designed to match their abilities, at least in theory. More recently, however, with the transformation wrought by globalization, we increasingly inhabit liquid times, in which "a stable identity [is] even more desperately sought after and more difficult to achieve" (Bendle 2002: 16). Past certainties have given way to a new flexibility in the workplace, accentuating feelings of insecurity and disorientation (Bauman 2000; 2007). This is accompanied by a new awareness that communities, once the bedrock of any society, are no longer indissoluble and welded together, but on the contrary are polycultural, variegated and shifting:

One becomes aware that belonging and "identity" are not cut in rock, that they are not secured by a lifelong guarantee, that they are eminently negotiable and revocable; and that one's own decisions, the steps one takes, the way one acts ... are crucial factors of both. In other words, the thought of "having an identity" will not occur to people as long as "belonging" remains their fate ... (Bauman and Vecchi 2004: 12)

A primary characteristic of the accelerating liquefaction of social frameworks is that it implies a process of "disembedding without re-embedding" (Bauman and Tester 2001: 89; Lee 2006b: 357). The "disembedding" of social institutions is viewed by Giddens (1991: 17) as a major influence on modernity. As the binding power of traditional social structures and ways of life ebbs away, agencies of collective action are swept aside by a new form of power, "increasingly mobile, slippery, shifty, evasive and fugitive" (Bauman 2000: 14). The new, unpredictable and inexorably transient world left in its wake is marked by "the falling apart, the friability, the brittleness, the transience, the until-further-noticeness of human bonds and networks" (Bauman 2000), disembedding or "lifting out" social relationships from their local contexts (Giddens 1991: 18), and instilling feelings of dissonance amongst the dispossessed (Bacharach *et al.* 1996; Hollinshead and Maclean 2007; Lee 2006b: 360). As Bauman puts it, this is a world which ultimately "goes back on its promises" (Bauman and Vecchi 2004: 52). The massive upheavals engendered by globalization are by no means restricted to the former communist bloc (Verdery 1996). But the socialist economies were particularly outmoded (Jowitt 1992), suggesting that the pernicious effects of the rapacious change driven by global capitalism may be felt there especially keenly. This was exacerbated in the case of Serbia due to the upheavals it had experienced, including the economic collapse of the country in the 1990s, UN sanctions, NATO bombings, and shock therapy privatization.

Habitus, for Bourdieu, is a system of lasting, transposable dispositions, informed by the earliest experiences of childhood. It serves as a system of cognitive and motivating structures which orient and direct the individual. As such it provides the individual with a practical sense of how to act, suggesting "procedures to follow, paths to take," albeit without entirely predetermining these (Bourdieu 1990a: 53; Emirbayer and Johnson 2008; Maclean *et al.* 2010). As a "product of history" (Bourdieu 1990a: 54), both individual and collective, being rooted in a present past which extends into the future, it is understandable that an individual's notion of habitus might be deeply affected by the growing instability of a post-traditionalist, individualizing society (Adams 2006). Habitus, Sweetman (2003: 532) observes, "is a product of our upbringing and more particularly of our class." Identities, in this sense, are often "classed" (Bourdieu 1977); though to identify with a class, one needs to prove one's membership continually through deeds, otherwise one risks becoming *déclassé* (Bauman and Vecchi 2004: 49). Viewed in this light, a more accurate definition of class or stratification, Bottero (2004) suggests, might be the ability or otherwise *to escape from the field*. In this regard, the experience and prospects of the subsidiary managers and the indigenous workers in our case study below are revealed as dichotomous. While the former are able to exercise a degree of choice and agency, and a measure of control over the direction and development of their careers, the latter lack both choice and agency, emerging as powerless to influence their employment (other than through the "Hobson's choice" of exit).

Relations between management and workforce, of course, are normally asymmetrical. The point to stress here, however, is that in a former socially owned production plant, this would not necessarily have been the case, the Yugoslav self-management model – characterized by state control yet endowed with a measure of decentralization and imbued with an ethos of equality – which prevailed during the Tito era being regarded as something of an ideal type in terms of employee participation.

In the elaborate setting of a transnational MNC, it is also clear that issues of power and control are rendered more complex across borders, giving rise to a subtle interplay of informal and formal power relations between parent and subsidiary (Bouquet and Birkinshaw 2008; Ferner 2000). Informal systems in the subsidiary and the power relations they represent are magnified in importance, since the MNC actually needs local managers to function, to occupy crucial bridging roles (as Fenton-O'Creevy *et al.* explore in the present volume) as "cultural go-betweens" or as "interpreters" of the local context (Ferner 2000: 530). This may result in a potential disjunction between the formal system of rules endorsed by the MNC and the practical operation of the system at local, subsidiary level. At the same time, low-power subsidiary actors may enhance their power resources vis-à-vis the parent company through such informal means, enabling them to increase their influence over time, potentially at least (Bouquet and Birkinshaw 2008).

Nevertheless, this cannot disguise the fact that in this relationship, and notwithstanding the tendency of the foreign-owned subsidiary to engage in strategies to enhance its influence with the parent over time, the power resources available to parent and subsidiary are inherently unequal (see also chapter of Ybema and Byun in this volume). Internal competition may exist between different sister subsidiaries, which are effectively in competition with one another for resources from the parent company. It may even suit the parent to allow a particular subsidiary to decline while the capabilities of others are strengthened through additional investment (Birkinshaw and Hood 1998). Ultimately, the parent may choose subsidiary divestment (Boddewyn 1979; 1983). All of this instills a fundamental asymmetry at the heart of the relationship between the two parties (Bouquet and Birkinshaw 2008). At Weisser, this asymmetry arguably existed on two main levels, between the MNC headquarters (HQ) and subsidiary management on the one hand, and between the subsidiary management and its workforce on the other.

Research process

The fieldwork for the present study was conducted by one of the authors of this chapter, with the assistance of a Serbian academic. The involvement of a native academic proved to be invaluable to the research process. Gaining access to organizations in transitional economies is often difficult for western "outsiders." Local participation helped the western researchers to adjust to the culture and politics of the company under investigation, with the Serbian academic acting as a cultural informant, while enhancing their acceptability to insiders (Clark and Michailova 2004; Soulsby 2004). The Serbian academic also assisted with simultaneous translation during interviews with employees – thereby slowing down the questioning at times, and allowing the researchers an opportunity to observe respondents' reactions to particular areas of questioning (Soulsby 2004) – while helping to authenticate ideas and findings emerging from the research.

Invariably, the researchers themselves contribute to the milieu of the research environment, impacting on the social contexts under study (Johnson and Duberley 2003). This is, arguably, particularly the case in conditions of societal transience. Soulsby (2004) argues that it is important not to stereotype respondents as passive beings, whilst assuming the researchers to be neutral, unobtrusive observers to proceedings. The reality may be starkly different, with the researchers occupying a critical position in the research process which deserves to be acknowledged (Steger 2004), at times even creating quite a stir in the transitioning case organization, becoming "objects of curiosity and discussion" among the workforce (Soulsby 2004: 50).

The fieldwork for the present study was based upon three sets of semi-structured interviews, conducted in Belgrade and the brewery in Pančevo, ten miles from the capital, in the course of three separate visits to Serbia during 2004 and 2005. The first set of interviews took place in Belgrade in May

2004, and involved five in-depth semi-structured interviews with Serbian experts and government officials in the privatization process. The purpose of these interviews was twofold: first, to gain technical insights into the privatization process; and second, to acquire qualitative observations regarding the speed of privatization and the principle and practice of foreign ownership in a country where, until recently, all industry had been state owned (see Howard 2001). Insights provided by interviewees, and derived from related published material, helped to sharpen the authors' understanding of the political and economic setting of the case study (Lofland and Lofland 1995).

The second set of interviews was conducted at the Weisser Brewery near Belgrade in February and March 2005, and involved semi-structured interviews with senior managers, including the human resource manager, company lawyer, production manager and the sales manager. These managers served as key internal informants, providing valuable information on the case study organization, and acting as "guides to insider understandings" (Lofland and Lofland 1995: 61, cited in Soulsby 2004: 50), especially necessary in a post-socialist transitional setting. The purpose of these interviews was both to acquire factual information concerning the organizational effects of the takeover by Eden, and to obtain reflective observations from the managers concerned regarding their personal experience of the joint venture, and the nature of the strategic relationship between Weisser and Eden. The interviewees spoke in English, an indication of their education and international experience, obviating the need for translation.

The final set of interviews took place at the Weisser Brewery in May 2005, involving six lay representatives of the trade union Nezavisnost, which represented a majority of the workers. The purpose of this interview (which involved all six individuals concurrently) was to gather worker perceptions as to the organizational implications of the takeover at shop-floor level, and to elicit their feelings as to the future prospects of Weisser. Interviewing low-power actors in an MNC in a post-socialist transitional setting in this way is relatively uncommon (Bouquet and Birkinshaw 2008), and strengthens the grass-roots, bottom-up aspect of the present study (Clark and Soulsby 1999; Michailova and Clark 2004). The interviewees spoke in their native Serbian, with simultaneous translation provided by the Serbian academic. The approach adopted by the researchers in all cases was informed by Weber's notion of *Verstehen*, seeking to access the different cultures of respondents through a heightened understanding, thereby gaining first-hand insight into their perceptions, interests and contexts (Johnson and Duberley 2003).

Following Czarniawska (1998: 47), we believe it is important to hear and heed the "voices of the field." Kostera (2002: 113) gives poignant expression to the fundamental importance of doing so, stressing the need to "give voice to the fears, dreams and struggles of people who have entrusted me with stories about them." This is especially necessary in a world which, as Bauman highlights, seems intent on going back on its promises – as exemplified by the subsequent demise of the Weisser brewery in 2008, its few remaining employees subsumed into the sister subsidiary at Zaječar.

The internationalization of brewing

The brewing sector has seen dramatic shifts in ownership in recent years, away from indigenous interests and towards internationalized cadres of professional managers. Serbia represents an increasingly important market for Europe's major groups, not least because per capita consumption is still relatively low, with scope for improvement. Total Serbian beer consumption per capita stands at around 60 liters per annum, compared with an equivalent volume in neighboring Croatia and Slovenia of around 75 liters and 100 liters respectively. There were twelve breweries in Serbia at the outset of this study, all previously state or socially owned, but which rapidly became subject to foreign ownership; within a matter of years, however, several of these had closed. The Belgian MNC Interbrew entered a strategic partnership with the Apatinska Pivara brewery in Apatin in 2003, acquiring ownership of 50 percent of its shares. Interbrew also acquired a major stake in Niksicka Pivara. Carslberg and Celarevo Pivara became strategic partners in October 2003, with the Danish giant acquiring 51 percent of the brewery's shares. Belgrade-based Beogradsku Indusrija Piva (BIP), in combination with Vrsacka and Jagodinska breweries, was privatized and purchased by Dutch MNC Heineken. The Turkish-owned beverage group Eden, meanwhile, bought up two Serbian breweries in 2003–04: Weisser, the subject of this study, in August 2003, followed by a second brewery, Sava, at Zaječar the year after, which thereby became the sister subsidiary of Weisser. Within a short time of these takeovers, the total annual brewing capacity of the two breweries had risen to 1.4 million hectoliters – 0.4 million hectoliters in Pančevo and 1 million hectoliters in its sister subsidiary in Zaječar.

The joint venture

The parent: Eden

Eden is an 85 percent subsidiary of Turkish-owned food and beverage producer Eden Ark, a system of companies producing and marketing beer, malt and soft drinks across a territory ranging from the Adriatic to China, consisting of fourteen breweries, four malteries, and nine Coca-Cola bottling facilities across ten countries. To date, Eden Ark has exhibited a pronounced strategic orientation towards central and eastern Europe, its field of operations concentrating on Russia, Ukraine, Kazakhstan, Romania, Moldova as well as Serbia. State-of-the-art brewing facilities in Moscow were developed with the assistance of the European Bank for Reconstruction and Development (EBRD), which contributed a €20 million loan in 2001. The group is amongst the ten largest European brewers by sales volume. In 1989, Eden Ark group management set itself a long-term goal to generate fifty percent of its beer sales internationally by 2004, an objective it achieved in 2003, a year ahead of target.

The subsidiary: Weisser

At the time of our study, Weisser was the oldest brewery in Serbia, having been established in May 1722. A critical stage in its development occurred at the end of the nineteenth century, when a German family, Weisser, took charge and developed the first steam brewery. The brewery's international connections were useful in learning brewing techniques from abroad, particularly from Austria and Germany.

During the Tito era, Weisser was nationalized, family ownership giving way to the socialistic organizational form of "social ownership." Accordingly, while the state remained a powerful actor in the process, the brewery was nevertheless owned by the workers themselves and managed by their representatives. In 1970, the brewery became a subsidiary entity within the Hamis holding company, which also possessed interests in agriculture and other sectors. In the 1980s, Weisser enjoyed rapid development and increased capacity, serving markets in Serbia, Montenegro, Macedonia and Croatia through the establishment of distribution centers in these regions. In June 1989, Weisser became a legal entity through the provisions of the first law on companies.

During the 1990s, however, in common with other Yugoslav enterprises, Weisser suffered as a result of war and UN sanctions. Indeed, the community surrounding the brewery was particularly badly affected by NATO bombings, which caused the local refinery to leak carcinogens into the environment. As well as losing valuable markets as the former Yugoslavia disintegrated, the brewery was unable to attract new investment from government or to import new technology and equipment. Nevertheless, there remained a sustained demand for beer throughout the period of crisis, and local producers had a stranglehold over the market.

In 1991, the brewery became one of the first privatizing organizations in Serbia, with shareholders acquiring 60 percent of socially owned capital. This figure was raised to 90 percent seven years later, in 1998, as a result of the new privatization and transformation law. Accordingly, although the general assembly overseeing the company continued to be made up of appointed individuals, the general manager operated in a relatively independent capacity, with a primarily professional, as opposed to political, orientation.

The process of merging

Heralding the new joint venture, Eden-Weisser (hereafter referred to in its shortened form as Weisser), in August 2003, the president and CEO of Eden Ark, Mahmed Kari, stated: "We will integrate Weisser's 250 years of brewing heritage with Eden's proven technological as well as marketing capabilities to be a leading brewer in Serbia. We will act with speed to fully leverage our advantage of being the first international brewer to enter Serbia." Eden acquired a 63 percent stake in Weisser through its acquisition of €6.5 million. This was followed in 2004 by a further investment of €5 million. The new owner also repaid the brewery's debt to the state of €3 million. Fresh capital injected into the joint enterprise was used to enhance product quality and the technical infrastructure of the brewery. Subsequent important developments included the introduction of pasteurization, product rebranding through the use of a new logo, the reshaping of bottles and crates, and the introduction of new plastic bottles. In December 2003, the company's main "Weisser" brand was relaunched, followed by strong marketing support.

In the case study which follows, we pick up the story following the implementation of a "technological surplus agreement" in 2003, which had the effect of reducing the workforce from 368 to 235 employees in the first instance. In agreement with Nezavisnost and a smaller independent trade union recognized at the brewery, and in accordance with the relevant labor laws and collective agreements, surplus staff were redeployed or transferred wherever possible. Eden set aside €1 million to pay the 133 redundant workers, each of whom received €330 (before tax) for every year of service at the brewery.

Contesting social space from grounded perspectives

The locus of our study in Serbia, which may be considered an "extreme variant" of other post-socialist settings (Eisenhardt 1989; Hollinshead and Maclean 2007), arguably offers the potential for distinctive, and perhaps idiosyncratic, analysis of the structuring of the strategic interactions of the social actors involved in the international joint venture (Crozier and Friedberg 1980). As highlighted by the present volume, recent departures in the study of MNCs depict the MNC as a site of micro-political contestation and pluralistic tension (Dörrenbächer and Geppert 2006; Dörrenbächer and Geppert 2009; Morgan and Kristensen 2006), rather than as a nexus of bounded rationality – the result of a "clash between different actors within the firm utilizing resources derived from their institutional and organizational context to pursue their own agendas" (Morgan and Kristensen 2006: 1468). In keeping with this theme, we seek to expose the basis for micro-political "game playing" (Doz and Prahalad 1991) on the part of key organizational actors by reflecting upon their primary interests and grounded positions.

The parent: cost and cultural consonance

While access to senior managers of the Turkish parent company, Eden Ark, was not available, the authors were able to gain insight into the strategic motivation of the Turkish-owned "red" MNC from secondary and web-based sources. In a published interview with the company's marketing director in October 2002, the following statement was made:

We are the major player in Turkey, but that will not be enough in the future. Especially when Turkey eventually becomes part of the EU and we will not have the protection of the monopoly system. We already produce Becks and Miller beer under license in Turkey, as one means of avoiding too many competition concerns when Turkey joins the EU, but we need to do more to ensure that our business continues to thrive after that date. We have focused on eastern Europe for one main reason – money invested there goes a lot further than it does in the west. Of course, Turkey has also had traditional links with that part of Europe as well, so it makes it the ideal place to start expanding sales of Eden. (FoodandDrink.com 2004)

The importance for cultural consonance between home and host environments is underlined also by Barrett (2002: 21), who points out that whereas US or European investors were put off the entire Balkan region by repeated televised images of war, investors from more proximate countries, in contrast, formed a more realistic picture of the possibilities for doing business there. As Barrett explains, "The whole environment was more familiar to them. They had historical links – the Hapsburg Empire once stretched into today's Croatia, Bosnia and Serbia, while Turks occupied much of the area for hundreds of years. History fosters cultural links that facilitate contacts and even trust between business people" (Barrett 2002).

In analyzing the strategic intent of Eden Ark in Serbia, it is evident that the potential for building a normative "bridge" through the subsidiary provides a powerful rationale for initiating the joint venture. This corroborates the assertion by Martinez and Jarillo (1991) that "cultural consonance" serves to lubricate the dynamics of the parent–subsidiary relationship, particularly given the contextual specificities of the Balkan region. It is, of course, also the case that Eden Ark's interest in the area is driven by a powerful economic logic: the lure of cheap, skilled labor (Barrett 2002). A concomitant of this economic rationality, however, is an underlying political "asymmetry" in the power relationship between MNCs and local stakeholders, including government, in the post-socialist region (Clark and Geppert 2006). The structural weighting of power in favor of the MNC is heightened in the Serbian case by the retarded macro-economic status of the country and the general climate of political volatility. This was borne out by our interviews with privatization officials, who revealed that a primary governmental concern was to relieve the debts incumbent upon the state by selling off publicly owned enterprises to foreign buyers at artificially low prices as rapidly as possible; Eden was a direct beneficiary of this process. The Serbian government unquestionably falls into the bracket of "low-influence national governments" referred to by Bouquet and Birkinshaw (2008: 478). As a low-power actor in its own right, in need of funds from privatization and inward investment, it can do little to bolster the status and influence of indigenous actors in foreign-owned Serbian subsidiaries.

Local management: managing in a zone of uncertainty

As the protocol for merging was formulated, a "transition team" of senior managers from Eden Ark and Weisser were appointed to steer the process of organizational integration, replacing the former senior management team.

The team included the former general manager at Weisser, as well as legal, sales, technical and finance managers. It was joined, on a project-by-project basis, by temporary expatriate experts who offered assistance and advice on matters such as information technology and quality control.

At the time of the first set of interviews at the premises, eighteen months after the takeover, the transition team had been replaced by a new team of managers at what was now called Eden Weisser, following the joint venture. Although the general manager, appointed immediately after the establishment of the joint venture, was of Belgian nationality, having been recruited from the senior ranks of the Belgian-owned MNC Interbrew, the majority of the senior management team at EW was of Serbian origin, from Belgrade, with good local knowledge of the region. Three out of the four top managers interviewed (excepting the company lawyer who was a time-served employee at Weisser) were relatively young business graduates of Serbian higher educational institutions. All had "worked their way up" in other MNC drinks producers based in Serbia, one (the human resource manager) at Coca-Cola and two (the plant manager and sales manager) at Interbrew. The plant manager had acquired significant international managerial experience in the sector, having worked for some time for Interbrew in Belgium and the UK. All three were fluent in the English language. In classifying the new cadre of managers at Weisser, they were clearly professional and specialist practitioners, who, although Serbian nationals, had acquired through their international experience extensive command of their functional areas. Their appointment effectively marked a final end to the legacy of worker self-management which had characterized the brewery during the Tito era.

Our primary focus in interviews with local managers was on their perceptions of the degree of control exerted by the parent on the subsidiary, and their consequent room for manoeuvre with regard to initiatives (Birkinshaw 1997). All management interviewees were asked about the frequency and form of contact they experienced with representatives of the parent in Istanbul. The production manager, who was also responsible for coordinating the financial investment from Eden, contrasted the rigorous scrutiny he had experienced whilst working at Interbrew with what he described as the greater room for flexibility and autonomy permitted by Eden: "We discuss everything with them, but they leave us to develop things for ourselves, and for me that is the right way of doing things, because I know this market much better than people sitting in Eden." This was due, he maintained, not just to the smaller size of Eden Ark (it owned 14 breweries at the time as opposed to the 300 owned by Interbrew), but also to the cultural compatibility resulting from

Eden Ark's eastern European origins and zone of operations. According to the plant manager, a "positive" form of monitoring by the parent was apparent whereby it always "kept an eye on you." This was understandable, he explained: "They are never going to leave me alone, because this is a property of theirs." At the same time, the parent had confidence in the work of local managers, and was prepared to delegate to them and allow them to "formulate their own strategies." The plant manager explained that he had frequent conversations with his line manager at Eden, which were typically cordial, covering subjects such as the weather and holidays, but which were also focused on the achievement of pre-set targets and deadlines, betraying the existence of a tighter leash. This included "reporting to them every day about how much we sold yesterday."

Despite the Weisser team being able to develop plans and policies "in a personal way," the group sales manager at Eden monitored results rigorously, expecting daily reporting on sales volumes. In addition, if the subsidiary wished to stage a large promotion or event, costing in the region of €100,000, it was necessary to gain Eden approval. There is clearly a tension here between what the subsidiary managers describe as decentralized control and evidence of quite detailed surveillance by HQ.

Whilst the above conversations indicated that, at the very least, a "soft" form of corporate control was being exerted by the parent over subsidiary managers in an organizational climate of relative cultural consonance (Larsson *et al.* 2004), it nevertheless became clear that local managers were mobilizing tacit and culturally specific non-transferable knowledge resources to optimize their organizational legitimacy (Gertler 2003). The following observations from local managers are instructive in this regard.

According to the sales manager, it was necessary for him to convey to his team that the Serbian market was different from the rest of the world. Macro-economic and political instability created an environment which was highly charged and rapidly changing, with a high risk of inflation and devaluation. Furthermore, it needed to be understood that business dealings were not always conducted with propriety, a major problem being delays in payment for delivered items: "Payment conditions are 60 days or 90 days, and I'm collecting my money in three months, but I have to pay tax and excise in advance." Since his appointment in 2003, the sales manager had concentrated on building up the sales profile of EW from a very low base, Weisser having been in debt, and having failed to invest in branding and marketing. In conjunction with the previous human resource manager, the sales manager had recruited a sales force from scratch by 2004, covering all major Serbian subregions, and embracing Bosnia, Montenegro and Macedonia. Members of the sales force were typically inhabitants of major Serbian cities, who had experience and a good track record in sales, and who were committed to forming a "chain" between EW and customers in a direct and personal fashion. One activity, for example, was to visit stores to observe and negotiate the position of Weisser beers on shelves: "You have to fight for the market every single day, to get a good position on a shelf in a store." In gradually building the market, it was necessary for the EW sales team to be acutely aware of distinctive Serbian tastes in beer, which could be discovered through market research and "blind" tasting. According to the sales manager: "You have to adapt to the market if you want to survive; if you do not you will die in two months."

The human resource manager and company lawyer had been primarily involved in introducing the program of employment changes at EW following the takeover by Eden. The single most significant development had been the technological surplus agreement, which involved a workforce reduction of over one third. This agreement had been implemented with adherence to Serbian employment law and established collective agreements, as mentioned, which require consultation on matters such as redundancy and levels of compensation, as well as providing for the redeployment of redundant workers where possible for a period of three years. Thus a number of redundant workers retained their association with the brewery, including former drivers who bought trucks with severance pay and thereafter operated on a self-employed basis.

Thus a vital strategic contribution of the Human Resource team had been to ensure that Serbian employment law was properly applied in change programs, the law remaining the primary determinant of the substance of the employment relationship. Accompanying the administration of the more technical aspects of change, the newly established HR department devoted considerable attention to communicating and explaining new policies to workplace representatives in a manner which took account of distinctive Serbian expectations and sensibilities. Thus, following Clark and Geppert (2006), a vital attribute to enable local managers to negotiate and uphold their social space within the enterprise was aptitude for learning. This strikes a chord with the arguments presented in the chapter by Williams and Geppert, who underline the importance of national resources, including employment laws, to provide actors with social space in MNCs. In the Serbian plant, however, this space seemed rather limited, despite their protestations to the contrary. These managers were walking something of a tightrope, having to combine effectively two distinct forms of knowledge. First, through their dealings with the parent, and through their accumulated experience of western companies and educational/training institutions, they needed to demonstrate ideological acceptance and proficiency in the application of "universal" western management concepts in the fields of strategy, production, human resource management and so on. Second, in order to functionalize the peculiarities of operating in the "insecurity zone" (Crozier and Friedberg 1980), they needed to capitalize on the rare, tacit and inimitable knowledge resources derived from their subjective experience of the uniquely challenging and potentially impenetrable Serbian institutional and cultural milieu (Gertler 2003). It was through the competent personal mixing of these discrete knowledge repertoires that the Serbian managers could maximize their organizational status and career opportunities.

Thus, in seeking to understand the micro-political "game-playing" occurring between parent and subsidiary management groupings, we should recognize that, in an organizational and macro-political climate of considerable asymmetry, local managers were nevertheless seemingly able to protect some valuable social space within the enterprise by mobilizing two primary knowledge-based resources. Firstly, westernized managerial and technical acumen was required to ensure competitiveness in the new market-orientated business environment. Demonstration to the parent of profitability would allow indigenous managers considerable latitude within a relatively high-trust, culturally consonant parent–subsidiary relationship (Ferner 2000). Secondly, in pursuit of the above, local managers could bolster their positions in inimitable fashion through the interpretation (Dörrenbächer and Geppert 2006; Ferner 2000) of universalistic fields of managerial knowledge in the highly particularistic Serbian business context.

Employee interests: the expression of dissonance

While the social space between parent and subsidiary managers possessed a "loose–tight" dynamic, a conditional degree of latitude being permitted to host country management, within the enterprise itself a widening gulf of contested social space was opening up between local managers and the organizational rank and file. It was the latter grouping that bore the brunt of the asymmetrical power distribution by the parent and its associated cost-cutting agenda, the victims of a "hollowing out of democratic institutions and the privatization of the public sphere" (Bauman and Vecchi 2004: 5), which they were effectively powerless to resist. While the particularistic and tacit skills of the elevated managerial cadres in the enterprise were of value to the parent, the technical skills and proficiencies of (particularly older) production workers were viewed as dispensable. It is instructive to reflect briefly on the "workers' story," conveyed during the third phase of fieldwork and second visit to the brewery.

Taking issue with management's perspective on the takeover, the worker representatives stated that a climate of secrecy had prevailed at Weisser, with little information having been forthcoming on specific work changes or the future direction of the business. Indeed, it was alleged that important financial data had been manipulated to bolster the interests of the incoming management. The lay officials of the union Nezavisnost asserted that the Weisser brewery had been undervalued to reduce its purchase price, thus lessening the value of payments due to workers according to their status as "social owners." At the same time, Eden had allegedly changed the product, reducing the quality of the beer, which likewise had the effect of lowering the value of the factory. Furthermore, it was alleged that the profitability of the enterprise, now highly productive according to the workers, was continually underestimated in order to justify low average pay for workers (approximately €150 per month, a sum too low to live on, compared to €1,300 for managers).

Turning to the technological surplus agreement, although severance pay had been acceptable by Serbian standards, allegedly the process of selection had been far from ethical. According to these representatives, "psychological pressure" had been brought to bear on many older workers to quit; these time-served individuals, who possessed greater legal and social protection at work, being replaced with student workers denied pension or employment rights. "New" machinery that had been introduced was in fact second-hand, as one employee reported: "A lot of what is coming is used machinery, it's not new. It's imported from Germany or somewhere. It's all used. Only the plastic bottling machine is new." The temporary workers employed in the subsidiary were ill equipped to use this machinery, producing inefficiencies and creating something of a hazard.

Turning to broader issues concerning organizational culture, the worker representatives referred to the higher, managerial stratum of the brewery as "Eden," indicating a perceived dichotomy in identity between themselves and the incoming professional cadres, despite their predominantly Serbian nationality. If the new and youthful management grouping were offensive to a workforce steeped in the principles of self-management, this was exacerbated by the removal of social benefits which had been enjoyed prior to the takeover. According to the representatives: "We used to get free sport and other welfare assistance, but now there is nothing."

Thus, at a micro-political level, profound changes had occurred in the configuration of social spaces within the enterprise following the merger. Previous notions of egalitarianism and collectivism in the enterprise, binding management and workers together as a legacy of socialism, had given way to a polarization of power and status. Although a productive and reciprocal normative relationship was now enjoyed by parent and subsidiary managers as a product of newly negotiated knowledge repertoires, workers tended to operate in a cognitive and normative organizational "black hole," giving rise to feelings of helplessness. A comment by one shop steward is insightful, revealing the workers as feeling adrift and bereft following a string of broken promises:

Before Eden came there was good communication in the factory. We all decided together, management and workers, about everything ... now we are happy to have the possibility to work, end of story. We can't plan anything. Nobody knows what will happen tomorrow. Social security doesn't exist. Although we have been promised everything, including apartments and schools, nothing has happened. We have had a bad experience with promises.

At the same time, the representatives pointed to the sister subsidiary at Zaječar, Sava, which had received very different treatment from the parent company, and where the workers had benefited from far higher redundancy payments: "Eden bought another company in Serbia, and the workers were much happier. The workers in other companies had a better agreement, a better deal, averaging €40,000 based on shares. But Pančevo workers didn't get the shares. They got some shares, but the value of them was very small, around €300." By the time of our third field visit to the brewery, the plant had become much less active, prompting the researchers to reflect that things could not go on in this way.

Discussion and conclusion

This chapter contributes to our understanding of MNCs as complex micro-political systems, dominated by the interplay of power and politics, by turning the spotlight on a "red" joint venture in Serbia, which manifests both universal as well as particularistic tendencies in international organizational behavior. Reflecting on "cultural consonance" as a lubricating force in the devolution of strategic authority, it is clear that the normative factors that contribute to such consonance possess regional specificity. Thus a Turkish-owned corporation was prepared to overlook ethnic tensions and political volatility as a serious risk factor in the host environment, in a situation where a western corporation might have demonstrated a more cautious approach, highlighting the power of history and the cultural empathies it spawns as a precursor to international business activity and understanding, suggestive of a strong country-of-origin effect (Ferner 2000; Harzing and Sorge 2003; Tüselmann *et al.* 2009). The Turkish-owned company was clearly prepared to give the brewery the benefit of the doubt in its investment decision. However, in a context of political and institutional fragility, our study would suggest that the MNC is bound to place a particular, perhaps exceptional, reliance on locally based and tacit indigenous knowledge. Viewed in this light, the MNC may be particularly compelled, perhaps counter-intuitively, to devolve strategic authority to "savvy" local managers in politically and institutionally uncertain environments.

Returning to our first research question specified above, it is clear that the power base of Serbian managers in the subsidiary was essentially fivefold. In the first place, the indigenous managers demonstrated prodigious language proficiency (cf. Ferner 2000). One, indeed, had begun his career as a translator, a role he abandoned as soon as practicable, but which had nonetheless served as the basis of his corporate career. In contrast, language proficiency was something the workers were singularly lacking, confining the latter to a relatively low-power position in the enterprise (Bouquet and Birkinshaw 2008). Secondly, the local managers possessed a striking familiarity with western management discourse, demonstrating a formidable mastery of its concepts and practices. The "tool kit" of western managerial concepts which they had built up and assimilated allowed them to converse fluently, employing up-to-date management rhetoric in their day-to-day roles with reference to strategy, marketing and human resource management, as evinced by their use of such terms as "key performance indicators," or a new style of work based on "polyvalence." The third source of power on which local managers were able to draw was their wide-ranging experience, combining internationally acquired knowledge of new techniques to do with, for example, downsizing with their aforementioned fluency in management rhetoric. This experience had been acquired through management training programs as well as through time served with other MNCs. Fourthly, they were able to consolidate their power base through their local knowledge of the Serbian market, as exemplified by the sales manager's efforts to secure top-shelf positions for

Weisser beer in local supermarkets. In contrast, expatriate managers from the parent company would have been incapable of managing the realities of selling the product at this practical, grass-roots level, essentially giving local managers a monopoly in this regard. And finally, the Serbian managers had accumulated varying degrees of social capital acquired during their employment at Eden or other drinks MNCs, providing them with an international network of useful contacts and acquaintances on which they were able to draw (Burt 1997; Granovetter 1973).

The local subsidiary managers interviewed were able to exploit this repertoire of power sources in various different ways. In particular, they were able to marry together their grasp of newly acquired, "western" managerial techniques with a deep-seated tacit knowledge of local culture, and, at the same time, a more traditional, Serbian, pluralistic concept of enterprise. This was underlined in particular by the human resource manager, who at interview displayed a strong grasp of concepts such as downsizing while simultaneously engaging with a local union representative at every stage of the conversation; or by the sales manager, who stated that one of the workers at the brewery was also his neighbor, suggestive of a pre-existing, implicit equality between the two despite the asymmetrical salary differentials which now divided them.

This brings us to our second research question, namely to what extent might the relationship between subsidiary managers and workers be regarded as asymmetrical, founded on a habitus which is no longer shared but dichotomous? Habitus, as Bourdieu (1990b: 116) observes, is not set in stone but, on the contrary, can be transformed and transcended "by the effect of a social trajectory leading to conditions of living different from initial ones." As the examples cited above imply, the habitus of workers and subsidiary managers which used to be indivisible and shared according to the spirit of the traditional Serbian model of "social ownership," emerges now as both shared and dichotomous, with the two co-existing in an ambivalent fashion. While the workers were displaced, marginalized and dysfunctional, the managers required their continued cooperation to shore up their own position, being in need of the workers' skills and knowledge of the local market. The local, subsidiary managers therefore had to pursue something of a double agenda, undertaking the cost-cutting measures required of them by senior managers at Eden, while maintaining good relations with the workers at Weisser. Workers who had been made redundant through cost-cutting measures designed to maximize efficiency were therefore regularly re-employed in the enterprise, albeit on a different contractual basis. Likewise, cordial relations with the workers were maintained as before, since these represented a *sine qua non* to the ability of the managers to implement the cultural shift required by Eden, which required the transference of international practices on to the domestic mentality. The degree of cordiality in evidence in the human resource manager's office, for example, as she chatted with an in-house union representative (a time-served employee who might well have been at the brewery during the Tito era), was an essential prerequisite to securing the workers' cooperation concerning the introduction of the new measures.

Moreover, while the managers were able to negotiate their patch with the parent company, at least to a degree, there is a sense in which the subsidiary managers and workers were "all in the same boat," the local managers themselves being also relatively low-power actors in the sense implied by Bouquet and Birkinshaw (2008), albeit less so than the workers. The disadvantaged position of workers in the new micro-political "game" being played out in the Balkans would suggest that, even in a "red" joint venture, apparent cultural consonance is partial in its embrace of organizational actors, and is powerfully compromised by the imperatives of capital accumulation and profit maximization. Likewise, in a fundamentally stratified world, the local managers, although needed by the parent company, may have little credibility ultimately with senior managers at Eden, partly because operations at Weisser are so small (Birkinshaw 1999). Though production had increased at the brewery, it did not exceed 0.4 million hectoliters annually, less than half of that produced by the nearby brewery, Sava, in Zaječar. So while the subsidiary managers were clearly able to strengthen their relative position vis-à-vis the parent company by having recourse to the various power sources enumerated above, at the same time they too were operating under the severe constraints of the volatile Serbian macro-economic and political environment, where issues to do with the destabilizing effects of inflation and devaluation and the extradition of war criminals, over which they had no control, loomed large over their collective future, undermining their view of their own position.

Nevertheless, what differentiates the local subsidiary managers and workers most of all is their *ability to escape from the field* (Bottero 2004). Ultimately, the subsidiary managers have the wherewithal to escape their current fate, through their university degrees, language proficiency, international experience, social capital and transferable skills. The workers, in salient contrast, being rooted in the field, have far fewer options, starkly illustrated by their re-employment on less favorable terms following redundancy. This underlines the fundamental asymmetry in the relationship between management and workers: while the former had exit options, the only real exit option available to the latter was redundancy.

In January 2008, it was announced that Heineken and Eden were to merge their breweries in Serbia from June 2008, forming a new joint venture, Ujedinjene Srpske Pivare (United Serbian Breweries), with Heineken becoming a 72 percent majority owner of the joint venture, and Eden having a smaller 28 percent stake. At the same time, it was announced that the brewery at Pančevo would close in October 2008, its remaining employees being transferred to Sava, its sister subsidiary at Zaječar; a sad end to the oldest brewery in the Balkans, which had survived for almost 300 years, only to succumb to the hostile winds of change brought by globalization.

At the time of our visit to the brewery, productivity, as mentioned, had risen and profitability, according to the workers, had also increased. However, where there is internal competition for resources from competing subsidiaries, it is not always clear how the rules will be interpreted by senior, host company managers. As Morgan and Kristensen (2006: 1479) observe: "It is a common story in the closure of multinationals that the local plant did everything that was asked of it and yet still became the victim of the MNC's axe." Conformity to the new rules set by the parent company does not mean that subsidiary managers will keep their jobs (Dörrenbächer 2007). Nor does it guarantee survival. Head office support is a necessary condition for subsidiary development; but on its own it may not be sufficient (Birkinshaw and Hood 1998). "Boy Scout" behavior on the part of subsidiaries eager to please is as likely to result in parent-driven divestment as more "subversive" strategies pursued by alleged "misfits" or "problem children" (Boddewyn 1979, 1983; Delany 1998; Morgan and Kristensen 2006). Parent companies, as Mueller (1996) points out, often attempt to play subsidiaries off against one another in pursuit of further investment or preferential treatment. Clearly, Eden had demonstrated considerable commitment to Weisser in the initial stages of the joint venture, paying the company's debts, installing a transition management team, purchasing new equipment, and so on. But centrality to the parent company is not guaranteed in perpetuity, and is bound to evolve over time. While some subsidiaries will improve their centrality, strengthening their influence vis-à-vis the MNC – perhaps through the use of local and national resources to create spaces for local actors to shape events, as illustrated by two other chapters (Sorge and Rothe; Williams and Geppert) in this volume – others will find on the contrary that "in the face of changing environmental contingencies … their connections may tend to vanish over time" (Bouquet and Birkinshaw 2008: 486).

Foreign subsidiaries may be established for a number of reasons, as Birkinshaw and Hood (1998) assert; and it is by no means clear that the subsequent development of the foreign-owned subsidiary is necessarily viewed as desirable from the parent company's perspective. Subsidiary evolution can lead to the depletion of the foreign-owned subsidiary's capabilities, which may be allowed to atrophy, and ultimately to the demise of the subsidiary itself. The dynamics of internal competition between individual subsidiaries are a decisive factor in the prosperity or failure of individual subsidiaries (Almor and Hirsh 1995). Despite the positive statement by the president and CEO of Eden cited earlier in this chapter, namely that Eden intended to build on Weisser's capabilities to ensure that it became a leading brewer in Serbia, it is clear that the brewery in Pančevo was competing internally for parent company resources with its sister subsidiary in Zaječar from an early stage of the joint venture. There was not necessarily any hidden agenda on the part of Eden to merge the two sites. Eden had, after all, given the brewery five years to return to profitability. It is also unlikely that early integration of the breweries was politically blocked, the Serbian government being too weak and impecunious an actor to take such a stance (Bouquet and Birkinshaw 2008). The market for beer was clearly crucial in what transpired. Serbia is a small market, and primarily a wine-drinking region to boot, and one can surmise that with two sister subsidiaries in close proximity to, and in competition with one another, the writing may have been on the wall for some time. Weisser was the smaller of the two, producing less than half the volume of beer produced by Sava, and equipped with outmoded machinery, with the exception of a German pasteurizing machine (which the workers claimed was not new, but had been purchased second-hand) and a new bottling machine. An awareness of the other subsidiary at Zaječar was constantly present. Notably, both subsidiary managers and employees at interview expressed their fear regarding the future: as one union representative bluntly put it, "We're scared, we live in hell." One could argue that the seeds of decline were already detectable in the levels of dissonance and suspicion felt by the workers; the widening gap between subsidiary managers and employees in terms of salaries and status; and the expedient replacement of time-served employees with temporary workers, with few rights.

By the time of the closure of the brewery in October 2008, the numbers of employees there had been whittled down to just thirty remaining workers. With many former employees displaced and dispossessed by the chill winds of globalization, our Serbian case study emerges as potentially archetypal. The corollary of globalization is frequently a "lifting out" of social relationships from their local contexts (Giddens 1991), an all-too-familiar process of disembedding without re-embedding (Bauman and Tester 2001), in a world which constantly rescinds on its promises (Bauman and Vecchi 2004). In our Serbian case study, this entailed a severing of links with the local context and the disconnection of managers and workforce, despite the former legacy of worker self-management.

One question which arises is why some individuals are more likely to become the "atomized" subjects – as Bauman puts it – of powerful forces beyond their control, while others are better equipped, through education, skills, experience or new technology, to emerge as winners in what Habermas (1990) terms the "catch-up modernization." Examination of this issue must be the preserve of future research. Nevertheless, it is important to observe that in a post-socialist country such as Serbia, which saw rapid and extensive privatization, the competence of unions remains a concern. Unable to adapt to market liberalism or to withstand unilateral management decision-making, untrained in negotiation, losing their membership, yet stuck in the mentality of a bygone era, the protection they offered workers was ineffectual, leaving a vacuum in terms of worker representation.

The case study we have presented here provides a poignant illustration of the vicissitudes of globalization. Weisser was not the only Serbian brewery under foreign ownership to close in the past few years. It may be the case that Eden effectively made use of young, Serbian managers to secure a relatively smooth transition in ownership and in the execution of HQ plans. The volatile Serbian context seemingly provides limited political resources for local actors to construct a power base they could truly exploit. Ultimately, largely due to factors beyond their control – including the Serbian market for beer, and decisions being taken elsewhere, in Istanbul or Amsterdam – the joint venture failed.

The dangers of Balkanization, however, are not limited to the region which gave the term its name (Meštrović 1994). Our story doubtless resonates with British and US readers in particular. We conclude this chapter with a warning from Bauman of what may lie ahead if such issues are not addressed:

And what are the abandoned, desocialized, atomized, lonely individuals likely to dream of, and given a chance, do? Once the big harbors have been closed or stripped of the breakwaters that used to make them secure, the hapless sailors will be inclined to carve out and fence off their own small havens where they can anchor and deposit their bereaved, and fragile, identities. No longer trusting the public navigation network, they will jealously guard access to such private havens against all and any intruders. (Bauman and Vecchi 2004: 46)

Acknowledgement

The authors wish to thank Professor Ankica Borota Tišma of Belgrade Business School, the research participants who agreed to be interviewed, and the British Academy for funding research visits. We also wish to thank the editors and reviewers for their insightful comments.

REFERENCES

Adams, M. 2006. "Hybridizing habitus and reflexivity: towards an understanding of contemporary identity?," *Sociology* 40: 511–28

Allen, J. 2003. *Lost Geographies of Power*. Oxford: Blackwell

Almor, T. and S. Hirsh 1995. "Outsiders' response to Europe 1992: theoretical considerations and empirical evidence," *Journal of International Business Studies* 26: 223–39

Bacharach, S. B., P. Bamberger and W. J. Sonnenstuhl 1996. "The organizational transformation process: the micropolitics of dissonance reduction and the alignment of logics of action," *Administrative Science Quarterly* 41: 477–506

Bachmann, R. 2001. "Trust, power and control in trans-organizational relations," *Organization Studies* 22: 337–65

Barrett, L. 2002. *Business in the Balkans: The Case for Cross-Border Cooperation*. London: Centre for European Reform

Bauman, Z. 2000. *Liquid Modernity*. Cambridge: Polity Press
  2004. *Wasted Lives*. Cambridge: Polity Press
  2007. *Liquid Times: Living in an Age of Uncertainty*. Cambridge: Polity Press

Bauman, Z. and K. Tester 2001. *Conversations with Zygmunt Bauman*. Cambridge: Polity Press

Bauman, Z. and B. Vecchi 2004. *Identity*. Cambridge: Polity Press

Bendle, M. F. 2002. "The crisis of 'identity' in high modernity," *British Journal of Sociology* 53: 1–18

Birkinshaw, J. 1997. "Entrepreneurship in multinational corporations: the characteristics of subsidiary initiatives," *Strategic Management Journal* 18: 207–29
  1999. "The determinants and consequences of subsidiary initiative in multinational corporations," *Entrepreneurship Theory and Practice* 24: 9–36

Birkinshaw, J. and N. Hood 1998. "Multinational subsidiary evolution: capability and charter change in foreign-owned subsidiary companies," *Academy of Management Review* 23: 773–95

Boddewyn, J. 1979. "Foreign divestment: magnitude and factors," *Journal of International Business Studies* 10: 21–6
  1983. "Foreign and domestic divestment and investment decisions: like or unlike?," *Journal of International Business Studies* 14: 23–35

Bottero, W. 2004. "Class identities and the identity of class," *Sociology* 38: 985–1003.

Bouquet, C. and J. Birkinshaw 2008. "Managing power in the multinational corporation: how low-power actors gain influence," *Journal of Management* 34: 477–508

Bourdieu, P. 1977. *Outline of a Theory of Practice*. Cambridge University Press

    1984. *Distinction: A Social Critique of the Judgement of Taste*, translated by R. Nice. London: Routledge and Kegan Paul

    1990a. *The Logic of Practice*, translated by R. Nice. Stanford University Press

    1990b. *In Other Words: Essays towards a Reflexive Sociology*, translated by M. Adamson. Stanford University Press

Burt, R. S. 1997. "The contingent value of social capital," *Administrative Science Quarterly* 42: 339–65

Child, J. and S. Rodrigues 1996. "The role of social identity in the international transfer of knowledge through joint ventures" in Clegg and Palmer (eds.) *Producing Management Knowledge*. London: Sage, pp. 46–68

Clark, E. and M. Geppert 2006. "Socio-political processes in international management in post-socialist contexts: knowledge, learning and transnational institutional building," *Journal of International Management* 12: 340–57

Clark, E. and S. Michailova (eds.) 2004. *Fieldwork in Transforming Societies: Understanding Methodology from Experience*. Basingstoke: Palgrave Macmillan

Clark, E. and A. Soulsby 1998. "Organization-community embeddedness: the social impact of enterprise restructuring in the post-communist Czech Republic," *Human Relations* 51: 25–50

    1999. *Organizational Change in Post-Communist Europe: Management and Transformation in the Czech Republic*. London and New York: Routledge

Clegg, S. R., D. Courpasson and N. Phillips 2006. *Power and Organizations*. London: Sage

Crouch, C. 2005. *Capitalist Diversity and Change: Recombinant Governance and Institutional Entrepreneurs*. Oxford University Press

Crozier, M. and E. Friedberg 1980. *Actors and Systems: The Politics of Collective Action*, translated by A. Goldhammer. University of Chicago Press

Czarniawska, B. 1998. *A Narrative Approach to Organization Studies*. London: Sage

Delany, E. 1998. "Strategic development of multinational subsidiaries in Ireland" in Birkinshaw and Hood (eds.) *Multinational Corporate Evolution and Subsidiary Development*. London: Macmillan, pp. 239–67

Djelic, M.-L. and S. Quack 2003. *Globalization and Institutions: Redefining the Rules of the Economic Game*. Cheltenham: Edward Elgar

Dörrenbächer, C. 2007. "Inside the transnational social space: cross-border management and owner relationship in a German subsidiary in Hungary," *Journal of East European Management Studies* 4: 318–39

Dörrenbächer, C. and M. Geppert 2006. "Micro-politics and conflicts in multinational corporations: current debates, reframing, and contributions of this Special Issue," *Journal of International Management* 12: 251–65

    2009. "A micro-political perspective on subsidiary initiative-taking: evidence from German-owned subsidiaries in France," *European Management Journal* 27: 100–12

Doz, Y. and C. K. Prahalad 1991. "Managing DMNCs: a search for a new paradigm," *Strategic Management Journal* 12: 145–64

Economist Intelligence Unit, 2008. *Country Report: Serbia* London: EIU

Eisenhardt, K. M. 1989. "Building theories from case study research," *Academy of Management Review* 14: 532–50

Emerging Europe Monitor. *South East Europe Monitor 2009.* 16: 10

Emirbayer, M. and V. Johnson 2008. "Bourdieu and organizational analysis," *Theory and Society* 37: 1–44

Ferner, A. 2000. "The underpinnings of 'bureaucratic' control systems: HRM in European multinationals," *Journal of Management Studies* 37: 521–39

FoodandDrink.com, *From Turkish number one to European Player* 2004 (last accessed 29 May, 2008)

Geppert, M., K. Williams and D. Matten 2003. "The social construction of contextual rationalities in MNCs: an Anglo-German comparison of subsidiary choice," *Journal of Management Studies* 40: 617–41

Gertler, M. S. 2003. "Tacit knowledge and the economic geography of context, or the undefinable tacitness of being (there)," *Journal of Economic Geography* 3: 75–99

Ghoshal, S. and D. E. Westney 1993. *Organization Theory and the MNC Corporation.* Basingstoke: Macmillan

Giddens, A. 1991. *Modernity and Self-Identity: Self and Society in the Late Modern Age.* Cambridge: Polity Press

Gordy, E. 2004. "Serbia after Djindic: war crimes, organized crime, and trust in institutions," *Problems of Postcommunism* 51: 10–17

Gould, J. A. and C. Sickner 2008. "Making market democracies? The contingent loyalties of post-privatization elites in Azerbaijan, Georgia and Serbia," *Review of International Political Economy* 15: 740–69

Granovetter, M. S. 1973. "The strength of weak ties," *American Journal of Sociology* 78: 1360–80

Habermas, J. 1990. *Die nachholende Revolution.* Frankfurt am Main: Suhrkamp

Hadžić, M. 2002. "Rethinking privatization in Serbia," *East European Economics* 40: 6–23

Hardy, C. and S. R. Clegg 1996. "Some dare call it power" in Clegg, Hardy and Nord (eds.) *Handbook of Organization Studies.* London: Sage, pp. 622–41

Harzing, A.-W. and A. Sorge 2003. "The relative impact of country of origin and universal contingencies on internationalization strategies and corporate control in multinational enterprises: worldwide and European perspectives," *Organization Studies* 24: 187–214

Hickson, D. J., C. R. Hinings, C. A. Lee, R. E. Schneck and J. M. Pennings 1971. "A strategic contingencies theory of intraorganizational power," *Administrative Science Quarterly* 16: 216–29

Hollinshead, G. 2006. "Educating educators in a volatile climate: the challenge of modernizing higher business schools in Serbia and Montenegro," *European Journal of Education* 41: 123–41

Hollinshead, G. and M. Maclean 2007. "Transition and organizational dissonance in Serbia," *Human Relations* 60: 1151–74

Hollingsworth, J. R. and R. Boyer 1997. *Contemporary Capitalism: The Embeddedness of Institutions.* Cambridge University Press

Howard, J. 2001. *The Treuhandanstalt and Privatization in the Former East Germany: Stakeholder Perspectives.* Aldershot: Ashgate

Johnson, P. and J. Duberley 2003. "Reflexivity in management research," *Journal of Management Studies* 40: 1279–303

Jowitt, K. 1992. *New World Disorder: The Leninist Extinction*. Berkeley and Los Angeles: University of California Press

Kaya, I. 2004. "Modernity, openness, interpretation: a perspective on multiple modernities," *Social Science Information* 43: 35–57

Kostera, M. 2002. "Control: accounting for the lost innocence" in Kelemen and Kostera (eds.) *Critical Management Research in Eastern Europe*. Basingstoke: Palgrave Macmillan, pp. 111–27

Larsson, R., K. R. Brousseau, M. J. Driver and P. L. Sweet 2004. "The secrets of merger and acquisition success: a co-competence and motivational approach to synergy realization" in Pablo and Javidan (eds.) *Mergers and Acquisitions: Creating Integrative Knowledge*. Oxford: Blackwell, pp. 3–19

Lee, E. 2006a. "Open tinderbox: toward lasting peace in the Balkans," *Harvard International Review* 28: 11–2

Lee, R. L. M. 2006b. "Reflexive modernization vs liquid modernity vs multiple modernities," *European Journal of Social Theory* 9: 355–68

Lofland, J. and L. H. Lofland 1995. *Analyzing Social Settings: A Guide to Qualitative Observation and Analysis*. 3rd edn. Davis, CA: Wadsworth

Maclean, M. and C. Harvey 2008. "The continuing diversity of corporate governance regimes: France and Britain compared" in Strange and Jackson (eds.) *International Business and Corporate Governance: Strategy, Performance and Institutional Change*. Basingstoke: Palgrave Macmillan, pp. 208–25

Maclean, M., C. Harvey and R. Chia 2010. "Dominant corporate agents and the power elite in France and Britain," *Organization Studies* 31(3): 327–48

Martinez, J. I. and J. C. Jarillo 1991. "Co-ordination demands of international strategies," *Journal of International Business Studies* 22: 429–44

Meštrović, S. G. 1994. *The Balkanization of the West*. London: Routledge

Michailova, S. and E. Clark 2004. "Doing research in transforming contexts: themes and challenges" in Clark and Michailova (eds.), pp. 1–18

Morgan, G. and P. H. Kristensen 2006. "The contested social space of multinationals: varieties of institutionalism, varieties of capitalism," *Human Relations* 59: 1467–90

Mueller, F. 1994. "Societal effect, organizational effect and globalization," *Organization Studies* 15: 407–28

  1996. "National stakeholders in the global contest for corporate investment," *European Journal of Industrial Relations* 2: 345–68

Nojonen, M. 2004. "Fieldwork in a low-trust (post-)communist society" in Clark and Michailova (eds.), pp. 157–76

Obradovic-Wochnik, J. 2009. "Knowledge, acknowledgement and denial in Serbia's responses to the Srebrenica massacre," *Journal of Contemporary European Studies* 17: 61–74

Ohmae, K. 1990. *The Borderless World: Power and Strategy in the Interlinked Economy*. London: Collins

  1995. *The End of the Nation State*. London: Harper Collins

Pettigrew, A. 1973. *The Politics of Organizational Decision Making*. London: Tavistock

Quack, S., G. Morgan and R. Whitley 2000. *National Capitalisms, Global Competition, and Economic Performance*. Amsterdam: John Benjamins

Ristić, Z. 2004. "Privatisation and foreign direct investment in Serbia," *South-East Europe Review for Labor and Social Affairs* 2: 121–36

Rothman, J. and V. J. Friedman 2001. "Identity, conflict and organizational learning" in Dierkes, Berthoin Antal, Child and Nonaka (eds.) *Handbook of Organizational Learning and Knowledge*. Oxford University Press, pp. 582–97

Sklair, L. 2002. *Globalization: Capitalism and its Alternatives*. Oxford University Press

Soulsby, A. 2004. "Who is observing whom? Fieldwork roles and ambiguities in organizational case study research" in Clark and Michailova (eds.), pp. 29–56

Steger, T. 2004. "Identities, roles and qualitative research in Central and Eastern Europe" in Clark and Michailova (eds.), pp. 19–38

Sweetman, P. 2003. "Twenty-first century dis-ease? Habitual reflexivity or the reflexive habitus," *Sociological Review* 51: 528–49

Tüselmann, H.-J., F. McDonald, M. Allen, S. Golesorkhi and D. Filiou, 2009. "Cross-border transfer of employment relations approaches: country-of-origin effects and the level and type of industry internationalization" in Ibeh and Davies (eds.) *Contemporary Challenges to International Business*. Basingstoke: Palgrave Macmillan, pp. 52–67

US Commercial Service Serbia 2009. *Doing Business in Serbia*

Verdery, K. 1996. *What was Socialism, and What Comes Next?* Princeton University Press

Vujadinović, D. 2004. "Democratic deficits in the Western Balkans and perspectives on European integration," *Journal for Institutional Innovation, Development and Transition* 8: 4–22

Whitley, R. 1999. *Divergent Capitalisms: The Social Structuring and Change of Business Systems*. Oxford University Press

World Bank 2008. *Doing Business 2008*

Part V

Conclusions

Reflections on the macro-politics of micro-politics

Glenn Morgan

Introduction

The study of politics and power inside multinationals has made significant strides over the last decade. No longer is it possible to treat MNCs simply as rational unitary actors pursuing efficiency logics in competitive markets and selecting appropriate forms of organizational structure depending on the contingent characteristics of particular sectors. Instead, we now have a view of MNCs as consisting of different types of social actors with differing interests and power derived from their distinctive institutional origins. These interests and powers are embedded within the particular strategic and operational positions that subsidiaries and actors occupy within the MNC and the places which they take up within global value chains. In turn this is embedded in the dynamics of global competitive markets that provide the performance outcomes crucial to the survival and growth of firms. Internally, therefore, MNCs are shaped by the ways in which different actors are constituted as collective interests and identities by these processes and how they interact with other actors inside and outside the MNC. From this perspective, the MNC is neither a Weberian rational legal bureaucracy nor an "internal market" but rather a "contested terrain" (Collinson and Morgan 2009; Edwards and Bélanger 2009). Many of the chapters in this book and other recent papers by the editors and authors have contributed substantially to extending our understanding of these processes (Becker-Ritterspach and Dörrenbächer 2009; Blazejewski 2009; Dörrenbächer and Geppert 2006, 2009; Gammelgaard 2009; Geppert *et al.* 2003; Geppert and Matten 2006; Geppert and Williams 2006). They establish a strong agenda for future research, which will offer important insights into the workings of multinationals. Through case studies, they reveal the ways in which actors' mobilize resources from organizational and institutional contexts in order to develop a collective voice and identity which enables them to pursue their interests.

As the chapters in this volume make clear, there are many different theoretical resources that are now being drawn on in order to understand the MNC. However, crucial to all these discussions is identifying the specificity of the multinational as an organizational form; what is it that makes a multinational different from any other type of organization? From my perspective, within what I will describe as the "comparative institutionalist" approach (see Morgan *et al.* 2005, 2010), the answer lies in how the specific process of organizing and coordinating activities across the borders of distinctive national institutional contexts creates a new and distinctive level of complexity in social and organizational relations. Where does that new level of complexity lie? Comparative institutionalist analysis identifies this in the existence of different practices, processes, actors and legitimatory discourses across distinctive national settings. It is of course simple enough to note, as scholars of organization studies have done, that any firm is characterized by what Edwards and Wajcman describe as the "politics of working life," i.e. processes of conflict and compromise over structures of control and coordination (Edwards and Wajcman 2005). In the institutionalist study of multinationals, however, analysis of the politics of working life is embedded in the potential clash of processes, practices and legitimacies that derive from the different institutional contexts brought together in the MNC (Almond and Ferner 2006; Kristensen and Zeitlin 2005; Morgan *et al.* 2001). Kostova's concept of "institutional duality" (Kostova 1999; Kostova and Roth 2002; Kostova and Zaheer 1999) describes this in part, even though the theoretical resources on which she draws are distinctive from those used in this chapter. In a situation of institutional duality, actors are subject to two opposing pressures. On the one hand, senior managers from the head office may seek to transfer to subsidiaries practices and processes that conform with the institutional practice of the home base; local subsidiaries are therefore pressured to confirm to head office practices. On the other hand, actors in local subsidiaries have to engage with other actors in the local context and with the institutions that are taken for granted in that context. Thus the pressure towards institutional isomorphism comes from different sources and has profoundly different impacts on local subsidiaries. Both these pressures are in an institutionalist sense "legitimate": i.e. they derive from embedded expectations about appropriate forms of behavior that are accepted in their different social contexts as legitimate claims on how business and management "should" be done. Since Weber, the claim to legitimate authority (and the source of that claim) has been central to understanding organizational relations. The distinctiveness of the MNC lies in the existence of multiple competing forms of legitimate authority and the impact that this has on the internal and external relations of the MNC. The study of multinationals is therefore about how organizations are impacted on by the process of managing in multiple institutional contexts. What does this mean for the traditional questions of organization studies about the forms and structures of control and coordination that exist amongst different firms? Case studies of micro-politics inside MNCs, such as those published in this book and elsewhere, contribute to this task.

However in this chapter, I argue that the focus on the micro-politics of multinationals must be accompanied by a "macro-politics" of multinationals where the MNC as a whole is brought back into focus. In particular, I want to emphasize first the diversity of the MNC and the need to contextualize any particular MNC and any particular process of micro-political engagement within a "map" of the diversity of the MNC. I do this through a theoretical discussion of the concept of "transnational social space" (Morgan 2001, 2006; Morgan *et al.* 2001) and develop it in relation to a series of examples of the forms of diversity which exist in the nature of MNCs. Second, and countering the diversity theme, I want to emphasize elements of unified power in the MNC particularly deriving from legal ownership and financial control. Finally, again on the theme of unified power, I want to consider the construction of global management cadres within the MNC and how this relates to the broader reconstitution of economic elites and power in the contemporary world order. The goal is to provide an initial framework for a macro-politics of the MNC as a distinctive organizational form. In doing so, I aim to open up fertile areas of inter-disciplinary research which are in danger of being ignored when the focus becomes highly micro. I therefore seek to embed the micro-politics of the MNC into a macro-politics which draws on political economy, sociology and critical accounting studies to complement an organization theory approach.

The multinational as a distinctive organizational form and its relationship to comparative institutional analysis

In the previous section I have described the issue of "institutional duality." In this section I develop this further and link it to the idea of the MNC as a transnational social space. Crucial to this is having a perspective on the nature of national boundaries and how they enclose and shape institutions to create forms of legitimate practice. If, as the journalist Tom Friedman has suggested, we are living in a "flat world" (Friedman 2005) or in what Kenichi Ohmae described as the "borderless world" (Ohmae 1999), then national boundaries are increasingly irrelevant and the problem of the MNC simply dissolves into the broader problem of organization per se. The contributions in this volume make it obvious that this is not what is happening; that differences in national contexts are far from disappearing.

However, where do these national differences come from and how are they reproduced? In comparative institutional analysis, social life in general and economic organization in particular is shaped by institutions, i.e. expectations and rules of how to behave in particular contexts. These expectations arise out of particular historically and spatially constituted patterns of interactions and social relationships, which become embedded in particular routines and practices as well as in discourses of legitimation. What makes the comparative institutionalist approach distinctive (compared, for example, to organizational institutionalism as discussed in Greenwood *et al.* 2008) is the role that it assigns to focusing on the society-wide aspects of these processes and through this the particular role played by the modern state. The modern state is in this perspective the ultimate guarantor of social institutions through, in the classic Weberian definition, its monopoly over the legitimate use of force within limited geographical boundaries. In this role it is the state which ultimately defines, monitors and sanctions deviant behavior. The formation of the modern nation state in Europe, the USA and Japan involved the creation and embedding of key society-wide institutions such as property rights, markets and their regulation, financial provision and governance, industrial relations, and education and training systems, as well as systems of political representation and implementation. The state which was created penetrated into the social and personal relations of its citizens in ways which had never previously been possible (see e.g. Hall 1986). It stood behind and reinforced the institutions of economic life as the ground rules of social order – leading to the formation of what have been variously called "varieties of capitalism" (Hall and Soskice 2001) and "national business systems" (Whitley 1999; 2007) among others.

The entry of the MNC into a state requires the recognition of the existence of the institutions of the host society, making institutional duality endemic in the everyday processes of managing the MNC and its subsidiaries. However, the nature of this institutional duality can vary. Some institutional aspects are obligatory and legally sanctioned whilst many others are informal. Thus the incoming MNC does not have to convert all its practices to that of the host society; it may seek to impose some of its own practices, and it has to be ready to accept some of the more formal and legal rules of the host society, but between these two positions exists the arena for negotiating around dual legitimacies. Which legitimacy is to count? It is in this negotiation that uncertainty, change, hybridization, diversity and the like occur at the level of the individual and the organization, with consequent impacts on home and host country institutions. It is in this interaction that micro-politics is revealed and enacted because the MNC, by definition, encloses a variety of institutional spaces within its boundaries, each of which has a level of legitimacy in its particular context. Research by authors in this book and elsewhere is giving us an excellent picture of the sorts of factors which influence these processes, showing the importance of the power available to different actors depending on the internal structure of the MNC and the external context, as well as the significance of the tactics, rhetorics, voice and networks deployed by groups in these processes.

It is important, however, to think more broadly about the nature of the transnational social space which is being created. In particular, my interest here is in the managerial complexity of coordinating the different sites of the MNC and the shape which the MNC takes. I therefore want to make more visible the degree of institutional differentiation within the MNC. Kostova's concept of institutional duality effectively breaks the MNC down into sets of dyadic relationships between the home country and the host country. However, beyond the smallest of MNCs, there are not just two parties involved but many and this is likely to impact on how the transnational social space is organized. In the following section, I focus on understanding more explicitly the range of institutional diversity within the MNC's transnational social space. What range of local social spaces is bounded into the MNC's transnational social space and with what effect?

The multinational as transnational social space: structures and processes

Measuring the internationalization of MNCs is problematic (Dörrenbächer 2000; Hassel *et al.* 2003). Some theorists such as Rugman have used sales turnover as a means of getting at the issue and on this basis, Rugman has constructed categories of different types of MNCs, differentiating particularly around the issue of globalization and regionalization (Rugman 2005). Dividing the world into three regions and measuring the degree of sales turnover a company has in any of the regions leads Rugman to argue that there are few truly global firms (i.e. with a significant presence in all three regions) and slightly more bi-regional firms (i.e. significant presence in two out of three of the regions), but by far the most populous type of MNC is regional, i.e. with the great bulk of activities concentrated in the home region. For all their detail, however, Rugman's measures precisely conceal the diversity of the transnational social space because there is an assumption about a homogeneity amongst the national contexts within single regions. Clearly a comparative institutionalist approach insists there is diversity within regions even across quite short distances. Therefore if we want to understand the degree of institutional diversity experienced in the MNC, this cannot be done on such a macro-regional perspective and instead a more fine-grained analysis is required.

In this respect the various efforts of UNCTAD in the World Development Report are more informative, even though they remain flawed for the purposes of this chapter. The most basic measure which UNCTAD has developed is its transnationality index (TNI) (unless otherwise stated the data in this section is taken from UNCTAD 2009). The TNI score for a particular company is an aggregation of three measures and the proportion of home/overseas in each measure. These measures are assets, employment and sales. For current purposes, it is the first two dimensions which are most significant. Assets reflect the degree of investment which the MNC has overseas; employment varies independently of assets and can in some circumstances reflect relatively low investment in technology and highly labor intensive activities, e.g. in retailing or simple commodity production as in the mass drinks industry. The TNI is relatively blunt as it only offers a contrast between home and overseas, and provides no differentiating mechanisms in terms of different overseas locations. Nevertheless this measure can still have some interest in terms of micro-politics because it suggests how significant overseas activities are to the MNC in general.

Take, for example, the profile of General Electric (GE), which is ranked number 1 in terms of the absolute dollar value of its foreign assets in the 2009 World Investment Report from UNCTAD. In spite of this, GE has a TNI of 51.4 percent, ranking it only 76th of the top 100 non-financial TNCs on this dimension. This reflects the continuing importance of its US base in terms of assets, employment and sales, and by implication the continued strength and significance of US management practices and processes in the MNC as a whole. GE subsidiaries are therefore likely to be characterized by strong home country influence and subsidiaries are likely to have to adapt to that context, shaping a particular pattern of micro-politics. On the other hand, top ranking on the TNI for the largest MNCs is generally associated with one of the following characteristics.

The first is the small-country effect; origins of the company in a small country (such as Switzerland, the Netherlands, Finland, Sweden) make the firm dependent on overseas growth and therefore in terms of proportions of assets etc. overseas, these are the most internationalized companies. As Katzenstein (1985) showed, small countries in the European context have been generally characterized by forms of corporatist governance both at the state and the corporate level. This suggests that they may be strong on export-ing their institutional practices when they internationalize. However, they have also tended to be open outwards and more dependent on international markets for longer than countries where the internal market has been large enough to sustain a productive base. Such companies also have a relatively small cadre of potential MNC managers to call on and although they have expanded that cadre by developing their educational infrastructure, it still means that they are likely to be more reliant on nationals from other coun-tries for management and technical expertise than those companies from larger economies. This suggests that the allocation of roles within headquar-ters and amongst subsidiaries may take a different form in these MNCs than in large-country MNCs with consequent effects on how institutional duality is perceived, managed and adapted.

The second group of large MNCs with high TNI scores arises from an effect mediated through industry structure, i.e. the degree of depend-ence on overseas resources (particularly significant in the oil, mining and agricultural production sectors). There is no doubt that these MNCs tend to face a different sort of institutional duality than others. The sorts of resources which they require are fixed; there are fewer opportunities to "regime-shop." This creates a strong dependency on the local environment. It frequently draws these MNCs into the politics of the country and the region. This may be a matter of dealing with contexts where corruption is endemic, a situation that may be stable over a long period of time or may be part of short and medium-term processes of destabilization, civil war and state collapse. In such contexts, MNCs get drawn into processes that undermine institution building at the state level, a process which they may try to repair at local level in order to ensure continuity of supply. Key skills in such contexts are political, being able to find allies in the local context and support in the home country where negative publicity may be highly damaging and needs to be avoided. Even in stable contexts, however, this sort of MNC may become highly politicized (e.g. BP and the Gulf of Mexico oil spill) and governments become involved. In these MNCs, local actors frequently become key because they have access to the powerful people and can smooth the way. Head office managers have to be able to trust such actors but to guard against allowing them too much autonomy in areas which may reflect back on the reputation of the MNC. Thus these managers, too, have to have political skills, contacts and networks both in their home contexts and in the areas where their assets are most significant. This creates a distinctive sort of transnational social space that requires more investigation.

The notion that the transnational social space varies in distinctive ways can be developed more generally in relation to MNCs in order to compare them and consider the role of this structure in shaping the framework of micro-politics. Sony, for example, proclaims itself a global company and is ranked 43rd in terms of the dollar value of foreign assets and 49th in terms of the TNI. Looking at this more carefully, however, a significant influence on the TNI is overseas sales which constitute around 75 percent of its total sales; and foreign employment is 66 percent of total employment whilst foreign assets are only 41 percent of total assets. This suggests that the most capital-intensive activities are kept in Japan and a substantial proportion of foreign employment is in assembly and low value-added areas. Therefore the way in which the subsidiaries relate to Sony HQ is likely to reflect this subordinate role and this is likely to be reflected in the form of micro-politics which arises.

A further element in this is the degree to which transnationality is dependent on heavy investment and employment in a small number of areas or in more limited investment spread across a large number of locations. UNCTAD has developed measures in an effort to clarify this. The simple starting point is what is termed the Internationalization Index (II). The II is the ratio of the number of foreign to total affiliates. In a 2007 paper, UNCTAD reported that "on average, more than 65 percent of the affiliates of the top 100 TNCs are located abroad ... the II, like the TNI, is highest for the top TNCs from small countries (such as Belgium, Finland, Ireland and Switzerland)." The II reveals differences between companies in the same sector and from the same national context. For example, Toyota, which is in 9th place when ranked according to the dollar value of its total foreign assets, is ranked 68th on the TNI with a score of 47.3 percent and 94th on the II because it has only 124 foreign affiliates out of a total of 330 (37 percent). By comparison, Honda is 19th on foreign assets, 21st on the TNI and 35th on the II where it has 102 foreign affiliates out of 130 (77 percent). Nissan is closer to Toyota except on foreign assets, where it is ranked 45th compared to rankings of 63rd for TNI and 91st for II. The degree of variation across MNCs in the same sector and from the same institutional context is therefore significant and creates different sorts of transnational social spaces with head offices having different levels of significance.

This method of analysis also reveals the substantial difference which exists between manufacturing and service sector firms. For example, the largest accounting, banking and management consultancy firms are likely to have offices in most countries in the world. This is because they are firms where the main fixed costs are incurred in the production of centralized systems and processes. Once these are in place it is relatively inexpensive to leverage those systems across as wide a set of customers as possible; their main costs are associated with employing labor whereas manufacturing MNCs, whilst also engaged in leveraging, usually require significant investment in new fixed assets. In their search for customers to sell standardized and customized products to, service MNCs are driven into many different settings where set-up costs can be kept relatively low and contained, as can closure costs if the business fails. So the possibility for upside gains and downside losses tends to favor expansion and proliferation.

The result of this is also a much greater differentiation in the scale and significance of overseas offices in these service sector MNCs than is likely in manufacturing MNCs. Many service sector MNC offices will be small and highly dependent on reputation, knowledge and infrastructure facilities funded and maintained by large offices in other contexts. They can be created ad infinitum almost as clones of an existing model; once the model has been developed it costs very little to extend it. At this level, therefore, the transnational social space in the clones is likely to be dense, filled with processes and procedures common across the MNC as a whole. On the other hand, there may be a relatively small number of powerful national offices in the service sector MNC that came together initially through federation or agreed mergers in order to create a global brand for international clients; these offices may be likely to be strongly embedded in national contexts (Morgan and Quack 2005). This creates a potential schizophrenia in such firms between those offices which are clones of a transnational model and those which are nationally distinctive, yet in theory cooperating on creating a global service to international clients. The micro-political dynamics of these organizations resembles in some way a colonial system in which the imperial powers (the strong large offices) dominate the weak, peripheral offices by transferring to them their existing rules and processes. However, the imperial powers (the big offices) are in rivalrous relationships to control the colonies and to keep their own national clients.

Manufacturing MNCs, on the other hand, are likely to develop a different dynamic because of their structure. This involves smaller numbers of subsidiaries with higher levels of investment, creating a stronger lock-in effect for the MNC top managers, an effect which can be increased where the subsidiary offers particular skills and knowledge to the MNC and its global markets. Particularly where the MNC is the outcome of multiple merger and acquisition activities, which is the case for many firms particularly from the USA and the UK, the ability to create a dense transnational social space will come up against embeddedness in local contexts where continuities of relationships inside and outside the firm may be strong, at least in part because of the precariousness of relying on what might prove temporary links with corporate networks.

A further relevant consideration here is the size of the MNC itself. Most of the discussion so far has focused on the largest MNCs. As has been frequently explored, a key element in this process is the home base of the MNC. However, this in turn requires a broader analysis than has often been the case. For example, it may be surprising that the country with the most parent corporations based in it is Denmark with 9,356. Although Denmark has a number of large multinationals, none of them features in the world's top 100 non-financial TNCs as ranked by foreign assets in 2007. This is clearly because many of them are small and medium-sized enterprises with relatively limited overseas investments. It is interesting to note that a number of other countries in Europe known for their strong SME sectors have somewhat similar profiles, e.g. Italy with 5,750 parent corporations (in 2005), the Netherlands with 4,788 (2008) and Germany with 6,115 (2007). In comparison, the UK has 2,360 parent corporations based in the economy (in 2005), the US 2,418 (2002) and France 1,267 (2002). In Asia, Japan has 4,663 parent corporations (2005), China 3,429 (2007) and South Korea 7,460 (in 2008).

These figures suggest a number of important issues for the study of micropolitics of MNCs. There is clearly a need to differentiate more carefully between MNCs in terms of their size. There are many SME multinationals, presumably with a much smaller average number of subsidiaries than bigger multinationals and yet there is very little specific knowledge about how they deal with issues of institutional duality. This is likely to impact on the way in which transnational social space is constructed in such settings. For example, issues of subsidiary "voice" and "issue-selling" are likely to occur very differently in small multinationals than they are in large ones, purely because of issues of scale and visibility.

Finally, it is also important to consider the host location in more detail. One particular aspect of this which has been underplayed relates to the numbers of foreign subsidiaries in a particular location. Top of this list is China (excluding Hong Kong) with a total of 286,232 affiliates, approximately 35 percent of the total of all foreign affiliates (in 2007). By contrast, the USA had only 5,664 foreign affiliates (2002). Other major sites of foreign affiliates are in eastern and central Europe with 71,385 affiliates in the Czech Republic (1999), 26,019 in Hungary (2005), 89,911 in Romania (2002), and 14,469 in Poland (2001). In western Europe, the largest sites for foreign affiliates are the Netherlands with 17,521 (2008), Spain 14,767 (2008), Sweden 11,944 (2007) and the UK 13,667 (2005). Other countries with large numbers of affiliates include Mexico with 25,708 (2002), Turkey 21,079 (2008), Malaysia 15,567 (1999) and Singapore 14,502 (2002).

Numbers of foreign affiliates have obvious impacts on the host society where the host society is dependent on overseas MNCs and FDI for economic growth, because it lacks key local capacities for growth such as risk capital, new technology, international marketing skills and networks, and a large consumer market. Thus the high dependence of relatively small economies like those of central and eastern Europe on foreign affiliates is noticeable. This feeds into the importance for the host society of continuing to be attractive to such investments. In such contexts, pursuing an environment which supports MNCs may lead to institutional changes that undermine existing forms of local embeddedness. Some societies are therefore more likely to be open to institutional change stemming from outside, such as from MNCs. In the current period, MNCs and other powerful external actors can have significant influence on institutional change. Thus the transnational social space of the MNC may extend outwards into the wider society, either explicitly through the MNC advising or lobbying governments on how to reshape local institutions or implicitly through providing templates for local contexts to copy (Morgan 2010). This inter-relation between the MNC, the local subsidiary and the local state is another set of factors shaping the terrain of micro-politics.

In conclusion, micro-politics occurs on the terrain of macro-politics in the transnational social space of the MNC. It is therefore important to understand the nature of that social space and its determinants more effectively in order to contextualize micro-political activity inside the MNC. Key issues concern (1) the extent of the transnational social space in terms of the number of national institutional contexts contained within the firm; (2) the size of the MNC; and (3) the degree of dependence of the national context on MNC activity. Such information and analysis should provide invaluable background to understanding the power and significance of various actors and subsidiaries in the MNC and their ability to engage in and influence micro-political activities in particular contexts.

The MNC as a unified legal and financial entity

The previous section used the institutionalist perspective to emphasize the diversity within the MNC and the importance of analyzing the degree and nature of this diversity in MNCs. Where then does the cohesion of the MNC come from? If we take the lesson of the micro-political studies in this book and elsewhere, the ability of the structure of control and coordination established by the head office to produce cohesion is frequently subject to disruption and uncertainty. For this reason, it is important to look beyond organizational structure per se. Instead, I suggest that it is useful to address two other issues. The first is the MNC as a legal and financial accounting entity that has a continuity and existence separate from the manifestation of the MNC in particular subsidiaries or organizational structures. The second, which is examined in the next section, is the continuous formation and reformation of an elite cadre of MNC managers.

The identity of the MNC as a legal and financial accounting entity is fundamental to its existence, and whilst it may be contested in various ways, without this basis, there would be no such thing as the MNC. This requires reaching out to interdisciplinary studies in the fields of accounting and law in order to understand how these processes work. Clearly, comparative institutionalist analysis has much to say about the nature of the firm in different contexts and how this is instantiated in particular laws, regulations and practices of corporate governance. There is a vast literature which explains how systems vary in terms of the legal nature of the corporation and the rights and obligations which particular groups of stakeholders, particularly financial stakeholders (shareowners and bondholders), creditors and employees hold under these different systems. These differences shape and constrain how firms are structured, the strategies which they follow in various markets, the risks which they take and the forms of alliance and cooperation which they build with other firms. It follows that the institutional context for the MNC influences how it deals with subsidiaries in its transnational social space. These are all very well-known aspects of the comparative institutionalist approach to MNCs (see e.g. the overview by Goyer 2010).

However, my focus on the legal and financial aspects of the MNC aims to open up a different perspective on the macro-politics of the transnational social space. It is useful to begin such an analysis by considering the MNC as a financial and accounting entity because this illustrates clearly the way in which the specific transnational nature of the MNC creates particular forms of social action that are distinctive. One simple example is the phenomenon of intra-firm trade inside MNCs. Intra-firm trade within multinationals is defined by the OECD as consisting of the trade between a parent company and its affiliates abroad. In a 2002 paper exploring inter-industry and intra-firm trade, the OECD noted that "intra-firm trade accounts for a large share of trade in goods" (for example, around one third of exports from Japan and the USA and a similar proportion of all US goods imports and one quarter of all Japanese goods imports). Furthermore, taking the example of US MNCs, the degree of intra-firm trade with selected trading partners varies. For example, in 1999, 44.3 percent of all US MNC exports to Mexico were intra-firm compared to 12.3 percent to eastern Europe. Conversely 73.7 percent of imports from Japan into the USA were via intra-firm trade compared to just 17.6 percent of Chinese imports.

The significance of intra-firm trade for micro-politics is that it involves transfer pricing, the fixing of prices for goods and services which are internal to the MNC but which cross national boundaries. How are these prices fixed? Since they lack certain elements of competitive markets, the answer lies in forms of estimation that are influenced by conventions and rules of accounting. As accounting research has shown, the application of conventions and rules is never mechanical; it requires the social construction of norms which in turn is influenced by powerful actors (see e.g. the recent collection by Chapman *et al.* 2009). Similar issues arise with other aspects such as the pricing of corporate overheads, how these are allocated across the various parts of the MNC as well as how certain assets, particularly intangibles such as intellectual property rights, are accounted for and allocated. These processes unify the transnational social space of the MNC since all parts are subjected to the same procedures in order to produce a set of accounts that are visible to and legitimate in the eyes of governments, regulators, shareholders and others.

There are two interconnected elements which need consideration here: the first is the relationship between intra-firm trade, transfer pricing and taxation; the second is the impact of these processes on the distribution of wealth and power within the MNC. MNCs seek to economize on tax liabilities and part of this process involves using the possibilities of transfer pricing to ensure that profits appear where they are subject to the most favorable tax environment. The ability to do this, however, is not unconstrained. Many of the largest tax authorities led by the USA and supported through the OECD have sought to develop clear rules about acceptable transfer pricing policies, building these around two principles. The first principle is that "each government taxes the worldwide income of its residents and the domestic source income of its nonresidents" (Eden 2001: 601). When income is repatriated from subsidiaries post-payment in the source country, "a foreign tax credit is granted for the corporate income taxes and withholding taxes paid in the host country up to the level of the home country tax" (Eden 2001: 601). Thus the home base of the MNC has a priority in tax terms, as it also does in terms of accounting for its financial activities in its shareholder reports or similar. Again, the multiplicity of activities in its subsidiary all have to be unified and calculated according to the financial and accounting principles embedded in that context. The second principle governing transfer pricing is that intra-firm transactions are priced according to the "arm's length standard," i.e. as though they were occurring on the external market and the price was being set in normal market conditions.

Both of these principles allow for plenty of ambiguity and negotiation. Pricing intra-firm transactions, whilst subject to a number of accounting techniques (see Eden 2001), remains highly contentious and complex. Eden states that "at the national level, most bargaining games occur behind closed doors between "large case" tax auditors and MNE tax departments. The negotiations take place over several years, from the date of the first tax audit through to the completion (win, lose) of enormously complicated tax court cases that can cost millions of dollars" (Eden 2001: 610). In terms of the residence principle, varied rates of taxation, but particularly the existence of tax havens and the ability of MNCs to defer the repatriation of income from subsidiaries, offer multiple possibilities for MNCs to manage their tax liabilities to their best advantages over prolonged periods of time (Palan *et al.* 2009). The fact that the standards of tax authorities in terms of freedom from corruption differ significantly across the world further undermines some of these principles.

From the point of view of the micro-politics of the firm it can be seen that these negotiations and processes place a great deal of power in the hands of the MNC HQ, which is the prime mover in the negotiation process, alongside its legal and financial advisers. It is the MNC HQ that has the legal responsibility to produce audited accounts and to present these to its shareholders and the broader community.

In engaging in these processes, the MNC HQ is also simultaneously engaging in a struggle over the identification of profits in subsidiaries and their distribution. Decisions on transfer pricing, on the allocation of overhead costs and on the profits of intangible assets are crucial to efforts to identify the profitability of particular subsidiaries. This in turn has a major impact on the self-identification of the subsidiary as a success or failure, and on the ability of the subsidiary to retain control of discretionary funds that might enable it to develop new products and processes. One can anticipate that this may lead to conflict with subsidiaries, particularly at moments when issues of local profitability emerge, e.g. where a subsidiary is being told that it is unprofitable compared to other subsidiaries and will have to close. At this point, accounting systems which may have appeared as neutral technical instruments "reflecting" an underlying reality may be challenged and presented as shaping that reality because decisions have been taken about how to distribute costs etc. Critical accounting research has emphasized the role of such systems not as representing an underlying reality, but as giving visibility to a particular version of reality. However, there is no doubt that in many contexts, accounting is treated as solid, as representative and difficult to take issue with. At crisis moments, actors in subsidiaries can start to challenge and unpick accounting conventions and show how they have created a particular representation. This may involve allying with other local actors; it may involve trying to win visibility with the investors in the MNC and even engaging with other MNCs to assess appropriate fits in other businesses. The power of expert knowledge reinforced by the power of legal ownership means that most of the time this element of the MNC macro-political terrain remains invisible.

Transfer pricing and taxation is therefore inseparable from the way in which the transnational social space is constructed. In relation to the previous discussion on the nature of the transnational social space, it would therefore be helpful to have more studies on how processes of accounting are conducted in particular subsidiaries, the role of head office experts and processes versus local managers and experts. This would reveal the degree to which the different groups managed to ally interests, especially against outside tax authorities. It would also reveal how the taken-for-grantedness of these accounting processes shapes the transnational social space and in particular provides a powerful mechanism for complementing the diversity of the transnational social space with a drive towards uniformity. As discussed earlier, this drive towards uniformity is not the same as the drive to impose a single system of control and coordination. It is more concealed than that, going right to the heart of the existence of the MNC as a legal, financial and accounting entity and empowering the MNC headquarters in ways that enable it to override and overcome many of the diverse institutional pressures to which it is subjected by its subsidiaries. It is in this sense a macro-political process of setting the terms on which micro-politics can occur.

Global management in the transnational social space

The final element in this analysis is a clearer focus on the actors inside the MNC and in particular the actors which span the transnational social space, move around it, reinforce it and most importantly cross its boundaries into the emerging institutions of transnational governance. I am less concerned, then, with organizational definitions of these managers and more concerned with their elite position – a position which is partly inside the organization but also frequently in broader "transnational communities" (Djelic and Quack 2010) that engage in shaping and reconstructing national contexts. The regeneration of elite studies in recent years (e.g. Savage and Williams 2008) has generally emphasized the fragmentation of elites, e.g. between arenas of political life (such as parliament, the civil service etc.) and arenas of social life (e.g. cultural elites, economic elites), between different levels of the society (the local and the national), between different economic groups (the financial elite embedded both in large organizations and in small private ones such as hedge funds and private equity on the one hand and the corporate elite dependent on organizational position on the other), between top members of different expert groups (lawyers, accountants, management consultancies) and between elites from different countries as well as between country-based elites and transnational-based elites (in transnational organizations such as the World Bank, IMF etc.).

Within this diversity of elites, who is the corporate elite in MNCs and what difference does this make to our understanding of micro-politics? The literature on expatriates has something to contribute here if, rather than focusing on all forms of management transfer across boundaries, it focuses more specifically on how MNCs identify and groom their top managers. Who are these people? Where do they come from and what do they do in order to move up towards becoming part of a global management elite with an influence and power that extends beyond the MNC? There is remarkably little systematic research and remarkably little effort to theorize about their significance (see Maclean and Hollinshead in this volume for an exception to this).

An initial starting point for this argument is understanding the way in which position in a national institutional context can be leveraged into position in a wider transnational arena of activity. The complexity of this process has been revealed in a series of Bourdieu-inspired studies of national elites by Dezalay and Garth (1996; 2002a; 2002b). What these authors show across a variety of contexts is a two-step process – firstly into the national elite, a process achieved through the use of existing social and cultural capital, secondly into the international elite. In the first stage, therefore, the comparative institutionalist approach remains central as it explains how different societal structures shape the creation of various national elites and in particular the development of a corporate elite. In contexts dominated by small firms (and small MNCs), for example, such an elite may be more difficult to identify than in contexts dominated by big and powerful MNCs. This may reflect greater social solidarity in local contexts and a resistance on the part of managers in these contexts to identify a significant distinction between themselves and others, so that even where the opportunity to move away from the locality arises, the manager may reject it. In other settings, elite distinctions may be constructed in education and reinforced in the organization, as is the case in France, in contrast to the UK where elite positions, whilst partly defined by education and expertise, seem also dependent on the choices individuals make in the workplace and how they leverage opportunities to move up or across organizations at crucial moments.

Passage into the global elite requires an expansion of existing capital through a range of processes, e.g. acquiring qualifications beyond the home country, such as gaining a postgraduate degree in law or economics from an elite institution in another country (often the USA), or building networks of contacts at the international level (within the MNC and outside it), or gaining a position as an intermediary, a translator between the national and international level. These processes occur based on the possession of social capital (in terms of appropriate ways of behaving and living in such circles), financial capital (having the money to participate in these processes) and expertise (having forms of specialist knowledge that are internationalized in their application).

Meyer and colleagues using sociological neo-institutionalism add an important element to this picture through their analysis of the emergence of "world society" and its associated practices and processes (Drori et al. 2006). In particular they identify the commitment to a world characterized by scientific rational legal authority in which legitimacy is embedded in conformity to norms and standards. These norms and standards are increasingly established in their view in the international arena by epistemic communities sharing a similar background in terms of expert knowledge, elite education and transnational social networks or transnational communities (Djelic and Quack 2010; Djelic and Sahlin-Andersson 2006). International standard-setting organizations interact with national institutions, smoothing out differences and developing common standards, e.g. in codes of corporate behavior, in systems that rank performance by similar criteria, thus inducing competition and imitation.

The concept of global management in MNCs thus refers to those managers, whatever their current position in the MNC, who are oriented to building their career in these ways. It is not that they have disengaged from their original national institutional context; on the contrary it is often essential to their ability to move into the global management category, that they have proved themselves successful in their home contexts. What is distinctive is the "double" trajectory – the trajectory up and the trajectory out – both of which must be continually reinforced and combined to become an effective member of global management.

In terms of understanding the transnational social space of the MNC, then, the question arises as to which managers make this transition. Which managers become part of transnational communities inside and outside the MNC? How and with what effect? Is the MNC dense with potential global managers, or is it dominated still by managers that are primarily embedded in their national institutional context? In Japanese MNCs, for example, the predominant influence remains Japan; few Japanese managers are educated outside Japan; on expatriate assignments, they tend to mix predominantly with other Japanese. By contrast, there is evidence that increasing numbers of German managers (and to some degree in recent years, French managers) are educated in part overseas and that overseas assignments are seen as opportunities to develop international networks. National and international elite formation processes interact with organizational and inter-organizational career-building developments to create particular propensities towards the growth of global management elites in different countries and in different types of multinationals. Micro-political processes need contextualizing in terms of these wider macro-political contexts if we are to understand more about the outcomes and consequences of particular forms of transnational social space inside MNCs.

Conclusions

The purpose of this chapter has been to acknowledge the contribution of the micro-political approach to MNCs whilst at the same time suggesting that there is now a need to go further. In particular, I have argued that the micro-political context needs to be complemented by a macro-political approach. This macro-political approach I associate with the idea of the MNC as a transnational social space, a contested terrain in which the shape of the terrain must in itself be analyzed in order to understand how micro-political spaces are pre-structured. In undertaking this task, I have sought connections with adjacent disciplines, fields and concepts that can open up new ways of understanding the MNC – with political economy, sociology and critical accounting.

First, I have emphasized that the structural configuration of the MNC and its subsidiaries needs to be further examined if we are to understand the diversity of institutional contexts and the sort of transnational social space which emerges. Issues such as the distribution of assets and employment, the nature of the industry, the size of the MNC and the degree of dependency of the host society on MNCs – all of these provide the macro-political terrain on which micro-politics occurs.

I have also made the argument for a stronger connection between the study of micro-politics and the study of the MNC as a legal, financial and accounting entity. The power of the MNC headquarters over transfer pricing, tax liabilities and the identification of profit is a crucial countervailing power to the diversity of the transnational social space. In many ways it is the ultimate power inside the transnational social space since it is where decisions about disinvestment and closure (as well as merger and acquisitions) are taken, determining the nature of the MNC's boundaries. There is too little research on micro-politics which obeys the classic injunction, "Follow the money!" Including this perspective into micro-political studies takes us to the heart of the relationship between capitalism, MNCs and institutional contexts: how is profit produced, how is it measured, how is it distributed and how is it transferred across national boundaries? This must surely lie at the center of most micro-political conflicts even if the issues are wrapped in other discourses.

Third, I have argued that the transnational social space of the MNC is increasingly being populated by global management. I have explicitly linked it to the notion of the emergence of new forms of international elites which are increasingly occupying not just the transnational social space of MNCs but also the sphere of transnational governance. I have emphasized that access to this group is conditional on access to national elites, but in addition other processes are required that create a further differentiation but not separation. Instead, the global management cadre become intermediaries between the sphere of transnational governance and that of national institutional context.

They also engage in transnational institution building that sets standards and frameworks which are imposed on other actors. These sorts of actors play crucial roles in the transnational social space of the MNC, setting standards and frameworks and engaging with actors in national contexts in ways that impact on the outcomes of micro-political struggles. Research that links more broadly issues of elite formation in national and transnational contexts and how this works out in the sphere of global management would therefore constitute an important complementary strand of research to that undertaken in this book.

In conclusion, the study of micro-politics and power in MNCs has progressed substantially in the last few years, as this book testifies. It has established itself as a legitimate and important approach to the study of MNCs. It is therefore now time to look beyond the purely micro and to look for complementary perspectives on the macro-political terrain of the MNC. This, in turn, requires looking outwards to other disciplines and research traditions which can provide new ways of looking at MNCs. I have suggested three perspectives which can be drawn on to create this form of complementarity. No doubt there are more that could be considered. This book provides a stimulating source of cases and theories to help begin this task.

REFERENCES

Almond, P. and A. Ferner (eds.) 2006. *American Multinationals in Europe*. Oxford University Press

Becker-Ritterspach, F. and C. Dörrenbächer 2009. "Intra-firm competition in multinational corporations: towards a political framework," *Competition and Change* 13: 199–213

Blazejewski, S. 2009. "Actors' interests and local contexts in intrafirm conflict: the 2004 GM and Opel crisis," *Competition and Change* 13: 229–50

Collinson, S. and G. Morgan (eds.) 2009. *Images of the Multinational Firm*. London: Wiley

Chapman, C. S., D. J. Cooper and P. B. Miller (eds.) 2009. *Accounting, Organizations and Institutions: Essays in Honour of Anthony Hopwood*. Oxford University Press

Dezalay, Y. and B. G. Garth 1996. *Dealing in Virtue: International Commercial Arbitration and the Construction of a Transnational Legal Order*. University of Chicago Press

  2002a. *Global Prescriptions: The Production, Exportation, and Importation of a New Legal Orthodoxy*. Ann Arbor: University of Michigan Press

  2002b. *The Internationalization of Palace Wars: Lawyers, Economists, and the Contest to Transform Latin American States*. University of Chicago Press

Djelic, M.-L. and S. Quack (eds.) 2010. *Transnational Communities: Shaping Global Economic Governance*. Cambridge University Press

Djelic, M.-L. and K. Sahlin-Andersson, K. (eds.) 2006. *Transnational Governance: Institutional Dynamics of Regulation*. Cambridge University Press

Dörrenbächer, C. 2000. "Measuring corporate internationalisation: a review of measurement concepts and their use," *Intereconomics* 35: 119–26

Dörrenbächer, C. and M. Geppert 2006. "Micro-politics and conflicts in multinational corporations," *Journal of International Management* 12: 251–65

2009. "A micro-political perspective on subsidiary initiative-taking: evidence from German-owned subsidiaries in France," *European Management Journal* 27: 100–12

Drori, G., J. W. Meyer and H. Hwang (eds.) 2006. *Globalization and Organization: World Society and Organizational Change*. Oxford University Press

Eden, L. 2001. "Taxes, transfer pricing and the multinational enterprise" in Rugman and Brewer (eds.) *The Oxford Handbook of International Business*. Oxford University Press, pp. 591–621

Edwards, P. and J. Bélanger 2009. "The multinational firm as a contested terrain" in Collinson and Morgan (eds.) *The Multinational Firm*. Oxford: Wiley-Blackwell, pp. 193–216

Edwards, P. and J. Wajcman 2005. *The Politics of Working Life*. Oxford University Press

Friedman, T. 2005. *The World is Flat: A Brief History of the Globalized World in the 21st Century*. London: Penguin Allen Lane

Gammelgard, J. 2009. "Issue selling and bargaining power in the intrafirm competition: the differentiating impact of the subsidiary management composition," *Competition and Change* 13: 214–28

Geppert, M. and D. Matten 2006. "Institutional influences on manufacturing organization in multinational corporations: the 'cherrypicking' approach," *Organization Studies* 27: 491–516

Geppert, M. and K. Williams 2006. "Global, national and local practices in multinational corporations," *International Journal of Human Resource Management* 17: 49–69

Geppert, M., K. Williams and D. Matten 2003. "The social construction of contextual rationalities in MNCs: an Anglo-German comparison of subsidiary choice," *Journal of Management Studies* 40: 617–41

Goyer, M. 2010. "Corporate governance" in Morgan, Campbell, Crouch, Pedersen and Whitley (eds.), pp. 423–52

Greenwood, R., C. Oliver, K. Sahlin and R. Suddaby 2008. *The Sage Handbook of Organizational Institutionalism*. London: Sage

Guillen, M. 2001. *The Limits of Convergence*. Princeton University Press

Hall, J. A. 1986. *Powers and Liberties: The Causes and Consequences of the Rise of the West*. London: Penguin

Hall, P. and D. Soskice 2001. *Varieties of Capitalism*. Oxford University Press

Hassel, A., M. Höpner, A. Kurdelbusch, B. Rehder and R. Zugehör 2003. "Two dimensions of the internationalization of firms," *Journal of Management Studies* 40: 701–19

Katzenstein, P. J. 1985. *Small States in World Markets*. Ithaca, NY: Cornell University Press

Kostova, T. 1999. "Transnational transfer of strategic organizational practices: a contextual perspective," *Academy of Management Review* 24: 308–24

Kostova, T. and K. Roth 2002. "Adoption of organizational practice by subsidiaries of multinational corporations: institutional and relational effects," *Academy of Management Journal* 45: 215–33

Kostova, T. and S. Zaheer 1999. "Organizational legitimacy under conditions of complexity: the case of the multinational enterprise," *Academy of Management Review* 24: 64–81

Kristensen, P. H. and J. Zeitlin 2005. *Local Players in Global Games: The Strategic Constitution of a Multinational Corporation*. Oxford University Press

Morgan, G. 2001. "Transnational communities and business systems," *Global Networks* 1: 113–30

2006. "Transnational actors, transnational institutions, transnational spaces: the role of law firms in the internationalization of competition regulation" in Djelic and Sahlin-Andersson (eds.), pp. 139–60

Morgan G. 2010. "Globalization, multinationals and institutional diversity," *Economy and Society* 38: 580–605

Morgan, G. and S. Quack 2005. "Internationalization and capability development in professional service firms" in Morgan, Whitley and Moen (eds.), pp. 277–311.

Morgan, G., P. H. Kristensen and R. Whitley (eds.) 2001. *The Multinational Firm: Organizing Across National and Institutional Divides*. Oxford University Press

Morgan, G., R. Whitley and E. Moen (eds.) 2005. *Changing Capitalisms?* Oxford University Press

Morgan G., J. L. Campbell, C. Crouch, O. K. Pedersen and R. Whitley (eds.) 2010. *The Oxford Handbook of Comparative Institutional Analysis*. Oxford University Press

Ohmae, K. 1999. *The Borderless World: Power and Strategy in the Interlinked Economy*. Revised edn. London: HarperBusiness

Palan, R., R. Murphy and C. Chavageaux 2009. *Tax Havens: How Globalization Really Works*. Ithaca, NY: Cornell University Press.

Rugman, A. M. 2005. *The Regional Multinationals: MNEs and "Global" Strategic Management*. Cambridge University Press

Savage, M. and K. Williams (eds.) 2008. *Remembering Elites*. Oxford: Blackwell Publishing

UNCTAD 2007. *The Universe of the Largest Transnational Corporations*, United Nations Conference on Trade and Development, New York and Geneva, http://unctad.org (last accessed January 19, 2010)

UNCTAD 2009. *The World Investment Report*, United Nations Conference on Trade and Development, New York and Geneva, http://unctad.org (last accessed January 19, 2010)

Whitley, R. 1999. *Divergent Capitalisms*. Oxford University Press

2007. *Business Systems and Organizational Capabilities*. Oxford University Press

Index

For EU product safety concerns, contact us at Calle de José Abascal, 56–1°,
28003 Madrid, Spain or eugpsr@cambridge.org.

www.ingramcontent.com/pod-product-compliance
Ingram Content Group UK Ltd.
Pitfield, Milton Keynes, MK11 3LW, UK
UKHW012200180425
457623UK00020B/324